THE

ANCIENT WORLD

Vincent M. Scramuzza

Paul L. MacKendrick
UNIVERSITY OF WISCONSIN

HENRY HOLT AND COMPANY   NEW YORK

To My Mother
V.M.S.

Preface

SHORTLY before Professor Scramuzza's lamented death on December 3, 1956, I had agreed with him to complete his *The Ancient World,* abridging it, bringing it up to date, and supplying maps and photographs. I should emphasize that the book's plan and four-fifths of its contents are Professor Scramuzza's; my role has been subsidiary; I have leaned heavily on the authorities starred in the section "Suggested Additional Reading" (pp. 758–764) and, for Ancient Near Eastern dating, on the works of Professor James B. Pritchard. I am aware of following scholars with a point of view different from Professor Scramuzza's in the sections on early Athenian constitutional history (Chapters 16 and 17) and on the Augustan principate (Chapter 46).

The abridgment was made in the interest especially of the general reader and of courses treating ancient history or classical civilization in a single semester. The aim has been to provide a succinct survey of cultural and political history from the Stone Age to the fall of Rome. The survey includes ancient Egypt, Sumer and Akkad, the Hittites, Syria, Palestine, and Phoenicia, Assyria, the Persian Empire, classical and Hellenistic Greece, the Roman Republic, and the Roman Empire. There is special emphasis on cultural history: literature, philosophy, science, art, the theater, Judaism, Christianity, and Roman law.

Professor Scramuzza's desire was to concentrate, with intensity and depth, on the most characteristic aspects of the civilizations treated. He gave Roman history a larger treatment than Greek, because he held that Rome has had a larger share in shaping Western civilization, as exemplified in language, nationalities, religion, customs, methods of land tenure and farming, law, literature, and art. He wished to present the material in such a way that while the reader was at grips with aspects of ancient history, he would be induced more or less unobtrusively to relate them to modern problems. To him, ancient history was not something remote, separate, or alien, but the first act in the indivisible drama of Western civilization. He saw unity from Homer and Archilochus to Milton and Walt Whitman, from Pericles and the Gracchi to Franklin Roosevelt. In the last fifteen years the college curriculum has tried under various names to lead the student back to the roots of Western culture. This book is a conscious and systematic effort toward that goal.

A special effort has been made to supply new, unhackneyed photographs, many never before published in a work for the general reader or beginning student. Developments in the field are rapid: the book takes account of the decipherment of Linear Minoan B, the discovery of the Dead Sea Scrolls, work in progress on the Karatepe bilingual, recent excavations at Isthmia, Serra Orlando, Cosa, and Sperlonga, and the new papyrus of Menander discovered in 1957.

Professor Scramuzza would have wished to thank especially Mr. Louis Cohn Haft of Smith College and Professor Nels Bailkey of Tulane University for helpful criticisms. My prime debt is to Messrs. Holt's anonymous reader, but I should like to thank also Dr. Ernest Nash for throwing open to me the incomparable resources of his Fototeca, now housed in the American Academy in Rome, and Mrs. Gladys D. Weinberg, Editor of *Archaeology*, for making available cuts from that admirable journal. The maps have been made especially for this volume by Giuseppe Tilia of the University of Rome. Mrs. Mary E. Bakken, secretary of the University of Wisconsin classics department, supplied expert typing above and beyond the call of duty. The Research Committee of the University of Wisconsin Graduate School and the John Simon Guggenheim Memorial Foundation have placed me deeply in their debt by supplying precious leisure for more monographic labors, now in progress, the interstices of which have been occupied with preparing this book for the press.

P. L. M.

American Academy in Rome
March 21, 1958

Contents

Part IV/THE ROMAN REPUBLIC

Part V/THE ROMAN EMPIRE

Illustrations

Maps and Diagrams

Part I / THE DAWN OF
CIVILIZATION

Chapter 1 / IN THE BEGINNING

The Progress of Primitive Man

Civilization is not improvised. It is complex, fragile, slow-growing; it neither moves in a straight line, nor climbs indefinitely upward, nor advances—or recedes—at the same pace on every segment of its jagged front. The first signals indicating its birth are so early and so faint as almost to escape detection. They can be accepted as incontrovertible evidence only on assuming tangible form as artifacts, that is, tools and weapons clearly conceived by human intelligence and shaped by human hands. Driven always to seek a better life, man began in the Old Stone (Paleolithic) Age to fashion various stone implements, numbers of which are constantly being excavated throughout the world. Roughly chipped, first by percussion, then by pressure, these tools evolved slowly toward higher efficiency and specialized forms. When man fashioned his first tool, technology was born, however humble in processes or crude in results. In the Old Stone Age, too, esthetic appreciation began. The wild-animal drawings with which Stone Age Man adorned his caves have real artistic merit. The New Stone (Neolithic) Age saw a revolution in methods of making a living; man turned from food gathering to stockbreeding and agriculture; gained skill in creating and handling textiles and ways of constructing earthen vessels, first by hand, later with the earliest machine ever made, the potter's wheel. More significantly still, he organized the first political society of which we find definite records, his village, ruled by the clan chief. (Earlier, tribes had existed.) Gradually he elaborated moral values and religious practices, some of which postulate an incipient belief in immortality.

Some Problems, Chiefly about Time

The astrophysicists tell us that our earth split off from the parent sun as a fiery mass at an incomprehensibly remote time. At the point when the fiery chip cooled off, the geologist takes up the story. He examines the once-celestial material transformed into rock, sea, soil and various deposits; next comes the paleontologist, to study fossilized plant and animal remains, so as to reconstruct the appearance of life and its rich, varied development. Life apparently began with various microscopic organisms which appeared when the earth cooled, hundreds of millions of years ago. Plant life probably evolved from rudimentary algae, and animal life, including man, has grown from these organisms through variations, mutation, geographic isolation, and other more or less hypothetical processes. Still another science, anthropology, unfolds before us the drama of man's appearance on earth, his physical characteristics and mental attitudes, the culture he has created, and his diffusion over the globe.

Before looking into man's remote past we ought to clear it of some of its enveloping mist. First of all, how do we know what we know? For example, how do we arrive at geological ages and dates? Patient scientific observation has worked out, chiefly from rock formations and soil deposits, a sliding scale of time sequences. One can understand the nature of these problems from observing, when driving on a road fresh cut through a hill, the original layers of rock, clay, or sand. Geologists fix the earth's age at hundreds of millions of years.

Second, the claim that man first appeared on earth one or more million years ago is now discarded. He may be 300,000 to 500,000 years old. New measuring techniques have corrected assumptions long current even among respectable scientists; for instance, they have demolished the myth of the Piltdown Man, once proudly called the first Englishman, which turns out to be a modern skull retouched and planted in an ambiguous collection of fossils. Whereas most geologists and physical anthropologists had fixed man's earliest date at 600,000 years ago, a new instrument, measuring the fluorine content of bones, showed an alleged 600,000-year-old specimen to be no more than 50,000 years old. Another test, carbon dating, has produced more devastating results. Organic materials—men, animals, plants—contain Carbon 14, which specially fitted Geiger counters can measure, in amounts diminishing in ratio to the time elapsed since their death. Thus the Geiger counter has scaled down the age of the Pyramid of the Sun in Teotihuacán, Mexico, to about 1200 years. Unfortunately the best tests thus far devised do not register beyond 30,000 years. More sensitive instruments will solve many of the mysteries shrouding man's remotest past.

Third, different sciences, or different schools of the same science, look at a given time from different angles. Geologists call the age of man's first appearance the Pleistocene, which is the sixth epoch of the Cenozoic era—from the Greek *kainos,* new, and *zoe,* life. The Cenozoic is the last of five eras, each lasting millions of years.

Those who measure time by climate postulate an initial period too hot to sustain life, a gradual cooling off to tropical temperatures, and then, in Europe and most of the earth, four ice advances, each followed by a retreat which produced a period of warmer weather. These four advances occurred in the million years of the Pleistocene epoch. These scholars tell us that the first man—more ape than man—appeared at the end of the first glaciation, about 500,000 years ago. The last glaciation occurred about 110,000 to 25,000 years ago. Different forms of man came and went between the end of the first ice age and the end of the last. Eventually the evidence for early man becomes clear enough for us to trace the principal stages fairly accurately.

Fourth, laymen wonder by what magic scholars can tell how ancient man looked, how he lived, what his occupations, beliefs, and ideals were. There is no magic, only scientific deduction. For instance, if stone tools, clearly man-made, surround the skeleton of Neandertal Man, the inference is, first, that Neandertal Man made them, and second, that he was intelligent enough to reason out that with proper weapons he could kill more animals for food. Charred wood or ashes in a cave-dwelling show that its occupant knew the use of fire. The animal bones lying about are the refuse of the kitchen. Scientists can identify them as those of hairy mammoths, reindeer, and other arctic animals, and conclude, therefore, that Neandertal Man was a hunter. Other evidence shows that he gathered wild fruit and made useful tools from bones, especially reindeer bones. In brief, scholars can reconstruct ancient man's life from the nature of the remains around him. The technique of collecting, classifying, and interpreting these remains is called archeology.

Paleolithic Times in Western Europe: The Invention of Tools

During the interglacial periods, elephants, hippopotami, rhinoceros, and other warm-climate animals roamed over what is now western Europe. Bears, foxes, and other arctic animals flourished in each ice age. So also with the flora: subtropical plants and trees alternated with arctic or temperate-zone ones. This climatic seesaw, with each ice age lasting 40,000 to 90,000 years, caused changes in vegetable, animal, and human life over much of the earth, and also changed the character of geologic deposits and of the earth's surface itself. With the advance and retreat of the glacier, land bridges were formed in areas now covered by water (for instance, the English Channel) and present land areas were submerged.

Early in the Pleistocene epoch, about 600,000 to 400,000 years ago, an anthropoid creature, *Australopithecus,* showed a tendency to stand erect and may have used crude stone tools. During the next several hundred thousand years, a number of increasingly manlike creatures (Pithecanthropoids) appeared.

One of the earliest and most apelike was the Java Man, who spread over to mainland Asia and Africa. The few extant .parts of his skull and skeleton, reconstructed, show a creature about five-and-a-half feet tall, with a head not quite erect, but with some manlike traits and a 940-cubic-centimeter brain (the brain of the Australian bushman is 300 cubic centimeters larger). Java Man apparently used unworked stones for hammering and cutting; hence his period is called Eolithic (Greek *eos,* dawn, and *lithos,* stone). Some skeletons found in China, near Peking, represent a second apelike type. Archeological evidence suggests that the Peking Man was a trifle more erect, intelligent, and human-looking than his Java cousin. He lived in caves, as protection against the rigors of climate, the terrors of nature, and the attacks of men. He hunted wolves, tigers, buffaloes, bear, deer, sheep, camels, and elephants, eating their flesh and their marrow. He used fire and may have cooked his meat. Apparently he also ate wild fruit and vegetables. He developed tools, chipping quartz into broad scrapers, cleavers, and knifelike implements, all without handles; his strong grip was his handle.

The earliest Neandertal was probably the Heidelberg Man, who may have lived between 275,000 and 120,000 years ago. Superior to the Peking Man in ingenuity, he made his tools with keener edges. He was able to produce by percussion (hitting with another stone) an edge on one or both sides of a stone. With his commonest tool, the hand-ax, or fist hatchet, shaped like a flattened pear, he could cut, cleave, scrape,

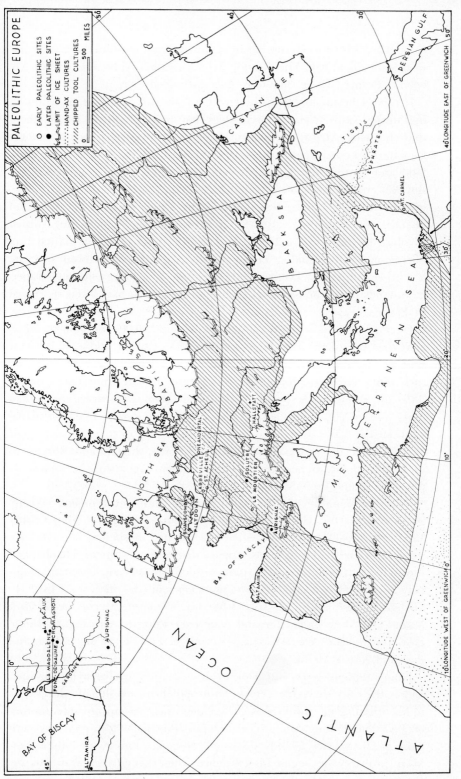

Fig. 1a. Map of Paleolithic Europe. Inset shows early cultural centers.

or whittle. These tools survive in quantity, for they blunted easily and were soon discarded. These crude axes are called Abbevillian from Abbeville, France, where they were first discovered.

It should be noted that primitive man's history can best be followed in Europe, since scientific archeology has been practiced longer there than in Asia, Africa, or America, resulting in correspondingly fewer gaps in our knowledge. In Europe, the fullest evidence comes from England and France, though much evidence is now coming from Czechoslovakia and Russia.

Abbevillian technique was improved by a finer method of percussion (named the Acheulian, after St. Acheul, another French site), which involved hitting the rough flint with a stout stick or crude mallet, producing more and smaller dents and less jagged and uneven surfaces, a sharper hand-ax, a keener blade, a point, or a more efficient scraper. Thousands upon thousands of such improved flints have been recovered in France.

During a warm interglacial period, about 200,000 or 150,000 years ago, the Acheulian technique spread as far east as India and as far west as England, then joined to Europe by a land bridge. Over 10,000 such flints have been found at Swanscombe, on the south bank of the Thames, a few miles from London. The men who made Acheulian flints hunted elephants, horses, bison, and rhinoceros. Their principal weapon may have been a wooden spear whittled to a point with their efficient bifacial scrapers. They built themselves shelters and wore skins in winter. Some archeologists consider them precursors of Homo sapiens, or Homo sapiens himself.

The next notable step in Paleolithic cultural development was apparently also taken by the Neandertal group. Neandertal Man existed 120,000 to 70,000 years ago, sometimes living in sheltering caves. He stood erect and had a brain as large as that of modern man. He changed the Acheulian technique. His tools (called Mousterian, from Le Moustier, France) have a smoother and more efficient edge than those hitherto discussed; these flake tools used what was formerly the residue of flint. Neandertal Man spread far and wide over Europe, Africa, the Middle East, and Central Asia. His traces survive in Europe, Western Asia, and East and North Africa.

Homo sapiens is far superior to any of these earlier types of man and is the only surviving genus. Anthropologists are sharply divided as to his origin. Some think he is early Paleolithic, perhaps a contemporary of Java and Peking Man. If so, he probably had close relations with most of the species already discussed, and may have wiped them out. More probably he began his existence when Neandertal Man was declining. It is not yet clear whether he was an entirely new species or a

Fig. 1.1. Altamira. Prehistoric cave painting of wild boar, dated 40,000–20,-000 B.C. Some fifty caves adorned with prehistoric painting are now known in southwest France and northeast Spain. The superb technique is evidence that history is not simply an evolution from "savagery" to "civilization." "One cannot paint better; he can only paint differently." (Carthaillac & Breuil, *La Caverne d'Altamira à Saintillane près Santander*. Monaco, 1906. Plate III.)

transmuted descendant of Neandertal Man. During the latter part of the ice age and afterwards, he moved across Europe, peopling it from the North Sea to the Mediterranean, and across North Africa from Morocco to Egypt. Slowly he filled the whole earth.

The earliest evidence of Homo sapiens comes from in and near Cro-Magnon, in southern France, though future excavation may produce earlier traces. Cro-Magnon Man improved Paleolithic techniques by substituting pressure for percussion. His flint instruments had more and smaller flakings and gave faster and smoother results. He left abundant traces of his industry all over southern France, especially at Aurignac, Solutré, and La Magdalène. Each site shows the percussion technique evolving in ever more advanced stages.

If progress is measured by man's power to provide light and heat for himself, Cro-Magnon man may justly be called its first pioneer. His realistic and animated groups of animals carved on horn or bone, high reliefs of galloping horses, and sculptured figurines show a real esthetic sense. Even more remarkable are his cave frescoes on both the French and Spanish sides of the Pyrenees, especially at Font-de-Gaume, Lascaux, and Altamira, representing the animals he chased, chiefly reindeer and bisons. The burial of his dead reveals his beliefs. He laid the body doubled up in a foetuslike position. Did he perhaps imagine that, composed in that fashion, the dead would be born again? He also scarified the bones of the dead, then painted them red, perhaps simulating human blood and intending magic to help the dead return to life. Such practices suggest a belief in a future life.

World-wide Paleolithic culture may be the result of European penetration of Asia, Asian penetration of Europe, cultural diffusion, or independent parallel cultural evolution.

The Neolithic Age: A Progressive Era

Compared with the previous age, the Neolithic Age, beginning about 5000 B.C., its characteristics first appearing in western Asia, was a progressive era. By the time it ended, about 3000 B.C., implements, housing, means of subsistence, and social organization had been revolutionized. Man had discovered new methods of finding food. He added to hunting and fishing the domestication of animals, especially cattle, sheep, goats, and swine. In time he made oxen, horses, asses, mules, and camels work for him, pulling the plow, carrying burdens or, until the wheel was invented, dragging them. Meanwhile the old food-gathering economy had been replaced by agriculture: sowing, planting, tending, harvesting, and storing. The first agricultural implement was probably the dibble-stick, a pole used for making holes in the ground; later, the hoe and then the plow were introduced.

Agriculture revolutionized man's life: it allowed him to become really settled. The earliest huts had been half buried; later they were built entirely above ground. Their shape—rectangular, circular, oval, or octagonal—varied by regions. For walls and roofs they had a structural skeleton of poles, the walls interwoven with wattle and the roofs with thatch. Hut size and grouping give evidence of family and village life; cemeteries with some tombs more impressive than others (megalithic) suggest social structure, clan chiefs, and possibly slaves. Against his enemies, Neolithic Man fortified hills with palisades and ditches, sometimes enclosing twelve to seventeen acres.

Progress touched clothing, too. Skins were still used but, having learned to make baskets by plaiting reeds and other pliable plants, man went on to process flax fiber, spin it, and weave it into clothes. Later he was to spin sheep's wool into thicker and warmer material, both linen and wool being dyed and decorated with bright geometric designs.

Constantly expanding his wants and finding practical ways of satisfying them, Neolithic Man waterproofed his baskets by daubing them with clay and then used these reed-and-mud receptacles for cooking vessels. In time he omitted the reed skeleton altogether, making pans, cups, and dishes entirely of clay. Gradually he improved them by firing them in a kiln, decorating them with painted designs. The later Neolithic period saw hand-turned pots superseded by the products of the potter's wheel, which produced thinner-walled, more symmetrical pottery that could be produced faster and therefore more cheaply.

These baked utensils supply invaluable historical evidence. While time and the elements damage or destroy wood and metal, fired clay is virtually imperishable. Vast quantities of the potter's output lie buried with the refuse and debris left by generations of men, under accumulated sand, mud, or decayed vegetation. Even pottery fragments (sherds) are useful to the archeologist, for if vases of the same clay or shape, the same ornamental style, or the same firing technique are found hundreds of miles apart, one can legitimately infer a common origin or the existence of trade relations. In addition, decorative fashions furnish precious data on the development of art.

The Study of History

We have thus come to the point where we can understand what prehistory means. Until two or three centuries ago "ancient history" meant a written account, like Herodotus' for Greece or Livy's for Rome, and little was known beyond the written sources. But writing started only yesterday—not much more than 5000 years ago—when man had already existed for some 95,000 years. This amazingly long period antedating the art of writing and known only from surviving artifacts is prehistory or preliterary history.

At first reading, our presentation will seem dismayingly vague. The vagueness has two causes: first, evidence from newer excavations makes reconstruction valid only for a season, since, paradoxically, not even modern history receives almost weekly such quantities of documentation, and is therefore so subject to new interpretation, as the study of ancient man. Second, there is the nature of history. History is not merely a collection of facts and dates, for dates by themselves are meaningless and facts are like corpses. At best they make a chronicle, the raw material of history. But history is much more than that. In a narrow sense it is interpretation, the meaning distilled by the historian from the raw material; in a larger sense it is evaluation of all the forces—often subtle and elusive, or lying almost invisibly deep—of which the "facts" are but shadows and symptoms. Furthermore, history at its best can be written only by men who, besides a full knowledge of the past, have a clear understanding of why and how man and societies act. Thus history is largely a product of judgment. This is precisely why it may seem arbitrary, especially to the beginner. For one thing, no two individuals' judgment is exactly alike. For another, every generation, living in a different climate of opinion and with a different set of values, rewrites history in the light of its own time. Under these circumstances, no dogmatic conclusion, valid for all time, is possible, and it is the reader's understanding of this that will make profitable his study of history.

Part II / THE ANCIENT NEAR EAST

Chapter 2/EGYPT: THE

OLD KINGDOM

From Clan to National State

Ancient Egypt, like its modern successor, was a narrow valley bordered on the north by the Mediterranean, on the east by the Red Sea, on the south by Nubia, the modern Sudan, and on the west by the Sahara Desert. It was bisected lengthwise by the Nile River, which from the heart of Africa flows northward into the Mediterranean. This mighty stream has dug through solid rock a canyon five hundred miles long and three to five hundred feet high. The upland on each side of the canyon is a melancholy expanse of rocky hills and red and yellow dunes melting away into the horizon. Since no great civilization could possibly grow in this desert, the rich and varied history of Egypt is to be sought entirely in the Nile Valley (that is, the canyon floor, six to twelve miles wide, where the river flows between two strips of land green in the growing season, golden when the harvest is ripe) and the alluvial plain, which, starting where the canyon ends, fans out in three directions—north, east, and west. The ancient Egyptians called the canyon Upper Egypt, the plain downstream Lower Egypt (called the Delta by the Greeks). Summer breezes from the Mediterranean

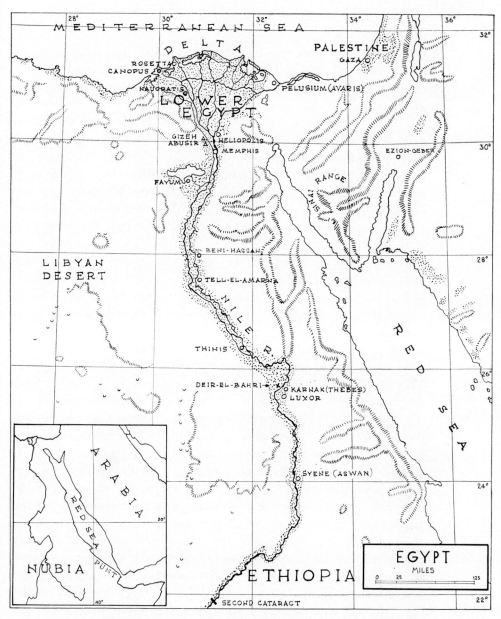

Fig. 2a. Map of Egypt. Inset shows perimeter of Red Sea.

Sea give the Delta a climatic advantage over the walled-in semitropical trough of the Nile.

In Paleolithic times, when the bottom was as yet uninhabitable, the people of Upper Egypt lived in comparative comfort as roving cliff dwellers, supporting themselves by hunting and fishing. The Delta people, lacking the advantage of high elevation, met the challenge of the swamp by building huts of reeds and mud, clustered together in hamlets on slightly high ground, a technique which eventually spread to Upper Egypt. After a series of unusually devastating floods, the Delta Egyptians began to experiment with villages built on artificial mounds and linked together with causeways, thus keeping dry and maintaining communications while the country lay deep under water. In inventing and using tools they followed roughly the pattern described in the preceding chapter.

Neolithic Egyptians learned to exploit the resources around them more intensively, thus developing agriculture and industry. They raised barley, wheat, and millet; ground flour, kneaded dough, baked bread; increased their food supply by breeding herds of horned animals; trained oxen to draw the plow and asses to carry loads; fashioned tools of polished stone as well as of bone and ivory; contrived sharp weapons, wove cloth, plaited reed mats, and made vases of stone or baked clay. They learned to navigate the river in canoes made of papyrus reeds, with evident consequences for the development of commerce.

They advanced in social and political organization. Grouped in clans, they, or rather their chiefs or priest-kings, discovered the value of teamwork for protection from floods and for enlarging the tillable area. By the concerted efforts of the whole clan, they built dikes to keep the river within bounds and dug irrigation canals. In the dry season they lifted the precious water from the river in buckets hung from poles in the manner of the colonial sweeps of New England. By compelling obedience and exacting cooperation, the clan chiefs secured order within and security at the border—a double necessity if men were to work, accumulate wealth, and advance in civilization. Thus the state was born. The authority of the clan-state, or rather of the chief impersonating the state, was expressed by a symbol: a dog, a falcon, a scorpion, a solar disk; in brief, some sign around which men might rally. When one clan overcame another, it expressed its superiority by placing its own emblem above that of its victim.

The dwellers of the Two Lands were peoples of different strains. Those of Upper Egypt, who resembled the Gallas and Somalis of today, migrated from Nubia or Ethiopia, perhaps even from southern Arabia. Those of Lower Egypt, a folk of small stature, long head, black eyes, and black hair, were probably a branch of the so-called Mediterranean stock, with or without Negroid admixtures. Finally, Semitic tribes from Syria or northern Arabia made their way into Lower Egypt either through the Sinai peninsula or after a long sojourn in Libya. Gradually these strains merged into a composite but culturally homogeneous people, the Egyptians of historical times, each contributing its share to the growth of Egyptian civilization. The Semites, for example, furnished certain linguistic elements as well as the worship of the sun-god Ra, while the Negroids gave the great god Horus who, according to legend, slew Anu, the hero or god of alleged aborigines.

Down to Neolithic times each clan had occupied a district of its own with its own village or town where the government had its seat, craftsmen plied their trades, families lived, and men retired at night after the work in the fields was done. Gradually these districts went through a process of amalgamation until the point was reached, some time in the fifth millennium B.C., when there emerged two kingdoms, Upper Egypt and Lower Egypt.

After living side by side for more than 1000 years as separate and independent states, now in peace, now at war, the two kingdoms were joined together by Menes, a legendary king of Upper Egypt. This important event, which may have taken place about 3100 B.C., was symbolized by joining the White Crown of Upper Egypt with the Red Crown of Lower Egypt, the White above the Red, and by adopting the emblem of the falcon perched on the head of the sovereign, symbolizing divine descent and power. This noblest of birds sailing the Egyptian sky had originally been a symbol for the god Horus. When Horus and Ra became in the popular mind a single divinity, the falcon still remained its emblem.

The original clan-states survived as nomes or administrative districts into Roman times, the original diminutive royal capitals becoming the equivalent of our county seats. The clan emblems acquired new significance. Since the emblems had borne a close relation to the founders and heroic chiefs who were worshiped as gods, when the latter vanished from memory, they themselves, that is, the dog, the scorpion, the elephant, the thunderbolt, became objects of worship. This accounts for one of the salient features of Egyptian polytheism.

Flowering of Neolithic Culture

The long slow process culminating in the union of Upper and Lower Egypt was a religious and intellectual experience as well as a political one. To the ancient Egyptian mind, which never conceived of a secular side of life separate from the religious, the king was both human and divine. His office was the heart of national life, the mainspring of civilization itself. His was the power joining heaven and earth together into one indivisible whole. Through him the cosmic forces fulfilled their role, men lived, then went to another existence. The rotation of the seasons, the alternation of day and night, the rain and the sunshine, the sowing and the reaping, the yearly growth of the flora, the generations of the fauna, in short, the whole of life on earth, above, and below was associated with kingship.

As understood by the Egyptian mind, the cosmos started with Horus-Ra, King of Heaven, who begot the Air; the Air begot the Earth; the Earth begot the Nile; the Nile begot the land of Egypt. The Nile itself was identified with the god Osiris, while the Land, annually fertilized by it, was equated to the goddess Isis. Osiris and Isis, envisaged as husband and wife, also as brother and sister, remained the most intelligible and popular Egyptian divinities to the end of pagan times. The Egyptians were remarkably near the truth in imagining that, after the Land had been formed, they had lived on it forty to sixty thousand years. They also imagined that during that span of time they had been ruled by several dynasties of gods, demigods, and heavenly heroes until at last the kingship fell to an earthly man, the Menes of tradition.

More remarkable than these concepts themselves is the fact that they were worked out as far back as the Neolithic age. Indeed the whole context of Neolithic culture, especially in Lower Egypt, is a noble chapter in the history of mankind. Living was no longer a brutish struggle for the bare necessities, but was for the ruling class gracious and elegant. Artists developed an unerring eye for beauty. Their pottery has seldom been surpassed in the fineness of the clay, the thoroughness and uniformity of the baking, or in design and coloring. No less admirable are the vases carved out of stone in this same age, the Neolithic. Nothing like them in fresh, rhythmical, and harmonious beauty or perfect craftsmanship has since been produced.

As the nerve center of national life, the king drew around him the energies of his people in administration, agriculture, industry, religion, thought, letters, and the arts. For example, there was in vogue a luxury utensil, the palette, usually an oblong slate on which green malachite was ground into fine powder. Men and women painted their faces with this substance. Court artists adapted the palette to a new use in the service of the king, as a commemorative tablet, engraved with figures and symbols expressive of his achievements, especially his victories. They also carved portrait-statues of the king and his courtiers and servants which, shapeless at first, after long experiment succeeded in conveying a sense of movement and acquiring lifelike expression.

A people who could not think of national life separate from their kings grouped the latter into dynasties with distinct characteristics or programs. According to a list handed down by Manetho, a Greek-speaking priest of the third century B.C., there were about thirty such dynasties. The first three dynasties, which ruled some five hundred years (*c.* 3100–2650 B.C.), strove for the twin aims of Menes or whoever it was that founded the united kingdom: to protect the state from the desert tribes and to unify culturally the Two Lands. The principles and methods they evolved in carrying out these plans became the master mold that was to shape government, religion, culture, public administration, social and economic life, in brief, every institution of ancient Egypt.

With the title of pharaoh, which meant "The Great House," the king fixed his capital at Thinis. His power was absolute, but he was assisted by a council of wise men and experienced officeholders who theoretically represented the nation but actually represented the aristocracy. Although intensely autocratic, the pharaoh was aware that he had obligations towards the poor; indeed he regarded himself as divinely appointed to protect their rights and to secure justice even for the lowliest members of society. Conscience had developed to such an extent in Egypt that the pharaoh's laws imposed justice as the norm of conduct on every subject, high and low.

A highly departmentalized bureaucracy reached down to the smallest hamlet and the humblest shack, watching over the king's interests, especially the collection of rents, taxes, and other dues, and keeping a check on the subjects' ability to pay by periodically taking a census. Taxation was in ratio to the volume of the Nile floods: the higher the river and consequently the thicker its deposit of fertile mud, the higher the tax.

Religion taught men to approach the kingdom of death with that same ceremonial thoroughness to which the god-king had accustomed them in life. In both Paleolithic and Neolithic times the dead were buried curled up in shallow oval graves lying upon the left side, the head resting on the knees. The body was usually smoked or dried. With the deceased were buried his weapons, the reed mat on which he squatted, his palette, and his pots and pans. That is, he went to the next world supplied with the same equipment he had used in this, in order that he might feel at home in the strange realm beyond. But towards the close of the Neolithic period, about 3000 B.C., the aristocracy developed a new method of burying the dead: the bodies were mummified and laid out full length. By 2500 B.C. the common people had adopted an inferior grade of the new fashion.

The organization of the national state was surpassed by another achievement, the art of writing, derived perhaps from Mesopotamia. At first a crude picture was used to represent a simple object (cow or snake or bird). Then a series of continuous pictures signified an association of objects, that is, a chain of objective ideas. When this stage was reached, the ground was cleared for expressing abstract ideas. This pictographic, or ideographic, system evolved into a second stage, the phonetic, or syllabic, when pictures or signs denoted, no longer objects, but sounds, and the joining together of sound-signs formed words. A third and final stage was reached when the syllable was split into its component consonants, thus creating the alphabet. The infinite possibilities of grouping alphabetical letters to express any word, old or new, enabled man to record every shade of his thought. The alphabetical system was fully developed before the merger of the two kingdoms (3100 B.C.).

After the alphabet was invented, the lettering itself passed through three stages: hieroglyphic, in which each letter was represented by one of the original pictographic signs; hieratic, in which the old signs were simplified, each becoming shorter and almost linear or cursive; and demotic, a true cursive script. By 600 B.C. the hieratic was practically abandoned, the hieroglyphic used almost exclusively for religious texts, and the demotic for all other purposes. But in the succeeding centuries all knowledge of these signs was lost. During Napoleon's expedition to Egypt the discovery of a basalt tablet in the town of Rosetta promised a solution of the mystery, since its inscription was written in three different alphabets, hieroglyphic, demotic, and Greek. The Greek text was a decree of Ptolemy V, dated 196 B.C.; but although it was rightly thought that the Egyptian texts were versions of the same decree, all attempts to decipher them yielded only meager results. The key to the mystery was found in the 1820's when the French scholar, Jean François Champollion, in studying a recently discovered obelisk, noticed that the Greek names of the kings Ptolemy and Cleopatra, enclosed in ovals, seemed to be repeated also in ovals in the hieroglyphic text accompanying the Greek. By a comparative study of the obelisk and the Rosetta Stone he at last was able to decipher not only the hieroglyphic but also the hieratic and the demotic writing systems. Thereafter Egyptian grammars, dictionaries, and translations appeared in rapid succession.

The early dynasties invented the 365-day calendar, designed to reconcile for record-keeping purpose the Nile year with the lunar year. Over the centuries the Egyptians kept records of the number of days between each high Nile, worked out an average, which came close to 365 days, and worked out an arbitrary year, pegged to an annual phenomenon, the appearance of the Dog Star on the eastern horizon at dawn. We owe a debt to the Egyptians for the observations and calculations by which, nearly 5000 years ago, they invented the direct ancestor of our calendar year.

In sum, a line of powerful kings, led by Menes, unified Egypt as an autocratic divine state, commanding the allegiance of every inhabitant and controlling his thought, his labor, and his life. Thereby Egypt was transformed from a peasant culture into a highly developed civilization, with written records, a calendar, an appreciation of beauty, and a fresh and majestically original explanation of the universe.

Paralleling this magnificent march towards civilization, if not actually underlying it, was the introduction of metals. The art of smelting gold and copper and the use of copper tools antedated the First Dynasty. Men learned to mix copper with tin somewhere in southwestern Asia, not long after 8000 B.C., thus producing a harder alloy, bronze. The knowledge of this discovery, so momentous for the future of mankind, soon reached Egypt. In the course of a few generations, large-scale use of bronze tools increased the product of man's labor. But it increased also the power and wealth of the state, and it gave greater incentive to the creative imagination of man.

The Old Kingdom: 3100–2200 B.C.

At the beginning of the Dynasties, the seat of government had already been transferred from Thinis in Upper Egypt to the apex of the Delta, in order to watch more closely, from a more centrally located capital, both sections of the united kingdom. But since Memphis, the new metropolis, was a seaport like London or New Orleans, it was more fully exposed to outside influences, especially from Phoenicia, Palestine, and Crete. Egypt's new links with the world in this period are evident not only in its exploitation of the mines of the Sinai peninsula, the commercial relations with the Punt (Somaliland) by way of the Red Sea, and the exchange of goods with Crete, but especially in its armed struggle with Libya, Palestine, and Syria. By 2500 B.C. the pharaohs had established commercial relations from the Delta to Lebanon, gaining thereby two indispensable materials, timber for their ships, and copper. An Egyptian temple in the Phoenician city of Byblos suggests an Egyptian commercial colony there, but the Old Kingdom was not imperialistic in a political or military sense.

The king was still a benevolent theocratic despot. He was assisted by a prime minister, who acted as chief adviser, deputy chief justice, supervisor of all the departments, and controller of the administration of the nomes; by a treasurer, by a minister of public works (chiefly irrigation), by a commander of the armed forces, and by a purveyor of military equipment. Under these department chiefs there was an army of clerks, secretaries, stenographers, accountants, bookkeepers, tax collectors, managers, messengers, and confidential agents. These servants were given every opportunity to work their way up, until the most capable among them, no matter how humbly born, filled the highest offices. They received salaries in the form of goods in kind which kept on flowing into the royal stores as rents, taxes, or perquisites. The higher officials were given also perpetual land leases from the king's domain as well as concessions, immunities, and privileges of various kinds.

Every petition or grant, every order and the acceptance of every order, every receipt and disbursement in the nomes as well as the capital was transmitted in writing and deposited in official archives, which survive by thousands to give us masses of information about Egypt.

The archives inform us, for example, of the king's vast wealth. Since all the land was his personal property, great lords and humble peasants alike paid him rent for it, in kind, so that he owned immense stores of wheat, barley, olive oil, wine, beer, fruit, and other produce. Moreover since he held a monopoly of all trades, he received a percentage of all profits, and sold all surpluses on the open market or exported them abroad.

Just as written documents give us a full picture of the royal administration, so miniature statues buried with the dead enable us to reconstruct most phases of Egyptian life in the post-Neolithic period. The Egyptian lived, of course, by agriculture, raising wheat and barley, breaking the ground with a simple plow drawn by a team of oxen, scattering the seed by hand, cutting the crop with flint scythes, and threshing by the tramping of asses or oxen. The commonest crops were cereals, flax, vegetables, and fruits, especially figs and grapes. Wine was obtained by tramping grapes in a trough; the mash was then put into a sack and pressed by twisting the sack between two sticks. Cows and she-goats furnished meat and milk. Cattle, chickens, and geese were fattened in enclosures. The swamps teemed with geese, ducks, cranes, herons, and fish, while in the desert professional hunters trapped or killed wild oxen, gazelles, lions, panthers, and hyenas.

Surviving artifacts show skilled artisans at work: weavers of cloth, curtains, tapestries, baskets, carpets, and mats; ropemakers, shoemakers, carpenters, stonecutters, potters, makers of stone vases, bronzesmiths, goldsmiths, jewelers, sculptors, and painters.

Men wrapped around their waist a piece of white starched cloth, held in place with a sash and falling to the knees, but the rest of the body was exposed. On the head they wore a skullcap. The rich and the noble dressed much like the common people, except that they wore sandals made of papyrus or leather, had their heads shaven and covered with a wig perfumed with a greasy substance, and wore false beards and massive necklaces. Women wore a close-fitting garment strapped over the shoulders and reaching from below the breasts to below the knees. The hair was kept in place by a fillet and greased with perfume or scented oils. They wore jeweled metal bands on the arms and ankles. Expert manicurists and pedicurists kept milady's hands and feet in trim.

House furniture was simple. The common people squatted or crouched on reed mats; the rich sat on stools, and at meal time on chairs or love seats, eating from dishes placed before them on small round tables. They slept on high beds provided with mattress, pillow, and covers. Clothes and other articles were kept in chests.

Transportation and communication were easy. Great lords traveled on litters, while goods were carried donkeyback. Flood embankments served as convenient causeways, not only in high water, but also after the crops were sown, for laws were enacted against tramping on sowed ground. But the best means of transportation was the river and the numerous irrigation canals which were increasingly plied by skiffs, wherries, and larger boats, usually propelled with oars or with sails rigged to a mast, while a common oar took the place of a rudder. From drawings and paintings of every period of Egyptian history one can follow the evolution of shipbuilding from open boats to decked ships, larger sails, and better piloting devices.

Popular religion clung to the Stone Age pattern, that is, the worship of the nome-founders. These legendary kings had not only been metamorphosed into gods, but given the shape of the bird, animal, or reptile emblems under which, while living, they had won the loyalty of their people. Each was supreme in his nome, attracting around himself the other local gods in a functional hierarchy, as his wives, children, companions, or servants.

These local divinities entrenched themselves so deeply in the affection of the common people that they were never displaced by the cosmological gods who appeared at a later time as the product of a more advanced culture: the moon-god, La; the earth-god, Jeb; above all, the sun-god, Ra, who, identified with a local god, Aton, had a splendid temple at Heliopolis, where he was worshiped as god not of a nome, nor even of Egypt, but of the universe, the supreme being who made all things, even the gods themselves. He was believed to travel unceasingly in his sky-ship, giving light and sustenance to the living during the day, visiting the world of the dead at night.

Another god singularly fortunate in the account his priests gave of him was Jeb's son, Osiris, whose cult survived into the Greco-Roman world. The priests taught that he was drowned in a furious flood, but that his magic-working wife, Isis, recalled him to life. He returned from the womb of the earth, revivifying all growing things in the process. But while he was the god of food-bearing nature, he was also the god of the dead. Food and Death—there were no more important values than these for the Egyptians.

Fig. 2.1. Pyramids of Gizeh, air view. The Great Pyramid (Vth Dynasty, *c*. 2500 B.C.) contains 6,250,000 tons of stone, yet the casing-blocks fit to ⅟₅₀th of an inch. The Egyptians sought stability; the Pyramids endured. (Photo courtesy Trans World Airlines, Inc.)

The solar temples were on a scale commensurate with the grandeur of a universal god. One at Abu-Sir was an unroofed terrace (300 feet by 240 feet) in the form of a truncated pyramid, surmounted by a 100-foot obelisk with a great altar in front. The walled precinct was approached from the east as befitted a sun-god's shrine; outside, in brick, was Osiris' solar boat.

We know much about funerary architecture. Two types of masonry tombs were in fashion, the earlier *mastaba* and the pyramid. The *mastaba* was a small truncated pyramid, usually containing two chambers, a chapel and the repository for the mummy. Gradually these chambers received elaborate architectural and sculptural ornaments.

As the kings increased in power and wealth and architects grew in experience, ability, and daring, more imposing royal tombs were built. At first one *mastaba* was superimposed on another in step-backs or terraces. The tapering effect of this construction led to another step, the full-fledged pyramid. But *mastabas* continued to be built to receive the remains of members of the royal family and the grandees of the realm.

The greater pyramids, which required millions of man-days to build and as an engineering achievement are still the wonder of mankind,

Fig. 2.2. King Mycerinus and His Queen, IVth Dynasty, *c.* 2525 B.C. The stiff frontality of the figures lends them great ceremonial dignity. (Boston, Museum of Fine Arts)

were built by the kings of the Fourth Dynasty. That of Khufu is the tallest (480 feet). That of Khafra, still set off at the end of a majestic portico which starts at the bank of the Nile, is the most magnificent, but that of Menkaura might have been still more beautiful if it had only been finished. The squarish blocks of stone, precision-cut, are joined together by no mortar. A pyramid was more than a tomb; it was the eternal dwelling place of the dead, and the inside of a pyramid is a place fit for a king, an amazing ensemble of corridors, staircases, chambers, chapels, and repositories. Someone has rightly called a pyramid an act of faith, faith in a life beyond this, in the Pharaoh as an incarnate god, in his right to exact that tremendous expenditure of capital, talent, and toil which went into its making. The pyramid of each king was surrounded by the *mastabas* of the great personages of his court, for it was part of Egyptian mortuary theology that those who had served the king in life should attend him also in death.

A temple for the worship of the king-god stood near the pyramid where he was buried. What remains of these temples as well as what is seen in the pyramid chambers themselves tell the story of the architectural triumphs of the Memphite era. The Egyptians were already acquainted with most of those elements which we are apt to think of as typical of Greek and Roman architecture. They used columns fluted and slightly convex in the lower part of the shaft, as well as the engaged column, that is, a pilaster, attached to a wall for decoration rather than for function. Beautiful capitals, carved with motifs from the native flora, chiefly the lotus flower, the palmetto, and the papyrus, surmounted these columns, while above the capitals ran an architrave of huge stones. The temple walls, like those of the pyramid chambers and of the earlier *mastabas,* were decorated with painted bas-reliefs, the central figure of which was the king.

Round sculpture, too, was in fashion, not only for the miniatures representing the army of workers, servants, and courtiers in attendance on the king in his tomb, but for life-size and lifelike statues, which are characterized by a massiveness and solidity which seem to defy time, a frontal posture which, although intentionally rigid, conveys the idea of motion, and an endeavor to draw an accurate likeness and give it individuality. The crouched scribe of the Louvre, the diorite Khafra at Cairo, and the bronze Pepi are among the noblest examples of statuary in any age. Yet these pyramid stones, these columns and statues were cut and carved with instruments of stone, copper, or bronze, for iron was still unknown. Painting had to wait several centuries before reaching its highest point.

Chapter 3/SUMERIANS
AND SEMITES

*

Early Sumer

We shall now examine the ancient civilization of the flatland, between and to either side of the Euphrates and the Tigris rivers, called Babylonia (from Babylon, its chief city) or Mesopotamia (Greek: the land between the rivers). Mesopotamia emerged substantially in its present form about 20,000 years ago while Paleolithic Man was building his civilization not only in Egypt but in the surrounding countries: Palestine and Syria to the west, Armenia to the north, Asia Minor to the northwest, and Kurdistan to the east. Alluvial deposits and sand washed from the sea formed this land and has since operated so steadily that the site of the city of Ur, which about 2000 B.C. was a seaport, today lies 125 miles inland.

Of the first Mesopotamian homeseekers we know nothing except that they came in Neolithic times, left a record of their existence in a thin-walled greenish-gray pottery, and disappeared about 5000 B.C., apparently driven out by invaders of Semitic stock. One such group, probably from Syria, settled well north of the Persian Gulf, eventually building such famed cities as Agade (hence Akkad), Babylon, and Kish, and (chiefly because they had copper, like the fine cast lions' heads

* Top of stele bearing Code of Laws of Hammurabi. (Paris, Louvre)

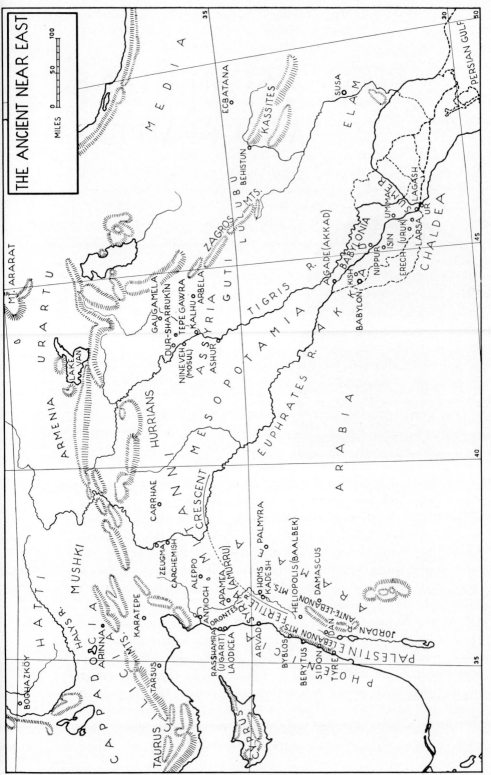

Fig. 3a. Map of the Ancient Near East

found at al-Ubaid) developing a superior culture. Another group—from Arabia, a great reservoir of manpower since the dawn of history—occupied the southern plain close to the Gulf of Persia.

While the Semites of Akkad rose to world power, the descendants of the Arabian immigrants succumbed in the fifth millennium to a new wave of dark-haired invaders, the Sumerians, after whom the Gulf Coast was named Sumer. From the fact that their private and public buildings in Sumer, although constructed of brick, resembled wooden structures and from their custom of worshiping their gods on the top of high towers, it has been inferred that in their premigration days they had lived in a forested and mountainous country. About 4500–4000 B.C. a common civilization existed from Susa in the foothills of the Iranian Plateau to Anau in the Russian Turkestan, and it seems likely that the Sumerians came from some point in that area. A Mesopotamian myth that invaders, half man and half fish, came to the coast of Sumer and introduced agriculture, metallurgy, and writing might very well mean that the Sumerians came to their new home by sea.

Our knowledge of Sumer comes mainly from archeology, and that of the last hundred years. Graves, skeletons, weapons, implements, and objets d'art unfold the essential traits of Sumerian life. Especially revealing are the fine arts: buildings, statues, reliefs, paintings, jewels, and the ubiquitous seal used as a signature to authenticate documents. Made of one kind or other of hard stone, in the shape of a cylinder a little more than an inch long and less than an inch in diameter, these seals bear deep designs which leave their imprint when rolled over a tablet of fresh clay. The receiving clay, the negative of the cylinder, becomes practically indestructible when baked. There are tens of thousands in existence, for every people exposed to Sumerian culture, even if as indirectly and remotely as the Persians, made use of this device. The best artists tried their hand at these fascinating miniatures. But the historian's interest is less in their artistic or esthetic quality than in the rich variety of subjects: gods, heroes, warriors, kings; agriculture, industry, and commerce; the animal kingdom and the kingdom of fable; legends, epics, theology; the development of the arts and sciences. Indeed it would be possible to reconstruct nearly every aspect of Sumerian life solely from the study of these precious little documents.

We have also the Sumerians' own words, written in their own hand, to tell us more fully of their deeds. The Sumerians invented a pictographic script, which developed into a syllabic system with a basic wedge-shaped (cf. Latin, cuneus) sign, hence its name cuneiform. Some three hundred combinations of this simple sign express every Sumerian syllable. The difficult problem of deciphering the script and the language was solved about 100 years ago in three stages through the accumulated contribution of several generations of scholars. The first cuneiform language to be deciphered was Persian. Philologists worked back through several links, from modern Persian to medieval, to ancient, up to the language of the earliest portions of the sacred books, the *Avesta,* composed long before the founding of the Persian Empire. The techniques developed in this search, and the knowledge gathered while exploring certain linguistic byways radiating from their main path, helped scholars in the second step—the rediscovery of the two most important ancient Semitic languages, Assyrian and Babylonian. Here the starting point was the use as steppingstones of known Semitic tongues, chiefly Arabic, Biblical Hebrew, Phoenician, and Aramaic. Finally Sumerian itself was deciphered, the more easily because Sumerian culture was the parent of most civilizations of the Near and Middle East.

Upon reaching their new home south of Akkad, the Sumerians converted it into a series of city-states—self-governing and independent communities, each centering around a town. The effect of the rise of cities can scarcely be overestimated. Suffice it to say that within the city defenses it was easier for men to find safety, practice the arts, accumulate wealth, and exchange ideas.

Since lower Mesopotamia contained neither stone nor wood, the Sumerians invented a new building material, brick—at first sun-dried, later baked. And since the whole country was exposed to floods, they built their towns and villages on artificial mounds. Gradually these mounds were made higher for defense. Thus rose the Mesopotamian walled towns, perched high above the surrounding flatland, centers of government and business and wartime refuge for the folk who in peacetime dwelt in open hamlets.

The most distinctive feature of the Sumerian cities was the *ziggurat,* a building rising to the sky in several tiers approached by staircases or ramps. The ziggurat was a substitute for the mountains of the ancestral homeland, on the summit of which was the altar for the worship of the chief local god. As fully developed, a ziggurat looked much like a modern stepped-back skyscraper or like a jagged pyramid. Highly impressive were these terraced structures, especially when viewed from a distance; the city-mound seemed both to provide a broad base and to emphasize their height. The best preserved ziggurat has been found in Ur. That of Babylon, built probably 2000 years later, may be called a larger edition. The Greek historian Herodotus, who saw it while traveling in search of material for his *History of the Persian Wars,* describes it as eight superimposed towers, 600 feet square at the base, ascended by a winding ramp, with seats for resting halfway up, and a sanctuary at the top served by a god-selected priestess. The sanctuary had no cult-statue, only a great richly-adorned bed and a golden table.

Fig. 3.1. The Tower of Babel, model. The Biblical edifice was a great temple-tower or ziggurat in Babylon, already ruined in the time of Alexander the Great. (E. Chiera, *They Wrote on Clay*. Chicago, 1956. Page 123.)

This architectural triumph, so symbolic of Sumero-Semitic civilization, appears in the Bible as the Tower of Babel, an accurate folk-memory of the Hebrews' Sumero-Semitic ancestors. The confusion of tongues with which God punished the builders is a symbol of the diffusion of the various later languages.

The ziggurat's chief priest had great power, not merely because he administered the wealth of the ziggurat and the other official temples, nor yet because as priest he could regulate the life and thought of the people, but chiefly because he was the god's representative. Since the god was the real king of the city, the chief priest was his *ishakku,* that is, priest and governor, the official in whose person church and state were combined as an indivisible whole. Each government was therefore a theocracy.

Irrigation was of vital importance in a country where the rainfall was scanty. By digging canals, some of which went from the Euphrates all the way to the Tigris, and by apportioning the increased water supply to the needs of every farm, the Sumerians converted the desert into the early paradise of the Bible. But since the canals of one city-state often interfered with those of another (indeed, at times some city-state left insufficient water for another city-state farther down the river), the Sumerian governments were continually at war, despite attempts to preserve peace by establishing hegemonies, a system by which certain city-states forced upon the others a kind of federal control combined with home rule and religious tolerance, in the latter case making a virtue of a necessity, since each Sumerian state was fanatically devoted to its local gods.

The earliest noteworthy stage of Sumerian civilization is the first Dynasty of Ur, the contents of whose royal graves reveal the culture of the period. We gather from the study of them that even before 2500 B.C. brick-making had become a big industry, masons built arches and vaults, jewelers worked carnelian, inlay workers produced beautiful decorations in shell, mother-of-pearl, and lapis lazuli, and goldsmiths made gold ornaments, vessels, weapons, and figurines. Silver artifacts were abundant, and copper was in everyday use. The craftsmanship displayed is so skilled as to postulate centuries of apprenticeship and technical development, while the revealed luxury and tenor of life presupposes a civilization of long standing, older and more developed than the contemporary culture of Egypt.

The contents of the royal graves at Ur prove the import of raw materials from abroad: gold from Elam, Cappadocia, or Syria; silver from Elam or Cilicia; copper from Oman or the Caucasus; lapis lazuli from the Far East; even the cement and limestone for the royal tombs and other substantial buildings were imported, as well as alabaster and diorite for the carvings with which they were adorned. And we find Sumerian goods and influence in every surrounding country: imitations of Sumerian mace-heads, and cylinder seals dating from about 3000 B.C. in Syria; buildings of Sumerian design in Assyria; jewelry in the Sumerian style southeast of the Caspian Sea. The Sumerian economy of the late fourth millennium was therefore based on close intercourse with the outside world, and imports were paid for not only with grain, dates, and other agricultural products, but also with luxury goods.

Sumer after the Flood

At some time after the beginning of the third millennium B.C., a catastrophe befell Sumer. A flood, immortalized in the Bible, descended upon the whole valley, destroying all but the highest towns, drowning men and beasts, dislocating life. The magnitude of the disaster was confirmed in a recent excavation by the discovery of a thick layer of mud, deposited by the flood, which would seem to indicate that the waters rose sixteen feet above the plain. The havoc was even greater in low-lying Akkad. Before long, a legend took form that the flood had been let loose by the heavenly powers to annihilate mankind.

Life was disrupted, whole regions abandoned; certain Sumerian rulers whose cities had been relatively undamaged took advantage of the catastrophe. They usurped the right to appoint the rulers of the cities they now controlled. One leader penetrated into Akkad itself, where he established a dynasty of his own in Kish, the largest Semitic center. That Sumerian civilization had preceded the conqueror is clear from the antediluvian palace at Kish, which was typically Sumerian in its monumental stairs, its massive brick columns, and its walls of inlaid slate. Sumerian rulers now first dominated a free Semitic people. Each conqueror called himself king, *Lugal* in Sumerian.

Military strength made possible the growth and expansion abroad of Sumerian culture. Surrounded by Semites, a hardier, more virile and warlike stock, the Sumerians were forced to self-defense. Pictorial and sculptural remains enable archeologists to reconstruct the Sumerian army. As early as the fourth millennium B.C. the army was composed of three corps, cavalry, infantry, and archers. The cavalry fought from four-wheeled chariots drawn by four asses, each chariot carrying beside the driver a warrior who threw light spears from a quiver attached to the front of the chariot. The infantry, wearing conical copper helmets, leather kilts, and long, heavy protective cloaks, fought phalanx-like with short-handled spears. An archer corps is inferred from arrowheads and fragments of decorated bows. Other weapons in use were pike-heads of copper two feet long, maces with pear-shaped stone heads, and sharp cutting adzes. Eventually the chariot was used for transportation only, not for fighting. But the phalanx had become a more compact machine, consisting of six close ranks of men, helmeted and armed with pikes and axes, the front rank carrying rectangular shields designed to protect the whole body. Though citizen levies made up a Sumerian army, its core was the king's guard of paid volunteers. Defeat usually meant annihilation: prisoners, soldiers and civilians alike, were enslaved, slaughtered or held for ransom, while a captured town was stripped bare and then destroyed. This ruthlessness, of which the chief sufferers were the Sumerian city-states themselves, probably contributed to the decay of Sumerian civilization.

Why did Sumer fall? The most important reason was doubtless the perennial wars. No suzerain-city was strong enough to suppress all opposition among the vanquished, while no subject-city was so weak that it might not in turn overthrow its master. Second, the Semites of Akkad, once they absorbed all that the Sumerians had taught them, asserted themselves as equal or superior to their teachers. The Semitic city of Kish, for example, three times acquired hegemony over Sumer, only to lose it each time and to see its native princes replaced with Sumerian kings. Third, the hill peoples of the north and northeast, especially Elam, took a hand in the game of war, succeeding more than once in casting off the yoke of both Semites and Sumerians and in establishing their own dominance over Akkad and Sumer alike.

Relations between two cities, Lagash and Umma, illustrate inter-Sumerian rivalries. Lagash began to assert itself in proportion as its earlier suzerain, Ur, was decaying. Abandoning the title *patesi,* meaning local ruler and priest, its rulers took that of *Lugal.* The first Lugal, Ur-Nanshe (*c.* 2600 B.C.), fortified the capital and dug new irrigation canals. His grandson Eannatum subdued Umma, which had repeatedly interfered with the canal system of Lagash, conquered Ur, Uruk, and Kish, and came to dominate so many Semitic cities that he could boast of being lord of Sumer and Akkad. But Umma rebelled, seized the key canal and defeated Eannatum's successor. When finally the next Lugal of Lagash, Entemena, recaptured the rebellious city, he forestalled further rebellion by depriving Umma of home rule. Not long afterwards both Lagash and Umma became vassals of Kish. Subject to a common master, they lived in peace and enjoyed reciprocal rights and privileges.

Since the suzerain was far away, the clergy and gentry of Lagash, grossly misabusing their powers, began to oppress the poor. For example, the high priest would, as a document puts it, "come into the garden of a poor mother and take wood therefrom," or "gather tax in fruit therefrom." At last, sometime about 2500 B.C., a strong leader, Urukagina, with lower-class support, revolted against the king of Kish, who had tolerated these exactions, and, proclaiming himself king, legislated against them. He reduced burial fees by four-fifths, forbade the clergy to use temple lands as their own, and defined certain inalienable rights of the poor. A poor man was given protection against forced sale or sale at less than a just price. Urukagina's own words, "he gave liberty to his people," aptly summarize his humanitarian endeavors.

But Lagash was not allowed to enjoy peace for long. It fell before a sudden and unprovoked attack by Lugal-zaggisi, the patesi of Umma. As told in a plaintive song which has come down to us, the men of Umma burned every district, killed many of the inhabitants, carried away the precious metals and stones, desecrated and set fire to the shrines. They even slew Urukagina, making off with the image of his special protector, the god Ningirsu; and the poem closes with a curse upon Lugal-zaggisi.

Despite this indictment from Lagash, Lugal-zaggisi was a constructive and intelligent ruler. Since, like Urukagina, he was a vassal of the king of Kish, his attack upon Lagash was open rebellion. Having conquered Lagash, he pressed his advantage until he ruled all Sumer, partly by taking a leaf out of his rival's book and championing the poor against the priests and landowners. He upheld Sumerian nationalism against Semitic Akkad. He moved the seat of government from the upstart city of Umma to the more ancient and holy city of Erech. By this gesture towards national union, he won over those who realized that only by abolishing local feuds could the Sumerians hope to remain a free people before the growing power of Akkad. Feeling stronger than any previous Sumerian king, Lugal-zaggisi raided the countries north and west as far away as Syria. He may have reached, or at any rate come near, the Mediterranean Sea, for in the exaggerated language of Oriental kings he boasted that he had subdued all the lands from the Lower Sea (Persian Gulf) to the Upper.

The Clash between Semites and Sumerians

This national policy might perhaps have saved Sumer had it not been for Sargon. This Akkadian, who allegedly had been exposed as an infant, rescued by workmen, and brought up as a gardener, about 2350 B.C. made himself patesi of Agade, threw off the overlordship of Kish, and became king of all Akkad. His next act was the conquest of every country east, north, and west. He then moved against his strongest enemy, Sumer. The wisdom of Lugal-zaggisi's policy now became apparent, for, in the great struggle of Semites against Sumerians, no less than fifty Sumerian city-states stood fast by him, although to no avail. The Semites were stronger and Sargon more able. Sumer paid for its centuries-old rivalries by becoming a province of Sargon's Semitic empire.

Sargon and his successors, chiefly because Semitic culture was essentially Sumerian, tried to conciliate the Sumerian cities, especially their priests and ruling class. For nearly two thousand years the Semites had dwelt within the orbit of Sumerian civilization, adopting as their own the Sumerians' arts, sciences, legends, literature, even their religion. As the Romans borrowed Greek culture to disseminate it over the Mediterranean world, so the Semites spread a form of Sumerian culture throughout their empire, over Palestine and Syria, to the upper Euphrates and Tigris, to Assyria, Elam, and beyond. From Sargon's time, Sumerian culture exerted a more profound influence over the whole Middle East.

Although Sumer profited from Sargon's benevolence, it never acquiesced in his rule. It revolted against Sargon himself and against his son, Naram-Sin, administrator and soldier, whose victory over some Zagros mountaineers, the Lulubu, is commemorated by a handsome stele.

A day came when the Guti from the northeast destroyed the Sargonid empire. Anarchy ensued, but eventually the Guti consolidated their power both in Sumer and Akkad. If they came and conquered, they were in turn conquered by the superior culture of Sumer, for before long they too adopted the Sumerian gods. Moreover, perhaps because they had no flair for administration, they restored home rule, appointing Sumerians as patesis.

The archives of Gudea, one of the patesis of Lagash under the Guti regime (*c.* 2070 B.C.), reveal that these local governors made commerce and the building of temples their chief job. Gudea itemizes temple material imported from every country between the Persian Gulf, the Mediterranean, the Black Sea, and the Kurdistan highlands, while business documents of the same period show that Sumerian patesis had again internationalized industry and commerce. But although prosperity returned, Sumerian nationalists, unreconciled to any foreign domination, expelled the Guti, and once more Sumerians, the third Dynasty of Ur, ruled over Sumer and Akkad.

This meant that for the third time the governors of Ur succeeded in becoming kings. Ur-Nammu, the founder of the line (*c.* 2060–*c.* 1955), realizing that the Semites were a majority and were better soldiers than his own Sumerians, opened all state offices to his erstwhile enemy, granting the Semites equality. To improve agriculture and commerce he rebuilt the entire irrigation canal system and excavated four new ship-canals. Ships from the gulf or river ports could then unload at the docks of imperial Ur. He also built or restored temples in every city, almost in the same spirit in which medieval cities built their cathedrals. His most pretentious buildings were the city walls of Ur and its mighty ziggurat.

Following an old precedent which deified the living king, Ur-Nammu demanded worship as a god. The capital obliged, for a document described him as "the merciful lord who brought prosperity to Ur," but Erech and most other districts refused. His son Shulgi (2038–1990 B.C.), however, was acknowledged a god both by his fellow-Sumerians and by the Semites of Akkad.

Shulgi continued his father's policies, keeping the warlike border states well in hand. Susa, the chief city of Elam, for instance, was loyal throughout his fifty-eight-year reign. But Babylon, as yet a town of no importance, must have caused him serious trouble, for he laid waste its chief temple. Quantities of brick and numerous foundation-tablets bearing his name, found throughout Sumer and Akkad, show that he was a great builder.

Shulgi's long reign affords an opportunity to study the empire's organization. From his capital at Ur, the king set policy and appointed local minor officials and governors, who were left wide discretion. Except in Nippur, the holy city where the chief Sumerian god, Enlil, was worshiped, the governorship was no longer hereditary, an indication that the central government had become stronger. The regular dispatch of imperial couriers from the capital to every part of the empire implies that the roads were kept in repair and that the post was probably developed as a method of imperial control. Over these same roads every district sent to the capital and to the chief national temples its taxes, paid in kind, which demanded uniform weights and measures. These were supervised by Nannar's priests at Ur, in the interest of both taxpayers and government. These policies betoken a renascence in industry and trade and more prosperity than in any previous period of Mesopotamian history. Private business records preserved in clay tablets fully substantiate this view.

Half a century after the death of Shulgi, barbarians from the north and east destroyed the empire. While new Semitic groups from Amurru (Syria) overran Akkad, the Elamites devastated Sumer in revenge for their many years of servitude. Ibbi-Sin (1972–1947 B.C.), last king of the glorious Third Dynasty, was taken captive, and Ur itself was laid waste.

The history of Sumer as an independent people ended with Ibbi-Sin's fall. For a hundred years or longer two cities, Isin and Larsa, vainly strove to restore the nation. Having wasted its youth in fratricidal wars, Sumer in its old age died for lack of blood. Yet it may be that its extinction was due even more to the enervating effect upon mountaineers of the low, heavy, torrid atmosphere of a sea-level plain.

Thus it was easy for a new conqueror, Hammurabi, to crush Isin and Larsa and to annex Sumer. But even in its last years Sumer continued to cultivate arts and letters. Its architects could still produce beautiful buildings, its sculptors carve statues of delicate though decadent craftsmanship, and its scholars compile from ancient sources a record of the nation's achievements, especially in religion and politics. Sumer is now but a memory, but the seeds it sowed continue to bear fruit in the world.

Sumerian Society

Sumerian society embraced three classes: the nobility; a broad second class comprising professional men, traders, merchants, farmers, and laborers; and slaves. The principle of *noblesse oblige* worked two ways, for while a crime against a noble received harsher punishment than one against a simple burgher, while a noble injuring a non-noble was punished more severely than a law-breaker from an inferior class. In general, however, the law of an eye for an eye and a tooth for a tooth probably regulated the awarding of punishment.

Slavery as it existed in Greece, Rome, or the United States was unknown in Sumer. At its worst it resembled serfdom, since the so-called slave could own property, engage in business in his own name and for profit, borrow money, and buy his freedom, and his evidence before the law was as good as a freeman's. A debtor might in default of payment indenture his wife, son, or daughter to his creditor for a three-year period. Parents might, by mutual agreement, sell their children as slaves.

The Sumerians worked out humane and progressive legal principles. For instance, a rebellious slave was merely sold, whereas a thousand years later, in the Semitic kingdom of Hammurabi, he had his ears cut off. The courts of law were either civil, under king or governor, or ecclesiastical, under the priests of the temples. Verbal evidence was permissible, but the perfect proof was the tablet, the original written record of the sale, loan, contract, legacy, marriage, or adoption under dispute. Every sentence was recorded in writing and filed in the court's archives. Once the verdict was so recorded, a judge could not reverse it, although appeal was allowed to the king's superior court.

The position of women was, for that age, dignified. The family elders arranged marriages. As a survival from wife-purchase, the bridegroom gave his intended father-in-law a gift of money. The wedding ceremony was simple, merely recording the contract in writing under seal. The bride controlled her dowry absolutely and was not responsible for her husband's premarital debts, but only for those contracted after their marriage. Like unmarried women, a wife could engage in business for herself. The husband could divorce her easily, especially if she were barren; on the other hand, divorce for her was difficult unless she could prove that she was a good woman. The Sumerian attitude towards adultery is a comment on the evolution of ethics. A peccadillo in the earlier days, adultery had become by the time of the Third Dynasty of Ur a capital offense punishable by drowning.

If a woman, divorced for sterility, instead of returning to her father, continued to live with her husband and he remarried, the second wife was regarded as socially inferior, for she might be asked to wash the first wife's feet and carry her chair to the temple. To forestall her downfall, a sterile wife might, without imputation of eccentricity or unconventionality, give her husband one of her own slave girls as concubine. At a man's death, his property was divided equally among his wife and children, although a son might claim his share of the inheritance in his father's lifetime, as did the Prodigal Son.

The gods too had families, Sumerian style. Pious women attached themselves to a god's household, for Sumerian gods were anthropomorphic, with human needs. The sisterhood had three orders, the first of one woman only, the legitimate first wife of the god, a lady of the highest rank, considered too holy to set foot in a tavern. Thus the great king Sargon married one of his daughters to the god Nannar of Ur. In the second order were the god's concubines, living in the convent next the temple but allowed to marry mortal men and engage in business.

The sisters of the third and largest order were temple prostitutes, whose status was a development of a woman's ideal of dedicating her virginity to the god.

The Sumerians believed in a multitude of benevolent, immortal, heaven-dwelling gods who, like the earth, the sea, and the stars, were made in the process of Creation. The gods' design might be thwarted by evil spirits. All the gods were worshiped everywhere in Sumer, but each city had chosen one as its special king and protector: a sky-god Anu in Uruk, a weather-god Enlil in Nippur, a moon-god Nannar in Ur, and so on, stood out above the others, since each had for his province one of the three principal parts of the cosmos: Anu, Heaven; Ki, the Earth; Ea, the Sea. There was also a minor triad everywhere reverenced for its power: a moon-god Sin, a sun-god Shamash, and a storm-god Adad. Of the other gods Ishtar, the daughter of Anu, was under one aspect the most lovable, for she was "the kindly," goddess of fertility and pleasure, but also of war when war became a common business of the Sumerian states.

A god's supremacy did not depend so much on his own attributes or functions as on the power of the city-state which had adopted him. It is therefore difficult to speak of any clear-cut or permanent hierarchy of gods. Divine supremacy shifted with the shift in political supremacy. This is best seen in the fortune of Marduk. When Hammurabi made Babylon the imperial state, he exalted its god Marduk. Clearly Babylonian supremacy would be more glorious, more solid, and more readily acknowledged if all other gods bowed to Marduk. Accordingly there rose a new theology to explain how Marduk inherited the power. Through cowardice, Anu lost his supremacy, failing to execute his father's command to tame Tiamat (Chaos). But Marduk vanquished chaos; he produced order. In moral terms, that meant that he established justice. The admiring gods held a banquet to celebrate his victory and, while drunk, elected him their chief. He outranked any previous god, as Babylon outranked any previous hegemon.

A city's chief god was its real king and protector. Since he was thought to have all men's needs and to live a man's life, his temple was an enlarged replica of a Sumerian house, with altar, rooms for worship, sleeping, and dining, offices, counting rooms, and storerooms for donations and taxes in kind. Some temples included shrines of other gods, regarded as servants of the chief god.

Since the gods would do no favor unless coaxed with gifts or magic, public and private sacrifice was central to the worship. Public sacrifices of meat, bread, dates, milk, beer, or wine were offered daily. Private sacrifices were infrequent but expensive. The animal was regarded as a substitute for the sacrifice of the worshiper himself.

The upkeep of the larger temples, with their multitude of priests, assistants, and servants, was expensive, and the priests were often greedy. Some of the priests could conjure away evil by magic; others were soothsayers who read omens from the shape and peculiarities of the liver of sacrificed animals, from any kind of accident, or from unusual phenomena, all of which were classified in a complex and allegedly infallible science. Astrology was practiced too, although its heyday was to come much later, in the Second Babylonian Empire.

The Sumerians developed the idea of sin, regarded rather as a secular offense against society than as a theological one. Goodness, too, was a secular virtue, an action which promoted social well-being. If the chief god rewarded virtue and punished sin, he did so chiefly as king of the city. But since the Sumerians with their genius for religious speculation were bound to evolve a higher morality, their concepts of virtue and sin were subject to change. One of their penitential psalms begins: "Lord, my sins are many and my faults are grave."

The rewards for virtue were strictly material. Punishments were temporal, too, for although the Sumerians had notions of immortality, they had no concept of Heaven or Hell, thinking of man's spirit after death as living like a ghost. It was good insurance to place food and drink in the graves, since if the spirits were hungry, they might haunt highways and attack travelers. The deified kings were regarded as benevolent forces. When the tendency spread of regarding the chief god as the Sun, it was thought that kings after death became stars.

The Sumerian gods in time shed their primitive materialism to become providential and cosmic. In Sumer we first encounter the myth of the vegetation goddess, who dies each year when the rivers are low, plants wither, and winter comes; but rises when the buds swell and springtime returns. She it is who restores fertility to nature and sustenance to the human race. As religious concepts became more refined, litanies and invocations became more tender and delicate; some are deeply moving. We read them in countless clay tablets and hear their echo in the earlier books of the Old Testament.

Sumerian temples were centers of both religious and secular education. The Nippur temple had a large theological and liturgical library. Of Sumer's many contributions to theology, two deserve special mention: the elaboration of the doctrine of the Mother-Goddess and the development of the belief in the wrath of the gods, envisaged as a person sent down to chastise man. As a counterpart of this belief there was developed in the temple school of Ur the doctrine of a savior who interceded for men, identified as Ibbi-Sin, the last king of the Third Dynasty of Ur.

The training of scribes was the principal aim of education. Since commercial transactions to be valid had to be recorded in writing and since written records were indispensable in the law courts, literacy was prized. School tablets, found among the ruins of temples, reveal the progressive stages of the writing course for future scribes, which arranged the signs and their respective phonetic values, as we should say today, alphabetically, with short simple sentences, honorific titles and business formulae, grammar-rules, principles of copying, Sumerian-Semitic dictionaries, lists of weights and measures, multiplication and division tables, and tables of square and cubic roots. Geometry received special attention in this land crisscrossed by canals and in need of resurvey when floods obliterated property lines.

Among the professions we find surveyors of canals and estates, architects who have left plans of houses and towns, geographers who drew maps for the kings, doctors acquainted with the virtues of herbs even though they might depend on magic to exorcise human and animal ills, surgeons who were often punished by law if their crude operations failed.

The Sumerians were an ingenious and resourceful people whose wits were sharpened by their extensive business experience and, even more, by their relentless struggle to keep their mighty rivers in check. Their greatest practical achievement was the reclamation of the desert. They showed extraordinary skill in digging and building canals, many of which were navigable. Their greatest engineering problem was to transfer the surplus water of the mighty Euphrates to the shallow bed of the Tigris in order to irrigate the Tigris valley. The masters who conceived and executed this plan deserve an honorable place in the roster of the world's engineers. Talent, organization, vigilance were the keys to the Sumerians' prosperity; the smooth working of the endless miles of canals depended on the efficiency of an army of surveyors, engineers, builders, diggers, watchmen, and supervisors. The place of the government in this conquest over nature is obvious: by it and through it the energies of the individual as well as of the whole nation were harnessed to the common good. For example, each owner had to keep up the canal bank abutting his property, just as the grantee of royal land in Spanish Louisiana had to maintain the levee in front of his concession.

Whether or not the Sumerians invented the wheel, one of the most revolutionary inventions that has ever affected the life of man, they certainly used wheeled carts for transportation and wheeled chariots for war; and to date there is no evidence of the wheel before their time. They also seem to have been the inventors of a plow with a seed distributor attached, to do two jobs at once. They imported gold, copper, ivory, fine woods, and precious stones which skilled craftsmen turned into goods of exquisite artistry. Their merchants had representatives in distant lands, transacted business by correspondence, transferred accounts by letters of credit, and sometimes commissioned their sales to brokers who received a share of the profits.

Sumerian literature was essentially religious. It abounded in epic poetry with the usual heroic repertory of journeys to unknown lands or to the nether world, of brave deeds and breath-taking exploits, of gods and goddesses coming to the hero's assistance, of strife among men and among gods. Its best work is the *Epic of Gilgamesh,* which contains the story of the Flood. In it, the angry gods decide to destroy the human race, but the god Enki betrays the secret to Utnapishtim, advising him to build a boat to save himself, his family, and his goods. The account, like the Biblical one, tells of taking animals aboard the ark and sending forth a bird (not a dove but a crow) whose non-return presages the end of the flood.

In the story of the *Descent of Ishtar* into the nether world, Ishtar passes through seven gates before being admitted to the place assigned her in the Land of No Return. At each gate the gatekeeper strips her of a part of her dress until she stands naked in the cold of winter. These imaginative scenes are, of course, an allegory of the process by which nature, as winter deepens, is denuded of leaves, loses warmth, and all but dies.

The remains of Sumerian literature have not yet been fully recovered, for there are still tens of thousands of tablets to be deciphered, in a slow but steady process, which constantly adds to our knowledge. Perhaps when all have been read, the Sumero-Semitic world will be known as fully as the Egyptian, and the new evidence may very well prove that the Sumerian people stand second to none as builders of civilization.

By 1950 B.C. the Sumerians had begun to disappear. They had tutored the Semites in the ways of civilization only to perish at their hands. But something of Sumer proved imperishable. Its culture lived on in the religion, thought, art, and institutions of its destroyers. Indeed Sumer did not die until it had Sumerized the Semites. We shall see other nations dying politically but living in the culture of their conquerors, for example, Greece and Rome. The Sumerian language continued to be studied as classic until about the time of Christ. Much of Sumerian thought and literature, of religion and ethics, carried westward by those Semitic tribes later known as Hebrews, has been transmitted to modern nations. Other elements of Sumerian culture have come down the ages through other channels unrelated to the Bible, for example, the arch, the strange science of hepatoscopy (the examination of the livers of sacrificed animals) which the Etruscans carried over to Italy, the syncretism of Ishtar and Aphrodite, the lunar calendar, the division of the circle into 360 degrees, and the splitting of the hour into sixty minutes.

Hammurabi

Five descendants of those invaders from Amurru who had seized the principality of Babylon had ruled over that city when in about 1728 B.C. a prince of the same line, Hammurabi, ascended the throne. An extraordinarily able man, he broadened his inconspicuous kingdom into a larger and more powerful empire than that of any Sumerian king before him. His first step towards the attainment of this goal was the absorption of Akkad, where, since he was of Semitic stock, the people accepted him as one of their own and, when he went on to attack Sumer, gave him their unstinted support, regarding him as a heaven-sent leader in the centuries-old struggle with their Sumerian rivals. The joint victory of Hammurabi and Akkad, which eventually embraced Elam, Mitanni, Assyria, and the lands bordering on the Mediterranean, marked the end of the Sumerian era and the definitive ascendancy of the Semites in the Mesopotamian plain.

The administrator in Hammurabi was as good as the general. He did not introduce any new method of government: his genius was rather to adapt, expand, or consolidate the institutions handed down by his Sumerian and Semitic ancestors. His correspondence with his provincial governors show him giving the most varied instructions on finances, management of the royal estates, troop-movements, law, religion, or canal maintenance.

His genius is seen best in his famous code, a compilation of 285 laws governing Babylonian society. The stirring discovery of this document by the French in 1901 at once unrolled a new world before our eyes, the world of Hammurabi. Later discoveries have shown that Hammurabi's compilation is a larger, revised edition of previous Sumerian codes. This code shows justice being administered by a court system allowing appeal to the court of the king, where he himself presided, assisted by a jury of elders. The courts admitted evidence either by witnesses or by the parties to the suit under oath.

Punishment is minutely detailed: sometimes corporal, sometimes financial, frequently drowning, crucifixion, or burning at the stake. The death penalty had been rare among the Sumerians; its frequency in the heterogeneous kingdoms of Hammurabi may denote either lower morality or more absolutism. It was inflicted for banditry, robbery, adultery with a married woman, incest, harboring runaway slaves and false accusation, besides a number of lesser crimes. Punitive retribution in kind (an eye for an eye) was regarded as a deterrent of crime: for father-beating, amputation of fingers; for striking a superior, sixty lashes. Punishment was applied even in cases in which there was no criminal intent, but only negligence or bad luck: death for the builder whose house collapses and kills the owner; if it kills the owner's son, the builder's son too must die. The ferocity of these penalties may imply that they represent a maximum or that they are not compulsory. Perhaps the judges could use discretion, awarding a lighter punishment when they saw fit.

Property and commerce were fully protected. A landlord received two thirds of the crop, the renter one third. While the latter was responsible for any impairment of the estate and for any ill-treatment or loss of the stock, the landlord was responsible for maintaining the canals and ditches passing through his property. Since these were community assets, the care of them could not be shunted from renter to renter. If floods or drought caused crop failure, the farmer was forgiven debts and interest.

The code regulated relations between employer and employee, chiefly by establishing maximum wages, service-charges, and penalties for bad work: if a surgical operation results in the patient's death, the surgeon must die; if the patient loses an eye in an operation, the surgeon loses his fingers.

In general, townsfolk were better protected than farmers, for craftsmen could legally set up guilds, and bankruptcy regulations were mild. Thirty-three percent interest was allowed on loans of grain and produce, and 20 percent on loans of silver bullion. Coinage was unknown.

Monogamy was the only legal form of marriage. Woman was a free agent, much freer than she was in Greece or in early Rome. Her dowry was always hers, to dispose of as she pleased. She could appear as witness in a court of law. She had her own dignity and rights in marital relations. If a husband divorced a barren wife, he had to return her dowry. If her husband's cruel slanders caused her to refuse him her favors, she might divorce him and receive back her dowry. But she might not sin with impunity; if she neglected her house or belittled her husband, he might either divorce her without return of dowry or reduce her to maidservant and take another wife.

The code established three categories of population: free, semifree, and slaves. As in Sumer, this hierarchy of social status entailed a corresponding scale of rights and duties. For example, if a free man was killed in a brawl, the homicide was obliged to pay the family half a mina; if the victim was semi-free, a third of a mina. The cost of a surgical operation on a free man was ten shekels, on a semifree man five, on a slave two.

Most slaves were taken in war. They were the absolute property of their masters, who could sell them or free them at will. They were branded, but they had certain rights. With savings accumulated from gratuities or outside work in their spare time, they might buy their liberty. If a male slave married a free woman—which was legal—the children became free automatically at his death.

Hammurabi had an effective means of keeping lawbreakers in check; he held responsible both the officials and the community where the offense was committed. For example, if the city failed to capture a brigand, his victim was compensated. The penalty for an altered judgment was twelve times the fine assessed in the original verdict, plus expulsion of the judge.

While Hammurabi's laws are less humane than the laws of Sumer, they are in turn more humane than the laws of Assyria, which represent a later development of the parent Sumerian code.

Chapter 4/DECLINE AND REBIRTH OF EGYPT,

2200–1344 B.C.

*

Feudal Age and Middle Kingdom

About 2200 B.C. signs appeared that the hold of the Memphite kings was weakening. There was in the making a revolution, that once its full course had run, changed the character of Egyptian society and of the monarchy itself. The king lost the power to appoint his ministers and therewith the capacity to control their actions. The prime ministership became hereditary and increasingly independent of the crown, with expanded prerogatives and new functions, until the king became a figurehead.

The nome superintendents began to rule for life and to appoint their sons as successors, each incumbent usurping more power, calling himself not royal agent but governor, count, or prince. By forced donations, simulated purchase, or undisguised usurpation, these local political rulers became also owners of all the land in their nomes, finally emerging as minor kings under the nominal suzerainty of the helpless pharaoh. The temples, too, usurped royal powers and developed into

* Pillar from Temple of Karnak, section.

principalities where every farm plantation, village, and person was fiscally and politically subject to them. In brief, royal absolutism was superseded by a feudal system.

Having assumed royal power, the ruling princes and priests were looked upon as incarnate sons of the gods and as heavenly providence itself transplanted on earth to watch over the people's welfare. The local ruler, not the king, now supplied the sanction for oaths and became the object of prayers. Unchecked by the weak central authority, these local chieftains raised bands of mercenaries, chiefly from the Semitic populations of Arabia, Palestine, and Syria, to enlarge their kingdoms or to strengthen their defenses. Thus the unity of the kingdom was broken; the Two Lands split from each other and within themselves.

Gradually, however, certain powerful warlords gained the upper hand over a number of nomes. The most successful was a prince of Thebes who, having acquired pre-eminence over most of Upper Egypt, usurped the name of Horus and the title of Son of Ra, thus becoming *de facto* king. By 2000 B.C. the XIth Dynasty had regained the southern kingdom. The final and formal integration of the two sections was effected by Amenemhet II of the XIIth Dynasty (1929–1894 B.C.). The pharaohs of this dynasty advanced the border for a better protection against Nubians, Semites, and Libyans; improved irrigation, especially in the Fayum; made the country more prosperous than it had ever been before; fostered the arts, especially architecture, and, in short, were mainly responsible for that glorious material and intellectual renascence frequently called the Golden Age of Egypt.

A new monarchy and a new Egypt rose from the turmoil of the feudal age. Even though the king reduced the local lords to obedience, his authority was no longer absolute. Compromising with the new forces, he allowed the feudal lords to retain the land they had appropriated and the troops they had raised, on condition that they give him a share of the revenue and the use of the troops on demand. Before long he was strong enough to punish recalcitrant vassals, to suppress their new titles, and to make them realize that loyalty to him was to their advantage. His riches, too, multiplied, chiefly because his chancery, in full control of an expanded bureaucracy, discovered new sources of taxation and more effective controls over the nobles. On the frequent occasions when from this time on the census was taken, the landlord had to register the number of his houses and the names of himself and his entire household, including serfs, to provide the king with a complete up-to-date inventory of all houses and men, with their fiscal and military obligations.

In his effort to break the princes, the king won the support of the masses, tired of the robbery, bloodshed, and general insecurity of the feudal period. The literature of the time shows how strongly the people hoped, if not for actual relief in this life, at least for some form of compensation in a life to come.

Human dignity was envisaged in Egypt in terms of immortality. During the Old Kingdom the king alone was considered immortal, for he alone enjoyed the benefit of certain magical rites through which he was, after death, identified with Osiris. Hence those time-challenging monuments, the pyramids, which preserved his body forever in godlike grandeur. Gradually, as the king allowed his family and court to build their tombs around his, the belief prevailed that those who received this favor received also the gift of immortality. They too became Osiris. The grant of immortality entailed the rare privilege of disposing of one's landed estates at will, that is, of bequeathing them to one's family.

The local potentates of the feudal age usurped religious as well as political rights, serving the chief local god as priests and, as such, becoming incarnate sons of that god, and controlling the holy formulas which, by identifying them with Osiris, made them immortal. Like the former kings, they granted this prerogative to their families and administrative officers. By these steps all nobles acquired the divinity and immortality formerly monopolized by the king.

Finally even the common man achieved posthumous divinity and immortality. No elaborate or costly ceremony was needed; it was enough to inscribe his name on a wooden tablet or an inexpensive vase of clay together with the words, "Osiris justified, lord of fealty." Since with the grant of divinity went its twin right of disposing of one's plot of land, both state and Heaven confirmed the last will of every Egyptian. This was progress for the common man. There was still class inequality during the Middle Kingdom, but religious equality and its corollary, personal freedom, had been achieved. The peasant had the guarantee that his property would remain in the family; the artisan was no longer a slave in the factories of king, prince, or temple.

With this improved status of the masses, the pharaoh came again into his own. As guardian of the rights of both rich and poor, he commanded universal loyalty. The restored national monarchy thus assumed a constitutional aspect.

Art and Literature in the Middle Kingdom

The age of civil wars was not conducive to the creating of great art, but when peace and prosperity returned, art flourished anew. Funerary architecture followed the Old Kingdom style, but pyramids were smaller, sometimes with unbaked brick cores. The porticoes, courts, chapels, and temples connected with the new pyramids became more pretentious and complex. The landed barons of Upper Egypt had their tombs excavated in the rock of the steep cliffs flanking the river. Since every man was now immortal, the number of substantial tombs increased. Even the common man spent all he had to make his last resting place as beautiful and comfortable as he could.

Of temple and palace architecture of the Middle Kingdom there remain but few examples, chiefly because later pharaohs destroyed the monuments of this period to make room for their own grandiose structures. Temples were built on the Old Kingdom plan, but a new type of column-capital was introduced, consisting of two or four heads of the god Hathor with cow ears, above which stood a flat abacus. Karnak was the greatest architectural center of the middle period. The temple of Amon with its "proto-Doric" columns was the most conspicuous monument of the twentieth century B.C. Sculpture was not unworthy of the best Old Kingdom traditions. Still, as always, at the service of the king and the court, it continued to produce realistic personal portraits. Painting was freer and less conventional than in the previous era. Many scenes illustrate the wars of the feudal lords among themselves and those waged by the king to reassert his authority.

Whereas we depend chiefly on art to reconstruct the life and thought of the Old Kingdom, we can study the Middle Kingdom from a considerable body of surviving literature. Prose and poetry are already differentiated. Poetry is more lyrical, with recurrent alliteration and symmetrical phrasing or parallel ideas, and usually religious, thus preceding by a thousand years the Biblical poetic pattern. In the poem *Dialogue of a Despairing Man with his Soul,* the soul argues that death should cause no fear and asserts that rich tombs, magical formulas, and funerary offerings are all vanity. This marks an intellectual advance over earlier materialism. In a number of prophetic poems a wise man comes before the king to warn him that calamities will fall upon the land but that a successor will arise who will bring back the good times.

The Song of the Harpist has a light and clearly secular tone: "Where are the kings of yesteryear? No man has ever returned from his grave to apprise us of his fate. Since all things are vanity and life is fleeting, let us enjoy pleasure." In a half-moralizing, half-satiric prose genre called *Instructions,* a father tries to instill wisdom into his son, and the scribe's occupation is glorified.

Popular literature is represented by adventure stories, like *The Story of Sinuhe,* a romantic tale of an Egyptian prince who conquers the bravest Syrian warrior in a duel. It is a nationalistic story, glorifying the pharaoh and bringing out the cultural superiority of Egypt over

Asia. In *The Story of the Shipwreck,* the direct ancestor of Sinbad the Sailor tells what befell him during a trip to the mines and his shipwreck at the Serpent Isle off the Punt, and his joy in returning home to his children. *The Story of the Two Brothers* tells of a certain Biti, who was hounded by his brother's wife for having refused to sleep with her, and how, after a series of adventures, he is incarnated as the king's son, finally ascending the throne. Other stories tell how humble peasants gain the king's ear and tell him of their hard lot. One fable tells of the quarrel between the head and the body over their respective importance—anticipating by many centuries the apologue of Menenius Agrippa to end a strike in Rome.

The adventure stories reflect among other things the enlarged horizon of Egyptian enterprise. Having restored central authority, the Theban kings began to expand abroad. In their struggle against the feudal barons, they had rebuilt their army around a corps of conscript levies and well-paid loyal mercenaries. The army's chief function was to restrain the barbarous Negro and Negroid nomads to the south and to keep open the roads which from the first cataract at Aswan radiated towards Nubia and the Red Sea. To satisfy the luxurious and wealthy court taste, an uninterrupted flow of gold, ivory, skins, and ostrich feathers from Nubia was required. We have evidence that Egyptian merchants made large profits in this trade. Twelfth-dynasty pharaohs waged aggressive war against Nubia, expanding ever further, first with the establishment at the second cataract of forts to protect shipping and to guard desert roads, than with the conquest of the region between the second and the third cataracts, the establishment of fortified towns, and the stationing of twelve garrisons.

Under royal protection, Egyptian merchants sailed down the Red Sea to the Punt to buy ivory, gems, incense, and myrrh. The copper mines and turquoise fields of the Sinai were exploited intensively; as the natives were organized in robber bands, the precious freight had to be convoyed homeward with troops. In the broad neck of land where Egypt is connected with Asia, Amenemhet I (1991–1961 B.C.) built a wall to keep Semitic marauders away from the rich Delta crops. When the wall proved ineffective, the energetic Senusret III (1878–1840 B.C.) led an expedition into Palestine to attack the foe in his lair. Peaceful commercial relations continued with Byblos, the busy port of Phoenicia whence came indispensable olive oil and timber. These commodities were imported also from the country of the Keftiu (Crete) sometime before 2000 B.C. Egyptian prosperity under the Theban kings attracted not only foreign warriors bent on lightning-like raids or foreign traders interested in the peaceful exchange of goods, but also homeseekers. On a tomb at Beni-Hassan there is depicted a scene of thirty-seven Asian, probably Canaanite, immigrants, men, women, and children, seeking admission to the land of the pharaohs.

Indo-Europeans and Hyksos

Somewhere between the Rhine, the Danube, the Baltic Sea, and the Caspian Sea, there lived in the third millennium B.C. a group of peoples linguistically akin, nowadays known as Indo-Europeans. The Indo-Europeans were not of one stock, but although they differed in stock, they had a common patrimony of language, institutions, and religion. For instance, since Sanskrit, Lithuanian, Greek, Latin, Irish, High German, and English all have related words for *sheep* and since the word for *ox* is similar in Sanskrit, Avestic, Armenian, Greek, Latin, Irish, and English, it may be inferred that the original tribes shared, as a common experience, a pastoral life.

In addition, they must have been an agricultural people, since the terms for *plow, sickle, honey, cereals* are common to most of them. They domesticated the horse, invented or borrowed the wheeled cart, and knew the use of copper. They lived in villages (*vic* in Sanskrit, *vicus* in Latin, *oikos* in Greek), were grouped in clans (*gens* in Latin, *genos* in Greek, *janas* in Sanskrit), and were ruled by clan or tribe kings (*râj, râjan* in Sanskrit, *rex, regis* in Latin, and *rig* in Celtic). In time of war they took refuge in a fortified height which later developed as the city (*polis* in Greek, *pilis* in Lithuanian).

The word for divinity, too, has the same root in all the Indo-European languages. The sky was worshiped as god or father, and therefore called sky-father in several languages derived from pro-ethnic Indo-European.

About 2500 B.C. the Indo-Europeans began to migrate in all directions; Brahmins to India; Iranians to the Turkestan Plateau, later moving southwest to found Media and Persia; Kassites to the east of Assyria and Babylon, principally along the Zagros Mountains; the Hurrians (whose ruling class, at any rate, was Indo-European) to east Asia Minor, Palestine and Syria, and north Mesopotamia, eventually founding the kingdom of Mitanni; Lowites to the south coast of Asia Minor; Hittites to central Asia Minor and north to the Black Sea; Achaeans or proto-Greeks to the Greek peninsula; Italici, Celts, and Germans to Italy and northwest Europe; Illyrians and Albanians to the east of the Adriatic Sea; Slavs and Balto-Slavs to the wide plains stretching from the White to the Black Sea.

The Indo-Europeans were able to spread over so vast an area in so comparatively short a time because of a unique advantage over the peoples they conquered—their use of the horse. So far as we know they were the first to invent, or at any rate to use, two-wheeled horse-drawn war chariots. It is no accident that a treatise on horse training was discovered in the royal archives of the earliest Indo-Europeans to establish a civilized kingdom, the Hittites.

The coming of the Indo-Europeans had profound influences on Babylon and Egypt. Babylon immediately after Hammurabi was caught between the Hittites and other Indo-European invaders along the northern border and the so-called Sea People, a piratical Sumero-Semitic folk from the Gulf coast. It was raided during the reign of Samsu-Iluna (c. 1685–1648 B.C.), a son of Hammurabi, by the Kassites, Indo-European aristocrats. Though they soon withdrew to the Zagros range, the Kassites so sapped the vitality of the ancient kingdom as to leave it helpless before the blows of Hatti, the Hittite nation. For over a century the Hittites pressed heavily on Babylon, but having taken their plunder, they too withdrew. Five more generations of Babylonians lived in chaos and poverty until the Kassites returned to rule for the next several hundred years.

One of the peoples awakened by the coming of the Indo-Europeans was the Hurrians from east of Lake Van in Armenia. Kikkuli, the author of the manual on horse training, belonged to this group. Led by Indo-European princes, soon after 1950 B.C. the Hurrians trekked southward, making their presence felt everywhere from Asia Minor to Egypt and eventually organizing the powerful kingdom of Mitanni between the Euphrates and the Tigris to the north of Assyria.

For a century or longer, Indo-Europeans and Hurrians pressed on the Semites of Upper Mesopotamia as well as those of Palestine and Syria, including the Hebrews, pushing them towards Egypt, the line of least resistance. The story of Joseph, son of Jacob, who found wealth and renown in Egypt, is probably an episode of the Hebraic infiltration of this period into the rich land of the pharaohs. The most warlike invaders were mixed bands of Semites and Hurrians with a sprinkling of Aegean, Asian, and Indo-European freebooters under Hurrian leaders, carrying all before them with their war-chariots and iron-pointed swords. The swords showed the use of the new metal smelted in the mountains abutting on the Asiatic coast of the Black Sea. Aiding the Semitic and Hurrian advance was the fact that Semites long settled in the Delta fraternized with their kinsmen. Egypt fell easily before the invader and the Middle Kingdom, with its flourishing culture, ended. A period of national disorganization ensued, and by 1730 B.C. control of the country had passed over to the foreigner. The Egyptians called their new masters *Hyksos,* that is, *rulers of countries.*

The Hyksos, culturally inferior and followers of strange gods, were hated by the natives. Though they gradually adopted some Egyptian ways and even restored some of the ancient temples, they clung to the worship of gods like the Semitic Baal and the Hurrian-Hittite Teshub and refused to accept the supreme Egyptian god Horus-Ra, so that they appeared to the natives as sacrilegious intruders.

The Hyksos' capital was neither Memphis nor Thebes but Avaris in the northeast corner of the Delta, a fortress as close to the Asiatic mainland as possible, a bridge over which new Asian recruits might be drawn unhindered to keep the army of occupation at full complement, and which, if worst came to worst, might afford a safe escape.

The Empire

After more than a century of Hyksos rule, a national hero from upper Egypt, Ahmose I (1570–1545 B.C.), led a successful revolt and again unified the Two Lands. The dynasty he founded (XVIIIth) was the most dynamic in the entire history of Egypt. Ahmose not only dislodged the Hyksos from the whole Delta, including the fortress-capital, but started a military offensive which was to affect both Egypt and Asia for the next thousand years. He pursued the Hyksos army first into Palestine, where he bottled it up in a fortress west of the Dead Sea and, after a siege of three years, compelled it to surrender; then he went on into north Syria, the seat of the Hurrians' kingdom. He thus foreshadowed the future policy of his country—the subjugation of Palestine, Syria, and parts of Asia as the best method of securing peace and liberty at home. Thus military defense led Egypt to enter the paths of empire.

With liberation came reconstruction. Since to the Egyptian mind national renascence could be built only on the cornerstone of religion, both Ahmose I and his son Amenhotep I (1545–1525 B.C.) reinstated in splendor the worship of Amon-Ra. The temple at Karnak was restored, enriched with superb decorations, and endowed with new land grants and revenues, while the priests were given added honors and powers. In politics, the pharaohs of this dynasty, while willing to heap honors on the nome-governors, proceeded to trim the prerogatives of this group, taking into their own hands the conduct of diplomacy, the army, and the treasury. The vigor of this line of pharaohs is perhaps seen best, however, in the unrivaled grandeur of the monuments they built.

Meanwhile conditions in Asia were chaotic enough to invite intervention. Although the Kassites held Babylon, their power was so weak that the five or six hundred years of their domination bear the marks of profound torpor. Syria and Palestine were thoroughly unsettled by the return of the Hyksos. The Hittites were in decadence; at least, their history of this period is shrouded in obscurity. Only the Hurrian kingdom of Mitanni had vigor. Extending from the Tigris and Euphrates to

Fig. 4.1. Hatshepsut's rock-cut temple at Deir el-Bahri, model. XVIIIth Dynasty, 15th century B.C. Originally embellished with statues and reliefs, it was sacked and mutilated by Thutmose III's faction. (New York, Metropolitan Museum of Art)

Lebanon, and interfering steadily in its neighbors' affairs, it was a power as great as Egypt. Its decision to conquer Assyria brought on interminable wars exhausting to both sides.

While Asia was divided and weak, Egypt had three assets: the people were united in their hatred of the Hyksos, the army was efficient, the pharaohs were able generals. Borrowing Hyksos war techniques, Egyptian archers had driven the conquerors out of the country by shooting them down from fast-moving chariots. Thrown into confusion by the arrows, the enemy ranks were then completely broken up by the chariots bearing down on them at full speed. With these same tactics the pharaohs advanced to the conquest of Asia.

Credit for the conquest belongs chiefly to Thutmose I (1525–1495 B.C.). Following the plan of offensive initiated by the liberator Ahmose I, Thutmose I pushed past Palestine and Syria into Mitanni, whence the Hurrians had headed the invasion, reaching the Euphrates and erecting on its bank a commemorative stele. His son Thutmose II (1495–1490 B.C.) made several expeditions to consolidate these gains, but then came a temporary change of policy.

Thutmose III (1490–1436 B.C.), later a veritable Egyptian Napoleon, spent the first twenty-two years of his reign eclipsed by his remarkable aunt and stepmother, Hatshepsut, whose monuments call her king. But documents from her reign say nothing of military and imperialist expansion, while Thutmose vaunts his conquests and his efficiency as an empire-builder. She built temples and developed Egypt internally and commercially; he expanded Egypt with military genius. Imperialism ended Egypt's isolation and ultimately brought the characteristic Egyptian culture to an end.

The Empire in Asia consisted only of the city of Gaza when Thutmose III began to reconquer it country by country. The account of his first twenty campaigns is engraved on the walls of Amon's temple at Karnak. He won his most spectacular victory on the Plain of Megiddo, the Biblical Armageddon, which guarded the route to Syria. He reached this key fortress through a difficult defile which his enemies thought he would never take. Later, in his sixth Syrian campaign, by a flank attack he overwhelmed the defenders, who finally surrendered at Kadesh. Another great victory at Carchemish on the Euphrates opened up the whole of Mesopotamia. Thutmose III was now master of Asia.

Although allowed home rule, each city or kingdom had Egyptian garrisons quartered on it, and the pharaoh appointed royal inspectors, chosen from among native leaders, whose business it was to check on any trouble that might arise. To cultivate the friendship of the native princes, the pharaoh educated their sons in Egypt and took their daughters into the royal harem or married them to Egyptian princes. To show these future rulers the greatness of Egypt, to instill in them a healthy respect for its might, and to imbue them with Egyptian ideas was shrewd policy—one which has been successfully copied by other, later empires. To sum up, every state from Cyprus to the Zagros Mountains, from Sinai to the frontier of Armenia, paid tribute to Thutmose and his successors, sent ambassadors, or sent messages to assure Egypt of its loyalty. For a century, Egypt's will was law in both these cradles of civilization, the valleys of the Nile and of the Euphrates and Tigris.

But the pharaoh still faced problems. Let us mention just one, the departure of the Hebrews from Egypt. The exact date of this event is not known; it may have taken place in the later 1400's B.C. Although represented in Hebrew tradition as a miraculous victory over a reluctant pharaoh, to some scholars the Exodus appears to have been an expulsion by Egyptian nationalists in retaliation for the Hebrews' welcome of the Hyksos.

Gods and Power Politics

While the pharaohs' power was being challenged in Asia, there came to the throne a young man, Amenhotep IV (1369–1353 B.C.), who nearly succeeded in a novel method of unifying the nations his ancestors had won by the sword. An idealist and mystic, he sought to accomplish this aim through the adoption of a new religion acceptable to all, Egyptians as well as subjects. He would supplant the Egyptian Amon with a universal god, Aton, who, worshiped in Egypt since the fifth millennium, was held in honor also among Egypt's Semitic subjects in Asia; indeed it may have been Semitic immigrants who originally brought him to the Nile. Aton therefore was fully qualified for Amenhotep's design. Although he had been worshiped as a falcon, the reforming king decided to represent him under a new form, a sun emanating rays symbolic of his gifts to mankind. This representation of the sun which rises not for one nation only, but for all mankind, bringing life to man and beast and nature, could be understood easily by all races. So fervent was the young king in his reforming zeal that he changed his name from Amenhotep (Amon-is-satisfied) to Ikhnaton (Serviceable-to-Aton). His beautiful sister-wife Nefertiti shared his religious enthusiasm.

Ikhnaton's reform may have been further motivated by a desire to emancipate the throne and the country from Amon's clergy, whose wealth and influence had risen beyond all bounds. Possibly he realized that it would be easier to break away from the national church than to reform it. At any rate he founded a new capital on the site of Tell-el-Amarna, leaving the clergy of Amon to languish in the obscurity of the abandoned old capital, Thebes. Ikhnaton himself composed a *Hymn to the Sun* which, in a strain of mystic exaltation, sketches the main lines of his new theology. Certain passages show a striking parallelism to the 104th Psalm.

Immersed in religious contemplation, Ikhnaton neglected the defense of his Asian empire. Armies, not hymns, were the need of the hour. Since early in the reign of his father, Amenhotep III (1398–1361 B.C.), treachery, revolt, and assaults by foreign powers had weakened Egypt's hold over a number of cities from the Jordan to the upper Euphrates. Although Amenhotep had gone personally to his Asian possessions to see with his own eyes and to correct with his great authority, he had been able neither to restore order nor to protect the frontier. In a letter to his son, preserved in the royal archives of the new capital, he gave the bitter news, "The lands have fallen into the hands of the Khabiri (Hebrews)."

By the time Ikhnaton ascended the throne, the situation had become nearly hopeless. The main difficulties are revealed in more than three hundred letters in the Amarna archives. These letters are written on clay tablets in Akkadian, the *lingua franca* of the ancient Near East for a thousand years following the fall of Sumer. Some were sent by Kassite-Babylonian, Assyrian, Hittite, and Mitannian kings, all of whom protest friendship and goodwill, seek the pharaoh's support against their enemies, or try to cover their own misdeeds, for the Asian kings were in awe of Egyptian riches. The Kassite king of Babylon asks repeatedly for the building of a costly temple, for "gold is as common as dust in thy land."

Fig. 4.2. Queen Nefertiti, 14th century B.C., painted limestone with eyes of rock crystal. Ikhnaton's consort is not idealized but is rendered realistically as a beautiful woman just beginning to lose the bloom of youth. (Berlin, Staatliches Museum)

But it is with the chaos in Syria, Palestine, and Phoenicia that most of the letters have to do. The moment that Egypt's vassals in that part of the Empire sensed Ikhnaton's disinterest in military affairs, they went on a feuding rampage. The Thutmoses had forced cities and principalities to suspend their ancient struggles for lands and markets, but when, under Ikhnaton, the suzerain's hand faltered, the old rivalries and ambitions were revived, and subject peoples struggled for liberation.

The discovery and publication of the Amarna collection, with its exposé of international intrigue in the fourteenth century B.C., created a sensation in the latter half of the nineteenth century. The collection is a course in diplomacy. Some of the writers, while professing to be loyal to Egypt, were in reality intriguing against it. Enemies put on the cloak of friendship, aggressors pleaded that they were being attacked, while loyal vassals, denounced and lied about, found it difficult to establish their innocence or to have their advice accepted. Again and again these loyal princes warned Ikhnaton about the treachery of false brethren and the machinations of foreign kings. Their requests for armor, for money, for experts to train local militias, above all for troops, recur with pathetic insistence.

A series of letters from Ribaddi, governor of Phoenician Byblos, shows how he was being attacked by his own and the pharaoh's enemies, the Amorite princes, Abd-Ashirta and his son Aziru. Ribaddi, shut up in the city, caught with his people "like a bird in a net," cannot defend himself, as the pharaoh had suggested in one of his perfunctory replies, without his lord's assistance. He needs food, men, horses, chariots. "What dogs the sons of Abd-Ashirta are! And they act according to their heart's desire, and cause the King's cities to go up in smoke." To be sure, the offenders send their version of these affairs, a marvel of plausibility and distortion. They represent their attack on the cities of Phoenicia, not as the hostile act it was, but as a service to Egypt, a protective measure to prevent the pharaoh's possessions from falling into the hands of the Hittite king.

In a sense, it was true that the real villain was the Hittite King Suppiluliumas. Ruler of a small empire which in its last fifty years had made considerable gains (see next chapter), he decided to take a little more of the earth while Ikhnaton was gazing at heaven. Undetected most of the time, he used money and devious diplomacy to undermine the loyalty of the pharaoh's vassals and to bring about the ruin of the powerful states around him. He had secret or open agents among the rulers of Syria and Phoenicia. One of them had urged a neighbor to give up his Egyptian allegiance: "Come with me to the King of Hatti." But the importuned prince stood fast, at least for a while, protesting to the pharaoh: "Even if I die, I shall not go to the King of Hatti, for I am your servant." The king of Ugarit wrote that he was afraid of some surprise from Hatti. A *deus ex machina* in a large plan to oust constituted authority as far as his sword could reach, Suppiluliumas had encouraged Amurru, a kingdom in Upper Syria, to snatch the cities of Phoenicia from the pharaoh—only to steal them for himself. He engineered an alliance with the king of Hurri for a joint attack on Mitanni, Egypt's chief ally in Asia—Suppiluliumas to march from the west, the Hurrian from the east. In vain did the Mitannian Tushratta send frantic appeals to the pharaoh. He was murdered at the opportune moment by one of his own sons. Part of the kingdom fell to the Hurrian, part to the Hittite, but the bulk of it to Assyria, its vassal for two or three centuries. The ancient kingdom of Mitanni was reconstituted as the kingdom of Carchemish with the son-in-law of Suppiluliumas as king.

A dreamer occupied the throne of the pharaohs when a strong man was needed. Apparently Ikhnaton had no taste for military action nor talent for administration, at a time when action and administration were demanded to preserve the empire. Having made love a cardinal virtue of his religion, he presumably recoiled from acts of bloodshed. He died, probably of a stroke, at the time the empire was falling to pieces. Execrated by patriots, vilified by the clergy of Amon, Ikhnaton at last found a champion in an American scholar, the late James H. Breasted, who called him "the most remarkable figure in early Oriental history" and saw in him "such a spirit as the world had never seen before." The modernism and universalism of Ikhnaton's attempted revolution permanently affected Egyptian literature and art.

Ikhnaton's reform was the first casualty in the civil war which broke out after his death. The priests and followers of the old god Amon joined with the patriots to undo by revolution what the late king had done. The clergy's enormous wealth may be one reason for Ikhnaton's failure. Gifts from rich and poor had accumulated through the centuries, and innumerable royal grants in the form of properties and revenues had made Amon's wealth second only to that of the king. An inventory taken on the death of Ramses III (1164 B.C.) shows that the temple owned, among other things, 65 towns and villages, seven of which were in Asia; 433 gardens and orchards; 700,000 acres of arable land; 81,000 servants, slaves and dependents; 420,000 head of cattle; 83 ships; and 46 factories. During the reign of Ramses III the god had received 310,000 sacks of grain, 12,000 pounds of gold, 2,200,000 pounds of silver, 5,200,000 pounds of copper. It may be assumed that the temple wealth in Ikhnaton's time was not substantially less. At best Amon stood to lose a great deal if Aton triumphed. His clergy fought his battle.

But Ikhnaton had admirers who apparently accepted the challenge. His successor and son-in-law, Tutankhamen (1352–1344 B.C.), tried to reconcile the parties, evident from the fact that while the emblems on his furniture are those of Aton, his official name is taken from Amon. But Tutankhamen was swept from power, and his very tomb obscured until 1922 when it was opened to reveal dazzling riches. A new dynasty was installed and the capital moved back to Thebes. The clergy of Amon were restored to their former place of pre-eminence while the memory of the "criminal Ikhnaton" was consigned to oblivion.

Chapter 5/THE HITTITES
AND THEIR STRUGGLE
WITH EGYPT

Early Hittite History

Shortly after 2000 B.C. a new civilization, the Hittite, arose in the high,
arid plateau of Asia Minor. Asia
Minor, which was to play so important a part in ancient history,
is fringed by hills and mountains,
with fertile coastal strips where later the Greeks settled. The highest
mountain ranges are the Caucasus in the northeast and the Taurus in
the south. Generally, in antiquity as now, the rivers were not navigable
and the roads were poor. The land is chiefly suitable for farming and
pasture; only 20 percent is arable. Here the Hittites dwelt, principally
around the royal city of Hattusas (modern Boghazköy), east of the present Turkish capital, Ankara. The kingdom's early growth took place
while Sumer, exhausted after three thousand years of progress, was
yielding to Hammurabi, Egypt was reviving under the Middle Kingdom,
Babylon was in full decline, and Crete was on the eve of its greatness.

Hittites is the English term for the inhabitants of a region previously
subject to Akkad under the name of Hatti. Akkad withdrew when
anonymous Indo-European invaders entered Asia Minor. Few in number,

the warriors who conquered became a ruling aristocracy. The term *Hittite* therefore denotes not a group nor nation, but a conglomeration of culturally-related peoples dwelling in and around old Hatti.

Hittite culture was an amalgam of native Asian elements, Sumero-Assyrian influences, and Indo-European contributions brought by the invaders from their northern homeland. From the natives it received a number of local deities and certain religious practices connected with agriculture and shepherding, such as the practice of worshiping the gods on mountain tops. Having made their home in a country long exposed to Mesopotamian culture, the Hittites borrowed from the latter its cuneiform script, its science, its sculpture, and some of its gods and laws. But the Hittites were also in touch with and borrowers from the west. Thus their architecture was derived more from Minoan than from Mesopotamian models.

After the Hittites had had their day in the sun, all memory of them was lost, save for a few references in the Old Testament, for instance, to Bathsheba, "the wife of Uriah the Hittite," or to Hittite women in Solomon's harem. Other bits of information about the Hittites were gleaned during the second half of the nineteenth century, especially from the Amarna archives. Then at the turn of the century desultory investigations in and around the village of Boghazköy brought to light a number of architectural and inscriptional remains, appropriate to a capital, Hattusas, to which the Amarna archives repeatedly refer. In 1906 came the exciting news that the German Hugo Winckler had discovered among the ruins overlooking the village some 2500 cuneiform clay tablets in eight languages datable to the thirteenth century B.C.

In this polyglot empire, only Hittite and Akkadian were official languages. In 1915 the Czech Friedrich Hrozný published his discovery that Hittite, in inflection if not in vocabulary, was Indo-European, written in a cumbersome cuneiform syllabary better suited to Semitic. But Hittite was also written in hieroglyphics; the decipherment (since 1948) of a bilingual text from Karatepe in Phoenician (a known language) and hieroglyphic Hittite is leading to knowledge of this hitherto unread tongue, just as the Rosetta Stone's Greek text led to the decipherment of Egyptian hieroglyphics.

Upon their arrival in Asia, the Indo-European conquerors set up a number of principalities. The first prince deserving of notice was Pitkhanas, who thought of himself as the favorite of the storm god. He adopted a style of war new in the recorded experience of man, descending upon a rival state in the dead of night and capturing its king, but, in his own words, treating the inhabitants with the consideration due to "fathers and mothers." The title "Great King," adopted by his son Anittas, implies that he bound other kings to him by varying ties of allegiance. The Old Kingdom of Hatti was apparently the creation of Anittas. By the seventeenth century B.C. the federation had become a solid accomplishment. In about 1560 B.C. the Great King Mursilis I took two important steps. He established his capital at Hattusas, connecting it with the lands which previous Indo-European conquerors had brought under Hittite culture. He pushed the empire south, conquering the distant city-state of Aleppo, much of northern Syria, and some of the domains of the Hurrians. He even raided the ancient kingdom of Hammurabi, then in full decline, and sacked Babylon itself.

There follows a sorry period of palace intrigues, murders, invasions, and anarchy, a darkness, like that of Mesopotamia and the whole of western Asia in the same period, due probably to an invasion of this whole area paralleling the Hyksos invasion of Egypt. About 1525 Telepinus established order and adequate frontiers. Light breaks once more at the time of the Egyptian push into Asia, when Egypt and Hatti were friends, perhaps even partners. When, in driving the Hyksos northward, Thutmose III invaded Mitanni, Hatti looked on with pleasure, not indeed at the prospect of having the giant of the Nile next door, but because of the humiliation to the Hurrians, barons who from their Mitannian kingdom had brought devastation on Hatti by organizing expeditions on the Hyksos pattern. When the pharaoh took Carchemish (1459), the Hittite king sent congratulations and gifts. He himself profited from Mitanni's misfortunes, especially from its loosened grip on northern Syria and its neighbors. Indeed he grew to such power as to cause a diplomatic revolution, for the Pharaoh Amenhotep II (1439–1406 B.C.), in fear of Hatti, made an alliance with Mitanni. Now the tables were turned. With Egyptian help Mitanni grew again in strength while Hatti grew weaker. But about 1390 B.C. the greatest statesman-warrior in Hittite history, Suppiluliumas (1390–1354 B.C.), ascended the throne. Let us look at the organization and culture of his kingdom.

Hittite Civilization

A system of hereditary succession to the throne had been established by Telepinus; before him, ambitious nobles had contested royal authority. Though no living Hittite king was deified, titles like Great King (implying dominion over lesser kings), My Sun, and Hero attest his power, as supreme judge, priest, and general. As priest the king visited in rotation the main cult centers. His fief-kinsmen held the highest state offices; his sons governed the provinces; his daughters made dynastic marriages; vassal princes bound to him by oaths ruled the subject kingdoms. Kings and kinsmen, as an exclusive caste, gradually usurped the function of the original native assembly of peasants and craftsmen, now degraded to second-class citizens. Serfs could own property and had legal rights. By the early 1200's B.C. this hierarchical state was on terms of absolute equality and reciprocity with such great powers as Egypt.

The kingdom's economy, despite the hard climate of the Asia Minor plateau, was primarily agricultural, with metallurgy an important factor. The Hittites cultivated grapes, olives, apples, pomegranates and pears. They raised barley for bread and beer, as well as peas, beans, and flax. Mules were the most valuable domestic animal, followed by horses, oxen, cows, sheep, and goats. Mines produced copper, silver, and lead; iron was a precious metal. Bar silver was the medium of exchange; for weights and measures the Hittites used Babylonian standards. International trade involved the exchange of Hittite copper for Mesopotamian cloth and tin.

Hittite law and institutions were codified but not stagnant. The court of first instance, from which there was the right of appeal to the king, consisted of local elders, supervised by a royal officer. Great trouble, unique among oriental peoples, was taken to ascertain the facts, carefully and without bias. Hittite law is comparatively advanced in that retribution (an eye for an eye) plays an inconspicuous part; for citizens, only rape, bestiality, and rebellion are capital offenses; for slaves, disobedience and sorcery are added to the list. Cruel bodily mutilation, normal in Hammurabi's code, is here reserved for slaves. For all other offenses by freemen (assault, black magic, homicide) compensation or retribution is ordered. Except in rare cases—usually religious—personal, not clan or family, responsibility was the rule. The Hittite family was patriarchal. Marriage, prohibited between near relatives, but not between master and slave, involved bride-gift and dowry; the couple might live together or the bride remain in her father's house; an adulterous wife might be put to death. As to land tenure, royal fiefs but not artisans' lands were entailed.

In warfare the Hittites maintained predominance by the use of the war-chariot, with a three-man crew. Infantry wore kilt and helmet and carried a short sword and battleax; there is no evidence of cavalry or navy. Reading of omens preceded military operations, in which the Hittite kings proved themselves masters of strategy and tactics, yet free of the Assyrian lust for torture and cruelty. The capital, Hattusas, where natural defenses of gorge and crag failed, had a strong double wall, with towers, battlements, and a tunnel under the rampart for surprise sorties.

In religion, as in politics, the Hittites allowed a degree of local option, subject to royal supervision. But centralized government brings with it syncretized religion, with an attempt to evolve an orderly pantheon, and the rise of national divinities and a state cult, with elaborate ritual and mythology. The great rock sanctuary of Yazilikaya ("inscribed rock"), near Boghazköy, pictures the national gods in relief, winged, holding a weapon or implement in their right hands, a symbol in their left, and standing upon a sacred animal. Most characteristic is the weather-god Teshub, the ax his implement, the lightning his symbol; he drives a chariot of bulls; the Romans worshiped him centuries later as Jupiter Dolichenus. His consort is the matronly Hebat, who appears in art standing on a lion; their son is Sharma, symbolized by a pair of human legs. The goddess Shauska (syncretized with Ishtar), Hattusilis III's patroness, is pictured as winged, standing on a lion. At the holy city of Arinna the sun goddess Wurusemu predominates; we hear also of Tele-pinu, the fertility god, who is resurrected like Osiris. We know too of a rural god represented holding a hare and a falcon, and standing on a stag. The Neo-Hittites worshiped the weather-god Tarhund, who reap-pears in Etruscan cult as Tarchon.

Temples were many-windowed complexes of numerous small rooms, serving as offices and warehouses, grouped around a paved court, with the holy of holies in a side room. The cult statue was of precious metal or plated wood. The temple was the god's home, the priests his domestic staff. Ritually pure, they bathed, clothed, and fed him, gave him beer, and entertained him with music and dancing. As lord and master, the god demanded lavish offerings of first fruits and occasionally, especially after a Hittite defeat in battle, human sacrifice. In a typical festival the king and queen washed from a golden jar, took napkins, had a veil removed from a table, and ate a ceremonial meal, after which the ground was ceremoniously swept. Sometimes a mock battle was enacted before the god, or he was escorted in a procession, riding in a chariot beribboned in red, white, and blue and accompanied by temple harlots bearing torches.

Though gods were invisible and immortal, they were conceived of as in all other respects human. When their vigilance lapsed, plague ensued; they punished sin; their will could be divined by examination of entrails, by augury, by casting lots, or by consulting oracles. Hittites resorted to magic, ritual curses, and the use of scapegoats. Elaborate funerary customs, at any rate for royalty, included cremation, extinguishment of the pyre with beer and wine, deposit of the linen-wrapped bones in a silver jar of oil, and a funeral feast, a ritual closely resembling that of the Homeric Greeks. The common people, of different stock, buried their dead.

Surviving Hittite literature is mainly official; legend, myth, and ro-mance occupy a subordinate place. Official literature includes royal speeches, annals, charters, deeds of gift, royal letters settling disputed frontiers or indicting traitorous vassals, minutes of courts of inquiry, and standing orders for officials. The style, in contrast to the flamboyance of Egyptian or Assyrian documents, is straightforward and factual, free of oriental exaggeration and boasting.

No Hittite poetry survives; the sole surviving purely Hittite legend describes a siege in Syria. Myths are mostly borrowed; one which may be native tells of the slaying of a dragon, a ritual contest between a divine hero (the weather-god) and the forces of evil, in which the dragon is outwitted by being offered too many barrels of strong drink. Another possibly native myth is that of the missing god (Telepinu, the fertility spirit) who abandons man's world in a temper; blight and famine ensue; a bee, after searching over hill and dale, finds him; he returns on eagle-back, is appeased, and the fields once more become fruitful.

The most remarkable myths are Hurrian, including the gods' struggle for kingship and the epic *Song of Ullikummi,* a tale of rebellion against the weather-god; Ullikummi, finally defeated, is the rebel god's son, a monster made of diorite stone. Greek parallels exist in Hesiod's *Theogony* (*cf.* the myth of Typhon). Though the myths are primitive, even infantile, they are of the greatest interest as part of the history of religion; their parallelism with the myths of other Indo-European peoples is also significant.

Finally, we turn to pre-Hittite and Hittite art. Pre-Hittite tombs contain animal figures, jugs and goblets in silver and gold, primitive stone idols, and fine handmade polychrome pottery with geometric designs, superseded in the Hittite age by wheel-made, polished red ware. Cylinder seals were a highly developed art form. With the Empire, monumental stone bas-reliefs, inscribed with hieroglyphics, came into use to ornament the lower part of a wall-face; they often represent the king worshiping. The great gallery of Yazilikaya depicts, apparently in two converging processions, every Hittite god. The gods wear a fluted conical headdress, short belted tunic, and upturned shoes; goddesses wear a long pleated skirt, loose upper garment, and a mural crown. The goddesses are shown, for the first time in Oriental art, in profile. Finest of all the bas-reliefs is the great divine figure carved on a gateway at Boghazköy. Other sculpture shows musicians playing lute and bagpipes, shepherds, with flock, and hunting scenes. Sculpture in the round is represented by sphinxes, lions, and a few exquisite miniatures in metal. In architecture, Hittite temples in Syria are characterized by a porch, with columns resting on animal bases, leading into a wide shallow hall.

In sum, the civilization of the Hittite ruling caste was advanced in its methods of warfare, political structure, and legal institutions. Literature and religion, though interesting, were primitive and unoriginal. Hittite kingship, from beginnings in military leadership, later developed

Fig. 5.1. Boghazköy. Relief of a god in war panoply, from Royal Gate. (Berlin, Staatliches Museum)

religious functions. In art the Hittite genius, as shown in the powerful rock carving of the later Empire, probably reflected rather the rulers' taste than the sculptors' inspiration.

The Struggle for Asia

Suppiluliumas took from Egypt its possessions north of Palestine without actually going to war with the pharaoh (as mentioned in Chapter Four, Ikhnaton's help to vassals who offered resistance was inadequate or nonexistent). Ikhnaton hastily agreed to the loss of Syria; his administration and his nation were clearly paralyzed. Suppiluliumas bound to himself by those ties of vassalage customary in the Hittite federation the cities of Syria, the ex-kingdom of Mitanni, now renamed Carchemish, the kingdom of Aleppo, and all his other conquests. In his reign there was yet another sign of Egyptian decadence and Hittite power: the boy king Tutankhamen having died, his girl widow asked Suppiluliumas to send her one of his sons for husband. When Suppiluliumas died, shortly after this event, he left an empire stronger, though not richer, than its rival on the Nile. An international revolution had thus taken place; the new prevailed over the old, barbarism, so orthodox Egyptians felt, over civilization.

The expanded federative system through which the king of Hattusas controlled his allies and vassals may be compared to a center (the old kingdom of Hatti with its capital at Hattusas) surrounded by concentric circles. The Hittite sub-kingdoms of central Asia are the nearer circles; the more distant non-Hittite states are the peripheral ones. Each circle has its own kind of obligations and ties. The sun in this constellation increased in brilliance under Mursilis II, a younger son of Suppiluliumas, as he added new satellites to the system.

Meanwhile in Egypt the final curtain was being brought down on the XVIIIth Dynasty. The patriot-orthodox league which had revolted after Ikhnaton's death proclaimed a new dynasty with recapture of lost Asian possessions as the first point in its program. Seti I (1302–1290 B.C.) and his son Ramses II (1290–1224 B.C.) pursued this goal with an energy and intelligence worthy of a Thutmose III. After strengthening his position in Palestine, Seti reconquered the Lebanon and most of Phoenicia, sacrificing scores of war prisoners on the altar of the fully-ascendant Amon. Ostensibly an attempt to placate the god with the blood of oath-breakers and traitors, this was in reality an act of nationalistic revenge. Seti immortalized his exploits in numerous works of art. He restored the statues and buildings of the XVIIIth Dynasty as a public manifestation that he would restore the nation to the splendor of its best days. At Abydos he built a temple to himself and the empire's gods that despite the ravages of time remains one of the most grandiose achievements of Egyptian art. He filled the land with monuments advertising his reign as the apogee of Egyptian civilization. His dream of greatness came, fortunately, just at a time when Egyptian artists in various media had reached the highest degree of skill, a happy combination which has occurred not more than five or six times throughout history. To quarry the stone for his monuments, Seti employed thousands of Asian war captives, and also native Egyptians, whom he treated with a generosity remarkable for those days: daily rations of four pounds of bread, roast meat, and two vegetables, and two changes of clothing every month. He rests in the Valley of the Kings, that awe-inspiring cemetery of the pharaohs among the cliffs west of Thebes. In the tomb which he excavated for himself, seven staircases lead down from gallery after gallery to large rooms and pillared halls, which serve as chapels for his statues, furniture, and magnificent sarcophagus.

The reconquest of Syria was left to Ramses II, who, despite his ability, failed at this task. The Hittite kings had tightened the bonds of the federation and, foreseeing a showdown, carefully built up their army.

The list of the allied and vassal states in the Boghazköy archives shows the extent of the Hittite empire: Amurru beyond the Jordan, Carchemish in the upper Euphrates, Aleppo, or Naharin, in Syria, Arvad and Kadesh in Phoenicia, and practically every Asian state from the Black Sea to the Cypriote shore. Equally significant are names pointing to the emergence of hitherto unknown peoples who before long were to clash with the Greek invaders at Troy: the names on the Hittite monument recur in Homer's *Iliad*. Whether these western co-belligerents of Hatti were vassal-allies or simply mercenaries, the Hittite King Muwatallis faced Ramses with an army of about twenty-five thousand men, collected from nineteen or twenty different countries. Herein may have lain the Hittites' weakness: they depended on allies and subjects more than on their own native strength.

Egypt took first advantage, for Ramses II was able to proceed far into northern Syria. But Muwatallis, the better strategist, stopped Ramses at Kadesh-on-the-Orontes in the bloodiest battle in the history of Egypt (1286 B.C.) . Ambushed by the Hittites, Ramses would have lost everything if his cool head and fierce courage and his army's excellent discipline had not enabled him to cut his way out. He saved his skin and most of his army, but the battle was a setback, not a victory. This did not prevent its glorification in official accounts, in architecture and the plastic arts, nor its role as the subject of legend and the theme of poetry.

If Egypt needed peace, the Hittites, now under King Hattusilis III (1293–1270 B.C.) needed it even more, for while new migratory movements threatened the empire's frontier in the west, in the east Assyria was seeking to conquer its allies in the Euphrates valley. To keep Assyria in check, the Hittites needed peace with Egypt. Ramses II, for his part, knowing he was not strong enough to reconquer Syria, was ready for a reconciliation. Mutual need then led to a Treaty of Friendship (1279 B.C.) . Its terms are as well known to us as are those of any modern treaty because they have been preserved in inscriptions in the Karnak temples as well as on a clay tablet in the Boghazköy archives. Hattusilis is recognized as "The Great King" and treated as Ramses' equal. No boundaries are defined, but the two contracting parties (a) pledge themselves to peace and friendship forever, (b) promise to respect the integrity of their respective states, (c) bind each other to mutual assistance in case a third power [Assyria] attacks either, (d) promise mutual aid in case of internal revolution, and (e) lay down humane rules of extradition from one state to the other. The better to keep the peace, Ramses took as his chief wife one of Hattusilis' daughters. Hattusilis' state visit to his son-in-law, following the treaty, was commemorated in sculpture as far south of Thebes as the second cataract.

This *entente cordiale* came too late, however, to save either Hatti or Egypt. Recurrent waves of Indo-Europeans in search of homes or booty flooded over Asia Minor and upper Mesopotamia no less than over Europe. About this time Italic and Celtic tribes were invading western Europe, while the Dorians were occupying the Balkans before descending on the Greek peninsula. One of these Indo-European peoples, the Mushki, under King Mitas, perhaps the remote ancestor of the Phrygian King Midas of the golden touch, supplanted the Hittites as the dominant power in Asia Minor shortly after the death of Hattusilis (c. 1270 B.C.). Even though permitted to retain their Euphrates provinces, the surviving Hittites declined so fast that within sixty years we hear no more of them.

Egypt, too, declined rapidly after the reign of Ramses II, like Hatti, succumbing to the Indo-European flood, though the rapacity and dogmatism of the organized priesthood also contributed to its disintegration. The Libyans, who had made repeated incursions into the Delta, were now stronger and better organized, and were using as paid recruits or allies some of the new invading peoples—the Shardana (Sardinians?), Lycians, Achaeans, and Etruscans. Ramses III (1195–1164 B.C.) could not, for all his victories, stay his country's decline. He merely postponed the catastrophe. The Mushki, after overrunning Hatti, caused Phoenicia to fall away from Egypt; Ramses III is the last pharaoh whose name is recorded on Asian soil. In turn, Palestine was overrun by the Philistines, the vanguard of the new homeseekers.

The Egyptian homeland itself lay open before the invading sea peoples, including Philistines, Teucrians, Sicilians, and Danuna (Homer's Danai), who overran Anatolia, Cilicia, Cyprus, and North Syria, setting up camp somewhere in the northern Syrian plain. Ramses III was unable to prevent hordes of armed immigrants, men, women, and children, from crossing the border in their wagons (an ancient version of our prairie schooner) carrying with them their belongings, and driving their herds before them. He met the main body of barbarians at his Asian frontier, where he defeated them by land, and in the river mouths of the Delta in a great sea battle.

After the death of Ramses III, Egypt's decline was swift. As in the feudal period, the pharaohs became mere figureheads. A dynasty of priest-kings took over Upper Egypt while Lower Egypt lay prostrate under foreign domination.

Egyptian Culture under the Empire

The nation's imperial experience profoundly influenced Egyptian culture under the Empire. The character of this culture is best seen in Thebes, the capital whither flowed the trade and wealth of the tributary

Fig. 5.2. Egyptian women weaving, model. XIth Dynasty, *c.* 2135–2000 B.C. From Deir el-Bahri. (New York, Metropolitan Museum of Art)

nations. The Isthmus of Suez had become a great highway over which caravans brought spices and aromatic woods from the East, weapons and vases from Phoenicia, and tribute of gold and silver from the kings and princes of the Empire. A stream of galleys from Asia and the Aegean world converged upon the Delta to ascend the Nile and unload their cargoes at the principal cities. The luxury shops of the capital displayed elegant imported wares, among which Mycenaean products held pride of place. In the Cretan tradition, Mycenaean art appealed strongly to Egyptian taste and affected native art, especially pottery and frescoes. New facial types appearing in sculpture and painting indicate that the influx of visitors on imperial business, of slaves and free immigrants from the Semitic countries, of foreign mercenaries and merchants led to considerable intermarriage. Thebes changed from a strictly Egyptian city into the first cosmopolis in history.

The nobles lived on their estates in mansions set amidst semitropical formal gardens. The frescoes of this period show them hunting, fishing, supervising the administration of the estate, basking in beautiful groves, eating and drinking to the accompaniment of music and dancing.

The lower-class living standard improved. Scribes and artisans were more numerous than at any previous time, as we infer from the quantity of their output and the amount of literature devoted to praising their profession and adjuring schoolboys in training not to frequent beerhalls or run after women, but to stick to their books and become officials of high repute.

Trade and its influence flowed out of Egypt into other lands. Wares of high quality, principally vases, were exported to Knossos, Mycenae, Rhodes, Cyprus, Asia, and Sicily. Egyptian religious elements were introduced into Crete and Egyptian hieroglyphs influenced Minoan writing, while Egyptian motifs and forms inspired Mycenaean artists.

Generously subsidized by the pharaohs and with skill derived from two thousand years of technical experiment and progress, Egyptian architects were writing a new chapter in the history of their craft. They erected huge temples like that of Amon at Karnak and that of Amenhotep III at Luxor, in both of which the ceiling—higher over the central nave, lower over the lateral ones—is supported by rows of gigantic columns. They built smaller, flat-roofed, rectangular sanctuaries, thirty or forty feet long and fourteen feet high, raised on a high podium or platform, with columns on all four sides, the façade slightly recessed, and the front door opening between two graceful columns—examples of the oldest type of structural simplicity, a dream of beauty realized by architects of genius. Portraiture in stone was still in the best tradition, reflecting the subject's character with fresh and vibrant realism. Painters delighted in crowded scenes of action and movement telling a continuous story.

Just as Egyptian imperial art lost serenity, so imperial literature became lively and attractive, showing an awareness of strange lands, written in the vernacular, addressed to the *bourgeoisie;* its romantic love songs rejoice in nature and the open air. History shows a vein of biting humor, irreverently mocking what had once been sacrosanct. The pharaoh is caricatured; the gods are objects of farce. They sulk, they grow senile and drool, they go on picnics, they practice bribery, they change themselves into hippopotamuses. Earlier Egyptians had occasionally humanized their gods, but during the Empire the mockery became broad. Religion, hitherto so central to Egyptian culture, was showing signs of weakness. An art or a literature which holds nothing sacred is a disintegrating force.

Chapter 6/SYRIA, PALESTINE, AND PHOENICIA

Canaanites and Phoenicians

With Egypt exhausted and the Hittite empire disintegrated, Syria, Phoenicia, and Palestine became independent. Incapable of coalescing into a national body and located between Asia and Egypt in what has been for ages a battlefield of empire, these small countries were fated to play a largely passive role. It was only when the big powers fell that they could rise. So in the interlude from the twelfth to the ninth century B.C., after Egypt and Hatti fell and before Assyria rose, the Canaanites, Phoenicians, and Hebrews established themselves. Foreign invaders, the Philistines, also exploited the situation, settling on the Palestinian coast.

Syria, Phoenicia, and Palestine skirt the Mediterranean Sea southward from Asia Minor to Egypt. Ancient or Northern Syria lay east of Cilicia, south of the Taurus Mountains, west of the Euphrates elbow, and north of the Lebanon Mountains. At the latter point it was joined by the three parallel strips of Phoenicia (*Coele Syria* in Greek), the Mediter-

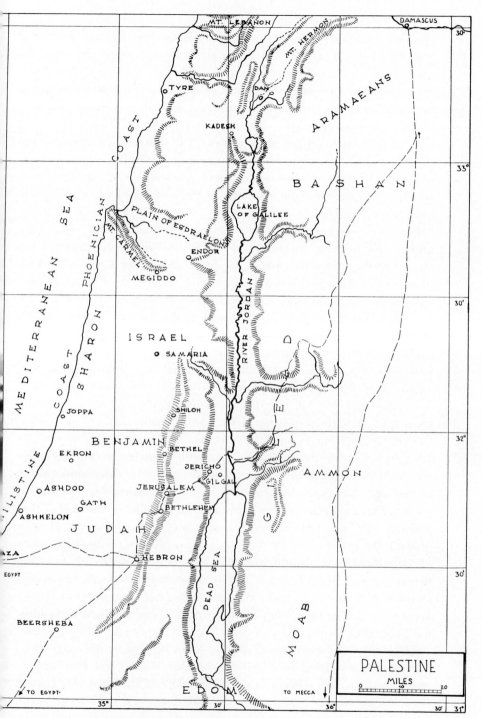

Fig. 6a. Map of Palestine

ranean coast, the Lebanon, and the Ante-Lebanon. Two rivers bisect the valley between the two Lebanons, the Orontes flowing northward and the Jordan southward to the Dead Sea. Palestine extends from the southern tip of the Lebanon to the southern end of the Dead Sea.

Inhabited in Paleolithic times and in constant development from the Neolithic to the Bronze Age, the area was settled by various strains of the Semitic stock as early as 3000 B.C. After 2000 B.C., when the main lines of its history become more distinct, its culture was Canaanite. Canaan is the Biblical name of Palestine before the Philistine and Hebrew invasions. Historically, however, Canaan connotes the wider civilization which flourished from the southern foothills of the Taurus to the approaches of Egypt.

French excavations at Ras Shamra (ancient Ugarit) since 1929 have greatly enriched our knowledge of Canaanite culture. Ras Shamra lies on the seashore directly east of the finger-like tip of Cyprus. There a plowman at work discovered some ruins, a mound of superimposed cities, the earliest of which goes back to 4000 or 4500 B.C. But the site flourished around 1400 B.C., the period of the Amarna archives, which had already revealed that Ugarit was a small city-kingdom, caught in the struggle between Egypt and Hatti, invaded by Aziru, the unscrupulous king of Amurru, and finally conquered by Suppiluliumas. The Ugarit tombs, sculptures, gold objects, jewels, the king's palace and ivory throne, above all, the temple with adjoining school and library constitute our clearest picture of Canaanite civilization.

The library deserves special notice. Its hundreds of cuneiform clay tablets express for the first time a Semitic language by alphabet, not syllabic signs. Twenty-nine letters reproduce all the consonants. There are no signs for the vowels, since these were supplied mentally by the reader. Two languages were written in this alphabet, a Hurrian dialect and Ugaritic or Canaanite, which is practically the same as the Hebrew of the time of Moses. In the tablets religious themes predominate: temple administration, hymns, liturgical rubrics, and myths of gods and heroes. Three epics, *The Loves and Wars of Baal and Anat, The Courtship and Marriage of King Keret,* and *The Saga of Aqhat, Son of Daniel,* are outstanding in their length, literary beauty, and the light they throw on Canaanite culture.

Although its elements were preponderantly Semitic, this crossroads culture was a melting pot. It had borrowed Hittite and Hurrian elements, mainly from settlers in northern Syria. It also showed Egyptian elements, principally from Byblos, the long-time Semitic colony of Egypt. Essentially, however, it was the product of several Semitic strains, influenced by the Amorites, natives of Canaan or immigrants from a nearby eastern or northeastern district late in the third millennium; the later arriving Akkadian and Assyrian merchants and craftsmen; lastly, the great wave of the Aramaeans (about 2000 B.C.) . These Semitic groups, closely akin, had a common core of beliefs, customs, institutions, and thought patterns. The Canaanites consequently formed a homogeneous society with a homogeneous culture.

They were organized in city-states, ruled by kings, and perpetually at war with one another. Their economy was agricultural. Their industry and trade were local; Egypt and Crete dominated the international markets. Their primitive religion conceived of many gods (*elim, baalim*) , whose principal concern was food, drink, and sex. One El or Baal was supreme. The Ugarit tablets tell of Bel seducing two women whose lips are sweet as grapes. Though they bear him two children, Shahru and Shalmu (Dawn and Dusk) , Bel drives them into the desert from his paradise at the source of two rivers. Later he appears as the thunder-voiced storm-god, the "Rider of Clouds," dwelling on a northern mountain. He marries his sister Anat. She and two other goddesses, Astarte and Asherah, are always pregnant, yet always virgins. Borrowed from Sumerian prototypes which emphasized motherhood, the Canaanite version of these goddesses emphasizes the flesh. They are worshiped as sacred courtesans by a prostitution ritual, practiced in or adjacent to the temple. Anat, Astarte, and Asherah (later merged) were also goddesses of war, delighting in the sight of blood. The god Kothar was a smith, the originator of the arts and crafts, the possible ancestor of the Greek smith-god, Hephaestus.

The Ras Shamra tablets have confirmed the view that Canaanite culture was the parent of Israelitic. The parallelism of Ugaritic poetry— "The heavens rain oil, the rivers run with honey" or "The mountains will bring thee much silver, the hills the choicest of gold"—is duplicated in the Bible. Besides poetic forms Israel borrowed ideas. For example, in *The Saga of Aqhat* Daniel calls down on the place where his son was murdered the curse of drought, just as four hundred years later David curses the place where Saul and Jonathan were slain.

The stage of Canaanite civilization best known to us is the later Phoenician one. Whereas the Hyksos incursions did not seriously disturb life in Canaan, those of the "People of the Sea" (about 1200 B.C.) caused serious changes.

Hatti, as we have seen, disintegrated under the maladjustments produced by these western invaders. Egypt declined rapidly. Troy was another victim. Mesopotamia felt the effects of that wide migration of races. Canaan itself was no exception, as we can see from the Ras Shamra ruins. Not only does local art show traces of Mycenean influence; a tablet even records a revolt against the foreign rule of Ionians, or proto-Greeks. With the arrival of more "Peoples of the Sea," Ugarit declined, and by 1100 B.C. it had fallen.

But Phoenician life went on, of course conditioned by the country's natural resources. The Lebanon foothills form, at the shore, sheltered coves and inshore islands ideally suited to the growth of maritime cities. Since the coastland was too small to grow all the food they needed, Phoenicians sailed the seas in search of fish and trade. They had a valuable asset in the cedars of Lebanon with which Egypt had built its fleets and which Solomon was later to use for his temple. The business relations between Solomon and King Hiram of Tyre were typical of Phoenician trade: in return for Hiram's timber and the loan of craftsmen, Solomon traded grain, olive oil, wine and other agricultural products.

By conquering the fertile valley between the Lebanon and the Ante-Lebanon, the Phoenicians were able to increase their food supply and profit from exporting the gums, spices, and medicinal products with which the valley abounded. They manufactured cloth, buying the wool from the flock-tending desert nomads and obtaining the dye from the gorgeous purple of the murex, indigenous to their own shores and, should the home supply be exhausted, obtainable in the waters of Asia Minor, Africa, and Greece. Once they had learned metallurgy—whether from Crete, Sumer, or Egypt—the Phoenicians manufactured copper, bronze, and iron tools, farm implements, household utensils, and weapons and armor such as the Achaeans used in the *Iliad*. They learned glass-making from XVIIIth-dynasty Egypt, and their cities remained the largest centers of this craft down to Roman times. They made gaudy jewels of semi-precious stones, cheap pottery, coarse and flimsy ornaments, and hardware. They dealt in another commodity, human cargoes, buying slaves or kidnapping free men—and especially women—on every Mediterranean seacoast and selling them at a profit.

In the east, Phoenician merchants traded hundreds of miles inland, in the bazaar towns touched by caravans from Arabia, Sumer, Akkad, Assyria, Elam, and beyond, from the kingdoms and baronies of Asia Minor. To obtain the local good will and immunity from desert-robber clans, they were willing to pay tribute out of their fat profit, passing the added expense on to the consumer.

More significant were Phoenicia's activities westward. Its shipyards launched seaworthy ships which, as early as 1100 B.C., linked east and west in a network of sea lanes. After Minoan times nearby Cyprus was exploited for the sake of the purple murex, and for timber, cattle, and copper. Before long there rose on its shores Phoenician cities which kept their Semitic character down to the Hellenistic Age. Phoenician sea captains sailed as far west as Gibraltar long before 1000 B.C. With their eyes always open for business opportunities, they explored incessantly, discovering bays, coves, harbors, and rivers, and opening commercial relations with the natives along the coast. They even entered the Atlantic, sailing along the Iberian coast after tin, possibly as far as Britain. Later they touched the Cape Verde Islands, and probably traveled as far west as the Azores. They were in a sense the first builders of Europe, for they helped to bring together the peoples whose lands they visited and whose products they exchanged. In former ages the Minoans had linked southeastern Europe with Egypt and Asia, but this link was broken. The Phoenicians' role was larger: they wove the Near East, southern Europe, and North Africa into one economic fabric.

As their interests were chiefly commercial, Phoenicians did not as a rule plant colonies, that is, settlements of men, women, and children. They made little attempt either to penetrate the countries the shores of which they visited or to garrison their places of business. They simply established trading posts for unloading cargo and loading the commodities gathered by their port agents. There were few of these trading stations on the south coast of Asia Minor; none on the west coast, which the Greeks monopolized. Rhodes, Crete, some of the lesser islands, and the Greek mainland itself had a few such posts, founded in or shortly after Minoan and Mycenean times. Two or three trade centers were established in Sardinia, others in the Maltese and Lipari islands and in Cadiz, beyond Gibraltar in Spain, probably about 1100 B.C.

Regular colonies were planted in the middle and western Mediterranean: Solus and Panormus on the northern and Motya and Lilybaeum on the western coast of Sicily, and several in North Africa, among which were Utica, Lixus, Hadrumetum, the two Hippos, and the greatest of all, Carthage. Founded by Tyre in 814 B.C. and dependent upon it for nearly two hundred years, Carthage became more powerful than any other Phoenician city, and itself founded colonies. Wherever they went, the Phoenicians and the Carthaginians established a ruthless monopoly: they sank at sight the ships of their Greek and Etruscan competitors.

No people receives merchandise from another without receiving also cultural elements. The Greeks could testify to that, for their words for *gold, camel, brick, jasper, cherry, spelt, sesame, terebinth, naphtha, cinnabar, marjoram, sack, mina, shekel,* and other items imported from the Orient were not Greek, but Oriental—either Phoenician or transmitted by Phoenicians. The worship of the Sumerian goddess Ishtar had spread first to the Minoans and then to the Achaeans and the classical Greeks, who called her Aphrodite. The Phoenician sailors, whose ships touched every Greek waterfront and who flirted with Greek women who came to buy the goods displayed at the beach, helped to popularize still further the cult of the goddess of love. The legend of Adonis, her young lover, killed in a hunt by a boar, is probably of Phoenician origin, or at least transmitted by Phoenicians. And Phoenician Melkart is the Greek Herakles.

Though Mycenean Greeks wrote using a Minoan syllabary, the classical Greek alphabet was a gift from Phoenicia, adopted somewhere between the 1100's and the 700's B.C. The 22 consonant signs of the Phoenician alphabet were in turn a simplified adaptation from the Akkadian, Egyptian, and Minoan scripts. The Phoenician alphabet was more efficient, for, whereas the syllabic methods in vogue until that time needed as many hundred signs as the language had syllables, the Phoenicians could express with a mere twenty-two letters not only all the syllables, but also all the words, of their language.

Until the sixth century B.C., the Greeks, like the Phoenicians, wrote from right to left. They remedied the inadequacy of the Phoenician system by adding vowel signs.

The Philistines

The Philistines, an Aegean people driven from their homes by northern invaders, were among the roving "Peoples of the Sea" who contributed to the downfall of Ugarit and the other civilized states of the Near East. They settled between Phoenicia and Sinai, on the coast, for they were a seafaring people, and the native Canaanite farmers stoutly disputed their penetration inland. But when their seacoast settlements, Ashkelon, Ashdod, Ekron, Gath, and Gaza grew overcrowded, the Philistines pushed eastward to the Jordan River.

The trek to the Jordan valley brought them into conflict with another set of newcomers, the Hebrews (the name means "those from the other side"), who, after being freed from their Egyptian bondage, had at last arrived in Canaan and staked out their claim to it. A thousand years earlier, their ancestor Abraham had migrated thereabouts from Ur. His prolific descendants, in need of more pastures for their flocks and of more land for their plows, claimed the land by ancestral God-sanctioned squatters' rights. In the century-long struggle the Philistines at first had an easy victory. For while the Hebrews fought with stone and wood weapons, and without armor, their enemies, Goliath, for instance, were as well equipped as the Homeric Achaeans at Troy—brass helmet, a heavy coat of mail, brass greaves and a buckler, and a spear like a weaver's beam.

Although, like the Achaeans, the Philistines normally fought from chariots, they discarded them in favor of archers on the hilly Canaanite terrain. Another reason for their series of victories as reported in the Bible was their knowledge of iron. The Hebrews, having none, were forced to hide from this enemy "in caves, and in thickets, and in rocks, and in high places, and in pits," and the Philistines captured the Ark of the Covenant, the Hebrews' most sacred relic, defended though it was with fanatic bravery.

By 1100 B.C. Philistia had reached its fullest development. Each of the five original cities was an autonomous state, ruled by the local aristocracy under a *seren,* or "tyrant." The serens formed a federal council in charge of national affairs; the subject and allied cities and the few colonies had no part in the council, but wielded only local authority.

Philistine civilization was a mixture of Minoan and Canaanite elements. For example, the Philistines added Canaanite to Cretan gods, identifying the Semitic goddess Ishtar with their own Mother Goddess. They adopted the Canaanite language, but kept the Minoan script. They brought from Crete the grapevine and the olive tree, advanced the urbanization of Canaan at a time when the Hebrews had not even reached the full agricultural stage, and used efficiently the advantages accruing from the occupation of the routes between Egypt and Asia. Excellent soldiers, they hired themselves out as mercenaries throughout the Near East. Like their Minoan teachers they had theaters in which the sexes mixed freely. They relished acrobatic games, but, possibly as a result of Etruscan admixtures, developed gladiatorial tastes: Samson, the strongest man in Israel, was exhibited before an audience of 3000 men and women in the theater of Gaza. Their metal products, architecture, and pottery were degenerate Minoan types. Greatly outnumbered by the natives, in relation to whom they were a ruling aristocracy, they at best laid a veneer of Aegean culture over a Semitic base.

After King David expelled them from both the hinterland and their own state of Gath, the Philistines declined rapidly (*c.* 1000 B.C.). Some of them became tributaries of a revitalized Egypt. Then they lost their identity, becoming indistinguishable from their Hebrew conquerors. Only the port cities were left to themselves, probably because they supplied ships and sailors which brought foreign goods indispensable to the Hebrews.

The Hebrews to the Fall of Israel

We shall now speak of a people whose influence on the modern world has been more profound than that of any hitherto discussed. They are the Hebrews, a branch of the Semitic stock, who developed a character of their own only after their departure from Egypt.

Long before settling in Egypt the Hebrews had dwelt in Canaan along the Jordan River between the seacoast and the desert, a land given by God, they claimed, to their ancestor Abraham when he came from Ur with his wives and children, relatives, retainers, and flocks. They traced their descent from Abraham through his son Isaac and Isaac's son Jacob. The twelve historical Hebrew tribes descended, they believed, from Jacob's twelve sons, as recorded in their oldest holy book, *Genesis*.

Swept out of their Canaanite pastures by their kinsmen, the Hyksos, most of Abraham's descendants wandered into Egypt, where they continued to live until about 1300 B.C. When they finally left Egypt, Moses was their leader and Canaan their destination. But since hostile tribes blocked the road, and the "Promised Land" was in the hands of peoples (Edomites, Moabites, Ammonites, Canaanites, and Philistines) in no mood to be dispossessed, the conquest lagged. Generations of Hebrews fought and perished before sighting the land of their fathers. By the late 1200's, however, they had established themselves in parts of the "Promised Land," as we know from the Pharaoh Merneptah (1224–1214 B.C.), who boasts of defeating "Israel," among others, in the land of Canaan.

Despite this setback the Hebrews continued to expand into the hills southwest of Jerusalem and towards the Jordan valley. But as they coveted also the rich Philistine coast as well as its extension, the Plain of Sharon, they audaciously attacked two peoples stronger than themselves, the Philistines and the Canaanites. For nearly a century their task was hopeless, for whereas their weapons and tactics were almost those of Neolithic nomads, their enemies were superior to them in tactics and equipment and, still more, in political strength. They succeeded only after they united, first under Saul (1020–1005 B.C.), then under David (1005–965 B.C.).

Had Saul done nothing more than to accustom the autonomous tribes to cooperation and national rule, his place would be secure in the honor rolls of Israel. But he also wore down the Philistines, preparing the way for David's final victory. Unfortunately he fell out with the conservative religious leaders of Israel when he displayed some degree of humanity towards the enemy.

Superior to Saul both in military prowess and statesmanship was David. This remarkable man, portrayed as in youth subject to more than the ordinary array of human frailties, including cheating, adultery, and treachery, seems to have grown up to unique moral stature. Indeed, in his conversion from sinner to saint he uttered in some of the *Psalms* cries of repentance and sentiments of faith and hope that have ever since been the inspiration of men struggling towards virtue. Incidentally the story of his life as told in *II Samuel* (composed, like the *Iliad*, about the ninth century B.C.) is a model of historical writing. In vividness, accuracy, and detachment, nothing in all ancient literature is superior to it.

When David finally took Jerusalem, a stronghold controlling communications, the struggle for the "Promised Land" was over. Moreover, since Hatti's sun had set and Assyria's not yet risen, the mastery of Palestine meant control over a wide area from Sinai to Euphrates, from seacoast to desert. David converted his kingdom into an empire to which the neighboring states of Edom, Moab, and Ammon, the Syrian city of Damascus, and the Aramaean states to the north paid tribute, and with which the powerful Phoenician city-states found it wise to be friendly. Jerusalem, key to his power, was made the capital.

Solomon (965–925 B.C.), son of David, could afford to be a king of peace. He did not oppose Egypt's claim to suzerainty over Israel, for peace with Egypt meant profits from extensive international trade. He is even said to have taken a daughter of the reigning pharaoh as one of his chief wives, to insure Egyptian backing in his foreign relations. His control of the great international caravan roads depended on peace, and he knew it.

Solomon allied himself, as we have seen, with a business magnate, Hiram I of Tyre. He borrowed from Hiram the services of masons, stonecutters, bronze workers, and other artisans to build the royal stables for 480 horses, the governor's palace, and the city walls at Megiddo, as well as for his great constructions in Jerusalem. When the balance of trade turned hopelessly against him, Solomon ceded to the Phoenician king a strip of territory in Galilee containing twenty towns. Jointly these royal merchant-adventurers equipped a fleet for commercial operations on the Red Sea and the Indian Ocean.

Recent excavations have shown that Solomon's port of entry for Red Sea commerce was at Ezion-Geber, at the head of the Gulf of Aqaba, which divides Arabia from the Sinai Peninsula. Ezion-Geber also controlled the spice trade route from Arabia to Phoenicia and Syria, as well as Araba, between the Dead and the Red seas, rich in copper and iron. A smelting plant, making Ezion-Geber the Pittsburgh of Palestine, has been discovered there. The copper used in Solomon's buildings probably came from Araba. Evidence is continually mounting that the export of copper and copper articles was the cornerstone of Solomon's foreign trade. At Ezion-Geber the Queen of Sheba probably disembarked on her visit to Solomon from her south Arabian kingdom. Perhaps she made the voyage attracted not so much by the fame of the king's wisdom as by the glamor of his wealth. She brought spices, gold, and precious stones, in return for which she took in goods "all that it pleased her to ask." Her story probably romanticizes a commercial alliance.

Tribute, tolls, and returns from his flocks and fields Solomon applied in Oriental fashion to the upkeep of his harem and court in Jerusalem and the maintenance of a large army. Though the luxury of his court was a scandal to the puritan prophets, Solomon expressed his piety by

Fig. 6.1. Solomon's temple, model by E. G. Howland. Front view. At left, "Molten Sea" (*I Kings*, 7; *Ezek.*, 43:13–17). Right, "Altar of Burnt Offering." (*Archaeology* V, 1952, p. 165.)

building a temple to house the Ark of the Covenant and to honor the great Jehovah for Israel's prosperity. The temple was one in a series of royal buildings planned for the capital as a city within a city. Its three main divisions, vestibule, holy place, and holy of holies, all sprang from Canaanite practices. One of the architects was Uram-abi, the son of a Hebrew woman and a Phoenician bronze worker. The splendor of Solomon's temple was a tradition elaborated chiefly in the imagination of latter-day Judaism during the nostalgic years of the Babylonian captivity.

Lower than the House of Jehovah, to the south, rose the House of the King. Like the temple, it was inside a court, and close by it lived the pharaoh's daughter. A Hall of Justice and the houses of priests, officials, and secondary wives completed the royal precinct. These structures, too, in concept and in such details as the masonry pattern, the use of capitals (which the Greeks also borrowed from the Phoenicians two centuries later), and the style of gateways, were Phoenician adaptations.

But it is neither by studying Moses who led them out of Egypt, nor Joshua who brought them to the border of Canaan, nor Samuel the greatest of the Judges who ruled after Joshua, nor any king, that we can understand the people of Israel. The central place in Hebrew history and life belongs to Jehovah (Yahweh), god of the tribes of the Exodus and giver of the Ten Commandments. At Mount Sinai, or possibly at Mount Horeb on the border of Canaan, the Israelites swore allegiance to Him and He in turn vouchsafed to prosper them as His chosen people as long as they remained faithful. These Jehovah-worshipers may have been Arabians settled in south Palestine. The northern tribes, more akin to the Aramaeans[1] of Syria, at first had worshiped other gods, but finally they also adopted the Jehovah of their southern brethren. Jehovah had become the god of all the Hebrews at least by the time they were conquering Philistia and Canaan. The visible sign of His dominance was the Ark of the Covenant, a tent sheltering the holy chest containing the two stone tablets of the Ten Commandments, Jehovah's fundamental law to His people.

As the Hebrews evolved from roving pastoral tribes to a settled agricultural people, a serious problem arose for Jehovah's priests, indeed for all pious Hebrews. When the Hebrew pioneers learned from their Canaanite neighbors how to raise grain, cultivate fruit trees, and make olive oil and wine, they also necessarily learned the magic accompanying the religious ceremonies. Since Jehovah, essentially a pastoral god, knew nothing about agriculture, the Hebrew farmers saw no way out but to adopt the gods of Canaan. Thus they worshiped both Jehovah, the national leader and champion of the army, and the gods (baalim) of Canaan, who granted grain, fruit, and good wine and oil. In the end, Jehovah triumphed: as unseen captain of the host, He conquered and held sway over the land of Canaan and its gods, absorbing their powers and functions and taking over their sanctuaries and ceremonies.

Jehovah's triumph was due chiefly to two separate groups, the priests and the prophets. The priests possessed the art of divination, knew the rules of the clean and the unclean, and remembered the ancient national customs. They served in the tribal sanctuaries, as at Bethel, Dan, Gilgal, and Shiloh, forming independent guilds, tending to acquire a monopoly of the sacrificial rites and to charge fees for their services.

But then a contrary trend set in from Jerusalem. With the twofold purpose of serving the nation's interest and nationalizing the worship of the national god, the king and the clergy of the capital joined hands in making their temple Jehovah's only sanctuary. It took centuries of ruthlessness to realize this aim, since it involved the destruction or

[1] The Aramaeans are of importance beyond the space which can be devoted to them here. Nomadic in origin, they occupied Syria and blocked Assyrian access to the sea. Absorbing cultural influences from both Hittites and Egyptians, they built great cities, the most important being Damascus. Merchants like the Phoenicians, they spread their convenient alphabetic language (the language spoken by Jesus) as a commercial lingua franca throughout the Near East.

abandonment of every tribal shrine. The final act did not take place until 638 B.C. The temple's increased prestige brought the priests both increased authority and many vested interests, and a stake like that of king and aristocracy in the *status quo*.

The prophets differed from the priests in being neither trained nor commissioned for their task, but in their opinion they were called to it by the divine spirit. They formed a numerous profession with a mission to announce God's will as revealed to them. The worst of them, the false prophets, were fanatics or demagogues adept at exciting themselves and their listeners to religious delirium. But most were honorable, devoted to the people's and Jehovah's cause. During the Philistine wars, indeed in every national crisis, one prophet or another would arouse the masses. Repeatedly they used their control of public opinion to dictate to the government itself.

The heroic prophets recorded in the Bible—Elijah, Isaiah, Jeremiah, Micah—were far above average in statesmanship and intelligence. Endowed with rare understanding of the nation's needs and feeling themselves moved only by the spirit of God, they preached and battled to establish Jehovah's dominion over His people. They courageously attacked the wrongdoer, whether priest or layman, rich or poor, even the king himself. They were the voice of the national conscience. They defended the oppressed, setting up a supratemporal rule to which the nation itself had to bow: the will of God. They represented, too, the right of free speech. The strongest king turned a deaf ear to a prophet at his peril. Prophets deserved much of the credit for Jehovah's victory over the Canaanite *baalim*, and they had fostered the growth of a national monarchy, which in their view represented the will of God.

Separation and Foreign Rule

Under Solomon the monarchy reached its height and began to decline. His revenues did not cover the expenses for building the royal citadel, for maintaining the court and Jehovah's cult, and for fulfilling his diplomatic and trade commitments. Most shocking to his people was the percentage of the royal income budgeted for the gods of his foreign wives. Solomon levied oppressive taxes and imposed corvées in the Egyptian style. In assessing taxes he unwisely favored the southern tribes of Judah and Benjamin. He could truthfully plead that justice underlay this apparent discrimination, for the tribes of the mountainous south were mainly pastoral and poor, whereas the northern tribes, with richer soil, had become prosperous farmers. But since Solomon's ancestry was southern, the north turned this act into a political issue. When Rehoboam, his son and successor, failed to redress this grievance, the northern tribes seceded, forming the Kingdom of Israel, later called Samaria. Left to themselves, the two southern tribes constituted the Kingdom of Judah, with Jerusalem, the holy city, as capital.

The secession of the north was in many ways unavoidable. The tribes had been united only loosely and briefly. The north contained larger alien elements, especially Canaanites. It was agricultural, and, lying in close contact with commercial states like Phoenicia and Syria, and on the routes to Asia, Mesopotamia, and Egypt, it had also become commercial and urban, while Judah, though close to wealthy Egypt, had remained backward and pastoral. In short, while Israel developed a comparatively rich and prosperous society, Judah remained a land of poor and conservative shepherds.

Cosmopolitan Israel was so tolerant in religious matters as to arouse the prophets' anger. Its kings, moreover, fostered national sanctuaries to rival Jerusalem, set up new guilds of priests in competition with those of Solomon's temple, and allowed the worship of Jehovah as a bull, contrary to the first commandment, but in agreement with an old Hebrew practice. They even tolerated the public worship of the *baalim*. Eventually the religious conservatives, headed by the uncompromising Elijah and his disciple, the fanatic Elisha, who organized a conspiracy among army officers, reformed Israel. Through the efforts of these two prophets and their successors the official cult was purified. Even so, new divergencies continued to crop out between Judah and Israel. While Judah claimed that it alone kept the Holy Laws, Israel could assert that in most respects it was more faithful to tradition, whereas the prophets and scholars of Judah were guilty of interpolating Scripture. Echoes of this cleavage sound in the low repute of Samaritans in the New Testament, an implication that the tribes of Israel were heretical.

But in spite of differences, religious fellow-feeling was still strong enough for 200 years after David to preserve the consciousness of a common origin and a common destiny between Israel and Judah. The Judean shepherd-prophet Amos preached in Israel, and the Israelite Hosea in Judah. This unity rose also from similar social conditions in each kingdom. By the 700's B.C. the small freeholds allotted at the conquest to most of the population had fallen, through mortgage and foreclosure, to a few landowners. The upper classes, enriched by the expansion of trade, even in Judah, built palatial homes and lived in luxury, while the poor, unable to keep up with the increased cost of living, sank into serfdom or slavery. Merchants and army officers, stationed in foreign lands, married foreign women who brought with them foreign gods, tastes, and ideas. Thus apostasy and injustice were rampant among the chosen people. The priests themselves, in Judah as well as Israel, accepted the benefits of tainted prosperity, since the more victims they were commissioned to offer and the more incense to burn, the larger was their income. The blaring music they permitted at the festivals and their own resplendent vestments antagonized the devout. Indignant at the general corruption, especially at the presumption that God could be bribed with mere ceremonies into condoning evil-doing, the prophet Amos makes God thunder for justice and right instead of this hypocrisy. This conception of a moral God satisfied with nothing less than justice and righteousness was basic to all later development of Jewish ethics. Isaiah made the obligation of public morality more compelling by showing that God is all-powerful, laying pride and arrogance low in the dust, and that men and nations can be great only through faith in Him and compliance with His will. To this idea that God can break the strongest, Hosea adds another, that God is also love, and if He chastises man and society, He will also restore their strength. The entire development of Jewish religion as a strictly ethical monotheism grew out of the lofty conceptions of these great thinkers.

Amos, Isaiah, and Hosea saw the rebirth of the Assyrian Empire (eighth century B.C.). Amos, the eldest, was first to understand its significance, for he spoke of it as God's chosen instrument to afflict Israel for its sins. Ancient rivalries among the states of Syria and Phoenicia, between the Philistines and their Hebrew overlords, and between the Hebrew kingdoms themselves, made it easy for Assyria to enslave them all. Repeatedly Assyria's support was sought in interstate or factional quarrels. In Israel, for instance, after the reigning king, Zechariah, was assassinated, the successful pretender, Menahem, paid tribute to the Assyrian King Tiglath-pileser III to continue in office.

But Menahem's pro-Assyrian son was murdered in a new revolution. And when the murderer ascended the throne he refused to pay tribute and joined the king of Damascus in a coalition against Assyria. In vain Isaiah and Hosea warned Israel that this was suicidal. They went up and down the land, like Amos before them, predicting that God, the maker and breaker of nations Who uses one to punish another, would make Assyria His avenging angel. Their prediction was fulfilled to the letter.

Tiglath-pileser III came in 734. After taking Damascus and deporting its population, he marched against Israel, now too torn by internal dissension to offer much resistance. The kingdom would have fallen had not the pro-Assyrian faction done away with the king responsible for this train of evils. They installed Hosea as king to carry on as a faithful vassal of Assyria. When Hosea was persuaded by the nationalists to rebel and refuse the tribute, the new Assyrian king, Sargon II, ended Israel's independence. He destroyed Samaria, its capital, carried off into exile 27,000 leading Israelites, and annexed the kingdom as a province (722

B.C.), assuring obedience by repeopling the land with settlers from elsewhere in the Empire who could be counted on to discourage any reawakening of independence. Thus ended the northern kingdom.

The kingdom of Judah learned nothing from Israel's experience. One of its kings at war with Damascus had, against Isaiah's advice, asked for Assyrian help. Assyria came—and stayed. When the next king, backed by Egyptian gold, foolishly defied Sennacherib, Sargon's son, the latter sacked Judah, carried off 200,000 prisoners, and besieged Jerusalem (701 B.C.). Judah, too, would have perished but for some unforeseen event, perhaps a plague, which forced the Assyrian army to lift the siege. Sennacherib's own account of the campaign mentions besieging forty-six cities with battering-rams and earthworks, carrying away countless domestic animals as spoils, keeping King Hezekiah a virtual captive in Jerusalem. Hezekiah was forced to plead for mercy and to send to Nineveh, the Assyrian capital, thirty talents of gold and 800 of silver, together with cosmetics, jewels, ivory in bulk and ivory furniture, his daughters, his harem, and his musicians, male and female.

Despite these substantial losses of territory, population, and wealth, Judah retained a large degree of self-government. Its end did not come until after the fall of Assyria.

Chapter 7/ASSYRIA

From City-State to Empire

Philistines, Phoenicians, and Hebrews, even Egypt and Hatti, lost their independence to Assyria. The earliest history of this nation is hidden near Mosul, in Iraq, in a number of conical mounds marking urban centers containing shops, temples, and public buildings—refuges from floods and fortresses in war. War, or internal decay, destroyed the buildings, then wind and vegetation buried the whole level under sand and soil. Centuries later other men were to build above this deposit, and another phase of civilization emerged with its shops, temples, community buildings, and protective wall—itself to die and be buried by the same process, and in time to become the foundation of still another settlement.

In 1927 American archeologists began to excavate the largest of these Mesopotamian mounds, Tepe Gawra. What they discovered has profoundly modified our knowledge of early Assyria, adding four millennia to its history. Twenty-six layers of human habitation were concealed in that mound.

Ashur, the Assyrian capital, was built on the banks of the Tigris, some eighty miles south of Tepe Gawra. Its founders were Semites from the south who had received their culture from Babylon. But they were not the first community to settle in the neighborhood, for at that time Tepe Gawra had risen to level six, that is, it had seen the rise and fall of twenty civilizations. The earliest of these had flourished about 6500 B.C.

* Relief from the palace of Ashurbanipal. (Paris, Louvre; Giraudon photo)

Level six was Sumero-Akkadian in culture, living largely by trade, not only with Ur, Elam, and Armenia, but with Asia Minor, Palestine, and Syria, with the Cyclades and Central Europe and India. Clearly, other Semites had preceded the founders of Ashur up the Tigris. But Ashur had such vitality that within a century or two of its founding it absorbed Tepe Gawra. Accordingly, levels five to one fall entirely within the Assyrian period and form part of Assyrian history. The earliest buildings of Ashur were of Sumerian design and construction. Religion, the social and economic structure, the kingship and the constitution followed Sumerian models. Documents in clay were as indispensable for business and public administration in Assyria as they were in Sumer or Akkad; they were written in cuneiform and in a language only slightly different from Babylonian. Though some of these documents have preserved the names of kings who ruled as far back as the Sumero-Akkadian era, we know little about the early history of Ashur. Only this is clear: the Assyrians continued to expand enough to plant a colony in far away Cappadocia.

Assyria was unstrategically located. Between it and Akkad to the south was a plain where no invader could possibly be stopped except by stronger forces. The precipitous Zagros range to the east and the formidable Armenian plateau to the north, both sloping towards Assyria, made attack from those directions easy but defense difficult. The western steppe was no effective barrier either, for it was as easy for a foe to traverse as for Assyrians. In its early history, and intermittently afterwards, Assyria was therefore ruled by foreign invaders. Successively, Sargon I of Akkad, the Third Dynasty of Ur, Babylon under Hammurabi and under the Kassites themselves, as well as Mitanni and Hatti and even distant Egypt, held sway over it.

There was only one means to overcome these geographical handicaps, a strong army. Assyria therefore proceeded to build up the most powerful military machine the world had yet seen, and to use it not only for defense but for expansion abroad. But unlike the Roman legions, which were formidable even when led by mediocrities, the Assyrian army depended for victory on brilliant generals, so that Assyrian power depended on the prowess of the king.

The army relied mainly on archers and pikemen, some very lightly armored, some protected by a cuirass and a conical helmet, and carrying a short sword for close fighting. Coordinated with this infantry was the cavalry, which at first fought from chariots, three men to a chariot—a driver, a warrior, and an orderly manipulating a shield to protect the other two. Later on, when the warrior rode the horse (about 700 B.C.), he had the infantryman's bow and spear. Still later came the most original Assyrian contribution to the art of warfare, siege artillery. No fortified city could withstand the assault of Assyrian engines. A choice body of troops fought beside the king, but it was the foot-bowmen who wrought havoc on the enemy. A number of sculptured reliefs give a good picture of the Assyrian army in action. A description by one of the later kings gives as good a picture: telling how the infantry built roads through the rocky mountains, making them "fly in splinters like a mason's stone." The king at the head of his chariots, cavalry, and body-guard flies over the mountain like a bold eagle, followed by his engineers, camels, and draft-asses, and he encamps at the summit.

The Assyrian army's power cannot be entirely explained by the bravery of the individual soldier, the competence of the king-general, or the sheer numerical strength so easy to attain in a country where every able-bodied man was subject to military service. Perhaps it is better explained by the theory that the Assyrian used iron extensively, though excavators find more iron agricultural or household implements than iron weapons. Indeed something like a revolution in the metal industry apparently took place under Sargon II (722–705 B.C.) when he invaded Urartu and exploited its iron mines. Cunning, too, aided Assyrian armies: an efficient espionage and intelligence service was conducted by royal governors and bureaucrats in the provinces and centered in the king's palace. Frequently when the troops entered a country they were aided by carefully organized fifth columns.

Lastly, according to the Assyrians, the great god Ashur himself and his divine consort Ishtar gave the army their special protection. He was the keystone of Assyrian strength. The city and the state were named after him, and most rulers adopted his name, combining it with their own. As a warrior-god he not only claimed authority over the four corners of the earth, but was appeased by nothing less than the destruction and death of the enemy. With Ashur's blessings militarism and cruelty became a fixed state policy. Heraldry itself shows this. Whereas the symbol of Egypt under Ikhnaton was a disk scattering rays benignly, that of Athens an owl, symbol of wisdom, that of Rome a she-wolf to represent that city as nurse of civilization, the symbol of Assyria was the war god as archer. Even more revealing of the Assyrian character are hunting scenes in which animals, transfixed by arrows, writhe in agony. Indeed Assyrian art reached its highest expression in scenes of bloodshed.

With their new army the Assyrians of the 1300's B.C. began to attack and wear down their western overlord, Mitanni. Emboldened, they sacked Babylon (1247 B.C.), the ancient holy city which had given them their religion and culture. The world of that day was shocked by Assyrian ruthlessness on that occasion, for not only was the city razed to the ground, but Marduk's temple was despoiled and, still greater sacrilege, his statue was carried off to Ashur as if he were a mean prisoner.

Assyria became a world power when a statesman king, Tiglath-

Fig. 7.1. Dying lioness from palace of Ashurbanipal, Nineveh (668–633 B.C.). Characteristic Assyrian cruelty, accentuated by the delicacy of the workmanship, is revealed in this rendition of animal suffering. (London, British Museum)

pileser I (1114–1076 B.C.), stepped boldly into the vacuum created by Hittite decline, conquering, as he records in a boastful inscription, forty-two states. When Phoenicia and Syria acknowledged his overlordship, he directed his chief archer to dip his weapons in the waters of the Mediterranean as a symbol that this sea was his. He created the permanent pattern of Assyrian kingship, a combination of military glory and the promotion of culture. He lived a strenuous life, chasing sharks, hunting lions, above all, conquering cities and peoples. But he also practiced the peaceful arts, building temples and palaces, opening pleasure-gardens and parks for himself and his court, introducing new plants, distributing new farm lands, and expanding his profitable ranches.

With Tiglath-pileser's death Assyria's early prominence ends. For some 350 years little is recorded but the cruelty of Ashurnasirpal II (883–859 B.C.), the embodiment of Assyrian ruthlessness. He punished his enemies by flaying them alive and nailing their skins up along the highways, or by adorning his city gates with their severed heads. It was his practice to destroy a captured city by fire. He was merciless towards the inhabitants, cutting off the hands and ears of the men, putting out their eyes, stacking them up in rows—like cordwood—to die. The children were burned alive and the chiefs taken to Ashur for more refined tortures. Small wonder he could write, "Over the ruins my shadow rested; in the gratification of my wrath I find contentment." Despite this terrorism Assyria declined again. The warning of the Hebrew prophet, Jonah, "Yet forty days, and Nineveh shall be overthrown," seems to refer to this period of Assyrian cruelty.

Assyria at the Height of Its Power

Assyria reached its peak under Tiglath-pileser III (745–727 B.C.). He reconquered the lands which had once fallen to his famous namesake, including Syria, Phoenicia, Philistia, and southwest Arabia. We have seen how he treated Israel. He is credited with originating, or refining, two methods of imperial control. If he doubted a vassal king's fidelity, he replaced him with an Assyrian governor, thus turning a semi-free state into a province. Secondly, he would transplant the inhabitants of a rebellious state to other parts of his Empire, replacing them with new settlers. Practiced on a larger scale by his successors, these wholesale deportations became the chief scandal of Assyrian imperialism. But inhuman though it was, it meant more than the mere elimination of rebels. Often the displaced groups developed an interest in their new homes, becoming permanent and contented citizens. The Empire gained in the mingling of races and the interpenetration of cultures.

Sargon II (722–705 B.C.) produced another innovation in imperalism, one followed by the Romans, the settling in subject areas of Assyrian colonists, to farm or fight for him as need arose. Like the Sargon I of legend he had no pedigree; like him he seized the crown and became a world conqueror. He extended the Empire in every direction: to central Armenia, to a number of states east of the Tigris, to the Persian Gulf and across Arabia, to the border of Egypt, to the Mediterranean coast, including, as we have seen, Israel, to Cyprus, and to Asia Minor as far west as the Halys River. For defense he built a chain of blockhouses, like the later Roman Limes, on the border against Elam. Since comparatively small garrisons could thus ward off incursions, he was able to conserve Assyrian manpower. The resurgence of Babylon was his most difficult problem.

Most Assyrian kings had been builders on a large scale. Not content, like Pericles, Augustus, or, later, Napoleon, with beautifying their capital, they built whole cities. This is the reason why the pre-Sargonid kingdom had at least three capitals, Ashur, Kalhu, and Nineveh. To rival his predecessors, Sargon II decided to build the perfect metropolis, one which in size, strength, and beauty should express to the full Assyrian power.

Dur-Sharrukîn, or Sargontown, was primarily a fortress, surrounded by a wall seven or eight stories high and as wide as a six-lane highway, with towers every hundred feet. There were eight strong gates, each dedicated to a god. Around the wall was a moat; on the far side of the moat

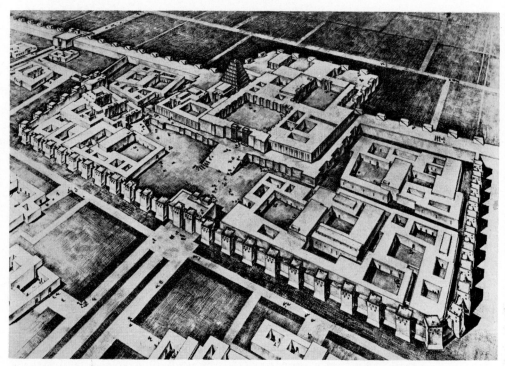

Fig. 7.2. Sargon II's fortified palace, Dur-Sharrukîn, reconstruction. Built in the late 8th century B.C., it contained 700 rooms, on a platform over 1000 feet long and nearly as wide, with 28-foot exterior walls. It was destroyed by the Babylonians, 612 B.C. (Chicago, Ill., Oriental Institute)

was a battlemented parapet. Inside the wall stood the palace, a colossal bastion covering twenty-five acres. A tower built on superimposed terraces like a modern recessed skyscraper rose about twelve stories. The mansion proper contained a series of courts, reception halls, lodgings for civil and military officials, the servants' rooms and of course the king's apartments. Like its Sumerian prototype, it was of brick, ribbed with pilasters and faced with enameled brick and glazed frescoes. Particularly striking was a series of alabaster reliefs of winged animals symbolic of Assyrian strength, portraying the great personages of the Empire in procession and glorifying the king's achievements.

Sargon founded a dynasty of extremely able rulers. His son Sennacherib (704–681 B.C.) had shown talent as general and governor before he ascended the throne. As king he called a halt to conquest. Instead of wasting the Empire's strength in new adventures, he strove to consolidate its gains and, breaking new ground, to establish confidence between himself and his vassals. Unfortunately he failed, not only because Assyrianism and his personal policy were mutually exclusive, but for two other reasons as well: the growing power of the Chaldeans and the intractability of the kingdom of Judah.

Sennacherib emulated his father's passion for building. He returned the seat of government to Nineveh, which he reconstructed magnificently, opening new quarters on reclaimed land, and building an "incomparable" new palace. He opened large squares to relieve the crowded streets, brought in a new supply of spring water in open canals from some nearby hills, and created a farming suburban area where experiments with new plants were made and cotton introduced. The iconographic stone friezes of the palace record his military and civil achievements. They also show that, despite a wider acquaintance with the outside world, native sculpture still attended in the old way to careful detail and to portraying human and animal figures with remarkable vigor and naturalness.

Sennacherib himself deserves much of the credit for the flourishing state of the arts: not only was he a good administrator, but he assured prosperity to the common people and took a personal interest in literature and technology. He enlarged the library founded by his father. He took credit for having discovered a new process of bronze casting, boasting that he spared workers much groaning. He stimulated a revival of Sumerian studies, took Sumerian names for his most pretentious monuments, and encouraged the collection of Sumerian classics, especially the Creation Epic. He also encouraged the study of Aramaean and Hebrew as indispensable languages for an imperial race.

Sennacherib's *Annals* are written in a style so inflated as to conceal the dubiousness of some of his "successes." The description of the battle of Halule (691 B.C.), for example, tells of the enemy host raising a dust like storm clouds. But the gods favored Sennacherib, who is pictured in his chariot, armed with coat of mail and helmet, bow and javelin, raging like a lion, roaring like the storm god as he decimates the foe, cutting their throats and making "their gullets and entrails run down upon the wide earth," while the war horses wade in blood and the royal war chariot is bespattered with it. Such was Assyria at its height; small wonder that so many nations thirsted for its fall.

The Problem of Chaldea

About 1100 B.C. Semitic groups called Chaldeans reached Babylon from the Persian Gulf and took Babylonia without much fighting, for the ruling Babylonian nobility was decadent, while the people's will to fight had been weakened by the infiltration of another group of Semites, the Aramaeans. Unless checked, the Chaldeans bade fair to occupy the entire Babylonian plain up to the very gates of Assyria.

Luckily for Assyria, the five Chaldean tribes were disunited. It was not until 722 B.C., the year of Sargon's accession, that a great statesman,

Merodach-baladan, fused the tribes into a nation. Then, having engineered an alliance with the king of Elam, who had what the Chaldeans lacked, an army almost as good as Assyria's own, he made himself king. The natives accepted him largely because four centuries of living together had made Chaldeans and Babylonians practically one in speech, religion, and culture.

To have so ambitious a prince on the Babylonian throne worried Sargon, for such was the éclat of that throne since the days of the great Hammurabi and such the prestige of Babylon that no Babylonian king worth his salt could fail to aspire to imperial grandeur. The parallel of Rome comes to mind, where the memory of past greatness and the very sight of ancient monuments have spurred popes and lay statesmen into trying to revive its glories. Clearly no Assyrian king, least of all Sargon II, could tolerate a usurper as ambitious as Merodach-baladan ruling from a dynamic center like Babylon. And so in 709 B.C. Sargon drove Merodach-baladan out of the city, allowing him to retain control of that part of Babylonia above the Tigris-Euphrates junction.

The expulsion of Merodach-baladan from the capital did not stop the Chaldeans' ascendancy. So deep were their roots in Babylonian soil that in less than a century they were to produce the best flowering of Babylonian culture. The old Babylonian stock was so rejuvenated that neither the unreconciled Babylonian nobility nor the mighty Sennacherib himself, who had meantime succeeded Sargon, were able to prevent Merodach-baladan's return.

In the end, however, Sennacherib got rid of the usurper and then sought to win the confidence of the Chaldeans by leaving in their hands as much self-rule as Assyrian interests would allow. But the uncompromising Chaldeans formed a new alliance with Elam and most of the old Sumero-Akkadian states and massacred the whole pro-Assyrian party. Sennacherib now had no alternative but to punish the rebellious city. He took it after a difficult siege, destroyed fortifications, diverted the canals to flood houses and temples, deported its inhabitants, and even carried away the god Marduk. The battle of Halule was an episode of this war. Sennacherib carried off a total of 200,000 Chaldeans to other parts of the Empire, replacing them with an equal number of exiles from Judah, Phoenicia, and Syria. Deprived of its leading men and its capital, Babylonia became a reduced Assyrian province.

To further his campaign Sennacherib had built a fleet to speed up troop movement along the Gulf coast, the rivers, and the canals. He built another fleet in the Mediterranean to neutralize the troublesome influence of Egypt.

After Sennacherib left Babylon a swamp, Esarhaddon, his son (680–669 B.C.) , rebuilt it for sentimental reasons, strange as sentiment may seem in an Assyrian king. He could not forget after all that Babylon was Assyria's mother-city, and he wanted to gain the good-will not only of the Chaldeans but of the entire Semitic world which reverenced the holy city. He felt that a strong city there was to Assyria's advantage, as a barrier against Elam and a link with the Persian Gulf. Lastly he needed to have peace near home while campaigning against Egypt. But it was necessary to prevent the new Babylon from setting itself up as a rival.

Ashurbanipal III (668–633 B.C.), Esarhaddon's son, tried to solve the problem by turning Babylonia into a family appanage, installing his brother, Shamash-shum-ukin, as vassal-king. For seventeen years lord and vassal lived in peace, but finally circumstances forced Shamash-shum-ukin to choose between Assyrian allegiance and Babylonian support. He entered an alliance with the nationalist party of Elam, then at war with Assyria. But the implacable Ashurbanipal moved so swiftly that his brother finally set fire to his own palace, perishing in the flames (649 B.C.). The victor assumed the Babylonian crown.

Elam, the other party in the anti-Assyrian coalition, was allowed to retain its dynasty provided it suppressed the nationalists and prevented further raids on Assyria. When it failed to do so, the dynasty was replaced with pro-Assyrian princes. This experiment too was a failure. When the nationalist party induced the new king, Teumman, to revolt under threat of dethronement, Ashurbanipal captured him in a short campaign and had him beheaded. A bas-relief in the British Museum shows the palace garden with the victor banqueting with the Elamite queen near a tree from which hangs the head of her husband.

Egypt and the Fall of Assyria

Though Babylon was subjected and Elam cowed, Assyria's perils were not over. There still was Egypt. Since the reign of Ramses III (1195–1164 B.C.) this country had become, except for short intervals, a third-rate power. Feudal interests, priestly intrigues, and civil wars had again split it into the two kingdoms of Upper and Lower Egypt. In the former the high priest of Amon had usurped the throne. Driven out by revolution, he founded a kingdom in Ethiopia the resources of which enabled him to rule Upper Egypt through puppet pharaohs. Confusion was worse confounded in Lower Egypt, now split into quasi-feudal principalities. At one time four or five princes contended for the title of pharaoh. Unity was restored only during Sennacherib's reign in Assyria.

A united Egypt seemed destined to take a hand in the affairs of Syria, Palestine, and Phoenicia. Promises of Egyptian help had lured Judah into challenging the rule of Sennacherib. Egyptian gold also had induced Sidon and other Phoenician cities, irritated by Assyrian commercial competition, to revolt. Esarhaddon, who had succeeded Sennacherib, made an example of Sidon (676 B.C.) destroying it and peopling its successor with Chaldean war prisoners. But to reach the real troublemaker, he invaded Egypt, conquering the Delta, destroying Memphis (671 B.C.) , and lodging Assyrian garrisons in the more important centers. His plans to subjugate Upper Egypt as well were cut short by death. His successor, Ashurbanipal III, tried at first to control Egypt by conciliating native princes but, when they revolted, he captured Thebes (661 B.C.) and sacked it, deporting its inhabitants and recolonizing it with Elamites. Here Assyrian militarism reached a peak, but it did not hold it, for by 652 Psamtik, an Egyptian national savior, had driven the foreigner out.

Psamtik (663–609 B.C.) founded the XXVIth (Saite) Dynasty. He curbed the feudal princes and freed the country from its dependence on Libyan soldiers who, though Egyptianized, had sided with the feudal lords and kept the kingdom weak for fully five hundred years. He built a new army, composed of loyal Greek mercenaries, chiefly Ionians, Carians, and Syrians. Greek merchants grew so prosperous and so hated that one of Psamtik's successors, Ahmose II, found it politic to concentrate them in a colony, Naucratis, on the Canopic branch of the Nile (565 B.C.) . Either Psamtik or an immediate successor allowed Hebrew refugees to plant another colony, on the island of Elephantine, in upper Egypt. Psamtik averted future usurpation by the clergy of Amon by appointing women of the royal family as high priests.

Psamtik's reforms brought prosperity and a revival of culture along with political stability. The pyramids were repaired, antique trappings and titles resurrected, ancient rites and beliefs reintroduced, and archaic literary and artistic forms revived, though without the ancient originality and vigor, portraiture especially being empty, uniform, and childish. Only technique improved: statues of the period are highly polished; the bronzework and pottery are competent if not inspired.

Driven out of Egypt, Ashurbanipal turned his attention to Elam, where revolt continued despite Teumman's execution. About 646 B.C. the capital, Susa, was destroyed, the population transplanted, the kingdom reduced to a province. The Assyrian conqueror posed as Sumer's heir and avenger, bringing back to his capital Sumerian statues, spoils of age-old Elamite raids on Ur.

Victory over Elam closed the military career of Ashurbanipal. According to legend, he spent the rest of his life in the pursuit of pleasure. The name Sardanapalus—a corruption of Ashurbanipal—is still a term for one who wastes his time in the gross pleasures of sensuality and gluttony. But he, like his antagonist Psamtik, was also a patron of the arts. He built and restored palaces, temples, and military constructions. His palace at Nineveh marks the highest development of Assyrian architecture and sculpture. Its reliefs of men and beasts in glazed brick are not only good art, but a rich historical document of the vitality of this warlike people and the grandeur of their empire. They acquaint us with the king's pageants, festivals, and hunts, his campaigns, conquests, and triumphs at which captured kings dragged him in his car to Ashur's temple for jubilant thanksgiving.

The British Museum now has in its possession Ashurbanipal's additions to the libraries of Sennacherib and Sargon: tens of thousands of clay tablets containing letters, reports, statistics, political, military, and administrative documents, books on magic, astrology, mathematics, and medicine, and grammars and annals, all giving us a broad view of the last phase of the history and civilization of this remarkable people.

Shortly after the death of Ashurbanipal internal discord and the combined blows of Chaldeans and Medes caused his Empire to crumble. While his successor was involved in a bloody struggle with a pretender, the Chaldean general Nabopolassar seized the Babylonian crown, and, having consolidated his power, allied himself with the Median King Cyaxares to destroy Assyria. The Medes, with other Indo-Europeans, the Cimmerians from Asia Minor and the Ouman-Manda from the Armenian highlands, had been waiting five or six centuries to lay their hands on the riches of the great empire. Assyria had no leader capable of staving off disaster. Civil and foreign wars had sapped its vitality. Its yeoman population had dwindled to the vanishing point, and its army consisted chiefly of non-Assyrian conscripts. Nor did the subject peoples care to help, so thoroughly had they been alienated by the Assyrian policy of destruction. When Nineveh, the destroyer, fell (612 B.C.), its contemporaries recognized the end of an era.

But if Assyria had destroyed, it had also built—and enduringly. It suppressed the opposition of local and national units, and it tried to destroy their culture. But in return it evolved a supranational society, only in part created in response to imperial greed or royal ambition. For a long time the city-states and tribes of the Fertile Crescent had been practically one in blood, language, religion, culture, production, and exchange. The need of also uniting them politically, by conquest, federation, or any other means, was evident, at least to the Assyrian rulers. Assyria succeeded where Egypt and Hatti had failed. More important for the stream of history, its success, limited and short though it was, served as model for a more gifted and humane people, the Persians.

Chaldea and the Fall of Judah

The quasi-annihilation of Judah at the hands of Sennacherib (701 B.C.) produced in the stricken nation a deep searching of heart. No nation could suffer, as Judah had, the loss of half of its citizens without asking what was wrong with itself or the world, or why God had forsaken it. Many inhabitants turned to new gods. The government played safe, officially adhering to the old ritualistic worship of Jehovah, but also permitting the Phoenician worship which involved burning children alive at the altar of Moloch and equating Moloch with Jehovah.

Two steps were taken to bring the people back to the pure worship. One was the extermination of every alien cult. Although by no means easy, this reform was largely successful. The other step was the resumption of the eighth-century movement to destroy every tribal sanctuary of Jehovah, however time-honored. Henceforth only in the temple at Jerusalem could sacrifices be offered, festivals kept, and the priests allowed to officiate. Josiah, the king, supported this program. He demolished the last remaining shrines (*c.* 621 B.C.), removing the priests to Jerusalem, attaching them to the temple, and supporting them by its revenues. The principle behind this reform, that Jehovah, the one national god, must have only one national sanctuary, had been inherent in the teaching of Amos and the other eighth-century prophets. But the seventh-century program proposed more than a mere purification of the worship; it prescribed a higher standard of human relations. Justice was not enough; God also demanded charity.

In spite of these efforts Judah suffered Israel's fate; it eventually lost what self-government it had been allowed after 701 B.C., and then ceased to exist altogether. God's instrument in this case was Babylon, which, by treaty with the Mede Cyaxares, had inherited the defunct Assyrian Empire's southern and western provinces, including Judah. Judah was at first a loyal vassal of Babylon. It recognized the Chaldean overlord as the rightful heir of Assyria, not simply out of expediency, but because the prevailing party headed by King Josiah identified the Babylonian claims with the national interest and Jehovah's glory. Indeed when the Egyptian Necho (609–594 B.C.), Psamtik's son, reached out to dominate Palestine, Judah's army opposed him (608 B.C.) in a fierce battle at Megiddo. Unfortunately the defenders were crushed and Josiah himself fatally wounded. Necho now imposed on Judah an indemnity corresponding to $2,500,000, and forced upon it a new king, Jehoiakim.

Under this puppet king (608–597 B.C.) the clergy was pro-Egyptian, but nobles and the people followed the pro-Babylonian prophets Jeremiah and Ezekiel, on the ground that God had decreed that Babylon should triumph and subject both Egypt and Judah. The issue was settled at Carchemish (605 B.C.) where the Chaldean crown prince Nebuchadrezzar ended Necho's expansionist dreams. As a result of this battle, every city, kingdom, and principality from the Taurus to the Egyptian border paid homage to the new master.

With unusual moderation, Nebuchadrezzar left Jehoiakim on his throne on condition of his loyalty to Babylon. Jeremiah for his part urged Jehoiakim to abandon his allegiance to the doomed Necho. He also prophesied that the Lord would punish Judah if Jehoiakim continued to condone heathen practices and the oppression of the poor and the weak.

But Jehoiakim could not read the signs. When he revolted under the pressure of the pro-Egyptian party, Nebuchadrezzar's vengeance was swift. Jerusalem was invested (597 B.C.) and the king apparently slain. The defenders were so demoralized that they left his body unburied.

Although Jehoiakim's successor surrendered to save the city, he was made prisoner and taken to Babylon after a reign of only three months, and with him were carried his mother, his wives, the chief civil and military authorities, and thousands of artisans who were to help build Babylon into a magnificent capital. Also among the exiles were the leaders of the clergy, among them the prophet-priest Ezekiel, friend though he was of Babylon.

Nebuchadrezzar now appointed as king Zedekiah (597 B.C.) who, despite his oath of loyalty to Babylon, allowed the Egyptian party to come back to life. Judah was again a house divided, torn asunder by the pressure of rival empires. So-called "false prophets" promised that God would shatter Babylon's "wooden" yoke, while Jeremiah declared that the yoke was of iron, God-wrought, and that Jehovah had appointed Nebuchadrezzar a scourge to chastise his people.

The "false prophets" carried the day. They persuaded the weak Zedekiah to join certain other states in a hopeless revolt, assuring him of Egyptian help. But Egypt proved of little assistance, most of the allies withdrew, and Judah paid the full penalty. Jerusalem was besieged and taken in 586 B.C. The royal palace, the public buildings, the houses of the rich, and the mighty city walls were levelled, the temple profaned and destroyed as a center of intrigue. The fleeing Zedekiah was captured, his sons were killed in his presence, and his eyes put out (the standard treatment for a rebel) ; he and the ringleaders were taken in fetters to Babylon.

After this catastrophe Judah lay for a time inert, its remnants of population bereft of direction and spirit, its towns levelled, its leaders and artisans in imposed or voluntary exile, its traditions forgotten. Yet out of the chastisement of the nation and the advent of simpler social groups it was possible to shape the Hebrew religion along the lines traced first by Amos and later by Jeremiah and another prophet, the so-called Deutero-Isaiah.

The Israelites and Judeans who went to Assyria, Babylon, Egypt, and other lands initiated the movement known as the Diaspora, that is, the scattering of the Chosen People in groups or colonies in almost every city of the civilized world.

The Babylonian Exile has been called the supreme test of Hebrew vitality, and the Judeans the only people of antiquity known to have been taken wholesale into captivity and still to have retained their religious and social identity. The Exile proved that the spiritual community could adapt itself to and develop under the most adverse conditions, and adversity bred leaders in the highest prophetic tradition.

Transcending all else was the loftier concept of God which evolved from the nation's downfall. Only the shortsighted could say that Jehovah had been vanquished by Babylon. The people as a whole accepted the prophets' teaching that whatever had happened had been willed by Him. He became in their thought the maker of history and the author of the moral order, guiding individuals and nations, causing the rise of Assyria to punish heathenish Israel, then calling upon Babylon to chastise faithless Judah. When within two generations Persia in turn destroyed Babylon and set the exiles free, it seemed clearer than ever that Jehovah used the great empires as instruments of His holy will.

This was the theme of the prophets, that from the ruin of Jerusalem and the flames of the temple a new era would arise for Israel. Historically the tragedy of those who lived in exile by the waters of Babylon, and those who were left behind under the foreign yoke, purified the nation. Both groups emerged from their ordeal less nationalistic and warlike, and with a better understanding of the spirituality and universality of the Kingdom of God. But since the exiles were culturally more advanced, when the Persians let them come back they were the leaders in reshaping the national life on the prophetic pattern. Having lived abroad, they were more aware that Israel was merely part of the wide world, with no more control over its destiny than its masters seemed to have over theirs. Subject and master, province and empire, each was working out God's plan. This new generation of Hebrews henceforth we call the Jews, and their thought and way of life Judaism.

Chapter 8 / THE PERSIAN EMPIRE

The Medes and Persians

The Medes, who had contributed most to the overthrow of the Assyrian Empire, had long lived along Assyria's eastern fringe and had fought the Empire as early as 837 B.C. They were kin to the Scythians and the Cimmerians; while the latter attacked Lydia, the Medes engaged Assyria.

Their ancestors, the Iranians, are known at least as early as 2000 B.C. Their land, the Iranian plateau, connects westward with the Anatolian plateau and eastward with the high plateau of Afghanistan. To the north and northwest the plateau rises to form mountain ranges, perpetually snow-covered, where rainfall is abundant, but in the center and southeast there are vast sand and salt deserts, roamed over by nomadic tribes. Here the days are hot and the nights cool. The south coast is low and subtropical. The rivers serve less for navigation than for irrigation, which produces abundant crops, especially wheat.

Settling first in Turkestan, the Iranians later moved southwest along the Caspian, to the Tigris and the Persian Gulf. Their name, a variant of *Aryan,* long in disuse, reappeared in the nationalist upsurge after World War I to designate the area held by their descendants. By the 800's B.C. when they fell foul of Assyria, the Iranians had split into two branches:

the Medes in the north around Ecbatana and the Persians in the south around Pasargadae.

The seminomadic Median tribes, addicted as they were to raids and living in near-anarchy, offered constant temptation to Assyria to intervene in their affairs. At last a chieftain, Deioces (708–655 B.C.), organized them and made his peace with Assyria, but at the price of vassalage. He made Ecbatana the capital and fostered Assyrian culture among the wild tribesmen. One of his innovations was destined to affect deeply not only the Medes and Persians, but later peoples in both Europe and Asia. He adopted the Nineveh court protocol, making the royal palace a forbidden mansion where the king, divinely set up above men, could neither be seen, heard, nor addressed by the ordinary subject. Phraortes, a son of Deioces, added the Persian tribes to the kingdom (mid-seventh century B.C.) .

Media became a great power under Cyaxares (633–584 B.C.), at whose accession Assyria was disintegrating. His first task was to strengthen the kingdom by uniting Medes and Persians both politically and militarily. Like Deioces an admirer of Assyria, he reorganized the war machine on the Assyrian model, building up a compact infantry armed with sword and pike, and developing a skilful archer-corps trained to shoot on foot or horseback and from all positions, even in retreat. And since on their wide fertile uplands they had bred horses extensively, the Medes and Persians had more cavalry than did Assyria or any other nation. Cavalry remained the most distinctive fighting force of both Medes and Persians, even centuries later when, under the name of Parthians, their successors fought the Roman Empire.

Having reorganized the army, Cyaxares made ready to conquer Assyria, in spite of his failure to form an alliance with Nabopolassar, King of Chaldean Babylon (c. 625–605 B.C.), an alliance he had tried to cement by giving his granddaughter in marriage to Nebuchadrezzar, the Chaldean crown prince. As we have seen, in 612 B.C., the Medes and Babylonians destroyed Nineveh, and in 605 B.C. Assyria ceased to exist. While Babylon took over its southern and western provinces and the Asia Minor district fell to Lydia, Assyria proper, with its northern and eastern possessions, became subject to Media. But, like Chaldean Babylon, Media itself was short-lived.

While the Mede Phraortes was subjugating the Persian tribes, a tribal subgroup, the Achemenid clan, migrated to Elam, apparently to preserve its freedom. There it brought new vigor to the local Iranian groups which had existed since the Kassite invasion. Before long an Achemenid chieftain conquered the principality of Susa, but as vassal of the Median king, Astyages. Finally the Achemenid Cyrus revolted against his suzerain, conquered Ecbatana, and seized the crown (549 B.C.) . He allowed the vanquished king to live in honor as a prisoner of war, a humanity

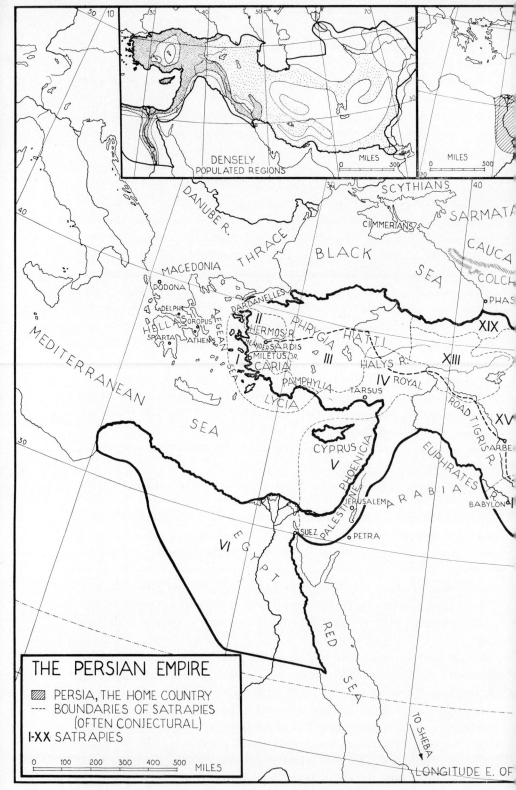

Fig. 8a. Map of the Persian Empire. Insets show population distribution, Assyrian

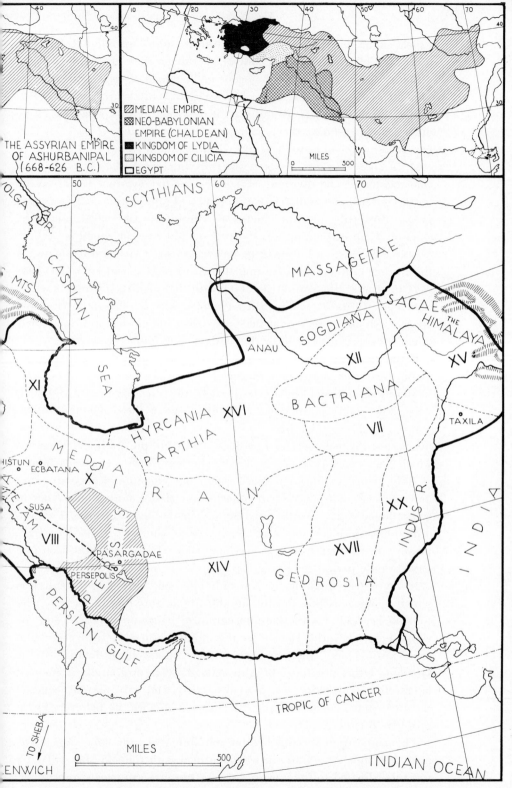

THE ASSYRIAN EMPIRE
OF ASHURBANIPAL
(668-626 B.C.)

MEDIAN EMPIRE
NEO-BABYLONIAN
EMPIRE (CHALDEAN)
KINGDOM OF LYDIA
KINGDOM OF CILICIA
EGYPT

MILES
0   500

Empire of Ashurbanipal, and early kingdoms of the Ancient Near East.

which augured well for the fate of future subject-peoples. Roles were now reversed, the Persians in control, the Medes their associates.

The Persian tribes were homogeneous in blood, speech, and religion, but had attained different levels of civilization. While six tribal groups had settled down to an agricultural way of life, four were still pastoral. Like other Iranian peoples, they subdivided their tribes into clans, each clan governed by a chief assisted, as in early Greece and Rome, by a council of elders. When the Persian state was fully organized, the tribes and the clans became feudal divisions, attached, some loosely, some firmly, to the central government and socially differentiated into peasants, warriors, and priests. Both tribe and clan chiefs were considered, and called, kings; the chief of the united nation was styled King and King of Kings.

Like their western kinsmen the Greeks, Latins, Celts, and Germans, or their other kinsmen who became the aristocracy of India, the Persians were in general frugal and temperate, with that dignity of manners which their cousins, the Romans, called *gravitas*. The Greeks, those close observers, were impressed by the Persians' strong and musical speech, by their talent for government, and by their private and public virtues.

Both Medes and Persians worshiped natural forces, that is, the sun, moon, earth, fire, water, and winds. To these deified cosmic forces they sacrificed animals slain by a priestly caste, the Magi, originally a Median tribe. The Magi's power apparently grew out of their monopoly of funeral rites. They supervised the exposure of the corpse, which was not buried until it had been torn by dogs or birds of prey, a practice against which later Persians reacted, covering the body with wax before burial.

This change in burial practice is but one example of a much wider movement, away from Magian concepts, towards a more refined view of god and god's place in the universe and in the hearts of men. This reformation was chiefly the work of Zoroaster, who lived in eastern Iran, possibly in the eighth century B.C. or earlier. His doctrine has been preserved in the part of the Persian scriptures (*Avesta*) called the "Gathas."

In Zoroaster's teaching there is only one god, Ahura-Mazda, unrepresented by images. He is not the sun, but the mighty lord of the sun, who controls heavenly bodies, the alternation of light and darkness, and the whole physical world. He guides the moral world also, since from him come justice, piety, good thought, welfare, and good ordinance of the kingdom. Other attributes of Ahura-Mazda have profoundly influenced later religious thinking. He is man's judge, who will one day conduct the great judgment to reward with his own immortality believers in his prophet Zoroaster.

This Zoroastrian doctrine became contaminated with older Magian elements. In time Ahura-Mazda was identified with the sun and still later was subordinated to the morning star, Mithra, the sun-god's forerunner.

Another Persian belief was in the guardian spirit, similar to the Roman belief in the genius or the Jewish and Christian faith in the guardian angel. The Persians believed also in evil spirits, *Daivas,* led by Ahriman, lord of darkness. Ahura-Mazda and Ahriman are seen in perpetual conflict, light against darkness, good against evil. Man, who has free will to choose between them, by positive action can help the forces of good to prevail against evil. Man can produce good in the physical world around him, changing the wilderness, for instance, into parkland and orchard: into a paradise, to use a Persian word. He must replace evil with good, especially within himself; for this Ahura-Mazda will hold him accountable on Judgment Day. These doctrines decisively influenced postexilic Judaism, Manichaeism (a religion which enlisted the youthful Augustine among its votaries, representing Satan as coeternal with God), and heretical Christians, like the Gnostics. Their emphasis on justice and self-improvement, coupled with their innate humanity and liberalism, combined to make the Persians a nation of upright citizens and wise and tolerant rulers.

The Kingdom of Lydia

Having liberated the Persians from the Medes, Cyrus set about empire-building. His first foreign war was with Lydia, a kingdom in the valleys of the parallel rivers Hermos and Meander in western Asia Minor. After the fall of the Hittites, Lydia had expanded eastward to the Halys River. Its population included several Asian groups, principally Carians, Phrygians, and Lycians, besides a few Indo-Europeans, mostly Hittites and Urartics. The real history of Lydia starts with Gyges, a tribal prince, who usurped the central power (about 683 B.C.) and united the country. Herodotus, connoisseur of good stories, tells how Gyges' predecessor Canduales, proud of his beautiful queen, insisted on showing her naked beauty to the captain of the guard, Gyges. The offended queen revenged herself by forcing the captain to kill her husband and marry her. Candaules had aimed at turning to good account Lydia's key position between Mesopotamia to the east, which with its ancient culture had much to teach, and the young Greek world to the west, which was eager to learn.

Relations between the Lydian kings and their powerful neighbor, Assyria, were not easy. Although dictated always by the instinct of self-preservation, Lydian policy changed from decade to decade, or from year to year, as the situation shifted at home or abroad. Gyges was ally, not subject, of Assyria when two aggressive Indo-European peoples, the Cimmerians (invaders from the Crimea who settled in the region around Lake Van in eastern Asia Minor) and the Medes, were menacing the northern frontier of both countries. When this threat receded, Gyges had a share in weakening his former friend: he sent mercenary forces to Egypt to help Psamtik shake off the Assyrian yoke. When a little later Gyges was killed in a new Cimmerian war, his son and successor Ardys acknowledged the Assyrian Ashurbanipal as overlord.

The rise of the Medes posed a new set of problems to Lydia, especially since their occupation of the northern provinces of the erstwhile Assyrian Empire had brought them to the eastern gates of the kingdom. The Medes, however, failed to conquer it. Greek mercenaries in Lydian service exchanged blows with the Medes, each getting to know and respect the other. After six years' fighting, the frontier stood on the Halys River. An extraordinary event, the solar eclipse of May 28, 585 B.C., furnished an excuse for a *status quo* peace, arbitrated by Nebuchadrezzar, a noteworthy episode in which Greeks were in contact with Medes, while Lydia, a Mediterranean power, and Media, bordering on the Indian Ocean, submitted their quarrel to the judgment of the ancient kingdom of Babylon. A Greek scientist, Thales of Miletus, foretold the eclipse; he had learned his astronomy from the Babylonians, and Lydia was the channel through which that science had reached the Greek world. These are illuminating examples of the close interrelation of east and west. Lydia and the Medes continued friends till they both lost their freedom to Persia. The last king of Media, Astyages, and the last king of Lydia, Croesus, were brothers-in-law.

Croesus (560–546 B.C.), famous in Greek legend, unified Asia Minor from the Halys to the Aegean. He was competent enough politically to keep the freedom-loving Greek cities of Asia as willing subject-allies. From some he exacted tribute or military service, some he made harmless by dismantling their fortresses, and some he annexed outright. Although he gave the city-states home-rule, he limited it by placing a Lydian adviser in residence or through setting up local tyrants.

Despite this interference, the Greeks admired Croesus, for he was a magnificent patron of their temples, especially the national shrines of Delphi, Dodona, and Oropus; of their scientists and poets, for instance, Thales and Aesop; and of Greek leaders of public opinion, for instance, the Athenians Alcmaeon and Miltiades, king of Thrace and uncle of the victor of Marathon. In his house, always open to Greek visitors, he is said to have entertained the philosopher Pittacus and the statesman Solon. A well-educated man, and an innovator in music, Croesus vigorously carried out Gyges' policy of making Lydia a cultural center. His keen mind reached out for Greek learning while the Greeks on their part tapped eastern culture through Lydia.

Croesus could well afford to play the prince bountiful. An excellent organizer and administrator, he was one of the world's first big businessmen. He exploited Anatolian mineral resources. Gyges probably coined the first money, but Croesus made these handsome coins international exchange media, simplifying trade and increasing its volume. He reorganized the customs service to increase his revenue from tolls on goods in transit to and from Lydia and the East. Thus for the first time a model of the solidly financed state stood at the door of Europe.

Only one cloud darkened the sky for Croesus—Cyrus, whom he suspected of a design of world conquest. Feeling certain that the Persian intended to attack him, Croesus decided to attack first. He was confident of victory, for he had an understanding with Sparta, the strongest Greek state, and alliances with the kings of Chaldea and Egypt. To make sure of heaven's favor, he asked the Delphic oracle what Apollo thought of a Lydian war with Persia, receiving a reply the subtle meaning of which escaped him: "If you go to war with Persia, you will destroy a mighty empire."

In one summer (546 B.C.) the war was lost. Cyrus' crack Persian army marched over a thousand miles to the Halys to meet Croesus before he received reinforcements from his Egyptian and Babylonian allies. Moreover the Persian had adopted new tactics, chiefly the element of surprise. Lydia fell to the Persian Empire and Croesus was captured. According to one legend, the humane victor let him live as an honored guest in Ecbatana, where he died a wiser man in 525 B.C. But now that the Great King's dominion faced Greece across the Aegean and the Dardanelles, Greece began to fear for its liberty.

Conquest of Chaldea and Egypt

Having conquered Lydia, Cyrus moved towards the vast steppes and plateaus which end at the Indus River. The conquest of Babylon too was on his program, but he did not care to expose his back to the Bactrians and Sacae, who, profiting by his absence, might invade Persia and nullify his plans. In six years (545–539 B.C.) he tamed them and made them his faithful subjects. He drew great strength from these young and vigorous peoples who henceforth fought valorously in every Persian battle.

Having subdued the east, Cyrus turned to Babylon. Its weak king, Nabonidus, an esthete and antiquarian, had encouraged Croesus in his struggle against Cyrus, realizing that the rise of Persia boded ill for the established empires. Although he did not send the Lydian king the promised aid, his intrigue gave Cyrus an excuse to attack Babylon. Nabonidus and the crown prince Belshazzar stored a heavy supply of food in the capital and made other preparations to withstand a long siege, but Cyrus' genius outwitted them; he diverted the Euphrates, which flowed through the city, then marched his army across the dry river bed into the great metropolis. This astounding feat destroyed the Chaldean morale, already undermined by the clergy and the nobles, who had been offended by the king's religious policy. These influential classes hailed Cyrus as savior and deliverer. Their fervor warrants the suspicion that he was there on their invitation. At any rate Cyrus boasted that he took the city (539 B.C.) as a gift of Marduk "without fighting a battle." The Biblical story of Belshazzar and the handwriting on the wall refers to this Babylonian disunity. As the chosen one of Marduk, Cyrus had himself crowned king of Babylon. His rule was in keeping with his claim to legitimacy, for he treated the vanquished kindly, sparing lives and leaving the city unscathed—except by tribute. With Babylon fell also its Empire, including Mesopotamia, Syria, Palestine, Phoenicia, and Arabia.

Characteristically and sensationally, Cyrus liberated the men and gods who had been war prisoners. He sent most of them back home, including some of the Jews, whose part in facilitating his capture of Babylon has remained problematical.

Cyrus died in 529 B.C. while consolidating his conquest of the northeast, menaced by wandering Scythian tribes. His accomplishment was incredible; he had unified the world from the Indus to the Dardanelles, from central Asia to the Egyptian border. More remarkable still, this empire was built on hitherto untried foundations: tolerance for beliefs and traditions of subject peoples, respect for national feelings, charity towards the vanquished. If liberty was lacking, so was Assyrian cruelty.

Cambyses II, Cyrus' son and successor (529–522 B.C.), took the next step and conquered Egypt in a short campaign. A usurper, Ahmose (Amasis) II, had freed Egypt from Babylonian and Greek influences just as Persia was conquering Babylon. To Cambyses the issue was clear: as king of Babylon he was also suzerain of Egypt. Victorious, he had himself proclaimed pharaoh, and Egypt remained a Persian satrapy for four generations.

Darius and His Empire

The childless Cambyses' death, whether by accident, assassination, or suicide, was the signal for certain provincial governors to seize power. But they were disposed of by Darius (521–486 B.C.), Cyrus' son-in-law and the most legitimate aspirant to the throne, not least because he had proved himself a statesman standing for unity of the empire against the pretenders' selfish separatism. To these assets he added two more: recognized military ability and the loyalty of the leading Persian princes. The six principal Persian families, which with his own had made up the King's Council, stood solidly behind him, realizing that this was a crucial moment for their nation. With their help Darius suppressed his powerful antagonist, Gaumata, who was trying to exalt Media and, as a matter of fact, had reigned for several months. These six families henceforward occupied a special position in Persian society; from them the great king regularly chose his consort; they ruled their great estates like independent princes.

Darius' own statements show that his rivalry with Gaumata was suprapersonal; he interpreted it as a struggle between Persia and Media and as a victory of Zoroastrianism over the Magi. He championed a version of the former, and fostered the Mazdan cult, for its emphasis on virtue and the war against evil appealed to him as the right equipment for a nation aspiring to rule the world. Darius was a practical idealist; he sought to educate the Persians, both high and low, not only to hate "the Lie" and to love Ahura-Mazda the True, but to identify the ideal servant of the king with the ideal servant of the truth.

Darius enlarged the empire Cyrus and Cambyses had built, annexing new provinces in northwest India and exerting a profound influence on Western civilization by the conquest of Thrace and the impact of that conquest on the Greeks. He may have turned to Europe to subdue the Scythians who were annoying Persia, as they had Assyria, with their constant raids on the border across the Black Sea and the Caucasus. He crossed the Danube with no less than 50,000 soldiers, but that he ventured as far east as the Volga is mere legend. He pursued the Scythians into the southern Ukraine, but they eluded him by retreating deeper into those friendly open spaces which modern Russians have ungratefully called their "greatest enemy." Darius never caught up with his quarry. Like Napoleon and Hitler, he retreated empty-handed, but he had established his power as far north as the mouth of the Danube. His empire was the largest known to history up to that time, almost as large as the United States and, extending over parts of Asia, Africa, and Europe. But more significant than its size was the policy upon which the Empire was built, the association of scores of races, under one government, yet with each guaranteed its national tradition and culture.

The organization of the Empire stemmed from the king, who based his power on hereditary right but claimed also divine sanction, the grace of Ahura-Mazda. As a ruler over Egyptians and Babylonians, he sought also the sanction of their gods. Although theoretically his power was absolute, in practice he consulted his nobles, especially the six or seven men of the King's Council, while in legal matters he took counsel with native experts.

Darius' dominant concern was to keep his widely heterogeneous subjects obedient and yet content. The interests of the Empire were of course paramount. As the ruling nation, Persia was tax-free, while the subject nations paid tribute, gave military service, and obeyed the orders of their foreign master. Yet their master consulted their welfare. Following Cyrus' example, Darius tried to understand his subjects' character, respected

Fig. 8.1. Immense, 36-columned audience hall of Darius and Xerxes, at Persepolis, with Darius' palace in background. In the staircase reliefs (center) are four alternating Persian and Median guards, flanked by triangular panels with a rearing bull attacked by a lion. Delegations of tribute-bearers from the nations of the Empire are carved on the inner staircase wall. (Erich F. Schmidt; Chicago, Ill., Oriental Institute)

their customs and laws, recognized their gods, and sought to conciliate their priests by giving gifts, privileges, exemptions, and honors. So all gods and peoples in exile in Babylon and not yet freed by Cyrus, including the Jews, were allowed to return to their native lands. Under Darius the Jews were first allowed to return to Palestine (though the mass movement occurred under Artaxerxes I, 464–424 b.c.). Here they rebuilt the temple at Jerusalem, for which Darius contributed generously, and lived again a semi-independent national life. Moreover, Darius personally paid for the temple sacrifices for his health and his sons'. This is one of the reasons why Cyrus, Darius, and Persian rule are referred to favorably in the Bible.

Persian garrisons in important cities and strategic points assured the loyalty of the vassal nations. Sufficient in peacetime was a skeleton army of Persians and Medes, like those placed alternately in the staircase frieze at Persepolis. A regiment contained a thousand men, and ten regiments made up a division. The core of the war-machine, the cavalry divisions and the ten thousand specially trained "Immortals" recruited from Persians only, thought of themselves as a master race. The generals were usually Persian, but Medes and some trusted non-Iranians could rise to this coveted rank. In war time all the nations of the Empire had to furnish their fighting quotas.

A specialized education prepared young men for an army officer's career or for the high administrative posts of provincial governor or satrap, minister of state, king's counsellor, or other responsible offices at the capital and in the satrapies. Each satrapy and the royal court itself had a school where boys from the foremost Persian families were trained to ride, to shoot, and to tell the truth, the three R's of a Persian gentleman. Plain living and this kind of training were thought to foster in young officers the vigor and the virtue of a conquering race. But Darius wanted his young noblemen to equate their two duties, to him and to god.

To keep the army supplied with good recruits, the Persian kings fostered the growth of a class of hardy peasants and mountaineers. To encourage the simple life, they sought to keep the nobles close to their ancestral acres and folkways. But the extent of the empire and its obligations thwarted this policy. Thus the capital was not on Persian soil, but in foreign Susa. Here were built the great treasuries, where millions of pounds of gold and silver were laid up, and the chief imperial palace with its immense, 250-foot-square room. In summer the court went north to lofty Ecbatana, the ancient capital of Media. In winter it moved to semi-tropical Babylon or some other southern city. Persia remained only the sentimental center of the empire: all the kings were buried there even though in life they might scarcely have visited it.

From the Assyrian and Babylonian empires the Persians had inherited a provincial system of satrapies. As finally organized, the Persian empire had twenty satrapies under royally appointed governors or satraps. A satrapy was normally an entire kingdom, like Egypt, Lydia, or Media; but sometimes it was a subdivision. The satraps were the highest nobles, often the king's sons or brothers, not bureaucrats, but viceroys, with courts nearly as luxurious as the Great King's own. In theory there was no limit to the satrap's authority. He could coin money, appoint diplomats, or wage war against barbarians, even against other satraps, without asking permission from the Great King. He was in office a number of years, frequently a lifetime. Sometimes, as in Cilicia, an abdicated or defeated king continued as satrap, a tribute to Persian sense of honor and conciliatory spirit.

In practice the king could supervise the satrap. At his elbow sat or stood a royal secretary, the link between king and satrap, since all correspondence between them had to pass through his hands. Although the satrap was theoretically commander-in-chief of his own forces, the Persian corps commander stationed in the satrapy was appointed by the king directly. Then too the king had the satrapies inspected periodically. There was a plenipotentiary inspector called "the King's Eye," supported by a contingent of the king's own troops. To keep full control and ensure quick handling of every emergency, royal roads were built and a royal postal service established. Messengers carrying orders from the capital to all parts of the empire, or taking satraps' reports to the king, or asking for instructions from him could be seen riding day and night along those roads to Susa. Invisible to the desert traveler, the traces of most of these roads can be clearly seen today from the air. Finally, since the king's views on the problems of a satrapy could be quickly learned, the satraps were almost compelled not to do anything of special importance without first informing the king and learning his pleasure.

Darius also regularized the treasury, surveying imperial resources to determine the amount of taxes each satrapy should bear. There were three kinds of taxes to which each satrapy was subject. First was a fixed sum in money or precious metal. This source alone yielded 14,560 silver talents, estimated at $17,500,000 in gold, or, in modern purchasing power, about $500,000,000. Second was a tax in kind—wheat, barley, fruit, horses, mules, or sheep. This produce supported the army and so was stored in great depots along the imperial army highways. The third tax was tolls on the movement of goods and commodities. Burdensome as these assessments were, they were moderate compared with those of Assyria, and in return the subject peoples received good government, peace, and security.

Chapter 9 / THE NEAR EAST IN RETROSPECT

In our mid-twentieth century there can be no doubt of the importance of the Near East; the preceding chapters have been an attempt to interpret its past as an aid to understanding its present. Egyptian conservatism, Babylonian invention of writing and codification of laws, Hittite simplicity, the Hebrew sense of being in God's hand, the Persian feeling of *noblesse oblige,* all these have their bearing on the attitudes of their modern descendants. For the Near East is the product of its ageless past; it cannot, it will not escape from its five thousand years of history.

The Near East today proudly recognized its unequalled span of recorded history; we in the west must appreciate this if we are to understand the feelings and assess the capabilities of the modern Near East, in which the force of tradition is strong and vital, and awareness of ancient heritage significantly persists.

First, perspective is important. When culture was raw in pre-Homeric Greece, it was already mellow and even overripe in the Orient, which had a history for as many years before Homer as have elapsed since, and that history is a cornerstone for western man.

Second, the ancient Near East was not only old; it was sophisticated; five thousand years ago it was the active center of enlightenment. Here civilized man began to work on the individual's place in the order of things. The vitality and dynamism of this culture can be judged from the fact that it has produced three great world religions: Judaism, Christianity, Islam.

Though wanton destruction and great changes in the locus of power accompany the life-and-death struggles of peoples and cultures, ideas survive, and of these the most important to us is the idea of the individual, about which two contrasting views emerge in antiquity, one in the Fertile Crescent, the other in Egypt.

The Sumerians and their successors spoke a language which has echoes in modern Hebrew and Arabic; their time reckoning and mathematics survive to modern times; but, most important, their society at its best respected the dignity of the individual, living under a free economy, protected by a law applying to rulers and subjects alike and providing a check upon absolutism. This was the first literate society of which we know and the first to evolve the concept of private property. We have seen how Sumerian law affected Hittite, and Sumerian literature the Hebrew Old Testament. And the ancient Hebrews learned from Mesopotamia to conceive of the civilized life as including conformity to law, which gives the individual a place in society and society a place in the universal order under a paternalistic God.

Egypt thought of the individual, society, and cultural heritage in another way. Here the king was god, absolute; here the concept of law as supreme had no place: the pyramids testify how far the pharaoh was above it. After its early technical and intellectual successes, its building of a nation, its early, later abandoned, concept of social justice, its organization of the first great empire, its belief in a universal god—after these achievements, Egypt petrifies. Twelve hundred years of stability is a weighty accomplishment, as is the skilled handling of mass in stone architecture, the portrait in art, the development of the calendar, strides in medicine. But the concept of social justice in Egypt did not survive; Egypt stood, in Greek and Hebrew eyes, not for justice but for dignity and ancient accomplishment.

The two major cultural inheritances from the ancient Near East, the rule of law and absolute monarchy, affected the Greeks and the Romans, and they are with us still.

History has had more practice in the Near East than anywhere else, and it may well be there that its future course will be set. The Near East long ago conceived of a society transcending national lines, and it has shown too in its 5000 years of history the essential interdependence of past and present, East and West, idealism and realism. Realization of the importance of that interdependence is one of the aims of ancient history, and one of the things that makes its study worthwhile. The lesson will be even clearer in our study of Greece, where we shall also find what Near Eastern culture lacked: great literature, original philosophy, true science, and the developed concept of the free citizen.

Part III / CLASSICAL AND HELLENISTIC GREECE

Chapter 10/MINOAN CRETE

Grandeur and Decline of Knossos

Three generations ago college students of Greek history started their course with the *Iliad* and the *Odyssey*, then the only available documents on ancient Greece. But in 1870, in excavations subsidized by American wealth, the physical objects themselves of that distant era came to light. As a schoolboy in Germany, Heinrich Schliemann had relived so intensely in imagination the adventures of Homeric heroes that he daydreamed of excavating the site of Troy. He emigrated to the United States and there made a fortune which enabled him to realize his boyhood dream. He actually disengaged from the dust and debris of centuries a city the walls, gates, and towers of which appeared to be the very ones described in the *Iliad*.

Next he excavated Mycenae, the city of Agamemnon, commander of the Greeks against Troy, as well as two other Homeric places, Tiryns and Orchomenos. His amazing discoveries revolutionized man's knowledge of early Greece. It was proved that Homer's world was fact, not fiction. Schliemann pushed back the frontier of Greek history a thousand years.

All the signs of this new old-world pointed to the island of Crete as the origin of Homeric culture, and this indeed had been an ancient view.

Crete then, beginning in 1900, became a field of intense archeological exploration. Sir Arthur Evans' findings at Knossos, the main Cretan site, surpassed in importance Schliemann's on the mainland. More millennia of Greek life were brought within the ken of modern man. Hence our study of Greece now starts many centuries before Troy, Mycenae, and Homer's heroic world.

Man began to inhabit the Aegean world in late Neolithic times, about 6000 B.C. A layer, twenty-four feet deep, of Neolithic deposits at Knossos shows that for three thousand years Cretan man progressed steadily, if slowly, in the ways of civilization. At first he lived in caves, supporting himself by hunting, fishing, picking wild fruit, gleaning wild grain, and domesticating wild animals; near his dwelling places have been found sea shells, bones of hares and boars, remains of sheep and cattle, and the rough limestone weapons with which he killed his prey. Eventually he built flimsy huts, discovered harder stone for his tools, imported obsidian, a vitreous rock which could be worked into thin, sharp knives and deadly arrow-heads, and made vases of baked clay. He fashioned female idols to represent the mysterious forces of fertility, showing that he had awakened to spiritual ideas. Spindle weights and bobbins show that the Cretans had learned to spin and to weave, and suggest that family labor was now divided, the men hunting, the women doing domestic work.

By 3000 B.C. both the Aegean world and the Asiatic mainland were astir with life. Peoples of different stocks but similar culture inhabited Asia Minor, Syria, Phoenicia, Cyprus, the Archipelago, and most of classical Greece. The similarities suggest close commercial relations and free migratory movements. Crete, almost equidistant from Sicily, Phoenicia, Troy, and Egypt and next door to Greece and its islands, early became a commercial center, receiving goods from surrounding countries and distributing them in all directions as soon as its inhabitants learned to build seagoing vessels.

Between 3500 and 3000 B.C. Crete acquired from Egypt or Asia knowledge of gold, silver, and copper. Although most implements were still of obsidian, copper tools began to appear. With these the Cretans could build larger ships, so that more people went to sea, and trade, as well as employment for craftsmen, increased. They learned to make copper and silver daggers with sturdy triangular blades, gold and silver jewelry, carvings of ivory imported through Egypt, polychrome stone vases, and pottery of fine baked clay. They next strove after new forms and effects. For instance, pottery at first was dark; later bright colors were used on a dark background, still later, dark colors were used on light. Imports from Egypt, Asia, and the islands increased, the home market expanded, ex-

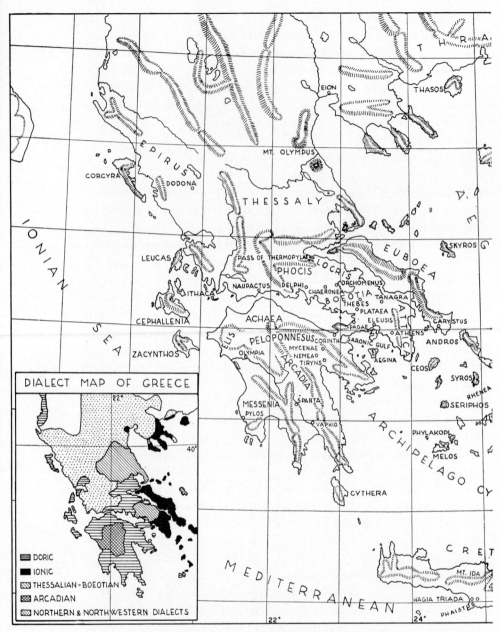

Fig. 10a. Map of Crete and Early Greece. Inset shows dialect map of Greece.

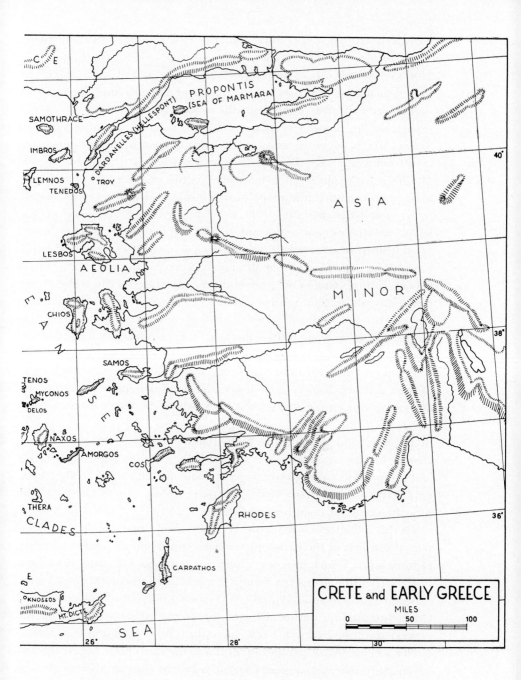

CRETE and EARLY GREECE

MILES

0   50   100

ports acquired new importance, and craftsmen, conscious of competition, began to identify their artifacts with seals like modern trade marks. By 2400 B.C. the necessity of keeping business accounts had led to the invention of pictographic writing. Crete, an island and therefore not easily invaded, could advance uninterruptedly in its arts.

Crete in the Bronze Age, about 2400 B.C., was as civilized as Egypt or Sumer. Merchants sailed westward to bring home the tin that came overland from Saxony and Bohemia or overseas from Etruria and Cornwall. Mixing it with copper imported from Cyprus, craftsmen produced magnificent bronze ware and weapons, which they sold in the nearby islands, in Syria, Palestine, and Phoenicia, in Egypt, Cyrenaica, and as far away as Spain. Jewelry, cameos, and beautiful polychrome pottery were exported.

Crete's best customers were on the Greek mainland, where the Achaeans, a people newly arrived from the north, were passing into the orbit of Cretan culture. Cretan soldiers and officials came in the wake of the merchants, and certain southern Greek cities were dominated culturally, and perhaps politically, by Crete. The Achaeans were allowed home rule, but mounting taxes upon them increased the magnificence of the court of Knossos.

The power and wealth of Minos, legendary king of Knossos, had three sources: industry, mastery of the sea, and domination of the market. Industry was concentrated in central Crete where the king's vassals or governors built stately palaces and large storehouses to deposit the proceeds of taxes in kind. A generally high living standard is attested by merchants' houses two and three stories high, with multiple apartments and ground-floor workshops where artisans manufactured goods for export. Every Cretan palace had a sanctuary for worship of the gods who brought the island wealth and power.

Yet this is not the whole picture. While central Crete remained wealthy, the eastern part of the island grew impoverished and eventually revolted. History is full of such instances where new techniques or shifts of location in industry bring prosperity to new districts and cause decay in old ones.

About 1700 B.C. an earthquake devastated Knossos and most of central Crete. Interpreting this as an omen, or simply taking advantage of the general confusion, eastern Crete successfully rose against the midlands. Under a new dynasty, prosperity returned, the court grew richer, the arts advanced further, and a more efficient syllabary (Linear Minoan A) was devised to replace the antiquated ideographs. Minoan civilization reached its highest peak in the post-revolutionary period, and the new palace at Knossos was the largest, most luxurious, and beautiful in all Crete.

The new regime was apparently a national government. The Greek legend that King Minos was the author of just laws suggests that the kings of Knossos improved social conditions. The prosperity of the east revived;

in the south, the fortunes of the city of Phaistos, facing Egypt and in close commercial relations with it, rose and fell with pharaoh's. When the Hyksos invaders isolated Egypt, Phaistos declined, but with their expulsion and the renewed prosperity under the Theban kings, Phaistos revived (16th century B.C.), apparently without fortification walls. This, if true (and if true it is almost unique in antiquity), is significant, for if Cretan towns of this period were open, it may be argued that they were friendly, peaceful parts of one national body, that all Crete was a single state, federal or otherwise, under the king of Knossos.

About 1450 B.C. misfortune overtook the island. The mainland Achaeans competed so successfully with their suzerain for eastern Mediterranean markets that Egyptian commerce began to abandon Crete for the mainland, and the pharaohs made treaties with Achaean princes. Like the American colonists, the Achaeans became conscious of their strength and unwilling to pay taxes to the mother government. In their revolt they attacked Crete repeatedly, burning the Great Palace at Knossos and the mansions of the rich together with the prosperous towns. Crete was sealed off, its commerce ruined. At last one Achaean war lord installed himself on the throne of Minos. But what a difference! The foreigner rebuilt only one wing of the palace, so modest were his means. Yet he adopted the local syllabary to the needs of his native Old Achaean language, and his surviving records, in Linear Minoan B, are therefore the first written Greek. Crete survived only as a shadow of its former grandeur. Then darkness and oblivion fell upon it until Sir Arthur Evans brought Minos' palace to light.

Economic and Social Life

The golden age of Crete is worth examination. Its political development was simple enough. About 2000 B.C. its cities were ruled, as they had been for centuries, from fortified castles by rival princes. Three hundred years later one ruler, the legendary King Minos, controlled the whole island. Nearly a hundred cities were the glory of the land, some small, some metropolitan, some thriving by agriculture, others by fishing, still others by industry and commerce, but all of them prosperous and apparently content with Minos' rule, for there is no sign of garrisons to keep them in subjection. Nor did they seem to fear danger from abroad, for the seacoast towns were as open as those inland. The fleet made them feel secure. With its aid Minos had freed the Aegean Sea from pirates, extended his sway over the Archipelago, and subjugated the mainland itself. Under its protection he sent abroad the products of Cretan industry and established trading posts and colonies from Cyprus and Syria to Sicily. The fleet was Crete's impenetrable line of defense; hence the lack of coastal fortifications. Crete is indeed a classical example of ancient thalassocracy, or maritime supremacy.

Life in Crete was geared to the sea. Timber was turned into ships, and seaboard towns' main streets led to the sea; that of Knossos was paved with stone to withstand heavy traffic of beast and wagon. Profits of overseas trade led manufacturers into mass production. The blue of the Cretan sea can be seen in Cretan frescoes. Potters' favorite motifs were sea rocks, marine fauna and flora; the cuttlefish was portrayed so accurately that modern naturalists can identify its species. Rings bear ships as signets. Even death was represented as a last sea journey. As Crete lived by the sea, so it perished by the sea, for the Achaeans came by ship.

Evidence of the wealth and power derived by the king from thalassocracy is best seen in the Great Palace at Knossos. It was an enormous structure, even compared with the Pentagon in Washington. Jars taller than a man, tapering down to a point, set row on row on the ground in appropriate receptacles and stored over several acres, hint at the royal revenue. Taxes, paid in kind, were stored partly to supply the court, partly for sale. Olive oil, wine, honey, wheat, and dried fruit were the principal items. Scores of secretaries and bookkeepers kept account of income and outgo on clay tablets, housed in appropriate archives. Of those in Old Cretan (Linear A) we can make out only the figures up to a hundred; [1] those in Linear B, which is Greek, can be read. Close by the palace were the royal craftsmen's workshops.

Cretan economic life blended agriculture, industry, and trade. The plains and valleys yielded wheat, barley, and other cereals; on the less fertile hillsides grew the olive tree and the grapevine, while the stony mountains offered pasturage for goats, sheep, and cattle. Dairy products, meat, ducks, pigeons, fish, game, and honey were staple foods. Flax kept the household looms busy. Saffron supplied yellows to supplement the red and purple dye from the sea-mussel. Flowers, especially tulips, hyacinths, iris, and lilies, grew in the royal parks and rich men's gardens. All this is written in Cretan vase and wall decoration, which, besides having esthetic value, are documents of social life.

Thousands of men found employment in industry as shipwrights, masons, carpenters, cabinetmakers, bronzesmiths, jewelers, gem engravers, painters, vase-makers, armorers, weavers, bleachers, and perfumers. Their output was sold at home, where prosperity and a keen artistic sense created a brisk demand, and abroad, over protected seaways. A commercial road linked Phaistos in the south, the port for Egypt and Libya, with Knossos in the north, the distribution point for the mainland and the Archipelago. To simplify business transactions, Linear A script used

[1] Late in 1957, Dr. Cyrus K. Gordon of Brandeis University published an article arguing that Linear A was Akkadian.

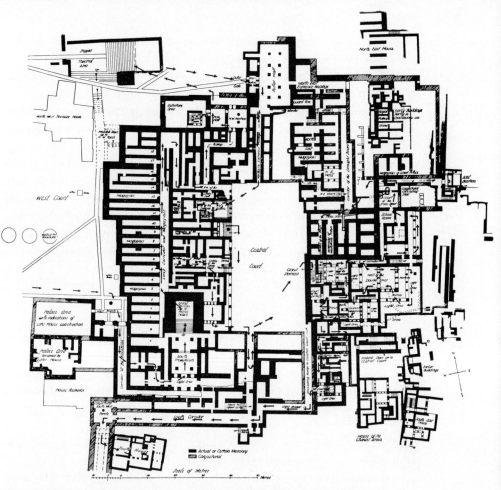

Fig. 10b. Plan of the Palace of Minos at Knossos. Earliest dated stage *c.* 1900 B.C. Continuously inhabited for six centuries. Unsymmetrical plan; many cross-walls were supports for upper stories. Noteworthy are the "magazines" where huge storage jars for oil and wine were found; the Throne Room, where excavators found the throne *in situ;* and the charmingly decorated domestic apartments (Hall of the Double-Axes, Queen's Megaron), equipped with baths and latrines with running water. (J. D. S. Pendlebury, *A Handbook to the Palace of Minos, Knossos.* London, 1954. Fac. p. 76.)

an Egyptian notation; coinage was based on copper ingots and on gold and silver plaquettes.

Cretans seem to have been humane, practicing neither large-scale slavery nor serfdom. Kindness to animals may be inferred from a fresco of men and women acrobats jumping and hurdling over a bull, endangering themselves but doing no harm to the animal. The living standard seems to have been comfortable, and life abounded in simple pleasures, like those illustrated on a black steatite vase from Hagia Triada showing a procession of happy harvesters returning from their labors, carrying the threshing flails, shouting, joking, laughing, and singing as they go. Another vase shows boxing and bull-leaping scenes. One fresco represents a monkey picking saffron and placing it in a basket. Another fresco shows men and women conversing at an afternoon party outdoors. The sexes mixed as equals, but they never appear nude either in painting or sculpture. Both men and women were tightly corseted, with wasp waists. Men wore also a closely fitting loincloth like a modern athletic supporter. Women wore hooped skirts and tightly fitting jackets, laced below the exposed breasts. Their hair was loose. Both men and women were bedecked with jewels. One portrait shows a young woman so charmingly sophisticated that nineteenth-century France dubbed her "La Parisienne." Indeed the hooped skirt, wasp waist, and full bosoms of these Cretan frescoes were so amazingly like the current fashion that some people in the nineties believed the finds were a hoax.

Art and Religion

The Cretans' feeling for beauty is evident in their unbroken artistic progress from Neolithic times to the Achaean invasion. Several factors converged to make the Cretans the most artistic people of antiquity— native ingenuity, an inspiring religion, a climate of apparent freedom, and the patronage of prince-merchants, especially the king.

The Great Palace of Knossos was the crowning achievement of Minoan architecture. It rose several stories high, tier upon tier of unevenly distributed terraces, terminating in flat roofs like our ultra-modern apartment houses. Its maze of halls and corridors leading to multiple office units and apartment suites gave rise to the Greek legend of the labyrinth. Its columns were thinner at the bottom than at the top (like those of Frank Lloyd Wright), perhaps a legacy from Neolithic times, when builders may have found the thinner end of a tree trunk easier to drive down. Outside rooms were provided with windows, those on the inside with light wells. Large and picturesque entrances, imposing staircases, and magnificent porticoes added to the monumental grandeur of this first royal palace of Europe. There was piped spring-water; baths and sanitary toilets with underground sewers ensured comfort and cleanliness. If these are marks of civilization, the Minoans were civilized indeed; Hellenistic and Roman architects practiced sanitary engineering, but after their time this art was lost. Neither the great Queen Elizabeth I nor the proudest queen of France in her Palace of Versailles had the conveniences of the queen of Knossos; not until the late nineteenth century did Europe and America have sanitary systems equal to that of Minos. As at Versailles, a smaller palace, like the Trianon, rose near the Great Palace. A theater for court entertainments completed the series of royal buildings.

Wall-painting was not in distemper, as in Egypt, but in true fresco where the design is drawn and the color applied while the plaster is still wet. Freshness, freedom, and naturalism are the qualities of the best period. Taste is always exquisite, colors vivid, design graceful, incident animated, execution sure. But the Cretans were never able to achieve true perspective—witness the *Saffron-gatherer,* the *Cup-bearer,* the *Toreador,* the *Parisienne,* or, to a still greater extent, the *Cat Stealing after a Bird,* the *Danseuse,* or the *Partridge and Peewits.* These murals are reproduced in many large American museums.

Another successful Cretan medium was the stucco relief, low-to-high in depth, painted over in colors, achieving an effect of roundness and chiaroscuro. An imposing figure of a priest exorcising an evil power is a good illustration of this technique.

Cretan sculpture, too, combines realism with delicacy of feeling. The chryselephantine *Snake Goddess,* the ivory *Bull-leaper,* and the faïence plaques of a wild she-goat and a cow feeding their young might well be the envy of the best Renaissance masters. Egypt itself never produced anything superior to Cretan intaglio ivories, jewelry, or inlay.

The best Cretan pottery (1600–1450 B.C.) is perfect in fineness of the clay, firing, shape, and decoration. Using the potter's wheel, the ceramists produced vases with eggshell-thin walls and interwove free lines, curves, spirals, sprigs, blossoms, and stars in a symphonic fantasy of light-on-dark designs. Several schools of pottery developed. A Knossos vase with white lilies on dark background is a beautiful example of stylized naturalism. One of the most important schools used the so-called Palace Style. Its motifs were drawn almost entirely from conventionalized but still realistic plant and marine life; a dark-on-light color scheme was used, and style and execution were admirable.

A people so proficient in art must surely have possessed other intellectual capacities. Although it has not yet been possible to decipher the Minoan language on any of the many thousand written stones, clay tablets, and other articles found in Crete, Cretan writing evidently progressed through several stages, from the pictographic to the phonetic. There are some 2800 clay tablets in Linear B, which is Greek, and some 255 in the undeciphered Linear A. Ink was apparently used both on clay and on some perishable material. It is hoped that the key to the Cretan language may be found in Cyprus, which, like Troy and other eastern Aegean settlements, received much of its culture from Crete. A number of Cypro-Minoan inscriptions (in Linear Minoan B), are, as we have seen, Greek written in a modified Minoan syllabary, but literacy in the Minoan language was restricted to bookkeeping purposes. The Cretan poetry which later became the basis of Greek epic and lyric was oral, not written. The Cretans had more than a rudimentary knowledge of music.

They played the flute, lyre, and sistrum; and they danced and sang, both solo and in chorus, to musical accompaniment.

Cretan art is practically our only source of information for Cretan religion. Through it we can discover the objects of worship and trace the development of the idea of divinity. At first the Cretans worshiped fetishes, that is, plain stones, meteorites, coarse sculptures, and other objects identified with the actual forces of nature. Later, when they came to believe that natural phenomena were caused by spiritual beings outside of the phenomena themselves, the fetishes were viewed first as indwelling places or visible forms of these spirits and then as mere symbols.

Among the principal symbols were the pillar, the double ax, the shield, and the sacred tree. The pillar or column came to symbolize a building or household, hence, the divine power which fosters the well-being of family or city. The double ax was a tool of vital importance. With it enemies were vanquished, trees felled, stones quarried, and animals killed. With it, too, victims were bled, their blood enriching by symbolic transfer the votary's life. Clearly then the double ax conveyed the idea of power over nature, a symbol of civilization. As time went on, the double ax was placed atop the pillar, making a sort of religious synthesis. The remaining symbols scarcely need comment: the shield for protection, the sacred tree as the emblem of life, fertility, and food.

Fetishes became symbols when divine powers were personified. The principal divine person was female, the Mother-Goddess, who, as we have seen, was worshiped in Mesopotamia, indeed in the whole Near East. In Crete she stood supreme and figured constantly in frescoes, statuettes, and seals. If other gods were worshiped in Crete, they stood much lower, except two who were inseparable from the Great Mother.

The earliest known representation of the all-ruling goddess, a roughly hewn stone from Phaistos, shows her in exaggerated female proportions to symbolize the deification of motherhood. Like other ancient peoples, the Cretans thought woman, more than man, possessed the creative powers of nature. The Great Mother therefore personified nature, which perennially brings into being men, animals, and vegetation. She was portrayed symbolically as a woman holding her breasts or as a mother watching over her child.

Her powers were supposed to encompass the universe, extending over field and forest where she brought forth food and even tamed lions and snakes; over springs, rivers, and lakes; and over the sea itself which she subdued with her boat. She dwelt in the sky, and the sun, the stars, and the air were full of her power. She sometimes flew from heaven to earth in the shape of a dove. The dove hovered around her or perched on her head or shoulders to carry her divine powers of generation and sustenance to man, animals, and plants. The exposed breasts of Cretan women rep-

Fig. 10.1. Snake goddess. Statuette in gold and ivory, only seven inches high, a miniature masterpiece of great delicacy and beauty. (Boston, Museum of Fine Arts)

resented no mere wordly fashion, but a religious idea, the honoring and propitiation of the giver of fecundity.

The Great Mother's power was seen as extending even to the nether world; she gave death as well as life. As death-dealer she was goddess of war and hunting. Life, death, rebirth; germination and harvest; winter and the return of spring—everything was under her dominion. She was the Queen of Heaven, Earth, and Hell.

By her side one often saw a "sweet maiden," Britomartis, her daughter, who was ardently pursued by Minos. To keep her virginity Britomartis leaped into the sea, but he rescued and ravished her. She was thus virgin and mother, virgin by intention, mother by superior force. At this point the "sweet maiden" and the Great Mother became one.

The Great Mother had a male companion, her son or lover, who died in the autumn and rose again in springtime. This, too, as we have seen, was a common Near Eastern myth. The pair represented the fullness of nature. In war the god mastered men, in peace he tamed the lion. He came down from heaven as rain to quicken the earth. His animal strength and male power were symbolized by the bull; as man he was represented as the king or legendary hero Minos, but in his complete essence he was the Minotaur, half man, half bull—to a Cretan not repulsive, but benefi- cent, combining wisdom and strength, man's mind and the fruit of his labor. His symbol was the double ax (*labrys*), and the labyrinth was his

Fig. 10.2. Hagia Triada, Crete. Painted sarcophagus with funeral scene. The deceased is at the right; three men bring him gifts: animals, and a ship for his final journey. Two ladies, accompanied by a priest with a lyre, are sacrificing (left) before double-axes. (Heracleion, Greece, Heracleion Museum)

home. He was honored by athletic festivals where, among other spectacles, male and female toreadors baited, but did not kill, a bull.

The number three held a religious significance. Pillars, doves, trees, flowers, crosses appear repeatedly in threes. The cross, used throughout the East as a charm, was apparently worshiped in Crete and was widely sculptured, painted, or carved in the shapes which become familiar later in Christian times: Greek cross, Latin cross, St. Andrew's cross, St. Anthony's cross, and swastika.

Cretans worshiped in caves and outdoors, in the home, in the Great Palace of Minos, and in small intimate shrines, but never in temples, of which none existed in Crete. Priestesses officiated, sacrificing animals, offering first fruits, purifying by water, milk, or wine, and burning incense. An adjunct of worship was the public games: wrestling, gladiatorial combats, gymnastics, foot and bull races, dancing, singing, plays, and, as mentioned above, bull baiting.

The dead were inhumed, and the graves and tombs show various forms, all apparently intended to assure the dead a continuation of earthly life; buried with them were food, drink, and their earthly weapons, tools, and jewels.

The development of Minoan civilization may be summarized as follows. In the Early Minoan Age (3000–2200 B.C.) ideographic writing was in use, as well as metalworking in copper, silver, and gold. The Middle Minoan Age (2200–1600 B.C.) marks the peak of early Cretan civilization. It produced exquisite pottery, naturalistic art, a matriarchal religion, and linear writing. In the Late Minoan Age (1600–1200 B.C.) pottery, bronze, and inlaid work were further refined, but the center of culture shifted to the Greek mainland, especially to Mycenae, Tiryns, and Pylos.

Chapter 11 / EARLY
GREECE

Achaean Mycenae

When an Indo-European people reached the Greek mainland in about 2000 B.C., they found a challenging terrain and climate. The area of continental Greece is only about 50,000 square miles, hardly twice the size of New England. Its maximum length is some 250 miles, its maximum breadth 180. The sea and the mountains profoundly affected Greek development; few parts of Greece are more than 70 miles from the sea. The mountains make land communication so difficult that the sea is the natural route; through the Aegean Sea the islands make natural steppingstones: one may sail from one to another and seldom be out of sight of land. The sea brought maritime trade, which early put Greece in touch with the outside world and prevented it from becoming provincial. Most of Greece is mountainous, with small swift rivers and some fertile valleys. The Greek terrain, which divides rather than unites, explains in part the growth of large numbers of small city-states and the difficulty Greeks found in achieving unity. The soil is thin, stony, and sterile; though Greece is and has always been an agricultural country (growing olives, grapes, and grain, the "Mediterranean triad") only 20 percent of its area is cultivable; its people have always been poor and frugal, and half its food must be imported. Though the Greek climate runs to extremes, with cold rainy winters and hot dry summers, for most of the year it is possible to live outdoors. This has helped make the Greeks an open, gregarious, socially-minded people, and may perhaps have influenced Greek thought; in that clear sparkling air the romantic murkiness of the foggy north is unthinkable.

To this land the homeseeking Indo-Europeans came from the north with their wives and children, driving before them their flocks and herds, the well-to-do among them equipped with weapons and with horses, which gave them a military advantage over the natives. These "Middle Helladic" peoples are the ancestors of the Greeks of historic times: Achaeans, Arcadians, Ionians, probably also Aeolians, and lastly Dorians. They settled first in the north from Epirus to Thessaly. After some centuries they moved southward into Boeotia, Euboea, Attica, and the Peloponnesus. Still later they poured over the islands and onto the Asia Minor coast. They brought to Greece the Greek language, wheel-made pottery, and the square megaron-type house, which was to replace the rough apsidal structures of the Early Helladic peoples.

But Achaean Greece for 150 years, from about 1600 B.C., owed much of its culture to Crete. The rulers of most cities—Mycenae, Orchomenus, Thebes, Tiryns, Athens—were vassals of the king of Knossos. Their dress, weapons, implements, houses, customs were largely copied from Knossos. The lords of Mycenae were by far the most powerful of the Greek rulers, since they controlled the roads between the Peloponnesus and the rest of Greece. Ensconced in an impregnable fortress, they derived their wealth from levies on goods in transit through their domain. The first great stage of Mycenaean civilization (1600–1500 B.C.), one of wealth, luxury, and refinement, is revealed to us by some royal shaft graves. The kings and their companions fought with bronze swords and daggers on which scenes of animal life, of cats chasing ducks, of marauding lions, of huntsmen pursuing wild beasts, were inlaid in gold. They drank from gold and silver cups that were shaped like ox-heads or lion-heads or engraved with vegetable motifs or war scenes. As discovered in their shaft graves by Schliemann, and more recently by George Mylonas, the Mycenaean princes were buried in gold-embroidered clothes, wearing gold diadems, gold breast-plates, gold bracelets and gold signets, their faces protected by gold masks, and with weapons and drinking-cups beside them. In one grave a baby, wrapped in gold foil, lay beside its queen mother amidst a profusion of gold ornaments: toilet vessels, diadems, play or magic disks, beads, and pins.

Wealthy houses were supplied with vases of local alabaster, copper caldrons, ivory carvings, faïence plaques, inlaid gaming boards, Egyptian furnishings, and costly Sicilian skins. By the late sixteenth century local artists, replacing Cretan craftsmen, rivaled their masters in representing

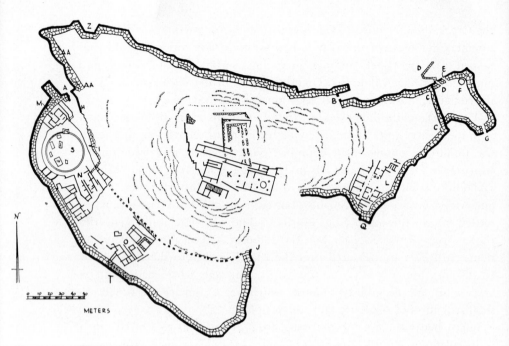

Fig. 11a. Plan of the Citadel, Mycenae. A. Lion Gate (*c*. 1250 B.C.). B. Postern. D. Opening to underground reservoir. G. Sally Port, I. Ramp. K. Palace (*c*. 1350 B.C.). L-O. Houses. S. Grave circle. A newly discovered second grave circle lies outside the wall to the west. (G. E. Mylonas, *Ancient Mycenae*. Princeton, 1957. Plate 7.)

scenes of extraordinary animation and in combining elegance with strength. The vase-maker was almost as proficient as the metalworker; although clay and firing techniques were still imperfect, shape and decoration were masterly.

The peak of Mycenaean civilization came in the 1300's B.C. Shaft graves were succeeded by beehive, or circular, and domed tombs which, although rifled in ancient times, still have a story to tell. They developed from an early group in rubble limestone to the neatly-sawn rectangular blocks of the so-called "Treasury of Atreus" (about 1350 B.C.). Its size is impressive; its inner diameter is 48 feet, its height 43. The single-stone lintel over the door weighs 110 tons. The "dome" is built of overlapping horizontal courses, with their faces cut to the proper curve; its exterior was decorated in red and green marble, its interior with bronze rosettes. Tombs of similar design and construction were built at the same time in other parts of Greece, sure indications that Achaean sister-cities were following Mycenae's lead.

The power of the lords of Mycenae is shown even more in their palace. It was planned as court, capital, barracks, and citadel all in one. Its entrance, or Lion Gate, is more than a tasteful monument; it symbolizes

Fig. 11.1. Mycenae. Lion gate, with blocks added in 1950. One of the earliest pieces of monumental Greek sculpture. The heraldic lions guard a pillar, perhaps symbolic of the Royal Palace. They were in place when Agamemnon passed through this gate on his way to Troy. (Photo courtesy Dorothy MacKendrick)

the hegemony of the ruler who from his impregnable palace-fortress dominated the nerve-center of Greece.

From these and similar Mycenaean remains scattered over Greece, of which the most noteworthy are those excavated by the American C. W. Blegen at Pylos, we can reconstruct the outline of an epoch-making upheaval. About 1450 B.C. the mainland Achaean cities, led by Mycenae, Tiryns, Athens, and Thebes, united against their Cretan master. Their challenge to a sea power shows (as do nautical terms on Linear B tablets) that the Achaeans had become a sea power themselves. While each city fought under its own prince, the supreme commander was the prince of Mycenae. The warlike Achaeans easily overthrew the government at Knossos which, secure behind naval force, had neglected to build up an army. They burned the palace and took over the island, chiefly by founding settlements of their own.

As the newly independent American colonies were free to shape their government and to regulate trade solely for their national advantage, so too the Achaeans, once rid of Cretan overlordship, reshaped their political and commercial relations. Mycenae, leader in the war of liberation, became the capital of the Achaean world. It still headed the federation when, two hundred years later, the Achaeans went to war against Troy.

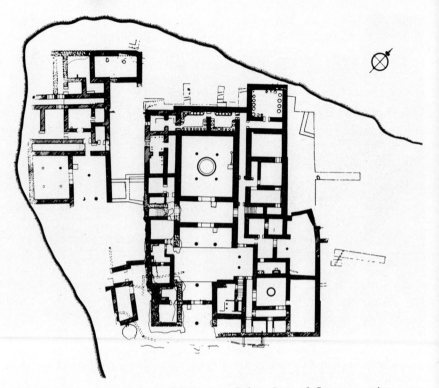

Fig. 11b. Plan of the Palace of Nestor at Pylos. Ground floor comprises some 46 halls, rooms, porticoes, stairways, lobbies, passages, and courts. The central room contains a great circular raised hearth, its profile painted with a flame motif; the rooms behind are storerooms. Hundreds of Linear Minoan B tablets were found in this palace. (*American Journal of Archaeology* LXI, 1957. Plate 39, Fig. 1.)

Achaean, or Early Greek, Society

Achaean society was essentially military. The ramparts and palisades of the Mycenaean citadels, the intricate palace passageways, in particular the postern and the partly subterranean exits, were elaborate defenses. Sherds from a Mycenaean tomb represent the defenders in a siege coming outside the wall to discharge a volley of arrows against the besieger; other sherds depict infantry on the march, each man helmeted, protected by breastplate, greaves, and an oval shield, and carrying a spear. The fact is that early Greek society was militarily insecure. Untamed individualists as they were, and heirs of ancient inter-city feuds, accustomed to regard loot from their neighbors as legitimate business profit, unrestrained by the central authority, and exposed to pressure from their Aryan cousins to the north, Mycenaean princes felt obliged to entrust their safety and freedom to their swords.

The smallest social unit was the family. A number of families, related

Fig. 11.2. Tiryns. Wall-walk, just inside east gate of citadel. About 1400 B.C. Small size of scale figure shows massiveness of construction. (Photo by Paul Mac-Kendrick)

by blood or drawn together by belief in a common ancestor, made up a clan (Greek: *genos*; Latin: *gens*). There were thousands of clans in the Achaean world, each practicing its own ancestral cult, guarding its members' marital purity, working the common land, and administering the common wealth. Since each clan was also responsible for its members' behavior to other clans, its control over them was total. The clans in turn were cells of a much larger organization, the tribe. Throughout Greek history the tribes formed the primary political divisions of the city-state. There came a time, possibly as early as the Mycenaean age, when for mutual defense the clans bypassed the tribes; they grouped themselves into phratries (Greek: *phratriai*), or brotherhoods, serving as army regiments or battalions. About 600 B.C. Athens had twelve phratries of thirty clans each. To belong to one of these groups of brothers-in-arms was a much prized privilege.

Farming and shepherding were the chief occupations. Farming is indicated by the Greek tradition that in heroic times Athena introduced the olive tree and Dionysus the vine into Attica, and Dionysus was worshiped in Mycenae as early as the thirteenth century B.C. A cup from Vaphio reproduces the capture of wild bulls; another, a peaceful rural scene with a bull as its center. Goats were raised to supply milk, cheese, and meat. Fishing added to the food supply.

The Achaeans engaged in household industry and they exchanged the goods they produced. Kitchenware and storage vessels were exported to most of the Mediterranean seaboard. These articles are carelessly designed, as though they were mass-produced. Bronzes, leather goods, articles of ivory, glass beads, alabaster ornaments, and such agricultural products as wine, oil, fruit, and cheese were shipped northward and eastward to Thrace, Troy, and Asia, southward and westward to Egypt, Sicily, and Spain. Each ship brought back its cargo: horses, harnesses, and cloth from Asia; armor and weapons from Phoenicia; paint, drugs, and luxury articles from Egypt; skins and slaves from Sicily; copper from Cyprus and probably also from Spain; tin from Britain. This wealth was inventoried on clay tablets. From a great store of these unearthed at Pylos and Mycenae, the young English cryptanalyst Michael Ventris was able to announce in 1953 that the language was Greek (Old Achaean) written in an adaptation of the Cretan Linear A syllabary.

Men and women dressed in the Cretan fashion, the men scantily, the women elaborately, with corsets constricting their waists and emphasizing their bosoms, tight-fitting jackets that left their breasts exposed, and flounced skirts reaching to their ankles. Their coiffure was elegant, curled over the forehead, knotted on the crown of the head, left hanging in the back in long tresses. They painted their faces and enameled their nails, wore necklaces and bracelets, and carried flowers and small vanity cases. The two sexes mingled freely—apparently as equals—at religious worship, and at secular fiestas and spectacles, or to view parades and, at harvest time, processions of field workers. They enjoyed parties in the open air. The men accompanied the women to social gatherings or to acrobatic performances and bull-baiting by professional male and female toreadors. Men hunted wild fowl and wild beasts; they rode horses and drove chariots over paved roads; they sailed to distant lands for business and pleasure. Bones and shells found near Mycenaean dwellings show that the Achaeans ate the flesh of goats, sheep, oxen, and pigs, of hares, deer, and boar, of fish and shellfish, especially lobsters and oysters, as well as the succulent land snails which Mediterranean people relish to this day. At their banquets the princes and nobles listened to itinerant minstrels singing to the accompaniment of the lyre about the deeds of gods and mighty heroes.

The archeological material illustrating Mycenaean civilization sheds little light on the life of the poor. However, Linear B tablets mention a number of occupations, including bowmaker, goldsmith, shipwright, mason, cook, baker, woodcutter, herald, longshoreman, oarsman, tailor, and shepherd.

Troy commanded the plain east and south and—more important—

Fig. 11.3. Linear Minoan B script describing three-legged vessel listed as *t-ri-po-de*. The matching of the syllabic values as posited by Ventris with the pictographic three-legged sign clinches the decipherment as sound. (*Archaeology* VII, 1954, p. 18, Fig. 3.)

the Hellespont, or Dardanelles, that narrow entrance first, to the Sea of Marmara (Greek: *Propontis*), and hence to the Black Sea (*Pontus*) and the wheat-growing regions of the Crimea and south Russia beyond. Troy's princes had grown rich on the tolls levied on every ship entering the strait, as well as, probably, on a tax exacted from every merchant attending the fair held annually outside the city walls.

The origins of Troy go back to Paleolithic times. Six stages as an inhabited center, discernible in as many archeological strata, had preceded Troy VIIa, Priam's city, which the Achaeans destroyed. By 1200 B.C., largely as a result of the Hittites' fall, Troy VIIa had extended its power over much of Asia Minor, on the European side of the Hellespont, and along the Black Sea coast. Many allies from these regions and from Asia were to fight for Troy and King Priam as members of a large federation over which Priam presided, some of them to settle old scores with the Achaeans. For more than a century Achaean pioneers had systematically been invading Asia. The aim of the Achaeans' decisive attacks against Troy was partly to open more land to Achaean settlers, but principally to free the sea from Troy's toll-levying ships. The Trojan federation fell before the pounding of the Achaean army which Agamemnon, king of Mycenae, had organized from contingents furnished by every Achaean state. Troy was destroyed (about 1180 B.C.), and Asia, the islands, and the Hellespont on both the European and the Asiatic side lay open to Achaean occupation. Ironically, however, those who came to settle on these shores were to be not conquerors but refugees who had lost their homes.

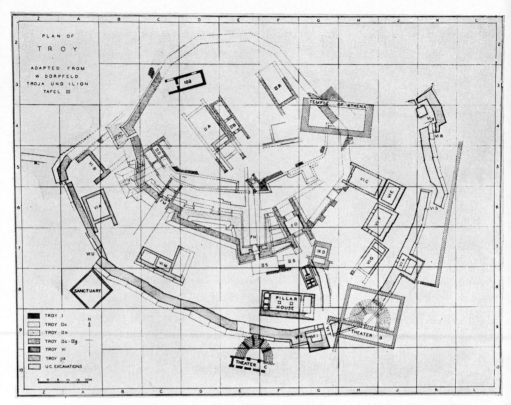

Fig. 11c. Plan of Troy. Troy I–II are Early Bronze Age (*c.* 3000–2600 B.C.); VI is Late Bronze Age (*c.* 1800–1275 B.C.); Troy VII (not shown) is Priam's Troy, destroyed by fire; Troy IX is Greco-Roman. Excavated by the University of Cincinnati beginning in 1932. (C. W. Blegen and others, *Troy,* vol. III, part 2. Princeton, 1953. Plate 446.)

The Dorian Invasion

The Achaeans could not exploit their victory for, while still exhausted by their long struggle with Troy, they themselves were attacked by a new wave of northern invaders, the Dorians. The Dorians were a kindred people who spoke a different dialect of the Achaean language. Their invasion caused no racial or cultural break, only a political disturbance in which the seats of the mighty were overthrown.

Scattered Dorian groups had settled on the western coast of the Peloponnesus before the Trojan War, but after the war they flooded the peninsula, looting everything in sight, burning the palaces of Mycenae and Tiryns, overthrowing the ruling dynasties, and occupying most of the Peloponnesus. The Achaeans fled before them, taking refuge in Attica and Euboea, crossing over to the islands, or spilling eastward over the Asiatic coast, now free from Trojan control. Some barricaded themselves in the Peloponnesus, that is, in Messenia and Arcadia—Achaean islands in a Dorian sea. Dorian bands settled in Thessaly, pushing the earlier inhabitants southward into Boeotia; others occupied the southern Aegean islands, including Crete and those along the coast of Asia south of the Achaean settlements.

The period following the Dorian invasion was one of gradual transition, not sharp break: pottery style evolved from Mycenaean through sub-Mycenaean and protogeometric to geometric; cremation gradually replaced inhumation, but this practice probably came from the east, not from the Dorians. (Troy, too, is now thought to be of eastern rather than northern origin.) The Dorians were adapters, not innovators. Even iron safety-pins seem not to have been their invention. But safety-pins revolutionized dressing; henceforward Greeks were to wear the *chiton,* a simple enveloping mantle, pinned on the shoulders and almost identical for men and women. In cold weather a cloak was worn over the *chiton.* This simplicity of dress gave to the lady a freedom which the Greeks believed had its effect on mind and manners.

The three hundred years following the Dorian invasion are, then, a "Dark Age" only because for them we have little or no evidence, archeological, historical, or linguistic. No undisturbed inhabited site of the period has been scientifically excavated. As systematic exploration proceeds, and as more Linear B tablets are discovered and read, the so-called Greek Dark Ages will lose their obscurity. Meantime there is a gap from the twelfth to the ninth century B.C., after which we see a settled civilization again in contact with east and west, and Dorian states like Sparta ready for their important role, competing with Ionian states like Athens in shaping the progress of Greek civilization.

Homer: A World in Transition

The period from the Dorian invasion to the dawn of the historical era (1100–800 B.C.) is best known through the works of Homer. It is a moot question whether Homer was a real person or a convenient symbol for a long line of poets who gave artistic form to popular legends of Achaean heroes. Mycenaean minstrels had sung their lays from court to court. After the Dorian invasion their successors, the traveling rhapsodes, recited these same songs at the banquets of the nobles; while retaining the original meter and "Aeolic" dialect (now known to be Old Achaean), they could not preserve intact the account of a vanished world, especially since in their hands some of the old lays were rephrased and new ones added. Finally, in the course of the eighth century, a rhapsode of genius, who may very well have been named Homer, welded this rich poetic literature into that matchless epic, the *Iliad.* Whether the *Odyssey* is by the same or a later hand is also an open question. But in dramatic narrative, eloquence, imagery, imagination, and precision of detail no other western poetry has surpassed the *Iliad* and the *Odyssey*, models for all subsequent epics from Vergil to Dante and Milton.

The *Iliad* and the *Odyssey* mirror this transitional period of Greek history. The former glorifies Achaean military exploits, the latter recounts their sea lore and adventures, while both illustrate their religion and practically every other aspect of Achaean society. The changes in Greek life are reflected in the dual subject matter of the Homeric poems. For instance, although weapons are usually of bronze, iron is used too; although warriors protect themselves with wasp-shaped leather shields covering the whole body, they appear also with the round bronze shield of more recent origin.

These disparities do not prevent our visualizing from the Homeric poems the society of that period as a whole. The Greeks lived in many tiny states, some of Mycenaean origin, some newly established, and almost all individualized by geography. The typical city-state was set in a small valley cut off from the outside world by a ring of mountains and opening on the sea. It was something like an early New England town: a small urban center, then a ring of villages, then open farm land, lastly pasture and woods. In the urban center was the modest house of the city chieftain (Greek: *basileus*, usually translated "king") , which served also as the temple of the founding god or hero; the market place, used for business and political assembly, and a high walled citadel. The city-state (*polis,* originally "citadel") was to remain the fundamental Greek sovereign unit, never in antiquity to be replaced by the nation.

Like their Achaean ancestors, the citizens of a Greek city-state were grouped into clans, subject to the disintegrating forces of population increase, clan warfare, and emigration.

For a time the clans sought strength by reinvigorating, perhaps by adopting for the first time, the phratry, which we have assigned to Achaean times. Apart from geographic determinism, it was the union of clans that chiefly operated to produce the city-state. The most potent, pious, or intelligent clan chief became chieftain or king of the *polis,* acting as supreme judge, commander-in-chief, chief priest, price regulator, and president of the council of clan-chiefs. Gradually his office became hereditary and was regarded as under divine guidance. But the monarchy was not absolute; it was limited by the council, which was summoned from time to time to discuss and act upon state affairs. The *basileus* had uncontested power only over his own clan, as a feudal king could enforce his will on his private domain only. He was thus a progressive force, for whereas each clan chief was, like a modern alderman, primarily interested in his own group, the king strove to promote the welfare of the entire population. The clan chiefs delegated to the king only such powers as would promote the general welfare, and those powers were comparatively as few as those originally delegated by the American states to the federal government. Otherwise, the chiefs retained almost intact the exercise of their ancient rights. Paramount among their functions was worship, especially of the founder-god or hero. Others were maintaining peace, certifying births, celebrating marriages, conducting funerals, administering justice, and managing the clan's landed property.

The people had no power, but were allowed to listen, each man in his tribal group, to debates of the state council and to approve its actions by acclamation or disapprove by silence. The *Iliad* describes several meetings of the council of the Achaean leaders, presided over by Agamemnon. Only once in the *Iliad* does a commoner rise up to speak. The poet, with an aristocratic audience in mind, represents the action as unprecedented, shocking, and bold. Thersites, the commoner, is represented as ugly, crude, vulgar, and insolent, babbling on, railing at the princes until Odysseus gives him a beating. A product of city life, Thersites represents the common people: they had duties, not rights; they were expected to serve, not to complain. He differed from his fellows only in having revolutionary ideas and the courage to express them.

Army organization reflected that of the state. The best soldiers were nobles, the clan, phratry, and tribe leaders. A battle was a duel between enemy chieftains who first hurled javelins from two-horse chariots, then dismounted and fought with bronze swords. The winner despoiled the slain foe of his armor, which had a high intrinsic value. Earlier, the infantry's role had been secondary, but the better captains were already training their men to meet the foe in serried ranks—"buckler pressed on buckler, helm upon helm, and man on man."

All land was divided into clan domains, administered by the clan chief, but held, with its domestic animals and equipment, as common clan property. All, including the clan chief and his sons, shared in the labor and in the harvest. The clanswomen, including the king's daughters, did the domestic work, washed the family clothes at a nearby creek, spun, wove, dyed, and sewed.

Homeric Religion

The religious beliefs of Homeric society were as simple as its social structure and politics. The gods were represented as men and women, but as nobles, not commoners, who ate, drank, loved, hated, hoped, feared, pleaded with their adversaries or intrigued against them like human beings and who had the beauty, charm, talent, and courage of the idealized aristocrat. But, unlike human beings, they were immortal. The more important gods had control over special spheres; Zeus ruled over the sky and Poseidon over the sea, while Athena was skilled in the arts and Demeter was the patroness of agriculture. Zeus was thought of as king of all the gods, although he did not always have power over them and had none at all over Fate. While the Homeric gods, called Olympians because they were believed to dwell on Mt. Olympus, were honored by the whole Greek people, each city-state worshiped one special god or hero—its putative founder—above all others. Other local gods swelled the total number, so that Corinth in classical times had 105 deities, and Attica over 300. But Zeus, Athena, and Apollo had the largest following. The Linear B tablets prove that most of the Olympian pantheon was not imported but was established in Greece as early as the fifteenth century B.C. Demeter is the Minoan Earth-Mother; Apollo and Artemis are pre-Hellenic gods native to Delos. Only Aphrodite is a Mesopotamian import. In general, the Homeric gods are partly sky-divinities from the Achaean-Aryan homeland and partly chthonic (subterranean) powers adapted from Minoan Crete. Thus mainland worship of the Minoan fertility goddess has a political dimension, coloring the concept of Hera, chief female deity and consort of the victorious king-god, Zeus. Tales of these deities were gradually unfolded under the graceful trappings of poetic myth. Thus classical Greek religion was the creation not of prophets, as in Israel, nor of lawyers, as in Rome, but of poets.

As the Greeks had no revealed religion and therefore no dogma to perpetuate, each generation could spin a new web of romance around the gods or transfer divine qualities from one god to another. Furthermore, since worship was a clan concern, there was no separate ordained clergy speaking with authority for the gods. The clan-chief was priest, offering to the gods fruit, milk, honey, and animal sacrifices, and the clan hearth served as altar. Without dogma and without clergy, the Greeks developed freedom of thought in the secular as well as in the religious sphere, attaining a level of political freedom not equaled again in Europe until the Renaissance and Reformation.

Primarily the protectors of communities—tribe, clan, city-state, hamlet, or neighborhood—the Homeric gods were more interested in group welfare than in individual salvation; that is, their role was chiefly social and political. They fostered local patriotism, civic morality, and group responsibility. Moreover, since all Greeks accepted them, they supplied a national unity negated by the independent city-states. Pilgrims from the whole Greek world visited the great shrines of Zeus at Dodona and Apollo at Delphi, where Greek met Greek to exchange news, ideas, songs, fashions, and customs. Slowly the shrines evolved into *asyla,* safety zones universally recognized as immune from warfare.

But Homer's gods did not entirely neglect the individual; they communed with him and worked for his benefit as well as society's. They protected strangers and rewarded hospitality, witnessed and safeguarded oaths, encouraged mercy, and sanctified marriage.

The Greeks of Homer's time had only vague notions of immortality. The underworld, abode of the spirits of the dead, was gloomy, and even those who passed the scrutiny of the infernal judge, Rhadamanthus, went on to an eternity which had none of the vitality or sensuous pleasures that both Greeks and their immortal gods enjoyed.

A better fate awaited the specially gifted. Since Greek gods were but human beings writ large and immortalized, a remarkable man was easily thought of as literally godlike, to be worshiped after death as a hero and eventually, if his fame and popularity grew, as a full-fledged god. Thus Asclepius, the mythical founder of the art of medicine, appears in Homer as a mortal, son of Apollo, heroized for his gift to men; by archaic times he is met occasionally as the god of healing, pre-eminent over Apollo; by the fifth century B.C. the hero has everywhere become a god. Thereafter his worship grew more and more popular, especially at his sanctuary at Epidaurus, and he was one of the last pagan gods to be rooted out by Christianity in the fourth and fifth centuries A.D.

Chapter 12/ ERA OF THE
ARISTOCRACY

Rise of Social Classes

Greek social structure, government, and culture as mirrored in the Homeric poems underwent radical changes. In the hands of the kings, the city-state became stronger and more trusted than its component units, the clans and tribes. To punish crimes and keep peace the city restricted traditional clan rights, taking over the public clan functions and subordinating its chieftains. But the process was slow. In Athens it took nearly five hundred years.

Unreconciled to subordination, but fully aware that the city could not be wished out of existence, the clan and tribe chiefs set out to capture the city government by usurping the king's authority. From some cities they expelled the king altogether; in others they reduced him to priestly and minor judicial functions. Only in Sparta and in the backward sections, as Thessaly, Macedon, and Epirus, did the kings retain their thrones. By 750 B.C., practically all Greek cities had become aristocratic republics, city-states where the franchise, magistracies, and priesthoods belonged exclusively to the aristocracy.

By aristocracy we mean the descendants of the clan chiefs who had originally joined the city-state. Although they gradually lost all political sovereignty over the clans, they salvaged for themselves and their sons several substantial privileges. They retained the lion's share of the clan lands, and they used their political experience, gained in the king's service, for personal and class advantage. When they reshaped the political system, they posited for its guidance qualifications they alone possessed: blood, land, and religious and legal knowledge. They called themselves the "beautiful and good," ruling over the herd of the "mean."

Wealth, which then meant property in land, gave them a significant advantage. They alone served as infantry since they alone could afford the equipment required: iron sword and spear, round shield, and greaves. Since to own and equip a warhorse was expensive, only the highest aristocracy formed the cavalry. Only aristocrats had leisure for athletic competition and for drill in the new close-rank strategy. In brief, conscious that they were the state, they served it on their own terms. Wealth gave them yet another advantage. The plain clan folk who had lost their lots, beasts, and customary right of support as clan members were now dependent on these chiefs as serfs or wage-earners. From being fathers to their clansmen, the chiefs became patrons; and the day was not far off when they would be exploiters.

Three classes, besides slaves, gradually emerged from the shapeless mass of the "mean." First, there were the small farmers, those few who, despite incredible obstacles, somehow acquired homesteads. With *polis* protection they could farm outside the clan domain or with luck might stake out portions of the domain itself. Their independence grew with every century, although for every man who succeeded, there were scores who failed. Forced to borrow from the wealthy at ruinous interest, with their property as collateral, most small farmers were squeezed out. Many pledged even their persons as security and thus, if they failed to meet their obligations, became slaves to their creditors.

Lower and more helpless were those men and women who had drifted away from their clans and become itinerant hired hands, employed by the year or for the harvest period; they were wretchedly fed and clothed, inhumanly exploited, unprotected by the state, and wholly at the mercy of their employer who might, and often did, sell them as slaves. These unprotected farm-hands were worse off than slaves, for at least slaves, as worshipers of their master's gods, came under divine protection. Then, too, since slaves were property, they were generally treated with care. The gang system had not yet degraded men and women to the level of beasts of burden. This may have been indeed as close as slavery ever came to a golden age, when slave boys worked in the fields, plowing, harvesting, or shepherding at the side of their master's sons, while slave girls did the family washing and knitted and wove elbow to elbow with their master's daughters. Odysseus upon reaching home greets his slaves as his son's companions and finds his father in an old slave-couple's care. There were probably plenty of slaves, supplied by war, piracy, purchase from Phoenician kidnapers, and from the rescue of exposed children.

In cities a third class rose. Building called for carpenters, masons, stonecutters, and other craftsmen, while the needs of urban life stimulated more specialized industries. Artisans or traders, the product of a new social world out of joint with the old, gradually broke loose from their ancestral clans. They formed a new class, meanest of the "mean," in a society which, glad to exploit their talent, allowed them no social reward and no legal protection.

Commerce and Emigration

Homer often mentions piracy as an occupation as honorable as war or husbandry. Though as old as navigation itself, piracy flowered when clan decay inched the cadets and bastards of the nobility out of land and influence (as early as the tenth century B.C.). Their energy and acquisitive spirit found an outlet beyond their home society on the seas and highways. The chief objects of robbery—the Greeks called it gain—were women, children, domestic animals, manufactured articles, and crops. Pirates ranged far and wide, as witness the *Odyssey*, the Argonaut legend, or authenticated Minoan-Mycenaean voyages to Egypt and Cyrenaica, the Black Sea, and as far west as Spain. But as a rule the Greeks dreaded the open sea and clung to the coastline, sailing in daytime, beaching their ships by night, and riding out storms in sheltered coves. Even with the improved navigation of later times, a trip through the islands always seemed risky to them even though familiar hills were constantly before their eyes.

Traders, at first suspected as enemies, gradually became guests and friends. In visiting a friendly community they displayed their wares on the beach for barter. Next day, if he passed by a community which, while hospitable to others, was unfriendly to him, the same merchant might turn pirate. But in time the profit motive led him to broaden peaceful relations. When finally his own city became interested in the wealth he brought home, he received official protection.

Religion encouraged peaceful commercial relations. Since Zeus protected strangers, they were entitled to hospitality, just as the early medieval Church protected merchants and pilgrims. The more the Greeks learned of the outer world the more they realized that despite local differences they were but one family in language, religion, and political system of free and sovereign republics. This realization brought tolerance. In brief, economic forces, religious sanctions, and a growing consciousness of kind combined to develop common usages which protected all Greeks everywhere.

Civilization is indebted to Greek pirates and traders, for in their quest for gain they discovered regions new to them, sailing eastward to Syria and the Asia Minor coast, northward to the shores of the Black Sea, southward into Egypt and Cyrenaica, westward to Sicily, in short, along the whole Mediterranean coastline, until they knew it as well as their own Greek shores. They did not fail to notice that many of these lands, which might be theirs for the taking, were rich in timber, abounding in wild grain and grapes, and teeming with wild cattle. The day was to come when mass migration thither solved certain problems bedeviling the Greek cities.

First among these problems was the poor soil, shallow, stony, stubborn, and sterile except in a few small valleys. Greece, ancient or modern, is probably the poorest farming country in Europe. It took sweat and back-ache for undaunted peasants to eke out the barest existence from a soil that in America would be rated lower than submarginal.

A second problem was overpopulation, or rather faulty land distribution. Since land was being concentrated into ever fewer hands, the number and poverty of the dispossessed increased, and, however much they loved their native cities, these discontented citizens preferred emigration to starvation.

Third was the inescapable necessity of borrowing. The man whose harvest was too scanty to support him was forced to borrow, since, with the whole harvest used for food, he had no seed for planting. Interest was so exorbitant that to borrow just once meant to be in debt for life.

Fourth was the plow. Scarcely more than a pointed stick with no plow-share, the Greek plow could not break the soil deep enough. Other available implements were equally inadequate.

Lastly, the rise of a money economy worked against the Greek common man. Barter was yielding to money as a medium of exchange; and since hoarding money is easier than storing commodities the rich became richer, and the gap between rich and poor grew wider. In brief, the poor, having insufficient land or none at all, entangled in a mesh of debt, excluded from the franchise and from legal protection, found an avenue of escape in emigration.

The poet Hesiod has drawn an unforgettable picture of the common man's despair in eighth-century-B.C. Greece. The son of a peasant, and himself a hard-working, sun-parched peasant, he had a down-to-earth view of life. Believing that mankind had steadily degenerated, he spoke of five ages: those of the gods, of the heroes, of gold, of silver, and his own, the worst of all, the age of iron. "Never by day will men cease to toil nor by night, as they decline and perish; the gods will give them hard troubles." He described the ruling class as ruthless grafters using their political power for self-enrichment— "gift-devouring princes." Justice has been expelled; a strong arm is the only right. The poor are disheartened, for they see evidence on every side that honest work brings the worker no profit; it only goes to make the rich richer. But Hesiod himself had hope. He wrote a didactic poem, the *Works and Days,* ostensibly to teach his fellow-peasants efficient farming methods, really to restore to them what they seemed to have lost, faith in work. Work, the poem says, has been decreed by the gods; it alone can keep the wolf from the door; it alone has dignity.

Hesiod documented a terrible and critical moment in human history. Gone were the days when kings' and chieftains' absolute authority was tempered by paternalistic responsibility for the welfare of the humble. Neither tribe nor clan offered solid protection; the family itself was splintering. Hesiod is frightening when he despairingly implores his own brother Perses to stand shoulder to shoulder with him in this jungle world they never made. In a sense the modern world was being ushered in—to Hesiod's agony and bewilderment—the world of the independent individual, free to make his own way, but free also to starve and die with no help from his fellow-men. But this was not exclusively a Greek problem. In words as poignant as Hesiod's, the prophet Amos indicated that a similar social revolution was plunging the Hebrew masses into misery.

The poor, led by disgruntled aristocrats, found relief from these social evils in a new start overseas. Any regime founded on privilege will create malcontents; so in the aristocratic city-states the traditional laws of legitimacy and primogeniture worked against the cadets and bastards of the nobility, who found themselves left out of clan-controlled city-state politics. Too high-spirited to submit but too weak to revolt, these malcontents sought abroad the opportunities denied them at home. They went to sea, group after group of them for four centuries, first as pirates and traders, later as planters of colonies. In the latter role they found more than material advantages, not simply better land, larger crops, or commercial profits, but renewed privileges: leadership, magistracies, priesthoods, scope for talent.

The propertied class and the party in power at home were only too glad to encourage emigration, recognizing in it a safety-valve against a social explosion that might unseat them. Their sense of relief contributed to the wave of good will which swept over a city on the eve of embarkation. Old hatreds and feuds were forgotten in a round of farewells; the whole city's population, headed by priests and magistrates, went down to the harbor to wish the pioneers godspeed.

Colonial Expansion

In the eighth and seventh centuries B.C., the Ionian cities especially tried hard, but unsuccessfully, to encourage migration to Cyprus, Syria, and the rich Anatolian hinterland. The dynamic Phoenicians stopped the colonists in Cyprus and Syria, while in Anatolia three powerful states, Phrygia, Lydia, and Assyria, proved a stone wall. Blocked to the east, homeseekers braved more distant perils around the Black Sea and (750–500 B.C.) westward. Every major city (except Sparta and Athens, for reasons which will appear later) sent out colonies: the following list is but a sample, recording only the more important foundations.

Miletus, the major Asiatic port, colonized, chiefly for trading purposes, the shores of the Sea of Marmara and the Black Sea. So did Megara, a small but enterprising city between Corinth and Athens. The most famous Megarian foundations were Heraclea in the Crimea, a link between Greece and the barbarians of southern Russia, and Byzantium, which after a thousand years rose to imperial greatness. Milesian colonies included Abydos on the Dardanelles, Cyzicus in the Propontis, Sinope and Trebizond on the southern Black Sea shore, Olbia at the Dnieper mouth, whence Greek products reached Central Europe, and Panticapaeum, a thriving market at the entrance to the Sea of Azov, where Greek artifacts were exchanged for Scythian furs, northern amber, and Siberian gold. But, most important of all, the Pontic colonies opened rich grain fields to the Greek world.

West of the Dardanelles lay Thrace, rich in gold, timber, and fisheries, and convenient to the tin mines of Serbia. The Greeks turned its good soil into fertile wheatfields, olive orchards, and vineyards. Here Chalcis and Eretria, Euboean cities, founded seacoast towns; the former gave its name to Chalcidice, the peninsula of the three promontories.

In the west, Sicily and southern Italy were tempting, for the soil was rich, the climate suitable, and resistance weak. Minoans and Mycenaeans had exploited the west commercially. Later Greeks had visited the area to exchange geometric pottery for native slaves and pelts. Much of the *Odyssey* deals with these fabled lands where sirens bewitched helpless mariners, the Sun pastured his cattle, and rams grew so big that Odysseus and his companions could hide under their bellies. Here, then, the Greeks came in endless waves, dotting the coastline with cities, turning forests and swamps into fruitful fields.

Cumae on the Bay of Naples is traditionally a Chalcidian foundation of about 750 B.C.; it in turn founded Naples; its alphabet the Romans adopted and handed on to us. In the 700's B.C. Chalcis planted colonies also in Sicily: Naxos, Catane, Leontini, and Zancle, later renamed Messana by Messenian refugees. Chalcis also founded Rhegium on the toe of the Italian boot. Chalcidians at Syracuse were soon expelled by colonists from Corinth; Syracuse was to become the largest of the western Greek cities and leader of the Dorians in this area. It founded some colonies and conquered others. North of Syracuse, little Megara founded Megara Hyblaea, famous for honey; this colony in turn planted Selinus in south-

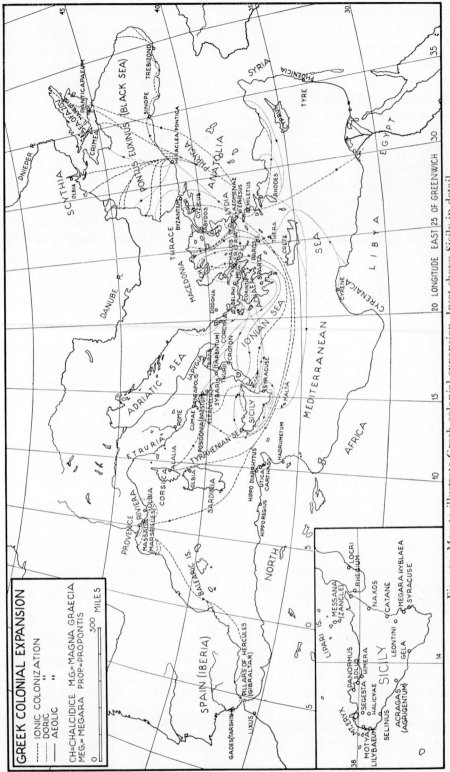

Fig. 12a. Map to illustrate Greek colonial expansion. Inset shows Sicily in detail.

Fig. 12.1. Paestum. So-called Temple of Poseidon (Neptune). About 450 B.C. The most beautiful and perfectly proportioned of surviving Doric temples in Magna Graecia. As in the Parthenon, imperceptible curves and deviations from the perpendicular contribute subtly to the effect. Recent excavations have established the cult-goddess as Hera. (Photo by Dorothy MacKendrick)

west Sicily as a check on Carthaginian expansion. The youngest Greek colony in Sicily was Acragas, or Agrigentum, founded in 580 B.C. Perched on a high hill amid extensive plantations, Acragas soon came to rival Syracuse. Its mother city was Gela, some 20 miles eastward, which had been founded by Rhodian pioneers. Thus Sicily was Ionian from Zancle to Leontini, Dorian from Megara Hyblaea to the south and west.

Settlers from Achaea in the northwest Peloponnesus colonized the south Italian toe, founding, for example, Sybaris and Croton, which prospered on farming and stock-breeding. Controlling both the Tyrrhenian and Ionian coasts, they could portage from sea to sea, avoiding the pirates who infested the Sicilian straits. Income from tolls and services made Sybaris a synonym for wealth and luxury. Both Sybaris and Croton sent out colonies which prospered. One such was Posidonia (Roman Paestum), the temples of which are today among the best preserved and most impressive Greek monuments in the West.

In the instep of the Italian boot rose Taras (Tarentum) allegedly founded in 707 B.C. by Spartan rebels or outcasts. These and many other foundations made south Italy a Greater Greece.

On the French Riviera the Greeks founded Massalia, where Cornish tin and Spanish metals were exchanged for Greek manufactures, a cul-

Fig. 12.2. Arcesilas vase. The King of Cyrene is seated aboard ship watching merchandise being stowed. Note the pet animals, monkey, and bird. The vase illustrates commerce between homeland and colonies in the 6th century B.C. (Paris, Bibliothèque Nationale, Cabinet des Médailles)

tural center whence Greek religion and ideas irradiated Provence and western Europe. Massalia too planted colonies of her own on the Riviera and along the eastern Spanish coast. Marseilles and its colonies, Taranto, Messina, Syracuse (to give them their modern names), were to affect Roman history significantly. Marseilles and Naples are still among the busiest ports in Europe.

Prevented from colonizing Egypt while the Assyrians held it, Greeks entered as mercenaries serving rebellious native princes, who, on achieving independence, rewarded the Greeks by admitting them as traders. One result was the Greek concentration already mentioned at Naucratis in the western Delta (about 565 B.C.).

West of Egypt, in what today is desert, rose beautiful Cyrene, founded about 630 B.C. by Dorians, many of whom came from the small volcanic island of Thera. Cyrene's wealth came from stock-breeding, commerce with the Libyan hinterland, and the raising and marketing of the valuable medicinal herb *silphium* (asafetida). Most of the above-mentioned colonies, though conquered by Rome and held to the end of its Empire, conserved their Hellenism. Greek colonization stopped in the 500's B.C., not because of increased prosperity or more equitable land distribution at

Fig. 12.3. Delphi. Theater and Temple of Apollo. 4th century B.C. The theater, with a capacity of 5,000, commands a magnificent view of the Sacred Precinct and the valley below. The temple, damaged by earthquakes, is approached by a ramp; before it (left) the Great Altar. Mt. Parnassus rises to the left. In the valley below the road can be seen the ruins of the *palaestra* (wrestling ground) with its round open-air swimming pool. (Photo by Dorothy MacKendrick)

home, but because of opposition from powerful states. Carthage blocked further expansion in western Sicily or Spain and had already staked out North Africa before Greek colonization began. The Etruscans denied the Greeks the Italian peninsula above Cumae, driving out those few colonists already settled in Sardinia and Corsica and preventing colonization eastward from Marseilles. In the 500's B.C., too, the rising Persian Empire stopped the Greeks in Thrace, the Pontic regions, Asia, and Egypt.

In general, planting a colony was a private enterprise, directed by a founder, or *oecist*, who was considered the creator of the new city, its laws, and its customs, and hence was honored by posterity as the colony's hero. The settlers took a brand from the sacred fire, always glowing on the public hearth of the old city, to kindle a holy flame in the new. They carried with them also the mother-city's culture (speech, customs, beliefs, religion).

The mother-city's role was active. It sent out exploratory expeditions, convoyed the emigrant ships, staked out spheres of influence for itself and its colonies, and fought interference. But the colony was a new *polis*, a full-fledged state, independent even of its mother-city, except for ties of sentiment. Sentiment and not law dictated that a colony founding a colony of its own should seek an oecist from the mother-city. Although not all colonies were homogeneous in population, the oecist accepted all on an equal footing with his own fellow-townsmen. Apollo's Delphic oracle strongly influenced early Greek colonization, making it not a furious and anarchic land-grab, but a comparatively orderly procedure. Apollo at Delphi had superseded Zeus at Dodona as adviser to the Greeks, for Delphi was central and Dodona inconveniently located in the far northwest. Before a colony was sent out, Apollo's oracle was consulted. The babble of a priestess in a god-inspired trance was interpreted by the priests as recommendations. The well-informed priests provided a central clearing house for colonial plans as well as for other policies. Thus the servants of Apollo, sending land-hungry malcontents overseas, staved off revolution in the homeland cities, and in the process Hellenized the Mediterranean from the rising to the setting sun.

Results of Colonial Expansion

Greek colonization affected world history profoundly. The Greeks, unlike the later Romans and English, clung to the coast. Centuries afterwards, the backland peoples, grown in culture and power, either absorbed those thin Greek fringes, or drove them out altogether, but not before the Greek colonies had revolutionized the surrounding barbarians, giving them literacy, religion, new ideas, wares, and weapons. In Sicily especially the Elymians and Sicels were thoroughly Hellenized, and in central and southern Italy most communities acquired Greek culture in externals and in spirit. Indeed, when Cicero called Rome the missionary of Hellenism, he spoke more truly than he knew, for Hellenism transmitted by Rome was to be the basis of all western civilization.

Colonization affected Greece itself no less profoundly. Since any Greek could by emigrating be free, self-respecting, and useful, the magic of family vanished: intelligence and enterprise began to count, and money too, called into being by the colonization movement and the resulting commercial expansion, became important. Henceforth value was placed not on blue blood, but on what a man was and what he had. Typical of the new men are Hesiod, an emigrant's son, and the full-fledged individualist Archilochus of Paros, a colonist who quarreled with the nobles at home, fell out with his fellow-colonists, and shamelessly proclaimed that he valued his skin more than his city. It was no accident, either, that individual rights were first recognized in the colonies and that the earliest stirring of the democratic spirit took place there. Tradition loosened its grip upon Greek frontiersmen, as it did upon American pioneers. Its hold was weakest in colonies of heterogeneous origin, for with no traditional bonds the one all-pervading interest was unity to make the new venture prosper. The average colonist, then, placed less emphasis on traditional social values than did the stay-at-home; his status depended on the strength he brought to the settlement, especially as shown in the common defense against the natives and in exploiting the new land's resources. Moreover, whereas at home the Greeks noted chiefly how different one city was from another, abroad, living in a new world with barbarian peoples, they were conscious rather of what all Greeks had in common. This new sense of unity prompted the division of all mankind into Greeks and barbarians, barbarians being non-Greeks, whether civilized or not. The Romans adopted the term to designate those peoples who, untouched by Greco-Roman humanism, represented a lower and more menacing culture.

Chapter 13/RISE OF THE COMMON MAN

Colonies and the Individual

As the kings had yielded to the aristocracy, so the aristocracy began to bow before the common man. The reasons were many. Increased industry, trade, and piracy, plus opportunities in new settlements, meant that any able man's economic status could rise. Successful commoners—an aristocrat would have said "the mean"—felt a new dignity and a growing desire to break the social and political monopoly of the aristocracy. The nobility was a closed corporation hostile to outsiders; nobility and commoners were bound to clash; this story is the history of the seventh and sixth centuries B.C. in Greece.

No longer did any Hesiod have to urge the poor to work; in this new day anyone could see the sure rewards of labor, especially in the colonies, with their limitless opportunities: swamps to be reclaimed, forests cleared, ranches, plantations, and small farms laid out, homes built, and indispensable industries started. In the old world a poor man could hardly keep from starving; in the new he could build himself a home. Even more heartening, he discovered his social usefulness. He himself was helping to fashion a society which quickly rewarded enterprise and industry, which needed every man and respected him according to merit, which drew its communal solidarity from the resulting sense of self-importance. In short, colonial conditions fostered social equality.

Indeed, as a founder of cities the common man was apparently surpassing the gods, heroes, or their descendants, the aristocrats of the motherland. Emigrant colonies soon equaled and often outstripped the mother cities in wealth, population, and culture. Croton, Sybaris, and Taras in southern Italy, Syracuse and Acragas in Sicily, and Massalia in Gaul were among the leading Greek cities; temples in Selinus and Acragas in Sicily were over twice the size of the richest in the motherland, and into their building went pride and hope as well as sheer massive grandeur.

Men who can turn the wilderness into rich and beautiful cities are not the kind to remain politically inactive. These transplanted Greeks put pressure on their new states to extend aristocratic privileges to the commoners. Several other factors prompted their challenging spirit and finally transformed Greek political life.

The Influence of Lydia and the East

One such factor was the influence of Lydia and the East. We have seen that the kings of Lydia had dominated Ionian cities by supporting merchants against the landowning aristocracy, thus making more democratic even cities under a local chief or tyrant answerable to the Lydian master. With the island and European Greeks, the kings were content to have commercial and cultural contacts. Croesus showed such generosity to Delphi, for example, that he was made an honorary citizen.

In Lydia the Greeks found not only the material advantages of employment and markets, but also invaluable cultural lessons: in geography, helpful for colonizing the Black Sea shores; in religion; in music (a new musical mode); in artistic motifs, applied to vase-painting and sculpture; in astronomy, leading to the development of the Greek scientific spirit.

The Lydian influence on the reawakening Greeks was rivaled by the Phoenician, which reintroduced the sea. In the *Odyssey* the Phoenician, not the Greek, is sea-captain, trader, pirate, and kidnapper, the man who has not the sense to stay on dry land, and so it was from the Phoenicians that the Greeks relearned shipbuilding and navigation.

From Phoenicia too the Greeks learned something decisive in western cultural history: an alphabetical script. Alphabetic writing had apparently been devised about 1900 B.C. by a Semitic-speaking people working the Sinai copper mines. In succeeding centuries this alphabet was developed and used in a variety of local forms by Semitic-speaking peoples of the Syrian coastlands, including the Phoenicians, from whom the Greeks borrowed and adapted to their Indo-European language an alphabet, the direct ancestor of every European alphabet in use today. To judge from the dates of the earliest known alphabetic Greek inscriptions, this development took place in the late eighth century B.C.

The alphabet's historic importance is worth considering. Civilized life requires writing. Recorded history means the history of civilization, which cannot exist without an ordered society which needs writing for archives, laws, contracts. The earliest civilizations, in Mesopotamia and Egypt, had different but equally complex writing systems requiring hundreds or even thousands of elaborate symbols for words or syllables. This meant that writing required long, specialized training, and was restricted to professional scribes, who thus became instruments of social and political control. In societies where writing is complex, the rule of the few over the many is inevitable.

The revolutionary significance of an alphabet is obvious. Instead of using numerous, complex signs, writing is reduced to some twenty-odd simple marks—the Greek alphabet has twenty-four—which can be easily learned. Thus anyone can become a merchant, a legal expert—or a ruler. An alphabet does not of course guarantee a society of equals, but it provides an essential precondition to such a society.

From various Eastern standards of weights and measures the Greeks had already developed two principal systems, the Euboic and the Aeginetan. Barter had begun to give way to the use of iron spits or copper pieces as media: an improvement, but still a cumbersome system, for at each transaction the metal had to be weighed and assayed according to one or another of half a hundred existing standards. Lydia had a better system, an official currency, the imitation of which by Greek cities about 650 B.C. opened a new era. Greeks also imported from Lydia electrum (70% gold, 30% silver). On a small pellet of this metal the city-states stamped their seals, later adding artistic emblems. This official guarantee of every coin's weight and fineness by a sovereign state interested in sound legal tender made coined money universally acceptable.

Within a century practically every Greek city had its own coinage, first of electrum and later of silver, often mined locally. The emblem stamped on the coins was usually the city's patron divinity or its basic commodity: *silphium* for Cyrene, a wheat-ear for Metapontum, a bull for Sybaris. The invention of coinage both stimulated business and gave status to those who lent money at interest. Here was, then, a type of wealth more profitable and easier to handle than land. Money began to compete with noble blood and landed property for principal control; and since it was easier to have money than to inherit noble blood, the expanding moneyed class competed successfully with the aristocracy. Of course, individual aristocrats too could make money; as a class, however, they began to lose to financiers and business men. The "self-made" man could not have the reverence his father had had for tradition.

Military Changes

Continental Greece was prospering too. In the period of wholesale emigration, its labor supply decreased while demand for goods increased. Busy taming the soil in new lands, the colonists had for a while to import from the old country their olive oil, wine, cheese, dried fruit, and a score of other essential manufactures and commodities. This expansion of commerce at home both profited established farmers and industrial workers and created new jobs. The cities better situated for commerce saw the new shipping industry expand by leaps and bounds, new shops and commercial firms rise along their waterfronts, and more men—employers and employees, native and immigrants—make a better living. Finally those newly enriched by industry and trade began to challenge the aristocracy's claim to rule either by divine appointment or because of the land they owned.

Simultaneously came a new method of warfare which shifted state defense from the nobility to the rising middle class. The farmer of moderate means, the trader and industrial worker who could afford the necessary heavy armor were drafted into the citizen army. The new system required drill, coordination and discipline, for a battle was no longer a series of duels among nobles, but the indivisible impact of closely serried infantrymen charging to hurl their spears. The nobles, forced to fight as cogs in this machine, were no different from their comrades in arms. At best their exclusiveness could be maintained in an élite cavalry corps. The common defense, perhaps more than anything else, brought the common man into his own, for equality to the aristocrat in war led to claims of equality in peace. The "mean" dared to demand a share in the privileges of the "beautiful and good." A new chapter was thus beginning in the history of Greece, a chapter of class struggle.

An aristocratic poet, Theognis of Megara, as late as the mid-sixth century B.C. could still not reconcile himself to this state of affairs. To his mind the world was topsy-turvy; it no longer made sense, for "the mean" had become "the good," and "the good" had become "the mean." Enraged at seeing the merchants in the saddle, he cried out, "Let me drink their blood." The new money-economy had dimmed the power and prestige of many of his fellow-aristocrats. Theognis had bitter words too for the nobleman unashamed to marry a low-born wealthy woman, or for the noblewoman who would stoop to marry a peasant for his money. Forty or fifty years earlier, another aristocratic poet, Alcaeus, had summed up this situation in the now famous cliché, "Money makes the man."

These were not isolated expressions. The struggle lasted long and evoked savage feelings. According to Aristotle, even in his day the aristocrats of some cities bound themselves by oath to hate the common people: "I will be hostile to the people and will plan whatever evil I can against them."

Intellectual Awakening: Philosophy

The social and economic forces and political trends just described combined to liberalize the Greek mind. Cultural awakening led to scientific questioning, first in Ionia, perhaps because the Ionian Greeks first felt the impact of those forces and had been longest exposed to the influence of the East. Thales, a scientist who flourished before 585 B.C., was a citizen of Miletus, a metropolis transcending the limits and outlook of the average city-state. In close contact with the progressive kingdom of Lydia and with Eastern cultures, Miletus was also the first Greek city to send out colonies. Its dynamism is especially evident from their number—about fifty—far more than those of any other city. Little wonder that throughout the eighth and seventh centuries B.C. Miletus was the largest manufacturing center and the busiest commercial mart of the Greek world.

Ionian thinkers, with an intellectual horizon wider than Homer's and a more realistic understanding of Nature and Nature's works, were no longer satisfied with Homer's cosmology. Thales declared that water as a cosmic element, not as the Homeric god Oceanus, was the one universal and eternal life-giving principle. That was a good beginning. What matters is not that Thales was wrong in identifying the origin of being, but that he came near the truth in conceiving some basic principle or element from which everything is engendered.

Another Ionian, Anaximander (born 610 B.C.), posited not any one concrete or visible universal generative element, but the "Unlimited" or "Infinite," a pregnant force which gives being to everything by a constant and eternal law inherent in its nature.

Influenced by these thinkers, a third Ionian, Anaximenes (fl. c. 546 B.C.) sought the primal element in air rather than in water, adding that Anaximander's eternal operative law resided in rarefaction and condensation, by which he believed all things to be created: fire, wind, clouds, water, the earth, and the gods themselves.

Pythagoras (c. 582–507 B.C.) had a different approach. Apparently a political refugee from his native Samos, he fled to Croton in southern Italy. A mystic and the founder of a monastic brotherhood, he thought that numbers were the key to the composition of the cosmos. A profound student of music and musical theory, he discovered a mathematical law in the relation of the lyre-string to the pitch of the tone that was obtained from it. From his knowledge of the mathematics of sound he argued a mathematical law of the universe. Since numbers for him were not symbols but realities constituting the essence of things, he developed the theory that the law or order regulating the cosmos consists of their interrelation or harmony. To him numbers were not merely a convenient language in which to describe natural phenomena; they were the actual force which brought about the observed events.

Pythagoras was the first Western thinker to direct philosophical investigation along new channels, to psychology and ethics. He or his disciples thought of a soul dwelling in man, the nature of which was harmony. They envisaged man's self-fulfillment as a process of becoming mystically like God through the practice of virtue. Virtues, or moral notions—for example, justice—are numbers, and virtue as a whole is the harmony of the different virtues, that is, the harmonious equilibrium of the soul's aspirations and practices.

In another city of south Italy, Elea, still another road to philosophy was opened by Xenophanes (born 570 B.C.), an immigrant from Ionia. He seems to have upheld rigidly the monism of his master, Anaximander. He allegedly took the position that everything in the universe is One and One is everything. He seems therefore to have denied the plurality of being, vaguely hinting that it exists only in man's imagination. He certainly denied the plurality of the divine being, remarking that Negro gods are black with flat noses and Thracian gods blond with blue eyes, while if horses and oxen could draw they would represent their gods as horses and oxen. Yet he strengthened the concept of deity when he taught that over the universe rules a supreme being, "all eye, all ear, all intellect," from whom everything takes its origin.

Ionian speculation, especially Xenophanes' teaching, had its impact on the Greeks of the turn from the sixth century B.C. to the fifth. About 500 B.C. Hecataeus of Miletus ridiculed the ancestral beliefs, shaking Homer's authority by the iconoclastic suggestion that the heroes commonly believed to be the offspring of gods were only bastards whose paternity their mothers assigned to Zeus, Apollo, or Poseidon in order to conceal adultery with plain mortals.

A few years later Parmenides carried one step further the germinal idea of his master Xenophanes about the oneness of being. Regarded as the true founder of the Eleatic school, he taught that what man sees as change or becoming, or differentiation and plurality, is pure illusion, since the senses cannot perceive and convey the truth. Only reason can be taken as guidance; opinion, or what man thinks he sees, is fallacious. Parmenides thus emerges as the first Western rationalist.

Intellectual Awakening: Science

The sixth century B.C. saw, mainly in Ionia, the rise of several sciences, as well as of philosophy. The Ionians, in contact with Eastern cultures, bound politically with Lydia and its successor, the Persian Empire, traveled freely among non-Greeks, some trading along the Black Sea shores and the Anatolian hinterland, others, especially architects, engineers, and physicians, entering the employment of Persian satraps or the Great King himself. One Scylax, in Darius' service, explored the Indus River and the Indian Ocean and wrote an account of his voyage. Wherever they went these Greeks asked questions, impelled by their characteristic unquenchable thirst to know and to understand. Then they wrote so-called histories of Lydia or Persia and books of geography. Meantime the Mediterranean had been colonized, thanks largely to increased knowledge of sea currents, safe lanes or dangerous shoals, headlands and river estuaries, coasts, harbors, islands. More or less systematically collected by observant pilots, this knowledge was handed down mostly by word of mouth, but sometimes by written descriptions or crude maps.

Historical writing was in its infancy. Its subject matter was the curious and the strange—what modern journalism was until recently—a hodge-podge of myths and legends, accounts of plagues, earthquakes, and monsters stalking among men, miracles and other supposed visitations from heaven. Such historical works were named "genealogies" since they dealt with the mythical origins of the more important Greek cities. They resembled somewhat the medieval monkish chronicles. Judging from the attitude mentioned above, Hecataeus of Miletus must have stood head and shoulders above his fellow "genealogists."

Progress in pure and applied sciences was more substantial. Pythagoras or his disciples formulated the multiplication table and, in geometry, the "Pythagorean" theorem. Pythagoras' idea of the interrelation of musical sounds could be easily applied to a better understanding of other arts, for instance, architecture or engineering. Progress in astronomy, much of it due to Babylonian influences, is evident from Thales' prediction of the eclipse of May 28, 585 B.C. Perhaps more spectacular was the Greeks' achievement in engineering. When Darius the Great invaded eastern Europe he looked to Ionian engineers to span the Danube River with a pontoon bridge.

Although riddled with superstition, medicine felt the effects of the Ionian scientific spirit. The Pythagoreans were aware of the value of diet and of a healthy mind in a healthy body. Their doctrine of opposites, for example, odd-even, single-multiple, coupled with their doctrine of numbers, cross-fertilized the thinking of Alcmaeon of Croton. About 500 B.C. he thought of opposites, cold-warm, dry-wet, and so forth, in relation to the human body, concluding that harmony or a just balance among them ensures health; its absence, illness. Alcmaeon is said to have been the first Greek to operate on the eye; he rediscovered the connection of eye with brain, which Egyptian physicians had known some 1500 years earlier.

By their efforts to reason things out and to apply practically the results of that reasoning, the sixth-century B.C. Greeks created an organized body of scientific knowledge. Better still, they honored reason above tradition. Every new generation contributed to this courageous undertaking. Following reason wherever it led, even if it led away from time-honored beliefs, scores of honest thinkers boldly renounced those beliefs. No more auspicious beginning could be asked for the growth of human knowledge.

Intellectual Awakening: Literature and Art

The same spirit of challenge and criticism is evident in literature. Homer never revealed his personality, but remained anonymous throughout. In the 700's B.C. Hesiod ushered in the age of individualism. He broke away from anonymity, announcing his name, his birthplace, his family, his social condition, his economic status.

The same period produced in Archilochus of Paros a full-fledged iconoclast who discarded the Homeric style and verse-form to which Hesiod had clung in favor of contemporary speech and new meters. His subject was himself, his rebellion against conventions which he thought no longer made sense—such as saving one's shield at the risk of one's skin. His invective was biting: a gentleman who had refused him his daughter in marriage because Archilochus was the son of a slave woman was driven to suicide by the public humiliation he suffered from the poet's written revenge. Archilochus founded a new genre, lyric poetry, which is still a poet's most effective medium for expressing his emotions.

Sappho of Lesbos (born c. 612 B.C.), greatest woman poet of antiquity, developed the lyric to an unrivaled delicacy. She describes a young bride:

Like the sweet apple which reddens upon the topmost bough,
Atop on the topmost twig—which the pluckers forgot somehow—
Forgot it not, nay, but got it not, for none could get it till now.

Alcaeus, her fellow-townsman, calls her "Violet-haired, holy, sweetly smiling Sappho." An aristocrat to the marrow, Alcaeus fought with pen and sword against democracy's advance. But like most Greeks he could forget civic strife; his views on wine are not those of a teetotaler.

Art, too, mirrors the new frame of mind. Greek ninth-century vase-decoration had been rigidly geometric, as exemplified in the Dipylon vases from Athens. In the eighth century, ceramists varied the old geometric designs with such oriental motifs as palm leaves, rosettes, sphinxes, and other animals in heraldic postures. These masters seem to be consciously trying to integrate the world of their fathers with the fascinating, newly-discovered world of the East. In seventh-century art, individualism asserts itself also. The painter's line is free-flowing; his subjects are men and animals reflecting the restless energy of the age. Proud of his work and eager to expand his market, like Archilochus in poetry, he asserts his authorship: the vases are signed. For the first time in history we can attach an artist's name to a painting.

By the mid-seventh century, B.C. Athens had begun to burgeon both commercially and artistically. Lively mythological pieces like the François vase are the product of citizen-craftsmen and resemble in spirit the sturdy work on twelfth-century cathedrals. In sculpture, too, Athens and the western colonies led in the new individualistic archaic style, exemplified in the Acropolis Moschophoros, youths and maidens, and in the metopes from Selinus and the archaic Heraeum near Paestum.

Legislators and Tyrants

During the seventh century B.C. the challenge to tradition also invaded politics. Traders, peasants, and shop workers began to agitate for a new concept in government—equality before the law. Greece had at that time no laws in modern sense of legislative enactments; only customs, precedents, and usages which an inner aristocratic circle—the eternal "ins" —was alone supposed to know. When a citizen came up for trial, the proper official would declare and interpret the applicable law, on what principle and at whose expense is evident from Hesiod's testimony. Men now came to think that if only the law were down in black and white they might know where they stood, and the poor man on trial have a chance against the rich. So the "mean" girded themselves to fight for what was to prove a characteristic Greek ideal, the rule of law against the whims of men.

The movement toward the writing down of laws began in the western colonies, where custom was less deeply entrenched and aristocratic control less complete. According to tradition, the laws were codified by an appointed or elected citizen acceptable both to the aristocracy and to the people. These lawgivers were almost certainly empowered also to insert new laws to remedy existing evils. The earliest recorded legislator was Zaleucus of Locri in southern Italy. His reform, while harsh, at least prohibited private vengeance: the state, not the injured party, henceforth might fix the penalty. Equally essential for the growth of democracy was Zaleucus' ban, under penalty of death, against coming armed to the people's assembly.

Charondas of Catania extended the state's authority and protected individual rights even further. He transferred from clan to state the protection of life and property and the guardianship of minors, thereby officially recognizing the individual as separate from the clan and the individual's welfare as a matter of public concern. The state here took the first step in replacing the private law of the clan with public law. The real loser was the nobility, which had controlled the clans. Many other cities in Greece, the islands, and Asia imitated Charondas' legislation.

Unwritten law seldom changes. But written law, representing the community's consensus at a given stage of its evolution, can be changed when the community's will changes. Thus codifying the law not only brought relief to specific seventh-century B.C. Greek needs, but opened the way for future generations to revise a law whenever it had become antiquated.

Those individualists, the tyrants, one-man rulers who bent existing laws and institutions to their own ends, also did spadework for the growth of law and eventually of democracy, even as they selfishly exploited the class struggle. While the aristocrat stubbornly defended his privileges, the well-to-do commoner insisted on a share in the government corresponding to his share in the common defense. The poor, ground into serfdom between greedy landlords and unscrupulous money-lenders, would follow any leader promising relief.

The introduction of money, the export of native farm products to better-paying foreign markets, and the shift of workers to industry combined to upset the social order. Supported by one or more classes hopeful of redress, the tyrants rode to power on this wave of general discontent.

From 650 to 550 B.C., tyranny flourished principally on the Greek mainland, where the city-state population was largest and worst treated, that is, where industry and commerce were displacing agriculture. Here the tyrants' power was based on exploitation of the discontented many against the wealthy and aristocratic few. Tyranny started first in Anatolian cities because they felt first the effects of the commercial revolution. It also lasted longer there because the Lydians and Persians supported the tyrants, thus keeping a finger in the Greek pie. In the western Greek cities, the typical tyrant was the indispensable general who defended the state against two formidable enemies, Carthage and Etruria. Among the most colorful tyrants were Thrasybulus of Miletus, Polycrates of Samos, Periander of Corinth, Pisistratus of Athens, and the Syracusans Gelon and Hiero.

None of the tyrants destroyed existing government or laws. Their power derived from their holding personally, or assigning to a friend or relative, an important city-state magistry and from their personal control of the armed forces. The city-state functioned as before, but the tyrant was its

Fig. 13.1. Dancing girls, full of delicate archaic grace, from the Temple of Hera (*c.* 500 B.C.) at the mouth of the Sele. (Paestum, Museum; Fototeca)

center and co-ordinator. Often, wanting more power and glory than the needs of a transitional period would guarantee, he tried to make his position hereditary and to perpetuate his power through a bodyguard, legally voted him by the popular assembly, and through residence on the acropolis or citadel, apart from and dominating the city.

The tyrants' domestic policy centered in conciliation of the masses at the aristocracy's expense, using a number of shrewd devices. For instance, the tyrants split or merged certain tribes which had become nothing but retainer gangs. Or they promoted new cults, chiefly those of Dionysus and Orpheus, at the same time snubbing the older gods, the source of the aristocracy's claims to privilege. In the city proletariat's interest they restricted slavery, which had begun to compete with free labor; they encouraged business—indeed some of the tyrants were big businessmen; and they constructed great public works like temples, market-places, and harbors. They built aqueducts to make work, to improve sanitation, and to facilitate urban expansion.

For the peasants' benefit they reduced taxation and rents, lowered the interest rate, or divided among the land-hungry the properties confiscated from unreconciled aristocrats. To assure the peasant some local control, they established local assemblies where his vote balanced the squire's. To relieve the peasants of time-consuming errands to the city (and themselves of interference), they established itinerant judgeships and enlarged the administrative authority of the rural wards.

The tyrants' foreign policy was to preserve peace. Earlier under the aristocracy and later under the democracy, Greece was almost constantly at war; under tyranny it experienced three prosperous generations of peace, during which the countryside blossomed with olive groves, orchards, and vineyards; cities became industrial centers; harbors were crowded with merchant ships. The people's activity was focused on colonization, trade, higher living standards, and beautification of the cities. Various tyrants established links of dynastic marriage and extended to citizens of other cities rights of residence, commerce, and intermarriage. In brief, under tyranny the Greek states were unified as never before or after.

Lastly, the tyrants stimulated cultural growth. They gave architects and sculptors opportunities to create some of the greatest glories of Greek art. Their courts were the rendezvous of poets, philosophers, and educators. Their promotion of civic and religious festivals on an unprecedented scale contributed greatly to the development of music, the choral dance, and the drama. In this respect they had much in common with the Italian despots of the eve of the Renaissance.

Chapter 14/GREEK LIFE
THROUGH THE SIXTH
CENTURY B.C.

*

Religion

The center of Greek life during the period we have been discussing was religion. In this archaic age the worship of the Olympian pantheon gave to Greece much of its unity, while local cults tended to defeat attempts to create larger political units. By the late 500's b.c. the chief deities, with their chief cult centers, were Zeus at Olympia and Dodona, Apollo at Delphi and Delos, Athena at Athens, and Poseidon at the Isthmus of Corinth. Zeus was the paternalistic maintainer of customary law, patron of aristocratic cities. Apollo was patron of the arts, and, through Delphic propaganda, prophet, adviser, and inspirer. Athena was patroness of craftsmen and craftswomen. Poseidon, god of earthquakes, was also god of seafarers, and, as god of horsemen, especially dear to the aristocrats. Clan gods became gods of city-states and the twelve Olympians were believed to dwell like aristocrats on their mountaintop, with tribal chiefs, exalted into heroes, in their train—a Heracles, a Theseus, an Asclepius.

These gods were addressed through public cults presided over by priest-magistrates, legalistically expert at the formula of a minutely precise

* Olive-harvest. Detail from an Athenian oil-jar, c. 525 b.c. (London. British Museum)

ritual performed before outdoor altars or in temples. The most important sanctuaries were those where gods gave oracles, advice to mortals. Zeus at Dodona spoke through the rustling leaves of an oak, Apollo at Delphi through the frenzied mutterings of a divinely inspired priestess. Besides the public cults there existed those of family, commerce, and handcraft: Hestia, the hearth goddess; Hermes, patron of trades—and thieves; Hephaestus, patron of metalworkers; the link between public and private cult was a priesthood reserved to a particular clan; thus at Athens the Eteobutadae supplied Athena's high priestess and Erechtheus' high priest.

Festivals, to be discussed below, were held in honor of the gods; some were local, some Panhellenic, but all had in common competitions in athletic sports, poetry, and music.

Of special interest for their ecstatic and mystic quality are two cults, the Dionysiac and the Orphic. Dionysiac ecstasy seized especially women, who, gripped by the god, raced over mountainsides, saw the god in a vision, and tore wild beasts to pieces. It took all the legalism of the Delphic Apollo to stem the Dionysiac tide; one of its more intellectualized forms is the drama-festival at Athens. The Orphic cult, named for the Thracian singer-prophet Orpheus, involved the myth of a suffering saint, a belief in the soul's primacy over the body, asceticism, purification for the righteous initiate, suffering in the underworld for the rest. Its center is the individual's guilt and atonement. Yet another mystery cult was celebrated at Eleusis, near Athens, in honor of the grain-goddess Demeter and her daughter Persephone, who returned in the spring from the underworld, to be greeted by sacred song, a revelation, and a sacred drama. The Eleusinian mysteries, like Orphism, involved notions of righteousness rewarded; they symbolized agriculture as the foundation of a civilized and peaceful life.

The State

Citizenship in the Greek world of 750–500 B.C., whether under oligarchy or under tyranny, was still a special privilege, depending at the very least on a minimum qualification in property or, later, in money. The state demanded of its citizens civil and military service, as magistrates and, typically, as heavy-armed infantry (hoplites). Throughout Greek history public service bulks larger in individual life than private business; this is a major difference between ancient Greek and modern life. Since in this period public service was unpaid, only the well-to-do could afford the luxury of holding public office; even if the constitution had allowed it, the poor could not have afforded the time or the money public service demanded.

The center of public life was the market-place, or agora, an open space in the center of the city, surrounded by religions and secular buildings and filled on market-days by a motley and colorful group of temporary stalls where all sorts of goods were on sale. Greeks have always loved conversation, especially about politics, and it was in the agora that many of these conversations took place. Formal political activity centered around the public hearth (called *prytaneum* in Athens), where ambassadors were entertained and the executive committee of the council met. Often the council-house adjoined it. The people's assembly met separately, usually outdoors, in the central space of the agora or in a less central meeting-place.

The citizen-soldier did his military duty from March to October, when weather permitted troop movements. He packed his knapsack, took down spear and shield from the chimney-piece, buckled on breastplate and greaves, put on his helmet, took his sword, and went off to join his comrades at the rendezvous. His job was usually to prevent enemy destruction of grain-fields or olive trees; since the olive tree takes eighteen years to mature, its destruction was particularly costly. In the archaic period military tactics were not highly developed; sheer weight of numbers was usually decisive. The victors set up a trophy; the vanquished asked for a truce to bury their dead. The citizen was liable for military service at any age between eighteen and sixty, with the youngest and oldest retained for garrison-duty only. Cavalry and light-armed troops were less important branches.

This was the period of the rise of navies, following upon Greek colonial and commercial expansion; the first recorded sea-battle took place between Corinth and Corcyra in 664 B.C. Navies did coast guard duty, patrolled against pirates, and convoyed merchant ships. Their upkeep was a community concern; in sixth-century Attica, subdivisions of the tribes, called naucraries, each had to finance one warship and crew. Since naval service required less outlay than hoplite armor, it attracted the lower class; naval successes by crews of poorer citizens were later to contribute to the rise of democracy, especially in Athens.

The Family

Generalizations about the family, and indeed about Greek life as a whole, apply to upper-class male Athenians, about whom our evidence is best. An olive branch hung on the doorpost announced the birth of a boy, tufts of wool the birth of a girl. From birth the male child was surrounded with affection; girl babies were held in far less esteem, and indeed were often "exposed," that is, set secretely in an earthenware vessel on a mountainside or in a temple, to die or to be brought up by others.

A child accepted by his father was given a name, often his grandfather's, formally registered in his phratry, and, until he was seven, brought up by his mother and his nurse, who sang him lullabies, told him nursery tales (of which Aesop's fables are an example) , and watched over him at his toys and games.

His education, discussed in more detail below, began where it should, at birth; it aimed at making the boy his father's image, a disciplined example of manhood and responsible citizenship. After the age of seven, the child was in charge of a slave "pedagogue," who followed him everywhere and helped to teach him modesty, reverence, manners, and self-restraint.

Before marriage the young man consorted much with young men of his own age or contracted close emotional relations with older men. Marriage was late, prearranged, and often distasteful to the man, since women were not educated to be intellectual companions. As part of her wedding ceremony the bride-to-be dedicated her girdle, took a sacred bath, participated, veiled, in sacrifice, banquet, and torchlight procession with song, and was then escorted to the wedding-chamber, henceforth to be her husband's chattel.

The house she managed, especially in town, was small, built of sun-dried brick, flat-roofed, its interior a series of cell-like rooms grouped around a central court. Women had separate quarters. There was no running water or central heating; oil-lamps supplied light. For living room the husband had the agora; woman's place was in the home, supervising the servants, spinning and weaving.

Diet was as simple as the living arrangements. The staples were fish, cheese, sausage, porridge, and barley-cake, with green vegetables and fruit, washed down with wine mixed with water. Oil served for butter, honey for sugar. Roast meat was eaten only on special, usually religious, occasions.

In the face of poor sanitation and undeveloped medicine, even this frugal life did not conduce to longevity. Proper burial was important; dirges were sung, and a ceremonial washing, anointing, and laying-out took place before the procession to the grave, where the body was cremated or buried, later to be surmounted by a monument, usually a marble slab sculptured with a life-sized relief portrait of the deceased. The arms, ornaments, toys, and vases buried with the dead enable the modern archeologist to reconstruct ancient life, so that we learn about Greeks living from Greeks dead.

Education

Greek education (paideia) embraced training of body, mind, and morals. Every boy, however poor, had the opportunity of instruction in gymnastic, music (including poetry), reading, and writing.

Gymnastic instruction was given in the sunny wrestling-ground (palaestra) on the outskirts of the city, where boys learned to wrestle, box, run races, and throw the javelin and discus. They exercised naked and anointed with oil; after exercise they scraped themselves with a strigil and took a cold plunge. Those who were to bear arms were trained in their use. The national festivals always included events for boys, who had been prepared for these events by their gymnastic training.

In music, boys were taught to play the lyre and sing to their own accompaniment; aristocratic young men were expected to play and sing at banquets familiar drinking songs (*scolia*).

In the grammar-school the boy learned to write, first with a stylus on a wax tablet, then, as he grew more proficient, with a reed pen on papyrus; in Athens, at least, illiteracy was very rare. The authors chiefly read were Homer and Hesiod, who were learned by heart; feats of memory were remarkable, and moral precepts in the works memorized influenced character indelibly. Teachers' status was low. Girls learned from their mothers or nurses the rudiments of literacy, but their education stressed housekeeping, spinning, weaving, sewing, and embroidery.

There was no formal instruction in foreign languages or in social or natural sciences, though boys in the port towns must have learned much from the tanned and bearded sailors, fresh back from voyages to the Pillars of Hercules and beyond; and there must have been a lucky few young men in Ionia who sat at the feet of Thales, Heraclitus, and other outstanding men.

Rich boys had no need of formal vocational training: they could learn estate management from their father and his bailiff or business in their father's counting-house. But tradesmen's sons were early apprenticed to their father's trade, and trained to be millers, bakers, dyers, fullers, tailors, tanners, jewelers, carpenters, masons, cabinetmakers, potters, armorers, smiths, or barbers. Smithies and barbershops were centers for lounging and conversation which carried indirect and interesting educational consequences.

In aristocratic Greek society, the artisan class was in disrepute; it was considered degrading to take pay for work, even painting, sculpture, playing instruments, teaching, and curing the sick. Commercial travellers and retailers were looked also down on; artisans and tradesmen, late arrivals on the Greek scene, found ideas of status already fixed, and this aristocratic bias is a pervasive note in Greek literature; the snobbery involved has seemed to many to be one of the most pernicious of classical inheritances. But aristocrats who learned their lesson well knew that their power involved them in social responsibility, and this lesson is one of the most precious, if unheeded, of our debts to Greece.

Making a Living

In spite of the growth of industry and commerce and in spite of the unsuitability of Greek soil, agriculture remained the most widespread source of livelihood. Land was irrigated, drained, and terraced; fertilizer was used, and the land allowed to lie fallow when it needed to recover its fertility. In Attica, ploughing was done three times a year. The ripe grain was harvested with sickles; it was then placed on a threshing floor and draft animals were driven over it until their hoofs had separated grain from chaff. After the winnowing, the grain was stored in earthenware jars and taken to the mill for grinding into flour when needed.

Wine was made by the barefoot treading of red and white grapes, as it is made in Greece today. Grapes were made into currants by being spread out to dry in the sun and wind, a practice still followed near Corinth, from which currants take their name.

Olives were beaten from the trees with sticks and pressed into oil. Some olive trees were sacred; the penalty for felling them was death. Greece was more heavily forested then than now, and forests provided ship-timber and charcoal. Grazing and beekeeping were other rural pursuits.

Industry had hardly progressed beyond the family-workshop stage; even at the end of the fifth century B.C., a shield factory with 120 workmen was considered large. Middlemen were important, as were artisans in the luxury trades, for example, goldsmiths, who flourished in Ionia, where they learned their craft from the East. Naucratis in Egypt was a typical Levantine industrial city, with its warehouses, temples, pottery works, and native quarter.

Toward the end of the seventh century B.C. metallurgy was revolutionized by iron-welding and hollow casting, but industry was not yet specialized; quarryman, mason, and sculptor's assistant were one. Pottery was the major industry, with a large market for household ware, receptacles for shipping, and special vases for display and religious use. When demand turned the Corinthian potters into mass-producers, the primacy passed to Athens, where art was reinstated in industry, but not without advertising: on an Athenian amphora the painter Euthymides writes, "Euphronius will never do as well."

The scale of price and wages is problematical, since evidence for the archaic period is scanty, and purchasing power was certainly greater then than now. But we know that in the early sixth century B.C. in Athens a sheep cost one drachma (eighteen cents) and an ox five, while later evidence shows that an allowance of three drachmas a day for feeding a family of five was considered extravagant. When pay for civil and military service was introduced, hoplites got a drachma a day, councilors five obols (an obol is three cents), jurors two or three obols, and cripples on government pension one. In this simple life, without luxuries or gadgets, an annual income of 300 drachmas must have sufficed to support a family, and many got by on less.

Recreation

In this age of transition from agrarian to urban life, rustic festivals like the harvest-home depicted on a famous vase still occupied country folk. For them, too, there were the pleasures of the hunt, usually with dogs, the quarry being the wild boar, fox, hare, deer, or wild goat. Birds were snared or caught with birdlime. Fishing was not regarded as a sport. Country folk also enjoyed country dancing and rustic work songs and play songs, like the lovely swallow-song sung in spring at Rhodes by children who went begging round the town, as our children do at Hallowe'en.

But the most glorified and sanctified recreation centered at Panhellenic festivals like the Olympic games, held at Olympia every four years in August. A truce to all hostilities for the duration of the festival made large attendance possible. The atmosphere was that of a great fair, with heat and dust and noise and color, and the festival was attended by all who wished, including slaves and barbarians but excluding married women. Here was focused what concept the Greeks had of unity, and here were all sorts of distractions, intellectual not excepted, for poets and thinkers came here to read their works.

The festival lasted seven days, of which the first was devoted to sacrifice, the last to a solemn procession and banquet, the central five to the competitions themselves. At the beginning, which tradition dated in 776 B.C., these included the footrace, the fight in armor, boxing, chariot-racing, and the javelin and discus throw. Later, seven other events were added, including the pentathlon and three events for boys. The games proper began with the footrace and ended with the chariot-race, which called forth much extravagant display on the part of princes, tyrants, and private persons. The prize was a crown of wild olive, but victors received special honors, and sometimes money, from their native cities.

The games were held in a sacred precinct, the Altis, in which were an archaic temple of Hera and a sanctuary of Pelops (a legendary charioteer), and treasuries of various cities and colonies, including at this period Sybaris, Cyrene, Byzantium, Selinus, Megara, and Gela, which thus monumentalized their new-found commercial prosperity. All the events but the chariot race were held in the Stadium, where the starting-blocks of a later epoch have been exposed. The great temple of Zeus with Phidias' gold and ivory statue, the molds for which were found in 1955, dates from the mid-fifth century B.C.

The Pythian games, held at Delphi in the high summer of the third

Fig. 14.1. Delphi. Sacred Precinct, model. The sacred way winds past Athenian Treasury (lower left), Bouleuterion (Senate House), and Portico of Athenians. In center, Temple of Apollo; above, left, theater. The precinct flourished in the sixth century B.C., but the model shows its state in the second century A.D. (New York. Metropolitan Museum of Art)

year of each Olympiad, featured musical competitions for a laurel crown. The Nemean games, celebrating Heracles' victory over the Nemean lion, were biennial; the prize a crown of wild celery. The Isthmian games, also biennial, had as prize a crown of pine. University of Chicago excavations since 1954 have revealed at the Isthmian site ingenious starting-blocks, a huge altar, and details of the ground plan. At Athens, Pisistratus was said to have founded the quadrennial Panathenaea, for which the prize was olive oil in a handsome amphora. All these games, like the Olympic, were Panhellenic and had a temporary unifying force.

Such was Greek life, public and private, religious and secular, about 500 B.C., on the eve of the great age of Sparta and Athens, to the historical background of which we now turn.

Chapter 15/SPARTA
THROUGH THE SIXTH
CENTURY B.C.

*

The Earliest Period

The Peloponnesus, the southern Greek peninsula, contained seven divisions: Arcadia, Laconia, Messenia, Elis, Achaea, the Isthmus of Corinth, and the Argolid. Of these, Elis is chiefly important as containing the site of the Olympic games; Achaea, except for a brief flowering in the age of colonization, and landlocked Arcadia did not become prominent until the Hellenistic Age; commercial Corinth flourished in the age of the tyrants and played an important part in the Peloponnesian War; Argos prospered in the seventh century B.C. and was to prove a thorn in Sparta's flesh in the fifth. But because the interest of the modern world centers in the struggle between democratic Athens and regimented Sparta, for us the rise of Sparta in Laconia and its conquest of Messenia are of paramount concern.

In the eleventh century B.C. Dorian conquerors occupied Laconia, the plain of the Eurotas River in the southeastern Peloponnesus. On the ruins of destroyed Achaean communities they built crude villages of their own, five of which in time federated into a city called Lacedaemon or Sparta. A true urban center Sparta never was; conservative by instinct

* A Spartiate, early fifth century B.C.

Fig. 15a. Map of the Peloponnesus through the sixth century B.C.

and resolved by calculation to base its wealth on land alone, it remained a coalition of rustic communities. Two clans stood out, the northern Agids and the southern Eurypontids. Their chiefs agreed on a balance of power and won recognition as joint kings of the united state. Unlike other Greek kings, they survived all aristocratic attacks, perhaps through unusually able leadership in constant wars against the Achaeans.

The Achaean nobility apparently was absorbed into the Dorian body politic, while the conquered masses formed separate interior groups. Some were *helots,* public serfs bound to the land, which had once been theirs, but which they now cultivated for the benefit of Spartan citizens; others were subjects, *perioeci* ("dwellers round about") with local self-government and minimum land allotments. The choicest fields were reserved to bring income to Spartan kings and Spartan gods. These arrangements operated smoothly in Laconia until about the eighth century B.C., when a high birth rate kept cadets or bastards from inheriting land and made this landless class a menace to internal stability. Sparta, instead of encouraging emigration as did other Greek states, turned these men loose against a peaceful neighbor, Messenia. After a futile twenty-year resistance (about 725–705 B.C.) the Messenians were reduced to serfdom, thus tripling the helot population.

Throughout this period Sparta was abreast of the most progressive Greek states in culture and economy, cultivating athletics, music, dancing, the gaiety of harvest and vintage, the joyful religious festivals, the social amenities. Choral singing, with its combination of poetry and music, had a special appeal. Poets were esteemed; some foreign poets received Spartan citizenship. One, Alcman, (*fl.* 654–611 B.C.) pictured the good life at Sparta. Luxury trades flourished, and Spartan goods were exported to the rest of Greece, the islands, the Asiatic cities, and even Lydia. Fine potters, wood carvers, smiths, jewelers, ivory cutters, weavers, and architects found profitable employment. Indeed it was in Sparta that some of the best sculptures and temples of archaic Greece were to be found. In this period the Spartans lived on the whole no differently from other Greeks.

This pleasant life ended abruptly when the Messenians rebelled. It took another twenty years—until about 620 B.C.—to prevail over the stubborn foe, but Sparta was determined that no Messenian uprising should ever again threaten its stability. To this end it was as merciless to its sons as to its slaves. Sparta mobilized permanently, regimenting its people to a comfortless, hard barracks life lacking individual freedom. Trade was shut off, money and profit outlawed, the arts and culture exiled as evils distracting the Spartan from his one and only business, instant military readiness. The one Spartan poet after Alcman, Tyrtaeus, was famous only for war-songs. Discipline, bravery, ruthlessness, dedication of one's whole life to the state: these were the virtues henceforth demanded of a good Spartan. Here was a planned society; liberty was sacrificed to security. In a certain sense, Sparta and the rest of Greece now parted ways. Most Greek states, having checked social unrest through emigration and expanded labor opportunities, could let their citizens live in an atmosphere of freedom. Sparta, however, from now on stood firmly anchored to a system where neither subject nor master was free.

Economic and Social Structure

To examine more closely this unique system which so appealed to Plato, Xenophon, and other Athenian thinkers perturbed by the defects they saw in Athenian democracy, we must start with the economic and social foundations, the binding of the helots, like medieval serfs, to the land. The land was mostly state-owned, assigned as warrior lots to support soldier-citizens. Although of unequal size, lots were large enough to be tended by several helot families, who plowed, sowed, and harvested, planning as they saw fit the lots to which they were bound, deciding on improvements and selling surpluses without hindrance from their masters. Good year or bad, the master received the same yearly amount of barley (about 170 bushels), wine, olive oil, and fruit. His income was therefore stationary, and he would not expand or contract his wants according to the success or failure of the crop. In this sense there were neither rich nor poor among the soldier-citizens, no difference of opportunity, no competition, no social strife. A warrior lot could not be sold nor given away nor worked by any but the helots born on it. In law the state owned it; only its usufruct was heritable. If the family died out, the usufruct reverted to the state, which assigned it to one on a long waiting list of the landless.

There were, nonetheless, inequalities of wealth in Sparta. Besides their warrior lots assigned by the state, the descendants of the original Dorian nobility had owned since pre-regimentation days land in the Eurotas valley which they held and could dispose of as private property. But they could not convert surplus crops into money or barter them for luxuries, for the warrior-citizen was strictly forbidden business activity or a luxurious home.

Economically the helot system was burdensome only in years of bad yield. The helots had an incentive to improve the land to which they were bound, since they could keep all produce above the portions due their masters; indeed they were better off than were free farm tenants elsewhere. But, being without civil and political liberty, they were always suspected of designs to revolt or run away and were therefore kept intimidated and isolated, each forced to live on his own lot or in hamlets. They were forbidden to bear arms, even for their own protection, or to assemble at night. They were under the constant, all-seeing eye of a secret police. At intervals the state authorized young Spartans to murder un-offending helots, in order to accustom untried warriors to the taste of blood and to keep the entire helot class well in hand. And yet the helots were not entirely without hope. They were conscripted in the army as orderlies to their masters and as soldiers in light-armed troops, which were probably composed of seven helots to one citizen. A helot distin-guishing himself by extraordinary bravery was rewarded with Spartan citizenship. In emergencies, helot regiments even shared with Spartiates, members of the ruling class, the common defense, to be later rewarded with citizenship.

Distinct from the helots were the perioeci. Broadly speaking, these were inhabitants of communities either of native Achaeans, or of fellow Dori-ans allowed to exist as dependent states, or were foreign refugees. There were about one hundred such towns of perioeci, protectorates round about Sparta, a ring of buffer states to absorb the first shock of invasion. Whatever their origin, the perioeci were free men, property-owners free to engage in cattle raising, agriculture, fishing, mining, industry, and commerce. They manufactured Spartan armor, equipment, and industrial articles, and they carried on trade with the outside world. They collected for Sparta the revenue from Spartan royal and temple lands within their territory, and paid tribute to the kings besides. They were bound to fur-nish half the hoplites Sparta mobilized in wartime, and they did naval service. Their cities enjoyed home rule with little Spartan interference, but they might not form federations nor follow any independent foreign policy. Lastly, perioeci could not marry Spartan women.

The apex of this complex structure was the Spartiate. The helots out-numbered them at least seven to one and the perioeci perhaps in the same proportion. They called themselves "peers" (equals) because, though some were richer than others and only older nobles could sit in the Gerousia or Council, all citizens were equally liable to military duty. Since family revenue was invariable, the state tried to keep the family size constant. Only healthy and perfect children were allowed to live; surplus, weak, or defective babies were rejected by a board of inspectors and eliminated by exposure. There existed also a class of "inferiors," who, though they had somehow passed inspection at birth, for one reason or another failed of full Spartiate status.

At the age of seven, the boys were taken from their mothers for group education in athletics and soldiery. Scantily fed, they had to steal to get enough to eat, but were thrashed if caught. They went semi-naked, slept outdoors on pallets of reeds, and subjected themselves to beating until blood flowed in order to develop the physical endurance, courage, and sense of sacrifice considered essential to the Spartan spirit. A few passages from the *Iliad*, a few moral verses, war songs, marching rhythmically to flute cadence composed their entire cultural fare. The emphasis was entirely military: expert handling of weapons and shield and mastery of manoeuvres made the Spartiate a synonym for invincibility.

At twenty, the young Spartiate, who now would live in barracks, was claimed by the army. At thirty he joined a company of fifteen mess-brothers, furnishing his own share of barley flour, wine, cheese, and dried figs; taking his meals with them, he formed with them an association knit by ties of devotion and honor stronger than family claims. During these long years of service, husbands visited their wives only by stealth. In the field, the mess-brothers fought side by side, protecting one another and competing in valor. At sixty, they quit active service, returning to their villages at last, to live with the women and children.

The only science studied in Sparta was military science; the Spartan army was efficient because Spartan military education produced men for whom disciplined courage was everything. We may idealize an education turned to a higher end and join Arnold Toynbee in criticizing Sparta as an "arrested civilization," but, given the inevitability of war in antiquity, we can understand why the Greeks admired the Spartan's willingness to die holding the ground he was assigned to defend, seeing it as the highest act of civic virtue and expressing their admiration by Simonides' epigram on the heroes of Thermopylae:

> Stranger, tidings to the Spartans bring
> That here we lie, their words remembering.

Government

In Sparta the kingship was hereditary in the Agid and Eurypontid lines, and the kings governed jointly. Before the First Messenian War they had been all-powerful, but afterwards, perhaps because they were accused of letting the war drag on, their powers were curtailed. Somewhat like John of England they saved their thrones by agreeing to rule by "established law." Five ephors, overseers, were set up to keep the kings to their constitutional pledges. Although by this reform the kings became mere figureheads in peacetime, they still enjoyed considerable prestige as priests, the links between gods and state and the judges expert in the ancestral rules. To the average citizen they still personified the ancient Spartan virtues.

In wartime, kings again came into their own as joint generals with power of life and death over every individual, although here too their powers were whittled down soon after the sixth century B.C. Mistrusting either kingly ability or kingly patriotism, two ephors in the field watched over their every move. A little later, perhaps for efficiency's sake, one king only, chosen by the ephors, led the army. Still later, by the mid-fifth century B.C., the king-general had a war council, or general staff, which planned the campaign, leaving him nominal power only.

Policy was decided by the Gerousia, the council of elders, which consisted of the two kings and twenty-eight life members elected by the Apella or assembly. To be eligible, one had to be a member of the original aristocracy, a man of moral merit, over sixty.

Theoretically, the Apella, including all citizens thirty years old and over, controlled both the kings and the Gerousia. In practice, however, the Apella had little power, since it could neither discuss nor amend the bills sent from the Gerousia—only approve or disapprove—and the Gerousia could override disapproval, declaring it foolish and perverse. The Gerousia really dominated the state. Thus the Spartan constitution neither insured political equality, nor was it, as has sometimes been stated, communistic; it aimed solely at preserving the more or less selfish vested interests of the older aristocracy.

The people, through the Apella, apparently tried to strengthen their power. Establishment of ephors as a check to royal authority was primarily their work, but it was the Gerousia which chose these officers; the Apella merely confirmed that choice. Every subsequent move of the Apella to enlarge its powers proved futile. Equally abortive were the attempts at reform by the Inferiors, who had no warrior lots and were probably not entitled to membership in the Apella. It was only late in the third century B.C., five hundred years too late, that the state was to be reformed.

The ephorate was the summit of the elective branch. The office was held for one year, but was all-powerful. The ephors presided over the Apella and fixed the agenda. They also attended meetings of the Gerousia; sat as judges with the kings and the Gerousia; apparently had the final word on custom, for Sparta had no written laws; executed the decisions of the Gerousia and Apella; and, as already stated, accompanied the army as inspectors-general. They could even fine, try, or imprison the kings.

Such was Sparta's government. Though most Greeks ascribed it to a traditional law-giver, Lycurgus, it was probably rather the force of circumstances which produced it. To hold down Messenia, Sparta had to resort to stern self-discipline, ensuring that each cog of the machine would function as planned. Eternal vigilance over helots, perioeci and the Spartiates themselves was the price of dominion. Both government and social structure were devised to ensure discipline and prevent change. Democracy, economic freedom, personal liberty, private wealth, the peculiarly Greek luxury of starting revolutions, all had to be sacrificed. But the system did not last. The temptations of empire, the collapse of discipline, and race suicide among the Spartiates combined, in the fourth century B.C., to bring about the rapid collapse of Spartan power, but what a modern writer has tellingly characterized as "the Spartan mirage" has remained to haunt totalitarian imaginations into modern times.

The Peloponnesian League

The Spartan soldier wrapped in his scarlet cloak, his long hair spread out behind like a mane, his plumed helmet making him appear even taller and more fearsome, was the most formidable instrument of warfare of his age. His interests, however, were not in expansion or aggression, but in perpetuating the Spartiate system. Thus, though Spartan soldiers were often in the field, they were there to fight a real or fancied threat to Spartan security.

The basis of Spartan foreign policy was the idea that the security of Sparta demanded that of the whole Peloponnesus, best assured by Spartan domination. Therefore, Spartan kings throughout the 500's B.C. in diplomacy and war aimed at a defensive coalition of Peloponnesian powers. The result was the Peloponnesian League, which became the largest and most effective permanent interstate organization in Greek history; without it the Persian invasion could never have been defeated.

Following an inconclusive war with Tegea, Sparta accepted its Arcadian neighbor as a subject ally about 550 B.C. Thereafter negotiations and warfare gradually brought the other Peloponnesian states into Sparta's alliance. Most of them were willing, for Sparta was not interested in meddling in its allies' internal affairs, especially since most of them were oligarchies already, and the prospect of Spartan military aid was an inducement to any city. Those that resisted incorporation into the League, either from suspicion of Spartan aims or because of devotion to independence, sooner or later yielded under threat of attack. Of the important Peloponnesian states, Argos alone, despite repeated smashing attacks, consistently refused to join, and the principle of city-state autonomy was so strong that even mighty Sparta did not dare eliminate Argos by annexation; it was allowed to remain the sole exception to Peloponnesian defensive unity, a permanent reminder that perfect security was impossible.

Sparta commanded the League in war and had sole right to summon and preside over its assembly. Each state had one vote, and a majority vote was required before Sparta could demand unanimous support in war. There was no regular tribute, but each member was pledged in case of war to send two-thirds of its entire military force.

Thus was Sparta's aim of Peloponnesian security guaranteed by its League. But its aims and those of other members did not always coincide.

One of Sparta's greatest rivals was Corinth. Located on its isthmus, with one harbor facing eastward to the Aegean, the other westward to the Corinthian Gulf and the routes to Italy and Sicily, Corinth was the major manufacturing and commercial city of the Greek homeland. Not Peloponnesian security but its own commercial prosperity was Corinth's aim. Since it was the focus for any land invasion of the Peloponnesus, Corinth was strategically as well as economically a key member of the League. Sparta had an interest in keeping Corinth satisfied—Corinth wanted Spartan military backing for its own complex and far-flung enterprises. We shall see later how this situation was to plunge all Greece into a devastating war from which only losers emerged.

Chapter 16 / ATHENS
THROUGH THE SIXTH
CENTURY B.C.

Early Athens

In the 2000's B.C., two or more racial strains inhabited Attica, that triangular peninsula northeast of the Peloponnesus. Then, between 2000 and 1500 B.C., Achaean migrants arrived, merging so thoroughly with the older inhabitants that later Athenians, having lost all memory of their earlier racial differences, described themselves as "autochthonous," that is, homogeneous aboriginal stock. The people of Attica also were affected by Cretan and Mycenaean influences, traces of which are evident in architectural and ceramic remains, the cultivation of the olive, sacred to the patron-goddess Athena, and the worship of Demeter, the Athenian Mother-Goddess. Despite their cultural debt to Crete, the men of Attica joined the other Achaeans in overthrowing Cretan domination, memorializing their liberation in the legend of their hero Theseus who, by slaying the Minotaur in the great palace of Knossos, delivered his city from a long-standing yearly tribute of youths and maidens.

The next stage in Attica's growth was the unification of its score or

* Comic mask of Silenus. (Athens, Acropolis Museum)

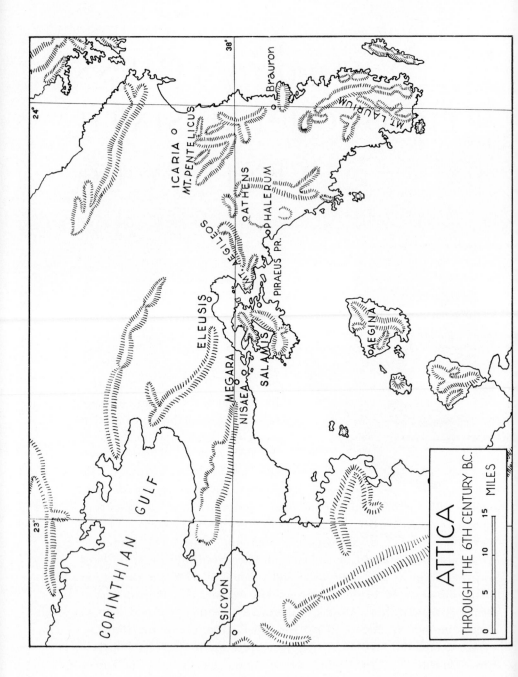

ATTICA

THROUGH THE 6TH CENTURY B.C.

0   5   10   15   MILES

ICARIA O
MT. PENTELICUS
ATHENS
PHALERUM
PIRAEUS PR.
MT. AEGILEOS
ELEUSIS
MEGARA
NISAEA
SALAMIS
ELEUSIS
CORINTHIAN GULF
SICYON
AEGINA
M. LAURIUM
Brauron

38°
24°
23°

more of warring village-states. Eleusis, Demeter's sanctuary, was one of the largest, Athens was another. Athens had geographical advantages: it was four miles from the sea, that is, near enough to profit by fishing and shipping, yet distant enough to escape pirate raids. Moreover it stood at the convergence of the principal Attic plains and the main roads, and it was close to progressive cities like Aegina, Corinth, and Sicyon. Above all, it lay in the shadow of the Acropolis, a natural fortress three hundred feet high. When the chieftain who controlled this fortress subdued the five or six villages nearest it, the city of Athens came into being. His successors merged the other Attic villages into administrative wards of one centralized state with Athens as capital. Here the king resided, the council sat, and the citizens' assembly met. By the eighth century B.C., the unification of Attica was complete.

As elsewhere in Greece, when monarchy was overthrown, the king survived only as an elected priest, in Athens called the king-archon. His military leadership passed to a new official, the *polemarch;* his judicial functions to another official, the archon, or regent. The archon soon became the most important magistrate, giving his name to the official year. He personified the interests of the aristocracy, guarding its property rights and its membership lists. Eventually six officers, the *thesmothetai,* were appointed to sit with the archon as assistant judges, so that in the end the traditional kingly functions were divided among nine annual archons—thesmothetai, polemarch, king-archon, and archon.

Upon leaving office, the archons entered the council, the Areopagus. Aristocratic in composition and controlling the appointment of archons, the Areopagus could and did choose only aristocrats for office. With life membership and representing a monopoly of wealth, privilege, and administrative experience, the Areopagus was stronger than all short-term magistrates and dominated the state.

Draco: The State above the Aristocracy

A social chasm separated the Areopagus from the people. Its members were the "well-fathered," the Eupatrids, who traced their descent from gods and heroes. Moreover, they owned the best land, extensive herds, and servants indistinguishable from slaves. As horse-owners, they dominated an army which fought from chariots. In time, when the army became a heavy-armed infantry equipped at individual expense, only these wealthy men could afford the cost. The richest landowners formed the best-equipped regiment.

Noble blood plus great wealth had more prestige than noble blood plus lesser wealth; nevertheless, the Eupatrids embodied tradition. They alone knew the law and sacred things; they alone filled public offices. In short, they controlled the property and liberty of every Athenian.

Most Athenians had little or no property and sold their labor for a pittance. Although theoretically free, actually they were at the mercy of their employer and easily fell into outright slavery from debt. This was the class of *thetes*. Though they could not afford heavy equipment, they still did army duty as light-armed auxiliaries or as rowers or marines. The least prosperous among them were the *hectemoroi*, share-croppers who paid their landlords one-sixth of the produce, or possibly as much as five-sixths if seed and equipment were provided. With the rise of trade and industry, more and more thetes worked as sailors and artisans at subsistence wages. Since in hunting for work they drifted away from their villages, they lost what neighborly pity or protection the peasant might still command. Among these, slavery took heavy toll.

The wealth some thetes acquired as manufacturers, shipowners, or merchants did not profit them politically: not being Eupatrids, they could neither be magistrates or Aeropagites nor even vote. Similarly lacking in political opportunity were the *zeugitae,* or teamsters, who plowed their small farms with a team of oxen.

In time all thetes, whether semi-slaves or wealthy and self-respecting, united to advocate a modest program: they wanted written laws. The Eupatrids agreed only to appoint the six thesmothetai to sit with the archon in judgment. They thought, with some reason, that seven judges would be more impartial and friendly to the people than one.

Establishment of the thesmothetai failed to conciliate the thetes; it only deepened a cleavage between reactionary and moderate Eupatrids. This double strife played into the hands of the reactionaries' leader, Cylon, who attempted in 631 or 628 to make himself a tyrant. Although he seized the Acropolis, the moderate Eupatrids, led by Megacles, with the people's help soon overpowered him. Cylon escaped, but his followers, who had taken sanctuary at Athena's altar and surrendered when promised on oath that their lives would be spared, were massacred to a man. This sacrilege, which involved Megacles' genos, the Alcmaeonidae, in a curse, is a commentary on changing Athenian values: political hatred had become stronger than fear of the gods. But Athenian public opinion veered against the Alcmaeonidae, and Megacles and all his fellow clansmen were banished. Even the remains of the Alcmaeonid dead were thrown beyond the border.

Violence poured new fuel on old feuds. A vicious circle of theft, arson, and murder, noble pitted against noble and clan against clan, reduced Attica to anarchy and terror until the reactionaries realized that public safety dictated their surrender to the demand to codify the law. They were even ready to accept new laws, if necessary, to protect life and property and to keep the peace.

There seems little reason to doubt the tradition that an experienced Eupatrid, Draco, was appointed in 621 B.C. to carry out the codification. To later ages his laws seem harsh—written in blood—but his task was to codify the laws, not to humanize them. Even so, the unprivileged classes benefited from Draco's work in that arbitrary verdicts were less likely when the law was written down and accessible.

Draco abolished the ancient right of the clans to take the punishment for murder of a clansman into their own hands. Henceforth they were forced to submit their feuds to state arbitrament, and the offending party had to accept the punishment the state decreed. By this reform the Eupatrids lost their most valuable means of controlling the clans while the state acquired an effective weapon for breaking aristocratic absolutism.

Solon

But Draco's reforms were no help to debt-ridden small farmers forced to forfeit their freeholds, sold into slavery abroad, or reduced to share-cropping at home. Though the dispossessed demanded land redistribution, it was realized that they might be induced to accept such political solutions for economic ills as were offered by Solon, a nobleman appointed archon (594/3 B.C.) and reconciler (perhaps in the 570's) to end Athenian civil strife. His rich and influential backers perhaps saw in the agrarian agitation an excuse to assume political power. Though Solon passes in ancient and modern sources as the father of Athenian democracy, it is more likely that he merely reformed, while carefully defining and limiting, the political organs of the aristocratic state.

He defined and limited, but did not alter, the Areopagus' traditional function in holding trials for homicide, impiety, and subversion, in leasing temple lands, in arresting and fining wrongdoers without being required to give reasons, and in hearing complaints of private citizens against magistrates. He probably did not institute any council other than the Areopagus nor alter, though he may have guaranteed, the power or composition of the popular assembly, which by now elected the archons, declared war and concluded peace, and made and modified laws. Solon probably instituted the Heliaea, the Athenian name for the people sitting as a court to safeguard against infliction of excessive penalties by magistrates; out of the Heliaea developed the popular courts of the Periclean age. Though Solon probably did not alter the assembly's composition, in the troubled years after his legislation, dispossessed farmers may have continued to attend though they had lost their property-qualification, while the landless may have attended without justification.

Magistrates' powers were limited and safeguards provided against their arbitrary extension, but they did not appear to have been democratized. Solon thus legally confirmed the functions of council, assembly, and magistrates, but he also transformed their composition (though in the case of the assembly the transformation was probably not what he intended). The aim was to wrest the monopoly of effective political power from its former holders; the means were not a formal constitution; Solon simply included in his code prerequisites for eligibility to Areopagus and magistracies which would attain his political ends.

What Solon did was to make wealth instead of birth the precondition for election to office, and thereby for passing into the Aeropagus. He set up four property-classes: Pentacosiomedimni, Hippeis, Zeugitae, and Thetes. The annual income of the Pentacosiomedimni was over 500 *medimni* (about 800 bushels) of grain, oil, or wine; of the Hippeis, over 300 medimni; of the Zeugitae, over 200; of the Thetes, less than 200. *Hippeis, Zeugitae,* and *Thetes* were traditional, meaningful terms indicating social status, but Solon's new scheme defined them more narrowly, and the tongue-twisting term *Pentacosiomedimni* seems to be his own coinage. A Zeugite did not need to own more than 43 acres, a Pentacosiomedimnos more than 110; yet, because of the sterility of Attica, the two highest classes probably did not include more than one-fifteenth of the whole citizen-body.

These property classes may have come to be used to determine military obligations, the first two classes supplying the cavalry, the Zeugitae the hoplites, and the Thetes the oarsmen for the fleet, but their main purpose at the start was to rationalize Solon's redistribution of political privileges. The chief magistrates were chosen from the first two classes only, and only the 500-measure men could be elected treasurers of Athena.

The gainers by this new arrangement, which was the core of Solon's political reforms, must have been landowners of seventy acres or more who had until now been blocked from office by the exclusiveness of a few dynastic noble familes. These beneficiaries may have included the ancestors of Pisistratus and Pericles; the rise of Pisistratus to power may thus be connected with the Solonian reforms. The Alcmaeonidae, laboring under their curse, may also have been interested in returning to prestige by an alliance with the new families against the old nobility.

At any rate the intent of the new alliance was to break the political monopoly of the old ruling families, for which agrarian agitation merely supplied an excuse. Leaders and masses had divergent aims, but in the name of civic security a fundamental change in the composition of magistracies and Areopagus could be managed, and, in fact, to bar influential landowners from office-holding must have seemed to Solon to threaten Athenian unity.

Solon broke the Eupatrid monopoly of political power, but his economic reforms were superficial. Though the masses were shielded from exploitation by his code, their main problems were economic. To solve these, Solon, who according to the view here stated was a typical conservative reformer, took only such steps as would postpone revolution, cancelling debts and abolishing serfdom, but doing nothing for ex-serfs or expropriated farmers. The reform of weights and measures attributed to him is probably to be ascribed to a later age. We shall see a similar combination of real political and spurious economic reforms in Rome's Licinio-Sextian laws of 367 B.C.

Solon's reforms were apparently the work of an alliance of rural squires and Eupatrid families eager to return to power. The price was the opening of the chief offices, and therefore the Areopagus, to non-Eupatrids. Popular discontent, mainly economic, was played upon to perform this political transformation. But while Solon satisfied the Eupatrids, the new families still had an interest in exploiting economic grievances. Solon's political changes could bring formal popular sovereignty into being if the assembly threw its weight to one or another of the rival Eupatrid factions. The people were now in a position, under powerful champions, to secure the reforms they wanted.

The Enlightened Tyranny of Pisistratus

The immediate result of Solon's reforms was not peace but war. The aristocrats felt that he had gone too far, the people that he had not gone far enough. Those who would yield nothing and those who demanded more went on a new rampage of violence. In some years the archons were elected illegally; in some years civic passions were so inflamed that no archons could be elected at all. The reforms of Solon were an unstable compromise, for the aspirations and interests of the parties involved were too divergent to be easily reconciled.

The political battles of the next generation were fought under the banner of a dynamic sectionalism that cut across tribal and clan lines. The landowning aristocracy of the plain of Central Attica (Pedion), where the best land lay and the largest estates were located, clung together as the party of the Plain, Pedieis, with the slogan, "Stand by the ancestral constitution," and the aim exclusion of their rivals from the archonship. The men of the Coast, Paraloi, were renegade nobles and non-Eupatrid landowners, backed by dependents and small farmers, who originally had supported Solon's legislation, but a dissident wing demanded revision. They called themselves the "men beyond the hills," Hyperakrioi; their nucleus was at Brauron in east Attica. This party drew into its ranks peasants who eked out a wretched existence from their fields of two or three stony acres, miners theoretically free but in fact indistinguishable from the slaves at whose side they sweated and starved, miserable charcoal burners, and poor herdsmen of a few sheep or goats. Poverty fused this motley crowd into a strong, active party. An ambitious aristocrat, Pisistratus, native of this region and its patron by family tradition, organized these forgotten men into a party demanding land, credit, and democracy. As polemarch in the war against Megara (shortly after 565 B.C.), Pisistratus had conquered Salamis, which added prestige to his program. Although he was twice driven out by a coalition of the Plain and the Coast, each time he made a dramatic comeback to give Athens a brilliantly productive experience with tyranny.

Pisistratus revolutionized the Athenian economy. He found land for the landless by dividing the remaining portions of the public domain and the estates of certain irreconcilable aristocrats who left Attica on his returns from exile. He ended the antiquated sharecropping system of land rent and apparently solved the agrarian problem so well that it was never again an issue in Athenian politics. He made vineyards almost as profitable as olive orchards. Since there was little available land left in Attica, this viticulture cut into the production of wheat, which had for some time been inadequate for home consumption. Pisistratus solved this problem by importing grain from the countries to the north —Thessaly, Macedonia, the Crimea, possibly also the Ukraine, and other Black Sea regions. To safeguard this policy he made treaties, built up the navy, brought part of the Hellespont (Dardanelles) under Athenian control, and sent Athenian colonists to the islands of Imbros and Lemnos to guard the Black Sea route. Henceforward Athenian foreign policy strove to assure enough imported grain for a growing industrial population; Pisistratus' policy set Athens on the road to empire.

To finance this expansion he opened up a number of silver mines, which he owned personally, in and outside Attica. The increased income enabled him to reduce the tax on crops from 10 percent to 5 percent. With the bullion he struck four-drachma coins (tetradrachms), with Athena's head on one side and her sacred owl on the other. The true weight and fineness of Pisistratus' silver pieces were so scrupulously continued in all subsequent Athenian issues that the "owls" became the most dependable currency of the Greek world. Pisistratus encouraged artisans and manufacturers to settle in Athens, and before long trade and industry supplied more wealth than agriculture.

By these enlightened policies, from which every class profited, Pisistratus entrenched himself securely. The small peasants who through him had become independent farmers and the merchants who through his energetic protection could compete successfully with their fellows of Miletus or Corinth were his staunch supporters. Even the landed aristocracy, finding more profit in oil and wine than in grain farming, were reconciled to his benevolent tyranny.

By breaking the hereditary jurisdictions of local dynasts, abolishing landholding as a prerequisite to citizenship, and exalting the rural Attic townships, or demes, Pisistratus prepared the way for democracy, in the face of the reactionary Eupatrids and the vindictive mob. Pisistratus saw that strong government was more necessary than new constitutional machinery, and he himself set an example of strict legality. For almost half a century, under his guidance and his sons', elections, that is, the normal assumption and relinquishment of office at the turn of each year, took place regularly, and the new organs of government—Areopagus, Ecclesia, and the people's courts—functioned without undue stress or strain. Under these normalizing influences, by the time Pisistratus' son was forced to abdicate, democratic institutions had taken root.

Growth of Athenian Culture

Pisistratus and his sons made Athens a great cultural center. During their reigns, ceramists created handsome black-figured vases which captured the markets not of the Greek world alone, but of Etruria, South Russia, and Scythia. When Pisistratus began his rule, Athens was little more than a village; by the time his dynasty ended it had become a beautiful city, adorned with temples, with statues, paintings, and sculptured mythological reliefs or friezes. More significant were public works, both civic and utilitarian, signs both of rising humanism and of rising prosperity: recreational gardens, improved athletic facilities, an abundant water supply, sewers, wagon roads, and monumental gates. The tyrants' court was a school of art, poetry, music, and the dance. Any creative artist might join the distinguished circle around the tyrants and be assured of their patronage. Anacreon, poet laureate of Polycrates of Samos, and Simonides, the lyric poet, both came to add to the brilliance of the court. That the Pisistratids sponsored a canonical edition of the Homeric poems, however, is now doubted.

The Pisistratids were master showmen. They gave, as we have seen, new luster to the Panathenaea, the festival of the goddess Athena. The aristocratic government, while preserving the customary annual panathenaea, had already begun to celebrate a superfestival, the Great Panathenaea, every four years. The tyrants, always one jump ahead of the aristocracy, made the quadrennial festival a Panhellenic event, containing new features and lasting from six to nine days. The presentation

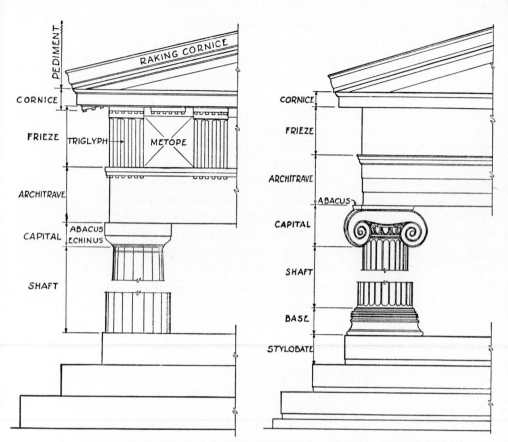

Fig. 16b *(left)*. Component parts of the Doric order. (J. I. Sewall, *A History of Western Art*. New York, 1953. Fig. 4.21.)   Fig. 16c *(right)*. Component parts of the Ionic order. (J. I. Sewall, *A History of Western Art*. New York, 1953. Fig. 4.25.)

to the goddess of a robe woven by Eupatrid maidens remained the devotional center of the festival; but it was surpassed in human interest by a procession of the arts, crafts, and professions—from warrior to shepherd—each bringing the goddess its own special offering. Then came a number of characteristically Greek contests: poetic recitations, musical compositions, and recitals by the best instrumentalists; athletic games testing mind and body, chariot races, boat races, and a parade of picked young men from each tribe.

Like other tyrants, the Pisistratids, in rivalry with the Eupatrids, promoted new cults, already mentioned (Chapter 14) but worth discussion here in greater detail. They revived the worship of Demeter for the sake of her intimate appeal to the farmers and her promise of happiness in the hereafter. For men were beginning to yearn for something in religion more satisfying than what was provided by the divine hedonists of Homer or the primitive local divinities. Lonely in an individualistic age, deprived of the sense of belonging once engendered by the clans, men found a substitute, a satisfying fillip to self-esteem, in the doctrine of regeneration and everlasting life imported from the East. Demeter's "mysteries," explaining the meaning of life and death in personal terms, gave solace to troubled souls.

Orphism gave even more. Orpheus—or the teaching which went under his name—endeavored to reduce the cosmos to some unity the common man might understand. It taught that Love (Eros), born from an initial cosmic egg, is the ever-present and everlasting force from which every-thing proceeds, including men and gods. Love also enables spirit (beauty and grace), to prevail over matter (brute force and degrading desire). The Pisistratids fostered Orphism at least to the extent of encouraging Orphic poets and Orphic preachers to edit the literature of their sect, a literature now unfortunately lost. Orphism grafted itself onto the myth of Dionysus, which thereby gained a new spiritual elevation. Originally a Thracian or Phrygian god, Dionysus is named on Linear B tablets (1500–1300 B.C.) recently found at Mycenae, and he is men-tioned twice in each of the Homeric epics as a minor divinity recently come into Olympus; but after 700 B.C. he took Greece by storm. He won popular affection because, besides being young, he was the giver of grapes and joy. Under his influence, worshipers felt spiritually exalted, purified of evil, at peace with the world and able to understand its mysteries. His very misfortunes were appealing: the myth records unjust persecution, imprisonment, indignities, and suffering. In brief, the com-mon man of the eighth and seventh centuries B.C. found in Dionysus' tragic life story and in Dionysiac emotionalism compensation for his daily afflictions and uplift from his low estate. Orphism emphasized the legend that the Titans had eaten flesh of the living son of Zeus, that for this wicked deed Zeus struck them with lightning and that from their ashes sprang a new being, man, who thus inherited two natures, that of the beastlike Titans and that of the divine Dionysus. Orphic theologians professed that through initiation and through acceptance of belief in the transmigration of souls they could free the god in man from the beast.

The cult of Dionysus was significant also because it sparked the drama into life. Probably as early as 700 B.C., groups of men, under the god's intoxicating influence, chanted hymns or recited episodes of his life in verse, sometimes improvising new ones, while dancing to flute-music. By the end of the seventh century B.C., poets had taken these popular song-dances in hand. Arion, who took up residence in Corinth, may have made the first major contribution. As librettist, composer, and choreog-rapher, he is said to have had a male chorus, stepping and skipping in a circle, sing the customary songs in a new pattern, a kind of repartee of gay turn, strophe, followed by gayer counter-turn, antistrophe. Thus the song-dance, dithyramb, was born. Long before Arion, the practice had evolved of dressing the chorus in goatskins to resemble the mythical satyrs who cavorted with the Arcadian shepherd-god Pan. Arion is said to have invented the Dionysiac dithyramb. Eventually the dithyramb became a robust and uninhibited dramatic piece, made to order for burlesquing gods and men.

We have already seen that the tyrants promoted the Dionysiac cult partly in order to detach the masses from aristocratic control. Pisistratus had an added purpose: raising the Athenian cultural level. He both revitalized the dithyrambic festival, later known as the Lenaea, which for some decades had been held in Athens in January, and founded a new, grander festival, the Great Dionysia. Celebrated each year in March-April, the Great Dionysia contributed significantly to the development of the drama.

At the Great, or City, Dionysia held during the "golden age" of Pisistratus, the god's statue was carried by night on a cart shaped to resemble a ship, under the glare of torches, from a shrine outside the city to his temple on the southern slope of the Acropolis. Beside the temple was a dancing-place, or orchestra, from which the Theater of Dionysus evolved. A chorus of fifty "satyrs" accompanied the god, whooping, singing, dancing, playing pranks, infecting young and old with a Mardi Gras spirit. Making merry and drinking Dionysus' gift of wine, spectators met the god along their way. Many joined the procession, carrying the symbol of the male generative power, the phallus, and singing phallic songs, for Dionysus was also the god of reproduction. The largest audience awaited him at the theater where, on his arrival at sunrise, a round of ceremonies began. The mob had its revelry, drinking, singing, and dancing; the elect delighted in lyrical contests, in the dithyramb, usually bawdy, and above all, in the dialogue between chorus and leader narrating and mimicking the experiences, both tragic and comic, of the lord Dionysus. Introduction of the god's attendants to the audience prompted lampoons of citizens, magistrates, political figures, and the gods themselves.

The Athenians did not invent these forms of amusement. The Dionysus-cult, the satyr chorus, the dithyramb could be found in most Greek cities. In Corinth, Sicyon, Syracuse, and elsewhere, imaginative poets, among them Stesichorus, were giving the dithyramb twists and turns until it gradually evolved into classical drama.

It is, however, in Pisistratid Athens that we may best trace the growth of drama. The chorus leader at the Lenaea had almost turned into an individual actor holding dialogue with the chorus when, in about 534 B.C. a revolutionary innovation was launched. The poet Thespis introduced an independent actor, the protagonist of Greek tragedy. He played Dionysus, engaging in dialogue with the strophic and antistrophic halves of the chorus and with their leaders, or "answerers" (*hypocritae* in Greek). Thespis, like many another actor in Greece, in Plautus' Rome, and in Shakespeare's England, himself wrote the plays he staged.

Thespis was probably a friend and protegé of Pisistratus, for besides being a man of talent, he came from near the tyrant's estates in Icaria; it was the poverty-stricken shepherds and landless peasants of this district who were Pisistratus' staunchest supporters. Pisistratus incorporated the Thespian invention into the Great Dionysia and was the first to award prizes for the best plays. The vitality he infused into dramatic competition was to last some three centuries and to bear fruit in some of the greatest of all contributions to the world's literature.

Before 500 B.C. the elements of drama were well developed: plot, characters, conflict, poetic dialogue, preponderant role of the chorus, subject taken usually from legend and myth. The essential features of the theater had likewise been fixed: the orchestra where the chorus sang and danced, the tiers of seats around it, the stage (originally a booth), costumes, masks, buskins with elevator soles to give the actor an awesome monumental stature. In a further development, the sole actor (Thespis or one of his successors), after impersonating Dionysus, would assume the dress and role of a second or even a third character, which meant that only one character could appear on stage at a time. One last outgrowth from the earlier satyr chorus was the emergence of three distinct genres, tragedy, comedy, and satyr-plays.

To sum up, the rise of Athens and the unification of Attica revealed patterns common also to the rest of the Greek world: conflict between wealth in land and wealth in money, codification of the laws, the rise after Solon of new political groups, prosperity and intellectual flowering under a tyranny. But Athens showed a difference, in part attributable to wise leadership and a tenacious people: the liberalization started under Pisistratus was to burgeon into a democracy which has been a model for the Western world.

Chapter 17/THE TRIUMPH
OF DEMOCRACY IN
ATHENS

The End of Tyranny

At Pisistratus' death in 527 B.C., his son Hippias took over the government, leaving to his younger brother Hipparchus the management of religious, artistic, and intellectual life. At first Hippias ruled as ably and moderately as his father, but after Hipparchus was assassinated (514 B.C.) in a plot from which Hippias himself narrowly escaped, he became suspicious and harsh, suspended the constitution, restricted Athenian liberties, and even reduced the citizen-army, putting self-protection above the public safety. Encouraged, the Eupatrid exiles attempted a forcible return, but the people, though disillusioned with tyranny, had no wish to restore the aristocracy. Even Harmodius and Aristogiton, the murderers of Hipparchus, had been motivated neither by love of liberty nor by patriotism, but by a private grudge. Nevertheless, legend heroized them as rousers of the people to regain liberty.

To Hippias' domestic difficulties, disturbing foreign problems now accrued. Eastward, Persia subdued Ionia and reached the Aegean, threatening the north and west Black Sea coasts. Nearer home, Thebes was building a Boeotian federation, prompting Athens to accept a proffered alliance with Plataea, unwilling to submit to Thebes. While Plataea thus would remain independent, Athens would have a buffer against further Theban expansion. This alliance was to be long-enduring, but Thebes' resentment was to bring on Athens a train of disasters. Sparta extended to the south and west the ring of strong powers being forged around Athens. Sparta had been strengthened when Corinth and Aegina joined the Peloponnesian League, the former none too friendly to Athens, the latter an avowed foe. Another enemy, commercial Megara, was soon to add its weight to the League.

Blamed by his countrymen for this encirclement and aware of their increasing distrust, Hippias made the mistake of turning to Persia, seeming to prove that he loved personal power more and Athens less. At this juncture the Delphic oracle played the game of the Alcmaeonid Megacles, an emigré from Pisistratid tyranny, by starting a campaign to rid Athens of the tyrant. Delphi looked especially to Sparta which, eager for primacy, was now posing as the champion of liberty, not however the people's liberty to govern themselves, but the aristocrats' liberty to supplant the tyrants. With foreign intervention, Hippias was expelled (510 B.C.) and fled to Persia. The aristocracy paid its debt to Sparta by joining the Peloponnesian League.

The aristocrats' triumph was short-lived. Their downfall was engineered by Cleisthenes, an ambitious democratic leader who could not tolerate the Spartan-aided ascendancy of his rival, Isagoras. Yet this was not the whole story, for Cleisthenes, an Alcmaeonid, quickly grew as a liberal statesman and a master of compromise. His family had a long antireactionary record and had collaborated with non-Eupatrids. Megacles, his great-grandfather, had overthrown Cylon; Megacles, his father, had turned against the Pisistratids. Cleisthenes fused the merchants of the Coast and the peasants of the Hill into one party to counterbalance the Eupatrids, reconstituted under Isagoras as the party of the Plain. His enemies counterattacked by again calling in Sparta, and Cleisthenes went into voluntary exile. The old curse on the Alcmaeonids was renewed, and the whole clan, with seven hundred other families, banished. The people were thus left leaderless, but when the Eupatrids, again with Spartan support, tried to set up an oligarchy, the people expelled the Spartan garrison, killed some aristocrats and expelled others, and recalled Cleisthenes to be again their leader.

The Constitution of Cleisthenes: Local Government

Now Cleisthenes revealed his political capacity: sobered by his and the city's misfortunes, he proceeded to build a government on firmer foundations than personal power. His reforms, while drastic, were so attuned to Athenian needs as to last for centuries. His government was less democratic in practice than in theory, but his reorganization of the citizen body prevented any aristocratic revival. In his new order there were still distinctions of rank, but they had little political importance. By affirming the new principle that landowning was unnecessary for citizenship, he converted at a stroke all earlier gropings toward popular rule into what the Greeks were to call democracy. He gave the government to all the people, that is, all free Attic males over twenty—peasants, shepherds and miners, fishermen and sailors, merchants, manufacturers, industrial workers and apprentices; even the aristocrats retained the vote and continued to be elected to magistracies, for Cleisthenes thought the people needed the guidance of the wise and should leave finance to those who were used to it.

Cleisthenes was interested in local as well as central government. Local units, with increased power, became the pillars of the central authority. The old country demes—almost 180 in all—were recognized as municipalities, and Cleisthenes created five new city demes. Each deme was self-governing, with patron god, temples, festivals, town hall, police, treasury, citizen- and tax-register. The deme's central authority was the town meeting, an assembly of demesmen to discuss local problems, vote local ordinances, and elect local officers. The deme was thus a school to train the citizen for his harder role in the central government at Athens.

Cleisthenes' registration of citizens by demes was a master stroke. Since deme-citizenship was prerequisite to state citizenship, control of the demesman-lists was crucial. Before Cleisthenes the clan chiefs had held control and built with it political blocs. Through these closed, obedient blocs the clan chiefs had long influenced elections, legislation, and the courts. When citizens were registered by residence and not by clans, discrimination against citizen and foreigner alike was much reduced. Cleisthenes thus carried forward Solon's and Pisistratus' liberal policy, offering citizenship to foreign merchants, artisans, and tradesmen to attract them to Attica. Cleisthenes' measure combined statesmanship with cleverness: it rewarded foreigners for their contribution to Athenian wealth and power; it enlarged democratic ranks in the perennial fight against the aristocratic party; it built up for him a new personal following.

The Constitution of Cleisthenes: Central Government

The Ten Tribes. Disregarding the four ancient Ionian tribes, Cleisthenes organized Attica into ten new ones, containing roughly 18 demes each. To make them rival the old ones in prestige he had them sanctioned by the Delphic oracle, which at his suggestion named them after ten Attic heroes. He gave them corporate personality: they became the basic electoral, judicial, and military units and the centers of Athenian religious and intellectual life. The new tribes were devised specifically to break the traditional tribal solidarity that permitted the aristocratic tribal heads to wield political power. Their make-up also discouraged regional pressure-groups, for the new tribes were not solid territorial blocks. Cleisthenes ensured against the rise of another Pisistratus who might play off one section against another by forming each tribe of three separate deme-groups, or *trittyes,* one from the city and suburbs, therefore of mixed occupational makeup; another from the coast, that is, chiefly maritime and commercial; the third from the country, that is, mostly agricultural. By thus creating a completely artificial tribal membership, he was able at once to destroy all the political influence of tribe, clan, and even family, and to submerge regional, class, and personal interests. Thenceforth the Athenian citizen's primary attachments were to his deme and to Athens.

The Council. Though Cleisthenes actually made few constitutional reforms and was far less democratic than is usually alleged, he probably did create a new council, the Boule, of 500 members, fifty from each new tribe; annually chosen by lot from a panel of nominees thirty or more years old, the number nominated being proportionate to the population of a given tribe. To prevent iteration in office, no one was allowed to be councilor more than twice in his lifetime.

The council had executive as well as legislative functions, amounting in practice to sovereignty: it instructed, supervised, and cooperated with magistrates, directed diplomacy, and controlled finance. Supervision of magistrates involved meticulous examination of their qualifications for office; control of finance involved auditing of magistrate's accounts.

To simplify business and fix responsibility, the council was subdivided into ten 50-man sections, prytanies, one for each tribe. By the mid-fifth century B.C., this arrangement had led to the introduction of a conciliar year of ten 36-day months, also known as prytanies. During its period of office the prytany received board and lodging in the official public hall, the prytaneum, so as to be ready for any emergency.

A prytany had the same wide authority as the council for which it acted; one important function was initiating bills, which it then submitted to the full council for further scrutiny, amendment, or rejection. If the majority of the council approved, the bill went to the assembly. The prytany introducing a bill was held responsible for it, so as to limit unconstitutional or shortsighted legislation. The bill's author was held directly responsible and was liable to prosecution for unconstitutional or mischievous proposals.

The prytany's chairman was chosen daily by lot from among its fifty members, so that in each prytany 36 out of 50 members took their turn at presiding; in a sense the chairman became President of the Republic, being custodian of the state seal and the keys to the treasury, having considerable discretionary powers, and presiding over the assembly if it met.

While the view that any citizen was competent to undertake any office belongs rather to the later radical democrats than to Cleisthenes, his system certainly presupposes a high level of Athenian political maturity and public conscience. These qualities were the more needed because the official in charge of any public business might be prosecuted if it miscarried. Prosecution was a major Athenian pastime. Since any citizen had the right to prosecute public officials, every Athenian was a potential district attorney. Any vindictive, envious, or notoriety-seeking person might for private reasons bring a public suit, alleging unconstitutional acts or malfeasance in office.

The Ecclesia. The ultimate sovereign power was theoretically the Ecclesia, the assembly of citizens. When he became eighteen, as Athenian presented himself to his deme to be enrolled as a citizen and assigned to his tribal regiment, from which after two years' service he passed into the reserves and took his seat in the Ecclesia. In Cleisthenes' time, Athens had perhaps 30,000 male citizens twenty years old and over; under Pericles, at Athens' height, it may have had as many as 50,000. Actually, not everybody attended the assembly: distance, work, sickness, old age, laziness, or apathy kept many away. Then, too, many were abroad on business, for the Athenians had become a nation of merchants and sailors; others were in the army and navy. Probably six thousand members formed a quorum in the Ecclesia.

The Cleisthenic Ecclesia met regularly, at least once a prytany, passed the final verdict in all capital cases, had the final voice on such important issues as peace, war, and alliance, and the last say on proposals submitted to it by the Boule. Whatever action it took was finished in one day, after which its decrees became the law of the land. Here was, for the first time in Western history, a people master over its government and, still more significant, over tradition itself. It dominated every phase of its own life, constantly reasserting itself and reshaping its course by the light or the mood or the prejudices of the majority. In this sense here was not the ancient world but the modern.

After Cleisthenes, the Ecclesia had the authority to ostracize: if Cleisthenes instituted the practice, there is no record of its use before 487/6 B.C. Yet tradition has it that, fearing a new Pisistratus, Cleisthenes had provided that the Ecclesia should vote to exile anyone suspected of tyrannical designs. Laws and institutions have a way of exceeding their original purpose, and ostracism became a device for eliminating the leader of the opposition. Safety and stability demanded that once

Fig. 17.1. Two *ostraka* scratched with name of Themistocles. Themistocles was ostracized *c.* 470 B.C. His name is misspelled on both sherds; on the second, the error is corrected. (Athens, Agora Museum; *Archaeology* I, 1948, p. 89.)

the people made up its mind on a public question, the resultant policy should be given a reasonable time for testing. On minor points a nation may safely change its mind often, but on major matters frequent shiftings may lead to disaster. For example, in time the Athenians had to decide whether to rely, against Persian encroachment, on the army or on the navy. Since armies and navies are not built overnight, to decide on the army one year and the navy the next would have meant waste and confusion. In 482 B.C. Aristides favored the army; Themistocles the navy. Themistocles convinced the Ecclesia, which then ostracized Aristides in order to permit his rival's policy to be pursued undisturbed.

The question whether or not to ostracize anyone was regularly raised, without debate, in the sixth prytany. If the vote was affirmative, the unlucky victim was selected two prytanies later, again without debate, a quorum of 6000 being required. The voters cut the name of their choice on a broken potsherd (*ostrakon*); the victim had to leave Attica within ten days and, theoretically, remain in exile at least two days' journey from Athens for ten years, but without loss of citizenship, property, or revenues. Ostracism was essentially a device to insure political continuity and stability; it meant neither punishment nor vengeance, and it carried no personal and scarcely any political stigma. It was the Athenian way of dealing with minority opposition. Frequently the person ostracized was allowed to return before the allotted time. Back in Athens, he might again wield considerable power, often reassuming the leadership of his party. He might even have the satisfaction of seeing his policy at last adopted.

The Magistracies. Civil magistracies were the least important organ of government. Cleisthenes made the secretary to the thesmothetai practically a tenth archon, to be able to assign one such official to every tribe. The chief archon and the polemarch were directly elected from the two top property classes until 487/486 B.C. when they and their colleagues began to be chosen by lot from a previously-prepared panel; therewith ended their political importance and that of the Areopagus into which they passed; few influential persons appear in the list of eponymous archons after that date. In 457 B.C. the office was opened to Zeugitae. Each of the archons presided over one of the ten law-courts, an exciting and enjoyable experience as well as a mark of honor.

The ten generals (*strategoi;* from 501/500 B.C.) furnished the steady element of leadership which neither the rotating prytanies, the annually changing Boule, the unwieldy Ecclesia, nor (after 487/486 B.C.) the random-elected archons could give. Each commanded his own tribal regiment or naval squadron. They were elected by direct ballot, not by lot, and could be re-elected year after year. The reason is obvious. Field command required specialists and could not be left to chance. Even the radical democracy did not alter this principle; indeed under Pericles, to assure competence, generals were elected by the whole people and not just by the vote of their respective tribes.

Since war was ever commoner than peace and since Athens was to become an aggressive imperialistic state, the board of strategoi was important in the coordination of policy, having a say in foreign relations, fiscal matters, industry, and trade, as well as in setting the size of army and navy. Furnishing data and advice, requesting funds, recommending long- and short-range plans, the strategoi were in constant contact with council and presiding prytany, helping to formulate almost every bill submitted to the assembly.

One strategos might surpass the others in political acumen, like Themistocles; or as a strategist, like Cimon; or in ability to sway the masses, like Cleon, or in integrity, like Nicias, or in the rare combination of gifts superlatively possessed by Pericles. Such a man would influence colleagues, policy-making organs of government, and electorate. All important business was referred to him and defended against possible opposition in the assembly. As leader, coordinator, and planner, the chief strategos was like a British prime minister or American president. But he had to stand for election every year, and his power sprang not from his office, but from his ability to persuade the sovereign Ecclesia, which could at will reject his proposals and leave him powerless.

The Courts. By the middle of the fifth century B.C., the popular courts, or Heliaea, had wider authority than the Areopagus. Neither Solon nor Cleisthenes had tampered with the jurisdiction of the Areopagus over murder and impiety. But as the secular spirit grew, much that formerly had been considered supernatural, religious, and holy was now regarded as natural, secular, and civil, and therefore subject to secular authority. The Areopagus, encased in its archaic mold, remained the least secular organ of government, scarcely touched by the humanism which altered the other branches. Against the fossilized Areopagus, the sovereign people, invigorated by Cleisthenes' reforms, asserted a greater judicial authority. Thus secularism and popular sovereignty converged to reduce the judicial powers of the Areopagus and to enlarge the jurisdiction of the jury-courts. Understanding of their role is the key to understanding the nature and practice of Athenian democracy, for they eventually became, even more than the Ecclesia, the symbol of popular sovereignty, of the absolute, even arbitrary power of the demos.

The Heliaea was probably left unaltered by Cleisthenes, but later, perhaps as late as 462 B.C., it was broken up into ten paid sections, or juries, to handle the crowded dockets. At the beginning of every year, 6000 citizens were selected as jurors, but, allowing for absences, only five thousand were impaneled each working day. Usually there was enough business to keep all ten sections occupied. A section consisted normally of 501 members representing all the tribes—the odd number would preclude a tie. A minor case would be tried by a 201-man jury; a major one by two to five sections sitting jointly. Pericles, for instance, was tried before 1501 jurors. Aristophanes, a consistent critic of radical democracy, caricatured the jury system in his comedy *The Wasps* (422 B.C.), mocking its regiments of jurors—usually, he says, dotards or shiftless fellows, attracted by the pittance, who trooped every morning to the court hoping to be impaneled for service. After the allotment, each juror, identified by a tablet inscribed with his name and the number of his allotted section, was admitted into the courtroom reserved for that section.

Jury service was an experience which, even though repeated day after day, never grew stale, for these buzzing judges (they are the "wasps" in Aristophanes' comedy) got not only a day's wages, but also amusement and a form of free education. These men of the masses, Aristophanes says, were drunk with their power over the honor, fortunes, and lives of resident aliens (metics), subject-allies, and fellow-citizens, for the court's verdict was final and a section was held to represent the whole sovereign people. The jurors had no legal training and were bound by no precedents or instructions from the presiding judge-archon. To prevent irresponsible prosecutions, a prosecutor failing to get 20 percent of the votes was fined. If the verdict was "guilty," the jury might choose between the penalty proposed by the prosecutor and that offered by the defendant. The commonest penalties were fine or exile; imprisonment and the death-penalty were rare. While political unpopularity or the jury's legal incompetence might be held to harm the defendant, the system made bribery difficult, the jury's numbers gave it confidence, and legal hair-splitting was much reduced. And the system as it developed showed great reliance on the ability of ordinary men to render substantial justice.

Chapter 18 / THE
STRUGGLE WITH
PERSIA

First Encounters

The Aegean islands and the Anatolian coast, opened to Greeks by the fall of Troy, were by 800 B.C. thoroughly Hellenic. Native resistance and Assyrian opposition prevented Greek penetration of the hinterland. When Assyria fell (612 B.C.), Lydia, as we saw, reduced these Asian Greeks to near-vassalage. In its drive to the Aegean, Lydia forced even powerful Miletus to open its port to Lydian commerce and its government to a Lydian protectorate. During Croesus' reign, nearly every Asian Greek city had recognized his enlightened overlordship.

When Croesus fell (546 B.C.), the Asian Greeks, with a few spirited exceptions, accepted the rule of Lydia's conqueror, Cyrus of Persia. Disunity and Milesian reluctance to revolt frustrated opposition. Fortunately, Persia's yoke was as light as Lydia's; it too controlled Greek states through local tyrants.

Even though Persia's interference was mild and generally acceptable to the Ionians, there was some feeling against it. The merchant classes were the first to grow restive, realizing that much of their share of the material advantages of this mighty empire was going to the Phoenicians, long their rivals, in Cyprus, Rhodes, and Asia itself.

The democrats in Ionia began to see that their real enemy was the Persian king, not the local tyrants. Their uneasiness increased when Darius undertook to establish a satrapy on European soil across the Propontis. The king had a double purpose. First, as long as there remained free Greeks in Europe, he could not feel sure of Ionian loyalty, since language, religion, and art, trade relations, political ideals, and the whole cultural pattern made all Greeks everywhere but one family, however disunited. From a European satrapy Darius could keep the European Greeks well in hand. Second, he also needed to watch the Scythians, who from south Russia imperiled his northern frontier as they had previously imperiled Assyria.

With a large Persian army and a fleet furnished by the Ionian Greeks, Darius set out (512 B.C.) to conquer the country between the Strymon and the Danube, organizing it forthwith as the satrapy of Thrace. He also, unsuccessfully, invaded Scythia: that he went as far as the Volga may be mere legend. The Greeks, however, believed that Darius actually tried and failed to subdue that region. His success in Thrace they ascribed to their own generous cooperation, especially to the prowess of their ships. More important was the service of Greek engineers who bridged the Danube. Once Darius and his army had crossed into Scythia, certain liberty-loving Greeks proposed to destroy the bridge and Darius with it. More cautious counsels prevailed and the bridge saved the retreating Darius. The event opened the Ionians' eyes to their intellectual and technological superiority, to their new political and military importance. They began to dream of driving the Great King from Ionia. They acted when they saw Darius methodically building up a Phoenician navy against them.

In 499 B.C. Ionia revolted. Aristagoras, its leader, who had voluntarily renounced the tyranny of Miletus, went personally to Sparta for help, but Sparta, seeing no threat to its own immediate interests, refused. Aristagoras had better luck in Athens, which feared that Hippias, the exiled tyrant, in league with Darius, was bent on recapturing the tyranny of Athens. With Hippias were allied also those irreconcilable Athenian oligarchs who had recently been gaining some ground at home and imperiling the Cleisthenic reforms. Athens sent twenty warships with which were associated five more triremes from Eretria—two thousand hoplites in all. With this token of pan-Ionian cooperation, in 498 B.C. the rebels marched into Sardis, the capital of the Lydian satrapy, which they burned to the ground, sparing not even the temples. But that was all. Desultory fighting continued for several years, but underestimation of the strength of Persia, lack of serious cooperation, and

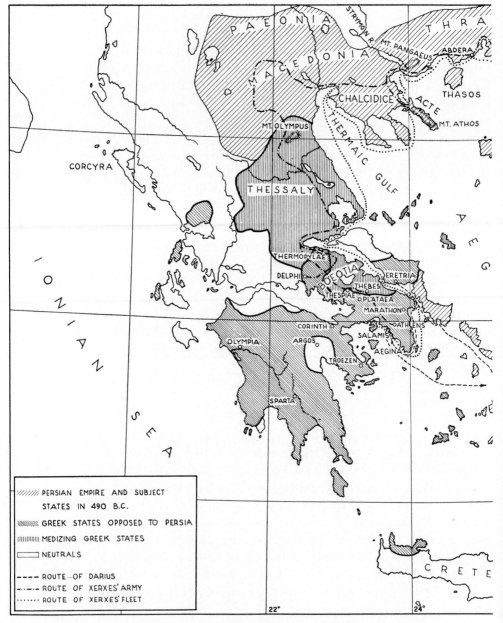

Fig. 18a. Map to illustrate the Persian Wars

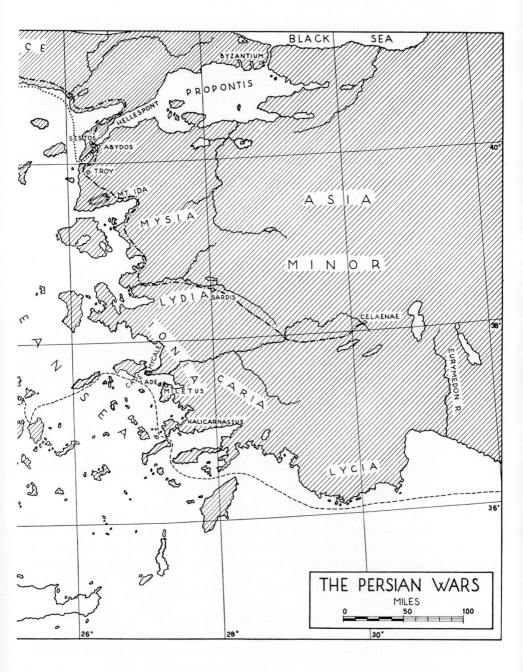

THE PERSIAN WARS

MILES

0   50   100

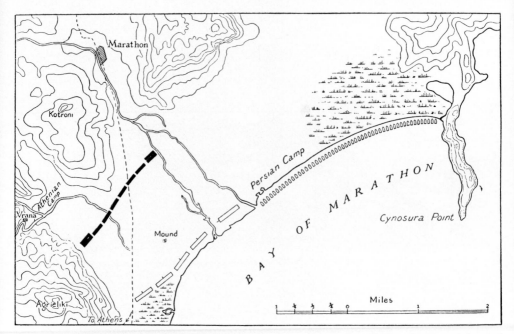

Fig. 18b. Plan of the battle of Marathon. Heavy dotted line shows positions of Athenians and Plataeans; the Persians face them with their backs to the marsh and the bay. Their ships are drawn up along the beach. (John L. Myres, *Herodotus*. Oxford, 1953. Page 205, Fig. 13.)

downright treachery led to disaster. After the combined fleets of Egypt and Phoenicia had routed the Greek forces at Lade, Miletus fell into Persian hands (494 B.C.). The city was burned in reprisal for the burning of Sardis; the men were mostly killed and the women and children sold into slavery in far-away Babylonia. With this terrible lesson the revolt collapsed. Every Greek city in Asia and Thrace fell again under the Persian yoke. The destruction of Miletus horrified every Greek. When the tragedian Phrynichus presented in Athens his *Sack of Miletus,* the weeping audience fined the poet for reviving bitter memories.

The Miracle of Marathon

Having subdued Ionia, Darius was ready to settle accounts with Eretria and Athens. But he aimed much higher—at the conquest of the whole Greek mainland. The Persian army, transported by sea across the Aegean, and its supporting Phoenician fleet easily overcame Eretria, which was delivered up by traitors after seven days of fighting. Like Miletus, it was sacked and burned and its inhabitants transplanted to Persia.

The Persians next sailed against Athens. Hippias, who was with them, advised them to land at the Bay of Marathon, believing that this region would declare for him as it had once declared for his father. But times had changed. Despite unreconstructed aristocrats' serious attempts to regain power, democracy was in control and resolved to fight for its life. The Athenians did appeal to Sparta, but Sparta was, as usual, slow. Athens therefore stood alone (490 B.C.) on the plain at Marathon. To the wonder of all Greeks and to their own no slight astonishment, they won a sweeping victory, dispatching 6400 Persians at a cost of 192 Athenian dead. True, the Athenians were fighting for their homes and their gods, and their general, Miltiades, was a remarkable strategist, but there were other reasons for their astounding success. No horse or archer could resist the mailed hoplites who, arrayed eight deep, elbow to elbow, moved on inexorably without breaking or bending. Moreover, democracy, by giving the average man human dignity and political power, had strengthened the whole state.

A Persian sea attack upon Athens itself was frustrated by the army's return only seven or eight hours after its triumph at Marathon, for Miltiades had reason to suspect treachery. After this second failure, the Persians could only withdraw to Asia. There Darius spent his remaining years planning and mobilizing for a new and more powerful expedition, but he died in 486 B.C. before the attack was ready to be launched.

In Athens the victory of Marathon had immediate political consequences. Irreconcilable aristocrats, preferring Hippias' return to the Cleisthenic constitution, were said to have flashed a signal from Mount Pentelicus to the Persian forces, indicating they were ready to open the gates. This charge is credible; it would not have been the first or the last time Athenian oligarchs used foreign aid to regain power. In fact, this became a Greek political pattern, especially during the Peloponnesian War. Immediately after Marathon the Athenian democracy rendered powerless oligarchic fifth columnists by ostracizing their leaders and, as we have seen, opening the archonship to election by lot. The general increase in wealth in the previous fifty years qualified hundreds, perhaps thousands, of citizens for this honor.

The Battle of Salamis

Darius' son, Xerxes (485–465 B.C.), prosecuted with foresight and determination his father's plan to punish Athens and conquer Greece. On the diplomatic front, he divided Greece by making alliances with those who cared least about national liberty and might hope to gain from a Persian victory, for instance, the Aleuadae, rulers of Thessaly, who were promised the headship of a new European satrapy. He isolated southern Greece by his alliances with Thebes and other Boeotian cities. Lying in the invader's path, these central Greek states preferred Xerxes'

Fig. 18.1. Stele marking site of battle of Marathon. Copy of original in National Museum, Athens. (Photo by Dorothy MacKendrick)

friendship to dubious promises of help from the south. He made another alliance with Argos, Sparta's persistent enemy, which had dreams of domination in the Peloponnesus. When the Persian army crossed into the Peloponnesus, Argos entered the war to knock out Sparta. Apparently Xerxes also had an entente with Carthage, which resented Greek expansion in the west. To prevent the Sicilian and south Italian Greeks from helping the homeland, Carthage was to carry war into Sicily while Xerxes attacked Greece proper. Briefly, the plan was to force all Greeks, east and west, into submission to these two empires.

On the military front, Xerxes organized the largest and best-equipped army the world had ever seen. The figures given by Herodotus—2,500,-000 soldiers and marines, or more than 5,000,000 men if sailors and camp followers were counted—are, of course, fantastic. It is more likely that the invading host did not exceed 180,000, plus an undetermined number of men to guard stores, roads, fortresses, and urban centers all the way from Asia Minor to Thessaly.

Impressive too were the organization and the techniques for saving time, avoiding risks, and ensuring success. Supplies for men and beasts, gathered from the whole empire, were transported by land and sea to five central storage points along the intended route in Europe. Across the Hellespont were built two pontoon bridges over which, Herodotus tells us, infantry, horses, orderlies, and baggage trains flowed like an endless river for seven days and nights. Similar bridges were thrown over the Strymon. The battle fleet and the supply transports—chiefly Phoenician, Egyptian, and Ionian squadrons—kept in close touch with the land forces. The expedition commander, Darius' son-in-law, Mardonius, took another precaution: he had a canal cut through the Acte promontory in the Chalcidice, to avoid another disaster like that of 492 B.C. when a bad storm had wrecked his fleet in an attempt to round Mount Athos.

Meantime Athens and Greece were not sleeping. Athens owed to one of her strategoi, Themistocles, her full preparation when Xerxes swooped down for the kill. A genius in statecraft, Themistocles was expert at waiting, daring, deceiving, and seizing opportunities. Moreover, his grasp of foreign affairs and his hold on Athenian hearts were equally firm. Many a thoughtful Athenian was convinced that Marathon was not the end but the beginning of the struggle with Persia, but Themistocles foresaw more clearly than anybody else that both Greek geography and Persian access to a fleet would ultimately make the struggle one of sea power—and he saw too that in such a struggle Greece need not be the loser. His task, therefore, was to convince his countrymen, who hitherto had made the army their chief bulwark, that only a navy could save them—a courageous facing of facts on the part of a man whose father was an Athenian noble. It was not too difficult to persuade the Athenians to abandon Phalerum, an open, shallow-beach harbor, for the Piraeus, a protected, deep-water haven. But it required consummate skill to break down the granite combination of prejudice, pride, and politics on which the army was founded. If the state were to make the fleet its main defense, the proud hoplites would inevitably lose their prestige to unromantic rowers, and propertied classes would be swamped politically by a tidal wave of thetes.

Themistocles' naval policy was helped by the discovery of a new vein in the state's silver mines at Laurium. When certain politicians proposed dividing the revenues among all the citizens, Themistocles argued for investing them in a navy. When recourse was had to ostracism to choose between Themistocles' farsighted navy policy and the army policy of Aristides, an incorruptible conservative, the former won, so that Xerxes in 480 B.C. had to face 200 Athenian triremes, fully equipped and efficiently manned. Thus did Athens, to use Herodotus' phrase, go down to the sea. Within three generations, it was to find on the sea, first freedom, then empire, lastly defeat and ruin.

Sparta now felt impelled to join the struggle, lest another stand against Persia by Athens alone bring Athens to leadership in Greek affairs. Also, Persian victory would mean primacy in the Peloponnesus for Argos. Still worse, it might spark a helot revolt. The lesser evil was to join forces with Athens.

At a congress of cities in Corinth, a Panhellenic League was organized for the common defense. Sparta received supreme land and sea command even though Athens had the largest and best-trained navy. Sparta no doubt merited this recognition as the leading Greek military power, but Athens deserves credit for accepting second place in the interests of national unity. This cooperative spirit helped to compensate for Argos' refusal to join the grand alliance, for the foreseeable defection of Thessaly and Boeotia, and for the eventual falling-away of Corcyra. The western Greeks, being occupied with Carthage, gave no help. Unity in the congress almost canceled the effect of appeasement propaganda from the Delphic oracle, which was suspected of yielding to Persian gold and had already weaned the Cretan cities away from the alliance. The League mobilized, nevertheless, some 35,000 hoplites and 40,000 light-armed troops, plus 333 warships.

Unable to defend the whole country, the high command abandoned northern Greece to the enemy, planning to delay him at the narrow Pass of Thermopylae, gateway to central and southern Greece. Themistocles' advice to the Spartan admiral frustrated a Persian attempt to land an army east of the Pass and take the defenders in the rear. On land occurred a minor disaster that became a heroic legend. Four thousand Peloponnesian hoplites, with some contingents from Boeotia and central Greece, held the Pass. The commanding general, the Spartan King Leonidas, dismissed most of his army when he saw that a smaller force could defend the Pass. But he made a serious error; he left practically unguarded the secondary but easier paths over the mountains to his left. The Persians, unable to force the Pass, followed the poorly guarded mountain paths and took the defenders in the rear. Trapped in the Pass, Leonidas, 300 Spartans, and 700 Thespians died to the last man, taking large numbers of the enemy with them. A contingent of 400 Thebans is said to have surrendered. Ironically enough, posterity has remembered Spartan valor only, leaving the men of Thespiae unsung.

No less remarkable was the courage of the Athenian people. On the heel of the news from Thermopylae and on the advice of Themistocles, they evacuated Attica, taking to their several refuges, Aegina and the small Peloponnesian city of Troezen, all their movable goods and animals, and leaving only a token force on the Acropolis. Themistocles knew that if the Athenians were to leave their ships in order to defend

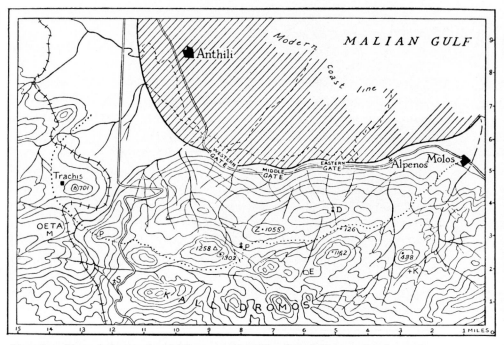

Fig. 18 c. Plan of the battle of Thermopylae. The dotted line marks the path where Ephialtes led the Persians to take Leonidas and his men in the rear. (John L. Myres, *Herodotus*, Oxford, 1953. Page 249, Fig. 15.)

their city they would meet disaster; for Xerxes could then destroy the Greeks piecemeal. The Athenian refugees on Salamis were to see their beloved city, homes, and temples go up in flames. The Great King had at last avenged Sardis.

The Persian high command had now only to invade the Peloponnesus. While the army attacked the Isthmus, the fleet was to land a force in their rear, repeating the strategy of Thermopylae. To implement this plan, the Persian fleet, so its admiral thought, succeeded in surrounding the Greek fleet in the Bay of Salamis. Athenians feared that the Spartan Admiral Eurybiades was planning to abandon Salamis to defend the Peloponnesus at closer range, but Themistocles, knowing that the narrow waters between Salamis and the mainland offered the best possible place for the smaller but more maneuverable Greek fleet to tackle the Persian armada, allegedly thwarted him by sending word to Xerxes of Greek panic and imminent flight. The Great Armada of Persia accordingly blocked the bay. Cut off from escape, the Greek fleet had to fight or surrender. Themistocles' ruse succeeded, for it was not a Persian-set trap but a Greek one. The Persians were bottled up in a sort of inner lake four miles long and one broad, in which their numerous and bulky ships found themselves in one another's way.

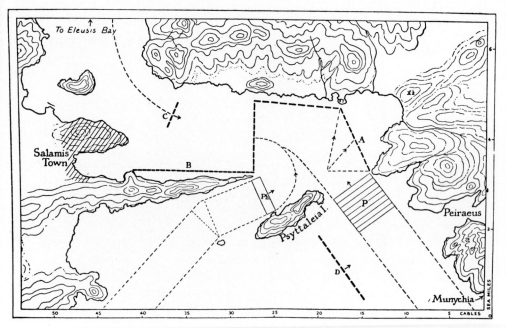

Fig. 18d. Plan of the battle of Salamis. A. Leading Greek squadron (Spartan). B. Rear Greek squadron (Athenian). C. Corinthian squadron. D. Aeginetan squadron. Ph. Phoenicians. P. Persian center. X1. Xerxes' seat (traditional). X2. Xerxes' seat (suggested). (John L. Myres, *Herodotus*. Oxford, 1953. Page 269, Fig. 18.)

Equally costly was the element of surprise; the Persian ships had no time to get into position. Salamis is justly counted as one of history's decisive battles, for to it Greece owed her salvation. Xerxes himself, watching from his throne on the headland overlooking the bay, recognized the magnitude of his disaster; he left Greece immediately, and fearing that his failure would encourage the Ionian cities to revolt and those of Thrace to cut the Strymon and Hellespont bridges, he dispatched whatever ships he could save to prevent either contingency. But his army was still intact on Greek soil, a formidable menace as long as he could keep it supplied by way of the precious bridges.

Greek Sicily played almost as important a role in the struggle between East and West. The Sicilian Greek cities had partly united, under Syracuse in the east, Acragas in the center. Gelon and Theron, tyrants of Syracuse and Acragas, were close friends and associates. Indeed, Gelon had married Theron's beautiful daughter, Damarete, who was to set a patriotic example by selling her jewels to buy arms in Sicily's hour of need. Carthage, holding the western tip of Sicily, now made a bid for the whole island. Recruiting an army from Phoenician satellites in Africa, Spain, and Sicily, and hiring whole regiments of North African and Western European barbarians, Carthage met the more disciplined and confident Sicilian Greeks on the narrow northern plain of Himera. With cavalry help (the Theban poet Pindar praises Sicily as a land of fast horses), the Sicilian Greeks won a victory, as great, in Pindar's estimate, as those of the mainland. Tradition places the battle on the same day as Salamis. The Carthaginian commander, Hamilcar, recognizing defeat, threw himself alive into the sacrificial fires. Gelon, the architect of victory, was hailed in art, poetry, and the grateful memory of generations of Sicilian Greeks as the liberator of his people.

Plataea and Other Victories

After the naval debacle at Salamis, Mardonius' Persian army wintered in Thessaly. The next spring (479 B.C.), it moved upon Plataea, the Boeotian city which for its loyalty to Athens at Marathon had, like Athens itself, been burned to the ground. Here Mardonius threatened both Athens and the Peloponnesus, outnumbering the Greek forces commanded by the resourceful Spartan regent, Pausanias. To drive the Persian out of Greece, Athens contributed 8000 hoplites under Aristides, who had been recalled from ostracism when the Persian invasion started. The appointment of this great conservative rather than of Themistocles, despite the latter's prestige as author of victory at Salamis, was quite logical, for Aristides was an army man.

Despite Mardonius' attempts at surprise attack and brilliant maneuvers for terrain and initiative, the Greeks won at Plataea as decisively as they had at Salamis. Mardonius himself was killed, and the remnants of his once proud army were hounded all the way to the Hellespont, while the Greeks admitted only 360 dead.

Soon after the battle, Plataea, the destruction of which reflected Theban rather than Persian enmity, was rebuilt, and all Greece guaranteed its freedom. But Thebes, which had "Medized," was reduced to impotence and forced to dissolve its Boeotian League. Its betrayal of Greece was to plague it for generations.

The last episode of this heroic struggle followed hard upon the victory at Plataea. In a joint land and sea battle at Cape Mycale, near Miletus, the Greeks burned such ships as the Persians had saved from Salamis and destroyed another Persian army. Destruction of a mighty empire in two short years was a unique achievement for a small country. The victory of Mycale sparked revolt all over Greek Asia and the islands. Indeed the Ionian Greeks, who had deserted Persia to achieve independence, deserve much of the credit for the success at Mycale. Over a number of years, one city after another drove out the Persian garrison, and, especially in Ionia, the democracies overthrew the tyrants, now denuded of Persian support. In their bid for freedom the rebels were abetted by

Fig. 18.2. Bronze charioteer. Part of a group, of superb archaic simplicity, dedicated about 474 B.C. by a tyrant of Gela in Sicily to commemorate a chariot-victory. (Delphi, Museum)

the Athenians, convinced by Pisistratus that their future was overseas and prepared by Themistocles for maritime supremacy. After Mycale, Athenians and Ionians together took Sestos, across the Hellespont, and destroyed the Persian refugees from Plataea. Pausanias cooperated by taking Byzantium. But the moment Sparta saw no further danger to the Peloponnesus, it withdrew from further expansion while the vigorous Athenian democracy went on to fill the vacuum created by Persia's collapse. But these are parts of another story, the rise of the Athenian empire. As for Persia, no peace was asked or offered; a cold war better suited both sides.

There were other victories besides Salamis, Plataea, and Mycale— victories of the spirit. Greece had triumphed once more over Asia, but whereas the ancient victories, when Heracles and Theseus defeated the Amazons, the Argonauts brought home the Golden Fleece, Europa was kidnaped, and Troy destroyed, were dim fables, the new ones were a living reality. The Persian ordeal quickened the tempo of Greek progress and heightened its quality, especially in Athens, where most had been lost and most gained. Democratic Athens' victory advanced the democratic cause in the whole Greek world. In Athens itself, faith in freedom grew, for Athenians believed the triumph of their government, their army, and their crews was due to the freedom, equality, and dignity which common citizens enjoyed and which defeat would have ended. This was the reason why the great Athenian tragedian Aeschylus, in his own epitaph, passed over his literary triumphs and boasted only that he had fought at Marathon. If other Greeks prized their share in victory as highly, we may understand why the national exaltation expressed itself in masterpieces of art and literature.

Socially, the Athenian thetes, despite their poverty, now enhanced their status, for, rowing the ships, they, above every other class, had saved Greece at Salamis. Commercially, Ionia, exchanging vassalage to Persia for federation with the islands and Athens, increased business with the thetes to the advantage of the whole Aegean area. In the west, the Sicilian Greeks profited materially from Carthage's defeat: war prisoners now worked Sicilian plantations, which thus competed with Carthage in producing olive oil, wine, and wheat. To the national gods, grateful worshipers heaped up votive offerings: jewelry, gold crowns, bronzes, statues, temples. With so many commissions, artists, as moved as Aeschylus by the transcendent national triumph, threw away archaic conventions. Preserving the severe archaic strength and beauty, they sought freer technique and forms and were able to attain new heights of pure beauty and idealism. National shrines like Delphi and Olympia became more than ever national treasuries and museums, displaying the myriad offerings made possible by Persian gold and silver left on the battle fields of Greece, Ionia, and Sicily. In short, the Greeks had become fully conscious of themselves and aware of their strength. Athens in particular was ready to embark upon a dazzling career.

Chapter 19/THE
ATHENIAN EMPIRE

Sparta's Dilemma

Though Persia was quelled, Greeks felt the need of organizing for safety. The Panhellenic League languished and died without Sparta, which could not afford Aegean entanglements when it had to be vigilant at home over the helots and Argos. Besides, Sparta had neither resources nor desire to build a fleet; it was a land power and needed hoplites, not sailors. But since the rest of Greece needed ships, Sparta realized its unfitness to lead the League; it was reluctant to risk the social and political changes which naval power would involve.

To be sure, some elements in Sparta were eager for revolution. Younger sons without warrior lots would find in an empire opportunities denied at home; but they were as yet no problem, for, having no arms, they had no influence. More dangerous to the *status quo* was Pausanias, whose victory at Plataea had made him a Panhellenic hero. His subsequent capture of Byzantium apparently inflamed in him an un-Spartan private ambition; men said he was plotting personal rule over the eastern Aegean with Persian help. His alleged willingness to betray Greece was to prove his undoing. For the moment his highhandedness toward the Ionian cities inflamed their resentment against Sparta itself, and isolationists at home had him recalled. For six or seven years

Pausanias continued intriguing with Persia and even, it was said, with the helots, to whom he promised freedom in exchange for their aid in overthrowing the Spartan government. He would then reform the constitution. The ephors and Gerousia moved warily against him. When evidence of his treason seemed complete, they prepared to arrest and try him. Warned of his danger, he sought asylum at the altar of Athena of the Bronze House. Unwilling to commit the sacrilege of tearing him from the sanctuary, the authorities had him walled up to die of starvation. As he was dying, they brought him out, to prevent the holy place from being polluted by his death. This trick, whereby Spartan authorities had flouted religion, was to be recalled later to deny Spartan claims of unblemished public morality.

Equally fantastic was the chain of events which led to the undoing of Themistocles, Athens' war hero. He had hoped to make Athens the head of a democratic United States of Greece, seizing for the realization of this hope a moment when tyrannies and oligarchies were everywhere being overthrown—in Ionia, now that Persia was eliminated; in Sicily and southern Italy, now that Carthage was crushed. In the Peloponnesus, too, Elis, Mantinea, and Tegea had democratic governments, and the submerged classes in Argos and elsewhere were acquiring political rights. Though Sparta objected, he built around the new Athens, now rapidly rising from its ashes, and around the Piraeus, with its all-important docks and warehouses, a protective wall, behind which Athens might safely pursue its own interests. Just then Themistocles, the democrat, apparently joined Pausanias, the would-be despot, in fomenting a helot uprising. If it succeeded, Themistocles thought, it would end Sparta as a great power and advance democracy everywhere. Impregnable behind its mighty walls of stone and mightier walls of ships, Athens, Themistocles urged, should unite all struggling democracies for protection in an east-west federation, and itself head a Greece conceived in democracy and dedicated to the ideal of Panhellenic unity.

Themistocles, however, was a practical politician first and an idealist second. To spike Persian opposition, he was willing to make a deal, letting the Great King control part of Ionia. But he was not allowed to fulfill his plan, for the championing of democracies everywhere was too risky for his more timid and less imaginative fellow citizens, while cooperating with Persia was repugnant to them. Moreover, aristocratic leaders, like Aristides and Miltiades' son Cimon, who meantime had come to power, opposed any anti-Spartan move, for in their view it was Athenian-Spartan friendship that had brought victory over Persia. Their policy, therefore was to live and let live; they claimed with some reason that Greece would be more peaceful and prosperous if Athens acquiesced in Sparta's primacy on land, in the Peloponnesian League,

Fig. 19.1. Reliefs from Themistoclean wall. The Athenians attached such importance to this hastily-built wall of 479–478 B.C. that they used even such superb works of balanced, realistic archaic art as this in its fabric. (Athens, National Museum; photo by Alison Frantz)

and among aristocracies, while Sparta left Athens a free rein eastward among maritime democracies. The Athenian Ecclesia adopted Cimon's policy of peaceful coexistence, and ostracized the over-adventurous Themistocles. His enemies later claimed that, like Pausanias, he had conspired with Persia; he was condemned *in absentia* and forced to flee from city to city until the Great King's court received him. There the victor of Salamis lived out a prosperous and influential life as the king's trusted adviser on Greek affairs. Greek history provides few more ironical twists in human careers.

The Delian League

Themistocles' plan, to have Athens liberate the Greek cities, in practice affected only Persian-dominated cities, for Persian garrisons still controlled much of Ionia, the islands, and part of Thrace. To dislodge them would take years, even if the Greek city-states could have agreed on policy. Whereas for mainland Greeks, mainland victories ended the Persian menace, the Asian and island cities could enjoy no security until the last Persian soldier had been expelled from the last square yard of Greek soil. They had come to realize that only by uniting under understanding and powerful mainland Greek leadership could they hope to win independence from Persia. Athens agreed. Its own prosperity needed freedom of the seas; its own sympathies dictated cooperation with the liberation movement. When Sparta disowned Pausanias and backed out of Ionian affairs, Athens was therefore eager to accept the vacant leadership. Consequently, in 478/477 B.C., the Delian League was established and the rise of imperial Athens began. Ironically, the task of organizing the League fell to Themistocles' archenemy, Aristides, a choice which suggested maturity rather than ingratitude on the part of Athenian democracy. The terrible war had taught the democrats that aristocrats too could be loyal and endure losses. Besides, the aristocratic and incorruptible Aristides was acceptable to the member-cities.

League membership eventually rose to about 200 states, some scarcely more than self-governing villages, others, like the islands of Chios, Samos, and Lesbos, powers of the stature of Athens itself. Members supplied either ships or money; most preferred to send money, which Athens used to maintain the fleet. Aristides' original assessment of each state is said to have called for 460 talents a year, the equivalent of 100 ships fully equipped and manned. The fairness of Aristides' assessments enhanced his reputation for justice, but his task was not difficult, since the quotas were based on the tribute each state had previously paid to Persia.

The League members assembled in Athens (476 B.C.) to ratify the terms of agreement. Its victories over Darius and Xerxes, its large navy —the largest in Greece—and its superior statesmen had given Athens such military and moral pre-eminence that it dominated the League from the beginning. The member states made their treaties of alliance directly with Athens, little realizing that this would eventuate in their subjection. Each state retained internal sovereignty; only its foreign policy was subject to the will of all member-states. Each state, however large or wealthy, had one vote, but Athens presided, commanded the federal fleet, and appointed its own citizens collectors of the annual federal revenue. The ships of the member-states were to assemble at Athens' call in Athens' harbors. The League Assembly met on the island of Delos, centrally located and consecrated to Apollo, patron god of the Ionian tribes, to which most of the member-states belonged. The federal treasury was placed in the god's temple for safekeeping.

The dynamics of the Athenian state soon nullified these terms. The mercantile economy of both Solon and Pisistratus had fostered in Athens the growth of a grasping middle class. The thetes from Themistocles' victorious navy had become Athens' strongest political group. The two classes complemented each other: employment for new thousands of citizens increased prosperity; the federal navy opened regions hitherto closed by Persian sea power and benefited both industry and labor. The Athenians could see the close relation among navy, expansion, and employment. So the middle class and thetes combined to make a profit from the Delian League. The member states themselves unwittingly played Athens' game by preferring to pay their quotas in money, leaving to Athens alone the task of building, manning, and servicing the fleet.

Cimon, Builder of the Naval Empire

The League's subjection to Athens was systematic and thorough. Secession was treated as rebellion and sometimes punished with loss of autonomy and demotion from ally to subject, as Naxos in 469 B.C., Thasos in 465–463 B.C., and the Euboean cities some time later discovered to their sorrow. Athens had its reason: every seceding state increased the financial burden on the others, and ultimately imperiled the League itself. The related question of procedure with neutrals also arose early and was settled with brutal finality. Carystus in Euboea had declined to join the League. Athens, arguing that Carystus' location gave it the benefit of the League's protection and therefore the duty of contributing to its cost, used its navy to force Carystus to join.

Membership in the League ceased to be a voluntary matter, and, since Athens collected federal quotas even after the Persian menace ended, dictated tribute replaced voluntary contribution. The planting of military colonies, cleruchies, in the territory of dissident states was an unmistakable warning that Athens intended to subject them all. Athens even meddled in their internal affairs, expelling refractory aristocracies and replacing them with accommodating democracies. Only democrats argued that the establishment of these democracies meant social and political progress; oligarchs elsewhere in Greece called it an outrageous infringement of the principle of self-determination, which they valued as highly as do modern nationalists. But to the masses in the Athenian Empire, as opposed to the oligarchs, Athenian democratic rule seemed neither politically oppressive nor economically predatory; for the masses, class feeling was stronger than desire for autonomy. They found Athenian democratic rule juster and more merciful than that of their own oligarchs; they preferred to have their cases tried in Athenian democratic courts rather than to submit to possibly oligarchic ones at home. They regarded political subjugation to Athens as the price they paid for escape from the tyranny of their own oligarchs. To the masses, the benefits of subjection seemed to outweigh the evils.

The sovereignty of member states was limited in other ways. Athens compelled suits between an Athenian and a citizen of a member state to be tried in Athens by Athenian courts. It also claimed the Ecclesia's right to judicial review of criminal cases already tried in local courts. It imposed advantageous commercial treaties on allies and subjects. It closed their mints, forcing them to trade with Athens to obtain silver currency, and incidentally simplifying commerce in the whole Aegean and making Athenian currency an international medium of exchange. Another innovation was removal of the federal treasury from Delos to the Athenian Acropolis (454 B.C.) ostensibly for protection, a not wholly insincere pretext. As Athens was also allowing the League assembly to lapse, no one doubted that the once-free alliance for Greek liberation had been converted into an Athenian subject empire.

Cimon was responsible for most of these developments. Elected admiral of the federal fleet, this son of the victor of Marathon freed both Europe and Asia of their last Persian garrisons. The capture of Eion (476/475 B.C.) at the Strymon mouth in Thrace and the conquest of Skyros (474/473 B.C.) made him the people's idol. Like Lemnos and Imbros, Pisistratus' island conquests which had been the modest beginnings of Athenian imperialism, and like the cleruchies in the Hellespont, Skyros was to guard the lifeline to the south Russian markets and wheatfields. For self-aggrandizement, Cimon had Theseus' remains, allegedly found on Skyros, transported to Athens amid patriotic enthusiasm, for this miraculous find seemed a good omen for the empire which the new Theseus was founding in the hero's own pattern. With these successes to his credit and with a pro-Spartan, anti-Persian program, Cimon's influence now surpassed Themistocles', and, as we saw, Cimon had him ostracized (c. 470 B.C.) . The principle of coexistence, Athens ruling the waves and Sparta controlling the continent, became official Athenian policy.

Cimon could now proceed with his war of liberation to detach Ionian states from Persia. Unattached cities were forced to enter the League, wavering or recalcitrant members to remain in it, and all but a few powerful states were persuaded into letting Athens alone furnish the ships, fight the battles, and reap the benefits. Then (468 or 467 B.C.) , at the mouth of the Eurymedon River in Pamphylia, Cimon won a land and sea battle over Persia's last-ditch army and fleet. The enemy lay exhausted; the Aegean became a Greek lake. All the islands and scores of Carian, Ionian, Lycian, and Hellespontine cities joined the Delian League.

Cimon's Spartan policy was less successful. Like most Athenian aristocrats, he considered Sparta the model aristocratic state, the natural prop of all aristocracies. Against Themistocles' view that democracy should be Panhellenic, and that to weaken Sparta was to strengthen Athens, Cimon's party advocated noninterference with the existing oligarchies since Greece still needed and might continue to need the hard core of Spartan military stability. This amounted, of course, to accepting Athenian democracy as a necessary evil, but advocating aristocracy for the rest of Greece.

Cimon soon had an opportunity to show his good will to Sparta. In 464 B.C. an earthquake destroyed Sparta, leaving 20,000 dead, and only five houses standing. The helots seized their chance and revolted, killing 300 Spartiates; a force of determined Messenians dug themselves in on Mount Ithome and refused to be dislodged. Meanwhile, ancient enemies began to threaten distracted Sparta, among them Argos, which now seized hegemony over several hitherto Spartan protectorates.

In its dire need Sparta applied to Athens for help. In the Ecclesia, Ephialtes, Themistocles' successor as radical democratic leader, argued that the time had come to let Sparta stew in its own juice. The gods themselves, he said, were showing their displeasure with it, and offering Greek leadership to Athens. Cimon, however, appealing to tradition and the memory of Sparta's stand against the Persian invader, pushed, as always, his principle of coexistence. Sparta's downfall, he argued, would maim Greece, for Athens alone was not enough to keep it straight and strong. Convinced by Cimon's argument, or yielding to his popularity, the Ecclesia voted to send to Sparta a relieving army.

So Cimon led the army of the most advanced democracy in Greece to suppress with bloodshed other Greeks fighting for liberty. The effort misfired. The Messenian stronghold held out against Cimon and his crack troops, and Sparta tactlessly called them half-hearted and pro-Messenian, finally notifying them that it had no further need of their services. Athenian democrats were infuriated. Here was a clear issue: national honor insulted by an ungrateful ally who was at heart an enemy. Tumultuously, they voted to ostracize Cimon as pro-Spartan and enemy of the people (461/460 B.C.). With Cimon fell aristocratic ascendancy. Radical democracy took over, to usher in for Athens an era of unbridled imperialism.

Pericles and the Land Empire

Ephialtes was mysteriously assassinated in his hour of victory, and Pericles, his successor as democratic leader, reverted to Themistocles' ideal: a democratic empire. But that ideal had been tarnished by tyrannical practices under Cimon, and Pericles may have yielded to the territorial ambitions of other prominent radicals. At all events, he later admitted that the Empire had been "unjustly gained." His mother was Cleisthenes' niece, his father had been in the thick of politics; politics was in his blood. The people apparently reasoned that since by family, wealth, and intellect he was their superior, his affiliation with them must be selfless. But perhaps it was his hereditary feud with the family of Miltiades and Cimon that prompted Pericles to court popular favor.

Whatever his motives, Pericles was a faithful and brilliant democratic leader, who succeeded where the more versatile Themistocles had failed. Perhaps his social status flattered the masses, perhaps his fellow-aristocrats did not strenuously oppose him, since after all he was one of them and, despite his apparent radicalism, at heart still a conservative. Moreover, thanks to Cimon, he had far greater public resources than had previous empire-builders. Lastly, he was practical, the first European statesman who methodically accumulated treasure to wage successful war.

An intellectual, Pericles enjoyed the company of artists and poets. At the height of his popularity he often left the conduct of day-to-day politics to faithful lieutenants, while he pondered metaphysics with philosophers, discussed Greek social problems with political thinkers, or listened to foreign ambassadors and settled with practical men the affairs of a thousand states. Even in his Olympian seclusion he had an intuitive sense of what the masses wanted, or perhaps his persuasive eloquence swayed the masses to want what he offered. In a model of understatement he once told the Ecclesia that he was as capable as anyone of devising and explaining a sound policy. Best of all, he knew how to idealize his program. He claimed hegemony for Athens, not merely on the ground of its navy, men, and money, but chiefly on the ground of its intellectual superiority, which made it "a model for Hellas."

As empire-builders, Pericles, or his party, had two aims: to extend Athenian hegemony over continental Greece, which of course meant war with Sparta, and to expel Persia forever from the eastern Aegean so as to exploit Asia and Egypt.

In 459 B.C., two years after Cimon's ostracism, while the Spartans were still exhausted, the democrats began their policy of extending the Athenian Empire on the Greek mainland, by treaties or threats where possible, by war where necessary. They made a series of alliances, some of which were to provoke the Peloponnesian League: in the north, with Thessalian cities; in the south, with Argos; in the center, with strategic Megara, Corinth's rival, with its two harbors, Pagae and Nisaea, facing respectively the Corinthian and the Saronic Gulf. Megara could keep Peloponnesian armies out of Attica and give Athens a short route to the west. With Athenian assistance, Megara now built a wall from Nisaea to Pagae to shield both itself and Athens from Peloponnesian land attacks. Athens itself built (458 B.C.) the Long Walls, two protective walls with a wide space between, all the way from the city to the Piraeus, where they joined the Piraeus defenses, started by Themistocles and finished by Cimon. Pericles now felt confident of Athens' invulnerability. The Long Walls made Athens practically an island which could be neither conquered nor starved, for its navy controlled the sea and its wall safeguarded the docks.

In the same fateful year, 459 B.C., the Athenian democrats had taken another warlike step: they settled at Naupactus, in the Corinthian Gulf, the Messenians who had finally been forced out of Mount Ithome. Corinth saw in that act a deliberate attempt to challenge its control of the Gulf and its long uncontested commercial supremacy in the western seas. The democrats had in fact revived Themistocles' plan of an

Fig. 19.2. Pericles. He preferred posing in his helmet, to conceal his exceptionally high forehead. (Rome, Vatican Museum; Anderson photo)

imperial drive to the west. Sparta, too, felt menaced by a free and democratic state of erstwhile helots, an Athenian protectorate to boot, at the gates of the Peloponnesus. Corinth first, and Epidaurus and Aegina soon after, declared war on Athens (459 B.C.). Sparta and the Peloponnesian League, Thebes, and most of Boeotia followed two years later, but Athenian resiliency blunted this coalition's striking power. A defeat at Tanagra (457 B.C.) did not weaken Athens, and the Spartans, though victorious, withdrew. Hence Athens, unopposed, subjugated Boeotia, Opuntian Locris, and Phocis, that is, all of central Greece except Thebes. Even Aegina surrendered (457 B.C.), yielding its navy, dismantling its fortresses, entering the Delian League, and paying thirty talents annual tribute. The last clause meant that this ancient commercial competitor was reduced to economic slavery.

The west itself heard the beat of Athenian oars. A timely naval demonstration in western waters, an alliance with Halyciae in Sicily, a more significant one with Segesta, long hostile to its neighbor, Selinus, and a friendly understanding with Naples (454 B.C.) were clear signs of intended Athenian westward expansion.

Lastly, in 459 B.C. Athens had started war on another front. Xerxes' death in 465 B.C. had prompted widespread revolts and disorders in the Persian Empire, especially in Egypt. When Egyptian rebels begged Athenian help, the Athenians sent a fleet of perhaps two hundred ships, though war with Corinth had started and it was possible that all Greece might become involved in the struggle. Such self-confident energy, such vastness of operations by a single city had no precedent in Greek history. Nor, perhaps, had such losses. An inscription tells tersely the price in blood and tears that Athens paid for its triumphs. In it a single tribe records casualties in a single year (459 or 458 B.C.) in land and sea battles a thousand miles apart:

> Of the tribe Erechtheis,
> these are the war dead, in Cyprus, in Egypt, in
> Phoenice, at Halieis, in Aegina, at Megara, in the
> same year.

Then follow the names of 177 fellow-tribesmen who fell to make Athens ruler of Greece.

But the Egyptian expedition failed. Though the Athenians gained control of the Nile mouth and occupied two-thirds of Memphis, its citadel, the key to all Egypt, forever eluded them and their native Egyptian allies. A naval disaster on the Nile (454 B.C.) and the Persian capture of a relief fleet shattered the dream of an Athenian empire in Egypt. Besides ships and treasure, 35,000 Greeks were lost, including 6000 Athenians. Only a few hundred men survived.

An immediate result of the Egyptian disaster was the transfer, noted above, of the treasury of the Delian League to Athens, for Pericles apparently feared that with most of the Athenian navy destroyed, to leave the treasury in Delos was to invite the enemy, Persian or Peloponnesian, to take it. Of greater consequence was the lesson that Athens could deal with but one enemy at a time. Cimon capitalized on this mood when, shortly after Tanagra, he was recalled from ostracism. Free again to espouse his pro-Spartan policy, he used his influence to arrange a five-year truce with Sparta and its allies. By this treaty Athens kept its gains in central Greece but had to become a party to Sparta's new Thirty-years' Peace with Argos; this removed Spartan fears that, in case of war, Athens would receive Argive aid.

Fall of the Land Empire

At peace with Sparta and the Peloponnesian League, Athens could now concentrate on the unfinished war with Persia. Athenian unity was reflected in Cimon's appointment to the supreme command. Democrats and oligarchs found agreement on the barbarian easier than on policy regarding other Greek states. But the hero of the Eurymedon had grown old and, in any case, could not perform miracles. He made no conquests, but Persia's naval losses led to the Peace of Callias (449/448 B.C.). Athens renounced its expansionist plans in the Persian Empire; the Great King, although he held Egypt and Cyprus, agreed to keep Persian warships out of the Aegean. He seems also to have recognized Ionian cities as independent within the Delian League framework. Thus if Pericles failed against Persia, he could at least claim Persian recognition of the Athenian Empire, which in itself was no mean achievement.

At peace with Persia, Athens turned to Greece, where Sparta, without breaking the letter of the Five-year Truce, had turned troublesome (448 B.C.). More dangerous loomed Thebes, which was defiantly abetting the return to their cities of the aristocrats of central Greece. These men Athens, moved by imperial interest as well as by ideology and sentiment, had exiled, turning over most city governments to local democrats, who parceled out the exiles' estates among themselves. The day of retribution came when, with the aid of Thebes, the émigrés recaptured the governments in Chaeronea, Orchomenus, and several other cities (447 B.C.). Athens not having recovered from the Egyptian disaster, its inadequate army was captured by the Boeotian oligarchs. To redeem these war prisoners Athens agreed to withdraw from Boeotia, saving from the wreck only its Plataean alliance. Without Boeotia, it could no longer hold either Locris or Phocis. Thus swiftly (446 B.C.) did Athens' brief hegemony over central Greece collapse.

There were other consequences. In view of the peace with Persia, some Delian League members sought release from their federal dues, claiming that the League was now unnecessary. Moreover, they had long resented Athenian interference, especially the presence of cleruchs who took their farms and confined their movements. Athens' Boeotian debacle heartened oligarchs, patriots, and malcontents throughout the Empire. The Euboean cities revolted; Megara, which had discovered that Athenian friendship was subjection in disguise, went over to the enemy, and Sparta, the Five-year Truce having just expired, sent an army across Megarian territory almost to the gates of Athens (446 B.C.).

The Athenian democrats dealt firmly with all these dangers. The Euboean cities were forced back to the fold, under even closer imperial control. Finally, in a Thirty-years' Peace with Sparta and the Peloponnesian League, Athens lost the Megarian harbors of Nisaea and Pagae and the Megarian alliance, but kept two worthwhile prizes, Aegina and Naupactus. Athens renewed its recognition of the Peloponnesian League, while Sparta and the Peloponnesians for the first time recognized the Delian League. Another provision allowed neutral states to join either

League while present members remained fixed, a provision which foreshadowed possible disturbance of the balance of power. All in all, the Peloponnesians could feel satisfied, for they had prevented the establishment of an Athenian land empire. Athens, too, could take satisfaction in having compelled the Peloponnesian League to follow Persia in formally recognizing its maritime empire. And Greece could look forward to what it hoped would be thirty years of peace.

Chapter 20/DEMOCRACY
AND IMPERIALISM

*

The March of Democracy

The Persian ordeal had slowed down the political struggle. Cleisthenes' new citizens put unity in the common defense ahead of political rivalry with the aristocrats, while the nobles proved no less patriotic. The credit for saving the city at Marathon belonged chiefly to the landed aristocrats, who served as hoplites and were led by an archaristocrat, but both parties shared in the trials and triumphs of the following decade. Themistocles' thetes, as rowers, won the victory of Salamis; Aristides' propertied men won at Plataea. Honors and dishonors were divided, too, in Athens' rise to imperial status. While Themistocles strove for supremacy over all Greece, Aristides brought the headship of the Delian League.

After such proofs of their wartime indispensability the nobles could not easily be ignored when relative peace returned. Cimon, Aristides' successor as aristocratic leader, could hypnotize the democratic Ecclesia into adopting his party's views. We have seen how, overcoming progressive democratic opposition like Ephialtes' and Pericles', he influenced Athenian intervention against the helot revolt. His ignominious failure gave Ephialtes a chance to unseat him. With Cimon's ostracism Ephialtes took a step towards realizing more fully the democratic ideals the old hero had so long opposed.

* Athenian tetradrachm, *c.* 470 B.C. (American Numismatic Society)

Another step was an attack on the Areopagus. Cleisthenes' reforms, though radical, had left this aristocratic citadel untouched, probably because it still passed for a semi-divine institution. As the pope's spiritual power after 1870 grew with the loss of his temporal power, so the Areopagus' spiritual prestige had grown after it lost its policy-making functions. Since until 487/486 B.C. its members were recruited from the age-old and noble ruling class, it enjoyed the highest respect. Again, it claimed precedence in authority over every other government organ. The ten tribes, Heliaea, Ecclesia, Boule, prytanies, army, navy, and board of generals, even the concept of democracy were comparatively recent and clearly man-made. But the Areopagus—who could tell when it started? Was it not born with the city itself, willed by the eternal gods as part of the eternal cosmos, appointed by Athena herself to guide her beloved city in the paths of justice and piety?

When Solon confirmed it as "inspector and guardian of the laws," the Areopagus assumed authority to determine whether the magistrates administered the laws according to the constitution. Their power of rejecting a law had made the Areopagus a supreme court and upper house combined and an ultimate check upon the democratic Ecclesia's sovereignty.

Realizing that democracy could not exist, much less enlarge its powers, as long as a superior organ could thwart the people's will, but aware also that a frontal attack would be difficult, Ephialtes, shrewdly taking advantage of Cimon's absence fighting the helots (465–462 B.C.), began to bring Areopagites to trial, indicting them for graft, corruption, and illegal practices. The jurors were mostly propertyless democrats, since the property-holders were with Cimon as hoplites. When, as a result of these convictions, the whole Areopagus fell into disrepute, Ephialtes had the Ecclesia deny it the right of review and veto; henceforth the Areopagus simply administered certain sacred properties and judged homicide cases. Shortly after this victory, the democratic leader was assassinated.

Pericles, his successor, who had learned practical politics as Ephialtes' understudy, put through reforms to make the man in the street the man in the saddle. From 446 B.C. on, Pericles was unquestioned leader, but his program was partly inherited from Themistocles as well as from Ephialtes, partly formulated by a sort of "brain trust" of practical business men, creative artists like Phidias and Sophocles, and advanced thinkers like Damon and Anaxagoras.

First of all, the archonship was opened (458/457 B.C.) to men of the third property qualification, the Zeugitae, and at their term's end the archons were to join the Areopagus, diluting it almost beyond recognition. At any rate, it could no longer threaten the people's liberties now that the people themselves were a part of it. In time apparently even the thetes were elected archons.

More important in democratizing government was the provision of pay for most officeholders, including jurors, whose original two obols a day in 425 B.C. was raised to three in order to meet the rising cost of living caused by the Peloponnesian War. The principle was soon extended to the five hundred councilors (*bouleutae*), and by 395 B.C. to the Ecclesia. The extension of the principle, coupled with the opening of the archonship to thetes, combined to extend the wage system to the archons themselves.

Of all the Periclean reforms, pay for public service was the most ferociously assailed by oligarchs and idealist philosophers. Pay for mental work, like teaching, was degrading and odious to conservatives. In the good old days, they felt, knowledge and virtue and the ability to govern were disseminated freely, usually from father to son: hence the aristocracy's monopoly in government and in setting the social tone. The conservatives accused Pericles of creating a personal following to perpetuate himself in office by corrupt and degrading means. They charged that questions of public morality, domestic or international, would henceforth be settled selfishly, not justly or on their merits. But Pericles felt that democracy was pure illusion unless it created a positive, real equality of opportunity for capable but poor citizens to share in officeholding with property owners. If public office did not support the holder and his family, he could not afford to hold it, and equality would simply not exist.

Lastly, the use of the lot was extended. The old system of applying the lot to a limited panel of nominees allowed manipulation and deals. To correct this evil, the lot was applied to the whole citizen body, thus securing for the common and the poor equal opportunities with the nobles and the rich. In brief, the amazing decade which started un-democratically with Athens' help to Sparta in putting down the helots saw the most advanced type of democracy firmly established.

A Closed Corporation

Citizenship in Athens was now a responsibility and an honor which made politics every man's concern. The government was not something above and apart from the plain citizens; they *were* the government, and, knowing this, with equal enthusiasm they fought for Athens in war, beautified it in peace, and profited from it in both circumstances.

Ancient religion plus political pressure produced the theory that the citizen body was one family, with public resources as common property to be used for the relief of indigent family members. In recent history, this theory has developed in times of economic depression; in Greece, it was widespread even in prosperous times, when the poor could advance unhindered socially and economically. It was not a social welfare concept but an expression of citizen solidarity.

This theory, plus the dogma that to the victors belong the spoils, caused many a Greek revolution to result in transfer of the losing party's—the aristocrats'—property to the indigent masses, who then showed unwillingness to extend the franchise and thus distribute more thinly the fruits of success. The Athenians themselves, though theirs was the most democratic community in Greece, did not conceive of democracy as capable of infinite growth. For them, it sufficed to have established equality before the law and the poor man's right to share office with the rich. So in the mid-fifth century B.C. the Athenians halted the naturalization of resident aliens, or metics.

Yielding to heavy pressure from the masses, Pericles proposed (451 B.C.) a law restricting citizenship to those who could prove descent from citizen parents. The Athenian commoner clearly thought there were too many metics. Soon after Athens became the federal capital of the 200-odd states of the Delian League and the center of Aegean commerce, thousands of immigrants—importers, investors, manufacturers, skilled and unskilled workers—had settled in the city or the Piraeus. If they became citizens, native Athenians would have to share with them such benefits as relief from distress and pay for officeholding. For example, during a famine, five years after Pericles' citizenship law was passed, the Egyptian pretender Psamtik II had presented Athens with a large cargo of wheat. Before this bounty was distributed, the citizen list was revised to conform with the law, and several thousand names were stricken off. Citizenship was too valuable to be offered freely.

Metics continued nevertheless to live in Athens as honored guests, protected as to person and movable property, free to prosper in business, but not to own land. Their work and taxes added to the city's wealth as did their underwriting as sponsors (*choregi*) all expenses of dramatic and gymnastic festivals. Wealthy metics won the respect that normally accompanies material success, including social recognition in high places, but they and their descendants could never be citizens.

This policy seems even more shortsighted, though fear of oligarchs might explain it, as applied to emigrants from the city-states of the Empire, who would have valued citizenship as some compensation for loss of or restrictions upon their sovereignty. A liberal citizenship policy might have assured the loyalty Athens was so desperately to need during the ordeal of the Peloponnesian War. Denial of citizenship humiliated metics and probably harmed the Athenians themselves. Under such a system neither Cleisthenes to whom Athens owed its democracy, nor

Themistocles, the preserver of its liberty, nor Cimon, the founder of its Empire, could have been citizens, for the mother of each was a foreigner. Ironically, Pericles himself had to appear before the Ecclesia to ask an exception to the law in favor of his own son.

Imperial Exploitation

Animated by such narrow self-interest, Athenian democracy capitalized on its imperial position. Though the material profit from the Empire to Athenian merchants, manufacturers, laborers, and farmers is incalculable, the tribute-income can be fairly accurately computed, an achievement of modern archeologists who have painstakingly reassembled the broken evidence of the buried past. A percentage of the annual tax, covering more or less completely the years 454/453–415/414 B.C. was inscribed on marble slabs, which survive in hundreds of fragments. Archeologists have fitted these jig-saw puzzles together to give us a picture of Athens' exploitation of its Empire.

Each state, these documents reveal, was taxed according to ability to pay, some a few hundred drachmas, others, like Aegina, a commercial rival, as much as thirty talents. A talent was 6000 drachmas, a drachma —worth twenty cents on a gold basis—had a purchasing power fifteen to twenty times as great. In a given year (443/442 B.C.), the Empire collected over 376 talents from 165 states. (Later, in 425/424 B.C., under stress of war, the tribute was much increased.) Though this figure exceeds Aristides' original assessment, each state in fact paid less, new states accounting for the increased total. Clearly, therefore, except for states punished for rebellion, the tribute was not high, but it was resented, especially by oligarchs, as a despotic exaction. With true Greek political supersensitiveness, the oligarchs felt keenly their demotion from partnership with Athens to the status of impotent subjects.

The revenues from Athens itself almost equaled the tribute. Their sources were many: from merchants as customs dues, sales taxes, or license-fees for certain businesses; from occupations requiring police supervision, for example, fortunetelling, juggling, or prostitution; from metics, freedmen, and slave owners (a poll tax); from court fees and fines; or from rent or lease of public properties—houses, market-stalls, farmland, forest, pasture, mines, quarries. No real-estate tax is included here; that was levied only in an emergency, chiefly war, to eke out revenues. In short, from both external and internal sources Athens raised about 750 talents a year, far more than any other Greek city.

Out of this pie over 17,000 Athenians sliced their living as public functionaries, a very high proportion of the whole citizen body, which is estimated at 43,000 adult males. Of this total, civilian services absorbed

7450 citizens: 5000 judges, 500 councilmen, 1400 administrative officials distributed between Athens and the Empire, 500 in the arsenal patrol, and 50 in the Acropolis guard. The military services accounted for 11,300: 2500 hoplites, 1200 cavalry, 4000 marines and sailors, and 2000 garrison troops, in addition to 1600 Thracian (noncitizen) archers. This list omits disabled veterans, orphans, widows and indigent parents of war dead, and poor citizens on relief (after 410 b.c.), all of whom received state pensions.

Payment for public service provided almost a living wage. The lowest paid, as we saw, were the jurymen at two obols a day, later increased to three; the highest were councilmen at five obols. Prytany-members received one drachma (six obols) plus free board and lodging. Hoplites received four obols; cavalrymen eight, four each for man and horse; marines and sailors three throughout the eight-month sailing season. Labor, skilled or unskilled, public or private, was paid one drachma a day.

These incomes were low compared with American wages, but so was the cost of living. We have seen that the typical Greek diet was bread, fruit, vegetables, cheese, fish, a little meat, olive oil, and watered wine. The cost of a year's living in the fifth century b.c. was approximately as follows:

Bread	15	drachmas =	90 obols
All other food and drink	45	"	= 270 "
Clothing and shoes	16	"	= 96 "
Housing	36	"	= 216 "
Incidentals	8	"	= 48 "
Total 120		drachmas =	720 obols

Since one drachma represented a normal day's wages, a bachelor working two days a week almost made his living; if he worked every day for six months, he had extra spending money; if he worked every working day of the year, he was well-off. A married man, however, needed 180 drachmas to support himself and his wife. If he had two children, he needed 240 drachmas. But if an elderly man unable or unwilling to work served as judge every court day (300 days), he would make 100 drachmas. If he lived with a son or daughter, he could pay almost full board and lodging. Pericles' program to make democracy effective by public pay for public work succeeded because the Empire financed it.

Two devices gave a share in imperialism's rewards to other thousands of Athenian citizens. One was the system of cleruchies, the Athenian or mixed garrisons planted during the Persian War. Pericles made this tool double-edged. He settled Athenian citizens as imperial militia on the domain of a rebellious or recalcitrant state. These cleruchs, mainly poor citizens, received the offending ally's best lands, usually taken by some compulsive method politely called a treaty. In extreme instances, when the Athenians wished to punish as well as control, the native population was reduced to virtual helotry, tilling for their Athenian masters the soil they had owned. Nearly a fourth of the Athenian citizens, some ten thousand men, benefited from this device.

The other was a vigorous building program. Pericles spent 3000 talents on public works, giving artisans at home a share of public funds rivaling that granted to civic, military, or imperial personnel. Even though 800 talents were spent abroad to purchase the gold and ivory for Phidias' statue of Athena, the balance was enough to provide jobs for 2200 workers at standard wages—one drachma a day in the dry season, that is, two-thirds of a year—for a whole quarter century. Even though many of these laborers were metics or slaves, Aristotle's estimate that altogether 20,000 Athenians were on the government payroll is not an overstatement.

Oligarchic Opposition

In Athens it clearly paid to be a democrat. Oligarchs elsewhere, however, found the democratic system offensive and called Athens a "tyrant state." Athenian oligarchs agreed, less out of pity for the exploited members of the Delian League than for domestic political purposes. The oligarchs, out of power since Cimon's fall, wanted a party issue. Athenian oligarchs, often intermarried with oligarchic families in the Empire, resented having their kinsfolk play second fiddle to democracy abroad as well as at home.

Instead of taking up arms against the ruling demos, the oligarchs acted as a loyal opposition. Not only did they dislike the people's perpetuation in power on the principle of a job for every voter, but they also had grievances of their own. After paying their share of ordinary taxes, they were saddled with other burdens. A tradition amounting to law required a well-to-do citizen to give banquets to the men of his deme and tribe, his wife to do the same for her sister demeswomen. He was expected to finance the competitive torch races of his tribe. He personally paid all expenses incurred by any diplomatic mission he might head, as well as those of the delegations led by him to the national oracles or Panhellenic games. Before metics became choregi, the oligarch alone provided and paid production costs for the plays which a host of brilliant playwrights was producing for citizen entertainment. These indirect taxes were called liturgies, that is, "services to the people."

The most onerous liturgy was the trierarchy. The state gave to the trierarch the hull of a trireme, with mast, sails, and minimum essential rigging. He had to furnish the remaining equipment, collect and organize the crew, give them a bonus over and above their pay from the state, keep the craft seaworthy for a whole campaigning season, and return it in good condition when the campaign was over. He had the honor of personally commanding the ship, but he received no compensation for his expenses, his time, or the consequent neglect of his business. An average trierarchy cost 3600 drachmas. In wartime this burden was imposed as often as every third year, but only on the wealthiest citizens.

No doubt a rich man felt partly compensated for the heavy financial burden of threescore liturgies in a lifetime. He had first of all the satisfaction of serving his country in the tradition of his ancestors. He found in liturgies many outlets for his varied talents. He earned the applause of both his deme and his tribe, which identified themselves with his successes. The feeling of self-importance which comes from shining in the public eye did not exclude sincere patriotism. Many a rich man saw in the liturgies a corrective of the economic difference between himself and the poor. Besides, he knew that these public benefactions would help him to secure a favorable verdict in the courts or to win votes for office. But great as these advantages and satisfactions were, his influence in the government was not proportionate to the time, energy, and money he put at the city's service. Politically he was the underdog in the kingdom of the common man.

In Pericles' time, the rich found their leader in Thucydides, son of Melesias. An old-line pro-Spartan aristocrat like his father-in-law Cimon, Thucydides, unlike Cimon, was anti-imperialist. Thucydides' strategy for unseating Pericles and restraining the radical democrats was three-pronged: forming a coalition of all discontented groups; securing full attendance of his followers at the Ecclesia; waiting for a favorable issue to take shape.

A single ostrakon bearing the name of Damon, Pericles' music teacher and alleged political adviser, has been used as evidence that Thucydides had Damon ostracized as a preliminary to a direct contest with Pericles. Perhaps he played on a certain disillusionment over Pericles' failure to extend the Empire. He sought also to capitalize on the restlessness among the subject-allies, which just then was serious enough to cause Pericles to reduce the tribute. In spite of the reduction, their discontent increased; we have seen how, since Persia had come to terms in the Peace of Callias of 449/448 B.C., the subject-allies resented the continuation of the Delian League. They hated above all the diversion of the federal defense levy to another purpose, financing public works in Athens.

Here was Thucydides' issue. Thucydides moralized: it was dishonest to have defense money diverted to adorn the city like a courtesan. More important were the things he left unsaid, chiefly the implied condemnation of making work with somebody else's money. But Pericles shrewdly kept the issue on the political plane. The Athenian navy, he replied, was still in being, bigger and better than ever, ready to defend the allies. As long as they received this service, it was no business of theirs to inquire how the money was spent. When the Ecclesia was finally called upon to decide the question, Thucydides was ostracized (443 B.C.). The school of Hellas, as Athens was later called by Pericles, had put self-interest above morality. Pericles remained the undisputed master. If that meant a continued repressive policy towards the subject-allies and a job for every democrat, it meant also the cultural flowering and the beautification of the city Aristophanes addressed as:

> O rich and renowned, and with violets crowned,
> O Athens, the envied of nations.

Chapter 21 / PERICLEAN CULTURE (I): THE ARTS

Peace and Idealism

Pericles was not yet fifty at the time of the Thirty-years' Peace (446 B.C.). Adverse results in the war for a land empire had profoundly modified his thinking. He had become more than ever aloof from the noisy crowds, absorbed in contemplation, seeking perhaps a new role for his city. Primarily responsible, as strategos-in-chief, for foreign relations, the aggressor of yesterday grew tolerant towards the states he had failed to subdue, avoiding offense and scrupulously living up to his treaty obligations. He now conceived the idea that if Athens renounced imperialism and became instead the intellectual leader of Greece, the next thirty years might well produce the fruits he had failed to harvest by war. Athens as "the school of Greece," the model of every civilized state—this was the new direction and Pericles' noblest dream.

But the dream was fulfilled only in part, for seeing in it a political trick, those states which may be loosely labeled Dorian, Peloponnesian, or aristocratic refused to cooperate. Those who doubt Pericles' idealism or magnanimity will sympathize with the Peloponnesians' wariness. Pericles' new program can be seen as a means to two practical ends: to put Sparta in a bad light if it refused to cooperate and to reassert Athenian leadership of the Delian League's maritime cities, which the peace with Persia seemed to make no longer necessary. Pericles planned several joint enterprises for the advantage of all Greece. His first attempt failed. Sparta did not even acknowledge his invitation to a Panhellenic Congress (447 B.C.) to discuss common problems: restoring the temples burned by the Persians, founding some spectacular festival to commemorate the common victories, ensuring the safety of the sea, and guaranteeing peace. Sparta cared nothing for restoring the temples, since its own, having escaped invasion, had suffered no damage. It felt that Athens, which was just beginning to rebuild the Parthenon and to beautify the Acropolis, would reap the chief advantage.

A second Panhellenic proposal (443 B.C.) to settle the decayed south Italian city of Sybaris found better reception. Several states cooperated and the city was renamed Thurii. But both the other founding states and Thurii itself resented Athens' attempt to dominate the young colony. In the coming struggle between Athens and the Peloponnesians, Thurii was to fight against Athens.

Then came the final disappointment and abandonment of these sterile endeavors. Pericles had set great store by another purely idealistic Panhellenic Congress. The Greeks' strong sense of superiority to the best barbarians—Etruscans, Carthaginians, or Persians—had prompted Sophocles in 442 B.C. to speak of man (and only the Greek was man; the barbarian was slave) as a miracle-maker: [1]

> Wonders are many, but there is no wonder
> Wilder than Man—
> Man who makes the winds of winter bear him
> Through the trough of waves that tower about him,
> Across gray wastes of sea;
> Man who wearies the Untiring, the Immortal
> Earth, eldest of the Gods, as year by year,
> His plough-teams come and go.
> The care-free bands of birds,
> Beasts of the wild, tribes of the sea,
> In netted toils he takes,
> The Subtle One.
> Creatures that haunt the hills, the desert dwellers,
> His cunning snares; he lays his mastering yoke
> On the horse's shaggy mane,
> On the tireless mountain-bull.

[1] Translated by F. L. Lucas, in *Greek Verse in Translation,* ed. by T. F. Higham and C. M. Bowra. New York, Oxford University Press, 1938.

Agriculture is one of this ode's themes, but a Periclean invitation to the Greek states to offer their first-fruits to Demeter at Eleusis was refused by all but the subservient states of the Empire.

Pericles' efforts to unite Greece spiritually were quite genuine, for, like his teacher Anaxagoras of Clazomenae, nicknamed *Nous,* "the Mind," he saw Mind as the prime universal force, pre-eminent over everything—birth or death, life or change, time or eternity—and the body, the city-state, the world as but instruments. This doctrine of Anaxagoras was now pivotal to Pericles' public career. Although he played the game of international politics, he sincerely believed that Athens should be the teacher of Greece because it had pushed farthest along the highroad of intelligence. He failed to persuade Greece to become a willing pupil, but he succeeded in fitting Athens for the role of teacher. Without him the city would not have lacked its Sophocles or its Phidias, its architects, painters, or ceramists of imperishable fame, or Socrates and, later, Plato, but he it was who with unwavering faith and as a matter of policy went about the creation of one of the most receptive environments for the nurture of the arts and sciences that any society has yet known.

No other Periclean enterprise reveals so fully the practicality of his idealism as his public works program. Besides providing employment, it asserted Athens' spiritual supremacy. Religion was then at the core of Athenian life. Most Periclean monuments were related to the gods, especially the goddess Athena, who men believed had nursed her city to greatness, freed it from the Persians, then made it imperial. She was the key to Athenian religious thinking and artistic achievement. Daughter of Zeus, sprung full-grown from his brain, hence regarded as goddess of wisdom and patroness of arts and crafts, Athena was revered also as giver of the olive tree, inspirer of valor, guardian of the city and its civilization and culture. She smiled always upon the Attica she had won in remote ages from Poseidon. The Panathenaic procession therefore brought her in thanksgiving lambs, kids, heifers, barley and wheat ears, jars of oil and wine, milk, cheese, and the fruits of the sacred land of Attica. For her, as Virgin Goddess, young maidens wove yearly a linen robe, choirs of men and boys sang hymns, and youths, well trained for war, rode the prancing horses their fathers had reared in the Plain. Her people, her beneficiaries, vowed to efface every disfigurement left by the Persian invader.

A spirit of competition was almost as important to Pericles' building program as was religion, for the Greeks traditionally competed in peaceful arts as passionately as in military ones. The religious revival and the patriotism inspired by victory over Persia exalted this ancient rivalry into a general movement for finer temples and civic centers, which in

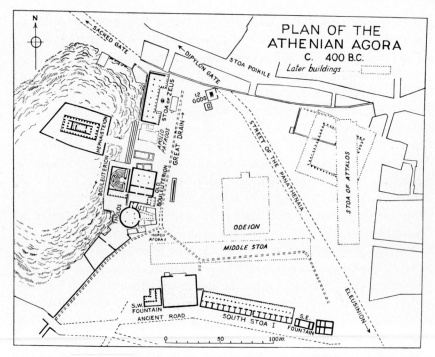

Fig. 21a. Plan of the Athenian Agora *c.* 400 B.C. (A. W. Gomme, *A Historical Commentary on Thucydides,* Books II–III. Oxford, 1956. Facing p. 54.)

turn stimulated artists to transmute Periclean ideals into works of undying beauty.

Athens in particular had every inspiration to artistic expression: unbounded self-confidence, sparked chiefly by its valor at Marathon and heightened by its imperial ascendancy; a noble artistic and literary tradition going back to Pisistratus and presently exemplified in Aeschylus' timeless poetry; a Pericles to incite it to become a model for Greece; wealth pouring in from subject-allies; architects, sculptors, masons, metalworkers, stonecutters, potters of native esthetic taste. Inspired by past Athenian glory and present Athenian greatness, Pericles and his chosen artists concentrated on making the Acropolis supremely beautiful, worthy of its gods and heroes, and symbolic of the imperial role for which Athenians had recently died.

The Parthenon

If the Periclean Acropolis is the most beautiful spot in Greece, the Parthenon is the crowning glory of the Acropolis. Foremost among its prototypes was the Doric temple of Athena Aphaia at Aegina, an achievement in austere beauty, Aegina's greatest contribution to art, and

Fig. 21.1. Athens. The Parthenon, floodlit. (Courtesy Olympic Air Lines)

Aegina had become subject to Athens. Aegina's marble pediments, sculptured with heroes of the Trojan War, were unmatched in Greece. The late archaic archer Heracles in the east pediment is a superb example of graceful tension.

The temple of Zeus in Olympia (c. 460 B.C.), was also Doric, the grandest structure in that religious and artistic center and the wonder of the thousands of Olympic visitors. A little later (c. 454 B.C.) Phidias made for it the previously mentioned chryselephantine cult statue, the embodiment of benignity and majesty. We have already mentioned the temples at Acragas, Himera, and Syracuse. Lastly, there was the stately temple "of Poseidon" at Paestum (see Fig. 12.1), which was to witness the rise and fall of the Roman Empire and which remains to this day the finest surviving example of a fifth-century Doric temple.

With such examples to emulate, the architects Ictinus and Callicrates, the sculptor Phidias, and hundreds of nameless craftsmen combined their skill to make the "Virgin's Temple," or Parthenon, at Athens a building that has ever since been acclaimed as one of the most perfect ever created by man. It occupies the site of an older sanctuary begun by Pisistratus and unfinished at the Persian sack. The new building was begun in 447 B.C., a year before Pericles called his first still-born Congress. Rectangular in plan, wholly of marble, the Parthenon is a Doric-Ionic synthesis, conceived to stress Pericles' striving for Greek cultural

Fig. 21.2 (*left*). The *Discobolus* of Myron. Roman copy (Antonine age) of an original of about 450 B.C., giving an effect of elasticity and compressed energy: that controlled excitement, miscalled "classical restraint," which is the essence of mid-fifth-century Athenian art. (Rome, Terme Museum) Fig. 21.3 (*right*). The *Doryphorus* of Polyclitus. Good Roman copy. A young winner in the javelin throw, represented in the ideal proportions painstakingly worked out by the sculptor. (Naples, National Museum)

unity. Subsequent generations have found it, in its incomparable setting, even though defaced and in ruins, the perfect expression of the Greek spirit. The front and back walls of the interior (cella) each abutted on a porch faced with six columns. Each porch and each lateral wall was flanked on the outside by columns, eight and seventeen respectively, to form a continuous portico.

The Parthenon's architectural beauty arises not from this stereotyped arrangement, but from harmony in proportions and certain subtle re-

Fig. 21.4. Lemnian *Athena*. Superb Roman rendering of original by Phidias, the only Athena without a helmet. The careful balanced treatment of contours approaches the techniques and intent of modern abstract art. (Bologna, Museo Civico; photo by Clarence Kennedy)

finements. Curves replace straight lines, and columns are tilted slightly from the vertical. The floor is not flat: higher at the center, it slopes imperceptibly outwards on all sides, partly for drainage, partly for esthetic effect. Nor is the entablature truly horizontal; it too curves up toward the center. The columns, besides the usual upward taper, have a delicate convex curve. The outside ones lean inward. These refinements correct the inadequacy of the human eye. But for them the building would seem to bulge at the top and its horizontal lines to sag. No less subtle than Ictinus' plan was the artisans' precise skill, unaided, we must remember, by modern machine tools and precision instruments.

The Parthenon sculptors also owed much to their predecessors and contemporaries. Within a generation after the creation of the Aegina pediments, those gifted masters had achieved a century of progress. For example, see the *Discus Thrower* of Myron, a Boeotian sculptor trained in Athens, working in bronze and interested in portraying strenuous action. The statue expresses not only youth, strength, and male beauty, but also the confident, self-disciplined mind, perfectly controlling the muscles with maximum efficiency and grace and minimum strain.

A slightly younger contemporary of Myron was Polyclitus, supreme in the Argive school, which worked principally in bronze studies of the athletic form. Unlike Myron, who sought to depict violent movement in an instant of arrest, Polyclitus modeled subjects standing in repose or with the right foot on the ground and the left rising and beginning to move. Aiming to represent the ideal human body, the Argive master studied it with infinite care until he worked out and published what seemed to him the rules of perfect proportions, embodied, for example, in the *Doryphorus,* the statue of a spearman in the prime of young manhood. That Polyclitus had in mind something slightly more impressionistic than mathematical formulas or naturalistic effects is evident from the squarish appearance of the head and shoulders of his statues.

A greater master was Phidias, who achieved the *ne plus ultra* of the Attic style. Before working on the Parthenon, he had probably finished his exquisite *Athena* at Lemnos, the epitome of womanhood. Apparently he had finished also the colossal statue of Athena the Protectress (*Promachos*) which could be seen above the surrounding buildings for miles around, especially from the sea. Acknowledged head of the Attic school, Phidias was appointed director-in-chief both of the Parthenon's sculptures and of building operations.

Phidias was past middle age at the time Myron and Polyclitus were perfecting their styles. He knew them well and admired both so much that in the Parthenon marbles he aimed at a blend and balance of Myron's rendering of physical strength, Polyclitus' ideal law of proportions, and the delicate grace of his own Attic school. Thus, while his friend Pericles was trying to unify the Greek states under Athens' intellectual leadership, Phidias was trying to integrate the different sculptural styles. The statesman's conviction that Athens was the teacher of Greece was probably strengthened by the general recognition of Phidias' preeminence as well as by the all-Greek character of the Parthenon marbles.

Phidias himself could not execute all the numerous Parthenon sculptures. He conceived the general plan and apparently designed a few of its statues and tableaux himself, leaving the majority to be designed by his helpers. So too with the carving. The finished pieces show the uneven ability of his assistants, some excellent, others mediocre.

Ninety-two metopes, panels high up on the entablature, each about four feet square, illustrate in high relief four legendary struggles: between Greeks and Amazons, Centaurs and Lapiths, gods and giants,

Fig. 21.5. Athens. Parthenon. Horsemen from west frieze. Handsome boys and spirited horses in a religious procession. *C.* 440 B.C. (London, British Museum)

Greeks and Trojans, all representing the eternal pattern of conflict and conquest with victor exulting over the fallen foe.

Fragmentary though it is, the pedimental sculpture seems to throb with life. Adaptation of human or animal figures to triangular spaces was a technique already mastered in the Aegina and Olympia pediments, but here again Phidias excelled his predecessors. The east pediment portrayed the birth of Athena. Its best-known figure is the so-called *Theseus*, rising from the couch, strong and graceful, with athletic muscles softly overlaid with flesh, and a handsome, intelligent, and alert head. *Theseus* embodies Pericles' ideal Athenian who could "adapt himself to the most varied forms of action with the utmost versatility and grace." As Pericles' Athenian epitomized the best Greek qualities, Phidias' statue epitomized the characteristics of the best contemporary schools.

The west pediment represented Athena's and Poseidon's contest over Attica. Poseidon, advancing with a retinue of gods and goddesses to take over the land, suddenly encounters Athena and her followers. The goddess' appearance startles him less than does her miraculous gift to the people he had hoped to rule: the olive tree through which Athena wins and Poseidon withdraws in vindictive rage to seek sullen vengeance by unleashing storms against mariners trespassing on his domain, the sea.

A continuous frieze in low relief encircled the cella walls outside, just under the ceiling of the four-sided portico. Executed by various hands, the frieze too is of uneven workmanship. The design, however, in its perfection throughout, suggests Phidias' own work. The subject is the Panathenaic procession. Amid standing spectators, Athena and other seated gods—her guests—await the pageant. With them are the magistrates, priests, and priestesses to receive the goddess' robe. Four hundred

Fig. 21.6. Athens. Propylaea. Monumental entrance to Acropolis, built from plans by Mnesicles, 437–432 B.C., of Pentelic marble; left unfinished at outbreak of Peloponnesian War. The left wing was a picture gallery. (Photo by Dorothy MacKendrick)

men and women and 200 animals participate in the joyful ceremony which unrolls in a marble scroll 500 feet long. Greek craftsmen never again produced so splendid a cooperative work.

The art of the Parthenon grows out of religious faith, a sense of community, and high artistic standards. With these incentives, Phidias' genius harmonized architecture and sculpture as it had already harmonized contemporary sculptural styles. Credit goes also to Phidias' co-workers, architects, sculptors, and craftsmen, moved by reverence for Athena and the desire to express in marble their city's pre-eminence, which playwrights had revealed in the theater, soldiers and sailors in battle, and statesmen in empire-building. They too were honest artisans, valuing their craft above money-making. For their talents they received the same pay as the top-ranking masters—Ictinus, Callicrates or Phidias himself—all of them, high and low, receiving one drachma a day.

The Athenian worshiper, stirred by the outward grandeur of the Parthenon and its sculptured story, was stirred even more when he beheld within the statue of the goddess filling the great hall with her presence. Two or three surviving small-scale Roman copies hint at the grandeur of the lost masterpiece. The statue, with the flesh in ivory, the drapery in gold, was so gigantic that a mere detail, the Winged Victory in its right hand, was taller than a tall Greek. The sight of the goddess within her shrine, dwarfing the spectator in her vast majesty, magnificently robed as befitted one radiating the power and beauty appropriate

Fig. 21.7. Athens. Nike Temple Parapet. Goddess tying her sandal. Circa 408 B.C. Informality is the keynote here. The free-flowing lines of the drapery transparently reveal the curves of the beautiful body beneath. (Photo courtesy Royal Greek Embassy)

to the daughter of Zeus and protecting her beloved city, awed the worshiper profoundly. Phidias made this statue with his own hands, and ancient writers considered it his masterpiece.

The Propylaea and Other Monuments

Eleven years after the cornerstone of the Parthenon was laid, the Propylaea was begun (437 B.C.) from designs by Mnesicles. Uniting Doric and Ionic even more boldly than the Parthenon itself, it was the monumental gateway to the Acropolis. The façade, looking westward, marked the end of the Sacred Way, which started at Demeter's Eleusinion, passed through the Dipylon Gate, entered the Agora, and, passing the Areopagus, ascended the steep western slope of the Acropolis to end in front of the Parthenon. A Doric colonnade provided five separate entrances. Through the wider central entrance passed sacred parades like the Panathenaic procession, and sacrificial animals. Through the Propylaea passed daily an endless stream of people, pilgrims, worshipers, tourists, or businessmen, who would not think of leaving Athens without having seen this famous and beautiful shrine.

On a bastion south and west of the Propylaea stood Callicrates' little shrine of Athena Nike, commissioned by Pericles but completed after his death. Its continuous frieze illustrated the battle of Plataea. Sculptured slabs formed a balustrade around the bastion supporting the shrine; they include the famous Victory adjusting her sandal, her thin drapery revealing the lovely form beneath.

Two hundred feet north of the Parthenon, to the left of the visitor proceeding from the Propylaea, rose the Erechtheum, the most exquisite Ionic structure ever designed by Greeks. It was begun probably about 420 B.C. and finished in 406 B.C., late in the Peloponnesian War. Built on two levels, its three halls and three porches symbolized its consecration to three divinities: Erechtheus, a mythical ancestor of the Athenian people; Athena Polias, guardian of the city; and Poseidon, still honored as a patron god of Attica despite his fabled loss of it to Athena. The building enclosed the holy spot where, legend said, Poseidon had brought forth a salt spring, and Athena the olive tree. On one of the porches the famous Caryatids, female figures used as columns, support the roof.

Commercial Art

Lest the beauty of the Acropolis leave the impression that Periclean craftsmen were impossibly perfect, we turn briefly in conclusion to the "minor" art of vase-painting. Its golden age was the time of the Persian Wars. By mid-fifth century B.C., though there were still some charming vases and a few great ones, the level was sinking rapidly. Potters and painters no longer signed their vases: their inferiority increased with the rising prestige of "major" artists like Phidias. And they were in a hurry: vases were mass-produced. In style they tried, and failed, to be three-dimensional, to compete with fresco-painting. Only the white-ground *lekythoi* (oil-flasks used in funerary rites) continued to show distinction; their elegiac charm contrives, in scenes of warriors' farewells, drawn with a classical economy of line, to take from death some of its bitterness, if not its inexorability.

But this is not a note to end on. The splendor of the Periclean age in architecture and sculpture is undeniable. Here magnificence did not degenerate into grandiloquence, nor patriotism into chauvinism. The greatness was inherent in the artists' intellectually controlled passion for clear, simple, generalized ideas, the same passion we are about to discover in Periclean literature.

Chapter 22/PERICLEAN CULTURE (II): THE INTELLECT

Tragedy and the Theater

Attic tragedy in the Periclean Age rivaled architecture in perfection. True, Aeschylus (525–456 B.C.) had been writing for nearly forty years before Pericles came to power. But the statesman's influence affected Sophocles (496–406 B.C.), a close second to Aeschylus, and the ideas of the age appear in the plays of a younger tragic poet, Euripides (480–406 B.C.).

We have seen that after 534 B.C. the protagonist introduced by Thespis impersonated two or more characters. Although this was progress, with but a single character on the stage at a time, action, conflict, or plot were handicapped. Aeschylus found the remedy about 484 B.C. when he added a second actor; Sophocles later added a third. Since each actor played several parts, the number of characters was multiplied. With more characters at work, with three actors on the stage simultaneously, poets could build more intricate plots, heighten the conflict, and in general widen the scope of the drama.

Since the thousands of plays produced in the rest of the Greek world in the fifth century B.C. have perished, our judgment of Greek tragedy

Fig. 22.1. Scene from Robinson Jeffers' *Medea*. (*Archaeology* I, 1948, p. 55.)

is based solely on 33 surviving Athenian plays. Here too, time has exacted its toll, for although Aeschylus wrote 90 plays, Euripides 92, and Sophocles 125—a total of 307—only some 10 percent survive. Other playwrights we know as mere names or fragments. Nor is it necessarily the best plays to which the fates have been kind. Although *Oedipus the King*, which fortunately survives, is generally considered Sophocles' masterpiece, the prize the year that it was presented was won by a lost tragedy by Philocles. *Medea*, perhaps Euripides' best surviving work, was awarded third prize in its year; the first- and second-prize winners have perished.

The same communal spirit which produced the glories of the Acropolis and the magnificence of the Great Panathenaea gave vitality to Attic drama. The people did not merely watch the plays; they organized and acted in them.

Most of Attica's 170-odd demes staged at least one tragedy a year, some also a comedy. On a humble scale these Rural Dionysia recruited their choruses, probably their actors too, from local talent. More sophisticated were the productions of larger places: Acharnae, Eleusis, the Piraeus, or Salamis. Athens produced the most brilliant of all in four annual festivals, Panathenaea, Hephaesteia, Prometheia, and Thargelia, in which dithyrambic contests, choral songs to Dionysus (see p. 198), were the main feature. In content, it was a medley of salacious scenes and subjects.

Two tribes joined to furnish a chorus of local talent, as in the Rural Dionysia. But no dithyrambic festival could compete in artistic worth or popular interest with the festivals offering tragedies and comedies, that is, the three-day Lenaea and the four-day City Dionysia.

The drama was as representative of its day as the epic and the lyric were of theirs. It rose in Athens with the rise of democracy, flowered as democratic government flowered. While the basic reasons for this parallelism are conjectural, few would venture to reject Pericles' suggestion that the democracy had created in Athens a favorable intellectual climate. Freedom of speech, for example, without which there can be no thorough probing of a people's problems, was the cornerstone of Athenian democracy. For an Athenian, life without the right of criticism was only half a life. He feared, to quote Pericles himself, "not discussion, but the want of that knowledge which is gained by discussion." Even in the midst of its deadliest struggle, the Peloponnesian War which destroyed its empire, Athenian democracy granted an avowed critic of democracy like Aristophanes full freedom to attack its war policy. In a way, the stage in both tragedy and comedy was a replica of the Pnyx, the meeting place of the Ecclesia. For example, though Aeschylus dramatized many episodes of the *Iliad* and the *Odyssey*, the give and take, the sharp argument and high controversy, even the impact and brilliance of language of his plays were inspired by the Ecclesia's debates and the democratic process.

The subject matter itself was communal, drawn from Homer's and Hesiod's sagas of gods and heroes. The Greeks' belief that they were the descendants of gods made this repertory a saga of the people themselves. Far from being a withering influence, religion and myth fecundated the imagination of poets and related the theater to life. Most Periclean Athenians were stirred by myths and legends of the long ago. Also, they had no regularly constituted clergy to formalize the national heritage, and their poets were prophets in whose hands the ancient myths were continually reinterpreted or adapted to new meanings several steps ahead of the communal mind and conscience. The tragedians in particular thus acted as a leaven of progressive thought and higher morality.

Progressive religion plus a democracy unafraid of controversy made Attic tragedy a vehicle of humanistic education. In the absence of such modern means of airing public questions as the town hall, the press, and television, the Athenians used the stage as a forum for discussing the great current public questions: religion, morality, education, international relations, patriotism, indeed any problem of public interest. This was true of every tragedy, but let one example suffice. Sophocles' *Antigone* poses the following problem: Should a citizen obey a law which reason tells him is unjust? In the play, King Oedipus having died, mastery of Thebes is contested by his two sons, Eteocles and Polynices. Both die in battle, Polynices attacking the city, Eteocles defending it. The new king, Creon, grants honorable burial to Eteocles, but denies it to Polynices. Creon's threat of death to anyone disobeying his decree does not deter Antigone's resolve to bury her brother, a resolve strengthened by her conviction that Creon's law is invalid, since it denies a basic law of humanity and violates the divine law that the dead be buried. Arrested for her simple act of piety, Antigone is brought before the king, admits her deed, accuses Creon of impiety, injustice, and insane self-conceit, exalts the unwritten law, and welcomes death in so lofty a cause.

Even comedy, as we shall see, throughout the fifth century B.C. concerned itself with community rather than individual problems.

Plays written for a school of adult education embracing the whole community required a theater large enough for most of the citizens. Women might, but usually did not, attend performances of tragedy; from comedy they were barred. Built and maintained at public expense, the theater was in the religious center of the city—on the south slope of the Acropolis under the shadow of the Parthenon. In its latest development the theater in Athens could seat 14,000 people. Pericles probably set up a fund to pay for seats for the poor, partly to reserve some seats for citizens as opposed to foreigners, partly no doubt for the sake of adult education.

Seating was on a communal basis. The best seats around the orchestra were assigned to magistrates, to the judges of the plays, to the priests of the official cults, to citizens distinguished in war or peace, and to war orphans. Each citizen sat in the section reserved for his tribe; that is, he went to a play in the same pattern in which he went to the Ecclesia or marched to battle.

State supervision emphasized the public character of Attic drama. For each festival a magistrate made a preliminary choice of a limited number of semi-finalists. For the Lenaea the king-archon selected two tragic poets to present two tragedies each, and two comic poets, who entered one comedy each. For the City Dionysia the chief archon chose three tragic poets, each of whom offered a trilogy and a "satyr" play, and three comic poets, who offered one comedy each. Thus there were twenty-one plays a year, and throughout the fifth century B.C. a play was staged only once; the first performance was also the last.

After choosing the poets, the archon gave each a sponsor, or choregus, who was more than a Broadway "angel": his financing of a play was not a loan, investment or speculation, but a gift. Only wealthy men were chosen, ten per year, one for each poet, one for each tribe. Taxes in Athens were moderate, and sponsoring a playwright was a form of taxa-

Fig. 22.2. Athens. Theater of Dionysus. Built against the south slope of the Acropolis. Transformed from wood to stone probably between 425 and 413 B.C.; completely rebuilt under Lycurgus (338–326 B.C.) to seat 17,000. (Photo by Dorothy MacKendrick)

tion. Although a burden financially, sponsorship was a much desired honor, principally because a sponsor whose production won first prize became scarcely less famous than the playwright himself and reflected credit on his tribe, or, in the case of metics, his birthplace, as well.

Supplying a chorus, until late in the fifth century B.C. an integral part of the play, was a sponsor's most important business. A comic chorus contained twenty-four men and boys; Sophocles fixed the tragic chorus at fifteen. The chorus represented some mythical, historical, or imaginary group connected with the theme. In reality however it personified public opinion speaking, the voice of common sense, "the moral tribunal of mankind." Its connection with plot and characters was intimate. It not only sang and danced to the lyrics assigned to it and followed step by step the plot's development, registering by mimicry its reactions— praising, reproving, warning, or exhorting—it also conversed with the actors and was therefore itself a composite actor. A chorus was made up of amateurs and gave experience to many. At least a thousand men and boys yearly acquired experience in the Rural Dionysia. Another thousand played in Athens in the four dithyrambic festivals, presenting twenty dithyrambs with fifty men each. A third thousand was needed for another twenty dithyrambs which, besides the regular dramas, were staged at the Lenaea and the City Dionysia. Thus in city and in countryside, year in and year out, Athens enabled no less than three thousand men and boys to appear in public to recite and to dance. The height of ambition was to dance at the Lenaea and the City Dionysia. Only 195 received that high honor.

Clearly Athenian drama was rooted in the very life of the people. A good proportion of the citizen body lived in and around the theater. Thousands had training in voice, declamation, singing, dancing, and acting, with the opportunity at rehearsals to rub elbows with the best actors and directors, often the poets themselves. Many Athenians were helped to become connoisseurs of the drama by the stage experience they had had as chorus members. Such an audience, knowledgeable, eager, keen, sympathetic, inspires actors and playwrights. The vitality and the beauty of Attic drama can be explained in part by the unquenchable thirst of an appreciative public for new and better plays.

To provide a chorus meeting the high standards demanded of a fifth-century B.C. poet and audience, the choregus spared no expense. He supplied rich costumes, hired the flute-accompanist, and had the ensemble trained to perfection. He also hired the actors and a stage director, as well as artists and mechanics for scene-painting and building the stage machinery. He did not choose the principal actor, since, to prevent any one choregus from cornering the most famous actors, the archon assigned him.

First, second, and third prizes were given; the award was communal, the prize-giving a city-wide solemnity. When the poet himself directed the production, his pecuniary reward was small. He attached more importance to his fellow townsmen's recognition of his poetic genius, not in cash, but with a modest crown. The choregus who had paid for a successful dithyrambic production received a tripod. A choregus under whose sponsorship a play won first prize might immortalize his victory with a monument. Moreover, his name appeared with those of the poet and the protagonist in an official marble tablet. This was glory indeed, for it came from a people who, in Pericles' words, "were lovers of the beautiful without loss of manliness."

A carefully selected jury made the award. First, ten judges were chosen by lot, one from each tribe. All ten sat as a panel, but to prevent even a shadow of favoritism, at the last moment five of them were again chosen by lot to make the actual award, subject to prosecution for a tainted verdict. Finally, in a special legislative session, the Ecclesia ratified the transactions of the archons who had supervised the festivals.

Religion

Periclean Athens was a unique melting pot of new ideas. The cultural groundwork had been laid as far back as Pisistratus. Athens had won immortal fame by defeating singlehanded the Grand Army of Darius the Great. Marathon became holy ground, its name a flame to fire men's imaginations. For two generations it catalyzed the naturally gifted Athenian mind. With renewed self-confidence after the triumph of Salamis, the Athenians liberated and attached to themselves the whole Greek world east of Attica. In less than a dozen years they turned their city into a seat of empire, the greatest center of wealth and the busiest international market of Greece in the fifth century B.C. But this is background rather than reason for that wonder of the world, the Periclean renaissance.

The fashion of higher education was a contributing factor, but Pericles' leadership accelerated its pace. With deep appreciation that his fellow citizens were "lovers of the beautiful," Pericles interpreted his leadership as involving the stimulation of Athenian intelligence and esthetic sense. As we have seen, he fused two ideas into a dynamic force: that intellectual values are civilization's core, and that Athens, the "school of Hellas," was best equipped to prove this thesis. He invited to his city artists, writers, scientists, and thinkers famed elsewhere, and he welcomed younger men with new contributions. This exciting circle of immortals-to-be met often like a club; their ideas cross-fertilized each other; they opened up each other's horizons. A partial list of these men reads like so many chapters in fifth-century B.C. intellectual history: Pericles himself, whose concept of democracy created a ground of utmost freedom for intellectual expansion; Anaxagoras the philosopher, who searched for the force that created and holds together the universe; Phidias the sculptor; architects like Callicrates, Ictinus, and Mnesicles; Sophocles the playwright; Herodotus the "Father of History"; Protagoras, humanist and political theorist; Aspasia, Pericles' beautiful and intelligent mistress, a woman from enlightened Ionia.

The great tragedians, Aeschylus especially, expressed the enlightened religious thought of the age. Like the early Hebrew prophets, Aeschylus was to refine the crudities of the inherited myths. Fiercely proud of his military record at Marathon, sensing more than most Greeks that Athens' victory over the Persians marked a triumph of civilization, Aeschylus exalted and humanized the stories he chose as dramatic subjects. He used the poet's freedom to reinterpret myths as a means of educating Greece to a deeper sense of morality and a higher concept of God.

His *Prometheus Bound* poses the problem of evil, how doers of good are rewarded with evil. The play opens with Power and Force carrying the Titan, by Zeus' order, to a cliff in the pathless wilderness of Scythia. Hephaestus chains him to a rock, to be parched by sun and numbed by frosts. This is Prometheus' reward for twice befriending man. First he foiled Zeus' plan to destroy the human race; then he stole fire from the gods and gave it to man.

In explaining the full meaning of this gift, Prometheus identifies himself with Civilization and Progress. He taught man to see, to hear, to understand; showed him how to build houses, discern the cycle of the seasons, count and read, tame the beasts, sail the seas. He invented medicine, appointed the modes of divination, and discovered earth's secret treasures—copper, iron, silver, gold. In so doing he had narrowed the gap between man and the gods. Through him man, like Adam about to be thrust from Eden, had acquired the knowledge of good—and evil. But Prometheus' friendship for man was treason to the gods; he had purloined their secrets. Hence his appalling punishment.

A selfless character and the personification of Wisdom, Prometheus is presented as a martyr for his benefactions to mankind. The villain of the piece is Zeus—cruel, capricious, selfish, and tyrannical. Aeschylus, a God-fearing man, appears to portray Zeus in repulsive colors because the *Prometheus Bound* is the only surviving play of a trilogy. In the last play, however, now lost, Zeus learned mercy and Prometheus self-restraint. The moral is that deity is neither pure Power nor pure Intelligence. "Justice without Force is impotent; Force without Justice is tyrannical." To Aeschylus, God's power and intelligence are indivisible. He thus begins that intellectual synthesis of the divine attributes which was to grow with the centuries.

In the *Oresteia,* his only extant trilogy, Aeschylus reveals more fully both his religious faith and his surpassing genius. A symphony in three movements, this masterpiece emphasizes the necessary harmonies between human conduct and divine justice. St. Paul's "the wages of sin is death" might be its subtitle.

In the *Agamemnon,* first play of the trilogy, the king of kings who had successfullly led the Greek expedition against Troy returns victorious to Argos, to be killed by his wife, Clytemnestra. She had taken a lover, Aegisthus; her husband had been unfaithful to her in Troy, and had brought home with him as mistress the Trojan princess and prophetess Cassandra. But Clytemnestra claims that it was her maternal instinct that pushed her to murder the king: he had slain their daughter on the altar of political expediency. The transport fleet to Troy, held up by contrary winds, had received a prophecy that only human sacrifice could release it, and Agamemnon had offered his daughter, valuing her, the queen says, as little as a sheep or goat. Since he had taken his daughter's life, his own was forfeit.

But no more than Agamemnon could Clytemnestra escape the consequence of her crime. In the second play, the *Libation Bearers,* her son Orestes kills her, abetted by his sister Electra. No other solution was possible under the old Greek clan law—blood for blood, life for life. Two tragedies were involved here. One was the personal tragedy of Orestes, impelled to the matricide not only by natural love for his father, but by an irresistible divine force. The other was the universal tragedy: spilled blood calls for vengeance, an inescapable doom, generation after generation. Aeschylus deliberately presents this example of Homeric Greek mores as an inexorable divine law.

The nightmare of endless bloody expiation continues in the third play, the *Furies (Eumenides)*. Orestes' conscience drives him mad. He is caught helplessly in a dilemma; avenging his father was a duty, but killing his mother was a sin. He wanders citiless from shrine to shrine, haunted, whether sleeping or waking, by the Furies' bloodcurdling shrieks, their unceasing demand for his blood. Reaching Athens in his flight, he seeks refuge at Athena's temple. The goddess now faces a problem. As goddess of enlightenment she has a higher mission, unsuspected by most Greeks; compassion and redemption. But since society cannot easily condone Orestes' crime, she refers his fate to the wise men of the Areopagus. Since the judges, torn between two ideals, strict justice and enlightened forgiveness, cannot reach a decision, Athena intervenes, casting the deciding vote, for mercy. Orestes had suffered enough. The goddess' influence humanizes the Furies; they become the Eumenides, the Kindly Ones. This startling denouement is uniquely Athenian. No other Greek city was more resolutely turning legal archaism into equity. Thus the *Furies* symbolizes the Athenian progressive spirit.

Even more than Aeschylus, Sophocles stresses the connection between religion and morality. In *Antigone* he proclaims the existence of absolutes, the eternal and inescapable law of God. In *Oedipus the King* he emphasizes another aspect of the same problem: man's moral responsibility for his actions, which no amount of intellectual prestidigitation (such as Ismene had tried in *Antigone*) can lessen or explain away. He sees connection between the divine laws and man's highest aspirations; the man who betrays them courts disaster.

Sophocles once remarked that whereas Euripides saw men as they are, he saw them as they ought to be. In the gods, too, he saw only the good. Although he lacked Aeschylus' Michelangelesque conceptions, he surpassed him in idealism. He saw, or preferred to see, only harmonies in heaven and earth. Moderation, serenity, balance: these were the ingredients of which those harmonies were made. The idealism of Sophocles paralleled in literature what his friend Phidias achieved in the Lemnian *Athena* or the Olympian *Zeus*. Like Phidias, he thought that the Olympian gods embodied man's highest conceptions about the spiritual world. Aeschylus saw no flaws in the gods, only in man's conception of them; Euripides showed them as a rascally lot. Sophocles, satisfied with his Periclean world, found the gods perfection incarnate.

Euripides denied this perfection. He liked to dwell on the absurdities of the Homeric gods, principally their immorality. The spectators grasped the meaning. They would be jailed or beaten if they behaved like the Olympian gods. Without apparent unorthodoxy, Euripides exposed the gods of popular mythology—liars, knaves, cheats, adulterers —so skillfully that Cleon, the most influential politician of the day, could not make an impiety charge stick against him.

But it was not just for the fun of being an iconoclast that Euripides undermined orthodoxy. He went beyond the position that reason determines the validity of religion and morality. He held up before his fellow citizens higher ideals than those attributed to the gods of Olympus or held by the fifth-century Babbitt. He pleaded for equality between Greek and barbarian. He wanted the dignity of women recognized, not merely the dignity of man. When Athens butchered the Melians for the crime of neutrality in the Peloponnesian War, Euripides advocated in his *Trojan Women* pity for all mankind and pictured an inscrutable divine power which, amid man-made carnage, prepares the ground for the sprouting of justice and righteousness. In *Helen* he couples two beliefs, immortality and divine justice.

In conclusion, Euripides, far from attacking religion as such, seems in the *Bacchae* to regard it as both necessary and uplifting. What he attacked. were gross and debasing myths. In the larger perspective, we can see that men had to be freed from their burden of mythological rubbish before they could rise to a higher conception of God and morality.

Philosophy, Education, and Science

During the fifth century B.C., philosophy branched out from Ionian cosmology into new fields: metaphysics, epistemology, or theory of knowledge, psychology, and ethics. Heraclitus of Ephesus (born *c.* 535 B.C.) held that substance was divine fire, regulating the universe as a moving spirit, *Logos*. He sometimes identifies it with Zeus. In his view, conflict shaped the universe, creating gods and men. Heraclitus' chief philosophical contribution was the doctrine of change. As opposed to Parmenides, he taught that change or becoming is the only reality and permanence merely an illusion of the senses. One cannot step into the same river twice. From life flows death, and from death life. Youth yields to age, waking to sleep, and whatever is contains within itself its opposite.

The Sicilian Empedocles (*c.* 493–433 B.C.) tried to reconcile preceding systems. His view of the cosmos posited four original and indestructible elements: fire, air, earth, and water. Two hostile forces, Love and Strife, distinct from those elements, bring them together or apart, thus generating the visible world. He modified Parmenides' theory of the inadequacy of the senses by denying change and plurality but holding that the original stuff of the universe is always the same and indestructible. From Pythagoras he accepted the doctrine of the transmigration of the soul.

Zeno of Elea (born *c.* 490 B.C.) expanded his master Parmenides' teaching. Zeno's rejection of sense-evidence involved denial of the existence of change, motion, space, and plurality. To prove the oneness of being and the illusoriness of the senses, he introduced two new tools, dialectical method and applied Pythagorean mathematics. To prove space nonexistent, he gave, using mathematics and logic, the now classic example of the race between Achilles and the tortoise: in a race, Achilles can never overtake the tortoise which starts out ahead of him; when he reaches its starting-point, the tortoise is a little farther on, and so on *ad infinitum.* In another demonstration, Zeno argued that a flying arrow does not really travel, for a simple reason. When a body is in a certain place, it is naturally at rest. The flying arrow is at any conceivable instant in a definite place; therefore it is always at rest. To think otherwise is to be tricked by the senses.

Such was the state of philosophical investigation when Anaxagoras of Clazomenae came to join Pericles' circle in Athens. He gathered around him pupils like Socrates, Euripides, and Pericles himself. His sharpening of the dualism implicit in both Heraclitus and Empedocles affected all subsequent metaphysics, classical and Christian. He supposed that out of an original amorphous mass of separate "seeds," an all-pervading Mind, *nous,* made the countless forms of the world we see. Anaxagoras apparently thought of this Mind as transcendent, simple, a being incorporeal, perhaps divine. It ruled itself, and it set the law and order of the whole universe.

With Anaxagoras' coming, Athens became, and remained for centuries, the center of philosophical studies. Philosophy took new directions, explored new fields, created new sciences. Protagoras of Abdera (born *c.* 485 B.C.) led a revolutionary movement that might be called the New Thought. His book *On the Gods* shocked the public. We have only a few words from it: "I cannot say whether the gods exist or not, or, if they do, what they are like. Many things hinder us from knowing;

principally the obscurity of the subject and the shortness of human life." Such sentiments, taken out of context, may have promoted his alleged conviction for atheism. Protagoras said also, "Man is the measure of all things," an idea dramatized as late as 1917, when the Italian Pirandello wrote *Right You Are If You Think You Are*. If man is the measure, truth is relative to individual belief, not based on absolute authority. Such doctrines have led to charges of undermining morality, but Protagoras may have been misunderstood. If he meant that mankind is the measure of all things, he is one of the first humanists. Protagoras' fertile mind questioned also the common belief in the divine origin of the natural laws governing men's social and political relations. Foreshadowing Rousseau, he thought of law mostly as a social contract. Pericles commissioned him (444 B.C.), as an expert political theorist, to write the constitution for the nascent colony of Thurii. He may have discussed his ideas before the Periclean group of intellectuals. We have some evidence of Sophocles' reaction. Enlarging Anaxagoras' concept of Mind regulating the universe to embrace the governance of the moral world, around the antinomy of God's law and man's law he developed the *Antigone* theme.

The Periclean circle's intellectual ferment percolated down to the masses, creating a demand for teachers in every field. Where the many governed and poverty was no bar to public service, an education was a public necessity. The aristocracy, which had guided Greece to its state of civilization, was still successfully running the domestic and foreign policy of many governments. Its ideal of mental, physical, and social perfection had been transmitted, not as now by school or church, but by the teaching and example of parents and friends.

Democracy, to compete, could not afford lesser ideals. But, not having inherited an educational tradition, it turned to professional teachers. The need was especially urgent in Athens where anyone could rise in the Ecclesia to amend or reject a pending bill or move a new one; could, as a prytany member for 72 days in his lifetime, be executive and legislator; and could have a two-to-one chance of presiding for two days over that body and the Ecclesia. Moreover, in these capacities, the citizen had to act within the letter and the spirit of the laws in order to avoid impeachment or lawsuits. He knew well for how trivial reasons his fellow citizens would destroy or besmirch his political reputation.

While some young Athenians sought a broad liberal education, more wanted a practical short cut to techniques by which they might shine in Ecclesia or prytany, win a lawsuit, become leaders. In response to this demand, teachers came forward who could give, they claimed, the key to success. Three principal types emerged: instructors in facts, instructors in how to think, how to handle the facts, and instructors in developing the well-rounded personality, integrated with the community group.

The members of the last group, the Sophists, began the diversion of investigation from the outer cosmos to the inward man. They thus created the earliest social sciences: ethics, politics, education, history, psychology. In their search for truth or for the better way they evolved some basic principles—often diametrically opposed to each other—with which Western civilization has been wrestling to this day. For example, whereas for Protagoras justice was simply general agreement, man-made, for his younger contemporary, Hippias of Elis, it was dictated by nature—Sophocles would have said, made in heaven. For Hippias, the law separates men, while nature made them all kin. Speculation about religion, politics, and shopworn conventions was encouraged, demolishing many an old fetish. Indeed some Sophists were creating the concept of culture as a humanistic goal, self-justified, detached from religion and often counter to traditional values. In so doing they incurred the conservatives' wrath.

All Sophists, those interested in improving their pupils' character and minds and those who peddled success, agreed that persuasive speech was essential. So Protagoras wrote the first European grammar to teach young Athenians to use Greek clearly and gracefully, while Prodicus of Ceos compiled the first dictionary of synonyms to help them speak precisely. When, in 427 B.C., Gorgias of Leontini came to Athens on a diplomatic mission, his speeches so captivated his audiences that he stayed as a teacher of rhetoric. Building on the principles of earlier Sicilian masters, Gorgias developed a stately, balanced, periodic, antithetic prose, brilliant in rhythm and cadence, and sophisticated throughout. Out of this concern with speech rose a new art, dialectic, which uses speech—question and answer—to pursue truth.

Helpful though the Sophists were in spreading education, they worked under some handicaps. The name "sophist" connotes "wiseacre" and evokes ridicule. The fees they received also gave them a bad name, for many thinking men, including Socrates, denied that virtue and learning could be bought and sold as a commodity. Though Protagoras' 10,000-drachma fee for wealthy pupils was above average, it is worth noting that in purchasing power this sum exceeds a Harvard professor's salary. Herodotus, too, is said to have been paid as much for one public lecture by vote and invitation of the Ecclesia. By contrast, Phidias, as we saw, was paid one drachma a day for his Parthenon sculptures. Honest men condemned the Sophists for claiming that winning an argument was more important than sticking to facts, using common sense, and having a scale of values. But only the worst of the Sophists made that claim, and, as we shall see, only later in the movement. Posterity inherits its dislike of the Sophists chiefly from Plato, who regarded even the best of them as none too good.

Scientific investigation registered a few successes. Polyclitus had measured the human body to determine perfect proportions. On this statistical basis he cast his *Doryphorus* in bronze and wrote his technical treatise. The painter Duris used the statistical method, perhaps somewhat unscientifically, in executing Sybaris' commission to paint a mural of Helen of Troy. He stipulated that, as his Helen would be a composite figure, he must have as models the most beautiful young ladies of the town. In optics, the Parthenon architects were sufficiently skilled to disregard the straight line in order to achieve the illusion of straightness. The architect Hippodamus pioneered in city planning, as the rectangular street-grid of the Piraeus still shows. He claimed that city government should be planned as carefully as city layout, and that he could do both. Empedocles was a reclamation and irrigation engineer. The story that he threw himself into Mount Etna's crater to find out what made the volcano burn, even though a satire, is significant as symbolizing the scientific curiosity of a whole generation. Atlases became common. Research sought some drug which would insure a painless death, and hemlock was selected; the Athenian Ecclesia adopted it for capital punishment.

Historiography: Herodotus

Historians too surpassed the late-sixth-century B.C. "genealogists." Herodotus of Halicarnassus was the pioneer. Among his other assets as historian was his awareness of the close interdependence of nations. He had too an unquenchable curiosity about every aspect of their everyday life as well as of their past. Born in Ionia about 484 B.C., he had heard since childhood the epic of Athenian and Spartan checkmate of the Persian advance. When, early in life, he decided to write the history of that mighty struggle, he felt that to deal adequately with it he must visit the cities, study the past, and examine the culture not only of the Persians themselves, but of all the tribes and peoples with whom they had come into contact and especially those they had conquered. He therefore traveled to Lydia and other parts of Asia Minor, Egypt, Mesopotamia, the countries north of Greece, and Greece herself. Notebook in hand, he observed how the people lived and what gods they worshiped, took measurements of such temples and public buildings as the pyramids of Egypt and the great zigurrat of Babylon, interviewed merchants, priests, or tourist guides, looked at inscriptions even when he could not read them, in short, tried to acquire the greatest possible amount of information. Finally he came to live in Periclean Athens and joined the Periclean circle of intellectuals. But there was a difference between him and the other stars of the Periclean firmament. He was little touched by the rationalism of his day; he never shook off the influence of the Homeric style and the Homeric mythology in which he had been reared.

Apart from his inimitable style, Herodotus' greatness as a historian consists in his development of a number of fundamental concepts which elevated his work above a mere chronicle or narration. He rightly evaluated the Greek victory over the Persians as one of the great events that change the course of world history. He thought of that conflict as the latest phase of an age-old struggle between East and West—Asia and Europe. Lastly, his observation that Athenian imperialism shaped the politics of every Greek state of his time probably suggested to him the idea that it was Persia which gave unity to world history in the period with which he dealt. Accordingly, taking the Persian Empire as a focal point, he grouped around it the history of Asia, Egypt, and Europe, the Greek known world. He thus created a unified design, satisfying to the intellect for its simplicity and logic.

Other aspects of Herodotus' historical genius are his broad human sympathy, his respect for other peoples' ways, his interest in their cultures: geography, climate, religion, folkways, diet, arts, and customs. In a very real sense he wrote a cultural history of all peoples, including the Greeks, who at one time or another had come under the domination of Persia. He is perhaps the most delightful storyteller in any language, himself delighting in the scenes he describes and the anecdotes he retails. He is not so uncritical as his less admiring critics would have us believe. His world view and his easy and delectable style combine to make him, as another great historian, Edward Gibbon, has said, a writer sometimes for children, sometimes for philosophers. Before Herodotus, the writing of history was a beginner's effort. He left it an accomplished art. A grateful posterity has called him the Father of History.

Chapter 23/THE
PELOPONNESIAN WAR

The Background of the War

In 432 B.C. the cities of the Peloponnesian League declared war on the Athenian Empire. By 404 B.C. the Empire was in ruins and Athens itself a Spartan satellite. The incomparable historian Thucydides calls this revolutionary struggle greater than any previous war. Never again were the Greeks to raise so many armies or equip so many fleets, shed so much blood or cause so much devastation as in the Peloponnesian War.

The war's immediate cause was, as we shall see, an alliance between Athens and Corcyra, a powerful city-state at the entrance of the Adriatic Sea. The underlying cause was a clash of principles and interests between imperialistic Athens and the conservative Peloponnesian League. The Athenian Empire's rise threatened the Peloponnesians' most precious heritage, city-state sovereignty. The unity Athens had imposed on the Empire seems good today; at least the Empire preserved peace within itself. To Greek oligarchs, however, unity was subversion, and peace by dictate was slavery. Naxos, Thasos, Samos were to them examples of the slave-peace the Athenian bully could demand.

Interference in local legal procedure was equally galling. Although Athens humanized and simplified the subject cities' judicial practices, Greek oligarchs everywhere viewed such innovation as tyranny.

Even more intolerable to the oligarchs was the overthrow of constitutional governments. Repeatedly Athens expelled aristocratic parties, replacing them with democratic regimes. Although this promoted the democratic cause, many Greeks saw no special virtue or superiority in democracy. Athens' aristocratic thinkers—Socrates, Plato, Aristotle—were no admirers of democracy.

Moreover, democracy as an ideal was quite different from Athenian democracy in practice. Like the Athenians themselves, their democracy was bold, aggressive, and ruthless. Aristocrats, naturally conservative and traditionally self-restrained, stood by the ancestral ways, which meant state sovereignty. To them, Athenian democracy seemed bent on upsetting the divine order. Aristocrats loathed seeing "the base and ugly" exploiting all Greece. Neither the subject-allies nor the members of the Peloponnesian League nor even neutrals felt safe while Athenian politicians vied in humoring the Ecclesia, which by nature and education could "neither be at peace itself nor allow peace to others."

Honest Athenian currency had spurred international trade. Athenian admiralty and commercial law helped standardize business transactions throughout the Aegean world. Many a Greek, however, was skeptical about these advantages—seen as calculated to divert business to the Piraeus.

The effects of Athenian sea power deepened this suspicion. Many Greeks would have preferred the return of piracy to the dominance of the Athenian navy, which tightly controlled and limited their foreign trade.

We have already seen how, through alliances with Naupactus, Achaea, and Megara, Athens had encircled Corinth, its greatest commercial rival. Though this pressure was later reduced, it was revived in aggravated form when Athens agreed to accept the Corcyrean alliance. The alarm spread to the other Peloponnesian states. It was not simply that this *démarche* violated the spirit of the Thirty-years' Peace. Since Corcyra had, next to Athens, the largest navy in Greece, the alliance would bring together an unrivaled armada.

The greatest tragedy of Greek civilization was now building up. Although he foresaw that the Peloponnesians would interpret the alliance as an act of war and although there were alternatives honorable to both Athens and Corinth, Pericles felt that he must go ahead with the plan. For Corcyra, if left unaided, would easily fall to Corinth, upsetting the balance of power in favor of the Peloponnesian League. In a last effort to save the peace, the Corinthian ambassadors begged the Ecclesia

Fig. 23a. Map to illustrate the Peloponnesian War. Insets show central Greece

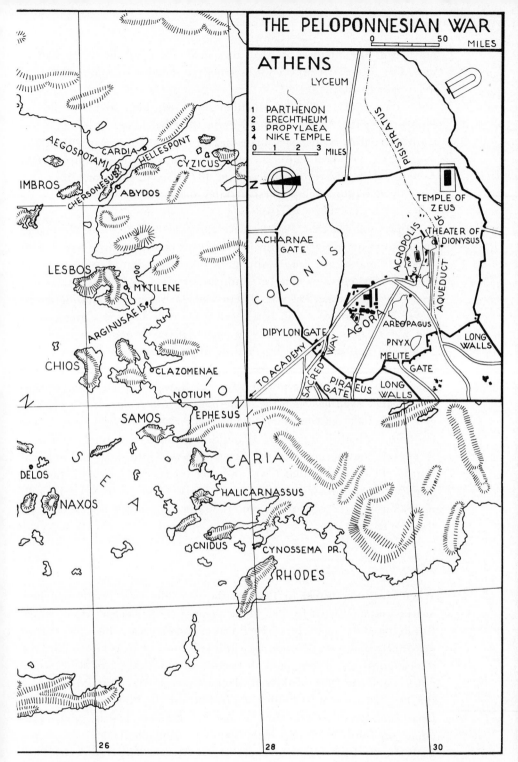

THE PELOPONNESIAN WAR

0   50

MILES

ATHENS

LYCEUM

1 PARTHENON
2 ERECHTHEUM
3 PROPYLAEA
4 NIKE TEMPLE

0   1   2   3

MILES

PISISTRATUS

AEGOSPOTAMI

CARDIA

HELLESPONT

CYZICUS

IMBROS

ABYDOS

CHERSONESUS

TEMPLE OF ZEUS

ACHARNAE GATE

COLONUS

ACROPOLIS

THEATER OF DIONYSUS

LESBOS

MYTILENE

AQUEDUCT

DIPYLON GATE

AGORA

AREOPAGUS

LONG WALLS

ARGINUSAE IS.

SACRED WAY

PNYX

CHIOS

CLAZOMENAE

TO ACADEMY

MELITE

GATE

NOTIUM

PIRAEUS GATE

LONG WALLS

SAMOS

EPHESUS

DELOS

CARIA

NAXOS

HALICARNASSUS

CNIDUS

CYNOSSEMA PR.

RHODES

S E A

26   28   30

in detail and plan of Athens.

not to vote the alliance, for that, they made clear, would surely lead to war. The fact that Corcyra was a renegade daughter-colony of Corinth did not help matters.

That same year, 432 B.C., Athenian and Corinthian troops clashed at Potidaea, on the Pallene promontory in the Chalcidice. Although a Corinthian colony, with Corinthian magistrates sent out yearly from the mother city, Potidaea had been forced into the Athenian Empire. When Athens, suspecting revolt, ordered the little city to dismantle its walls, Corinth and other Peloponnesian states sprang to its aid. Even so, no general war had been started.

To prevent just that, Pericles decided on a show of force. He placed an embargo on Megarian ships in every port of the Empire, less to ruin Megara economically for rejoining the Peloponnesian League than to warn Athens' enemies that he would never yield to threats nor be deterred by the prospect of war. There was also a personal consideration: if war had to come, it had better come while he had yet enough vigor (he was then sixty) personally to steer Athens through its perils.

But the policy of force miscarried. Menaced in their vital interests, Corinth and Megara goaded Sparta into declaring war for itself and the League. Sparta had come to regret its withdrawal from Greek leadership in the early seventies when the Hellespontine and Asian cities were begging to be liberated from Persia. It had let Athens take leadership by default, and Athens had gone on to build an empire, raise the largest navy in Greece, and accumulate the richest treasury—the first in European history. That empire, that navy, and that treasury were now a standing menace to every remaining free state. Fearful and, as Thucydides tells us, jealous of Athens' growing power, Sparta, after much hesitation, took the irreparable step.

Pericles' Leadership

When hostilities began in 431 B.C., the two sides were evenly matched. Sparta was supported by the whole Peloponnesus, except Argos, which still honored its own Thirty-years' Peace, and Achaea, which had turned neutral. By it stood, of course, Corinth and most of its colonies; Megara, the key to Attica; Thebes and all Boeotia except Plataea; most of central Greece; and the Dorian states of Magna Graecia. Athens could count on the over 300 cities of its Empire, on its faithful ally Plataea and the principal Thessalian states, on Naupactus, Ozolian Locris, and Acarnania, on Corcyra with its sister-islands of Cephallenia and Zacynthus, lastly on the Chalcidian states of Magna Graecia. Geographically then, Athens had the Peloponnesians surrounded. As most pro-Athenian states were Ionian, the war seemed to be one between Ionians and Dorians.

Eventually all Greece and some barbarians took sides. It was indeed the Greek World War.

The Peloponnesian League could equip about 100,000 hoplites and 200 warships. Athens, short on land forces (only about 30,000 soldiers), had naval preponderance with 100,000 sailors manning 500 triremes— 300 of its own and nearly 200 from Corcyra, Chios, and Lesbos, or Mytilene.

While the League had few financial difficulties, since each member-state financed its own contingents, for Athens this problem was serious. Still it faced the costs confidently. Assuming that the war would cost 1500 talents a year, Pericles calculated that by using the imperial tribute and borrowing from the tribute money in Athena's treasury Athens could fight six years without tax increases. If worst came to worst, the city could fight four more years by increasing taxation at home, emptying the treasuries of Athena and of the other gods, and selling the temple plate.

Pericles also laid down the strategy; the Athenians must let the Peloponnesian army wear itself out in frustrating movements simply by avoiding contact with it. Cattle, herds, and flocks were moved to Euboea; the rural families were brought, bag and baggage, inside the walls. Thus even if the land were devastated, the whole population would be safe, while sea-power would guarantee subsistence. Only a Pericles, however, could keep his infuriated compatriots from battle when they saw from the Acropolis their crops carried off and their farmhouses and orchards burned down.

For one reason or another, Pericles' miscalculated war exceeded his budget; it lasted twice ten years, its course was changed by a severe epidemic which killed, among others, Pericles himself, and when lesser men took over, it was incredibly mismanaged, to Athens' utter ruin.

In the first year of the war, Pericles delivered a speech at the state funeral of his fellow citizens fallen in their city's defense. He used the occasion to light up the entire panorama of the Athenian way of life. The Funeral Speech gives us insight into why the war was fought, what it meant to be Athenian, and why the Athenians preferred freedom to authority and democracy to other constitutions. It reveals, too, Pericles' intellectual quality. This precious document is preserved in Thucydides' version. Like Lincoln's Gettysburg Address, it will live through the ages for its formal, classical beauty and for its concept of democracy. A few passages are quoted herewith:

> We are rightly called a democracy, for the administration is in the
> hands of the many and not of the few. But while the law secures
> equal justice to all alike in their private disputes, the claim of excel-

Fig. 23.1. Mourning Athena, perhaps conceived as sadly reading the names of citizens fallen in defence of her city, but it has recently been argued, with many analogies from vase painting, that the relief is a dedication by an athlete. (Athens, Acropolis Museum)

lence is also recognized, so that when a citizen is in any way distinguished, he is preferred to the public service, not as a matter of privilege, but as the reward of merit. Neither is poverty a bar, but a man may benefit his country whatever be the obscurity of his condition. . . . In our private intercourse we are not suspicious of one another, nor angry with our neighbor if he does what he likes. . . .

Our city is thrown open to the world, and we never expel a foreigner or prevent him from seeing or learning anything of which the secret if revealed to an enemy might profit him. We rely not upon management or trickery, but upon our own hearts and hands. And in the matter of education, whereas they from early youth are always undergoing laborious exercises which are to make them brave, we live at ease, and yet are equally ready to face the perils which they face. . . .

If few of us are originators, we are all sound judges of a policy. The great impediment to action is, in our opinion, not discussion, but the want of that knowledge which is gained by discussion preparatory to action.

This manifesto of democratic ideals rings as true after 2400 years as if it had been issued by a modern—a Jefferson, a John Stuart Mill, a Lincoln. Reinforced by the living tradition of Anglo-Saxon liberalism, it has inspired thinkers and politicians on both sides of the Atlantic.

The capture of Potidaea (430 B.C.) was Athens' most substantial gain in the first years of the war. Reduced to cannibalism by a long siege, the inhabitants surrendered under a safe-conduct. Potidaea was repeopled with Athenians and their friends, bringing all Thrace under Athenian control. But for lack of space we must leave untold other moves and countermoves, or the acts of individual or collective heroism on either side and of individual or collective madness.

The Peace of Nicias

Besides the Peloponnesians, Athens had to fight its own rebellious subjects. After Pericles' death, Mytilene, an original member of the Delian League, joined the enemy. But, inadequately supported, it was forced to surrender unconditionally. Athens now decided to give a deterrent example of frightfulness. Cleon, Pericles' successor as democratic leader, carried the Ecclesia with a fiery speech urging death for the rebels and slavery for their families. As the Athenians considered their decision overnight, its enormity caused remorse which the moderates exploited by asking that the sentence be immediately reviewed. In the Ecclesia next day, one Diodotus argued that Athenian ferocity, far from quenching rebellion, would kindle it all over the Empire. The issue, he said, was not what Mytilene deserved but what was expedient for Athens. Diodotus carried the day, and a new set of messengers arrived at Mytilene just in time to save the inhabitants from massacre. The city however lost its independence. Its land rents were assigned to 3000 Athenian cleruchs, and its landowners reduced to helotry.

Cleon's setback served to identify him more closely with the party of war-to-the-death. Thucydides and Aristophanes, both aristocrats and hostile to the radical democracy, portray him as an ill-bred, evil-tongued, disreputable demagogue, a disgrace to Pericles' memory. The fact is that after Pericles' death a new type of leader emerged—men who climbed to office by the same rough-and-tumble methods they used in business. Cleon had been a tanner, and of his immediate successors Hyperbolus made lamps and Cleophon musical instruments. Although as commoners these new leaders were detested by men of Cimon and Pericles' class, some of them were able and honest patriots. Athenian democracy was now mature enough to develop its own leaders.

A comic-opera incident illuminates both Cleon's personality and post-Periclean democracy. The brilliant Athenian general Demosthenes had captured and fortified the peninsula of Pylos in southwest Peloponnesus, aiming to encourage a Messenian revolt and, by keeping Sparta on guard at home, to discourage its annual raids on Attica. But Sparta in turn blockaded Demosthenes by occupying Sphacteria, a small island

Fig. 23.2. *Nike* of Paeonius, perhaps dedicated after Sphacteria (425 B.C.) or the Peace of Nicias (421 B.C.). The goddess, originally on a triangular pedestal nearly 30 feet high, is represented just alighting upon earth. In lightness of treatment the piece anticipates the goddess of the Nike balustrade and the more famous Victory of Samothrace. (Olympia, Museum)

facing Pylos. When an Athenian relief expedition under Nicias failed to rout the Spartans, Cleon blustered before the Ecclesia that he himself, although no soldier, could teach Nicias how to capture the Spartan garrison in three weeks. Nicias was an aristocrat whose wealth came from the Laurium mines leased from the state and worked with slave labor. Incorruptible, almost superstitiously pious, and a believer in signs and portents, Nicias was a model of good citizenship. He had been repeatedly elected strategos by all who valued the old-fashioned virtues—as if mere respectability would make a general.

Now Nicias, resenting Cleon's aspersions, proposed to call the tanner's bluff and elect him general. Cleon tried in vain to wriggle out of this embarrassment. With astounding levity the Ecclesia elected him; actually, it took him just about his three weeks to capture the Spartan garrison and bring it captive to Athens (425 B.C.). A declaration that another Spartan raid on Attica meant death for the prisoners sufficed to insure immunity for the countryside. To these achievements Cleon added another. Excellent financier that he was, he trebled the tribute to an all-time high of 1460 talents. At the same time, to meet the higher cost of living he raised the jurors' wages from two obols to three.

The victory of Sphacteria, however, was neutralized by the loss of Amphipolis, an important Athenian colony on the Strymon. A Spartan general, Brasidas, captured it without unsheathing his sword, and from it he menaced both the Athenians' control of Thrace and the sea route to the Hellespont. The historian Thucydides, as admiral in northern waters, was rather capriciously exiled for not preventing Amphipolis' fall. Cleon, sent there in command of a strong expedition, was almost immediately killed in battle (422 B.C.), and Brasidas, also, suffered fatal wounds.

Cleon's death cleared the way to peace. Self-styled watchdog of democracy, he would have given no terms but those suiting the radical demos. Against him stood Nicias, solidly supported by the pro-Spartan oligarchs and by the conservative middle class whose business, farms, and investments had suffered most from the war. The democrats being leaderless, Nicias could compromise with Sparta on the basis of the *status quo ante bellum*. The Peace of Nicias (421 B.C.) was an Athenian triumph in that the Peloponnesians failed to achieve their war aim, the destruction of the Athenian Empire.

Pressing his advantage, Nicias concluded a Fifty-years' Alliance with Sparta. Most of Greece welcomed the prospect of a long peace. Since this new alliance meant, at least in principle, the elimination of the Peloponnesian League, Athens could congratulate itself. Aristophanes celebrated the event with a new comedy, *The Peace*. In a matter of months, however, it was discovered that Nicias had been outsmarted.

Alcibiades and the Demoralization of Democracy

The Peace of Nicias was signed by Sparta and most of the Peloponnesian states, but not by Corinth, which remained in a nominal state of war, nor by Thebes, which would neither restore war contraband nor return prisoners; and Thebes exasperatingly refused any agreement but a truce renewable for ten-day periods. Athens suspected Sparta itself of duplicity. Since Amphipolis refused to rejoin the Athenian Empire and Sparta claimed it could not force such compliance, Athens on its side refused to restore Pylos. A number of other clauses proved equally unrealizable.

That the Fifty-years' Alliance was precarious was proved when the signatory ephors failed of re-election and when Sparta signed a new pact with Thebes. True, this pact was aimed at protecting Sparta from now democratic Argos, whose Thirty-years' Peace with Sparta had just expired. But since Thebes was their uncompromising enemy, the Athenian democrats profoundly mistrusted the new alignment. Troubled also about Sparta's real intentions, they began to suspect that the Peace of Nicias had been a sham and a blunder. Making the Peace an issue, they refused to re-elect Nicias general, electing instead a young nobleman, Alcibiades.

Kinsman of Pericles, and brought up in his house, Alcibiades entered public life as a favorite of fortune. His brilliant mind and natural talents were sharpened in the sophistic schools. Contemptuous of conventions, irreverent towards the gods and insolent to men, he became the idol of the young set, who aped him in dress, speech, and manners. He was irresistible to men as to women, formidable in the Ecclesia, brave on the battlefield, dazzling in the display of wealth. The luxury of his household broke the frugal tradition of well-to-do Athenians. His good qualities—and he had many—won for him the friendship of the wisest man in Athens, the philosopher Socrates. A born leader, he seemed destined to play a leading role in Athenian affairs. But his persuasive charm and his genius for shaping the course of events led this supreme individualist to think of himself as exempt from normal human restraints, above laws and above constitutions. He could not be of the state—rather the state must be his to rule or to ruin.

Such was the man who, paying Sparta in its own coin, engineered a defensive alliance between Athens, Argos, Elis, and Mantinea. Argos, always angling for Sparta's place as leader of the Peloponnesus, attacked a Spartan ally, Epidaurus. Sparta came to its defense, and might well have succumbed to the Quadruple Alliance but for two circumstances. Democrats and aristocrats in Argos wasted Argive strength in a bitter class struggle, in which even a pair of aristocratic generals turned traitor. And in Athens, the oligarchs, in an effort to save the Spartan aristocracy, defeated Alcibiades for a third term as general (418 B.C.), re-electing Nicias instead. By this election the Athenian government served notice that it would not interfere too seriously; Sparta could thus have its showdown with Argos. Both Athenian and Argive events made clear that this was a class war, transcending state boundaries and superseding state loyalties. Although Athens could have tipped the balance toward democracy in the Peloponnesus—hence probably in all Greece—it failed as signally as in Cimon's time. In fact, political confusion followed Pericles' death. Aristophanes' attacks on democracy and those of that tough-minded reactionary pamphleteer, the "Old Oligarch," were beginning to tell. Caught in the crosscurrents, Athenian democratic leaders seem to have lost their bearings.

Despite his intention to help Sparta by remaining neutral, Nicias had to yield to the democrats' clamor for honoring the terms of the Quadruple Alliance. The help he sent, however, was too little and too late. Victory on the battlefield in 418 B.C. enabled Sparta to smother Peloponnesian democracy. Argos was forced to renounce its ambitions, accept an oligarchic government, and exchange its alliance with Athens for one with Sparta. Mantinea and Elis were dealt with more severely. The Peloponnesian League was revived, and Sparta re-emerged as the foremost Greek military power.

The democrats, seeing in Sparta's regained pre-eminence a new threat to the Empire, blamed Nicias' contradictory policy for their setback. Hyperbolus, the democrats' leader since Cleon's death, proposed ostracism. Alcibiades or Nicias must go: the former for engineering the Quadruple Alliance, the latter for betraying it. Hyperbolus felt certain that the electorate would vindicate Alcibiades, whose foreign policy matched the democratic party's. But Alcibiades, to make sure of the outcome, suggested to Nicias that they join forces against Hyperbolus. It turned out just as his fertile brain had contrived; Hyperbolus was ostracized (417 B.C.). This melodramatic twist brought ostracism into disrepute. The decay of this institution which had repeatedly insured steady policy was a symptom of the demoralization of Athenian democracy—leaders as well as electorate.

As junior partner to Nicias, Alcibiades found a way to spur the older man to action. The incorruptible Nicias declared war (416 B.C.) on the little island of Melos, which, to imperialist Athens, was enjoying the peace and prosperity provided by the Athenian League, itself contributing nothing. First an Athenian embassy tried to persuade the Melians of the wisdom of surrender. There are no more poignant pages in Greek literature than Thucydides' account of this conference, the Melian dialogue. The nobility of the Melians who reasoned that, since submission meant slavery, resistance was preferable, is contrasted with the Athenian boast that small states could not hope to defy Athens with impunity. The islanders' appeal to the Athenians' sense of justice and honor is countered with the cynical retort that justice and honor exist only among equals; small states should not invite risks when the path of expediency is safe. Melos should not forget that it is a law of nature that "the powerful exact what they can, and the weak grant what they must . . . This law was not made by us, and we are not the first who have acted on it; we did but inherit it, and shall bequeath it to all time, and we know that you and all mankind, if you were as strong as we are, would do as we do."

The Melians were easily overcome, whereupon their men were put to death, the women and children sold into slavery, and the land allotted to 500 Athenian cleruchs. This atrocity was intended as a double warning: to neutrals not to side with Sparta; and to the states of the Athenian

Empire not to dream of revolt. No other misuse of power brought on Athens more execration from the Greek world than this unprovoked attack on an innocent bystander.

The Sicilian Expedition

If the Melos affair was a crime, the expedition to Sicily a year later was a compound of genius and folly. By defeating Carthage at Himera in 480 B.C., Gelon, tyrant of Syracuse, had enhanced his city's prestige. In 474 B.C. his brother Hiero smashed the Etruscan fleet near Cumae. The prisoners and spoils of war enabled the Greeks of Magna Graecia to adorn their cities with architecture and sculpture and to enlarge their plantations and industries. Peace re-established, the dynasts had more leisure to compete at the Olympic Games in the chariot races immortalized by Pindar. But once the Carthaginian danger was past, the Sicilian Greek cities began to fight among themselves. At this point a democratic wave swept over the island. Syracuse and Acragas, even Selinus, now free from the Carthaginian incubus, became democratic republics.

The adoption of democracy did not prevent Syracuse from making a new bid for hegemony. In 445 B.C. it defeated Acragas. In that same year, the cavalry was doubled, the army reorganized, and plans made to add 100 triremes to the fleet. Worried by these developments, the cities of Leontini in Sicily and Rhegium across the Strait, both of Ionian origin, entered into an alliance with Athens. Two other cities, Segesta and Halyciae, had signed such a treaty earlier. Thus two groups developed in the West: one Dorian headed by Syracuse, the other mainly Ionian looking to Athens.

When the two groups came to open war in 427 B.C., with fortune on the Dorian side, the Ionians sent Gorgias of Leontini to Athens to invoke the help stipulated in the treaty. The talented orator and stylist easily persuaded the Athenians to send a few ships to restore Ionian morale. Unfortunately some Athenian incendiaries burned to convert Sicily into an Athenian domain. This threat prompted the Sicilian groups to bury the hatchet. At a conference held in Gela in 424 B.C. they agreed to the new policy of the Syracusan Hermocrates, that is, that amidst the perils of the Peloponnesian War their prime interest was peace. Sicily, a world to itself, should not get entangled in Greek mainland quarrels. This declaration of independence temporarily eliminated Athenian interference in Sicily. Even so Athens could congratulate itself that the Peloponnesians were equally barred.

The rise and fall of the Quadruple Alliance, the resurgence of Sparta, and most of all the frightful experience of Melos gave the Sicilian states, though neutral, cause for anxiety. And with reason, for Athens picked

Syracuse as its next victim on the pretext that, contrary to the Agreement of Gela, it had attacked two Athenian allies, Leontini and Segesta. Athens' real purpose was to prevent the western Dorian metropolis from aiding the Peloponnesian League in the event of a new general war. There was also the hope, first voiced by Cleon and recently repeated by Hyperbolus, of subjecting Sicily to Athens. Although Cleon was dead and Hyperbolus ostracized, the plan to attack Syracuse won assembly support. Nicias tried to discourage the expedition on the ground that while Athens was engaged in a distant war its subject-allies might revolt or the Peloponnesians attack at home. But practical reasons were dimmed by Alcibiades' vivid picture of the wealth and power that would come from a Sicilian war.

In 415 b.c. an armada of 130 supply ships, 134 triremes, nearly 7000 soldiers, and 20,000 sailors was placed under the joint command of three men of incompatible views—Nicias, a temporizer, Alcibiades, who optimistically foresaw a bloodless victory, and Lamachus, a professional soldier impatient to attack. The expedition was ready to sail when one night the hermae, or stone busts of Hermes and other gods, erected in the streets, were mutilated. This sacrilege, which in any case would have disquieted the populace, was exploited by Alcibiades' enemies who maliciously spread the rumor that he was responsible, intending to frighten the people and ultimately to overthrow the democracy. Foreseeing trouble for himself and the expedition if he set forth under this cloud, Alcibiades demanded an immediate trial, which was denied him through the maneuvers of the very parties responsible for the false alarm. They had reason to fear that a trial held while the sailors and soldiers who idolized him were still in Athens would result in acquittal. Alcibiades was forced to sail. The fleet ran into trouble when the Italian cities refused it admittance except for water and anchorage. The generals wasted time arguing over strategy. Lamachus' plan of attacking Syracuse at once was rejected in favor of Alcibiades' plan of winning allies in Sicily by parading the mighty armada off the coast. At this juncture the Athenian state galley arrived to summon Alcibiades to trial.

The mutilation of the hermae had meantime been traced to the members of an oligarchic club who testified in court that theirs was no sinister plot, but a drunken prank. But in the prevailing alarmist atmosphere a coterie of roistering blades was accused of burlesquing the Eleusinian Mysteries. Their conviction deepened anxiety for public safety and the preservation of the constitution. For it was an open secret that numbers of oligarchs, impotent since before Pericles' time to defeat the demos by the ballot, had gone underground in the guise of social clubs. Their plan was to confuse the public mind and soften morale by spreading rumors. Sophistic training enabled them to use propaganda to strike for power, even at the cost of betraying their country to Sparta. Conviction of the roistering band was used to build up popular clamor for trying Alcibiades also as its alleged leader. Alcibiades, however, while being escorted back to Athens, succeeded in eluding his guard and escaping to Sparta, where he ingratiated himself with his hosts and seduced the queen. He was now to bring a series of disasters on his native city by putting his genius at the enemy's disposal.

Meantime Nicias in Sicily moved camp from Catana to Syracuse where he defeated the Syracusan army, but instead of pressing his advantage, he went back to Catana into winter quarters. Although he had thus given Syracuse a breathing spell, when he returned in the spring of 414 B.C. he caught the enemy napping. Subsequent resistance, however brave and intelligent, was no match for the superiority of the Athenian army. Despite Lamachus' death in action, Nicias almost forced the enemy to surrender.

At this point Alcibiades tipped the scales against his own country by advising Sparta to do two things: send a capable general to Syracuse to rally the defenders, and station a permanent garrison at Decelea, in the center of Attica, for a year-round offensive, instead of the usual summer incursion. Gylippus, the commander sent by Sparta, quickly changed Nicias' position from besieger to besieged. The situation became so hopeless that in October (414 B.C.) Nicias asked Athens either to recall the expedition or to send a new armada as large as the first. In either event, he begged to be relieved of the command because of illness.

Before reinforcements arrived, Gylippus destroyed most of the Athenian fleet in Syracuse, bottling up the remnant in the Great Harbor. He also drove the army from its favorable position and seized the forts housing armor, food, and naval stores. The new armada was sent, seventy-three triremes and 8000 soldiers, but proved in the long run ineffectual. In July, 413 B.C., the Athenians abandoned the struggle. But Nicias delayed the departure some weeks while disease took its toll. On the night set for withdrawal (August 27), an eclipse of the full moon, which should have helped to mask their movements, was taken as an ill omen by most of the men, including Nicias. On his soothsayers' advice he put off the retreat for a month.

To prevent the Athenians' escape, Gylippus blocked every land and sea route. He narrowed the harbor mouth by anchoring a large number of ships broadside to prevent the Athenian fleet from making a dash for the open sea. When the breakthrough was finally attempted, it turned into a disaster; only sixty ships out of 110 got through. A worse fate was in store for the army. Although able to leave camp undetected, it found every road barred. Hemmed in on all sides, the Athenians were trampled by the Spartan cavalry and decimated in hand-to-hand encounters, so that they had no choice but to surrender. Seven thousand

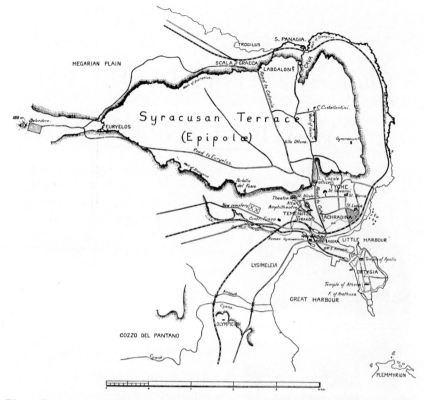

Fig. 23b. Syracuse. The great sea-battle of 413 B.C. was fought in the Great Harbor; the retreat was to the southwest. The Athenians had attacked also from the north, and a complicated system of walls and counter-walls was built on and about the height Epipolae. (*Klio*, Beiheft XXXVIII, 1938, at end.)

men, all that were left of nearly 50,000 soldiers and sailors, were brought captive to the city they had expected to enter as conquerors. No generosity was to be expected from a people exhausted from three years of siege and frequent near-capture. Nicias and his colleague, Demosthenes (who had commanded at Pylos), were put to death, the mercenary and allied troops sold into slavery, the Athenians herded into quarries to die from exposure, starvation, and thirst. The stench of their own filth and that of the dead which they were not allowed to remove made their agony more horrible. Spared were only a few who touched their captors' hearts by reciting some verses of Euripides. In the words of Thucydides, "Fleet and army perished from the face of the earth. Nothing was saved, and of the many who went forth few returned home."

The Sicilian disaster was the prelude to the fall of Athens itself, to which three interconnected causes contributed: the sophistic movement, exalting expediency over honor; rising anti-democratic sentiment in Athens; and the increasingly irresponsible policies of Athenian leaders, above all, Alcibiades.

Chapter 24/FALL OF THE
ATHENIAN EMPIRE

Constitutional Crisis

The Sicilian disaster produced a constitutional crisis, in which oligarchs and democrats combined to demand a change. In 412 B.C. the Boule, held responsible for the national calamity, was disbanded and replaced by a board of ten *Probouloi,* who, men hoped, would guide the Ecclesia more wisely. As a new fleet was the urgent need, the Probouloi raised funds by substituting for the old tribute an irritant, a 5 percent toll on the value of goods entering or leaving all Empire harbors except the Piraeus. At the angry protest of the subject-allies, the Piraeus' exemption was promptly cancelled. The gesture, however, could not prevent the revolt of most of the Empire. The rebels joined the Peloponnesian League which had continued fighting in Greece while the Athenians were engaged in Sicily. The latest policy had alienated even Athens' democratic friends and it paid the price exacted of tyrant-states that treat their allies as subjects instead of partners.

Persia's intervention at this point made the situation ominous for Athens. The Great King joined Athens' enemies through the plotting of Alcibiades. Finding Sparta unsafe after his affair with the queen, he fled to the court of Tissaphernes, satrap of the Anatolian coastal provinces. Alcibiades showed how Persia might gain by financing a fleet for Sparta, a fleet not large enough to make Sparta mistress of Greece, but of a size to exhaust both contestants and make Greece easy prey for the Great King. Alcibiades was playing a double game: taking vengeance on Sparta and laying the groundwork for his own return to Athens as savior. To the latter end he encouraged rumors that he could induce Tissaphernes to switch his support from Sparta to Athens.

Meantime the oligarchs, together with the landowners, whose estates the Spartans from Decelea were ravaging, and the businessmen, whose trade the loss of sea power had ruined, were plotting to overthrow the democracy. The poet Aristophanes had his share in raising doubts about the democrats' ability to handle a war. Early in 411 B.C. he produced two comedies, *Lysistrata,* a plea for peace, and *The Thesmophoriazusae,* an insinuation that the democrats had turned tyrants. The oligarchs pressed for a further constitutional change to save Athens. The Great King, they hinted, was willing to ally himself with the city, but not while it was run by the same radical democracy which through the Delian League had lost him his Asian and Aegean possessions. There was no question, they added, of abolishing democracy, but only of modifying it until the war was won. Even convinced democrats, troubled over colossal mismanagement, were induced to accept the change, disguised as a war measure.

In reaction against mob rule, active citizenship was limited to 5000, that is, to the wealthy, whose taxes had long paid the lower classes for jury and naval service. Since the government's blunders had made war finance the crucial problem, the wealthy demanded the sole direction of public affairs.

The conspirators were careful to make their *coup d'état* appear legal. They called the Ecclesia at Colonus, outside the city walls, exposed to Spartan attack. Thus only armed citizens attended, property-holders serving in the army. Without the masses, the conspirators could put over their plan practically unopposed. A council of Four Hundred took over the government and never summoned, or even registered, the five thousand to whom they were, theoretically, bound to refer all major decisions. Clearly the oligarchs had betrayed those well-meaning citizens who had followed them to Colonus.

This anti-democratic plot might have succeeded but for sailors and soldiers stationed at Samos who held that they alone were the legitimate government. Casting their lot with Alcibiades, chiefly to prevent his going over to the Four Hundred, they made him general, and he at once showed his uncanny genius. He persuaded the fleet and army to abandon their plan of forcibly ousting the Four Hundred, which would have meant civil war. Next he drove a wedge between the oligarchs, who to save themselves would gladly have betrayed the city to Sparta, and the moderates, who, although not whole-heartedly democrats, stood for Athenian independence. He thus peacefully eliminated the Four Hundred and got a new constitution adopted, midway between the oligarchic rule of the five thousand and mob-rule. The electorate was to number 9000, representing neither the few nor the many, but the middle class. One fourth of this body was to function each year as combined boule and ecclesia. Though the 9000 restored Athenian command of the sea and gave Athens, Thucydides says, the best rule it ever had, they were obliged to retire after only eight months. No force could stay the complete restoration of the Cleisthenean constitution.

A series of naval victories made unavoidable this people's government represented by men at Samos. In 411 B.C. the Peloponnesian fleet had been crippled at Cynossema and Abydos, and in the following year it was annihilated at Cyzicus, a success which brought Alcibiades triumphantly to Athens and democracy back to power. These exploits regained so solid a military advantage that no responsible democrat would accept a Spartan peace offer, fair though it was.

But the treasury was sadly depleted, the imperial revenue halved, and the income from industry drastically reduced. Wise management and a redistributed budget were the alternative to poverty. The lyre-maker Cleophon, schooled in Cleon's and Hyperbolus' tradition, became the financial genius of the hour. To create jobs, the Erechtheum was finished at this time. The daily wage—two drachmas, twice as much as the Parthenon workmen had received thirty-eight years earlier—suggests mounting inflation. Accordingly, the masses, now again in power, doubled the payment for jury service and other public employment. Cleophon also gave the unemployed two obols a day (*diobelia*), reflecting the growing feeling that the state owed the citizens at least a bare subsistence, an old idea to which impoverishment caused by war gave new impetus.

Determined to retrieve all their losses, the Athenians relied more than ever on Alcibiades. But the citizens knew he was not the ideal champion of democratic institutions. For he had betrayed his country, called democracy manifest folly, and declared that in this world the strong get what they want and the weak grant what they must. Since they saw no alternative, however, they sent Alcibiades (fall, 407 B.C.) to reconquer the rebel states.

Vae Victis

Unluckily for Alcibiades and for Athens, Darius II now had his son Cyrus instead of Tissaphernes as chief adviser for Greek affairs. Aiming to crush Athens at all costs, Cyrus subsidized Sparta to foment insurrections among Athens' remaining allies and built for it a bigger fleet than Athens could equal. Both funds and fleet were entrusted to the Spartan Lysander. Even so, the initiative was still with Alcibiades. But while he was absent on a mission, his lieutenant, disobeying fixed orders not to be drawn into battle, challenged Lysander at Notium (March, 406 B.C.) and was defeated. Alcibiades' enemies seized this excuse to destroy him politically. At the new elections they defeated him by charges that he had been tempted from his post by carnal pleasures. Fearing assassination, Alcibiades retired to his Thracian estates. His exultant enemies little knew that by destroying him they were destroying Athens itself.

With Persian subsidies, Lysander could offer higher wages to more than 30,000 oarsmen enlisted from all over Greece. To compete, Athenians took a series of emergency measures. They converted into coin the gods' silver plate; they stripped of their gold the statues of Victory and other gods to mint an unprecedented gold currency; taxed incomes ruthlessly; issued war bonds, that is, token money of copper redeemable at victory in silver; impressed metics and slaves as rowers, promising them citizenship; and even tried to make oarsmen out of ill-conditioned upper-class citizens.

The results were as magnificent as Athenian courage. At the Arginusae Islands (406 B.C.), the Athenian fleet sank 70 ships and disposed of 15,-000 sailors, almost half Lysander's forces. Even Callicratidas, Lysander's successor, lost his life. Unfortunately, in the hour of victory the sea rose and prevented the rescue of the crews of twelve unseaworthy Athenian warships. All of the eight commanding admirals were indicted for criminal negligence, even two who prudently had not come home. Two illegalities were involved: denial of separate trials guaranteed by Athenian law and the arbitrary decision that a conviction was to carry the death penalty. But the mob, misled by demagogues, controlled the verdict, and the mob hysterically threatened to try "by the same vote as the generals" everyone who counseled legality, moderation, or mercy. Only Socrates stood up to them. The mob voted "Guilty." The six generals present were executed, among them the younger Pericles. Not long after, however, the repentant Athenians decreed the prosecution of those who had deceived the people.

Even now, Sparta, troubled over its dependence on Persia, again offered peace. But its proposal to restore Decelea and then allow each side to keep what it had, met an unrealistic counterdemand that it relinquish also all it held of the Athenian Empire. So Sparta strengthened ties with Cyrus and restored Lysander to command, while Athens by a supreme effort equipped 180 more warships, manned by 6000 Athenians and 30,000 foreigners. To deter other Greeks from enlisting under Sparta, Athens amputated the right hand of every captured seaman.

Finally Lysander, in 404 B.C., placed his ships at the Hellespont entrance to starve Athens out and destroy its fleet. But before joining battle, he observed the habits of the Athenian fleet, operating from Aegospotami. He saw that after a sortie the men beached their ships and dispersed along the shore after food. Alcibiades, whose castle was nearby, came down to warn Athenians against this carelessness. But the leaders told him to mind his own business: they were generals now, not he; and so he went away. On the fifth day, when the Athenian sailors had dispersed as usual, Lysander made a lightning attack. He captured 160 warships, the biggest prize in Greek naval warfare, and seized practically every man. Only one of the generals escaped, Conon, with twenty ships. Three thousand Athenian prisoners, including all the other generals, were executed. In the words of Xenophon, when the evil tidings reached Athens,

> a bitter wail of woe broke forth. From the Piraeus following the line of the Long Walls up to the heart of the city, it swept and swelled, as each man to his neighbor passed on the news. That night no man slept. There was mourning and sorrow for those that were lost, but the lamentation for the dead was merged in even deeper sorrow for themselves, as they pictured the evils they were about to suffer, the like of which they had themselves inflicted upon the men of Melos. . . .

But the real outcome of the war was not so much Sparta's victory as the establishment of the vast financial resources of the Persian Empire as the decisive factor in Greek politics.

Lysander, in no hurry to storm Athens, left the Spartan army to besiege it, while he swept the sea of Athenian ships. Time and starvation would break down the defenders. In vain, Cleophon threatened death to anyone proposing surrender. Defeat, famine, discredit of the war party, political assassinations, and intensified oligarchic propaganda did Lysander's work for him. Formal negotiations opened after the firebrand Cleophon, victim of mob fickleness, was executed for evading military service. The terms were harsh: loss of every non-Attic Athenian possession, reduction of the navy to twelve triremes, tearing down of the Long Walls and the Piraeus fortifications, and reinstatement of political exiles. Athens, while retaining self-government, was made a Spartan ally, contributing men and money to its master. These conditions, no matter how onerous, at least permitted Athens to live. "After that," Xenophon tells us, "Lysander sailed into the Piraeus, the exiles were readmitted, and the fortifications and walls demolished with much enthusiasm, to the music of flute-girls, in the belief that that day was the dawn of freedom for Greece."

Once the walls were down and the city defenseless, the underground government came into the open. In a matter of months, the democracy was overthrown by the steady pressure of intimidation and murder, and most of all by the presence of Lysander's fleet in the harbor. A Commission of Thirty was set up, ostensibly to advise the Boule, actually to repeal the old anti-oligarchic laws hamstringing the Areopagus and creating the Heliaea. They aimed to put the clock back two hundred years. To forestall opposition to their future anti-democratic moves, the Thirty were delighted to have a Spartan garrison stationed on the Acropolis. Ousting their moderate fellow-members, they gradually unmasked themselves as lawless autocrats. They disfranchised, disarmed, and authorized the execution of all citizens and metics except 3000 pro-Spartan reactionaries.

In a few months of terror, the Thirty Tyrants executed 1500 Athenians and metics. They assigned the more odious arrests to men whom they wished to compromise, Socrates among others. But Socrates, tough timber at all times, ignored their orders. Thousands of citizens whose only crime was patriotism or democratic sympathies fled, only to be hounded by Lysander's agents and returned to the Thirty. Alcibiades himself, Lysander's bête noire, fell victim to the conquerors' vengeance. Thus after years of war Athens lost its fleet and its Empire, its independence and, for a time, democracy itself.

The Thirty were so hated and so clearly Lysander's tools that when an exiled patriot, Thrasybulus, reached Attica at the head of seventy men, every decent Athenian rallied to his banner. The presence of this little army divided the Thirty, the more moderate constituting themselves as the Ten. For some months Attica had three governments: the Ten in Athens, the Thirty entrenched in Eleusis, Thrasybulus' democrats in the Piraeus. Civil war suited Lysander. But Sparta, by now suspecting him of dangerous ambition, replaced him with King Pausanias, who offered general amnesty, with return of all exiles, and restoration of citizenship and property to every Athenian. Only the Thirty refused. Captured after nearly two years of resistance, they were executed, but their followers were granted amnesty. By the year 400 B.C., the terror and the civil war were over, and Athens was again a united state and a full democracy.

War and the Athenian Mind

The war did not stifle Athenian creative genius. During the war years were produced nine of the eleven extant comedies of Aristophanes (c. 450–385 B.C.) —masterpieces of wit, free speech, and outspoken criticism of radical democracy, whether for its bellicosity, toleration of graft, litigiousness, or overfondness for progressive education and *avant*

Fig. 24.1. Socrates. Here are the bald bulging forehead and the snub nose described by Plato, but behind the superficial ugliness the unknown Hellenistic sculptor has caught the fundamental gentleness and nobility of the inner man. (Rome, Villa Albani)

garde poets. Aristophanes was a good hater; his list included Cleon, Socrates, and Euripides, an ill-assorted group whose common claim to Aristophanes' detestation was an interest in new ideas. No one, it is said, dared to make the mask for the part of Cleon, whom the poet pilloried unmercifully in *The Knights* (424 B.C.), perhaps the most devastating political satire ever written. Socrates allegedly stood up in the theater, so that the audience could compare him with his actor-counterpart, throughout the performance of *The Clouds* (423 B.C.) which unfairly identifies him with the Sophists and which contributed twenty-two years later to his being condemned to death. *The Frogs* (405 B.C.) contains some side-splitting parodies of Euripides and a strongly-expressed preference for Aeschylus' old-fashioned morality. In *The Clouds* Aristophanes had been eloquent in praise of the old-fashioned pre-sophistic education, whose products were seen and not heard, went orderly to school under invariably arctic conditions, learned memory-gems and emphasized athletics, a eulogy which has been called perhaps the most charming invitation to the brainless life ever written. But for comic and lyric genius, for the insight they give us into the passionately partisan life of wartime Athens, Aristophanes' comedies are unequaled.

Through the whole of the Peloponnesian War waddles the paunchy figure of fifth-century Athens' most influential thinker, educator, and martyr, the philosopher Socrates (469–399 B.C.). His boundless curiosity, his intolerance of "sacred cows," his great moral and physical courage made him the idol of young men, who clustered about him as he sat in the palaestra, questioning the unexamined assumptions on politics, ethics, art and everything under the sun of politicians, artisans, and poets. He called himself a gadfly, and Athens did not realize how much it needed him. He asked upsetting questions but would give no comforting answers—the only valid educational method. His faith in man's essential goodness and in the immortality of the soul did not save him from the enmity of men whose self-conceit he had wounded. In 399 B.C. the Heliaea tried him for atheism and subversive activity and condemned him to death. While the charges had a basis in his association with aristocratic youth, that does not excuse the verdict. His defense as recorded in Plato's *Apology* is magnificently eloquent and courageous. Refusing the opportunity to escape from prison, he spent his last hours conversing with his friends and took the hemlock calmly and without rancor, confident that no harm can befall a good man in this world or the next. Athenian democracy made him a martyr, but his spirit is deathless; it lives on wherever men of outspoken courage are willing to die for what they believe.

The Peloponnesian War is fortunate in its historian, Thucydides (c. 460–400 B.C.), unique in historiography for his ability to generalize from the particular. Child of a sophistic age, influenced by the medical writers and by tragedy, his history is at once practical—intended as a political handbook—scientific, and artistic. In speeches, he derived from specific situations great generalizations. The plague at Athens became the symbol of disease in the body politic, civil strife in Corcyra an anatomy of revolution; arrogance at Melos was followed dramatically by disaster in Sicily. He believed that lessons could be learned from history; with rigid accuracy he drew conclusions from evidence, sought historical causes, austerely refused to romanticize history, which he saw for what it is—a naked struggle for power. We have seen how his treatment of Pericles' Funeral Speech makes that oration the eternal declaration of faith in democracy wisely led, tolerant, just, open, non-snobbish, generous, resting firmly upon active citizen participation. His history is a tragedy; for him the death of Pericles was the end of Athens' greatness. Though he was not without bias, hating Cleon and the masses, pitying Nicias, admiring Pericles, the austere incisiveness of his mind makes his history what he proudly claimed it to be: "A possession for eternity, and not a prize composition for the present moment."

Thucydides' work, as we saw, was influenced by the medical writers active in Athens in the Periclean Age and after, of which the chief was Hippocrates. A contemporary of Socrates, to him is ascribed the famous Hippocratic oath still taken by doctors today. He analyzed the symptoms of diseases as Thucydides analyzed those of war and, like him, was not satisfied with supernatural explanation. According to him, diseases of men and of society pass through crises; clinical study will help the physician—and the historian—to build up the patient's power of resistance. Physicians examined particular instances, wrote case histories, to reach valid diagnoses and new conclusions. The physicians treated their patient by diet, herbs, or operations—without anesthetic. Their descriptions enable us to recognize diphtheria, typhoid, epilepsy, and Cheyne-Stokes breathing. They set a standard of medical ethics which is still a model for the profession; within limits they were true scientists, with a sense of vocation suggested by the famous aphorism: "Life is short, the Art long, the occasion urgent, experience deceptive, decision difficult; yet the physician must be ready to do his duty, and patient, attendants, and circumstances must cooperate if there is to be a cure." Greece itself was now desperately ill; it will be our next business to analyze the course of the disease.

Chapter 25/LIBERTY

AND CHAOS

Lysander

Greece clearly needed unity so that men might live and work in peace. The victorious Lysander could have replaced the Athenian Empire with a confederation of autonomous cities cooperating in foreign relations. He might, for example, have imitated the Peloponnesian League, in which Sparta was pre-eminent, but without authority either to impose tribute or to interfere in member states' internal affairs. Or he might have learned a lesson from the scores of vengeful cities which rose to destroy Athens for the humiliation and injustice they had suffered.

But the opportunity that Lysander saw was for himself. The vacuum created by the Athenian Empire's fall seemed made to order for his rise as a Panhellenic ruler. Though arrogant and unscrupulous, he was a magnificent general, who, uniquely among Spartans, knew how to handle free men. As Themistocles 75 years earlier had envisaged an all-democratic Greece under Athenian leadership, so now Lysander conceived another kind of union, based on oligarchy and led nominally by Sparta, but actually by himself. He established in every city, as he had done in Athens, a decarchy, that is, he turned the government over to ten local oligarchs who disfranchised or exiled the democrats, confiscated their property or took their lives. Beside each decarchy he placed a Lacedae-

* Portion of the decree establishing the Second Athenian League.

monian harmost, governor in everything but name; and often he quartered on a city a Spartan-commanded mercenary garrison like the one he had lately established in Athens. He strengthened his position at home by sending there yearly a thousand talents, a fantastic bonanza for Sparta, representing the tribute imposed by the "liberator" on Athens' helpless ex-subjects. Lysander shrewdly collected it, not through Spartan agents, but through his compliant decarchies.

The ephors at Sparta winked at these practices, for the passions unloosed by war often make governments as well as individuals callous to injustice. But when it dawned on them that Lysander aimed to make himself the uncrowned king of Hellas, they resolved to strip him of power. In his megalomania he had sought to have the oracles of Apollo at Delphi and Zeus at Dodona declare him a second Lycurgus, godsent to remodel the Spartan constitution; to the same end he visited a third sanctuary, that of Zeus Ammon in Egypt. Failing to persuade divine revelation to connive at his self-aggrandizement, he concentrated on having his friend, the lame Agesilaus, elected king, confident that his beneficiary would make a complacent tool. But Agesilaus, with the ephors' support, relegated Lysander to private life within a matter of months.

The new king served Sparta well, but nowhere better than in Asia's war with Persia. We have seen that in return for wartime subsidies Sparta had agreed to hand over to the Great King the cities which had been Persian before Athens absorbed them. However, faced with the execution of the agreement, Sparta saw the difficulty of casting itself as both hero and villain in the same play, liberating Greek cities from Athens in one act and delivering them to Persia in the next. War by roundabout methods seemed a solution to this dilemma. Limited hostilities designed to help preserve the freedom of some Ionian cities became serious in 399 B.C. when 6000 roving hoplites who had good reason to be contemptuous of Persia enlisted.

The Ten Thousand

We must retrace our steps to identify these men. They were remnants of a fantastic expedition led by Cyrus, Persian viceroy of West Asia, two years earlier, against his brother, Artaxerxes II. Cyrus, who toward the end of the Peloponnesian War had substituted for Tissaphernes' Machiavellianism a genuine alliance with Sparta, had seen and admired at first hand Greek fighting qualities. Knowing that Persia could not match the hoplites' striking power, he decided at the war's end to hire Greek regiments and seize the Persian throne.

Dynastic rivalries had afflicted the Persian Empire ever since the death of its founder, Cyrus the Great. Repeatedly, two or three pretenders had provoked civil war over a vacant throne. Nor did the successful rival, once installed, enjoy impunity. The mighty Xerxes himself was assassinated; the murderer reigned until driven out by one of Xerxes' sons. These dynastic feuds would have dismembered the Empire but for the powerful administrative machinery established by Darius the Great. When Darius II died (405 B.C.), Artaxerxes II succeeded him, although the queen-mother Parysatis had tried hard to secure the throne for her younger son Cyrus.

Cyrus surreptitiously collected 10,000 Greek hoplites (401 B.C.) and 3000 light-armed troops, besides a Persian army. The Greeks were told they were to fight some nearby foe, perhaps Cyrus' implacable enemy Tissaphernes. The actual muster was entrusted to an exiled Spartan general, Clearchus—first of a long line of professional captains-for-hire—and four of his friends. Among the privates was Xenophon, an Athenian nobleman, once Socrates' pupil and later a prolific writer.

The phenomenon of thousands of Greeks enrolling as mercenaries in foreign or Greek civil wars deserves attention. It shows that, despite war losses, Greece had a surplus and impoverished population which sought sustenance by hiring itself out abroad. Industry, agriculture, and commerce, although expanding throughout the fourth century, could not absorb everyone. New colonies might have absorbed the excess, but the civilized world was guarded by strong powers, Carthage, Rome, Persia itself, and Macedon, while the uncivilized territories north of the Black Sea and east of the Adriatic held no attraction. The war had bred in thousands of men a lust for excitement and plunder. Moreover, many preferred military service abroad to political insecurity at home. The city-state itself, perennially in or on the verge of revolution, had ceased to enlist men's loyalty. There was also widespread disillusion about the ideals which had motivated the war. Had not Sparta become a worse tyrant than Athens? And was not the unholy alliance of foreign despots and local opportunists in hundreds of cities destroying liberty, property, and lives in the name of oligarchy? In the resulting restlessness, men of every class sought escape in mercenary service.

It was with such Greeks, veterans of many campaigns, ill-adjusted to the postwar world, that Cyrus marched over deserts for days, weeks, and months until he met the Persian army at Cunaxa, forty-five miles from Babylon. Although outnumbered, the hoplites smashed the enemy's infantry. But Cyrus' cavalry was inadequate, and hoplites, however brave, were no match for cavalry ten or twenty times their number. Even so, Cyrus succeeded in wounding the king, but was himself killed.

Persian weakness was now revealed; the king hesitated to attack the Ten Thousand trapped in the heart of the Empire. In contrast, according to Xenophon, the invincible Greek spirit, coolness, and discipline pulled the Ten Thousand out of a nasty situation. Giving a promise not to pillage in return for regular food deliveries, they accepted Tissaphernes' offer to guide them along the Tigris towards the Armenian wilderness and the friendly Black Sea coast. They distrusted the satrap, but Cyrus' death left them no alternative but to continue to rely on him. He invited Clearchus and his staff to a dinner party ostensibly to discuss way of escape, actually to have them arrested, sent to the king in chains, tortured, and put to death.

This was the worst crisis for the Ten Thousand; yet they faced it coolly by electing new officers, including Xenophon. The new staff had to lead the Ten Thousand among the perils of wild and unknown Kurdistan and South Armenia, not least of which perils was the hostility of uncivilized tribes. In time the Greeks found it safer to dismiss their Persian guides and trust to themselves. Through dense forests they marched, past deep gorges, over endless mountain passes, for seemingly endless months, aware that their only hope of safety lay in their own wit and courage.

Their reward came one memorable day when from a height the men in the van caught a glimpse of the Black Sea seventy or eighty miles to the north. ' "The Sea! The Sea!" they cried.' ' "The Sea! The Sea!" '— that is, civilization and home—was echoed amidst tears and laughter from company to company down the entire line. This dramatic account comes from the *Anabasis* of Xenophon, the historian of that incredible expedition.

Anti-Spartan Coalition

Back in civilization, few of the Ten Thousand returned to their homes. Hundreds enlisted under professional captains or in city-state armies. About 6000 joined the before-mentioned Spartan army which was helping the Asian Greek cities' fight for freedom from Persia. With their enlistment the war of liberation prospered. It turned into a crusade when, shortly afterwards, Agesilaus took command. At the head of these seasoned veterans, he overran the western satrapies at will, delivering one city after another from the barbarian's hold. Gradually as he learned from the Ten Thousand to scorn the strength of Persia and saw for himself its powerlessness, he aspired to conquer the great empire. But Sparta, by acquiescing in this plan, was faced with war on two fronts; in Asia against the Great King, in Greece against a combination of states impatient of tyranny.

The dual rule of local decarchies and Lacedaemonian harmosts does not exhaust the grievances of the cities of the ex-Athenian Empire. One and all were treated like conquered enemies instead of like liberated friends. The forced tribute, twice as much as under Athens, hurt much more than martial law or oligarchic misrule. Thoughtful Greeks saw that these levies, inconsistent with the Lycurgan system, marked an ominous change in Spartan tradition and character.

Spartan imperialism was evident chiefly in Athens where it had insured doubly against any democratic revival. The Thirty Tyrants ruled for Sparta, and a Spartan garrison ruled the Thirty Tyrants. Watching over people and government from its station on the Acropolis, the occupation force was a daily reminder that insurrection was folly. The democracy that succeeded the Thirty had no choice but to be equally subservient, since Athens had no fleet, no friends, and no walls.

Fortunately for Athens, Spartan refusal of a just share of spoils caused the Peloponnesian allies to fall apart on the morrow of victory. Corinth began to befriend openly every Athenian exiled by the Spartan-supported oligarchs. Theban expansion too was blocked. Had it been permitted to march northward towards Thessaly and subject certain eastward harbors, Thebes might well have overbalanced Sparta. Hence the latter's opposition to either move. But Sparta's rivals chiefly feared its possible use of its 1000-talent revenue to increase further its military strength.

Resigned outwardly to subservience, Athens was secretly contemplating revolt. The malcontents included the victims of the Thirty, the patriots smarting at the city's downfall, the unemployed ex-sailors, the merchants whose maritime trade had vanished, the cleruchs expelled from their homesteads and sent back home as beggars. Impressed by this wave of anti-Spartan feeling, Thebes entered into cordial relations with Athens.

A trival border incident gave Sparta a pretext for declaring war on Thebes (395 B.C.), which Athens promptly assisted. The Spartan campaign failed miserably. Lysander, recalled from retirement, was killed in battle before Haliartus; his death was blamed on the cowardly delay of Pausanias, one of the kings, whom the Spartans condemned to death. The king escaped by refusing to return to Sparta. These reverses prompted Corinth, Argos, and other states, supported by Persian gold, to join the Athenian-Theban alliance (395 B.C.). The coalition soon empowered Athens to rebuild its Long Wall and the Piraeus fortifications. Fearing an invasion of the Peloponnesus, Sparta felt obliged to recall Agesilaus from his Asian triumphs.

The struggle for Corinth (394–390 B.C.) was the most spectacular phase of the war. Sparta, so long as it held Corinth, could prevent the Athenian and Theban armies from joining those of Argos and Corinth. Conversely, the allies needed Corinth as an assembly point for invading the Peloponnesus. Corinthian traitors helped the Spartans to break through the city walls and occupy a section of the Isthmus. At this juncture, Athens, with a touch of its old bravery and inventiveness, recaptured Corinth's walls, which Athenian masons promptly repaired. But shortly afterwards Agesilaus bottled up Corinth effectively and awaited an early and total victory.

Corinth's plight led to an unparalleled development in Greek constitutional history, a union of Corinth with Argos, with common citizenship, government, and army. This auspicious achievement was followed by another. An Athenian general, Iphicrates, had trained a mercenary force in a new method of warfare. He equipped his peltasts (Greek: *peltē*, a small round shield) for greater speed and maneuverability and thus defeated the clumsier Spartan hoplites. Iphicrates' victories forced Agesilaus to abandon Corinth and return home to forestall a possible attack on Laconia (390 B.C.).

The military stalemate could be broken only by diplomacy, and Sparta took the initiative. It convinced Artaxerxes that, in view of the Athenian menace, a Spartan-Persian rapproachment would be advantageous to both sides. Indeed Athens' able democratic civilian administrator Thrasybulus, its admiral Conon, and its general Iphicrates had made it again a power to be reckoned with. Again solvent, Athens could withdraw from circulation the emergency bronze currency it had coined when it lost the Empire, minting instead the gold and silver Conon had procured from Persia. Persian gold had equipped for Conon a fleet, with which he had defeated the Peloponnesians in the battle of Cnidus (394 B.C.). Athens had reconquered its bases in Imbros, Lemnos, and Skyros and regained its pre-eminence in the Pontic wheat market. Through the recapture of Delos it again headed a maritime coalition of cities in the islands, the Hellespont, the Bosporus, and Asia Minor itself. And Conon was working like a new Themistocles towards a grand alliance with Cyprus on the east and Syracuse on the west which, if consummated, would have endangered Persia as much as the rest of Greece. Sparta pointed out, too, that radical democracy would certainly seek to recover all its former possessions, including the Asian cities ruled by the Great King. So Sparta gained by diplomacy what it had not been able to gain by force of arms.

Painfully aware that they could not beat a Spartan-Persian coalition, the allies accepted the Great King's summons to Sardis (387 B.C.). Here he laid claim to Clazomenae, Cyprus, and the Ionian mainland cities, demanded freedom from Athens for every Greek state but Lemnos, Imbros, and Skyros, and threatened reprisals with troops, ships, and money against any state that disliked his terms.

A general congress, called to Sparta the following year (386 B.C.), ratified the barbarian's dictate. In return for a free hand in Greece, Sparta abandoned to the Great King every Asian Greek city. "Freedom from Athens" meant in fact freedom to go on fighting as before, freedom to sink deeper into anarchy and chaos. No federations and no attempts at unity were permitted. Argos and Corinth were forced to dissolve their federal ties, Thebes to renounce its ambition of founding a united states of Boeotia, Athens to give up its reborn maritime league. But the Peloponnesian League was tacitly recognized, and Sparta permitted to assert supremacy under the hypocritical slogan, "liberty for every state." This was a far cry from the days of Leonidas and his fellow-Spartans who gave their lives for the preservation of Greece.

It humiliated the Greeks to think that these arrogant terms had been forced on them by a barbarian whom they had consistently beaten on land and sea. The Great King was master. Named with obvious irony the King's Peace, the Persian dictate was indeed the humiliation of Greece.

Sparta's Misadventures

After 386 B.C. the Greek world had three masters: Greece proper with the islands was under Sparta, Asia under the Great King, the West under Dionysius the Elder, tyrant of Syracuse. Sparta's problem was the most difficult, both because Sparta was inexperienced in empire and because the love of liberty was strongest in its sphere of influence. The Greek cities of Asia, both the "autonomous" ones and those which passed to Persia, submitted uncomplainingly to the power of the Great King. As members of the world's greatest empire, their market for agricultural and industrial products expanded. After the Peace they minted more silver, electrum, and gold, an index of increased prosperity. Dionysius, who, although not a signatory to the treaty, was apparently in league with Sparta, could without interference extend his kingdom from Sicily to the upper Adriatic.

Sparta under Agesilaus bungled as it had under Pausanias in the 470's and more recently under Lysander. Sometimes it would oust a legitimate democratic government and banish the leading democrats; again it would wage a kind of cold war, climaxed by a demand that a city surrender its citadel. To keep Greece disunited, it crushed a League headed by Olynthus in the Chalcidian peninsula. It compelled democratic Mantinea to dismantle its walls and resettle its citizens in open villages shorn of the dignity of city-statehood. After forcing Thebes to relinquish its sovereignty over Boeotia, Sparta recognized separate Boeotian city-states, each "protected" by a Lacedaemonian garrison. Thebes was thus encircled— in the name of liberty for every Greek. Sparta's real intention soon transpired. A Spartan captain en route to Thrace seized the Theban acropolis (Cadmea) on the day when the men customarily left it to a woman's festival. Although Sparta fined the captain to conciliate public opinion, it kept 1500 Lacedaemonian soldiers in the citadel. Then it re-

settled Plataea, abandoned since the Peloponnesian War, with its few surviving exiles and the descendants of the rest. Although most Greeks
thought this an act of justice long overdue, there was no altruism involved. A friendly Plataea on the Boeotian-Attic border made an excellent base for controlling both.

Theban patriots struck back hard. Theban exiles went about preaching
that, for the common good, Sparta must be stopped. Seven underground
leaders, including one Pelopidas, engineered a fantastic plot. Disguised
as field workers, they entered Thebes along with peasants returning home
at dusk. An accomplice, secretary of the Board of Generals, offered the
Board a banquet, promising them seven beautiful women, who turned
out, of course, to be the conspirators bearing concealed arms. The generals were killed, the imprisoned patriots freed, a call to arms raised,
and when other armed refugees entered the gates as prearranged, the
revolution was an accomplished fact. The Spartan troops holding the
Cadmea surrendered, and a democratic constitution was adopted.

Sparta resumed its offensive with a new piece of brigandage, this time
against Athens, though Athens had honorably explained to Sparta its part
in the Theban affair and had even executed a general for letting Athenian volunteers join the revolutionists. Even so a Spartan harmost from
Thespiae decided, possibly on his own, to capture Attica to compensate
for the loss of Thebes. But his plan to surprise the Piraeus by night
miscarried; sunrise caught him some ten miles from his objective. Though
this attempt at conquest was a breach of international law, Sparta ab-
solved its perpetrator.

Victims both of Spartan treachery, Athens and Thebes joined forces.
Meantime several maritime states, ex-members of the Athenian Empire,
tired of Spartan imperialism. Interpreting the victory of Cnidus and the
rebuilding of the Long Walls as foreshadowing Athens' resurgence, they
began to cultivate its friendship. The attempt on the Piraeus was an unmistakable warning that no state was immune from aggression; they
sought a common defense. The inscription survives recording the agreement (377 B.C.) "to compel Lacedaemon to let the Greeks enjoy peace in
freedom and independence with the lands unviolated." Before long the
states formed around Athens an alliance which included provisions to
prevent its being perverted into a second Empire.

Membership in the League was open to any state not controlled by the
Great King. Members were guaranteed freedom from outside interference,
foreign garrisons, tribute, or cleruchies; in turn, they promised mutual
assistance in war. In the League constitution, Athens avoided the mistakes
of its first Empire. A council (*synedrion*), in which each member had one
vote, met in Athens. The Athenian boule referred the synedrion's resolutions, especially those on war and peace, to the Ecclesia for ratification,

after which they became laws (*dogmata*). For finance there was a common war chest, supplied by voluntary contributions, not tribute, the annual amount being fixed by the synedrion and the Ecclesia after a budget request by the generals. This confederacy was the Greek's best effort at federation to date, and a first attempt at representative government. It lasted, with vicissitudes, until 338 B.C.

At first, especially with Thebes as one of its 70 to 75 members, the League was a great success. Athens made public an inventory of its own resources (6000 talents), and groups (symmories) of rich Athenians consented to an income tax (*eisphora*) in order to finance Athens' new major role in the world. Callistratus, the new Athenian leader, was talented; naval successes by the Athenian admiral Chabrias induced new cities to join the League, and prompted Sparta to accept an Athenian offer to treat for peace (374 B.C.). Within two years Athens broke the peace, but the League treasury was impoverished, and, in 371 B.C., by the Peace of Callias, the League induced Sparta to guarantee the autonomy of member states, to recognize the League's rights over Amphipolis and the Chersonesus, and to withdraw all garrisons. Thebes now weakened the League by withdrawing in a pique because Sparta would not recognize its hegemony in Boeotia. And as Sparta weakened, contributions to the League fell off, so that from 371 B.C. the League declined and Theban power rose.

Thebes now, through the genius of one Epaminondas, established the most democratic government in its history, built up the most powerful army in Greece, and centralized Boeotia into a federal state. Epaminondas, the inspirer of those moves, was a younger friend and admirer of Pelopidas, the patriot conspirator; he is said to have had all the Greek virtues and none of the Greek defects; he was a cultured gentleman, especially talented in music, a serious thinker, and a first-class general. Though a strong partisan and patriot, he was fair to oligarchs in Thebes and elsewhere. He spoke seldom, but when he did he impressed his auditors deeply. He was a politician who died poor—as rare an event then as now.

Epaminondas' dramatic withdrawal from the peace conference of 371 B.C. gave Sparta an excuse to force Thebes to break up its Boeotian League. But three weeks after the conference ended, Greece was stunned by the news of a Spartan disaster at Leuctra. The myth of Spartan invincibility was shattered in a day. A revolution in tactics had taken place, and Epaminondas was its author. The 12,000 Spartans, as disciplined and brave as ever, fought as usual in ranks twelve deep, but the Thebans, half their number, first puzzled the enemy with their maneuvers, then threw them into complete disorder. The Thebans attacked in a phalanx fifty men deep, spearheaded by the Sacred Band, a body of 300 daredevils, fighting in pairs, and sworn to win or die together. Baffled and crushed, the Spartans lost 400 peers, King Cleombrotus among them; and the losses of its Peloponnesian allies were still heavier. With the ruin of Sparta's prestige at Leuctra, its influence in Greek affairs was gone forever.

But Athens failed to see the significance of Sparta's defeat. It rejected a Theban alliance in favor of an attempt to win over ex-members of the Peloponnesian League, an attempt which entangled Athens hopelessly in Peloponnesian intrigues. Sparta, frightened of a direct attack by Epaminondas, proposed to its ancient rival (369 B.C.) an amalgamation of their two Leagues. Of this the synedrion took a doubtful view, and members began to fall away. Athens then turned to Dionysius, tyrant of Syracuse, and Jason, tyrant of Pherae in Thessaly, which antagonized its allies still further. It turned also to Persia, but Persia preferred a Theban alliance. In all these moves, Athens was thinking of itself first and the League second; it ignored the synedrion and infringed on the autonomy of member-states. Epaminondas, Mausolus of Caria, wars in central Greece, the rising threat of King Philip of Macedon, dealt successive blows to the League, which now appeared a pale reflection of the old Empire. Doomed to impotence from the beginning by the poverty of its resources, the lack of understanding among its members, and the narrowness of its aims, the League was broken by the intrigues of Persia and the implacable jealousy of Thebes.

Chapter 26/UNIFICATION
UNDER PHILIP
OF MACEDON

The Failure of Thebes

Its military prestige lost at Leuctra, Sparta could no longer maintain its pre-eminence either in Greece or in international affairs. Pelopidas and Epaminondas, the authors of its downfall, pressed their advantage. Although the Theban people favored peace, Epaminondas' eloquence persuaded them that this was their hour of imperial destiny.

Epaminondas planned first to subject central Greece, which lay close at hand, and teemed with men, horses, crops, and timber—the essentials of empire-building. Luck played into his hands. Jason of Pherae, who had unified Thessaly as preliminary to unifying all Greece for his own ends, was assassinated by one of his kinsmen. A family struggle split Thessaly into three or four warring camps until a prince, Alexander, restored unity. Thebes was fishing in these troubled waters when Alexander arrested Pelopidas during an interview the latter had solicited. Released a year later, Pelopidas resolved to repay the insult with interest. Alexander was a savage. His rule of terror drove the Thessalian cities to appeal to Thebes for relief just when Thebes was most eager to take them under its protection. Theban troops were pursuing the fleeing Alexander when Pelopidas galloped past his companions to get his man—only to be killed himself by the king's bodyguard. But Alexander was forced to surrender and permitted to keep only Pherae. The rest of Thessaly became a satellite confederacy under Thebes, and the whole of central Greece also soon fell.

The imperialists envisaged Theban control of the Peloponnesus, too. When the Peloponnesian cities realized that Leuctra meant the end of Spartan supremacy, they were successively rocked by revolution. Aristocracies could not survive without the help that Sparta had traditionally offered; the democratic spirit which had made the Theban government and army invincible spelled the doom of aristocratic government. Fortune's wheel had turned, and the Peloponnesus lay open to invasion. Thebes, like Sparta in the old days, could now overrun the peninsula with impunity. The Peloponnesian League itself, once a pillar of stability, had ceased to exist. Democratic forces now emerged in practically every state, expelling the Spartan harmosts, seizing the governments, and driving the aristocrats out or cudgeling them to death, thus demolishing the political and social structure which Spartan hegemony had held together for centuries.

Twice Epaminondas, with unprecedented effrontery, marched to the very edge of the city of Sparta, which meant real danger, for Sparta was an open city, purposely kept unwalled to assure the martial spirit of its sons. The danger of an internal upheaval was imminent, first, because the reactionary ruling class, clinging to the Lycurgan system, had let the number of warrior-citizens dwindle to a mere 1500; second, because the masses, disinherited and disfranchised, were ripe for revolution. But the day of reckoning was to wait for another 150 years. Though Agesilaus enrolled 6000 helots by promises of citizenship, several perioeci towns and innumerable helot villages went over to the enemy. Sparta was saved by Athenian reinforcements, for Athens, fearing Theban imperialism more than it feared Sparta, had changed sides. Sparta had repeatedly been considerate towards Athens. A powerful Spartan faction with a counterpart in Athens had always held that peaceful coexistence best served the interest of both cities. But Thebes had until recently been an uncompromising foe. Indeed when Thebans and other hotheads had wanted Athens wiped out at the end of the Peloponnesian War, Sparta had saved it.

Although Epaminondas failed to take Sparta, he curbed its power by helping its ancient enemies to regain independence. The Mantinean expatriates abandoned their drab villages to rebuild their city, endowing it with a democratic constitution, a theater, a market place, and impregnable walls. Arcadian cities formed a defensive confederacy against

Fig. 26.1. Messene: walls, towers, and battlements, the finest surviving work of their period in continental Greece.

interference from Sparta or anyone else. A brand new city, Megalopolis (the Great City, built 370–362 B.C.), served as federal capital and urban center for several rural communities combined as a city-state. The federal legislature had two houses: an Assembly, the Ten Thousand, comprising the citizens of the component city-states; and an elected Council of Fifty. Even Tegea, long a pro-oligarchic Spartan ally, joined the Arcadian Confederacy.

Messenia too gained independence. A new city, Messene, rose, partly on the spur of Mt. Ithome, a natural fortress. Encircled with a wall which still stands, it successfully combined military strength with architectural beauty. Long a helot rallying point, Mt. Ithome was at once the grave of shattered hopes and the symbol of undying faith in liberty. To it now came helots from all over Messenia, as well as the descendants of the heroic rebels of 464 B.C., chiefly from Naupactus. Invited by Epaminondas, talented architects and engineers erected the reborn city's splendid fortifications and public buildings, a testimonial to a people's will to live. For the many Greeks who believed that freedom is all mankind's birthright, Messene's resurgence was a major event. All Messenia, nearly as large as Attica, became one city-state. Sparta never again succeeded in subduing this people, who had kept liberty's spark alive despite 300 years of bondage. An independent Messenia was a calamity for Sparta also, for by its existence almost half the Spartan peers lost income-producing land.

The founding of these states—democratic, leagued with Thebes, and all ex-Spartan subjects not likely to forget Spartan cruelty and arrogance —surrounded Sparta for the first time with powerfully armed enemies. Yet Epaminondas, dissatisfied, burned to make the Corinthian Gulf a Theban lake. He forced the oligarchic states of the Achaean League, north of Arcadia, into a Theban protectorate. If he had stopped here, Thebes might have enjoyed longer an unequaled land empire, aping Sparta of old, but he sent harmosts into Achaean cities to promote "spontaneous" revolutions of democrats, seizing governments and exiling oligarchs. These puppet democracies, however, lacking popular support, were soon overthrown, and the restored oligarchies naturally became Sparta's allies.

In another reversal the Arcadian Confederacy went over to Sparta. The occasion appeared when Elis, a city off Arcadia's western frontier, took advantage of the confusion and weakness early in the Arcadian fight for independence to seize certain border lands. In the ensuing struggle Arcadian troops sacrilegiously occupied Olympia, sanctuary and town, just before the Olympic Games of 364. Elis tried to recover the sacred precinct during the actual games; times had changed; neither side had a monopoly on sacrilege. Worse yet, the Arcadians seized the sacred treasures and used them to pay their way. Elis of course allied itself with Sparta. A serious split developed within the Confederacy when Mantinea, supported by a majority of the Ten Thousand, condemned the seizure of the treasures as sacrilege and voted to return Olympia to Elis. When a minority, disavowing the Ten Thousand's vote, placed itself under Theban protection, Mantinea, although democratic and always anti-Spartan, joined Sparta, followed by other members of the Confederacy. But oligarchic Tegea, always before pro-Spartan by tradition and self-interest, now sided with democratic Thebes. Democratic Athens itself stood with Sparta. Briefly, deep-seated divisions in and between states, clashing interests, and plain opportunism had supplanted such decencies as had ever governed Greek society. By comparison with the kaleidoscopic shifts of this decade, fifth-century Greece had been a model of stability.

All these realignments were prompted by Thebes' imperialistic ambitions. Athens, though itself busy changing its Second Confederacy into a Second Empire, was deeply disturbed by Thebes' building a 100-ship fleet to contest Athenian ascendancy. The showdown came on the plain of Mantinea, where Epaminondas' Theban army, supplemented by Arcadian, Argive, Messenian, and Thessalian allies, faced the combined forces of Sparta, Athens, Elis, Mantinea, and Achaea (362 B.C.). Epaminondas won as handily as he had at Leuctra nine years earlier. Indeed the Spartan command, completely forgetting that lesson, allowed itself to be trapped into near annihilation by an identical strategy. But Epaminondas' death turned the Theban triumph into disaster. His dying advice was peace. Without him the Theban army was leaderless. Thebes' imperial design was in Epaminondas' own brain; its energy his energy. His death was the death of everything for which he had stood.

Even so Sparta was too weak to regain pre-eminence. And so was Athens which, breaking its pledges to its League, exacted tribute and, gambling to reconstitute the empire, deprived some states of autonomy. Athens, Sparta, and Thebes were now morally and militarily bankrupt, and there was no rallying-point for the still numerous peace-loving cities.

Philip II and His Kingdom of Macedon

Until this time Macedonia, north of Thessaly, had played only an intermittent role in Greek history. It had been more closely associated with Thrace to the east, Illyricum to the west, and Paeonia to the north, with all of which it had been constantly locked in a struggle for existence, so that it had barely achieved statehood by the beginning of the fifth century. Mountainous and heavily wooded, Macedonia lies between the Balkans and Greece proper. The Axius and Haliacmon valleys are fertile, though marshy near their mouths. Communication with Greece was by sea or through the lovely defile of Tempe into Thessaly. The coastal plain, protected by high mountains, was open to attack only from the sea or from the east. The Macedonians, busy with farming and horse breeding, had not looked beyond their borders. Whether or not they were Greeks, they and the Greeks probably sprang from the same origins, but Macedonian blood had indigenous admixtures, and Mediterranean influence is by no means marked. Some of the mountain dialects had little if any affinity with Greek. Their Balkan position had caused them to develop more slowly than the rest of Greece, and they never lost a certain barbarity of language and manners. They still kept a hereditary monarchy though without fixed laws of succession; it was kept in check by a powerful landed nobility living feudally. Social stratification was less marked than in Greece, but there were interminable and futile wars between district and district, sometimes resulting in anarchy, sometimes in union. Thus Macedon was an unknown quantity, but clearly vigorous, undisciplined, and fearsome. Its strength depended on its king.

We know little of the kings of Macedon before Philip II. They early freed themselves from Persia, and towards the end of the fifth century King Archelaus emerges as a great monarch, creating an army, building roads, striking handsome coins, moving his capital from the mountains to the plain of Pella, erecting monuments, entertaining at his court such illustrious guests as Euripides and the painter Zeuxis, and organizing gymnastic and musical contests. His relation with Athens were good, but embarrassed by an internal uprising. Nevertheless, in the last years of his reign, he penetrated into Thessaly and annexed Larissa. His assassination (399 B.C.) ushered in a new era of civil war, until Sparta set on the throne Amyntas III, who ruled till 369 B.C. His son Alexander II again intervened in Thessaly. The usurper Ptolemy reigned weakly, and with the death in battle of Perdiccas III (359 B.C.), Macedonia seemed on the eve of total dismemberment. Perdiccas' son was a minor, under the guardianship of his uncle Philip. Here at last was a Macedonian to reckon with.

Philip is one of the most remarkable figures of the ancient world: a true Macedonian, loving wine, women, and violent physical exercise, ambitious, energetic, able, evoking fanatic loyalty in his countrymen, knowing how to gain his ends without going too far, cunning, and unscrupulous. For him the end justified the means, whether the means were bribery or promoting treason. Sometimes brutal, sometimes charming, he knew how to make concessions in details without ever yielding the main point. While still a young man he had known unhappiness and exile, but his forced sojourn in Thebes had at least acquainted him with Epaminondas' phalanx tactics. He was a fearsome combination of soldier and diplomat. He used his power as regent to show his virtues and his vices; his nephew abdicated in his favor, and in 359 B.C. Philip became king. Greece looked on in astonishment at the meteoric rise of the man who in less than twenty years was to be its master.

Philip began by isolating his enemies and conquering them piecemeal. He bribed the Thracians and Paeonians to withdraw from conflict. To facilitate an attack on Illyricum, he allied himself with the king of the Molossians, whose niece he married, and negotiated with Athens; he took Amphipolis (357 B.C.), but promised to return it in exchange for Pydna, which had been compelled to join the Second Athenian League in 364 B.C. Next he turned to the Chalcidice peninsula, despite Athens' attempts at alliance with the kings of Thrace and the Bosporus. By spring 356 B.C. he had conquered the Illyrians and occupied Pydna, but still held Amphipolis. He took the Athenian cleruchy of Potidaea and razed it. Meantime a son was born, Alexander, later to be called the Great. Philip next refounded Crenides and renamed it Philippi. Thenceforward, the neighboring mines furnished him with an annual revenue of 1000 talents, from which he coined money which competed with the "owls" of Athens and Persian darics to buy him troops and friends. Athens, though then involved in the Social War, so feared Philip that it tried, though in

Fig. 26.2. Demosthenes. Roman copy of a bronze original of 280 B.C. Severe, thoughtful, a little sour, it faithfully expresses the personality of this dedicated fighter for Athenian freedom. (Rome, Vatican Museum; Fototeca)

vain, to encircle him by alliances with Paeonia, Thrace, and Illyricum. Philip, without for the moment pressing his advantage, set about reorganizing his kingdom. Among the nobles he attracted to his court he distributed civil and military posts; their sons became his pages. Everywhere he recruited collaborators, buying genius and energy for gold. To his loyal partisans the generals Antipater, Parmenio, and Perdiccas, he added an admiral, Nearchus of Crete, and a secretary, Eumenes of Cardia. Under his impulse Pella was turned into a true capital; he accustomed his people to urban life and gave each district its own new city; he colonized the interior. By the sole force of his will Macedonia became Hellenized. He ruthlessly transplanted whole tribes. He established his closest associates on lands near the frontier and gave them plantations in strategic spots. And, above all, he improved his army. The cavalry, already excellent, he simply domesticated. The king's household—the Companions—and the royal body guard (*Hypaspistae*) had now none but nobles in their ranks. Philip also developed the national infantry which Archelaus had established. Recruited by conscription in each district, the peasants were forced to serve in it, under nobles as officers, and it later served as a counterweight to the aristocratic cavalry. To give

these raw recruits confidence, Philip grouped them in the massive phalanx formation he had learned from Epaminondas, armed them with
the long lance (*sarissa*), and gave them heavy protective armor. Finally,
he equipped the army with a complete artillery. With this army, he
planned a strategy involving the complete destruction of the enemy. In
two years, Philip had set up an admirable war machine. He was ready
now to seize the first opportunity to test its efficiency.

Philip's Hegemony over Greece

Philip's intervention in Greece was to mean the political downfall of
Athens, but the Macedonian conquerors were to foster Athenian cultural
pre-eminence, and proceed to Hellenize the whole ancient world. When
Philip came down into Greece, he found Athens, Sparta, and Thebes
equally exhausted. Athens had exiled Callistratus, who stood for moderation and peace; an unsuccessful Thracian war had put its last outposts of empire in the Chersonesus in peril. Financially, too, it was exhausted; it had the ships but could not pay the crews. Besides Macedon,
Thebes and Caria threatened it. While Athens exhausted itself to save
the remnants of its League, it paved the way for Philip's easy victory.

One enervating effort was the "Social" War (357–355 B.C.). Three of
Athens' allies, Chios, Rhodes, and Byzantium, had revolted; in an effort
to quell them, the admiral Chabrias was killed, and Athens made peace
with the rebels. A wise financier, Eubulus, undertook to head Athens'
government, replenish its treasury, and strengthen its failing hold on its
few remaining subjects. It now renounced any struggle for hegemony.
With Sparta and Thebes equally weak, this might have been the hour of
autonomy for all, but Philip was to assure autonomy for none.

Of all the powers that watched Philip's progress, Athens was the most
anxious, for he was threatening its life-line to Black Sea grain. But
Eubulus counseled resignation, tax-reduction, and the financing of the
pleasures of the poor with the surplus in the budget, providing out of
this Theoric Fund free theater tickets instead of war preparedness. But
a majority of young men refused to acquiesce in decline and fall; among
these was Demosthenes (384–322 B.C.). We shall follow in Chapter 28
his eloquent appeals to Athenian patriotism; here suffice it to say that he
devoted himself, from 351 B.C. onward, to reminding his fellow-citizens
of the Macedonian menace. And Athens had need of him, for it was
about to plunge into another great war.

The Sacred War, religious only in its pretext, began in 355 B.C. Delphi
complained that its Phocian neighbors were cultivating the god Apollo's
sacred plain, and called its friends to its aid. At Delphi sat an Amphictyonic Council, with Panhellenic representations to hear complaints of

Fig. 26.3. The Lion of Chaeronea, erected over the mass grave of the Thebans of the Sacred Band who fell in the battle of 338 B.C. (Photo by Dorothy MacKendrick)

this kind. The council voted to expropriate the Phocians; the Phocians resisted, seized Delphi and its fabulously rich treasury, and threatened all northern Greece. The Thessalians, feeling themselves threatened, called in Philip. The Athenians chose the other side, and Demosthenes egged them on to become the champion of oppressed peoples everywhere, using the Theoric Fund to finance the necessary forces. His real target was Philip.

Since 353 B.C. Philip had had his eye on Chalcidice, to which the key was the city of Olynthus. Demosthenes pleaded in vain for forces to rescue the city, and in 348 B.C. Philip took it, razed it and sold its citizens into slavery. Athens, unable to find allies willing to join it against Philip, agreed to peace negotiations, which Philip allowed to drag on until he had attained his ends in the north, so that the Peace of Philocrates (346 B.C.) was a diplomatic defeat for Athens. Worse still, Philip suppressed the Phocians and forced them to hand over to him their two votes in the Amphictyonic Council. Once he was sure of a majority there, his control of central Greece was assured, the more because he had active fifth-columnists in every city.

Thebes, though allied to Philip, was restive; furthermore, Demosthenes crossed Philip's will by persuading Athens to offer Thebes an alliance. For six years Philip prepared his army and his intrigues; for six years Demosthenes defied him, while Philip's gold nourished Athenian traitors. Philip himself in these years subdued Illyricum, the Molossians, and Thrace, intrigued in the Peloponnesus, and concluded a treaty with Persia, while Demosthenes, diplomatically active in the Peloponnesus, obtained an alliance with Achaea, Argos, and Mantinea, to which he added Megara in 342 B.C.

The years between 343 and 340 B.C. saw intrigue and hostilities short of war between Athens and Philip. While Philip intrigued against Athens in the Chersonesus, Demosthenes proposed a program of arms and propaganda against him, and by bringing Byzantium back into the Athenian fold, he safeguarded once more Athens' trade route. By engineering alliances, supporting democratic regimes, using the navy skillfully and inaugurating a new Panhellenic League with 100 triremes and 12,000 mercenaries, Demosthenes earned the crown his grateful fellow-citizens awarded him in 340 B.C. In the same summer, Philip invaded the Chersonesus, besieged Byzantium, and deliberately provoked Athens to war by capturing some triremes loaded with gold and stores. Open war was now inevitable.

The Ecclesia put Demosthenes in charge of the navy and sent a squadron to Byzantium. Philip raised the siege, only to turn up unexpectedly at Elatea, the gateway to central Greece. Amid the ensuing panic, Demosthenes alone remained cool enough to persuade Thebes to an alliance. Philip seized Amphissa, near Delphi, and the Athenians and Boeotians resolved to face him on the plain of Chaeronea (338 B.C.). After a savage battle, Philip emerged victor. The Athenians lost 1000 dead and 2000 prisoners; Thebes suffered the annihilation of its Sacred Band. Philip, with no further resistance to fear, was free to impose his dictates on the whole peninsula.

On Thebes his dictates imposed a Macedonian garrison and autonomy for all Boeotia. Other Greek cities hurried to join Philip's triumphant cause. Athens prepared for the end. But Philip unexpectedly offered an acceptable peace and returned without ransom the prisoners from Chaeronea. Athens was allowed to keep a few small islands, but was forced to dissolve its maritime league and to pledge allegiance to a new league dominated by Macedon. Almost its last independent act was to decree to Demosthenes another golden crown.

Meantime Philip was arranging Greek affairs to suit himself. Having subdued the Peloponnesus, he called at Corinth a congress to establish a Panhellenic League with himself as head and the majority of votes assigned to his satellite-states. Though the League guaranteed the constitutions—mostly oligarchic—existing in each member-state at the time of joining, Philip's word was law. Behind its screen he partitioned the

Peloponnesus, ruined Sparta, and arbitrated disputes in his own interest. League members were bound to furnish Philip, as their generalissimo, troops and ships. After due allowance is made for Philip's selfish aims in founding the League, it remains historically important as an attempt to promote Greek inner harmony by means of a federal constitution. The League's first target was to be the Persian Empire.

Such a crusade, Philip thought, would unite the Greeks behind him. He spent the year 337 B.C. in preparing his own army and fixing the number of the Greek contingents, with a heavy fine for delinquency. In 336 B.C., when his forces were already in Asia Minor, Philip was mysteriously murdered as a result of a palace intrigue, and the fate of Greece and his Persian expedition hung in the balance. But his son Alexander was destined to assure that Philip's work would not die with him.

Chapter 27/THE WESTERN GREEKS

The Rise of Carthage

We saw that as early as the twelfth century B.C. Phoenician merchants had established coastal trading posts in North Africa and Europe. During the next 300 years they founded new stations and planted regular colonies, which were already prosperous when Tyrian colonists founded in 814 B.C. a city which they called Carthage, or Newtown (Phoenician: *Qart Chadascht;* Greek: *Carchedon;* Latin: *Carthago*). Situated on a small peninsula between the sea and Lake Tunis, Carthage had room to grow, an excellent harbor, and good land and sea defenses. Its situation south of Sicily at the narrowest part of the Mediterranean gave it control of that sea's eastern and western basins and made it a central emporium for shipments east, west, or north to central Europe via the Italian peninsula. In time, it established colonies of its own in Sicily, the Balearic Islands, Spain, and North Africa. By 600 B.C. it had outstripped all other Phoenician colonies in wealth, population, and power.

Carthage gained from two almost parallel developments in the outside world. The successive subjugation of Phoenicia by Assyria, Chaldea, and Persia left it as well as the other Phoenician colonies politically independent. Greek expansion, first from the Greek mainland and later from Massalia and Magna Graecia, forced Carthage's sister colonies to look to it for protection. And so, practically without design or effort, Carthage became an imperial city. Thanks largely to it, no Greek colonies were planted farther west. Cyrene in Africa was unable to extend its power, Acragas and Selinus in Sicily were too weak to expand west or north, while a naval defeat by combined Phoenician and Etruscan forces off Alalia in Corsica (c. 535 B.C.) stopped further Greek expansion from the Tyrrhenian Sea to the Straits of Gibraltar. In its heyday Carthage headed a great federation of city-states: twenty-two in North Africa along the Mediterranean; three or four in West Africa, facing the Atlantic; about twenty in Europe, principally in Sicily, Sardinia, and Spain. It ruled the natives in the hinterland as well as the Phoenician populations, demanding of them all military service, and taxes amounting to 25 percent of the grain harvest and 50 percent of the wine, olive oil, and fruit.

Since maritime trade was the cornerstone of its prosperity, Carthage had to keep the sea open to its ships. Hence a powerful navy was essential. Like imperial Athens, Carthage forced its subject-allies to pay tribute. Though their burden was heavy, they did receive full protection.

Phoenician colonies, including Carthage, resembled the cities of old Phoenicia. Since they had a large number of manufacturers, merchants, moneylenders, industrial workers, and seamen, they contained the nucleus of a strong *bourgeoisie,* largely free agents, even under kings. They had no local king, but were subject to the kings of their mother cities. When Carthage became independent of Tyre, it made itself a timocratic republic.

Two annually elected magistrates, called judges (*suffetes*) headed the state. The ruling class consisted of rich merchants who had invested their maritime profits in pastures and fertile plantations south of Carthage. A Senate of thirty life members, elected probably by the people, had deliberative and some executive powers. There was a Grand Council, probably of three hundred members, most of whom had filled the lower magistracies. The suffetes presided over both Senate and Grand Council. Measures became law if agreed to by the two bodies and the suffetes. Failing this triple agreement, questions were referred for decision to the people's assembly which had the right to discuss controversial matters. But the people were not master. The two councils, with their life members, guaranteed continuity of policy and political stability little affected by popular passion. Aristotle thought imperialism assured this stability, since the proceeds from exploiting the natives filtered down to the masses. Since the people knew that their material well-being depended on a stable merchant oligarchy, they almost never challenged their rulers. Moreover, since hard work and talent could lead to wealth and political power, the government had no fear of revolution.

The Carthaginian ruling class could feel secure also because the people, unlike the people of Athens, had no jury rights. Instead, 104 lifelong judges, all important ex-magistrates, kept vigil over the incumbent magistrates and the public administration in general. They could examine a magistrate's official acts just before the end of his term. But their chief function was to keep ambitious politicians or generals within bounds. Negligence or malfeasance in office, graft, or political venality were not prosecuted. Votes and exemptions from military service were bought and sold openly, without stigma.

The Carthaginians were pre-eminently an industrial people. They developed a favorable balance of trade by exchanging finished goods for raw materials, partly local, but chiefly imported. To supply their many looms with wool, they promoted shepherding in the semiarid regions between the coast and the Sahara. They expertly raised bees, cultivated grain, grapes, olives, and fruit, and wrote technical works on agriculture from which the Greeks and later the Romans learned much. They linked Europe with Africa in a vast network of exchange, importing amber, skins, and furs from the Baltic regions; copper, tin, and iron from Spain and probably Britain; timber and pitch from Spain; ivory, ostrich feathers, and spices from beyond the desert; and exporting beeswax, salt-fish, dyes, wool and linen clothing, metal and glass manufactures, and slaves. Shipping and shipbuilding furnished the most employment. Customs duty paid at seaports and the frontier furnished much revenue, 1000 talents a year from the port of Carthage alone; in later years the revenue from the Spanish mines exceeded that from customs. The Carthaginian flair for trade and habit of mendacity increased these profits enormously. Carthaginian astuteness, duplicity, and greed, though vouched for by hostile sources, are well established.

The original Carthaginian citizen army gradually was set apart in an élite corps. By 300 B.C. all fighting was left to mercenaries, Libyan, Spanish, Gallic, and Sardinian infantry, Numidian cavalry. Only the officers were Carthaginian citizens. With such a motley army did Carthage face Agathocles in the late fourth century B.C. and Rome in the third. This system had its advantages. It enabled the citizens to stay safely at their business. A mercenary army was cheaper, and a general of mercenaries could afford to risk his men and suppress insubordination more ruthlessly than could a general commanding citizens. The ruling oligarchy was well aware that mercenaries were safer in this respect than were citizens who knew their rights and were capable of mutiny. The one serious drawback was that an ambitious general might use his army to threaten the Republic. But the Board of Judges could dismiss an over-ambitious general or try one who lost too many battles and crucify him if he was convicted. Usually a mercantile society fails to produce good generals, but Carthage never lacked first-rate and loyal veteran commanders.

We know little of Carthaginian spiritual and intellectual life. Unlike their Jewish cousins, the Carthaginians had little intellectual curiosity or esthetic sense; they have left no literature. Then too the little we know about them comes from the Greeks and Romans, their bitter competitors in business, colonization, and conquest. We do know that their gods were Canaanite: the *Adonai* (lords), the *Baalim* (masters), the *Elohim* (gods), and the *Melekoi* (kings) of their Phoenician ancestors; in cohesive, stable Carthage their sway was always unquestioned; indeed, the Carthaginians had not the speculative capacity, originality, or critical power to question, as Greeks and even Romans did, their ancestral gods.

The chief goddesses were Tanit and Astarte. Tanit was sometimes identified with the moon; indeed when the Romans came to know her, they called her *Caelestis,* the Heavenly One. Astarte resembled the Greek Aphrodite. Her most famous temple outside Carthage was on Mt. Eryx in western Sicily where hundreds of women practiced sacred prostitution as part of her official worship, and sailors came from every land to invoke her and partake of her blessings. Sometimes she appeared as the wife of Esmun, the god who stimulates nature's cycles through those of his own life. Human sacrifices were part of the cult, especially in a national crisis. When the Sicilian Greek Agathocles invaded Africa, Diodorus Siculus reports that a great fire was lit around a colossal statue of a god and 500 children, 200 of them from the best families, were thrown into his waiting arms to perish in the flames. Although this information is probably exaggerated, that Carthaginians showed a barbaric streak is indubitable. By Hannibal's time, however, manners had become more refined; the would-be destroyer of Rome yielded to neither Greek nor Roman in humanity towards his civilized enemies.

Whereas in early times the men had their ears and noses pierced for gold and silver rings and wore wide flowing sleeves to prevent their hands from showing in polite society, Hannibal and his contemporaries dressed like the Greeks and Romans. But there were few other concessions to foreign influence. Religious dogmatism and racial exclusiveness kept Carthaginians from absorbing the subject races. In Sicily, Sardinia, Spain, and Africa itself the natives felt no common bond with their masters.

Carthaginian art was a blend of Greek and Oriental elements. Its best period—the fourth and third centuries B.C.—coincided with the attempted conquest of all Sicily and Italy. But the chief interest of Carthaginian craftsmen was not really art, but the production, chiefly for export, of cheap imitations of Greek, Egyptian, and Etruscan models. In art as in literature the Carthaginians were uncreative. Their technical treatises on commerce and agriculture are typical of their materialistic culture.

The Western Greeks and Their Struggle with Carthage

The pattern of Magna Graecia's history resembles that of mainland Greece, quarrels between cities, revolutions within cities, and, always, the barbarian on the borders. But it is a lively story, fascinating not least because the development of the western Greeks is curiously retarded. Not until the fourth century B.C. did the Dorian cities of Sicily reach their zenith and resume their war with Carthage, halted since 480 B.C. They were late, too, in developing political theory.

After defeating the Athenians in 412 B.C., the Syracusans had not been able at once to harvest the fruits of victory. Within, revolutionary democrats profited by the absence of the fleet in eastern waters to create dissension. Without, Carthage again threatened, profiting by a quarrel between Segesta and Selinus to intervene in Sicilian affairs on the invitation of the former. Carthaginian mercenaries hardened in African wars took and destroyed Selinus, enslaving its inhabitants. Then they turned to wreak vengeance on Himera (409 B.C.) where they slew 3000 Greeks.

Fig. 27.1. Acragas (Agrigento). So-called Temple of Juno. Doric; shortly before 450 B.C. Beautifully set on a high platform within the city's southeast wall. Its slight curves and structural refinements are like those of the temple at Paestum (Fig. 12.1) and of the Parthenon. (Photo by Dorothy MacKendrick)

Acragas narrowly escaped destruction and was forced into the Carthaginian Empire.

At this perilous juncture for the Sicilian Greeks, there rose in Syracuse a man of genius, Dionysius the Elder. Of humble origins, he had been stirred to indignation by the growing audacity of the Carthaginians and the incompetence of the democratic regime in Syracuse. Brave, intelligent, ambitious, and unscrupulously realistic, he contrived to accuse the incumbent generals of treason and persuade the Ecclesia to appoint others, including himself. Then he discredited his colleagues and had himself appointed general-in-chief, with a bodyguard which he used in the traditional manner to obtain for himself a tyranny. Faced with a revolt of the aristocratic cavalry, he made a peace (405 b.c.) with Carthage which recognized its conquests. Then he consolidated his power, and under him Syracuse enjoyed for forty years an incomparable prestige.

In domestic policy he recalls Pisistratus: he was scrupulously just in his dealings with private citizens; he preserved the existing magistracies, although reserving them for his friends and relatives; he encouraged his fellow-citizens to take to the sea. But Dionysius outdid Pisistratus in military genius. He created a fleet of 200 ships, became an expert in siege-craft, and fortified Syracuse with a citadel—not so much defense against the Carthaginians as against internal revolt. He built naval dockyards and on the height Epipolae behind the city, at Euryalus, a fortress. To meet expenses, he confiscated the property of his enemies, and those to whom he gave it became his faithful friends. Then he set out to subdue Sicily, both Carthaginian and Greek, and eventually the Italian mainland as well.

He first attacked some Sicel villages in north and northeast Sicily, allies of Carthage, and made them into protectorates. Then he turned to the Greek cities, occupying Catana, razing Naxos, and transferring the inhabitants of Leontini to Syracuse. This last act aroused the Carthaginians, who had exacted from him a promise to leave Leontini autonomous. Dionysius increased the provocation by massacring Carthaginian merchants and taking Motya, a Carthaginian stronghold in west Sicily. The Carthaginians, thoroughly roused, retook the city, destroyed Messana, defeated Dionysius in a naval battle off Catana, and had actually penetrated Syracuse Great Harbor (397 b.c.) when Spartan arms and a plague came to the tyrant's rescue. The defeated Carthaginians were allowed to ransom their lives for 300 talents. By 375 b.c. Dionysius was master of all Sicily. In 367 b.c., as, bent on vengeance, he was mounting attacks on Carthaginian cities in west Sicily, he died of a drug administered to cure a fever.

Between Carthaginian wars Dionysius found time to conquer and organize an empire. Campaigns in south Italy yielded him 10,000 prisoners,

Fig. 27.2. Serra Orlando, Sicily, the ancient Morgantina. The Great Stairs from the southwest. They overlook the Agora and may have been used for citizens to stand on in public assemblies. Unfinished, they are dated in the 4th-3rd centuries B.C. (*American Journal of Archaeology* LXI, 1957, Plate 53, Fig. 2.)

which he actually returned without ransom, thus eliciting from the grateful Italians golden crowns and offers of alliance, whereby he consolidated his power on both sides of the Strait of Messina. The conquest of Croton (379 B.C.) gave him control of its Adriatic colonies. Dionysius spread his influence by treaties with the Lucanians in the toe and Iapygians in the heel of the Italian boot, and with the Molossians across the Adriatic. And he made himself felt in Greece proper by lending Sparta his fleet.

Good fortune followed Dionysius beyond the grave. In 367 B.C. a tragedy of his won first prize at Athens. In his later years he had entertained at his court the philosopher Plato and other Greeks—poets, philosophers, and historians. His death closed a great epoch of Sicilian history. His son and successor, Dionysius the Younger, was less vigorous and energetic than his father, depending heavily on a mercenary army supported by exorbitant taxes and tolls. His long reign (366–345 B.C.) was marked by cruel sacking of cities, counterfeiting of money, and treachery to gain his ends.

Dionysius II had a half-brother, Dion, a pupil of Plato, who passionately desired the return of his master whom the first Dionysius had insulted and expelled. Dionysius II approved, Plato returned, and the whole court fell to studying geometry. But this era of good feeling did not last. The tyrant, suspecting Dion of revolutionary and even treasonable designs, exiled him and imprisoned Plato. Dion collected an army of 3000 mercenaries and took Syracuse during his half-brother's absence in Italy. In the resulting civil war Dion had to defend himself simultaneously against Dionysius II, against the people, who disliked him for his intellectual superiority, and against his own lieutenants. His unpopular oligarchic government ended in 354 B.C. with his assassination by stabbing. The Carthaginians profited by the ensuing anarchy by threatening Syracuse, which appealed to its mother city, Corinth; the result was the dispatch of the Corinthian general Timoleon.

Brave, antityrannical, philosophical, devout, Timoleon is a figure attractive to the moralist. He found himself obliged to fight not only the Carthaginians but Leontini and Dionysius II as well. He drove Dionysius II into miserable exile in Corinth. He divided and defeated his other two enemies (343 B.C.), tore down the fortress at Euryalus, restored democracy, recalled the exiles, and invited 60,000 colonists from the whole of Greece. When he attempted a similar clean-up and restoration in other Sicilian cities, Carthage sent against him an army in which even citizens served. Timoleon defeated it near Segesta, in a bloody battle which yielded 15,000 prisoners. Then considering his task accomplished, Timoleon retired (about 337 B.C.) to an estate pressed upon him by the grateful Syracusans, where he lived in semiblindness, but was consulted like an oracle. At his death, all Sicily mourned the only tyrant who had ever been its benefactor.

After Timoleon, Sicily enjoyed a generation of comparative tranquility, with cities rebuilt, civil wars lulled, and a boundary peacefully settled with the Carthaginians. South Italy enjoyed a period of twilight splendor, an era of materialistic Hellenism which was to have its effect on Rome.

Syracuse itself soon fell again into civil war, out of which (317 B.C.) emerged a new tyrant, Agathocles. Born of immigrant artisan parents, he had been a soldier who dabbled in democratic politics and was exiled. Returning with Carthaginian help, he rose quickly to power, for which he rewarded the people by remitting their debts and redistributing confiscated lands. Under him tyranny again subjected all Sicily but Acragas and Gela. Attacked by a now uneasy Carthage, he carried the war into Africa (310 B.C.). At the return of peace (306 B.C.) he ruled over all eastern Sicily as king. In this capacity he restored the Syracusan Empire in South Italy, and even expanded it to Corcyra. Agathocles died in 279 B.C., by his will restoring to Syracuse a liberty which its citizens had lost the capacity to enjoy.

Chapter 28/LIFE AND THOUGHT IN THE FOURTH CENTURY (404-322 B.C.)

Social, Political, and Economic Life

The fourth century B.C. has been called an age of individualism, cosmopolitanism, and a striving for synthesis. In art, literature, and philosophy, the keynotes were an emphasis on contrast, organic structure, and external detail. Gone were the self-sacrificing spirit of the men of Marathon, the unquestioned intellectual primacy of Periclean Athens, the philosophical pioneering of an Anaxagoras or a Socrates. Yet though the fourth century inevitably suffers from comparison with the fifth, the age of a Praxiteles and a Scopas, an Isocrates and a Demosthenes, a Plato and an Aristotle will challenge comparison with any but the very greatest in the intellectual history of western man.

In this as in the preceding age, the Greek city-state we know best is Athens. While Athens recovered remarkably from the Peloponnesian

War, its defeat had had profound social, political, and economic consequences; hence the fourth century in Athens was an age of failure of nerve and of fading tradition. For example, men put less faith in law, in duty, in the obligation of marriage. Race suicide and war losses had reduced the population from at least 40,000 adult male citizens in Periclean Attica to no more than 22,000 at the beginning of the fourth century B.C.

Another sign of the times was the new prominence of political and religious associations which inadequately replaced the close links of blood ties in the old clan and phratry. Since the revolution of 411 B.C. the oligarchic political clubs (*hetaeriae*) had come to wield a new and sometimes sinister political influence: they helped their members in elections and lawsuits, and they were hotbeds of antidemocratic plots. But they were intellectual centers, too; at club banquets their young members discussed with passionate interest the political and philosophical problems of the day. Late in the century, religious brotherhoods (*thiasoi*) united to worship gods sometimes quite outlandish, gave protection, a sense of belonging, and a decent burial to their members, often foreigners or slaves.

These were artificial groups, interest-groups, the product of class war. For this was the age of the newly rich; bankers like Pasion, who rose from slavery to leave a fortune of 40 talents, had a standard of values different from that of the pedigreed landed proprietors of a few generations back, and little sympathy for the mass of ruined small farmers and craftsmen. Intellectuals complained that the only thing all classes agreed on was the systematic, cynical persecution of all forms of superiority, whether of wealth or brain.

It was an age, also, of political exiles, mostly defeated soldiers willing to sell their sword to the highest bidder. Athenians and others were glad to hire these professionals to do their fighting for them, so that when the time came for an all-out effort the will to fight was gone, and on the field of Chaeronea Athenian citizens fled before the Macedonian army.

These were real problems; they evoked from thinkers more or less theoretical solutions: to redistribute wealth and property, abolish debt, let a philosophical élite rule, unite against Persia, revitalize the middle class.

Fourth-century politics saw the rise of Leagues, which we have already traced, and the retreat of democracy before oligarchs or demagogues, until in the end the city-state's political independence was much reduced.

A direct democracy like Athens is ever in uneasy equilibrium between increasing its prerogatives or diminishing its power. Men like Isocrates, Plato, and Aristotle argued for the latter alternative, substituting for democracy an élite; in practice, the Athenian democracy tried the former course and ruined itself in the process with persecutions for subversion, impeachments, and subjection of the boule to the Ecclesia. The Ecclesia was plagued by absenteeism, so that pay for attendance had to be introduced (first in the late fifth century B.C.) and successively raised, and more and more people lived on the state payroll. This venal body became the prey of professional politicians, themselves corrupt and venal, who kept their power by flattery, by bribes, of which the Theoric Fund is an example, and by inciting poor against rich. The rich were far from guiltless, evading taxes, avoiding the trierarchy, refusing to accept the responsibility which alone would justify their power. Such was the city which Demosthenes vainly tried to rouse against Macedon.

But while political life was in decadence, economic life flourished. The Piraeus prospered as never before, its warehouses crammed with imports and exports of arms, timber, salt, fish, grain. Athenian silver drachmas passed current all over the Mediterranean, and for a time the Second Athenian League guaranteed that Athens really ruled the waves.

Religion

The individualism and cosmopolitanism of the age is especially evident in its religious observances. Intellectuals continued agnostic, as during the Periclean enlightenment, and found their satisfactions in the philosophical schools, but in Athens and elsewhere the state rituals continued to be formally observed, sometimes, as by the orator and financier Lycurgus, with real pietistic fervor. The poor and the slaves turned after Chaeronea to Oriental religions, like that of Isis or the Mother of the Gods, which promised salvation, while the Eleusinian mysteries absorbed rich and poor alike.

For knowledge of the state religion's ritual, our chief source is inscriptions, which stress the just apportionment of parts of sacrificial animals, not forgetting an adequate share for the priest; in Athens late in the century the state received profit from the sale of skins of sacrificial animals. Provisions against priestly absenteeism suggest that it was not a deeply religious age, but in the Piraeus groups of humble folk, called *orgeones*, united for common worship of such gods as Asclepius, the god of healing, or the Thracian goddess Bendis, and welcomed slaves. And at Eleusis the ancient noble classes of Eumolpids and Ceryces (heralds) continued to subsidize the processions and to reveal to the initiates the secrets of the Mysteries, led in an impressive voice by the hierophant in his headband and long purple-dyed embroidered robe.

All over the Greek world individual benefactors and communities built humble shrines and splendid temples. In Halicarnassus, Herodotus' city, a wealthy donor, on the advice of an oracle, devoted his income from property to Zeus, Apollo, the Fates, the Mother of the Gods, and the Good Daemon, and in his will enjoined his sons to be priests. At Delphi through all the vicissitudes of this eventful century a magnificent new temple to Apollo was building, at a cost of over $632,000. Panhellenic contributions from the Black Sea to Cyrene, from Asia Minor to Sicily, made this a truly international project. We possess the building accounts, which record the architects' names, the construction details, and the administrative arrangements. At Epidaurus, between Corinth and Argos, Asclepius' sanctuary attained new splendor, with a new temple, porticoes, baths, a gymnasium and wrestling gound, a splendid theater and a large hotel. Inscriptions recording miraculous cures here are among the most fascinating preserved to us from antiquity. Toward the end of the period Alexander the Great dedicated at Priene in Asia Minor a great temple to Athena Polias, patroness of Athens. From every part of the Greek world the inscriptions record religious building activity and dedications: at Delphi, in the Piraeus, on Delos, at Eleusis, at Oropus on the borders of Attica (by a pious local historian of Attica) , in Athens itself; the list is endless, but the breadth and depth of the piety involved is hard to gauge.

The manner of worship varied little in this century from past practice. Sacrifice was the central point. In tributary sacrifice, the god was regarded as eating the offering or enjoying its savor; a banquet might be spread, with table and couches for him and his fellow gods. In piacular sacrifice, a sin was atoned for or accursed ground (for example, a place struck by lightning) was reserved to the god. In mystic sacrifice, magic was practiced upon the god: an animal in full vigor was sacrificed to him, that the crops too might be vigorous. The worshipers first mourned and then rejoiced, the god was resurrected, there was a solemn sacramental banquet. A garlanded priest performed the sacrificial ritual; the victim too was garlanded and his horns gilded. There was holy water, a sacred torch, a sprinkling of the altar, a holy silence, and prayers. The victim was sprinkled with barleycorns, a few hairs were cut from him and burned; then he was stunned, his throat cut, the blood caught in a sacrificial vessel and poured on the altar or sprinkled on the worshipers, who chanted throughout, sometimes to a flute accompaniment. Then the victim was skinned and cut up, the parts reserved for the god burnt on the altar, the rest roasted on spits and divided among the worshipers. Curses are a form of prayer; they were often inscribed on lead tablets; one from the Piraeus prays that the tongue of the object of the curse may turn to lead.

A pious Greek in this irreligious age, as in the sixth century, B.C., would include religious observances in almost every daily act; and public meetings of assembly, boule, or law court were opened with sacrifice.

Festivals were an important part of ritual. In the fourth century in

Athens the chief festival was the Panathenaea. The dramatic festival at the Dionysia continued, though with revivals of old plays, and the same names, including that of the playwright Sophocles' grandson, tend to recur on the lists of victors. Generals and metics vied with one another for the prestige of training a winning chorus, though many of the rich were reluctant to spend the money.

The credulous continued to consult oracles, of which those at Dodona and Delphi were the most famous. Barren wives asked if they might have children, advice was sought about a purchase of a house (should it be the cheap or the dear one,) or a sheep, the outcome of a journey, or a cure for an illness.

The most interesting fourth-century religious document is the record of alleged cures performed at Asclepius' shrine in Epidaurus, cures of barrenness, paralysis, dumbness, pockmarks, gallstones, pinkeye, blindness, lameness, baldness, dropsy, worms, tumors, ulcers, lice, migraine, gangrene, tuberculosis, gout, arthritis—all the ills that flesh is heir to. Unbelievers got short shrift: they were doubly stricken or were moved to pay the god a heavy fee in silver. A man whose mother-in-law gave him leeches to drink had them miraculously removed by the god; a boy nine days drowned was revived by the god's intervention; a lame man dreamed he climbed on a ladder to the very ridgepole of the temple; the god even mended for a slave a hopelessly smashed pot. The kick of a horse cured arthritis, licking by a sacred dog cured tumor, the nip of a goose cured gout. The credulity is remarkable, and it was not limited to those of low degree: a Molossian princess testified to being cured of barrenness.

Finally, there were the Mysteries, held with great pomp and splendor at Eleusis in the Telesterion, built by the architect of the Parthenon. We know that a ritual was recited, that sacred objects were shown, that a sacred drama was enacted, perhaps celebrating the return of Persephone to her mother Demeter after a sojourn in Hades, but beyond that the ancient initiates have kept their secret well. Perhaps there was no secret to keep, beyond that of a religious experience profound enough to have a permanent moral effect. Those initiated believed that theirs would be a happier afterlife, an individual consolation sorely needed by lonely and anxiety-ridden fourth-century Greeks. The new age was to see men turn to faith in their rulers as divine.

Art, Architecture, and City-planning

The individualism of the age comes out clearly in its sculpture, which humanizes gods (the *Hermes* of Praxiteles) and deifies mortals (Mausolus, Alexander the Great). Clear too is the emphasis upon contrast

Fig. 28.1. The *Hermes* of Praxiteles. (Olympia, Greece, Museum; Walter Hege photo)

(the adult Hermes and the baby Dionysus in Praxiteles' statue at Olympia), organic structure (the Alexander mosaic, copied from a painting of about 330), and external detail (Tanagra figurines).

In sculpture the great names are those of Scopas of Paros, master delineator of pain and passion; Praxiteles of Athens, portrayer of the exquisite and voluptuous, and their younger contemporary, Lysippus of Sicyon, the last great original sculptor of Greece, whose portrayal of vigorous movement made him Alexander's favorite. Scopas and Lysippus' work either does not lend itself to reproduction, is uncertainly attributed, or exists in bad Roman copies, though a fourth-century reproduction of a statue by Lysippus has been found at Delphi. But in the *Hermes* of Praxiteles, found at Olympia in 1877, we possess a treasure, the sole surviving original by a great Greek master. With the grace, gentleness, softness, and delicacy for which he was famous, Praxiteles portrayed the messenger god playing with his baby brother Dionysus, teasing him with

Fig. 28.2. Battle between Alexander and Darius. Mosaic. (Naples, Italy, Museum; Fototeca)

a bunch of grapes (now missing) which he held just out of the baby's reach in his outstretched right hand. It is a picture of idyllic play, rendered esthetically satisfying by the famous Praxitelean s-curve, the result of shifting the weight of the figure onto one leg. But it is a picture too of supernatural beauty and intelligence with its mind on something beyond the game. The work was probably commissioned in 343 B.C., to symbolize an alliance of Arcadia (of which Hermes was patron) with Elis (under the protection of Dionysus).

Of anonymous originals, justly the most famous is the *Nike* of Samothrace, probably commemorating a naval victory of the late fourth century. It is one of the most powerful renderings of movement in the history of art. The goddess stands on a ship's prow, wings spread, her drapery seeming to float miraculously on a sea breeze. One must imagine her holding a trumpet in one hand, a trophy from the enemy's fleet in the other. Recent American excavations on the island of Samothrace have unearthed further fragments of the masterpiece. Another lovely original, one in the soft Praxitelean tradition, is the exquisite head from Chios, now in the Boston Museum of Fine Arts. A whole series of funerary monuments in Athens present simple moving farewell scenes, the subjects presented as in life, men exercising, women spinning, children with their playthings. The charm of the fourth century is epitomized in the graceful little terra-cotta figurines from Tanagra in Boeotia, lively and elegant miniatures from daily life.

Painting on canvas does not survive, and fourth-century vases do not stand comparison with earlier work. Painting is best represented for us by later mosaic copies like that of the battle between Darius and Alexander from the House of the Faun in Pompeii, now in the Naples Museum. The main figures are skillfully made to stand out from the mass. Alexander, bareheaded, draws his lance from the body of a fallen Persian with intense desire to transfix Darius, who is portrayed as more anxious for his faithful comrades than for his own life. The slanting spears are used in masterly fashion to give depth and back boundary; in this composition organic structure is everything.

In architecture the center of activity moved to Asia Minor where the wealth was. Here were built in the fourth century two wonders of the ancient world, the temple of Diana of the Ephesians and the Mausoleum at Halicarnassus. The former, built to replace a structure dedicated by Croesus and destroyed by fire allegedly on the day of Alexander's birth, retained the foundations and some of the superstructure of the

Fig. 28.3. Tanagra figurines. These elegant Boeotian terra-cotta miniatures reproduce the types portrayed in New Comedy by Menander. (New York, Metropolitan Museum of Art)

Fig. 28.4. The *Nike* of Samothrace. Victory is poised for flight on the peak of a warship. The sense of breezy lightness is remarkable. (Paris, Louvre)

earlier temple, which meant that the new one, too, was vast (over 180 by nearly 360 feet) and the temple cella itself surrounded two deep by a veritable forest of enormous columns (one source mentions 137). In size, fluting, and decoration, these were exceptional variations on tradition, some 36 of the column drums and pedestals having figures in relief carved on them. The Mausoleum, a symbol of the glorification of an individual and the deification of a monarch, was a tomb built soon after 353 B.C. by Artemisia, widow of the Persian satrap Mausolus of Caria. It rose temple-like on a high base, carrying a stepped pyramid crowned by a chariot group. It was adorned with reliefs by the greatest sculptors of the age, including Scopas and Praxiteles. This is the most magnificent architectural concept of this century, and its fusion of Oriental and Greek feeling interestingly foreshadows the Hellenizing of the East in the age of Alexander and his successors, but it shows also an ostentation and vulgarity which give a foretaste of the most flamboyant of Roman work.

In Greece itself the new temples of Apollo at Delphi and at Delos and of Asclepius at Epidaurus have been mentioned. Scopas himself was the architect of the temple of Athena Alea at Tegea, the major and most beautiful temple in the Peloponnesus. At Nemea, south of Corinth, site of one of the four great international Greek festivals of games, the three surviving Ionic columns of the temple of Zeus show a slim elegant grace characteristic of this century. Round temples like the Tholoi at Delphi and Epidaurus use all three orders, Doric, Ionic and Corinthian, in ways which combine the touchstones of the period—contrast, emphasis on organic structure, and interest in external appearance. But it is characteristic also of this age that its most impressive buildings are secular. The meeting hall (Thersilion) at Megalopolis, the mushroom city founded in 370 B.C. to be the capital of the Arcadian League, was ingeniously planned to give the best possible view of the orators; here as rhetoric grew more and more histrionic, the influence of the theater began to supersede that of the Pnyx type of assembly place; it is to us perhaps more than merely symbolic that the Thersilion's south porch opens onto a theater.

The two great theaters of this period are the one at Epidaurus and that rebuilt by the pious Lycurgus in Dionysus' precinct at Athens. The beautiful Epidaurus theater, seating well over 7000, is a miracle of

Fig. 28.5. The Bartlett Aphrodite. Perhaps a Praxitelean original. Charming, pensive, intensely feminine. (Boston, Museum of Fine Arts; Clarence Kennedy photo)

Fig. 28.6. The Mausoleum of Halicarnassus, reconstruction. Built 353–350 B.C. Reckoned one of the seven wonders of the ancient world for novelty of design (pyramid supported on columns) and fame of its sculpture (Amazon, centaur, and charioteer friezes by Scopas and others). (W. B. Dinsmoor, *The Architecture of Ancient Greece*,[3] London, 1950. Plate LXIII(b).)

acoustics, and its design shows many subtle correspondences of measurement and some ingenious variations from convention; for example, the auditorium has two distinct slopes, the upper part being steeper. The Lycurgan theater with its statues of the Tragic Three may be taken as a symbol of the fourth-century canonization of the fifth-century golden age.

Finally, this was an age of city-planning. We have mentioned the new federal city of Megalopolis. Priene, a market town of 4000 in Asia Minor, was refounded in Alexander's time, walled, and exactly oriented, with straight streets and equality of blocks between them, most blocks divided equally among four houses with common party walls. The public buildings, including temples, and the open spaces were subordinated to the street scheme; this is in keeping with a secular age, but the rather rigid symmetry of the plan is a part of the somewhat inhuman striving toward synthesis which grows in foundations like Alexandria and the later plans of Roman colonies. American excavations at Olynthus, which Philip destroyed in 348 B.C., have revealed the city gates, street and house plans, and a business quarter which give us a picture of ancient life rivaled only by Delos, Ostia, and Pompeii.

Literature

The fourth century was an age of prose; its most important practitioners were the historian and essayist Xenophon (c. 430–354 B.C.), the pamphleteer Isocrates (436–338 B.C.), and the orator and statesman Demosthenes (384–322 B.C.).

Into seven major and seven minor works, all written lucidly and simply, Xenophon packed the varied and crowded experiences of an adventurous life. In youth an admirer of Socrates (*Memorabilia, Symposium, Apology*), he left Athens before his master's execution in order to take part in Cyrus the Younger's attempt upon the Persian throne.

Fig. 28a. Plan of Isthmia, one of the four sites of the Greek games. Temple of Poseidon and sanctuary of Palaemon excavated 1955–1957 by a University of Chicago expedition. Southeast of the temple, the starting-blocks of the stadium. In a crypt below Palaemon's shrine initiates performed secret ceremonies and took oaths in the name of the god. (Professor Oscar Broneer)

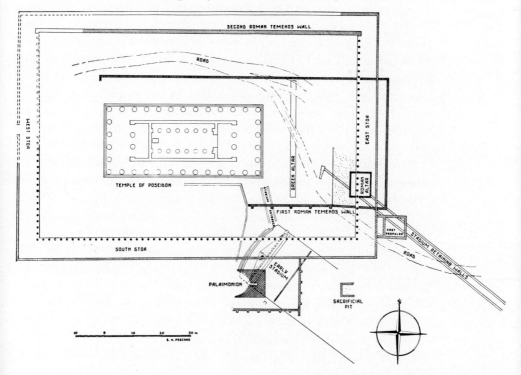

Fig. 28.7. Epidaurus. Theater. Modern performance of a scene from Aeschylus'
Persians. (*Archaeology* I, 1948, p. 115.)

Cyrus' death at Cunaxa, as we saw, left to Xenophon, among others,
the immense and exciting task of leading the army to the sea and home;
he tells the story in the *Anabasis.* The expedition foreshadowed Alexander's campaigns. Xenophon recorded his admiration of the Persians
in a romantic biography, *The Education of Cyrus.* He admired Sparta,
too, as he testifies in his *Agesilaus* and *Spartan Constitution.* He had
served with Agesilaus and was present on the Spartan side at the battle
of Coronea (394 B.C.). Exiled, he retired to Elis to an estate given him
by Sparta, where he lived like a country gentlemen (*Oeconomicus,*
Horsemanship, Hunting with Dogs) and in his leisure wrote his *Hel-
lenica,* a continuation of Thucydides to the battle of Mantinea (362 B.C.)
wherein Xenophon had lost his son, who had fought on the Athenian
side.

Hero worshiper, soldier, exile, squire, huntsman, aristocrat and conservative, would-be philosopher and historian, Xenophon epitomizes
in himself the life and attitudes of the century his works so valuably
record. He has had the misfortune to be judged by intellectuals and to
be compared with his betters, like Thucydides and Plato. Thus assessed,
he stands up ill, but if we take him for what he is, we find in him the
type of gentleman that Athenian aristocratic education turned out:
physically fit, good at sports and games, a fine soldier, well-bred, pious,
of interests rather wide than deep. His very superficiality typifies one
aspect of the fourth century, its interest in externals. In his virtues and
defects he anticipates Rudyard Kipling.

Isocrates' long life spanned the eventful century from Pericles to

Chaeronea. Trained by the great Sicilian rhetorician Gorgias of Leontini, he imbibed his teacher's highly colored style, his broadly cosmopolitan world-view, and his deeply conservative bias. Isocrates' style is
antithetic, carefully structured, and superficial, yet he founded the
concept of leisured educated prose, discussing serious issues against
a background of tradition. His chief influence was as an educator.
About 390 B.C. he founded a school which rapidly became the most
fashionable in the Greek world and a rival to Plato's Academy, number-
ing orators, historians, and princes among its pupils.

His weak voice drove Isocrates from the speaker's platform, but his
pamphlets simulating speeches influenced two generations. The pamphlets probably reflected his lectures. His ruling idea was Panhellenic;
he envisioned a union of Greeks all convinced that Hellenism was a
community of all civilized men. This unity, he thought, might best be
realized in a great crusade against Persia, whose weakness Xenophon's
expedition had exposed. For fifty years Isocrates turned from one power
to another in search of a leader for his crusade, appealing successively
to the Second Athenian League (*Panegyricus*, 380 B.C.), Jason of Pherae,

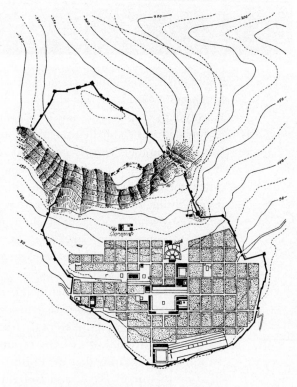

Fig. 28b. Plan of Priene. 4th century
B.C. Rectangular grid on terrace, with
agora in center and theater higher
up. The walls enclose an area large
enough for 4,000 people. The remains give a good idea of a typical
planned city of the period. (A. von
Gerkan, *Griechische Städteanlagen*,
Berlin and Leipzig, 1924. Abb. 9.)

Fig. 28.8. Olynthus. Villa of Good Fortune, model. A two-story, sixteen-room house of 348 B.C., with peristyle and mosaic floors. (*Archaeology* V, 1952, p. 232.)

Dionysius I, Archidamus III of Sparta, Evagoras and Nicocles of Cyprus, and finally Philip II. He did not live to see his dream realized, but Alexander's empire owes much to the ideas of this "old man eloquent."

For Isocrates Panhellenism was more important than domestic policy, but his pamphlets *On the Peace* and *Areopagiticus* (355 B.C.) show that he saw the connection between them. He was never willing to sacrifice Athenian autonomy to his ideal; in his *Panathenaicus* (339 B.C.) he asked Philip for a privileged position for Athens. Of his fellow citizens he asked moral reform, suppression of selfishness, and a return to the ancestral constitution supervised by the Areopagus. Like Xenophon, Isocrates had no faith in the Athenian democracy, which had been brutalized by irresponsible oratory.

Demosthenes, on the other hand, at least tried to rouse democracy out of apathy into action, to educate it up to a laborious outlay of civic virtue. His was the eternal struggle of the man of vision trying to convince his fellow citizens of the need to defend liberty against tyranny, in this case that of Philip of Macedon. Demosthenes is the hero in an epic of David and Goliath which is also a tragedy, for him and for his city. Familiar from Plutarch is his struggle against his wicked guardians and against his own defective voice, which he trained by declaiming with pebbles in his mouth. His resultant skill in speaking he used partly in private suits, over thirty of which survive, but his distinction in oratory soon involved him in politics. He began political life among the conservatives led by the financier Eubulus, but his position changed as he saw Philip's inexorable progress to primacy in the Greek world.

In his great *Third Philippic* (341 B.C.) Demosthenes argued that Athens no longer had a free choice between war and peace; with all Greece in the greatest peril, Athens must think of its great tradition (which to him was vital because it was rooted in the plain people who fought at Marathon) and lead the fight for freedom in the face of intrigue and corruption whereby Philip, using fifth-column methods, had gained a foothold throughout Greece. Demosthenes flayed Athenian selfishness, susceptibility to flattery, inertia, apathy, forgetfulness of ancient reputation, complacency, and self-seeking. His positive proposals included realistic financing to equip an army and astute diplomacy to form alliances. Athens was stirred, but too little and too late; three years later Philip won at Chaeronea.

His enemies' opposition to his grateful fellow-citizens' gift of the gold crown for distinguished service moved Demosthenes in his most famous speech, *On the Crown* (330 B.C.), to defend his private life and his public policy, arguing that his anti-Macedonian policy at the time of Chaeronea had been right, the only course possible, and that any other would have dishonored Athens. In an eloquent passage he took the men of Marathon to witness that it had ever been Athens' way to honor the brave, regardless of whether they found in battle defeat or victory.

Demosthenes won his crown, but his final reward for years of hard work not only in moving public sentiment and keeping up morale, but in running the city's finance, diplomacy, and military effort, fighting as a common soldier, and spending his own money on reinforcing the city walls, was accusation of bribery, imprisonment, and exile. In 322 B.C. he committed suicide rather than fall into the hands of his enemies among the Athenians. With him Athens died as a political power, though its intellectual primacy remained quite unchallenged for nearly another thousand years. Demosthenes and his policy had seemed to go down in defeat, but out of such temporary defeats the centuries make victories.

Philosophy

The names to conjure with in this century are those of its two great philosophers, Plato (*c.* 429–347 B.C.) and Aristotle (384–322 B.C.). Plato, imperious and authoritarian aristocrat, was devoted to Socrates' memory; apart from some abortive attempts to put his philosophy into practice in Sicily, he consecrated his life to teaching in his Academy (founded about 387 B.C.) and to writing his brilliant dialogues, of which

35 survive. Of these the most important are the *Apology,* on Socrates' trial; the *Phaedo,* on Socrates' death and the immortality of the soul; the *Symposium,* on love and its sublimation; the *Republic,* on justice in the individual and the state, the *Timaeus,* on the origin and system of the universe, and the *Laws,* on the practical organization of a real state.

Plato's dialogues state for the western world the idealistic or dualistic position: that mind is superior over matter, soul over body, and reason over the senses. His method he called dialectic: it involves precise definition, arrival at conclusions by induction, and education as Socrates had practiced it, by question and answer drawing from the pupil the truth that is in him. In metaphysics he argued for the immortality of the soul and for the primacy of what he called Ideas or Forms, which partake of the nature of our abstract conception of things, but have a real existence outside the world of sense; they are the unchanging reality behind the changing appearance. Plato thought of his Forms as in an ascending order, culminating in the Idea of the Good, the True, and the Beautiful. In ethics Plato held that all human action is directed toward some good, about the nature of which a man may err, but about which he may also be taught, for virtue is knowledge. It follows that a man does evil only through ignorance; the wrongdoer is more unhappy than his victim; the unpunished sinner more unhappy than he who pays for his crime. In esthetics Plato held that art, as a copy of mere material things which in turn do not adequately represent the Forms, is a mere imitation of an imitation. In literature he opposes those poets (Homer sometimes, Euripides always) who present the gods unworthily or overemphasize passion.

To the intellectual historian, Plato's most influential dialogue is the *Republic.* It opens with an analysis of current opinions on justice, those of the man in the street, the poet, the sophist (who thinks it is the interest of the stronger). Obviously the term needs definition, not only as it applies to the state, but, more important, as it affects individual conduct. But the state, being larger, is easier to analyze: in it, justice is found to consist in a harmonious division of labor in which each man does the job for which he is best suited, even if he has to be propagandized into it. If the just city is to be realized, there must be great innovations: women must be educated like men, the rulers must give up family life, and they must be philosopher-kings, educated in mathematics and dialectic, and aware of their duty to bring light to those who sit in darkness. By contrast, Plato described the unjust state and the unjust man, be he timocrat, oligarch, democrat, or tyrant. In the just state emotional and impressionistic art are to be condemned; in the end the rewards of the just life are great in this life and in the life to come.

The whole of modern philosophy has been described as a set of footnotes to Plato. His austerity, aristocratic bias, and insistence on the rule of an élite have prompted attacks upon him by liberals, and it is indeed clear that Plato takes no very optimistic view of the common man's capabilities, but it is in his desire to exalt and improve the individual's lot that his value lies: his very austerity, his insistence that man's reach should exceed his grasp, his exhortation that the philosopher-king should rule in us, have been an inspiration to the intellectual life for over twenty-three hundred years.

Almost equally great has been the influence of Plato's pupil Aristotle. Son of the Macedonian court physician and later himself tutor to Alexander, Aristotle came young to Athens and sat at Plato's feet for twenty years before founding his own school, the Lyceum. His works, terse as lecture notes, full of technical terms, precise and unadorned, form a complete and classified encyclopedia, synthesizing all the knowledge of his day. His method, which he invented, was formal logic: reasoning from a major through a minor premise to a conclusion. He divided knowledge into theoretical and practical: the former including metaphysics, mathematics, and physics, the latter embracing ethics, politics, and poetics. Rejecting Plato's Forms, he distinguished four causes: material (the marble of a statue), formal (the model), efficient (the sculptor), final (the sculptor's intention). In nature, observation of characteristics common to certain groups led him to classify plants and animals according to genus and species.

Our chief concern is with his *Ethics* and *Politics,* which, for him as for Plato, are connected. Ethics is the science of the good for man as an individual. Man's good is happiness, defined as an activity of the soul in accordance with virtue, "a state of character concerned with choice," lying not in a transcendental sphere, as for Plato, but in a mean. The Greeks distinguished four cardinal virtues: wisdom, justice, courage, temperance. Temperance, for example, lies in a mean between drunkenness and total abstinence, courage between rashness and cowardice, wisdom between pedantry and ignorance. Courage, temperance and justice are moral virtues; wisdom is intellectual virtue, best realized in the contemplative life, where happiness consists in uninterrupted intellectual activity. After a discussion of pleasure and friendship as related to happiness, Aristotle concluded that legislation is needed if happiness is to be attained not merely for the individual but for society; this is his transition to the *Politics.*

There is some evidence that the writing of *Politics* was preceded in scientific fashion by the collection of a large number of constitutions of actual states on which to base generalizations (Aristotle's *Athenian Constitution* survives, having been discovered in 1891). The *Politics* begins by defining the state as the highest form of community, aiming at the highest good. Its nature is to be formed by analyzing its smallest component part, the household. There follows a sharp criticism of Plato's *Republic* as incomplete and aiming at a unity both undesirable and, under his system, impossible. Next citizenship is defined as membership in jury court and assembly, requiring property and leisure. States may be ruled well or badly (the criterion being whether they are governed for the common good or the good of the ruler) by one, few, or many. The classification produces six types, the good being monarchy, aristocracy, or "polity" (constitutional government) ; the bad, tyranny, oligarchy, and democracy (defined as the rule of the poor and unleisured). The best claims to power are education and virtue. Aristotle then treated the various constitutions, with a fascinating and incisive section on revolutions, their cause (desire for power) and cure (the best cures are moderation and conciliatory public spirit). According to him, the best practicable state would be of medium size, the land neither all public nor all private, the citizens of the middle class, habituated to the life of reason by a systematic, universal, and public education.

Aristotle's *Poetics* suggest that he would not follow Plato in ejecting tragedy from the state; it serves a purpose, to purge the soul by an experience of pity and terror.

Aristotle's work in practical philosophy brings Plato down to earth, sets the ideal in this world, where it is attainable by effort, and not in the next, where it may seem unattainable, and exalts the solid, sensible *bourgeoisie*. His powerful logic produced a system which dominated the intellectual life of the medieval era, his keen observation reached conclusions of the greatest interest to modern science. In his impulse to synthesis, his concept of an educated, responsible ruling class, Aristotle was characteristic of the best minds of his age, but he towers above that age as the center of the revolution from the classical to the Hellenistic world.

In this century Athens, small as it was, became the cosmopolitan center of one world, where artists, sculptors, architects, orators, historians, philosophers met continually and struck sparks from each other in the process of working out the common attitudes which have been summarized as the emphasis on contrast, organic structure, and external appearance. There are dangers in each attitude, but we owe much to the creative artists of this century. Their total achievement is astonishing; this is the century of Praxiteles and Lysippus, of Isocrates and Demosthenes, of Plato and Aristotle. In this small city, in this interconnected world, artist and architect, orator and philosopher together elaborated a concept of human life which was passed on to Alexandria, to Rome, and so to us.

Chapter 29/FOUNDER OF THE HELLENISTIC[1] ERA: ALEXANDER

Philip's son Alexander, to be called the Great, carried on his father's work spectacularly well. He began his reign at the age of twenty, and in only twelve years and eight months marched his armies from Greece to India, revealing in the process supreme qualities of courage, organizational ability and leadership, and unique military genius, together with no little brutality and no little chivalry. He subjected the homelands of all the civilizations thus far surveyed in this book. He was Columbus and Cortez, discoverer and conqueror. He realized Philip and Isocrates' dream of uniting the Greeks against Persia. Dreamer as well as realist, he laid at frightful cost the foundations for a supra-national commonwealth. He was perhaps the first Greek to treat Greek and barbarian as equal. Death claimed him before he was thirty-three, but his legacy was one of civilization's most fruitful ideals: that of

[1] The term "Hellenistic" is used to describe Hellenism as spread by Alexander and his successors over the Near East and far into Asia. Alexandria in Egypt was the intellectual center of Hellenistic civilization. The era is characterized by monarchy and the rise of large states, by rootless cosmopolitanism and lonely individualism, by nostalgia for the past, and by the rise of science.

Fig. 29.1. Alexander. From Hadrian's Villa, copy of an original by Lysippus. The pose of the neck and head, the treatment of the hair, are those affected by Alexander, perhaps to give himself that lionlike quality exalted by Plutarch. (Paris, Louvre)

different nations linked by a common culture in peace under a common authority.

The Problem of Greece

Alexander inherited in intensive form both the good and the bad qualities of his father. An incomparable warrior, he could, like his father, kindle his men's imagination and arouse their devotion. Also like his father, he was sometimes brutal and violent. His Molossian mother Olympias, a new Medea in a Greek court, was boundlessly ambitious. A passionate Dionysiac devotee, she may have implanted in the youth that mysticism which led him to declare that sleep and sex impede man's fullest development. Sprung from such parents, he naturally thirsted for power and sighed—or so the myth-makers say—when there were no more worlds to conquer.

Alexander was fortunate in his teachers: first, his father who taught him war, statecraft, and how to handle men; then, Aristotle, an intellectual influence profounder than kings or conquerors. Aristotle stimulated the boy's eager mind to study ethics, politics, logic, metaphysics, and the natural sciences. Alexander was fascinated by Greek mythology and believed he was a descendant of Achilles and Heracles. He cherished an *Iliad* annotated by Aristotle for a course in rhetoric and kept it—and a dagger—under his pillow.

When the army had ratified his accession (336 B.C.) Alexander, in the first of his famous shortcuts to success, liquidated several possible pretenders as well as the disloyal Attalus, his father's general in Asia. His father's new wife and her infant daughter he left in the hands of Olympias.

Three short campaigns in Europe revealed Alexander's military genius. On news of Philip's death several states denounced the League of Corinth as a personal contract with Philip, which lapsed with his death. But Philip's son took them from behind and they changed their minds. The League, now permanently renewed, confirmed him as Greek generalissimo, commanding the projected war against Persia (336 B.C.).

Philip's death sparked revolt also among the barbarians surrounding Macedon. In defeating them—by quick thinking in a crisis—Alexander proved to himself and his army that his tactical ability matched his father's. In his fight against the barbarians of the northeast he demonstrated, not for the last time, an irrational impulse to probe the unknown. Determined to discover what lay beyond the Danube, he ferried across in one night 1500 horse and 4000 foot—in small boats and on sacks stuffed with straw. Early morning found the Macedonians assaulting the camp of the Getae, who in dismay collected their women and children and made for the northern steppes. As in previous campaigns against other barbarians, Alexander lost not a man.

In Greece Persian money was at work, reviving the parties still eager for autonomy. Demosthenes alone received 300 talents to promote insurrections and supply arms. Someone was produced to testify before the Athenian Ecclesia that he had seen Alexander killed in battle. The hoax electrified Thebes also, where patriots besieged the Macedonian garrison in the Cadmea. Several states sent reinforcements. Alexander reached the city with lightning speed. Rebuffed when he offered amnesty to all but the ringleaders, he took Thebes by assault (335 B.C.). With a precocious diplomatic wisdom he left its fate up to the League. A hastily called meeting, packed by pro-Macedonian states, voted to destroy the rebel city. Six thousand patriots fell, and there were left standing only the temples and the house of the poet Pindar, whom Alexander admired next after Homer. The democrats' party was wiped out, and 8000 men, women, and children were allegedly sold as slaves. This ruthlessness demoralized every Greek state, including Athens, which had sympathized with the rebels. But Alexander was lenient toward Athens, asking at first only the surrender of ten men, including Demosthenes, then relenting and leaving the matter to the Ecclesia.

Finally only one man was exiled; the rest left the city voluntarily. Demosthenes was left undisturbed.

The problem of Greece thus settled (fall 335 B.C.), Alexander turned to the war against Persia. He appointed his father's trusted friend Antipater viceroy of Macedonia and watchdog of Greece. Antipater re-established a tyranny or two which had existed at the time the states in question had joined the League of Corinth. This naturally antagonized the democratic masses. Though they felt that Antipater's policy violated Alexander's noninterference pledge, the Greeks were too cowed to break the peace.

Decline of Persian Power

Persia was ill-prepared for the attack. Its internal weakness increased during the long reigns of Darius II (424–405 B.C.) and his son Artaxerxes II (404–358 B.C.). Ministers and satraps turned traitor, subjects revolted, intrigue was rampant in court and army, and often in the king's own family; a king or heir apparent was lucky if he escaped poisoning or assassination.

Dissension in the royal family was matched or exceeded among the viceroys and satraps. Hardly a year passed without rebellion or civil war in the satrapies. War between satraps was not necessarily disloyalty to the throne. It might climax a series of misrepresentations of the victim of aggression as a traitor and the aggressor as defender of the crown. But even if its aim was to gain royal favor, its result was to weaken the monarchy.

In its impotence Persia lost its richest province, Egypt, which, after challenging Darius II's authority throughout his reign, at his death proclaimed independence. Three dynasties (XXVIIIth, XXIXth, and XXXth) prospered, defeating several Persian armies, once (361 B.C.) with the Spartan Agesilaus' help, and restoring the prosperity of Psamtik's day. At last Artaxerxes III (358–338 B.C.), using Greek mercenaries, brought the country to terms (343 B.C.).

The fourth-century kings antagonized the subject nations when they abandoned the former Persian policy of tolerating native traditions. Artaxerxes II's contemptuous treatment of Jewish holy books caused widespread Jewish resentment, reflected in *Esther* and *Judith*. When Artaxerxes III entered Egypt he turned the temple of Ptah into a stable, slew "the living bull" Apis, and served him up at a banquet. Offended nationalism nourished the hope of a Messianic deliverer. At the same time a rash of subversive acts broke out.

The subject Greek city-states of Asia and the islands were easily managed, for 250 years of servitude to Lydia, Persia, Athens, and Persia again had left little taste for independence. Then too their soft way of life was utterly unmartial. The record of challenges from Athens and Sparta proved to the Persian monarchs that the real danger was from Greece proper. Persian policy therefore aimed at keeping the European Greeks divided, a policy which required no Persian regiments, only bribes and the knack of playing one state off against another.

Greek weakness allowed the Great King to purchase Greek military manpower which a united Greece would have used against him. True, his enemies bought mercenaries, too: Cyrus the Younger to wrest the crown from his brother, the satraps to make their own wars. But the Great King could outbid his rivals. Economic distress among the masses made manpower a drug on the market. Greek mercenaries enabled Persia to recapture Egypt, Cyprus, and Phoenicia, put down the satrap revolts, and ultimately face Alexander the Great.

Artaxerxes III's death was a loss Persia could not afford. He had re-energized the administration and, despite his repressive religious policy, given the Empire a new cohesion. He was poisoned by his own prime minister, who proclaimed one royal son king and assassinated his brothers. Then in the critical spring of 336 B.C., while Philip was sending his advance army to Asia, the faithless minister murdered the young monarch together with his sons, giving the throne to a kinsman of Artaxerxes, Darius III, who promptly poisoned the kingmaker. When Alexander invaded Persia, he had an unknown ally in the dissensions of the central government.

Conquest of the Persian Empire

Except for a fleet, provisions, and money, Alexander's expeditionary force was superb. His cavalry numbered 5000: Macedonians, Greeks, and Thracians. His infantry numbered about 32,000 men: 9000 in the phalanx; 3000 light-armed hypaspists, a distinguished corps named from the shields (*aspides*) they carried; 7000 allies, chiefly barbarians; and 7000 Greek hoplites used for garrison duty, seldom in actual fighting, for they were present chiefly as hostages for Greek good behavior. Five thousand Greek and Asian mercenaries completed the regular army. A well-trained artillery corps distinguished this expedition from every previous one, except Dionysius the Elder's march against Motya and Philip's Greek campaigns. Unique too were a number of technical services: an intelligence and communications section manned chiefly by barbarians, a commissary, an ambulance group, and a small medical corps. A natural interest in, and 'layman's knowledge of, medicine, acquired under Aristotle's guidance, led Alexander to interest himself personally in this service. Alexander stressed, too, constant close liaison between the different services, especially in the hour of battle.

Alexander himself handled every crisis, ordering every movement,

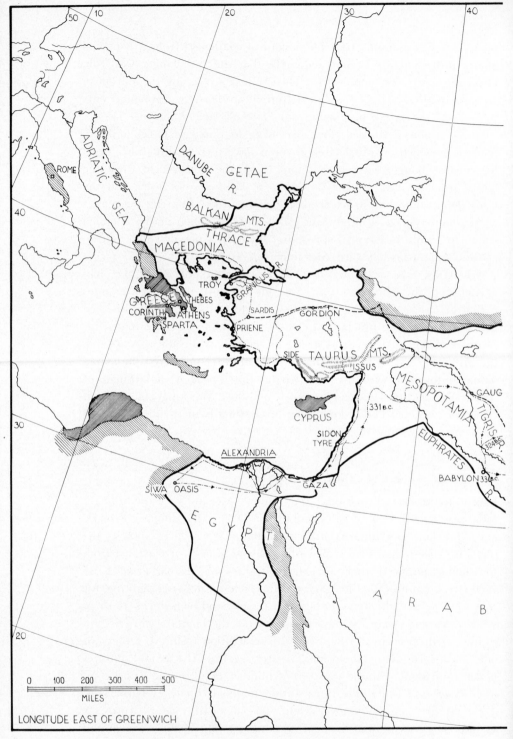

Fig. 29a. Map of Alexander's Empire

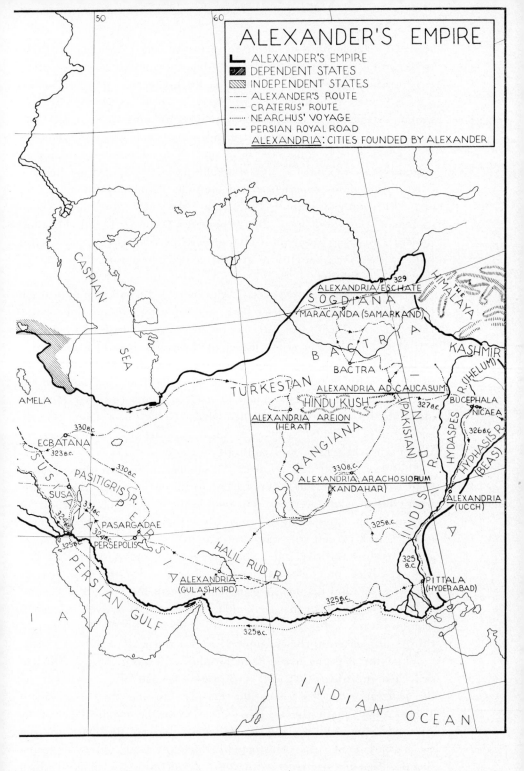

ALEXANDER'S EMPIRE

⌐	ALEXANDER'S EMPIRE
▨	DEPENDENT STATES
▨	INDEPENDENT STATES
—·—·—	ALEXANDER'S ROUTE
—··—··—	CRATERUS' ROUTE
········	NEARCHUS' VOYAGE
— — —	PERSIAN ROYAL ROAD
<u>ALEXANDRIA</u>:	CITIES FOUNDED BY ALEXANDER

CASPIAN SEA

AMELA

TURKESTAN

SOGDIANA

329
ALEXANDRIA ESCHATE
MARACANDA (SAMARKAND)

BACTRA

BACTRA

HIMALAYA

KASHMIR

HINDU KUSH

ALEXANDRIA AD CAUCASUM

ALEXANDRIA AREION
(HERAT)

DRANGIANA

ECBATANA
330 B.C.
323 B.C.

330 B.C.

SUS
SUSA
316 B.C.
PASITIGRIS R.
PASARGADAE
PERSEPOLIS
PERSIA
324

327 B.C.

BUCEPHALA
NICAEA

HYDASPES R. (HELUM)

326 B.C.
HYPHASIS R.
(BEAS)

ALEXANDRIA ARACHOSIORUM
(KANDAHAR)
330 B.C.

ALEXANDRIA
(UCCH)

325 B.C.

325
B.C.

PITTALA
(HYDERABAD)

325 B.C.

HALIL RUD R.
ALEXANDRIA
(GULASHKIRD)

PERSIAN GULF

I A

325 B.C.

INDIAN OCEAN

INDUS R. (PAKISTAN)

ready in a flash with a stratagem to turn near-defeat into victory. Blind to his brutal side, his admiring men, Macedonians and foreigners alike, were ready to give their lives for him, for his reckless courage and his personal interest in their welfare. After a battle he would make the rounds of the camp, visiting the wounded, listening to their tall tales of the day's events, never failing to praise their valor. Except for Napoleon's general staff, there has probably never been so brilliant an entourage as Alexander's, chosen by Philip, but retained by his son. They included his experienced chief-of-staff, Parmenio, staunch friend and wise counselor of both Philip and Alexander; Antigonus, whose diplomacy was worth more than regiments; Seleucus, Lysimachus, and Ptolemy, all kings-to-be; the Cretan Nearchus who was to make naval history; Perdiccas, the future regent; and Hephaestion, Patroclus to Alexander's Achilles.

On arriving in Asia (334 B.C.), Alexander led a military pilgrimage to Troy. For he was Achilles reborn, dedicated to a resumption of war with Asia. His men were infected by his sense of dedication. But he was also a new Agamemnon, leader of the Greek host to a showdown with the barbarian, even though his latter-day Greeks played minor parts. To avoid dependence on Greek cities, he had even skimped his fleet. Yet the Macedonian monarchy had long ago espoused Hellenic ideals, and the Macedonians themselves—Greek in religion, speech, and sense of Asian mission—personified Isocrates' intellectual view of Hellenism as not racial but cultural.

The Persians decided to meet Alexander on the Granicus, which from back of Troy runs east-northeast to the Hellespont. Though elsewhere the Persians were to rely on numbers, here the governors of the Anatolian satrapies, disdaining to use their large Greek mercenary force, hoped to end the war by themselves killing Alexander. Alexander reached the river on a spring afternoon and, disregarding Parmenio's advice, ordered an immediate attack. Across the swollen river went his men and up the opposite bank to give the Persians a beating (334 B.C.) from which they took eighteen months to recover. A Persian scimitar nearly split Alexander's skull, but one of the Companions, Clitus, surnamed the Black, jumped to his rescue.

While the Persians licked their wounds, Alexander was active. He dedicated in Athens 300 sets of captured Persian armor, symbolizing the vengeance he had taken for Persia's burning the Acropolis in 480 B.C. Diplomatically, he gave the Greeks the credit: "Taken by Alexander, son of Philip, and the Hellenes, all except the Spartans, from the barbarians of Asia." He then liberated the Greek cities, replacing the pro-Persian oligarchies with loyal democratic governments which he made members of his Corinthian League. The liberation of the Greek cities dovetailed with his maritime strategy. To prevent the

Persian fleet from cutting his communications with Europe, he marched along the Asiatic seaboard as far east as Side, occupying every harbor and supply base. The Persian fleet, defeated on land, eventually broke up.

During this unopposed march Alexander replaced Persian satraps with Macedonians. The story goes that at Gordium, in central Asia Minor, he was shown the relic of an ancient king, a chariot whose yoke was fastened in a complicated knot. The man who could untie the knot, it was said, would become master of Asia. Many had tried and failed. When Alexander's fingers failed, he took his sword and cut it.

Alexander had now decided on the conquest of Asia. On the far side of the difficult Taurus Mountains he reached the crossroads of the Middle East where for seven thousand years armies have clashed and empires risen or fallen. On the plain of Issus he unexpectedly met (333 B.C.) the Persian army, again on ground of its own choosing, and commanded by Darius himself. Alexander's onslaught sent the Great King fleeing in panic. Even so, the Persian army, especially its 12,000 Greeks, continued to fight bravely. Finally, however, it crumbled before the phalanx. Alexander, in the thick of battle as usual, was wounded, but he had won a decisive battle. Sitting in Darius' tent, in luxury unprecedented to a Macedonian, he said: "This, I believe, is being a king." Darius' mother and daughters and his beautiful wife, now prisoners, were courteously treated. The victory of Issus had far-reaching results: the spoils, including Darius' war-chest, solved Alexander's financial problem; the resultant prestige cowed recalcitrant Greek states; and from Issus Alexander could choose between two routes, toward Mesopotamia or the eastern Mediterranean coast.

Alexander chose to invade the coast, to destroy the seat of Persia's naval power and open the way to Egypt. Only Tyre, chief arsenal and recruiting center of Persia's navies, resisted his advance. Old Tyre was a mainland city, but probably as early as the eighth century its industries, shipyards, and docks had been moved to an offshore island which gradually became antiquity's most impregnable fortress. Alexander tried in vain to take it by building a causeway from the mainland. He then enlisted the services of 120 Phoenician warships, chiefly from Sidon, eager for the destruction of its ancient rival. The employment of fire and siege-engines and the ingenuity and doggedness of both sides still excite students of tactics. Tyre was eventually captured and made a Macedonian fortress. Whereas Nebuchadrezzar 250 years earlier had assaulted it for thirteen fruitless years, Alexander won success in seven months (January-July 332 B.C.). One more fortress, Gaza, blocked the road to Egypt. Alexander took it after a two-months' siege and made it too a Macedonian fortress. Then he marched unopposed into Egypt, to be welcomed by the natives as liberator and pharaoh (fall 332 B.C.).

At this point his mysticism reasserted itself. Though a decisive battle with the Persian army was urgent, he traveled 280 miles into the Libyan desert, to the Siwah Oasis, the home of a temple to Ammon, Egypt's principal god, whose oracle rivaled those of Delphi and Dodona in prestige among the Greeks. The Spartan Lysander, as we saw, had consulted it while scheming to become master of Greece. Although Alexander's interview was private, the story gradually spread that the oracle hailed him son of Ammon. This was to be expected, since Alexander was Pharaoh, therefore the god's incarnate son. But since the Greeks had long identified Ammon with Zeus, the oracle's greeting might easily be turned into a message to the Greeks that he was son of Zeus. Apparently this interpretation pleased Alexander, as an answer to those who doubted his mortal parentage. He himself perhaps helped foster the legend that Zeus in the shape of a snake had had intercourse with Olympias.

With Asia Minor, Egypt, and the lands between in his grasp, Alexander stabbed at the Empire's heartland, entering Mesopotamia (summer 331 B.C.) to meet the re-formed Persian army at Gaugamela, well east of the Tigris. He thwarted Darius' front line of scythed chariots intended to slice the Macedonian front into segments (October 1, 331 B.C.). The one serious gap that developed was stopped by the ever ready Companions. This was Alexander's slimmest victory, only assured by Darius' second shameful flight, which set the example for his army. Only the Greek mercenaries retreated in order.

Gaugamela was sign unmistakable that the Persian Empire was crumbling. Darius' staunchest supporters abandoned him, and one capital after another opened its gates to the conqueror: Babylon, Susa, Persepolis, Pasargadae, Ecbatana. Alexander burned Xerxes' palace at Persepolis as symbol to the Greeks that Nemesis had been served and that Achemenid rule was ended. The Great King's treasuries fell into his hands: gold, silver, jewels, and 120,000 talents in coins and bullion, the equivalent of 130,000,000 gold dollars, with a purchasing power of $4,000,000,000. This wealth staggered the imagination of frugal Macedonians and Greeks. After taking Ecbatana, Alexander pursued the fleeing Darius with a small force. When after eleven days the vanguard caught up with Darius, they found him dying—stabbed by men who despised him for his cowardice (July 330 B.C.). Alexander sent the body to Persepolis for burial and ascended the Achemenid throne.

Central Asia to the Indian Ocean

The period after Darius' death was militarily the most fascinating in Alexander's life and politically the most important. Instead of consolidating his gains, he pushed his armies on—for seven more years and some 5000 zigzag miles—into a world unknown to Westerners: Turkestan, Afghanistan, Kashmir, Pakistan, and the great watershed east of the Indus River. They saw fabulously strange civilizations, unspoiled by urbanism and fiercely independent. In all Afghanistan only one place, Bactra, even looked like a city. The Great King had never really controlled these frontier peoples; they acknowledged only their local lords. Although racially heterogeneous, they found in Zoroastrianism a common bond. The terrain—steppes, deserts, icy mountains, and a bewildering network of torrents and rivers—forced Alexander constantly to change strategy. Whether the Turkomans used desert tactics or the Sogdians guerrilla warfare, he could always beat them at their own game.

The army's quality matched their general's cunning. Scantily supplied, roaming through countries completely unfamiliar to them, they lived for weeks and months on a starvation diet. Snowblinded, they crossed and recrossed the freezing Hindu Kush, after the Himalayas the highest mountains in Asia, through passes 14,000 feet high. To take one fortress, some 300 volunteers climbed up a sheer cliff by driving iron pegs into rock and ice. They tramped over deserts, tormented by thirst and illness. Alexander himself fell ill from drinking bad water. They spent three years (330–327 B.C.) under these hardships to subdue regions of questionable value to Alexander. The men feared they were lost, thousands of miles from home, in an inextricable tangle of river, mountain, and desert.

Alexander's immediate objective was to capture Bessus, Darius' cousin and probably the chief instigator of his death, who had proclaimed himself King of Persia. Bessus aimed to wear the Macedonians out in the frontier satrapies of Bactria and Sogdiana. Even when, after two years, he was captured, the war was not over, for the Sogdian Spitamenes, Alexander's most resourceful enemy, took up the torch. He destroyed eight or nine Macedonian garrisons, decimated Alexander's army in open battle, and twice besieged Samarkand, which Alexander had taken soon after capturing Bessus. Alexander finally built a network of forts and isolated the Sogdian tribes. Finally a turncoat tribe slew Spitamenes and sent his head to Alexander as a gift. Meantime Bessus had been tried and executed for murder and usurpation of the throne.

Driven by an irresistible inner force, Alexander then spent two years (327–325 B.C.) trying to subjugate what is now Pakistan, ostensibly because the area had owed allegiance to Darius the Great, really to ascertain whether India, of whose extent he had no idea, marked the eastern end of the earth. Crossing the upper Indus River (326 B.C.), he exposed his men to still another and much different civilization and to more desperate fighting. In a battle with the rajah Porus they faced a terrifying wall of 200 elephants. As they advanced south beyond the Jhelum (Hydaspes) River, a main tributary of the Indus, they found the country more tropical. At the Beas (Hyphasis) River during the drenching winter monsoon, they balked. In rags, their weapons bent or blunted, their spirit broken, they told Alexander they had had enough. No appeal, no ruse could dissuade them; they had gone repeatedly beyond the call of duty; it was time to go home. Alexander had to yield, his dream of reaching the world's end shattered. But at least Porus, recognized as king, had become his ally.

The return west demonstrated anew Alexander's organizational genius. To explore the countries between the Indus and Persia, he divided his army three ways (spring 325 B.C.), fixing a rendezvous on the Halil Rud River, some 150 miles above the entrance to the Persian Gulf. One section, under Craterus, trekked westward from the middle Indus via Kandahar; another, under Nearchus, sailed down the Indus; the third, under Alexander, marched along its banks. Near Hyderabad (Pittala) the fleet and the third division parted company. Nearchus reached the Indian Ocean, then sailed west, hugging the coast while Alexander marched overland through an utterly strange and hostile region. At long last Craterus, Nearchus, and the king rendezvoused and then went on to Susa, the armies via Persepolis, the fleet traversing the Persian Gulf, then sailing up the Pasitigris River. In 323 B.C. the expedition reached Babylon.

Alexander the Statesman

Years of constant fighting amidst civilizations even stranger, more distant than legend had ever imagined put Alexander and his men under severe strain. Their heroism was heightened, but their nerves were frayed. The cases of Philotas and his father Parmenio illustrate the result. In Drangiana, gateway to central Asia, Alexander in 330 B.C. had Philotas, one of his ablest generals, executed for treason. Philotas had inexplicably concealed his knowledge of a plot to murder Alexander. Himself discovering the plan, Alexander had the general delivered up to the army for execution, in accordance with Macedonian constitutional practice. But the subsequent murder of Philotas' father had no legal—much less moral—justification. Parmenio, who had served both Alexander and Philip faithfully and well, was hardly the man to turn against his king because of his son's execution. But Alexander, taking no chances, had his faithful friend assassinated. One wonders whether the proofs of Philotas' guilt were really incontrovertible.

Three years later, while drunk, Alexander with his own hand killed another faithful follower. At one of those Macedonian banquets that usually turned into orgies Clitus the Black, also drunk, compared Alexander unfavorably to Philip. Twice forcibly removed by friends, he returned each time to remind the king that he had saved the royal life at the Granicus. Before the horrified assemblage, Alexander in a rage ran him through with a spear. Then, conscience-stricken, he shut himself up in his tent and fasted for three days. After the murder, the flatterer Anaxarchus allegedly told the Macedonian Zeus that kings are above the law.

Alexander antagonized his men when he decreed (327 B.C.) that all who approached him should prostrate themselves in the Persian fashion. The order was too much for sophisticated Greeks or simple Macedonians. Whereas for the Persians prostration was merely protocol, the Greeks and Macedonians knelt only before the gods, and Alexander, they knew, was no god. Alexander knew it too but, as we shall see, he had political reasons for wanting to be so regarded. The Macedonians laughed the royal order off as a joke. The Greek Callisthenes expressed his countrymen's reaction: he called the king's demand an act of Asian despotism. But Callisthenes soon found himself in difficulties.

Callisthenes, Aristotle's nephew and one of several intellectuals attached to the expedition, had been chosen by Alexander as adviser on Greek affairs and soon promoted to court historian or propagandist. (A more objective chronicle was kept by Eumenes of Cardia in the *Journal*, though the fragments we have may be a forgery. This was an official day-by-day account of personnel, commissariat, communications, reconnaissance, tactics, political developments, and the like, modeled on Philip's *Journal*.) Callisthenes' job was public relations; he shamelessly glorified his master, with exaggerated accounts of miracles, stating for example that the sea once prostrated itself before the king. From him too comes the information that the oracle of Siwah hailed Alexander as son of Ammon-Zeus. He used to boast that Alexander would be remembered not for what he did, but for what Callisthenes wrote. But the boaster was hoist by his own petard; Alexander's divinity as propaganda was one thing; taken seriously, it was another. Callisthenes recoiled from it as stubbornly as did the recalcitrant soldiers. Faced by this determined opposition, Alexander dropped the idea of prostration, but had Callisthenes put to death for conspiracy.

Three years after the prostration order was revoked, Alexander asserted an undisguised claim to divinity. From Susa, on his way home (324 B.C.), he commanded the cities of the Corinthian League to take back all political exiles. Twenty thousand displaced persons with wives and children were roaming through Greece, unsettling the region's peace and economy. Though eminently constructive, the order ignored the facts of Greek politics. Class hatreds and political practices, deep-rooted in

Greek tradition, could not be legislated away at one stroke, especially when the order was an invasion of city rights by a generalissimo who had no jurisdiction over internal affairs. To circumvent this constitutional obstacle, Alexander ordered the League cities to declare him a god. As god, bound by no human laws, he could compel obedience.

While agnostic intellectuals saw deification of a living man as a political dodge without religious significance, the masses, religious in almost every age, took it seriously. Alexander's world-shaking career might well, to them, appear godlike. Even Isocrates and Aristotle, with Philip and Alexander respectively in mind, had in hyperbolic phrases equated supreme success with divinity. Their thinking had affected Callisthenes and, doubtless, other intellectuals. The masses, even more deeply impressed, had the vote required to give Alexander the supraconstitutional position he sought. Even the Athenian Ecclesia fell into line. Moreover, when the vote came on this issue, the educated and the superstitious both knew that the would-be god, though thousands of miles away, was looking over their shoulders. Sparta, outside the League, alone refused him divine status. Alexander had Greece on its knees.

Alexander's claim to divinity was only a means to an end: the establishment of a world empire unprecentedly just, humane, and close-knit. Some of his steps toward that ideal, preceding the prostration order of 327 B.C., had angered his army. He had promoted a number of Persians, some even to the office of satrap. He had taken to wearing the tiara and other Persian royal paraphernalia. He had married Roxana, daughter of a Bactrian warlord, to conciliate East Iranian nationalists. He had revealed a plan to train 30,000 Persians as Macedonian soldiers, a move that would have equalized conquered and conquerors. Against this background the prostration order looked ominous.

Though the ordinary soldier grumbled over this confusion of conquered and conquerors, Alexander matured the idea of a fusion of Europe and Asia into one commonwealth. He disclosed further details during his stay at Susa (324 B.C.) shortly after he had ordered the Greeks to worship him. Intermarriage was to be the principal means of integration. He married Darius' daughter Barsine, and his friend Hephaestion married her sister; he had eighty of his principal officers wed Persian princesses, and 10,000 Macedonian rank and file married commoners. Education, too, he saw as a means to his end. He would spread Greek culture over Asia and India. Since to him Greek culture represented man's highest achievement, he relied on Greek language and literature, training in Greek athletics, the celebration of Greek festivals, the diffusion of Greek art to make of Asia a new Hellas.

Since Greek cities would spread Greek culture, Alexander founded and named for himself at least fourteen, possibly some twenty, more.

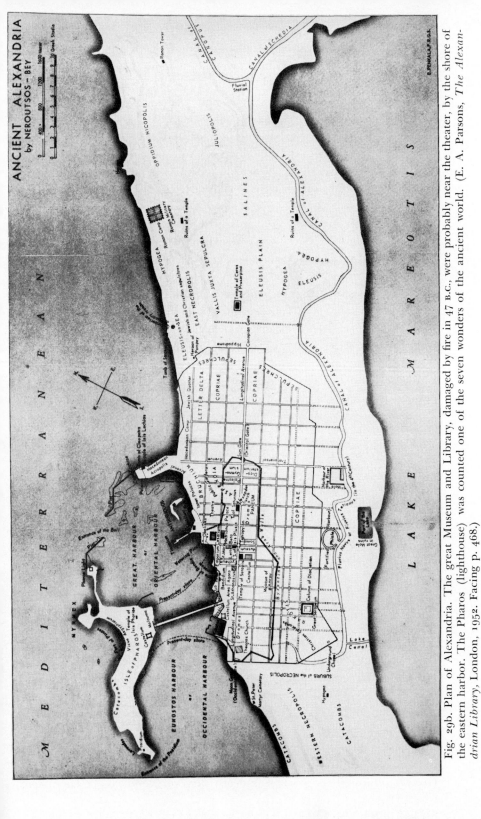

Fig. 29b. Plan of Alexandria. The great Museum and Library, damaged by fire in 47 B.C., were probably near the theater, by the shore of the eastern harbor. The Pharos (lighthouse) was counted one of the seven wonders of the ancient world. (E. A. Parsons, *The Alexandrian Library*, London, 1952. Facing p. 468.)

Several of these towns spread Hellenism hundreds of miles around, their influence affecting even Hindu art and thought. Their chief purpose however was military: to hold down native populations and maintain communications. The settlers, men and women, were preponderantly Greek.

Alexander, sharing with some important thinkers of his age an exalted view of the importance of economics, saw in commerce still another base for his empire. In 331 B.C. he had founded Alexandria in Egypt at the westernmost mouth of the Nile. Within a few years the city became the principal Mediterranean port. To promote east-west trade he built wharves, warehouses, and shipyards in Babylon and in Pittala in India. He planted another Alexandria (Gulashkird) where he, Craterus, and Nearchus had kept their historic rendezvous, to serve as a half-way station between Babylonia, Susiana, and India. He founded cities (military and trading posts) at the crossroads of central Asia: Alexandria Areion (Herat), Alexandria Arachosiorum (Kandahar), Alexandria ad Caucasum (Kabul), Alexandria Eschate (the Ultimate; Khodjend), Bucephala and Nicaea on each side of the Jhelum, Alexandria (Ucch) where the Jhelum flows into the Indus. He made Babylon the imperial capital, and, to assure its prosperity, deepened the Tigris and Euphrates, cleaned the canals, and renovated the irrigation system. Aware how the Pangaeus mines had profited his father, he had engineers survey a gold mine in India.

As a further encouragement to commerce, Alexander introduced an imperial silver currency on the Attic standard. From this Athens and the Aegean world were to gain most, for they became the financial and commercial hub of the Empire. Asia gained too, for the new coinage drove out the divisive provincial currencies. Alexander thus simplified commercial transactions between Europe and Asia and among the Asian nations and laid a good foundation for economic unity from the Adriatic to the Indus.

Alexander's New Model Empire helped to spread a new doctrine, the equality of man. Aristotle held a different view. His pupil, however, now master of the most diverse tribes and nations, perceived that the best binding force was political equality. If this doctrine was calculated statecraft (putting conquered and conquerors on the same level would simplify dominating them all), it was also high idealism. This was *homonoia,* concord or good will, between Greek and barbarian, between European and Asian, and, reasonably enough, between subjects and the imperial throne.

The expedition furthered science. Once he found himself deep in the Persian Empire, Alexander called for more professional men from Greece: philosophers, poets, engineers, surveyors, and, as we have seen, historians. He had Aristotle send him also geographers, botanists, zoologists to collect specimens. With a modern touch he set aside 800 talents for scientific research under his old master's direction. His soldiers were the first Europeans to discover petroleum in central Asia, while Nearchus' sailors came across a hairy people, the Fish-eaters, still in a Stone Age culture, and saw a school of whales, to them as terrifying as an army. Among the king's last acts was the organization of two naval expeditions, unfortunately canceled at his death, one to explore the Caspian Sea, the other under Nearchus to circumnavigate Arabia.

Disease, perhaps malaria, struck Alexander in Babylon. Overtired and still suffering from a chest wound received in India, he could not throw off his illness, which was not helped by the banquets and nightlong drinking bouts staged as a send-off to Nearchus. He died June 13, 323 B.C., having reigned only thirteen years. Perhaps he planned to conquer the West also, Magna Graecia, Carthage and Rome, and to establish a universal empire. Perhaps he would have returned east to explore the Indian subcontinent and the Caspian region and even to make contact with China. At any rate, the world he actually conquered was of unprecedented dimensions.

Alexander was a military genius, adept at exploiting victory and winning the allegiance of the conquered. The world-state he founded introduced into the West concepts of charity, tolerance, harmony, peace, and world-brotherhood. Without his life's work neither the Roman Empire nor the spread of Christianity would have been possible. His premature death and the resulting rivalry among the Macedonian nobles were to loose a welter of wars upon the Hellenistic Age.

Chapter 30/ HELLENISTIC
POWERS

Territorial Revolution

Alexander's Empire did not long survive his death, not because of uprisings, but because of the lack of central authority. Since Alexander had not settled the succession, the army designated as joint heirs Alexander IV, his posthumous son by the Bactrian Roxana, and his idiot half-brother, Philip Arrhidaeus. These broken reeds represented a compromise between the generals sympathetic to Alexander's ideals and the Macedonian peasant soldiery who were cool to new-fangled ideas of racial and cultural intermixture. The two kings did not last long. Arrhidaeus was murdered (317 B.C.) at the instigation of the bloodthirsty Olympias; Roxana was later killed at Cassander's instance; Alexander was murdered at the age of twelve, victim to a pretender's ambition (310 B.C.).

The chief generals became satraps of the choicest parts of the empire. History has seldom seen a group of more gifted men, simple Macedonian landowners who became prime builders of civilization: Antipater, Philip's last surviving general, and his brilliant son Cassander; Antigonus the One-eyed and his son Demetrius "Taker of Cities," whose military genius rivaled Alexander's; Perdiccas who for a while controlled most of Asia Minor; Lysimachus, threatening from Thrace both Europe and the East; Seleucus, satrap of Babylon; and Ptolemy of Egypt. Their loyalty, such as it was, to Alexander and his heirs yielded to political considerations. Each, except Antipater, aimed at royal power in his own satrapy and empire beyond. Two or three even tried to restore the empire and exact obedience from their peers. For twenty years they fought each other or combined against whichever one was for the moment dominant. A whole generation, east and west, bled to satisfy a half-dozen superindividualists' ambition. The decisive battle of Ipsus (301 B.C.), which saw an alliance of the successors against Antigonus, was a step on the way to a stability not fully achieved for another quarter-century. Antigonus was killed in action. Ptolemy emerged as king of Egypt and *de facto* ruler of Palestine and southern Syria, Seleucus as king of northern Syria and the lands from Mesopotamia to India, Lysimachus as king of Thrace and much of Asia, Cassander as king of Macedon and ruthless ruler of the Greeks.

The Persian Empire remained in Greek and Macedonian hands, all but the Indian provinces, which Seleucus traded for 500 war elephants. Alexander's territorial revolution was thus consolidated, and its kingdoms dominated world affairs until Rome emerged as an imperial power. While the struggle for old Greece and its manpower resources dictated third-century international relations, a new Greece took over the former Persian Empire. Three major states, Macedonia, Egypt, and Syria (Thrace disappeared as a kingdom when Lysimachus died childless), and somewhat later the smaller kingdom of Pergamum became the political, cultural, industrial, and commercial centers. Sparta was much reduced in importance, Athens a mere municipality—both monuments to history's vicissitudes. Kings, self-made and autocratic, not ancient constitutional communities, controlled events: the Ptolemies in Egypt, the Seleucids in Syria, the Attalids in Pergamum; Antigonid Macedonia managed to preserve constitutional government until the middle years of Philip V (221–179 B.C.).

These kingdoms had no cultural boundaries. Among them philosophers and men of letters, artists in every medium, professional men, traders, and clerical workers moved freely, making their living and trying to feel at home. Indeed they did as much as the kings to create the Hellenistic world, so different in spirit and form from the Hellenism of Pericles and Plato. Whether or not Alexander dreamed of one world based on Greek culture, such a world did develop out of his conquest. Though his generals partitioned the empire, they gave substance to this ideal by opening their kingdoms to Hellenic gods and Hellenic culture. Thus the known world became the home of civilization, the *oecumēnē*, where a simplified form of Greek, the *koinē* ("common speech") symbolized the rising universal community of Greeks and barbarians. Philosophy responded by evolving the concept of one world, the common home of all mankind.

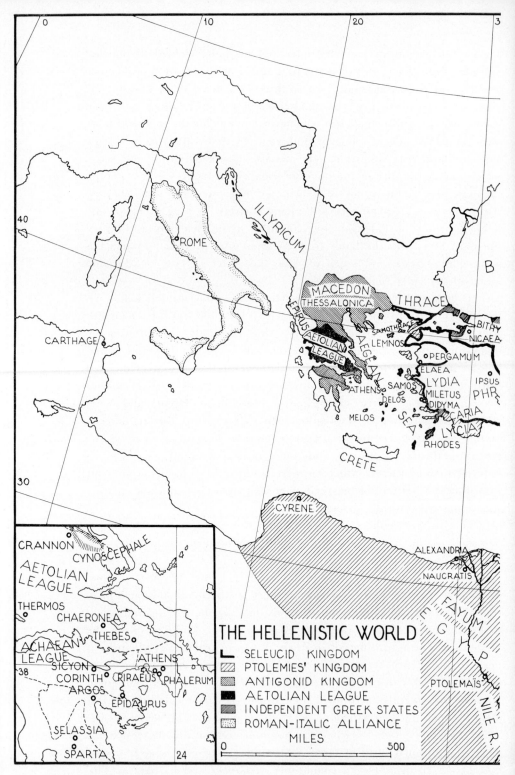

Fig. 30a. Map of the Hellenistic World. Insets show Aetolian and Achaean

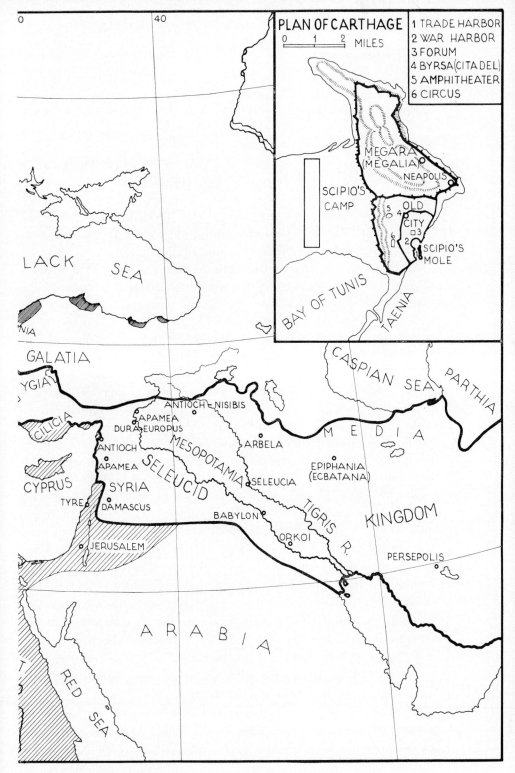

PLAN OF CARTHAGE

0   1   2   MILES

1 TRADE HARBOR
2 WAR HARBOR
3 FORUM
4 BYRSA (CITADEL)
5 AMPHITHEATER
6 CIRCUS

MEGARA (MEGALIA)

NEAPOLIS

SCIPIO'S CAMP

OLD CITY

5   4

□ 3

2

SCIPIO'S MOLE

BAY OF TUNIS

TAENIA

LACK   SEA

NIA

GALATIA

YGIA

CILICIA

CASPIAN SEA

PARTHIA

ANTIOCH — NISIBIS

APAMEA
DURA EUROPUS

M E D I A

ANTIOCH

APAMEA

MESOPOTAMIA

ARBELA

EPIPHANIA
(ECBATANA)

CYPRUS

SYRIA

SELEUCID

SELEUCIA

TYRE

DAMASCUS

KINGDOM

BABYLON

JERUSALEM

TIGRIS R.

ORKOI

PERSEPOLIS

A R A B I A

RED SEA

Leagues and plan of Carthage.

363

Ptolemaic Egypt

The Hellenistic age was a period of endless wars. Egypt, Macedonia, and Syria continued to encroach one on another. Egypt was the richest and, throughout the third century B.C., the strongest. Having inherited from the pharaohs a compact organization, the business-minded Ptolemies increased its scope and doubled or tripled its efficiency. The king was an absolute monarch unrestrained by constitution or public opinion. He was the state, his will was the law. Through military commanders and revenue-collectors he ruled the nomes (described in Chapter 2), where each *fellah* (serf) worked his full quota for the king in the fields, on the roads, dykes, or canals, or in the royal factories.

All Egypt was the king's estate. Half the land was his private property, planted mostly to wheat by sharecroppers, who, bound to their villages and indeed forbidden to leave them, lived on starvation rations. The serfs took the king's share of their crops to the royal granary in the village to be shipped to the nome capitals and thence to the giant warehouses in Alexandria to be sold in every Mediterranean country. The remaining land, although nominally the king's, was granted to various users: as temple lands to clergy, as revocable gifts to high officials, or as payment to bureaucrats. Since these beneficiaries shared their harvest with him, the king was the world's largest grain merchant.

The king enjoyed various monopolies. The most important was the production and sale of vegetable oils such as linseed and sesame. He determined yearly how much land should be planted to these crops, purchased the whole harvest, and had it processed by serfs, selling it at home and abroad at a 70 percent to 300 percent profit. High tariffs prevented oil imports. He took a third of the produce of gardens, orchards, and vineyards. Here too he imposed a protective tariff against Greek wines. He was the sole papyrus manufacturer, the sole clothmaker, took 25 percent of the yield of beehives and fisheries, had immense herds of livestock, and owned all the kingdom's quarries, mines, and salt works. He licensed other businesses for high fees. His taxes in money included an inheritance tax, a sales tax of 10 percent, a 5 percent tax on house rentals, a poll tax on every native, except the clergy. As the sole banker, with a central bank in Alexandria and branches in every nome capital and most villages, he made loans at 24 to 36 percent.

He regulated these multifarious activities through two tightly organized bureaucracies, one spying on the other. Wherever men toiled, his men took toll, keeping records and sending reports, each man counterchecked at every turn by another. As the third-century Ptolemies barred natives from political office and all but the lowest administrative echelon, Egypt became Eldorado for the Greeks. They flooded in as secretaries, inspectors, accountants, stenographers, surveyors, statisticians, tax collectors, census-takers, spies—in a word, as bureaucrats.

The Ptolemies' main interest was in increasing production. They opened the country to Greek, Jewish, and other immigrants to bring all Egypt under cultivation. They introduced the camel and initiated a camel service southward from Alexandria, improved sheep-breeding, developed olive orchards, and tried to acclimatize fir trees. They opened the Nile–Red Sea canal, rebuilt the irrigation system, and reclaimed the Fayum. Over most of Egypt, no tree could be cut down without their permission. They had no interest in promoting or maintaining liberty, even among Greek immigrants used to it at home. Their concern was to make every man work; their goal to make theirs the world's richest treasury. To close loopholes in the pharaonic system they replaced the regular courts with administrative ones in which tax collectors became also prosecutors and judges. They left the fellah only two freedoms, to breed—and to worship, a right more precious to him than life. But they kept the price of bread at a minimum. Even so, in desperation, the peasant sometimes went on strike.

Their enormous wealth enabled the Ptolemies to hire thousands of Greek soldiers and sailors, for soon after the conquest they disbanded the native army. They gained control of Palestine and southern Syria, whose timber they needed to build a merchant marine to carry their commodities abroad and a strong navy to protect commerce and convey mercenaries to Egypt. During the first century of rule the Ptolemies could contain both Syria and Macedonia, chiefly by controlling at one time or another key points in the Aegean Islands, the Asiatic coast, the Hellespont, and Thrace.

On discharge the Greek mercenaries received land grants which they had to cultivate themselves, to enrich the king still further. They settled mostly in the Fayum, once swampland but under Greek management especially fertile and a seat of Greek culture. City-states, however, were forbidden lest they interfere with Egyptian totalitarian government and economy. The Ptolemies built up only two cities, Ptolemaïs in Upper Egypt to counterbalance the local ecclesiastic power and Alexandria, their capital. But even these were not true city-states, for they were not self-governed. Apparently Alexandria had neither boule nor city council. Royal policy denied autonomy also to the old Greek colony, Naucratis.

Alexandria was the largest Hellenistic city. Its streets, laid at right angles and lined with shops, bazaars, and inns, were much admired, as were the royal office buildings and warehouses, the gymnasium, hippodrome, temples, courthouse (basilica), the Museum with its annex, the Library, the tombs of Alexander and the Ptolemies, the royal palace and park, and the mansions and gardens of the rich. Alexandria had two harbors, formed when Alexander joined the mainland with Pharos island. Beside the east harbor, the king's private port, stood his palace and park. The west harbor, connected by canals with a deep lake and with the Nile, could accommodate several hundred ships. Heavy maritime traffic required a lighthouse (Pharos), nearly 400 feet high (60 feet less than the Great Pyramid) with three stepped-back stories. In several European languages, the word for lighthouse is derived from this wonder of the world.

Alexandria was also, until Rome's Golden Age, the most cosmopolitan city of antiquity. Greeks were in the majority, and alone held citizenship. Macedonians, Cretans, Cypriotes, and others enjoyed varying degrees of semi-autonomy. The least privileged were the native Egyptians. Jews formed the largest immigrant group—by the first century B.C. there were 2000 to 3000 of them in the capital. These, and many more in the nomes, enjoyed freedom of worship, their own laws, and their own courts. To keep this melting-pot at peace was a problem; the Ptolemies solved it principally by denying any group complete self-government, placing a governor over all.

The Seleucid Empire

The Seleucid Empire ranked next to Egypt in the Hellenistic world. At peace or war with Egypt it shaped the course of international events. Internally it promoted Hellenism by founding cities, which siphoned off from continental Greece tens of thousands of settlers who, left at home, would have aggravated the country's economic distress and political instability.

At its greatest extent the Seleucid Empire stretched southward from the Aegean to the Indus, touching Arabia. Northward it approached the Black and the Caspian seas, whence it continued for some 1500 miles to the Indian provinces, later given up. The loss of other eastern provinces after the middle of the third century B.C. was not an unmixed misfortune, since it made the Empire more manageable. Besides, the loss was balanced by the conquest of Palestine and southern Syria (198 B.C.) and the consequent weakening of Egypt. Thus reconstituted, the Seleucid Empire embraced about twenty-five satrapies and 40,000,000 people. But the multiplicity of tribes and nationalities created for the Seleucids administrative and political problems which their rivals, the Ptolemies, were spared. Lastly, though the Seleucids could raise large

Fig. 30.1. King Euthydemus of Bactria. A Hellenistic anticipation (*c.* 200 B.C.) of Roman realistic portrait sculpture, this has been justly called one of the finest portraits in the world. The old king in his sun-helmet, his eyes squinting against the desert sun, his nose beaked like an eagle, his mouth hard and cynical, is the type of empire-builder in all ages. (Rome, Torlonia Museum)

armies, their revenues were considerably smaller than those of the Ptolemies.

The Seleucid Empire was a crazy quilt of cultures. One block, Asia Minor, was Greek on the Aegean coast, but in the interior Phrygian, Lydian, Carian, Lycian, and Cilician—of Hittite and native Asian origins, influenced by Hellenism in ratio to their closeness to the Aegean.

A second block, south of Asia Minor, embraced Syria, Phoenicia, and Palestine. Though all Semitic, their cultures differed. The Phoenicians and Syrians had an industrial and commercial economy and worshiped Canaanite *baalim,* while pastoral Palestine was faithful to Jehovah. Their languages too were different, though by the first century B.C. Aramaic had become the Semitic lingua franca from the Mediterranean to the Tigris and down to northern Arabia.

A third block, Mesopotamia, fanned out east of Syria to the border of Media and Persia. Sumerian, Old Babylonian, Assyrian, and Chaldean influences on its culture were not effaced until the rise of Islam in the seventh century of the Christian era.

The block farthest from the Aegean was Iran, embracing Media, Persia, Parthia, Drangiana, Sogdiana, and Bactria. Its economy was an independent and indestructible nomadism; its religion was an amalgam of Magian practices and Zoroastrian doctrines. One by one these countries broke away from the Seleucids, led or inspired by the Parthians, whose state succeeded Bactria as the strongest east of the Tigris—a continuing menace to the Seleucids and their Roman successors.

To unify these heterogeneous countries the Seleucids planted cities dominated by Macedonians and Greeks. We can count more than a hundred such foundations: some entirely new, some expansions or resettlement of decaying places, some large self-governing villages, some military posts transformed into civilian communities. At the principal crossroads of Asia Minor, where Greek merchants had traded for centuries without settling down, some fifty cities were planted. Another fifty were founded or refounded up and down Syria. (Some of these were Ptolemaic foundations.) On the river Orontes alone, at that time navigable and the most convenient link between north and south Syria, there were seven cities.

Mesopotamia too saw the rise of Greek cities. Twelve were founded along or near the Euphrates. One of these was Dura-Europus, on the west bank. Military operations rediscovered it during World War I, and Yale University expeditions have since excavated it. Its walls, streets, buildings, inscriptions, and paintings enable us to reconstruct its evolution from Macedonian garrison to a Hellenistic and later to a Roman city (Chapter 53) with a mixed population of pagans, Jews, and Christians. Ancient Uruk, refounded, became Orkoi, and Antiochus Epiphanes tried to Hellenize Babylon. Several cities were planted along the Tigris. Seleucia, with a peak population of nearly 500,000, was capital of the eastern satrapies. Media and Persia, hereditary foes of Hellenism, were now satrapies of a Greek empire. The Median capital, Ecbatana, was refounded as Epiphania, while Susa became Seleucia. Ten or twelve other cities rose eastward along the road to central Asia to hold down the natives and protect the luxury trade with India and China.

Since the Seleucids aimed in urbanizing the Empire to increase their revenues by promoting industry and trade, the logical next step was to set up a road network. They opened up the wild Asia Minor hinterland. Other roads connected the western and eastern halves of the Empire. One ran from Damascus via Dura-Europus to Babylon. Another, more northerly, linked Antioch-on-the-Orontes with Apamea-on-the-Euphrates, then with Antioch-Nisibis, Arbela, and Ecbatana. From Ecbatana it branched off, one arm to Persepolis and Alexandria Kandahar, the other to Bactria, Sogdiana, and India. The latter remained the trade route from India and China down to the Roman period.

To expand the economy the Seleucids persuaded the natives to use money instead of barter. Seleucid taxation resembled Egyptian, but was more humane. For example, whereas Egyptian orchards paid 25 percent in kind, Seleucid orchards paid only 10 percent, the same as wheat land. The result was peace in the country; we never hear of peasants' strikes. The king also levied customs dues and sales taxes. He had only one monopoly, in mining. But Seleucid wealth, as we said above, never rivaled Ptolemaic.

Expansion of the economy and the founding of cities involved a bold attack on age-old feudal land tenure, with which the Persian kings had hardly tampered. The Seleucids, however, in some parts of their empire relentlessly reduced the barons' holdings practically to the vanishing point. They encroached with equal determination in Asia Minor and Syria on the temple-states, where all the land belonged to the temple, the high priest was an absolute monarch, and the people were serfs. Gradually the dynasty secularized most such lands, leaving to the priest the temple, the village around it, and greatly reduced acreage.

These reforms were all part of the Hellenization of the East. The feudal and temple lands as well as the royal estates, often as large as an American county, were opened as freehold to new settlers, principally Greeks and Macedonians, on condition that they form self-governing communities on the Greek pattern. Since these cities were Greek in language, institutions, and culture, gradually—and partially—surrounding non-Greeks were Hellenized. The dynasty encouraged the process of Hellenization through gifts to new homesteaders of agricultural implements and through other incentives and by fostering the gradual absorption of non-Greeks into the Greek body politic. From the dissemination of Hellenism the crown expected that homogeneous culture which guarantees political strength and stability. In the city domains, native peoples for the first time enjoyed freedom and a sense of human dignity. Serfs became free men, although not necessarily citizens. But they could hope for citizenship as they assimilated Greek urban culture.

In their eagerness, the Seleucids tried to Hellenize even Palestine. Underestimating the Jews' aversion to alien creeds, they reduced Palestine from vassal to province, and undertook to make Jerusalem itself a Greek city. King Antiochus IV Epiphanes ("God Manifest"), the author of this policy, had no religious motive. He merely wanted to unify the Empire by lining up Palestine with his other provinces. He had the support of a well-organized Jewish party favorable to Hellenization. But when Judas Maccabaeus and his brothers saw Jehovah's Temple rededicated to Zeus, they called the nation to arms, filled Palestine with guerrilla warfare, and won friendship and alliance from Rome (c. 161 B.C.). Another piece of luck befell them when, soon after Epiphanes' death, the Seleucid Empire was rent by civil war. In short, the Maccabees not only reconquered the Temple, but won back Palestine's right to self-government, including freedom from Hellenization, although as a Seleucid satellite.

But Hellenization ultimately failed east of Syria, where the Greek settlements were mere islands in a sea of non-Greeks. Though the Seleucids gave Greek settlers land, money, cattle, and agricultural implements, the response, especially from women, was disappointingly small, for in the Greek homeland population was dwindling. For every two, rarely three, boys in a family, there was usually only one girl. For boys might support themselves as laborers at home or mercenaries abroad, but girls were a burden and only enough were reared to keep the race going. The surplus was exposed with no qualms of conscience. Therefore many, if not most, Greek settlers in the Seleucid Empire married native wives. Children and grandchildren with Greek names were not necessarily Greek by culture, for culture is often transmitted by the distaff side. Greek culture became too diluted to overcome the older cultures, at least in Mesopotamia and Iran.

The story was different in Syria and Asia Minor. Syria with its annex, Phoenicia, resembled Greece in climate and agricultural products and had had close relations with the Greeks for over a thousand years. Though Semitism there had firm roots, Hellenism penetrated it deeply and produced a new amalgam, especially evident in art. The Hellenization of some parts of Asia Minor was more thorough. Both in Asia Minor and Syria the full results of Seleucid policy showed after the end of the dynasty. From about 200 B.C. the Romans gradually whittled away Seleucid power until in 63 B.C. Pompey the Great annexed the whole East. But the break was political, not cultural, for the Romans themselves were Hellenized. Masters of Asia Minor and Syria, they carefully nurtured what Seleucids had planted. Indeed if Rome had not entered the East, Hellenism might have vanished both from the Seleucid Empire and from Egypt.

Although the Seleucids promoted Hellenism more than did any other dynasty, they created no cultural center comparable to Alexandria. Antioch, the capital and the Hellenistic world's second largest city, never attracted such poets, scholars, or scientists as adorned the Ptolemies' capital. However, it had a medical school, fostered a respectable school of sculpture in Scopas' tradition, and produced glass, mosaics, pottery, terra cotta, and metalwork. Its gay life made it a tourist center throughout Hellenistic and Roman times. The city very early embraced Christianity. Its ruins are scanty, but its beautiful mosaics in American museums show that the former Seleucid capital was prosperous even until the decline of Rome.

Pergamum

The third century B.C. marked for the Seleucid Empire a series of territorial losses. The dynasts of central and northern Asia Minor were resolved to keep Seleucid power out of their domains. The Ptolemies kept the Empire chronically weak by their alliances with the islands, by fomenting revolt among the Greek cities of Asia, but chiefly by waging several Syrian wars to keep their hold on Palestine and Syria. Amid these revolts and wars the Iranian satrapies easily broke away. Ultimately the Empire was reduced to Syria, Asia south of the Taurus, and the Mesopotamian satrapies. But there was one compensation. The Syrian wars ended with a Seleucid victory (200 B.C.) which gave them southern Syria and Palestine.

An unforeseen source of trouble was the Galatians, Celtic tribes related to those Gauls who shortly after 400 B.C. had spread terror in Italy. They had reached Illyricum when Alexander so terrorized that area that they sought his friendship and settled down. Fifty years later they were again on the move, 50,000 or 60,000 strong. The women and children traveled in carts with the furniture and loot. Plunder was their immediate aim; after that lands for settlement. On leaving Illyricum, they broke out in three directions. As in Italy, their first assault was the fiercest, but the Greeks had to learn this the hard way. The first wave invaded Macedonia, plundering at will and killing the king himself (279 B.C.) . Another wave overran northern Greece. Forcing Thermopylae, they were the first barbarians since Xerxes to invade central Greece. Although many cities united for mutual defense, the chief credit for saving the country belongs to the recently-formed Aetolian League. The third wave was invited into Asia by King Mithridates of Pontus and Nicomedes of Bithynia who were at war with the Seleucids. It met no organized resistance, for Antiochus I was immobilized by his Syrian wars, and the Greek coastal cities usually preferred to pay ransom. In an interval of his Egyptian war, Antiochus defeated it (277 B.C.) but a new Egyptian invasion prevented him from following up his victory. The Gauls settled at last in northern Phrygia, thereafter called Galatia, exacting yearly tribute from the Asian cities and princes and from the Seleucid Empire itself.

Out of the Gallic peril rose a new kingdom, Pergamum. An old Greek city, Pergamum lay on the lower Caicus river in western Asia Minor, with access to the sea through its port, Elaea. Its fortunes depended on the seesaw of power among Alexander's successors. After switching allegiance back and forth, it governor, Philetaerus, made a treaty with the Seleucids, thus keeping its prosperity intact. But his nephew Eumenes (263–241 B.C.) , bent on establishing an independent state, allied himself with Egypt.

Attacking Syria from the north while Egypt advanced from the south, Eumenes defeated the Seleucids on land and sea. With independence he won also larger domains and heightened prestige. Eumenes' successor, Attalus I (241–197 B.C.) , the Seleucids being immobilized by Egypt, liberated Asia from the Gauls and assumed the title of King. After two

Fig. 30.2. Pergamum. The Acropolis, model by Hans Schleif. A Hellenistic terraced site including theater with seats for 10,000, Great Altar (right center) with Athena's temple on the terrace above it, and in its precinct, the famous Pergamene library. At the top, the palace complex.

generations of Pergamene tribute to the Gauls, Attalus refused to pay, a gesture, sincere or calculated, to prove him the protector of Hellenism. The Gauls attacked; he routed them (c. 230 B.C.) and henceforward they behaved. The grateful Greek cities went over to him en masse. Because the Seleucids, though staunch friends of Hellenism, had sided with the Gauls, Attalus drove them out of Asia north of the Taurus. Although he soon lost his gains, the Romans restored them (188 B.C.) to his successor, Eumenes II.

Attalus I lavishly advertised his services to Hellenism. He enriched Athens with monumental sculptures, commemorating the triumph of Hellenism in four stages, the last his own: over the Amazons, Titans, Persians, and Gauls. He had the same theme treated even more spectacularly in the Pergamene Altar of Zeus, to be discussed in the next chapter.

Macedonia and Greece

The news of Alexander's death caused hopes to rise in Athens, which led a revolt, successful at first, but definitively crushed by Antipater in the battle of Crannon (September 322 B.C.). Athens had to pay indemnities and submit to a Macedonian garrison in the Piraeus and disfranchisement of 12,000 citizens. After Demosthenes' suicide an aristocratic puppet government took over, which lasted until Antipater's death (319 B.C.). The democracy that followed was short-lived; Antipater's son Cassander overthrew it, and installed as strategos Theophrastus' pupil, Demetrius of Phalerum (318 B.C.), an enlightened tyrant whose fate it was in his ten-year tenure to preside over a bankrupt Athens. His unpopular government was overthrown by Demetrius "Sacker of Cities" (307 B.C.), who took up quarters in the Parthenon itself and astonished even the sophisticated Athenians with his orgies. But Demetrius was defeated and his father Antigonus killed, as we saw, at Ipsus in Phrygia (301 B.C.) by a coalition of Ptolemy, Seleucus, and Lysimachus; he eventually (288 B.C.) lost even his precarious foothold in Greece. Imprisoned by Seleucus, he drank himself to death (283 B.C.).

Lysimachus, tyrant of Thrace, tried in vain, though lavish gifts of grain made him popular in Athens, to succeed where Demetrius and others had failed and to unify Greece under himself as ruler. At his death (281 B.C.) his kingdom broke up. Antigonus Gonatas (reigned 283–239 B.C.), Demetrius' son, a hero of the Gallic invasion, seized control in Macedonia and finally stabilized the situation. The world was now partitioned; a new epoch was beginning; after fifty years the last memories of Alexander's empire were to disappear, and Greece under Antigonus to embark upon the political decadence of its Hellenistic Age.

The decadence was political, not intellectual. While Macedon fostered Greek intellectual development, in politics, leagues, cities, and parties within cities wore themselves out in senseless struggles; cities that had been great, like Athens and Sparta, degenerated, and obscure districts, Aetolia, Achaea, Rhodes, come to the fore. King Pyrrhus of Epirus intervened in Macedonia, Greece, and as we shall see, in Italy, besieged Gonatas in Thessalonica, attacked Sparta, and was finally killed in a street fight in Argos (272 B.C.).

In Athens meantime all was confusion. The city changed hands seven times in forty-six years. Despite flirtations with Egypt, in whom it saw a more lenient master, it was forced to endure Macedonian garrisons all over Attica. The Ecclesia, Boule, and magistrates were Macedonian rubber stamps, though when Egyptian gold bribed its Macedonian garrison, Athens transferred its sympathies to Egypt (229/8 B.C.). Its coinage ceased, its Long Walls fell into ruins; it became, and remained to the end (A.D. 529), merely the intellectual capital of the Greek world, justly proud of its artists, comic poets, and philosophers.

Sparta remained the steadfast but impotent enemy of Macedon, for the Achaean League had become the great Peloponnesian state. Sparta's reactionary government and underpopulation were partly responsible. Recognizing this, King Agis IV (244–241 B.C.) unprecedently canceled debts, reduced mortgages, and was proceeding to land-redistribution when he was condemned to death by the reactionaries (241 B.C.). Ironically, it was Cleomenes III (235–222 B.C.), the son of Agis' ultraconservative colleague in the kingship, who continued his projects, redistributing the land, enlarging the citizen body, and allowing 6000 helots to buy their freedom. Sparta's high hopes of his regime were soon dashed; the Achaeans called in Antigonus III of Macedonia (224 B.C.), who crushed the Spartan King at Sellasia in northern Laconia (222 B.C.). Cleomenes fled to Egypt, and the proud city found itself, for the first time in history, occupied by an enemy.

Other states fared better. The Aetolians, brigands and pirates, brave men and poor, having acquired experience serving as mercenaries, set up a national army of 12,000 men, which beat the Gauls and supported the new Aetolian League (*fl. c.* 270–191 B.C.), with a sovereign assembly meeting twice a year at Thermos, a council of delegates, and a strategos. With a protectorate over Delphi and tolerance from Macedon during Gonatas' long reign, the League expanded from sea to sea. Its deadliest rival was the Achaean League across the Corinthian Gulf.

The Achaean League, successor to an earlier religious federation, was organized in 280 B.C. and gained importance by admitting non-Achaeans, of whom the greatest was its long-term strategos, Aratus of Sicyon (271–213 B.C.). The League had a primary assembly, the *syncletos,* and a *synodos* of uncertain function. The 60 member-states had voting strength varying with their size, and they shared a common coinage. Under Aratus, League armies took Acrocorinth (243 B.C.), repeatedly attacked Athens and Argos, and stood up to Macedon itself, but finally (220 B.C.) called in the Macedonian king, Antigonus Doson, against Spartan aggression, starting a relationship which lasted until the League went over to Rome (198 B.C.).

Macedon never succeeded in subjecting all of Greece, and itself was destined to succumb to the rising power of Rome. In the third century B.C., its treasury being limited (the Pangaeus mines were nearly exhausted) it had all it could do to protect its frontiers. In Greece, only oligarchs supported it, and its kings, Gonatas particularly, showed no respect for Greek liberty, so that democrats were glad to support King Pyrrhus of Epirus against him. But with Pyrrhus' death, Gonatas regained the ascendancy, and Greek cities again suffered Macedonian garrisons. A revolt by Athens and Sparta, the Chremonidean War, although it had Egyptian support, was crushed. Taking vengeance upon Egypt, Gonatas swept its fleets from the Aegean (258 B.C.). What Macedon acquired in his long reign it acquired painfully, but he and his successors held it; he protected Greece from the savage tribes north of his border, and at his death (239 B.C.) Macedonia was re-established as a nation.

Under Gonatas' successor, Demetrius II (reigned 239–229 B.C.), Macedon lost ground, and Antigonus Doson (227–221 B.C.) saw its sea-power pass to Rhodes; thanks to Antigonus Doson, however, at Sellasia Sparta found its Chaeronea. From the spoils Antigonus erected a monument to Apollo at Delos. He formed an Achaean alliance and revived the Corinthian League. At his death Macedonian power seemed reestablished in Greece.

Actually it was on the eve of crumbling, for his successor, Philip V, was a reckless adventurer who overtaxed his kingdom's strength. He antagonized the Aetolian League, which called in Rome. With the Roman's victory over him at Cynoscephalae (197 B.C.) the political history of an independent Greece and Macedon in antiquity comes to an end.

Chapter 31 / HELLENISTIC
CULTURE

Religion

Accompanying the political and territorial revolution which shifted the balance of power from the Greek mainland to the East was a considerable revolution in religion, philosophy, science, literature, and the arts. Zeus, Athena, and the other Olympian gods became often poetical allegories or at best occasions for civic pageants more glittering than pious. Undermined in the fifth century B.C. by the sophists, they tended to be a major casualty of the breakdown of the city-state in the fourth century and after. Since religion had permeated all city-state institutions —law, justice, the division of the electorate, the festivals, and the calendar—when the city-state decayed, the gods frequently became venerable antiques. Now that local patriotism had vanished in many places and the very term Hellene had a cultural rather than an ethnic connotation, the ordinary Greek lost his sense of direction. His life seemed empty and times were often hard at home. If he moved to the big Hellenistic cities, he was bewildered and lost.

While the educated classes were too skeptical to substitute one religion for another, the common man found warmth and sympathy in the more personal mystery cults. The idea of salvation, we have seen, was not entirely new to him. He had embraced it in his own Greek homeland when

Orphism emphasized the antagonism between the flesh and the spirit and the need of a mystic or sacramental experience as a corrective. Orphism flowered again in the Hellenistic Age.

To its votaries every mystery cult offered immortality and purification from sin. In each, the suffering god died young, rose again, and would transfer himself into the votary who after instruction underwent a series of purifications which made gods of destitute and hopeless mortals. Thus a new mystery—conversion or communion with a salvation god—solved the old mystery of life and death, the law of man's endless round of sorrows.

These mystery cults are Oriental religions. The oldest and most popular was that of the Egyptian Isis. She had made converts in Athens as early as the fifth century. She and her consort and son Osiris, who through suffering had secured immortality, were the prototype of the ordinary man and woman beset with life's usual problems.

Almost as popular as Isis was the Phrygian Great Mother, so vital in her appeal that her cult survived every foreigner who invaded Asia— Hittites, Minoans, Assyrians, Persians—then conquered the Hellenistic world, finally to become one of the chief sects of the Roman Empire. She had known the sorrow of a son's death. Syria too made its contribution, though not until the second century B.C.: Hadad of Damascus, a synthesis of many *baalim,* and his spouse Atargatis, whose descent may be traced from Babylon. Persian immigrants, even later, introduced the god Mithras into Egypt and Asia Minor, where he attracted natives and Greek worshipers.

The Olympian gods retained their hold, Zeus as a providential force, Aphrodite as the magic power behind love potions and aphrodisiacs. Asclepius, the healer, increased his following. The Epidaurus tablets recording his miracles grew more numerous as the Hellenistic Age ripened. But the most popular divinity of this period (though there is no evidence for a formal cult) was Tyche, the Romans' Fortuna—not a blind force, but rather Success, the reward of ambition and talent.

Many were drawn, from late in this age down through the medieval era, to Babylonian astrology. This pseudoscience assumed a correspondence between the course of the stars and the course of human events. According to it, an individual is the creature of his star, and an overpowering Fate holds him to a predetermined course. Experts professed to discover the future by casting horoscopes, basing their prophecies on conjunctions of celestial influences. Some present-day beliefs go back to Babylonian astrology—for instance, lucky and unlucky numbers or the mystic significance attached to the number seven: seven days of the week, seven gates of hell, seven heavens, the seven angels in *Revelation,* and apparently the seven deadly sins. Our language too reflects ancient astrological lore, for example, we "thank our stars" or call a man jovial, mercurial, or saturnine, thereby associating personality traits with planetary influences. Related to astrology was magic, associated especially with Hecate, the underworld Artemis of the crossways. Thessalian witches, some thought, could draw down the moon. Some believed in demons, stuck waxen images with pins, wore amulets, concocted potions, recited charms: the rational Greeks had their irrational moments.

Even the educated, no longer touched by rationalism, compromised with astrology and the salvation cults. Some syncretized (the first version of "one religion is as good as another"), holding that the same divinity reveals itself to different people in guises that are only superficially different; the Egyptian Isis, the Phrygian Great Mother, the Syrian Atargatis, the Greek Aphrodite, are really one goddess. Similarly they identified Zeus with the Syrian Hadad, with Teisbas of Commagene (the Hittite Teshub), and with Jehovah himself. Thus the Hellenistic world became the melting pot of gods. Others, especially the Stoics, posited one god governing man and the universe through lesser *daemones*, including the different national gods and the planetary powers.

Finally, ruler-worship appears in the Hellenistic Age, first associated with Alexander and then with the Ptolemies, Seleucids, and Attalids, who received dedications from individuals, worship from cities, a place in existing gods' temples, or official cult-honors sponsored by the dynasties. Its importance is more political than religious; it set a precedent for the deification of Roman emperors.

Philosophy

Religious syncretism and Stoic unitarianism were, basically, philosophies. Philosophy, reoriented, had neglected metaphysics, psychology, and logic for theology and ethics. It became a director of the soul. In an immeasurable, complicated, inexplicable world, which had lost the sense of belonging imparted by the city-state, philosophy undertook to provide a compass by which a lost generation might again find its bearings. Four principal schools held the field: Stoics, Epicureans, Cynics, and Skeptics.

Of these systems Stoicism was socially the most constructive. Its founder Zeno, a Cypriote of Phoenician extraction and possibly acquainted with Judaism, came to Athens in 313 B.C. and taught in the Painted Porch (*Stoa*—hence the term Stoic). Athens' respect for this cosmopolitan barbarian reflects its own cosmopolitanism in the Hellenistic Age. Stoics believed in one supreme power—Zeus, Nature, Destiny, or Providence—ruling the universe as Alexander might have ruled his empire. God was universal because all men were brothers, equal in His sight. He ruled according to immutable laws, which, deriving from his infinite

Wisdom, were the quintessence of justice and order. A Stoic would say that God's immutable decrees whereby the stars hold to their courses, kings and cities fulfill their mission, and history evolves, entail no determinism. For a wise man chooses of his own free will what God has foreordained—not because it is foreordained but because it is by its own nature good, which is why God has preordained it. To do God's will is man's supreme duty. This idea was given lofty expression in the *Hymn to Zeus* by Zeno's pupil Cleanthes.

Stoic duty was not a rigid concept, but an ever growing aspiration, an increasing detachment, leading away from bodily wants towards the inner life. Zeno's ideal of moral perfection was like Christ's 300 years later. For him, to think evil was to do it. Stoic virtue had another characteristic; it looked on self-improvement as a means to society's improvement. Thus, for the first time in Western history, Stoicism developed a social conscience, teaching kings how to rule and the rich how to alleviate poverty and all men to live for one another. Some Stoics in Asia, Sparta, and Rome actively advocated social revolution.

Epicurus aimed at raising ethical standards by concentrating on the individual. He opened his school in his native Athens in 306 B.C. He exposed himself to serious misunderstanding when, in teaching that happiness is man's supreme concern, he identified it with pleasure. But his notion of pleasure was not sensual but intellectual, the avoidance of pain and sorrow. So to live as to bring unhappiness neither on oneself nor on others was Epicurus' idea of virtue. In practice it meant discipline and renunciation, and ultimately freedom from passion—a serenity of mind like the Sophoclean ideal. Since withdrawal from active life conduced to this perfection, Epicurus and his disciples were the first to enter the ivory tower. In this they differed from the Stoics, who remained in the world to improve it. Epicurus' teaching is best known from the writings of the Roman Lucretius, especially his theory of a mechanical atomic world, knowledge of whose workings would free man's mind from the fear of the gods and of death. Lucretius' attack on the passion of love proves among other things that for Epicureans pleasure was not sensual.

The Cynics and Skeptics had a more limited appeal. The former were the mendicant friars of antiquity, roving from city to city, consorting with the poor, living on alms, and preaching against sexual immorality, a radical idea for that day. Their contempt for bodily needs, including cleanliness and hygiene, and for social graces led the genteel to call them *kynes*, dogs—hence their name. But Christians saw in them their own forerunners, selling their property, unconcerned with food, clothing, or shelter, and casting their lot with the poor.

The Skeptics, or Academics, whose viewpoint Cicero later found attractive, were heirs of the Eleatic school, since they questioned man's ability to acquire infallible knowledge. From this they drew a practical conclusion: since the line between certainty and doubt is blurred, one should never dogmatize. The wise man therefore should be tolerant; still better, he should be unconcerned. Through tolerance and unconcern would come that serenity of mind at which all Hellenistic philosophies aimed.

Science and Exploration

Many Hellenistic Greeks found science more rewarding than philosophy or religion. Building on Aristotle's works and the vast data from Alexander's explorations, they expanded known sciences or created new ones. For instance, they enlarged and perfected geometry. Euclid (*fl. c.* 300 B.C.) produced a systematic textbook which was standard until about 1900. Later scientists, chiefly Eratosthenes of Cyrene, Archimedes of Syracuse, and Apollonius of Apamea made geometry the key to algebra, quadratic equations, and trigonometry. Archimedes was a genius both in pure and applied mathematics. He invented the windlass, the double or compound pulley, and the endless screw to serve as water pump. He improved catapults and used concave glass to burn Roman ships besieging his native Syracuse and grapnels to dash them against the rocks. He applied the principle of the lever to launch by himself the largest ship built in ancient times. "Give me where to stand, and I will move the Earth." Since slaves were cheap, machinery seemed pointless. Even so, Hellenistic scientists invented the water-mill, water clock, and water organ, discovered the principles of compressed air, and used steam for motive power.

Greek astronomy learned even more from Babylonia when it became part of the *oecumene*. Babylonian astronomers had computed the length of the year to within 7 minutes 16 seconds. Building on Babylonian science, Aristarchus of Samos (310–230 B.C.) put forward the heliocentric theory, though he posited a circular, not an elliptical, movement and thought the sun was stationary. Most important, following Aristotle he emphasized observation as essential to science. Hipparchus of Nicaea (*fl.* 161–126 B.C.) calculated the mean lunar month within one second. Eratosthenes (275–194 B.C.), using astronomy, mathematics, and geography, measured the earth's circumference at the equator. Assuming the earth was round, he took the distance between two north-south points, that is, Alexandria and Syene (modern Aswan). Using two poles of the same length, and observing the length of their shadow on given days and hours in both Alexandria and Syene, he was able to calculate the earth's curvature between these points, and from that the circumference of the globe. His answer was 24,662 miles at the equator (the modern figure is 24,857) . His error arose from supposing Syene to lie due south of Alexandria, whereas it is 2½ degrees east.

Explorations, east and west, by traders and at the bidding of land-hungry kings enlarged the knowledge of geography. While Alexander was pushing his armies to India, Pytheas, a Massiliot Greek, ventured into the North Sea and possibly the Baltic, coasting along Scotland, Scandinavia, or both, and discovering the Arctic Ocean. He may have established the moon's influence on tides, as against Aristotle's view that tides were due to winds raised by the sun. The Ptolemies, eager for war-elephants, encouraged trade with India, both by sea and overland across northern Arabia from Mediterranean ports, in particular Tyre. Later they used African elephants, and limited Indian imports to spices, muslins, perhaps silks, and other precious articles for which Hellenistic and growing Roman wealth was creating an increasing demand. When they lost southern Syria, they diverted Indian trade to a new route, free from Seleucid interference, via the Indian Ocean, east Arabian ports, and the Red Sea. They established trading posts on the African coast as far south as Somaliland and possibly even farther. Carthaginian sailors explored the Atlantic as far west as the Azores and south to the Cape Verde Islands. A Greek or Carthaginian ship from Cadiz in Spain may have rounded the Cape of Good Hope, finally landing in Somaliland.

Eratosthenes, abreast of these developments, mapped Europe, Asia, and Africa as a single land mass surrounded by the sea. He may have suspected the existence of a north-to-south continent dividing the Atlantic. Eighteen hundred and fifty years later men were to call it America. Finally he thought of reaching India by sailing westward from Spain. Picked up by medieval scholars, especially Roger Bacon, and by them transmitted to the intrepid fifteenth-century navigators, this idea was partly tested by Columbus and fully by Magellan. Eratosthenes' world map, complete with lines of latitude and longitude, looked more like a modern one than any until the fifteenth century. Unfortunately, later generations returned to the geocentric concept of the universe, following Ptolemy, a compiler of the second century A.D.

Cicero's teacher, the Syrian Posidonius of Apamea (c. 135–51 B.C.) rivaled Eratosthenes as the greatest Hellenistic polymath. He undertook a *Summa Hellenistica* integrating all knowledge: science, philosophy, popular worship and a higher religion based on Stoic-Platonic ideas, Hellenic reason and Oriental mysticism, astronomy and astrology, gods and demons, men and beasts. For him, the earth was a copy or counterpart of heaven; and the entire mineral, vegetable, and animal kingdoms were directed from heaven. Man was both an earthly and a heavenly creature: a compound of clay and spirit while on earth, a spiritual or daemonic being after death. A Stoic Nature-Providence guided even

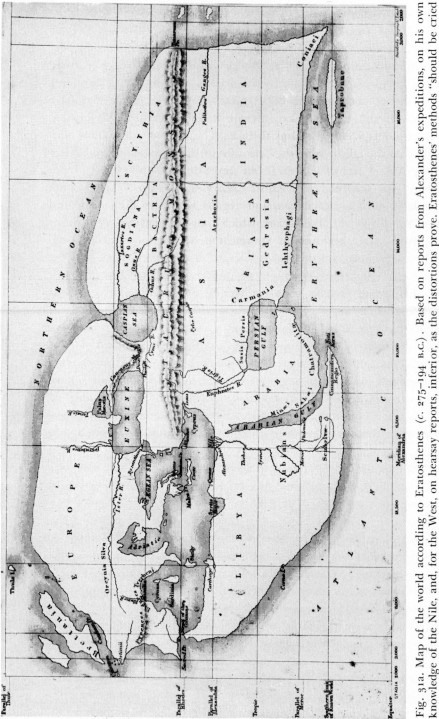

Fig. 31a. Map of the world according to Eratosthenes (c. 275–194 B.C.). Based on reports from Alexander's expeditions, on his own knowledge of the Nile, and, for the West, on hearsay reports, inferior, as the distortions prove. Eratosthenes' methods "should be cried from the housetops as the best thing in ancient science." (E. H. Bunbury, *A History of Ancient Geography* I, London, 1883. Facing p. 660.)

psychological phenomena, including man's thinking: both that based on fact and deduction and that which reflected his fears and hopes. The latter category included heavenly guidance by dreams, divination in all its forms (stargazing, hepatoscopy, bird flights, thunder and lightning), or magic and love potions. While Posidonius' serious influence rivaled Aristotle's, he also perpetuated superstition under the guise of encyclopedic science. His influence both good and bad on the Romans was enormous. In fact it was Hellenistic culture on which the Romans modeled their ideas, their arts, and their lives, and which they transmitted to posterity, though in time they also imitated the writers, philosophers, and the plastic arts of earlier Greek centuries.

There was progress in medical theory and practice. Hippocratic search for symptoms plus Aristotelian regard for observed facts produced the "Scientific School" of medicine, which flourished especially in Alexandria, under a royal endowment for research. Vivisection of animals and dissection of cadavers led Herophilus to important discoveries in the anatomy of the liver, the lungs, and the generative organs. He established that blood is propelled by the heart, and he contrived an instrument to measure pulse-beats. He almost anticipated William Harvey's seventeenth-century discovery of the circulation of the blood. He discovered the nerves and understood that they received their stimulation from the brain. He understood also the function of the spinal cord. Another school, the "Empiric," or practical, cured or relieved sickness by new drugs, including opium, and by dieting, cold baths, massage, and exercise. In short, Hellenistic physicians startlingly anticipated modern medicine. Surgery too progressed: new instruments were invented and more serious operations performed.

Aristotle's disciple Theophrastus (c. 369–285 B.C.), like his master, observed facts carefully and presented them in scientific treatises. His *Inquiry on Plants* deals with the problems and principles of methodology and classified scientifically all the varieties he knew. His *Ætiology of Plants* describes their physiology with a precision and acuteness remarkable without the microscope. Botany as an analytic science was his special province as zoology had been Aristotle's. Royal subsidies helped to establish zoological and botanical gardens in response to growing public interest, especially in exotic specimens.

Literature and Art

In this age literature, formerly written primarily to be read aloud, was produced to be read with the eye. This change had three contributing factors: the rise of an international, educated, leisured *bourgeoisie,* the emergence of publishers and booksellers, and, most important, the disappearance of city-state assemblies as agencies for deciding issues.

The availability of books produced bibliophiles—lovers, collectors, and commentators of books, men who wrote books on books, advancing the intricacies of textual criticism, and founding a new science, philology. This was the time when the text of the *Iliad* and other classics was established. One brand of commentator delighted in collecting—and manufacturing—scandals about great men: writers, philosophers, artists, statesmen. Typical of such gossip is Athenaeus' *Doctors at Dinner* (*c.* A.D. 200; from Hellenistic sources).

Kings had the largest book collections. The Attalids' collection at Pergamum, 200,000 rolls, was modest compared with that of the Ptolemies, which ultimately grew to 700,000. To house this treasure the Ptolemies built in Alexandria a new type of building, the Library, practically an annex of the Museum.

The Museum symbolized Hellenistic learning and research. Literally the home of the Muses, the Museum was more than an aggregation of buildings. It was the realization of one of Aristotle's dreams, a society of about 100 scholars, endowed by the king, each doing research in his own field, and all living together to open, each for the others, new horizons of knowledge. They dined together in a refectory, discussed literary, philosophical, and scientific problems in quiet indoor sessions or in the shade of tree-lined porticoes, and lectured on their researches in a special hall. Men of great learning served as President of Library and Museum, among others Eratosthenes and the poet Apollonius of Rhodes.

The writing of history was the literary form closest to life. Several conscientious histories recorded Greek events from Alexander to Pyrrhus, but all have perished. The best, Ptolemy I's biography of Alexander based on the conqueror's *Journal,* is known to us through Arrian (2nd century A.D.). Lesser writers, romanticizing Callisthenes' propaganda, influenced the Romans Curtius Rufus (1st century A.D.) and Julius Valerius (3rd–4th century A.D.) ; from the latter medieval historians concocted their version of the Alexander cycle, which vied in popularity with that of Charlemagne. Histories were written of Athens, Greece, Macedon, the Western Greeks, the Gallic invasion of Asia, and Hannibal's war with Rome. Although lost, they are reflected in Plutarch, Diodorus, and Polybius (*c.* 203–120 B.C.), the most important Greek historian after Thucydides. Biography became popular. There also appeared histories of art, medicine, mathematics, poetry, as well as geographies, of which the best was Eratosthenes' description of the world.

Journals and memoirs, books of science and adventure, utopias, state constitutions, imaginary conversations, and letters of famous men (mostly spurious) were published in great abundance. The utopias, inspired by

Plato, aimed at abolishing the epidemic of Hellenistic class wars. A predecessor of Campanella, Iambulus, wrote about a socialistic Sun-state. Of this large output only Theophrastus' *Characters* survives, a collection of psychological and social sketches. Political oratory decayed with the city-state. Rhetoric now concerned itself not with substance but with style.

The theater in Athens vegetated. Tragedies were many but undistinguished. Comedy fared better, probably because it developed a new slant, dealing now with the problems of ordinary individuals: ruffians and petty thieves, unwanted children, slaves who turn out to be long-lost sons, procurers hoodwinking inexperienced young men until they get thrashed by irate fathers. This is New Comedy, to be distinguished from the Old Comedy of Aristophanes which dealt with social and political problems. Menander (342–291 B.C.) is its best and most prolific representative. A new papyrus containing a complete play of Menander, *The Bad-tempered Man,* was discovered in the summer of 1957. Alexandria and most Hellenistic cities, however, preferred the mime, an indecent farce, spoken or sung, where mimicry gradually prevailed over the word and actors were free to improvise.

While comedy and philosophy were at home in Athens, Alexandria became the greatest center for poetry. There the sophisticated Syracusan Theocritus (*c*. 310–250 B.C.) wrote his pastoral *Idyls*. Perhaps homesick for his lovely native countryside, he sang of trees, flowers, and farm animals, of peasants, fishermen, unspoiled—and spoiled—country girls, with a genuineness of feeling unequaled in antiquity. He is the greatest poet between Aristophanes and Lucretius. Another Alexandrian, Callimachus of Cyrene (*c*. 305–240), polished that literary jewel, the epigram. A brief sketch, picture, or simple idea with a sting in its tail, the epigram tries to startle the reader. Apollonius of Rhodes (*c*. 295–after 247 B.C.), the librarian, composed an epic, *The Argonauts,* more learned than inspired, yet his Medea influenced Vergil's Dido, and proves that Apollonius really understood a girl in love.

The arts too revealed the spirit of the age. The rise of great capitals—Alexandria, Antioch, Seleucia-on-the-Tigris had each a 500,000 population—the founding and expansion of cities kept engineers busy for generations laying streets, building walls, constructing fortresses and arsenals, or improving harbors. A Hellenistic city had normally a rectangular or checker-board 'Hippodamian' plan (the Piraeus is a fifth-century example), although hilly terrain imposed modifications. Engineers made intelligent use of slopes and cliffs, and architects contrived beautiful vistas. The width of main streets averaged 30 feet, of secondary streets 15; Alexandria's main thoroughfare was 100 feet from house line to house line. There were no sewers or paving and open ditches took

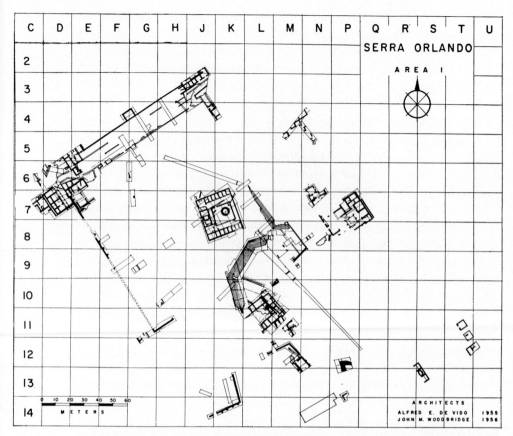

Fig. 31b. Plan of Serra Orlando (Morgantina), Sicily, early 3rd century B.C.
Site being excavated by Princeton University. North of the great Stair in the
center is a central shrine and market; to the northwest, a portico with shops.
Northeast of the Stairs, the ground rises to a Hellenistic house with peristyle.
(*American Journal of Archaeology* LXI, 1957, Plate 57, Fig. 1.)

care of drainage, but water supply was handled with care. Usually water
reached a city by gravity, but Pergamum supplied it to a hilly quarter in
metal pipes under pressure. Few Hellenistic houses had water; women-
folk fetched it from springs and public fountains as they had done since
Mycenaean times and as they still do in many Mediterranean areas.
Gymnasia in large cities had baths, but public lavatories were rare.

The decline in piety did not prevent the construction of grandiose
and sometimes beautiful temples. The Ionic temple of Apollo at Did-
yma, near Miletus, for example, measured 168 by 359 feet, with ten
frontal columns, compared with the Parthenon's eight. Its cubic volume,
eight times that of the Parthenon, shows that, in engineering, Hellenistic
architects had far surpassed fifth-century masters. Ptolemy II's queen, Ar-
sinoe (d. 270 B.C.), dedicated a circular temple at Samothrace, where
there was also an apsidal temple, foreshadowing the Christian basilica.

Every city had its theater, some also an odeon. Each had a gymnasium, used by the ephebate as chapel, exercise ground, and recitation hall. Publicly administered and supported, the ephebate gave citizens' sons the physical, intellectual, moral, and religious education to prepare for citizenship and preserve Hellenistic ideals. The stadium was another feature of the Hellenistic city. Theater, gymnasium, and stadium were, as in Hellenic times, adjuncts to religion.

A typical Hellenistic secular building was the stoa, a colonnaded portico giving shelter from sun and rain. One in the Athenian Agora, the gift of Attalus II of Pergamum, was restored with American help and dedicated in 1956. The basilica was a secular adaptation of the temple plan, used as market-hall and courthouse. With the rise of merchant princes and well-paid royal servants, private houses became larger and more luxurious. A peristyle round a central court formed a four-square portico. The rooms had plaster walls, painted at first in simple panels, later with garden scenes or vistas of streets and buildings to counterfeit the outdoors. Though architects experimented with them, the arch, vault, and cupola were never widely used. The only departure from an-

Fig. 31.1. Athens. Stoa of Attalus. Built about 150 B.C., restored in 1956 to house the Agora Museum and workshops. Each story accommodated 21 shops, with a continuous porch in front supported by two rows of columns. Here philosophers met their disciples, statues and paintings were exhibited, and crowds watched processions pass through the Agora on their way to the Acropolis. (Photo by Dorothy MacKendrick)

Fig. 31.2. The Belvedere *Apollo*. Roman copy of 4th-century B.C. bronze original, perhaps by Leochares. The elegant implacable young god has just shot, with effortless superiority, one of his infallible arrows. (Rome, Vatican Museum; Anderson photo)

cient types was the new Corinthian capital, with acanthus leaves enveloping the drum just below the Ionic volute.

Naval architecture prided itself on producing ships of enormous size. The most famous, the *Alexandria*, commissioned by Hiero II of Syracuse (reigned *c.* 270–215 B.C.) was the one launched singlehanded by Archimedes. Its displacement was 3310 tons, and it carried a crew of 600. It was lead-plated and had twenty banks of oars. Its marvels included mosaic floors, a gymnasium, a temple, stalls for ten horses, an aquarium, eight artillery towers, and enormous catapults capable of firing 173-pound stones and arrows 18 feet long.

The individualism of the age was best captured in sculpture. The masters show a capacity for rendering anatomy, drapery, and movement not far below that of the fifth and fourth centuries. They show too a new perception of human nature, especially in their portrayal of humble men and women. Kings are sculptured naked like heroes and gods, but with realistic portrait heads. There are visible the artificiality and flamboyance that often marks an age of sudden wealth and easy advancement. The Belvedere *Apollo,* probably a copy of a Hellenistic original, struts like a New Comedy actor. Even more theatrical and mannered is the *Laocoön* group, whose sculptor greatly overemphasizes agonizing bodily contortions. But the *Venus* of Melos, though a lovely woman rather than a goddess, has no peer but Phidias' Lemnian *Athena.* The naked *Aphrodite* of Cyrene, too, is human, all too human, in the Praxitelean tradition.

A number of statues of humble people surpass the statues of kings and gods. They are the work of artists abreast of such humanitarian tendencies of the day as the critiques of social utopians, the founding of societies for the redemption of slaves, and the organized efforts to bring comfort and justice to the poor, though some of these works are not

Fig. 31.3. *Laocoön.* The priest, for warning the Trojans against the wooden horse, was strangled by serpents, with his two sons. The emphasis on suffering seems excessive to modern taste. Late summer of 1957 saw the announcement of the discovery of an alleged new copy in a cave near Sperlonga; but far more fragments have since come to light than would make up one sculptural group, and the identification with Laocoön is more than dubious. (Rome, Vatican Museum; Anderson photo)

Fig. 31.4. The *Venus* of Melos. Sophisticated Hellenistic work, attempting to mix sensual charm with cold serenity. (Paris, Louvre; Archives Photographique)

without a sardonic cruelty. The *Market Woman* in the Metropolitan Museum of Art and *Fisherman* in the Vatican, privation and poverty written in the lines of their faces, were sympathetically treated. While the *Old Drunken Woman* by Myron of Tebes (2nd century B.C.) in the Capitoline Museum in Rome is a heartless portrayal of ugliness, the sculptor of the *Dying Gaul* approached his subject with compassion; the Gaul was to him not a barbarian but a human who died nobly in war. *The Boy with a Goose* is as true to the world of children as the third-century boy who wrote:

> Theon to Theon, his father, greetings! That was a fine trick, not to take me to the city with you! If you don't take me to Alexandria, I won't write to you, I won't speak to you, I won't say good morning to you. . . . I won't hold your hand or have anything more to say to you. . . . They kept me in the dark at home on the 12th

when you sailed. So please send for me. If you don't, I won't eat,
I won't drink! So there! Goodbye.

The wars and triumphs of the age that led soldiers and merchants to
seek fortune a thousand miles from home, even to found kingdoms, were
the theme of a dynamic, almost baroque sculpture. The chief impetus
came of course from generals and princes who paid to have their deeds
glorified: Attalus II paid the equivalent of $25,000 (gold) for a statue.

Some high personage had a naval triumph immortalized by perhaps
the most dramatic of Greek statues, the previously-mentioned Victory of
Samothrace. The hero of the victory may have been Demetrius Sacker-of-
Cities, commemorating a naval victory over Ptolemy I off Salamis on
Cyprus in 306 B.C.

But it was in the Altar of Zeus at Pergamum, erected by Eumenes II,
that the tumultuous character of the age was best expressed. Dominating
the city atop a majestic stairway, the monument, like the sculptures Attalus donated to Athens, proclaimed the triumph of civilization over barbarism. The theme was carved in a frieze over 400 feet long, as unlike
the Parthenon frieze as a feverish brain could manage. Men and Titans

Fig. 31.5 (left). *Old Woman Going to Market*. The realistic emphasis on old
age in this genre study is characteristic of Hellenistic sculpture. (New York,
Metropolitan Museum of Art)　Fig. 31.6 (right) *Old Drunken Woman*. An old
slave of unspeakable ugliness, unsparingly rendered, is seated on the ground
hugging a wine-jar. A genre piece typical of Hellenistic taste. (Rome, Capitoline
Museum)

Fig. 31.7 Pergamum. Altar of Zeus. Before 160 B.C. Commissioned by Eumenes II to emphasize the Pergamene defense of Hellenism against the barbarians, its theme is the battle of gods and giants, light against darkness, worked out with overwhelming variety in a frieze 450 feet long. (Formerly Berlin, Pergamon Museum; Marburg photo)

vying to possess the earth, races in turmoil and civilizations in conflict, violent action and daemonic energy marked these scenes as the culmination of Greek architectural sculpture. It stands as a symbol of the revolution Alexander and his successors had wrought.

Here ends our survey of Greek history. It has been a tale of violence, disloyalty, impotence to unite, and taste for anarchy, but let us not forget that these deeds were done by a people who were the originators, in government, literature, and art, of much of what we value in Western civilization. Captive Greece took captive its fierce Roman conqueror, and to that story we now turn.

Part IV / THE ROMAN REPUBLIC

Chapter 32 / PRIMITIVE AND ETRUSCAN ITALY

While Greek history focuses upon conflict and mutual enrichment between East and West, the focal point of Roman history is the building of a grandiose political structure unique in antiquity, the Roman Empire, which rose as much because of the discords of the vanquished as because of the might and greed of the victors. Conflict between victors and vanquished, gradual disappearance of racial antagonisms, class war between aristocracy and masses, the final breakdown of the Empire when the Mediterranean ceased to be the principal axis of world commerce—this is the stuff of the story. Add too the story of religion, how in the heart of the Roman Empire came the triumph of the religious revolution we call Christianity. To trace this story we must go back to the Stone Age in Italy.

Stone, Bronze, and Iron Ages

The boot-shaped peninsula of Italy, over twice the size of Greece, has higher mountains but is also more fertile. In the north the great wall of the Alps helps to protect the rich Po valley and to turn the Italians toward the Mediterranean rather than toward northern Europe. The Ap-

Fig. 32a. Map of Early Rome and Italy. Inset shows Republican Rome.

ennine range, the backbone of the peninsula, runs closer to the east than to the west coast, so that for commerce and conquest the ancient Italians naturally looked westward. The plains of Latium, encircling Rome, and of Campania, behind Naples, face west and, being mild in climate and rich in volcanic soil, early tempted invaders. Italian harbors are few, the rivers not easily navigable; silt prevents their mouths from forming good roadsteads; hence Italy turned late to the sea. The climate ranges from Mediterranean to subtropical; the scenery is sometimes rugged, sometimes soft, nearly always beautiful. The Mediterranean triad of crops—olives, grapes, wheat—flourishes, but minerals are scanty; such as there were the Etruscans early exploited. Off the toe of the boot lies Sicily, to control which the Romans successfully fought Carthage and divided the Mediterranean in two, conquering first the west and then the east. Thus Italy's central position assisted Roman imperialism, but human influences helped too.

Three influences shaped the Romans: Italic, Etruscan, and Greek. The first traces of Italic man go back to the Paleolithic Age.

Paleolithic man in Italy differed little in culture from the types described in Chapter 1. He used chipped tools, lived in caves, inhumed his dead. Neolithic man moved out of the caves into pole-and-wattle huts grouped into villages, polished his stone tools, made vases, baskets, and cloth, showed glimmerings of religious sense.

Bronze working was not known in Italy until after 1500 B.C. About the same time the first invaders must have appeared from the north, bringing with them the Indo-European languages. In the Po valley they lived in pile-dwellings (*terremare,* contemporary with the Mycenaean Age in Greece) and cremated their dead. About 1000 B.C. a new wave of northern invaders, the Villanovans (named for a district near Bologna where their remains have been found), swept down over Italy into Etruria and Umbria, but resistance in Picenum prevented their occupying the Adriatic coast. These peoples belonged to the stage of civilization called Hallstatt, the earliest iron age (contemporary with the period in Greece which followed the Dorian invasion). At Bologna, its center, traces of this culture persisted until toward the end of the sixth century B.C. Its artifacts spread into central Europe.

Illyrians from across the Adriatic also penetrated into Italy; the Messapians (Iapygians) in the south and the Veneti in the north were both of Illyrian origin. But between the two, Picenum passed straight from a Neolithic to an iron-age culture; its burials show a warlike people wearing wool garments fastened with iron fibulae (safety-pins) ; amber jewels were buried with them. These are ancestors of the Italian people whom Rome was to battle for the possession of the peninsula; the Marrucini, Frentani, Vestini, Paeligni, Marsi, Aequi, and Sabini. We call them all

Sabellians; their dialects were Indo-European; related to them were the Umbrians in the center and the Volscians spreading southeast of the Alban Hills. Greeks early occupied the south; Gauls the north, by the fifth century B.C. In the west lived the Ligurians, the Etruscans, Latins (with the Paliscans and Hernici), the Aurunci, and Oenotri. These diverse peoples it was to be Rome's destiny to rule.

The Etruscans and Their Civilization

Of all pre-Roman peoples the non-Indo-European Etruscans, who settled north and west of the Tiber (Etruria, now Tuscany) between 1000 and 800 B.C., left the deepest imprint on Italian history. Their origins are obscure, their language not fully deciphered. Artistic and linguistic evidence favors the view as to their origin expressed by Herodotus—that they came from Lydia. They were seafarers; in the late sixth century B.C. they provided for Rome kings who made the city something more than a village of mud huts. They gave their names to both Italian seas, the Adriatic and the Tyrrhenian. By exploiting iron mines on Elba and copper mines at Volaterrae (Volterra), they amassed enormous wealth, with which they bought so much Greek art that more Greek vases have been found in Etruria than in Greece; luckily, their golden age coincided with the best period of Greek ceramics. Their confederacy of twelve cities, among which Caere, Tarquinia, and Vulci were particularly splendid, expanded in the seventh and sixth centuries B.C. northward into the Po valley and southward into Campania, first encircling and then conquering Rome. Etruscan power did not fall until the Latins around Rome combined against it with the Greeks from Cumae, while simultaneously the Gauls invaded from the north (fifth-fourth centuries B.C.). They spread culture, built cities where there had been only villages, strongly influenced Roman religion, nomenclature, and symbols (the magistrate's toga, the lictor's fasces). Their mysterious language they wrote in the western Greek alphabet. In architecture the Tuscan temple of wood with unfluted columns and terra-cotta decor, which dominated Italy until late in the period of Republican Rome, was theirs in origin. Their political domination and cultural prestige unified Italy. On Etruscan and Greek culture Rome drew, and out of the amalgam made something of its own.

We know the Etruscans living from the Etruscans dead: their tombs, mostly excavated in the nineteenth century, with their colorful wall paintings and varied tomb-furniture, are more illuminating than their language. The many Etruscan sites in the Maremma, which malaria held static until recent times, are better preserved than those in the more progressive north. Rome itself is an Etruscan city, in its walls, its triple-

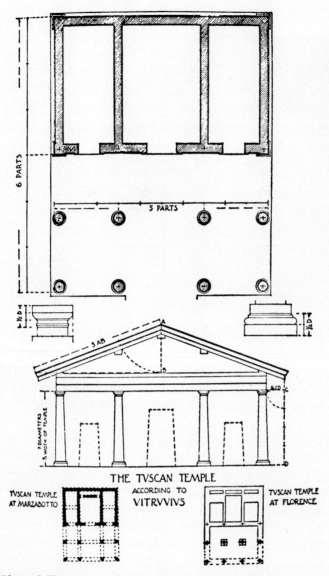

THE TVSCAN TEMPLE

TVSCAN TEMPLE AT MARZABOTTO

ACCORDING TO VITRVVIVS

TVSCAN TEMPLE AT FLORENCE

Fig. 32b. Plan of Tuscan temple, drawn according to Vitruvius' description. (J. I. Sewall, *A History of Western Art,* New York, 1953. Fig. 8.7.)

celled Capitoline temple, its constitution, its religion. Veii, on its high rocky spur only nine miles from Rome, is a typical Etruscan site. At Caere, in the seventh and sixth centuries one of the world's most splendid cities, the numerous tombs have produced a wealth of artifacts in gold, bronze, and terra cotta. At Tarquinia the Etruscan city-walls and a new temple have recently been excavated; the underground painted tombs have long been famous. The paintings reflect the gay life of the Etruscan overlords at their peak of prosperity and the gloom which settled upon them when the prosperity was past—first, scenes of ban-

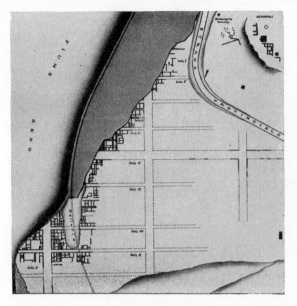

Fig. 32c. Plan of Marzabotto. An Etruscan grid, early 5th century B.C. Features creatively imitated by the Romans are the *arx,* or citadel (upper right), the rectangular grid, and the *insulae,* blocks of flats. (*Archaeology* IX, 1956, p. 127, Fig. 1.)

quets, dancing, music, hunting, fishing, circus-games; later, horrid winged blue demons armed with hammers carrying off the dead to the underworld. At Marzabotto, south of Bologna, an Etruscan city of about 500 B.C., with a grid plan, blocks of houses, and an elaborate sewage-system has been excavated. Recent excavation at Bolsena (Volsinii) has revealed an Etruscan walled town of great extent and importance.

Politically Etruria was a league of twelve cities with common religious and economic interests, dominated by whichever city was largest and wealthiest at a given period. The cities with the most impressive ruins, like Tarquinia and Veii, must have been political and cultural centers. The people may have been subdivided into tribes and the cities into wards (*curiae*). The early monarchy (Etruscans hated their kings even more cordially than Romans hated theirs) probably survived with a religious significance (as in Athens and later in Rome) after the political office was abolished. The Etruscan cities were oligarchies, their magistracies collegiate—that is, a corporate body of colleagues—short-term, and elective. There was a strong class differentiation, and genealogical and religious traditions were concentrated in aristocratic hands. There was probably a senate of clan chiefs and a popular assembly. In principle, to prevent the rise of a tyrant, power was parceled out, checked, and balanced. Inscriptions show a regular order of progression to the top magistracy, and a naming system involving personal name, father's name, and clan name, which the Romans borrowed. There is some evidence of plebeian revolts; the painted tombs show that the place of women was higher than in Greece.

The best-attested aspect of Etruscan culture is its religion, to which the

Romans were very receptive and which most strongly resisted Greek influences. It involved strict ritual, conformity to the gods' will, and dread of demons. There was a sky-god, Tin; a love goddess, Turan; a triad, Uni, Menerva, Turms, parallel to the Greek Hera, Athena, Hermes and the Roman Juno, Minerva, Mercury—Etruscan gods were as collegiate as their magistracies. Divination was important, especially that derived from the examination of livers (hepatoscopy), the flights of birds (augury), and the observation of the heavens at times of thunder and lightning. The rules regulating the interrelation of men and gods were rigid; the divine will was scrupulously asked. The Etruscans showed a desire which the Romans found congenial, to impose order and rigidity upon nature. Important was the orientation and division of space, a geometric survey of sky and earth, which the Romans called a *templum;* the crossing of main streets (*cardo*, *decumanus*) in a planned town and the survey of allotments outside it is religious in origin. The gods were placed, as it were, on a compass-rose and the desired sign came from the compass-point over which a given god presided. Thus, unlike the Greeks, the Etruscans had a powerful priesthood and no scientific rationalism; they superstitiously desired to prolong the life of the dead, and so, as in Egypt, an Etruscan tomb is an Etruscan house, with furniture, clothes, jewels, armor, food and drink, statuettes of slaves, and an incorruptible

Fig. 32.1. The *Apollo* of Veii. Painted terra cotta, creatively imitated by an unknown Etruscan master from the archaic Greek style, but with a personality of its own. The god is in rapid, decisive movement to regain from Hercules the sacred hind he has stolen. (Rome, Villa Giulia Museum; Fototeca)

portrait of the master. An inscribed tile from Capua suggests notions of beatitude which have nothing to do with morality; an inscription on a mummy-wrapping from Zagreb, in Yugoslavia, is a liturgical calendar which shows the formalistic, expiatory nature of Etruscan religion; numerous terra-cotta votive offerings suggest that Etruscan commoners participated.

Such Etruscan literature as survives is chiefly religious, though there must have been banquet songs and eulogies of the dead. Drama was introduced under Greek influence. As to music, wall paintings show Etruscans playing the lyre, double flute, trumpet, horn, and castanets. In architecture their temples differ from the Greek in material (wood), proportions (slightly larger than wide, half porch, half triple cella), and decor (terra-cotta). Their plastic arts we know chiefly from the tombs; much Etruscan art must have been religious and funerary, not monumental, historical, or civic. The only Etruscan artist whose name we know is Vulca of Veii, to whom is ascribed the remarkable and sinister sixth-century terra-cotta Apollo; Vulca did the sculptures for Rome's first Capitoline temple. Etruscan artists specialized in various mediums. The Conservatori "Brutus"—bearded, inflexible, stern, embittered, melancholy, typifying what the Romans wanted their ancestors to have been —exemplifies (whatever its date) Etruscan technique in bronze, as does the bronze she-wolf nurse of Romulus and Remus, in the same museum, with its mingling of convention and realism. The splendid winged horses from Tarquinia represent later Etruscan terra-cotta reliefs at their best; Etruscan artists specialized also in terra-cotta sarcophagus lids, laminated bronze chariots, vases unsuccessfully imitating Greek work, and bronze mirrors, chests (cistae), and buckets (situlae). Greek archaic art obviously influenced all this work, through imports of art and artists, but Etruscan art is not merely imitative: it is individual where Greek is typical. Etruscan art flowered as a regional creative variant of archaic Greek, realistic, formal, and orientalizing. It declined just as Greek art was passing from archaic to classical; the latter leaves no traces in Etruria. But a certain disproportion, a fondness for portraiture, and impressionistic technique remain characteristic to the end.

Etruscan life and customs we know mostly from the tombs. They give us a vivid picture of upper-class life, lived in rectilinear houses with double-pitched low roofs and a portico or atrium. Furniture was simple, as everywhere in the ancient world, but beds had lathe-turned legs and embroidered coverlets; there were wicker chairs and bronze candelabra. The Tomb of the Reliefs at Caere (fourth century, B.C.) shows on its walls a variety of domestic implements, including a rolling pin for making macaroni. Women used cosmetics, bleached their hair, and wore gold jewelry of barbaric lavishness; both sexes watched gladiatorial shows.

Fig. 32.2. Capitoline wolf. Etruscan bronze, perhaps of the late 6th century B.C., of the legendary she-wolf who suckled the twins, Romulus and Remus, who were to be the founders of Rome. (Rome, Conservatori Museum)

Finally, the mysterious Etruscan language. Since it is clearly non-Indo-European, it cannot be deciphered, as Linear Minoan B was, without a bilingual text. Texts in Etruscan are scarce and limited in content; our longest has only 530 separate words. The 10,000 inscriptions are mostly funerary or votive, brief and stereotyped. We learn something from the glosses (marginal notes) of ancient scholars, from Latin loan-words and place names, from Latin versions of, for example, surveyors' texts. It is significant that the Latin words for *yard-arm, actor, surveyor's transit,* and *fuller* (what we would call a dry-cleaner) are of Etruscan origin. Patient work has distinguished parts of speech and numerals, defined about a hundred words, translated simple texts which tell us something about Etruscan religion, funeral customs, family relations, political and social organization, household objects, buildings, and divisions of time.

These people, fascinating not least because we know so little about them, conquered Rome culturally before Rome conquered them politically, and made Rome an Etruscan town. Etruscan influence on Rome was at least as strong as Greek; it is simply less stressed, largely because Etruscan has no literature. But that influence went deep and lasted long; as late as 311 B.C. young upper-class Romans went to Etruria to school; Vergil's patron Maecenas had Etruscan ancestors, and the Emperor Claudius (reigned A.D. 41–54) still knew the language, though he was among the last who did. In short, it is partly owing to Etruria that Rome became Rome.

The Greeks

King Minos of Crete is said to have invaded Sicily, unsuccessfully, and Cretans to have settled in the heel of Italy, and archeology confirms these legends. There is no archeological trace of Greeks in Campania, on Ischia, and in Cumae until the eighth century B.C. In this century Italic civilization was transformed by massive importations from the Greek and Semitic East, from which we infer that commerce preceded colonization. We have seen (Chapter 12) how various mainland Greek cities planted colonies in Sicily and South Italy (Magna Graecia). The Dorians of Syracuse and Tarentum built the most durable political organizations, and Corinthian colonies, like Corcyra, on the Greek side of the Adriatic, had some effect on the Italian east coast. Greeks domesticated in Italy the vine and the olive, gave the Italians an alphabet, an art, and an architecture to be imitated which rivaled the Etruscan (itself Greek-derived), taught them the art of fortification and military tactics. But the immigrants had something to learn, too, from the natives. Neither Greek nor Etruscan civilization would have flowered in Italy without the support of an intelligent native population.

Through these influences and its own native energy, Rome united under its law every country bordering on the Mediterranean. Rome lay on the boundary line between civilization and barbarism; it still possessed its youthful frontier energy when the Greeks introduced it to the secrets of Eastern civilization. It contrived to rival the West in warlike spirit, the East in subtle intelligence.

Chapter 33/ MONARCHIC
ROME

For Rome of the kings the earliest extant literary account is 700 years later than the legendary date of the city's founding (753 B.C.). The sources on which this later history drew are biased in one or more of five ways: by rhetoric, by patriotism, or by family, party, or antiquarian spirit. Turning to archeology, we find that often the stones tell us little. Since the books are biased, sound method is to look for traces of documents or brute archeological facts, remembering always that modern rationalism is as fallacious as old myth, and not half so enjoyable. The legends of Romulus and Remus and the wolf, Horatius at the bridge, and the rape of the Sabine women are valuable as revealing the temper of those who accepted them and passed them on to future generations as worth having. Archeologically, the legends are frequently confirmed by the evidence of burial customs, building materials, and pottery.

The Founding of the City

About 1000 B.C. the Latins, a people of mixed stock who cremated their dead, settled south and east of the Tiber in the Alban Hills, the heights dominating the Tiber and Anio rivers, and several solitary hills in the adjacent plain. By the mid-sixth century B.C. this area, Latium, contained some sixty towns and villages, each with a diminutive domain seldom

Fig. 33.1. Rome. Forum. Archaic necropolis, 8th century B.C. Trench graves (for burials) have cut into earlier well-graves (for cremation). This is the archeological evidence supporting the literary tradition of two different peoples, Latin and Sabine, combining to found Rome. (Fototeca)

larger than ten square miles. By Lake Nemi the Latins built a shrine to Diana; on Monte Cavo, above it, was the sanctuary of their chief god, Jupiter *Latiaris,* for centuries the Latin religious center.

The Latins drained the marshy Campagna, sometimes cutting ditches through solid rock. Whether planned by Latins themselves or, more probably, by their sixth-century Etruscan overlords, this extensive drainage system indicates that Latium was supporting a dense population. Simple living and thrift characterized a people whose farms averaged a little over an acre. Repeatedly they faced starvation, especially when the Sabines, poorer than themselves, swooped down from the mountains across the Anio to steal their crops or their sheep.

Two or three Latin tribes were attracted to a cluster of hills, averaging some 140 feet above the plain, opposite a Tiber islet and about 15 air miles from the sea. Some of these hills were steep enough to be easily defended, for example, the Palatine, where in about 1000 B.C. a Latin village was founded, possibly in terramare fashion with two main streets intersecting at right angles. At the intersection the villagers dug a pit, filled it with religious objects, covered them with stones, and dedicated it to the tribal gods. This was the *mundus,* the center of the inhabited *Roma Quadrata.* Below the Palatine, northwards on the far

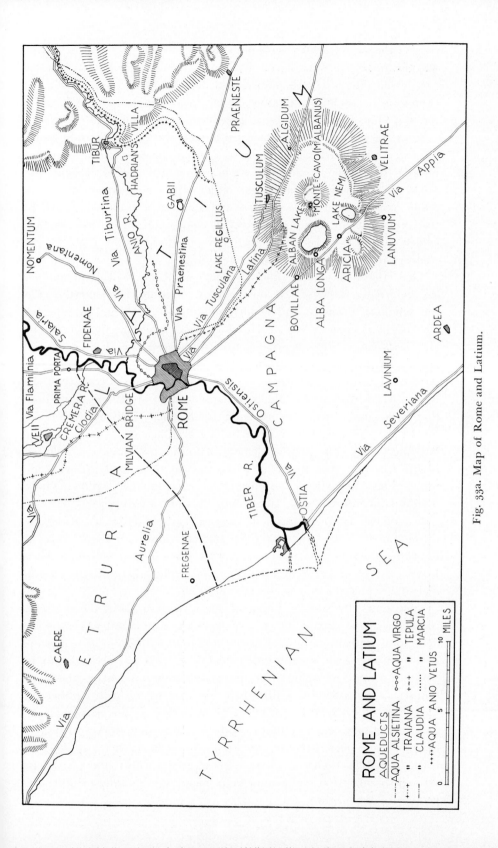

Fig. 33a. Map of Rome and Latium.

edge of the swamp which was later drained to make the Roman forum, was the cemetery. Since it contains early cremation and later inhumation burials, the inference is warranted that this was a joint cemetery of cremating Latins and inhuming Sabines, who had their own village on the Esquiline by 800 B.C. Thus archeology confirms legend.

Since the Sabines were simply a different branch of the Italic stock, the two strains fused easily. Before long seven villages—Latin, Sabine, or mixed—formed a religious association documented in historical times in the festival of the *Septimontium*. Gradually they merged into three ethnic tribes, the Ramnes, Tities, and Luceres of tradition, which in turn united to form the city-state of Rome. According to archeological evidence, this last event may well have occurred about 753 B.C., the traditional date of the founding of Rome.

The inhabited area of the city-state of Rome had its boundary (*pomerium*) ritually traced by the plow. Within the pomerium was the religious, business, and residential area. Its residents, full-fledged citizens, lived under a set of rules which were to become the core of the civil law. Apparently one condition of the merger was that no martial law might be enforced within the pomerium. This method of preserving the people's liberties proved effective until the last century of the Republic. Military rule could be exercised only outside the pomerium, that is, against foreign enemies. The man chiefly responsible for the merger may very well have been the Latin Romulus, chieftain of the Palatine village. The joint settlement of Latins and Sabines is reflected in the tradition that Romulus' successor was the Sabine Numa Pompilius. This alternation was repeated in selecting the next two kings, Tullus Hostilius, a Latin, and Ancus Martius, a Sabine.

Around 600 B.C. an Etruscan adventurer, Tarquin the Elder, seized the throne not by force but by political trickery. Traditionally, the first of his two successors, Servius Tullius, who after all may not have been Etruscan, was an excellent king, but the second, Tarquin the Proud, abused his power and was driven out.

Some time after the founding of the city, perhaps in the mid-fifth century B.C., the special interests of Ramnes, Tities, and Luceres were done away with by reshuffling them into four wards (*tribus urbanae*). The territory which Rome by then had conquered was divided into 16 *tribus rusticae,* each named for its chief landowner. During the sixth century B.C. King Servius Tullius had encircled his city with a protective wall, here of earth, there of masonry, according to the nature of the terrain; the surviving Republican walls of Rome date, however, from a fourth-century reconstruction incorporating some earlier stretches. In brief, from 1000 to 500 B.C. urban Rome grew steadily, though slowly, through immigration and a number of mergers, eventually to unite the peoples of the world.

Fig. 33.2. Rome. "Servian" wall near Termini, now dated, not to the age of the kings, but to about 378 B.C., after the sack of Rome by the Gauls. Its impressive tufa blocks testify to the rising power of Rome in the 4th century B.C. (Fototeca)

Society and Government

The ascension of an Etruscan dynasty to the throne of Rome was a phase of Etruria's expansion southward. When during the seventh century B.C. it conquered Campania, Etruria used Rome, nominally free, as a corridor to its southern dependency. Along that corridor passed Etruscan states-men and soldiers as well as Etruscan wares. When the Etruscan Tarquin the Elder finally took the corridor, Rome lost its independence but be-came a busy industrial city.

This was the work chiefly of Servius Tullius, to whom was credited a constitution so well adapted to the needs of the country that it con-tinued, except for a few changes, under the Republic. He it was who, building the defense wall, drained the marsh and first paved the Forum. The mouth of a later reconstruction of his underground *Cloaca Maxima,* the arched masonry storm sewer which carried the water to the river, is still visible. The old cemetery at the edge of the marsh now fell into disuse, and the whole reclaimed area became a civic and business center for the expanding city. On its eastern end was erected the *Regia,* or king's palace. The new Forum was connected with the old cattle market (*Forum Boarium*) west of the Palatine by a street, the Vicus Tuscus, named for the Etruscan smiths and merchants who opened shops there.

A traveler along this Roman Main Street about 550 B.C. would have met Etruscan gentlemen, Etruscan royal ministers and confidants, Etruscan lictors bearing the *fasces* symbolic of sovereign power, Etruscan architects, masons, and carpenters. He would have met Roman patricians followed by a handful of retainers, leaders of the Latin cities bound for a conference with the king, peasants from a friendly town like Gabii or an allied community like Lavinium come for the day to sell produce or to buy a few wares. He might even have noticed an occasional Greek immigrant from South Italy or Sicily: Rome's first barber was a Sicilian. He would have seen displayed at shop windows and in stalls a large variety of smooth, lustrous black vases (*bucchero nero*), bronze furniture and figurines, stout bronze armor, iron hardware and weapons, leather goods, mirrors, jewels, and luxury articles, all of Etruscan manufacture. He would have seen imported goods on display: small Corinthian oil and perfume vases, black-figured Athenian pottery, Campanian bric-a-brac, Syrian fabrics and glassware, and cheap utensils brought by Carthaginian sailors whose increasingly frequent visits to the Tyrrhenian coast were beginning to worry statesmen as well as merchants. Seaborne imports had increased so much that King Servius allegedly built a wharf at the foot of the Aventine. Legend says also that he organized around Diana's temple on the Aventine an annual fair, open without discrimination to Roman, Latin, Etruscan, Greek, and Carthaginian traders.

If our hypothetical traveler along the Vicus Tuscus happened to be an intelligent Athenian, he would have discovered many similarities to Athenian institutions, but also many differences from them. For example, social and economic relations between rich and poor in Rome were very like those in Athens before Solon's reforms. The patrician in the Forum with his satellites was the head of an aristocratic family. There were perhaps fifty or sixty such families in Rome of the kings, usually grouped in clans (*gentes*), each *gens* united by belief in a common ancestor. Less imaginative than the Greeks, neither Roman kings nor Roman gentes claimed descent from gods or heroes. That claim was both rare and late in Rome and borrowed from the Greeks.

The patricians, under the king, monopolized political, legal, religious, and economic power. They formed the Senate which elected and advised the king. At his death it appointed an *interrex* to supervise the election of a new king. Patricians alone were appointed to the religious boards and the military commands. They controlled public opinion, including the popular assembly's vote. They owned flocks and herds and most of the land, outright or by mortgage.

The other ninety-odd percent of the population, the *plebs,* had become semiserfs, sharecroppers on patricians' land. Needing protection before the law as well as in most private transactions, they willingly bound themselves to the patricians as clients to patrons. Thus they were relegated to an inferior class from which custom, religion, and a tight political system barred them from rising. To be sure, there were well-to-do peasants with homes, large fields, and one or more yokes of oxen or flocks of sheep. Merchants, artisans, contractors, workers were likewise plebeians—all socially inferior and politically unorganized.

Over both patricians and plebeians stood the king. Like an Etruscan overlord, on solemn occasions he rode in an ivory chariot, seated in a curule chair, clad in purple and attended by twenty-four lictors. He wielded the sovereign power (*imperium*) in the city and on the battlefield. The *fasces* carried by the lictors emphasized this prerogative. He enjoyed legislative powers, although custom required him to consult the Senate before enacting a law. As guardian of peace and justice, the king appointed arbitrators of disputes between citizens, a pair of judges (*quaestores*) to investigate and judge treason and murder cases. He personally led the army and conducted foreign affairs, but not without the board of *fetiales,* priests expert in the formulas for declaring war, making peace, and drawing treaties. As head (*paterfamilias*) of the people, he was head of Roman religion. As chief priest, he delegated some religious functions to several boards. The *flamines* headed the cults of Jupiter, Mars, and Quirinus. The *pontifices* supervised the canon law (*ius divinum*). A board of noblewomen, the Vestals, vowed to thirty years' virginity, tended Vesta's sacred fire. A board of augurs took the auspices before a Senate or Assembly meeting. The augurs could interpret the flight of birds, the feeding of sacred chickens, or the way lightning struck, as indicating divine approval or disapproval of the business on hand.

The king operated under a number of traditional usages, of which the most important was *provocatio*—in regal times, the appeal to the royal grace of a citizen sentenced to death; later, that citizen's right to appeal directly to the People, meaning not the plebeians as separate from the patricians, but the whole citizen body, high and low, officially assembled. Under the Republic, except in war time—and outside the city walls—when the strictest discipline was necessary, the consul had no authority to take the life of a Roman. It belonged to the family of the Roman people, whose solidarity was a greater force than even the sovereign power.

Before the so-called Servian constitution the People was organized into thirty *curiae*, ten for each tribe, and membership in a curia was prerequisite to citizenship. Each curia was functionally equivalent to a Greek phratry, a closed corporation with sole right to judge legitimacy, ratify adoptions, and witness wills. After the Senate had elected a new king, the People, assembled by curiae (*comitia curiata*), conferred upon him the imperium. The People also composed the army, each curia furnishing a contingent.

To sum up, the monarchical constitution was, at least theoretically, a partnership of the king, Senate, and People. In fact, the imperium gave the king strong coercive powers. But there were ways of preventing him from abusing it.

Early Roman Religion

A stock compounded of Indo-European and Mediterranean elements, the Romans had a composite religion. From their Mediterranean ancestors they inherited an awe for certain sacred stones believed to possess supernatural power. Such were the flints of Jupiter *Lapis* by which oaths were taken, and probably also boundary-stones (*termini*), for which the law-abiding Roman had enormous respect.

Religious taboos were many. Women might not worship Silvanus, the forest god; nor men the *Bona Dea;* strangers and slaves were excluded from other rites. There were also survivals of a primitive belief in magic. The Romans carried the "Dripping Stone" (*lapis manalis*) in procession during a drought to coax the rain to fall; in the *Lupercalia* youths (*Luperci*) dressed in goatskins, running through the streets, struck the women they met to make them fertile.

Roman religion was animistic, conceiving of noncorporeal beings (*numina*) endowed with will power. But while conceiving of these numina as spirits, the matter-of-fact Roman did not ascribe to them universal power or personify them as cosmic forces. Each numen's activity was limited to one particular grove, spring, field, or house. Or else each numen had a single function, being responsible for storm, sunshine, plant and animal health or disease, and many other blights and blessings. There was also a numen for each stage of man's life and for individual or collective activities: shepherding, agriculture, industry, government. Although individualized in their functions, the numina were not individualized or given sex as persons as Greek gods were. Finally, certain spirits were thought of collectively, for instance the hearth-spirits (*Lares*), pantry-spirits (*Penates*), or spirits of the dead (*Di Manes*).

The Romans thought a protective numen dwelt in each individual, insuring the preservation of the family: the *genius* empowered man to beget children; the *iuno* fitted woman to be a bride. The genius of the head of a household (paterfamilias) protected him and his entire family.

The Lares and Penates were invoked on all important occasions: engagements, marriages, births, sickness, and death; at plowing, sowing, weeding, or harvesting; on anniversaries and at other family festivals, at the beginning of each day and at the principal meal. Each household had an altar where its numina were worshiped by the paterfamilias acting as family priest, by his sons and their families, and by the family's clients and slaves. Janus who faced both ways, admitting friends to the house and excluding foes, and Vesta, the spirit of the hearth-flame, opened and closed the invocation of family gods.

Distinct from these domestic spirits were the Di Manes, the ancestral ghosts. Thoroughly repelled by death, the Romans cleansed their houses from the pollution of a corpse, took measures against its return as a spirit, and at the annual May festival of the *Lemuria* drove out kinless and hungry ghosts. But the parental spirits were regarded as kindly and beneficent. At the February feast of the *Parentalia* each family brought flowers, food, and drink to its ancestors' graves. The parental spirits, however, were neither worshiped nor prayed to, but simply invoked— that is, addressed with love and reverence (*pietas*).

The invocation of farm and storeroom numina make clear that Roman religion was agricultural. And so the whole neighborhood joined in public celebration of the field cult. Three main festivals occurred each year at the boundary-stones: the *Terminalia* in February as the growing season started; the *Ambarvalia* in May when the crops were up; the *Compitalia* in December when the harvest was in. These festivals and others like them were rest-periods for man and beast. In them prayer and sacrifices insured or preserved good crops and healthy flocks or protected the stored-in harvest.

Spirits once considered harmful came to be regarded as only touchy and unpredictable. Hence they might be propitiated with gifts offered at the right time and in the right way. The underlying assumption was that if man acted properly toward the spirits, they would act properly towards him. And so the Roman religious ceremonial was a rigid legal contract: the gods would respond if the prayer or ceremony honoring them had no flaw. Stress on the flawless formula tended to reduce Roman religion to mere formalism and to make relations between god and man much like those in a business deal.

The Roman city-state adapted to its own use the old field and family cults. Deities hitherto domestic and local now became national. Henceforth Vesta protected also the public hearth, Janus looked after national security, while the household Lares and Penates became the Lares and Di Penates of the Roman people. There even appears the Genius of the People and the Senate, personified on sculptured reliefs of a much later day.

Territorial Expansion

The Etruscan kings had a geographical advantage as they began Rome's territorial expansion. The Roman hills were both easier to defend and healthier than the surrounding plain, where receding Tiber floods caused malaria. Most of the plain, however, was fertile and well suited to the Mediterranean staples: grain, grapes, figs, and olives. Moreover, through the city passed the Via Salaria, the road from the Ostia salt-flats to the Sabine hill towns, which carried artifacts imported from overseas. The Tiber, too, though not very impressive compared to the Hudson or Mississippi, was adequate for cargo boats bound for Etruria and Umbria, returning with timber, charcoal, and other products for the markets of the Latin plain. The Capitoline and Palatine hills controlled this river route. Lastly, since Rome offered the easiest crossing of the lower Tiber into Etruria, it was exposed to the more advanced Etruscan culture.

Under the Etruscan kings Roman territory was extended by a series of guerrilla raids against the Latins further south. The Romans themselves had little interest in these excursions, which benefited only their Etruscan masters. The Latin towns were grouped into one or more federations, chiefly religious. The earliest known federation was headed by Alba Longa. Having fallen to one of the Etruscan kings, Alba Longa was destroyed, its inhabitants transported to Rome, and its territory annexed. Pursuing their expansionist policy, Rome's Etruscan rulers subdued another league led by Aricia. Servius Tullius defeated Aricia, and Rome then led the League. And since the Latin League had met at the Arician temple of Diana, a new temple to her was built on the Aventine, as the center of the Roman-dominated league. But there was more pretense than reality to Rome's claim of hegemony at this period.

Etruscan Rome moved also toward the Tiber estuary, attracted by the profitable Ostia salt-pans. It apparently controlled the coast from Ostia to Terracina, where Carthage was trying to get a commercial foothold. This control is inferred from a treaty with Carthage recognizing Rome's supremacy over the Latin seacoast. The treaty is traditionally of 509 B.C., but may be as late as 348 B.C. If it is indeed of early date, it reveals three important developments: Rome had begun to dominate central Italy; it had a protectorate over the Latins; and it was strong enough to earn Carthaginian respect.

Lastly, Etruscan Rome thrust eastward toward the hills where the Volsci were themselves expanding. This venture, following on the destruction of Alba Longa, the conquest of Aricia, and the resultant domination of the Latin hill towns, embroiled it in bitter wars, especially with the Volsci. Long after the last Etruscan king had been driven out, both the Aequi and the Volsci were still Rome's uncompromising foes.

Chapter 34/ THE EARLY REPUBLIC

The Magistrates

Having expelled the kings (traditional date, 509 B.C.) , the patricians established to their own advantage a class-conscious "republic," a gentlemen's exclusive club, whose members held office annually in rotation. The king had been expelled, but the concept of kingship was preserved in the persons of two annual magistrates (consuls) , of equal authority. They were sovereign in war and peace, in every department: military, legislative, administrative, and judicial. They recruited and led the army, conducted foreign affairs, declared war, made peace, and struck treaties. Their edicts had during their term the force of law; they convoked and consulted the Senate, filling its vacancies or enlarging its membership; they summoned the Assembly and directed its proceedings. They kept order and guarded the border. They presided over the civil and criminal courts and appointed arbitrators, judges, and prosecutors. They coordinated the activities of minor officials. Like the king, the consuls were nominated by an *interrex,* elected by the Senate (later by the *comitia centuriata*) , and confirmed by the comitia curiata. Like the king too, they sat on the *sella curulis* and were guarded by twelve lictors bearing the fasces; their ceremonial dress was royal.

* Brutus. (Rome, Museo Conservatori)

The patriciate wanted the consular authority to be absolute enough to insure domestic order and border security, but limited enough to preclude tyranny. Certain checks were devised. The first was limited tenure. A consul would ruin his prospects of a future senatorial career or of a later lucrative proconsulship if during his short year he should prove a traitor to his class or to the state. (Class and state were in effect one: the constitution was the governing class.) Second, either consul could veto an action of the other. Divided power was in itself a safeguard. The Senate and People acted as checks, too. The consuls inherited from the kings the precedent of always consulting the Senate in all but routine business. As for the People, the aristocracy itself conceded they held the ultimate sovereignty. But in the first century of the Republic, the People's will was effective only in securing or protecting life, liberty, and property—what Americans call the Bill of Rights. The magistrate's constitutional power to condemn a citizen to scourging, exile, or death was restricted by the citizen's right of appeal to the People. The right to liberty and property was reasserted, with guarantee of due process, in the Twelve Tables (traditional date, 451 B.C.), the result of a plebeian revolution. Lastly there was the *mos maiorum*— "the way of the fathers"—the system of precedents on which Roman conservatism was based. Like the English unwritten law, the *mos maiorum* was intangible, yet real: its roots were in the national experience.

Some time later (366 B.C.), when constant war preoccupied the consuls, a new annual magistrate, the *praetor,* was created to take care of affairs within the city. He too had the imperium, unlimited while the consuls were absent. In time the praetorship too became collegial—that is, pairs of officers held it. But by then the praetor's function had become chiefly judicial.

When Rome became a large city, the burden of petty administration was assigned (366 B.C.) to a new brace of officers, the curule aediles. There were already two plebeian aediles, originally superintendents of the plebeian religious center, the temple of Ceres on the Aventine; later they became custodians of public buildings and archives, and of public order in cult matters. It was established that while the original pair of aediles should be always plebeian, the curule aedileship was to alternate every year between plebeians and patricians. Henceforth the four aediles superintended streets, squares, water-supply, market places, public buildings, and temples. The next step was the assumption of police power, first over public, then over private, establishments: baths, inns, taverns, and places of amusement; next, added to their functions were price regulation, inspection of weights and measures, storage of wheat and other army provisions, and maintenance and distribution of the city's food supply. Gradually, from the supervision of games and festivals, evolved the aedile's most glamorous function, the financing of shows for the populace. The most lavish aedile was assured of the biggest vote when he ran for the higher offices of praetor and, in due time, consul. Julius Caesar was one who profited by giving extravagant games.

When the city's finances grew more complex the consul was assisted by another new officer, the quaestor, whose relation to him was as close as that of a father to a son. The earliest quaestors had been civil or criminal investigators. But when the praetor became chiefly a judicial officer, the quaestors gave up their investigative function to become, under the Senate, custodians of the treasury. The quaestors received revenues, made payments, and guarded the cash. A quaestor accompanied the consul in war as paymaster.

Military considerations led to the election every five years of two censors (instituted *c.* 443 B.C.). Rome's perennial wars required a draft. The army contained a cavalry company and several classes of light and heavy-armed infantry, and such non-combatant troops as musicians, artisans, and engineers to build ramparts, bridges, and roads. Since every man had to furnish his own equipment, the custom began of taking a census every five years of all male citizens according to age and property-qualification to determine in what class each should serve. This information it was the censors' job to obtain and record within eighteen months of their election, after which they went out of office.

Gradually the censors took on other functions. They kept records of all state properties, leased public lands, awarded building contracts for temples, markets, bridges, aqueducts, and streets, and farmed out the collection of rents and customs revenues. In their effort to control wealth in the public interest, they discouraged luxury and passed sumptuary regulations, thus slowly assuming authority over public morals. By this expansion of power they could strike off the list of knights or cavalry-men any disreputable member, and they came to have this power also over the Senate. They could even disfranchise a citizen on moral grounds.

In a military or political crisis, the Senate would advise the consuls to appoint a dictator. He had supreme powers (*summum imperium*) to direct the common energies to resolve the crisis. He appointed a Master of the Horse (*magister equitum*) to assist him. At the end of six months, the dictator normally relinquished his power to the regular magistrates. According to legend, one of the earliest dictators, Cincinnatus, was found at his plow when messengers notified him of the appointment and to his plow he returned when his task was finished.

Besides these functionaries, there were, as formerly, mixed civil and religious boards: flamens, pontifices, augurs, fetials, Vestals, no longer appointed by the executive, but closed corporations, coöpting their own members under general Senate supervision. Since the consuls did not inherit the king's office of chief priest, the direction of public cult and priestly "colleges" passed to one of the pontifices, who thereby became *Pontifex Maximus.*

The Senate

The deliberative body of the early Republic was the Senate, consisting of representatives from patrician clans (*patres*) and the plebeian (*con-scripti* or *adlecti*). Since the one class was politically as intransigeant as the other, the Senate continued as a bastion of conservatism.

The censors had the duty of drawing up the senatorial list, expunging the name of any one who had lost his good repute. By 200 B.C. they were giving membership *ex officio* to all ex-magistrates. After all ex-consuls, ex-praetors, ex-curule aediles, ex-quaestors, and (in the Gracchan age) ex-tribunes of the people had been enrolled, the censors added individuals eminent for wealth or birth. In the main, however, the Senate was at its best a body of experienced statesmen, profiting from the proven capacity of every decent man of property. Later Romans ascribed simple virtues and rugged honesty to the ruling class of the early Republic. Whether or not it deserved its prestige, the Roman Senate wielded great authority; a Greek observer remarked that it was like an assembly of kings. The Senate more than any other agency perpetuated the *mos maiorum.*

With the admittance of quaestors of plebeian origin—and their chief claim to membership was that they were as rich as the patricians—the Senate gradually became also a stronghold of wealth. Once they had arrived politically, the plebeian members forgot the interests of the class from which they had sprung, to play hand in glove with their enemies of yesterday. In the Senate, the struggle between classes was over. In sum, economic interests became the common bond of the patricio-plebeian Senate of the later as patrician birth had been of the earlier Republic. Hence the Senate regarded itself as the embodiment of the economic and political power of the nation and the guardian of the constitution, and it was determined to maintain its prerogatives unimpaired. Hence, too, few consuls dared to antagonize it, or even to disregard its advice.

Though apparently limited in function, the Senate was actually all-powerful. It did not elect magistrates, but it determined the nature and duration of their commands (*provinciae*). It did not make the laws, but, with the consuls, it prepared them, and its prestige influenced their content. It did not decide war and peace, but it controlled foreign policy and authorized troop levies. It made itself master of the treasury, and it alone could authorize withdrawals of money. In the official designation *Senatus Populusque Romanus* (SPQR), it is no accident that the Senate comes first.

The People

The People had at first little place in the Republican government. But they had numbers, a feeling of solidarity, and able leaders, so that slowly their influence grew at the expense of both Senate and magistrates. Broadly speaking, the People was the whole citizen-body, patricians as well as plebeians. The overwhelming majority were peasants owning an acre or two of freehold or leased land, or working as hired hands. Native tradesmen, craftsmen, and urban laborers were also members of the People. The comitia curiata, in which under the monarchy the People had a place, was able to increase its authority for a while under the early Republic, capitalizing on its authority to confer the imperium, which it then exercised annually instead of only about once a generation. This recurrence of authority awakened in the common man a certain sense of importance.

Technical and social changes brought the People new powers. The patricians ceased to be the main fighting force when, under the early Republic, the army was reorganized to include every able man. Since trade and industry were still limited, wealth was reckoned essentially in agricultural terms. This meant drafting property-holders—large and small. Since the state needed him, the smallholder came to realize that he was a political force. The principle finally prevailed that a man good enough to die for his country was good enough to help elect his country's magistrates and make his country's laws. Besides the comitia curiata there was now created another centuriate assembly (comitia centuriata) of the same Roman people, made up of all those who made up the new army. The censors placed each man, according to age and amount of property, in a specific unit (*centuria*) within a military class. For drill or battle, each man joined his particular group in the Campus Martius, the training ground outside the city walls. Practically the same procedure governed elections and enactment of laws. Each soldier, being at the same time a voter, joined his centuria in the Campus Martius as if marching off to war. Each centuria then marched a few steps to its own fenced-off section and voted for or against a candidate or a bill.

But this was not yet real democracy. It merely distributed the nation-in-arms into 193 centuries ranked according to wealth, with 18 cavalry centuries, 80 centuries in the first class, 20 each in the second, third, and fourth, 30 in the fifth, and 5 unarmed centuries unclassified. Since a century chosen by lot from the first eighteen was the first to vote, and since the knights and the first class combined could outvote the rest, this was clearly not a democratic arrangement. It was by their assembly by tribes (*comitia tributa*) with their tribunes at their head that the People gained such influence as they had in the Republic.

Origins of the Plebs

The common man's lot in early Rome was possibly harder than it had been at the corresponding stage in Greece. Against the aristocratic Republic he began to agitate in three areas: economic, to solve the problem of land and debt; political, to gain a share in the government; social, to break down the barrier between the patriciate and the plebs. Such success as the plebs achieved was gained by following with undeviating discipline a long line of responsible leaders. Not until 287 B.C. was their program full realized. This long quarrel, the "Conflict of the Orders," we should nowadays call a class struggle.

The Roman plebs included all nonpatrician citizens, regardless of wealth in landed property. Its most dynamic sections were the city workers and rural proletariat, especially landless peasants. The kings tended to befriend the plebs to counter patrician power. In the sixth century B.C., while the Tarquins were making Rome an industrial center, large numbers of craftsmen and tradesmen were attracted by the opportunities opened by this business-minded dynasty. The Tarquins' expulsion and their twenty-years' war to recapture the throne had disastrous effects on business. Communications were suspended, industry dwindled, and the prosperous capital became a poor municipal town, dependent almost exclusively on its own meager agricultural resources. Aggravating the distress from unemployment, Etruscan and Latin raiders stole or destroyed the crops. Famine ensued. The poor were forced into debt. The interest rate rose to 8 percent per month, and the creditor was empowered to seize the defaulting debtor's person, sell him abroad into slavery, even kill him.

The artisan and tradesman population had long lived on the Aventine just outside the old pomerium. Here they had built a temple to their patron gods, Ceres, Liber, and Libera (the Greek Demeter, Dionysus, and Persephone) —making it their guild headquarters and electing two keepers, the aediles (see p. 416). Gradually the aediles gained importance, administering temple funds, keeping guild records, finally, as guild leaders and arbitrators of commercial disputes, becoming spokesmen for the whole Aventine community. The aediles tried to acquaint the king with the grievances of the poor, but they had too little influence to bring effective aid.

The peasants made common cause with the artisans and tradesmen.

While the urban workers included many Greeks, Etruscans, and other foreigners, the peasants were native Romans. Some lived in the city, especially on the Aventine, going back and forth to their fields. More lived in the country. Both groups shared inferior economic, political, and social status. The average peasant, if he owned land at all, owned maybe two *iugera*, an area some 300 feet square. Even though he was allowed to pasture his ox, if he owned one, on the common, his tiny property would barely support his family. He wanted the right to lease a plot from the public domain (*ager publicus*). Rome's almost yearly wars steadily increased its public domain, for it would take about a third of a defeated enemy's land, theoretically to parcel it out among the citizens. But the aristocrats, who had long monopolized rented state lands, uncompromisingly opposed the peasants' demand. According to some sources, feeling was so strong that when the consular Spurius Cassius (*c.* 485 B.C.) proposed to share with the poor some sections of the ager publicus, he was murdered for exploiting public discontent to establish himself as despot.

The propertied peasant was in some ways worse off than the artisan or tradesman, for landholding entailed military service. Moreover, in early Rome's continuous wars his field was frequently ravaged. Then too a changing economy victimized him more than the artisan or trader. As money displaced barter, he was caught in a vise, borrowing a little today to keep alive, only to borrow more tomorrow. At this time he apparently could not put up his land as collateral, for property, as a joint family possession, was inalienable. His person was his collateral. Economic distress, then, impelled artisans, traders, and peasants to unite.

Since the farmers had slightly more prestige than the artisans, their leaders were correspondingly more influential. Also, not all plebeians were poor. The rich plebeians too had reasons for discontent. Their wealth gave them a standard of living so far above that of the average plebeians that they had little in common with their own kind except their social stigma, but they were excluded from patrician society, though in wealth at least they were its equals. The draft law, placing them in the same category as the rich, opened to them opportunities for wartime fellowship which the rich could not entirely ignore after their return to civil life. No less intelligent or patriotic than the aristocracy, they were made administrative officers (*tribuni militum*) in the legions. This position gave them much prestige with their fellow-plebeians and some respect and good will from the patricians themselves. In brief, early in the conflict of the orders, these rich plebeians emerged as natural plebeian leaders. Combining in a single program the grievances of the whole group with their own narrow aspirations, within two centuries they secured for themselves social equality and for their followers political emancipation. Economic betterment of the masses they were neither able nor anxious to secure.

Plebeian Gains under Tribunician Leadership

A time came when the plebs, assembled by tribes, elected from its own ranks two officers (later ten) as their advocates before the patrician government. They took immediate ascendancy over the aediles who usually collaborated loyally for the common good. The first incumbents were chosen probably from among the rich plebeian *tribuni militum,* hence, apparently, their title, *tribuni plebis* (tribunes of the people). The plebs took a solemn oath that it would execute anyone, even the consuls, who dared lay hands on its champions. It was this backing, reinforced by religious sanctions, that made the tribunes sacrosanct or inviolable, free to pursue their policies even when these impugned the magistrates' or the Senate's authority.

The tribunes' methods were unique. When they discovered that moderate agitation led nowhere, they conceived a bold plan. They ordered a general strike (traditional date, 494 B.C.) against the government. They marched off outside the city walls, very likely to the Aventine, long the rallying point of plebeian demonstrations, to secede forever from Roman community life and set up a government of their own. There is no reason to believe that they were bluffing. The patricians made considerable concessions to bring them back to Rome. The tribunes used the same technique successfully in later contests. Tradition records at least five secession between 494 and 287 B.C.

The earliest objectives of the class struggle were protection of the individual from the arbitrary authority of the magistrates, relief from intolerable burdens of debt, and sharing of the public domain with the peasants. Throughout his year of office a tribune's house was open day and night to afford both sanctuary and counsel to any citizen who asked for it. In the end this brought the ordinary citizen protection from arbitrary arrest and reinforced the ancient right to appeal death sentences to the People; indeed, it practically abolished the death penalty.

The need of protection from arbitrary exercise of the consular imperium and the desperate position of debtors brought a demand for a clear statement of the laws and legal procedure. Properly speaking, there was no law yet, but only custom and precedent as interpreted by the patrician Senate. Since the plebs was completely at the patricians' mercy, a more fundamental remedy was needed than the case-by-case protection of the tribunes. The movement thus arose to have the law collected in one book to acquaint every citizen with his obligations. But enlightened leaders, not satisfied with codifying primitive customs and aware of the more progressive laws of Greece and Magna Graecia, had a small commission sent out to investigate and report. On its return a larger commission of ten patricians (*decemviri*), headed by the consuls, was set up to codify the laws as described on page 416 above. To the original ten sections of the codification a new commission set up for the ensuing year added two more, one of which nullified part of the gains by confirming the prohibition of legal marriage between patricians and plebeians. According to tradition, when this reactionary group (which included plebeians) attempted to retain power, the plebs, fearing a worse tyranny than that of the consuls, seceded once again. Tradition says too that the plebs was infuriated when Appius Claudius, chairman of the decemvirs, lusting for the plebeian maiden Virginia, adjudged her to be a slave of one of his minions. To save her honor her father killed her with his own hands. Constitutional government was restored after this shocking incident.

In Roman constitutional and legal history the Twelve Tables were a great step forward. They of course reflect the society from which they emanated, an agrarian, not an industrial one. Most of the provisions concern rustic problems: boundaries, trespass, the upkeep of roads, the distribution of irrigation water. They reflect also the superstition of that age: magic potions, poisoning, the use of charms to destroy or spirit away a neighbor's crops. They reveal their double purpose, the preservation of the old and the introduction of the new. Thus, beside the recognition of the archaic law of retaliation, there is the legal acceptance of the plebeian common-law marriage. The Twelve Tables became the cornerstone of the later civil law, notably in the matter of legal procedure. For instance, the principle that if the plaintiff did not appear when his suit was called, the court should decide in favor of the defense, remained down to Imperial times, was incorporated in Justinian's Code, and has been accepted by our own courts in certain kinds of litigation. As late as Cicero's time, every student had to learn the Twelve Tables by heart, though their language was as archaic to him as Chaucer to us.

The problem of debt went unresolved, for the right of a creditor to the person of a defaulting debtor was confirmed. It was left for a future age to liberalize this barbarous practice. More favorable was the solution of the land question. The aristocracy could get rid of Cassius, the advocate of land for the landless, but not of the idea he championed. By the mid-fifth century B.C. the unoccupied portions of the Aventine were turned over to the plebs for building-lots. More significant was a later policy of settling colonies in conquered territories. The patricians saw an advantage in this, for it both siphoned off a turbulent element and guarded the frontier.

These were victories of considerable importance. But the fight had only begun; for the first taste of success encouraged the rank and file to rally more closely around the tribunes. The leadership was generally shrewd, often brilliant, but not always altruistic. But further advance was to come when the plebs had proved itself in war.

Chapter 35/THE
UNIFICATION OF ITALY

The Latin League

Tarquin the Proud and his fellow Etruscans were not resigned to losing strategic Rome, which controlled Latium and gave them access to Campania. They actually recaptured the city and allegedly denied the vanquished the use of iron except for essential farm implements. A legendary Sabine chieftain, Attius Clausus (*Claudius* in Latin), repulsed the Etruscans with five thousand clients; a grateful Rome rewarded them all with the right of citizenship and settlement.

Tarquin's expulsion in 509 B.C. was apparently the joint work of Rome and the Latin League. But after the monarchy fell, the League excluded Rome, taking advantage of Roman internal troubles. Rome's fruitless attempts to re-enter the League played into the hands of their common enemies, the Aequi, Sabines, and Volsci.

These hardy mountaineers had long been trying to seize the Latin and Roman lowlands. They had large flocks, especially of sheep, for which their mountainsides, healthy and grassy in summer, were ideally suited. But since in winter the mountains were icy, snow-covered, and grassless, the mountaineers coveted the plain, luxuriant with grass from November to May. Rome and the Latins were to learn that unless they combined they would both succumb. And so in about 493 B.C. Rome was accepted (*foedus Cassianum*) as the equal of the Latin League. Rome needed the mountains for summer pasturing as the Latins needed the plain in the spring, for the lowlands were malarial and drought-stricken from June through October. The alliance stipulated that Roman and Latin citizens should enjoy common private rights; this was the device by which Rome finally united Italy. There was to be mutual aid in war and equal shares in the spoils between Rome and the thirty Latin cities. The command of the joint army was to alternate each year between Rome and the League.

Soon after Rome made an alliance also with the Hernici, who, wedged between the Aequi and the Volsci, were threatened with extinction. It took the Latin League a hundred years to subdue the enemy. One of the chief means of victory was the founding of mixed Roman and Latin colonies, which relieved overpopulation at home and provided outposts against the enemy. During the long contest the dictator Cincinnatus gained his people's gratitude by defeating the Aequi (458 B.C.). Legend has it that he was eighty years old and, as we have seen, working behind the plow when he was appointed dictator. The Sabines were won over by a combination of friendship and force. Finally the Volsci too were subdued. The long campaign against them is associated with the name of Coriolanus, early Rome's only traitor, who, caught in certain antiplebeian intrigues, went over to the enemy. He was leading the Volscian army upon Rome until dissuaded by his wife and his mother who visited him at his camp. This tradition, perhaps intended to rationalize a Volscian assault on Rome, at any rate illustrates the strong influence of Roman women over their men.

The results of this war set the pattern for Rome's future behavior toward conquered peoples. First, a conquered tribe was forced to yield part, usually a third, of its territory, to Rome and the Latins equally, since each had contributed equally to the war effort. Roman and Latin landowners and stockbreeders could now double and triple their wealth by leasing for summer pasturage the new public domain being carved out in the mountains. Second, once Rome had taken its cut, it treated the conquered as equals. Third, Rome strove to dominate the League, for it was the greatest military power in Italy, and the city which controlled it had a future.

One other success contributed to Rome's dominance, the conquest of Veii. This was an Etruscan city, larger than Rome and much more civilized, situated on a well-nigh impregnable rock beyond the Tiber, and stronger militarily than the Aequi, Sabines, and Volsci combined. Veii, self-appointed avenger of Rome's expelled Etruscan kings, was a perpetual danger, the greater since it controlled Fidenae on the Roman side of the river. From Fidenae the Etruscan city not only hampered the Roman army in Latium; it could launch an offensive against Rome or the League. About 480 B.C. Rome, without League assistance, went to

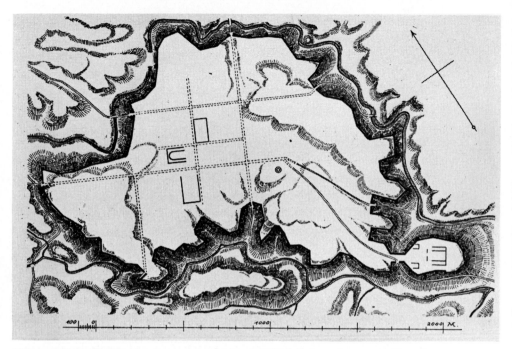

Fig. 35a. Plan of Veii, the great city which until its fall in 396 B.C. was Rome's rival. The grid shown, if it existed at all, was Roman. (A. von Gerkan, *Griechische Städteanlagen*, Berlin and Leipzig, 1924. Abb. 11.)

war with Veii and was defeated. Actually nearly every one of Rome's many wars began with one or more defeats; but Rome never accepted defeat and never made peace save with a vanquished enemy. Misfortune, more than victory, showed its mettle, its stubborn determination to see a thing through, whatever the sacrifice, and its capacity for self-criticism. This particular disaster, on top of the stalemated Aequian war, induced the Romans to reorganize their army.

The new army proved its worth, first, by capturing Fidenae (about 435 B.C.), then by taking Veii itself (396 B.C.). The legend that the siege of Veii, like that of Troy, took ten years shows what importance the Romans attached to this war. And with reason, for this victory was a turning-point in their history. Camillus, the dictator who finally took the city, cruelly massacred the population or sold it into slavery, the city was looted and razed, and its territory annexed as public domain (and soon afterwards formed into four new tribes, thus bringing the total to 25, and nearly doubling the size of the Roman state). Such vengeance became a regular practice whenever a besieged city refused to surrender.

The fall of Veii cleared the way for the conquest of southern Etruria. Within two years Capena and Falerii submitted to Roman hegemony. Another city, Caere, had refused to help Veii in the war and was later rewarded with the so-called citizenship without franchise. The war demonstrated Etruscan lack of cooperation: only two cities sent aid to Veii. This disunity which could not but be disastrous to them all, was inevitable at that particular juncture because the cities farther north were immobilized by a greater menace than Rome, the Gauls.

The Gauls

The Celts, an Indo-European-speaking people, extended at one time from Asia Minor to the British Isles. They were of mixed stock, included long-headed and round-headed groups, both fair- and dark-complexioned men. Apparently the predispersion Celts and the original Italic peoples before they entered Italy lived side by side and spoke practically the same language. In vocabulary and sentence structure, Celtic is closer to Latin than Greek is.

The Celts who invaded Italy were tall, with blue eyes, unkempt red hair, and long drooping mustaches. Although truculent and boastful, they were fearless and adaptable, nimble-witted and brilliant in repartee. Music, poetry, and wine were irresistible attractions; they loved to listen to bards singing the deeds of their heroes. They long preserved such savage practices as head-hunting and human sacrifice. At a man's funeral they slaughtered some members of his family, especially his women. They loved color and wore gay clothes. For convenience in riding they wore trousers in the Eastern fashion. Like most barbarians they had the women do the hard work while the men fought, feasted, or otherwise enjoyed themselves. The women were handsome, self-assertive even over their husbands, and ready to follow the men to the battlefield, inciting them with shrieks and curses. As late as A.D. 43 this custom horrified and fascinated the Romans who fought the Celts in Britain.

Whereas the earlier Celts fought from chariots, a few continental contingents fought on horseback. But infantry was the army's mainstay, its chief weapons the spear and a long sword, and its only armor a shield. The fury of the Celts' initial attack, without respite after lightninglike marches, the rush and war-cry of these wild naked giants at first struck terror into the Roman ranks. But once the Romans learned the enemy's tactics, they ceased to fear, learning like the Attalids that after the first blow a Celtic horde lost its impetus. Faced with cool strategy and strength in reserve, the Celtic method was bound to lose.

In religion the Celts believed in the soul's immortality. Possibly it was Pythagorean influences reaching them from Massalia that gave them their belief in metempsychosis and number mysticism. Though Celtic religion was polytheistic, its learned clergy, the Druids, gave it a strong philosophical tone, and exerted an overpowering influence on the family, society, the courts of law, and the state itself.

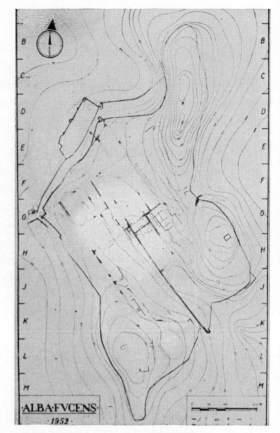

Fig. 35b. Plan of Alba Fucens, a terraced hilltop site for a Roman colony of 303 B.C., excavated by the Belgians in the 1950's. The Via Valeria runs through the city from north to south, forming the *cardo*. The typical forum layout (center) includes a basilica, market, and temple. The theater has been excavated since this plan was made. (*Archaeology* IX, 1956, p. 129, Fig. 7.)

This was, then, the people who about 400 B.C. debouched on the broad Po valley. The Etruscans, already in decline, could not stop them at the Apennine passes. This Etruscan decadence, evident in the expulsion from Rome in 509 B.C., the naval defeat at Cumae in 474 B.C., and the recent loss of Veii, the Romans ascribed to luxurious living and a general moral enervation. Perhaps a more cogent explanation is the social and political antagonism of fifth-century Etruscan cities, where aristocracies, though they could overthrow kings, failed to win popular support.

Besieged by the Gauls, Etruscan Clusium allegedly asked Rome to act as mediator. A tale of Roman envoys violating neutrality by fighting on Clusium's side sounds suspiciously like an attempt to explain Rome's subsequent fate as divine punishment. For the Gauls marched on Rome. A Roman army crumbled terror-stricken before their fury. The road to the city lay open; the Servian wall, long in disrepair, proved useless. The city was sacked and burned (390 B.C.); only the lofty Capitol was able to resist. Rome bought off the barbarians, who withdrew northward as suddenly as they had come. Joined periodically by other clans, they took from the Etruscans practically the entire country between Arno and

Alps, hence called Cisalpine Gaul. But they failed to master the Ligurians to the west or the Veneti to the east. Eventually they settled down to clear the forest, breed stock, and farm.

With Rome prostrate, its neighbors—the Latins, Aequi, Volsci, Hernici, even the enfeebled Etruscans—rose to regain their independence. In one summer Rome lost the hegemony over Latium which had taken a hundred years to build. Now it showed its real mettle.

Refortification of the city was the first task. The Servian rampart was rebuilt sturdier and higher, and enlarged to include the Aventine. The military system was overhauled, all lost territory recovered, and all enemies, including the Gauls, defeated in a long series of battles. By 350 b.c. Rome had re-established the Latin League, in which its supremacy was now unchallenged. The reconquered domain was converted into tribes of Roman citizens. Rome also, beginning about 338 b.c., founded at strategic places a number of garrison colonies to discourage insurrection and Romanize the surrounding districts. The new tribes and colonies again relieved overpopulation at home, eased political tension, and ringed the city at a distance with defences. They were to be as well bases for future expansion.

The Samnite Wars

East of Latium lived an agricultural folk, the Oscans, unused to wealth with its class distinctions. Their language was distinct from Latin, but they and the Sabines traced a common racial descent. Overpopulation sent some of the tribes seeking more fertile lands to the south. The Oscan tribes in the southern Apennines came to be called Samnites. Despite the isolation of their cantons they could at need improvise a military federation under an effective commander-in-chief. Those Oscans who moved farthest south were known as Lucanians; their new country, Lucania, was almost as hilly and broken as Samnium itself. The Oscans in Campania found broad fertile fields, a long growing season, and ripe civilizations—the Etruscan in Capua and the Greek in and near Cumae—which they were quick to absorb. Etruscans and Greeks buried their enmity and joined their new overlords in a league centered on Capua. The conquering Italic fused with the older elements into a single Campanian culture, industrialized and opulent. Campanian vases, though inferior artistically, offered stiff competition to the Athenian in the fourth century b.c.

While the Gauls were pushing against central Italy, Romans and those Oscans called Samnites were friends. But when the Gallic peril receded, the Samnites fell to raiding the Campanian cities of their own kinsmen. Capua appealed to Rome for help, and Rome in a sudden shift of policy made war against its Samnite friends (First Samnite War; historicity dubious) and then as suddenly made peace, leaving Capua in the lurch (341 B.C.). If the war is historical, the real causes for this peace will have been the army's unwillingness to serve far from home and public opinion in Rome which felt no urge to fight Capua's battles.

In any case the Samnite threat was growing. The Latins meanwhile were resentful of their unequal partnership in the revamped Latin League, especially since their territories were being carved into Roman tribes. Their resentment deepened in 348 B.C. when Rome in a treaty with Carthage insured the coast of Latium against Carthaginian interference, without mentioning the inland Latins who consequently feared they had been sold to the foreigner. Be that as it may, increasing distrust drove the Latins to Campanian alliances. The ensuing war (340 B.C.) ended in Roman victory. By 338 B.C. Rome was undisputed mistress of both Campanians and Latins, and the Latin League was dissolved.

The end of this war saw the beginning of a new chapter in international relations. With rare generosity Rome made Capuans and some other Campanians citizens without franchise, as a step towards full-fledged citizenship. Most of the Latins, Rome's closest kinsmen, were granted full citizenship. They became thus as fully Roman as the people of Texas became American when their state was incorporated into the Union. From such Latin cities came such typical Romans as Cato, Marius, and Cicero, to mention only the greatest.

Rome's successes boded ill for its relations with the Samnites. Foreseeing in Rome's incorporation of Capua an obstacle to their own expansion, they boldly occupied Naples. An important problem facing the Romans in the ensuing struggle, the Second Samnite War (326–304 B.C.), was how to adapt flatland tactics to mountainous Samnium. The technique they evolved of practically independent sections with gaps between man and man into which the enemy might be lured and despatched kept sectional and individual operations under perfect control along the entire line. Before this new system was fully worked out, two of the best Roman armies were destroyed. One was trapped in the Caudine Forks between Capua and Beneventum: each Roman was made to pass under a 'yoke' of spears symbolic of surrender. The other army was decimated at Lautulae on the seaboard between Campania and Latium. After these impressive victories the Samnites easily detached from their Roman alliance the Etruscan cities and the Hernici, Aequi, and Paeligni, and invaded the rugged Marsian country (now the Abruzzi).

But with its new tactics Rome beat the coalition. The Etruscan cities hastened to make peace on Roman terms; the prestige of their ruling aristocracies was broken and they became in effect Roman dependencies. Samnites were driven out of the Abruzzi and the revolting tribes reduced.

Fig. 35.1. Via Appia near Rome. A stretch of ancient paving, bordered with tombs and flanked by umbrella pines and cypresses. (Fototeca)

The Samnites were lucky to receive recognition of the *status quo* as of 304 B.C. Rome had now regained control of central Italy and extended it over all Campania. Moreover it had encircled Samnium on three sides with military colonies.

Rome's ability to contain the Samnites was due also in part to its superior communications: in 312 B.C. the censor Appius Claudius began to build the Appian Way. Paved with large stone blocks on a deep crushed stone foundation, it has withstood the bite of time. It stretched southward from the city over the Latin plain to the Apennine foothills and Samnite Capua.

But within six years the conflict was renewed. Rome and Samnium represented two mutually exclusive systems, life by the plow and life by raids destructive of the fruits of the plow. As the attack on Naples had precipitated the Second, so an attack on Lucania sparked the Third Samnite War.

Always resourceful, the Samnites attacked where least expected—to the north of Rome, where they enlisted Etruscan, Umbrian, and Gallic help. It took every ounce of Roman strength to overcome these allies. Manning its garrisons with older men and freedmen, Rome fielded an army of

40,000, the largest Italy had seen to that day. A smashing victory at Sentinum in Umbria (295 B.C.) broke both the coalition and the Samnites' will to carry on. Sentinum marks Rome's definitive hegemony over Italy. By treaties and by the planting of additional colonies, the peninsula south of the Po became Roman, except for its toe and heel. True, the Gauls resisted a while longer, but in the end were rendered permanently harmless. The contest with Samnium brought out the Romans' heroic capacity for endurance and survival. Never before nor after, not even when Hannibal came close to annihilating them, did they face a more courageous and disciplined army, one as good as their own. This is one more reason why the Samnite Wars are memorable. They were a school to Rome.

The Greeks of South Italy

The Greek cities of South Italy played no important part in the Samnite Wars. Like Greek states everywhere, they were both incapable of long-term cooperation and weakened by internal discord. Moreover, they were being engulfed by the rising tide of Italic tribes, chiefly the Samnites, Lucanians, Apulians, and Bruttians. Greek civilization in Italy had seen its best days.

Only Tarentum had managed to preserve its stability and influence. It had the largest navy in Italy and could field 15,000 men. Sheep-raising was the cornerstone of its wealth. Together with pottery and wine, Tarentine wool was exported to the Po valley and across the Alps. Desiring to expand their sheep-raising, the Tarentines eyed the Apulian plain, better watered then than now. But since the Apulians looked to Rome for help against invasion, and since Rome had founded a colony (291 B.C.) at Apulian Venusia, Tarentum came to regard it as a natural enemy. Matters worsened when, in response to Thurii's appeal against Lucanian invaders, Rome sent a few warships to the Gulf of Otranto. Alleging, apparently with reason, that this violated an old treaty, Tarentum attacked the Roman fleet without a declaration of war.

This sneak attack determined the Senate to subdue Tarentum. The Greek city appealed to the brave but unpredictable King Pyrrhus of Epirus to cross to Italy as champion of Hellenism. In their first contact with the Greek phalanx the Roman legions acquitted themselves well. Pyrrhus won two victories, but with such heavy losses that the phrase "Pyrrhic victory" has become a figure of speech.

When the Senate would not agree to his terms, Pyrrhus had to content himself with placing a garrison in Tarentum, leaving then to help the Sicilian Greeks in their historic struggle with Carthage. There too he defeated the enemy, but there too he abandoned his fellow Greeks without any solid accomplishment. When Pyrrhus recalled the garrison from

Tarentum and, shortly after, died (272 B.C.) , Tarentum capitulated. Like every other Greek city in Italy, it was compelled to receive a Roman garrison, although permitted to retain home rule. Lucania and Apulia having already become its allies, within six years of Pyrrhus' death Rome was not only mistress of Italy from the Alps to the Straits of Messina, but also one of the world's great powers, a fact already recognized (273 B.C.) when Egypt offered a treaty of friendship.

Chapter 36/CONQUEST OF
EAST AND WEST

The First Punic War

Rome's new interests in South Italy embroiled it in a deadly struggle with Carthage. The trouble started over the Mamertines, a band of Campanian mercenaries in the service of King Agathocles of Syracuse, who had (289 B.C.) treacherously seized Messana. When in 265 B.C. Hiero of Syracuse sent a force to expel them, they solicited help from Carthage. Desirous, as always, of driving the Greeks from Sicily, Carthage grasped at this new chance and sent troops to occupy Messana's citadel. Before long the Syracusans withdrew, but the Carthaginians remained, whereupon a Mamertine faction asked Rome to help dislodge the unwanted "protector." The Senate, unwilling to precipitate war, refused.

The people, however, persuaded by their leaders that intervention would increase the number of Rome's allies and decrease their own military obligations, took matters into their own hands and voted to intervene. Their decision marked the beginning of a struggle, lasting 120 years, which changed the course of world history. Henceforward popular hysteria and irresponsibility would sometimes overbalance traditional senatorial caution. Carthage was ultimately wiped out, while Rome emerged from this, its greatest ordeal, as the world's strongest military

Fig. 36a. Map of Rome and Italy, 227–70 B.C.

nation. But it was a Rome profoundly altered, and not always for the better, by the power and responsibility thrust upon it.

Having accepted the Mamertines as allies, Rome sent to Messana a detachment of troops small enough to discourage speculations of wide conquest. Rome wanted to prevent Carthage from dominating the Strait and sinking, as it regularly did, foreign ships venturing into what it claimed as its sphere of influence. Rome's concern was not for Roman shipping, which was as yet trifling, but for that of its Greek allies in South Italy. Rome also feared that Carthage might use Messana as an operating base against the Italian mainland. The idea of conquest grew gradually, for neither power wanted to see the theater of operations widen, but they had started something neither could control.

When Carthage would not withdraw from Messana, Rome sent out its first overseas army. Carthage won Hiero over by promising him a free hand in northeast Sicily. Thus Carthage and Syracuse, representatives of two perennially clashing civilizations, now joined forces against Rome. But Hiero made overtures to Rome and won an alliance to which he proved always faithful. Carthage assembled a 50,000-man army at Agrigentum (the Greek Acragas) but the Romans captured it after a brilliant siege (262 B.C.).

Having gained Agrigentum and dispersed the Punic forces, Rome decided to drive them from Sicily altogether. But Carthage was the world's greatest sea power, and Sicily was an island, while Rome depended for a navy on its Greek allies. It was ambitious and resourceful enough to build, within a few months, 150 warships of its own, with which it defeated the Carthaginian fleet off Mylae (260 B.C.), despite limited seagoing experience, and transported an army to Africa. But the African campaign failed, neutralizing two other naval victories. After a five-year lull the Romans again took the initiative and besieged Lilybaeum, the main Punic stronghold in Sicily. Although unsuccessful, the siege spurred Carthage to build another fleet and to attack. In a fierce battle off Drepana (249 B.C.) the Roman ships were captured, sunk, or lost in a storm.

The Romans were now on the defensive, especially after Hamilcar Barca launched guerrilla warfare from two mountain fortresses, Mt. Eryx above Drepana and Mt. Hercte above Panormus. But the war was decided at sea, off the Aegates Islands (242 B.C.), where a new Roman fleet of 200 ships annihilated the enemy. Carthage was forced to accept humiliating peace terms (241 B.C.) including withdrawal from Sicily. Thus Rome succeeded where the Greeks had failed in expelling the Phoenician from the Middle Mediterranean. By friendship treaties, it controlled the whole island. Rome exacted also an indemnity of 1000 talents cash and 2200 talents payable in twenty yearly installments. Four years later, while Carthage was occupied with a revolt of its Libyan

subjects and mercenary troops, Rome seized Sardinia, on the pretext of
Carthaginian inability to preserve order there. It levied on Carthage an
additional indemnity of 1200 talents. Carthage was too exhausted to resist. Its withdrawal from Sardinia left Rome free to occupy Corsica also.

Hannibal and the Second Punic War

Carthage had been weakened, not broken. Hamilcar Barca, the only hero
of the war, saw where it could compensate in Spain for Mediterranean
losses. Spain, cut off from Gaul by the Pyrenees mountains, has both Atlantic and Mediterranean coasts, as well as easy contact with Africa
across the Strait of Gibraltar. On and about its vast central arid plateau
lived the Celtiberians, Astures, and Cantabri, who were long to defy Roman arms. Greeks from Massalia, later to be ousted by the Carthaginians,
colonized its northeast coast and the Ebro valley, later called by the
Romans "Hither Spain." Carthage occupied the southeast, especially the
fertile Baetis (Guadalquivir) valley, center of the later Roman "Farther
Spain," or Baetica (now Andalusia). Spain attracted the Carthaginians
because it had gold, silver, iron, copper, tin, and lead mines, ship-timber,
and men. Carthaginians in Spain could, moreover, threaten the Romans
in Sardinia, Corsica, and perhaps Italy itself. Hamilcar, his son-in-law
Hasdrubal, and Hasdrubal's son Hannibal all successively—and successfully—exploited Spain.

Hannibal was a genius, a brilliant strategist and splendid organizer who
could mobilize Spanish manpower and resources, cross the Alps with
50,000 men, and bring the war to Rome's véry gates. A uniquely magnetic
personality, he inspired devotion in his motley army of Carthaginians,
Libyans, Spaniards, Gauls, Greeks. Not once in all the trials and sacrifices
of a sixteen-year campaign did his troops mutiny or falter in their support.
He personally unleashed the Second Punic War in the face of conservative reluctance. But once the die was cast, the conservatives too stood
by him loyally, if not always energetically.

Though Hannibal took a step he knew Rome would not tolerate, Rome
already feared Carthaginian power in Spain. Rome had recognized by
treaty all Spain south of the Ebro as a Carthaginian sphere of influence,
but when Hannibal picked a quarrel with Saguntum, 100 miles south of
that line, Rome honored the Saguntines' request for assistance, forthwith
demanding Hannibal's surrender and Carthaginian withdrawal from
Saguntum. One motive for this action, so clearly contravening the treaty,
was to protect Massilia (Greek Massalia), an old and faithful ally, who
saw in Carthage a military and economic threat. Possibly another was the
Roman nobility's desire to take men's minds off unrest at home by a brief
foreign war. In any case, Carthage's refusal of Rome's ultimatum was the
formal signal for the Second Punic War.

Rome's strategy was orthodox. It sent an army against Hannibal in Spain and was preparing to send another to Africa, feeling no danger for itself, since it had the Mediterranean's largest fleet, whereas Carthage had made little effort to rebuild its navy. Thus an attack on Italy from either Africa or Spain seemed unlikely. If Hannibal did risk a march on Italy, the combined Roman and Massiliote forces could stop him en route. But Rome did not know its man. Hannibal, eluding one of the consuls awaiting him near the mouth of the Rhone, led his army by back roads around Massilia and, with fearful loss, across the Alps.

Once in northern Italy (218 B.C.) Hannibal defeated a consular army at the Ticinus River and two other armies at the Trebia. By these victories he won over the Gauls. In a few months Rome had lost all the Po valley except Mantua and Patavium. In 217 B.C. Hannibal administered another staggering defeat at Lake Trasimene in central Etruria. The road to Rome lay open. Though Hannibal reached Rome's very gates, he made no attempt at siege, apparently for lack of siege engines. Instead he marched south, hoping to induce Rome's allies to desert. With their support he hoped if not to destroy Rome, at least to reduce it to municipal status.

The loss of three armies caused policy division in Rome. One group, led by the dictator Q. Fabius Maximus, held that Rome should study Hannibal's military technique to beat him at his own game. While Fabius commanded, Rome not only lost no more legions, but by guerrilla warfare prevented Hannibal from taking the initiative. But certain plebeian leaders, impatient with the Fabian policy and aiming to crush the enemy by mere weight, fielded an army of 80,000 instead of the customary 40,000 men. This only gave Hannibal twice as many Romans to slaughter. Not for 500 years did Rome suffer a disaster like that of Cannae (216 B.C.). The crisis evoked heroic measures. The patriciate and the plebs closed ranks; the Senate dramatically thanked the surviving consul "for not having despaired of the Republic" and forbade anyone to dress in mourning, though at least one man in every family was lost. Its determined courage in the face of near extinction is one of the most magnificent pages in Rome's long history.

Up to Cannae the Italian Federation had remained intact. After Cannae, however, some South Italian cities went over to the Carthaginian. Capua, Rome's oldest Campanian ally, was one; Tarentum was another. But Hannibal's hopes for the Federation's breakdown were to be disappointed. He underestimated both the Roman resiliency and the Italian temper. He mistakenly thought that the Italian Federation was a master-slave organization like the Carthaginian Empire. But with all its flaws the Federation was fair to its members; for instance, it was entirely free from taxation, whereas Carthage regularly imposed a 25 percent levy on agricultural products, not to mention levies on industry and commerce.

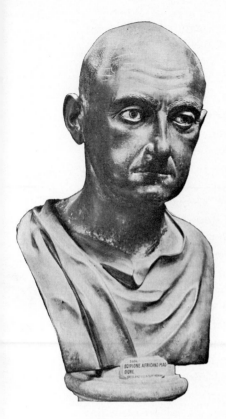

Fig. 36.1. So-called Scipio Africanus. From the villa of the Pisos, Herculaneum. The shaved head and the scar on the forehead, suffered when Scipio threw himself in front of his father to save his life at the battle of the Ticinus, supply the evidence for the identification. Some scholars believe the person represented to be a priest of Isis. (Naples, Italy, National Museum)

Besides, Hannibal personified an inimical oriental culture. Rome's decent treatment of its allies thus paid dividends in its hour of need; the few defections it was able to handle. Hannibal had one last weapon, but it too missed its mark. He had ordered his brother Hasdrubal to reinforce him from Spain. With this army advancing from the north and his own attacking from the south, he would squeeze Rome in a vise. But the Romans crushed Hasdrubal's army and captured Hasdrubal himself. His head thrown into the Carthaginian camp told Hannibal the game was up.

The war was won in Spain and Sicily as much as in Italy. By occupying Spain the Romans prevented new reinforcements for Hannibal; the brilliant young P. Cornelius Scipio won successes there which conquered for Rome eastern and southern Spain and its rich silver mines. In Sicily anti-Roman factions exploited King Hiero's death (215 B.C.) to hand Syracuse over to the Carthaginians, and most other cities followed suit. Marcellus, the hero of the Sicilian campaign, took Syracuse by storm despite Archimedes' burning-glasses and grapnels. In the ensuing sack Archimedes lost his life. With the acquisition of Spain, Sicily recovered, and Hannibal at bay, it was time to take the war home to Carthage. Young Scipio, the conqueror of Spain, was put in command. Hannibal escaped from Italy to command all Carthaginian forces. At the battle of Zama (202 B.C.) Scipio, a man of destiny, defeated Hannibal by the latter's own methods. In some regiments not a single Carthaginian soldier survived. Following Scipio's orders, the cavalry of Massinissa, a Numidian chieftain with a grudge against Carthage, hammered the Carthaginian center from the rear and contributed to the victory. When Carthage sued for peace, it was compelled to pay a 10,000-talent indemnity, reduce its fleet to ten ships, give up its African empire, and become a mere municipal town—the fate Hannibal had devised for Rome. It was not to be allowed to make war even in Africa without the Senate's consent. Hannibal, after a term as suffete, fled to Asia Minor.

In world history the Second Punic War established Rome's preeminence. The ultimate credit belongs not so much to Scipio and his army as to the Senate and the Roman people and the Italians who stood by them.

Relations with the Kingdom of Macedon

The Greek city-states of the Italian Adriatic coast, once vassals of defeated Tarentum and now left to shift for themselves, found themselves increasingly molested by Illyrian pirates. In response to the appeals of its allies—the South Italian Greek cities whose commerce was suffering— Rome rid the Adriatic of the nuisance. Soon, however, the Illyrian queen having compassed a Roman envoy's murder, the Senate (229–228 B.C.) declared some Greek coastal cities opposite the Italian heel a Roman protectorate. Rome's assumption of responsibility for peace on the Illyrian seaboard committed it to serious and unforeseen entanglements.

Philip V of Macedon, interpreting Rome's defeats at the Trebia and Trasimene as signs of exhaustion, willingly accepted Hannibal's proposal of alliance, though with no promise of military support in Italy. Philip had inherited a compact kingdom where the quality and devotion of the army were as strong as in Alexander's day. He led the Hellenic League (all Greece except Athens and the Aetolian League). Although Macedonian control of central Greece had earned him the enmity of the Aetolian League, Philip was the strongest king east of the Adriatic. Of the other two Hellenistic rulers, the Seleucid Antiochus III was too weak after the Egyptians defeated him at Raphia (217 B.C.) and too busy suppressing a usurper to be a serious rival, and Ptolemy Philopator of Egypt was also preoccupied by internal revolts.

Philip's first move after his Hannibalic alliance was to attack Rome's Adriatic protectorate, now wholly undefended. But Roman diplomacy procured him an unexpected war in Greece (211 B.C.) with the Aetolians joined by Pergamum and others. Though it ended favorably for Philip, gaining access to the Adriatic was poor compensation for universal Greek resentment at his attack on their sister cities of the Adriatic protectorate. The Greeks could now count on Rome's support against Philip. Why not too in their internal struggles?

In 203 B.C., during the Second Punic War, Philip had made an alliance with Antiochus III which alarmed both Pergamum and Rhodes. They convinced the Senate that Philip's next move might be a war of revenge against Rome. The Assembly voted a preventive war (200 B.C.). To strengthen its position, Rome came forward as champion of Greek liberties. But the skeptical Greeks, except for the Aetolian League, gave only nominal help.

Philip, abandoned by Antiochus, faced Rome alone. His best ally in this Second Macedonian War was the terrain from Epirus across northern Greece to Thessaly, where ridge after ridge of mountains ran north and south to impede the Romans' advance. After staving off the Romans for three years, Philip was finally defeated at Cynoscephalae in Thessaly (197 B.C.). More than the victory of a Roman proconsul, Flamininus, over a Macedonian king, this was the victory of the flexible manipular legion over the rigid phalanx. Cynoscephalae was the grave of the Macedonian empire, for Philip was permitted to retain only his ancestral kingdom. His Greek subject cities were freed, Thessaly organized into four small federations, and the Aetolian League rewarded by the cession of a few small states—as it turned out, too few for its appetite. No native hero in Greek history ever received a more delirious ovation than did Flamininus in Corinth (196 B.C.) when he announced to the assembled Greeks that cities and peoples hitherto subject to Macedonia were now free and autonomous.

The new freedom meant also new confusion for which not the Greeks alone but Rome also held responsibility, however unwittingly. Rome had become willy-nilly the protector of a free Greece, but the withdrawal of its forces on the heels of the proclamation, while giving notice that it had no imperialistic designs, left the field open to troublemakers. Actually Rome had many reasons for pulling out of Greece: for one, it had to subjugate Spain. Bloody and interminable Spanish wars occupied the Romans down to 133 B.C.; it was these, and not the easy victories in the East, which drained Roman and Italian manpower and contributed heavily to the social crisis to which the Gracchi were to seek a fateful solution. Besides, Carthage was recovering, and Rome's Italian yeomanry were war-weary. Furthermore, Rome had not yet found a satisfactory method of governing annexed countries, so it made no attempt to annex Macedon. It was enough to keep it weak, to prevent the rise of a powerful king who, like a second Hannibal, might harry Italy. The strongest reason, however, was the Senate's unwillingness to assume the traditional

Macedonian burden of defending the frontier of civilization from the trans-Danube barbarians. And before its third and final war with Macedon, fought on different terms and with different motives from the first two, Rome was to engage the armies of the imperialistic Seleucid, Antiochus III (192–189 B.C.). But though that struggle follows chronologically upon the Second Macedonian War, let us first pursue Rome's relations with Macedon and Greece to 166 B.C.

After Philip V's death, his son and successor Perseus further aroused the Senate's suspicions by posing as the friend of the Greek masses. After the first rush of Hellenistic eastward expansion, where the Greeks found undreamed-of opportunities, the homeland Greeks found themselves again caught in a vicious circle of low wages, high prices, and debt. Social revolution was in the air. Philosophers rationalized it; sculptors showed the pathetic lives of the slaves and the poor; playwrights dramatized man's distrust of his fellows, the struggle of the underprivileged, the inescapable web of oppression. Both Philip V and Antiochus had shrewdly exploited this charged atmosphere, encouraging the popular illusion that only a king could overthrow the aristocracies and oligarchies and set up municipal republics in the people's interest. Perseus too exploited this policy of divide and rule. But while the masses hailed him as savior, for Rome and the aristocracies he was the standard-bearer of revolution. The Romans were confused, for they could trust neither Perseus nor the Greek masses.

After the Second Macedonian War and again, as we shall see below, after the war with Antiochus, Rome wished to withdraw from Greece and Asia, to let them stew in their own juice. But in the years between the Second and the Third Macedonian Wars, a steady stream of Greek embassies importuned the Senate with requests to settle Greek internal quarrels; a Senate group, led by Cato, which loved Greece less than did the philhellenic Scipios, gradually turned Rome from a hands-off policy to one in which, impatient of Greek squabbles, it supported petitioners regardless of the justice of their case. Thus when Eumenes of Pergamum presented the Senate with an itemized list of Perseus' alleged acts of aggression against Rome and its allies, Rome declared the Third Macedonian War. The Roman victory at Pydna (168 B.C.) spelled the end of the Macedonian kingdom. The ancient monarchy, once dominant from the Adriatic to the Indus, was dismembered into four republics which, forbidden to negotiate with one another except through Rome, could no longer act as a nation. This ruthless decree, however, neither ended the confusion nor quenched the national spirit.

Macedon and Greece had since Alexander's day become so closely related that what happened to one necessarily affected the other. The war with Perseus bred new misunderstandings between Greece and Rome, for Rome compelled the Aetolian League to prosecute its pro-Macedonian members; but when the Achaean League refused a similar demand, Rome finally (167 B.C.) secured obedience by taking as hostages a thousand of the leading pro-Macedonian Peloponnesians.

Relations with Antiochus the Great

The Second Macedonian War had entailed complications with the Aetolian League and Antiochus III. The Aetolians, incensed at seeing an independent Thessaly which they coveted for themselves, invited Antiochus to free Greece from Roman interference. He accepted, only to find himself left in the lurch by the Aetolians and suspected by the other Greeks. The alarmed Romans rushed an army, stopped him at Thermopylae (191 B.C.), and forced him back to Syria. Their revenge on the Aetolians was a 1000-talent fine.

The Romans' alarm is understandable, for Antiochus was an empire-builder. Succeeding his brother when only nineteen (223 B.C.), Antiochus undertook to restore the Seleucid empire. He reconquered most of Asia Minor, then in a brilliant seven-year campaign took Armenia and the eastern dependencies, thereby earning the title of "The Great." Before long he wrested from Egypt Coele-Syria, its most valuable province. By shrewd dynastic marriages, he consolidated his power in his empire's most important vassal states and even in Egypt.

Rome had deliberately ignored Antiochus' alliance with Philip, assuming that their clash of interests would nullify their alliance. But it could not overlook Antiochus' sin of giving sanctuary to its archenemy, Hannibal. His constitutional reforms as suffete had made him *persona non grata* to the oligarchs, who told Rome he was planning a new war. When he heard that Roman commissioners were coming over to have him tried for disturbing the international peace, he fled to Antioch. His friendly reception there spread panic in Rome. Would Hannibal and Antiochus, the two empire-builders, organize Asian and African forces for an all-out attack on Italy? When Antiochus crossed the Hellespont and invaded Greece, Rome saw the expedition as a prelude to a projected invasion of Italy. The battle of Thermopylae, however, ended any dreams of conquest Antiochus may have had.

Lucius Scipio, Africanus' younger brother, followed Antiochus into Asia with an army whose real command lay with Africanus himself, present as his brother's adviser. Africanus decided to reach Asia overland via the Hellespont to avoid Antiochus' navy, now commanded by Hannibal. When finally the Roman admiral won control of the sea by a smashing victory over the Carthaginian, Antiochus lost the Hellespont, the Aegean Islands, and the Asia Minor coast.

The ensuing land battle of Magnesia (189 B.C.) sealed Antiochus' fate. The Roman army, including a few Pergamene troops and a small Macedonian contingent, numbered 30,000 men. Antiochus had 75,000, a larger force in men, horse, auxiliaries, elephants, and scythed chariots than had ever before fought in a Greek or Roman battle. And yet this mighty army was destroyed, and not simply through Africanus' genius, nor because of Antiochus' bad tactics, nor his elephants stampeding their own side, opening gaps into which the deadly maniples entered to cut at will. A truer reason was that it was untrained and uncoordinated. An even more basic reason was that the Seleucid Empire was weaker than its size would indicate. The heterogeneous population of civilized Greeks, sulky Jews and half-hearted Phoenicians, semicivilized tribes of central and eastern Asia Minor, and oriental barbarians from the Euphrates to the Indus lacked a national or spiritual bond to unite it in a crisis. Hellenism was spread too thin to be an effective binder. The only bond was the king's authority. But the provinces were normally more rebellious than obedient, while the Greek cities, a potential strong support, were congenitally antimonarchic.

The Peace of Apamea (188 B.C.) ended the war and opened a new chapter in Roman history. Down to 188 B.C. Rome's intervention in the Greek East can be explained by the intrigues of Hellenistic politicians. But after that date, when clearly the Hellenistic East presented no possible military threat to the Republic, Rome's eastern policy began to change. Henceforth Rome was all-powerful; endless embassies from Greece and the Greek East lay grievances before it; its attempts at settlements involved it in unpopularity, and it found intervention and eventually empire thrust upon it. Such is at least a partial explanation of the Third Macedonian War.

Although Rome annexed none of Antiochus' lands, it allowed its allies to help themselves handsomely. Rhodes, for its naval aid, received a large slice of southwestern Asia, increasing its domains fourfold. Pergamum acquired most of west and central Asia Minor, and the Thracian Chersonesus. This made it a European power, a buffer state between two troublemakers, Philip and Antiochus. The Asian Greek cities, Thrace, and the Aegean Islands were liberated under a Roman "Monroe Doctrine" which applied to the whole eastern Mediterranean. The Seleucids were now confined to Syria. Despite a more vigorous policy of Hellenism, it remained an Oriental monarchy. As it gradually lost its eastern provinces, chiefly to Parthia, Syria, and its other Mediterranean dependencies, gravitated towards Rome.

Although Rome took no lands for itself, it levied on Antiochus a record indemnity of 15,000 talents. It levied several thousand more on hostile or lukewarm Asian cities. It allowed generals, soldiers, bureaucrats, Italian merchants, bankers, and adventurers to extort from the helpless natives a fantastic booty in gold, silver, works of art, and slaves. Antiochus had his fleet reduced to ten warships and was forbidden to fight in the Aegean or Europe. To guarantee good behavior he had to give up twenty princely or noble hostages, including his own son, the future Antiochus IV. But Rome was cheated of its chief prize, Hannibal's unconditional surrender. Always elusive, he escaped and was hounded for six years from court to court until, feeling the net closing around him, he committed suicide (183 B.C.) .

Muddling Through to Annexation

The Senate refused to annex defeated countries—Syria, Greece, Macedon—less out of respect for sovereignty than from a reluctance to assume the burden of direct management. But in avoiding one problem, Rome incurred another, for to leave the vanquished nominally free, yet militarily impotent, was to frustrate them and invite troublemakers to profit from the general bankruptcy. Since most states, for fear of Rome, were unwilling to assume responsibility in their foreign relations, a paralysis set in all over the East. And so, scores of embassies and hundreds of petitions to intervene here, restrain there, and do something everywhere continued to come to Rome year after year. The Senate, usually not knowing what to do, followed the easy policy of letting well enough alone. Its annoyance was plain, but the cities' plight was tragic. Only rarely did positive action supplant the stagnation of muddling through, and then only when it suited Roman interests. For example, incensed at Rhodes for its anti-Roman policy, the Senate took away its Asian possessions. Worse still, the Senate also took Delos and made it a free port which shortly became the shipping center of the East, while Rhodes' annual customs revenues fell from 1,000,000 to 150,000 drachmae.

Again, when Egypt sought to recover Coele-Syria from Antiochus IV, he repelled the attack and invaded Egypt, hoping to turn it into a Seleucid annex and ultimately make the Hellenistic East a counterweight to Rome. The Senate, busy with the Third Macedonian War, could not hinder him for the moment. But directly after the war, it sent C. Popillius Laenas to bid Antiochus withdraw from Egypt. When Antiochus tried to argue, Popillius, tracing a ring around him, demanded that he answer yes or no before stepping out of the ring. Antiochus left Egypt posthaste. Again, in trying to unify his dependencies around a common Hellenistic culture, Antiochus locked horns with his Palestinian Jewish subjects. He tried to make them worship Zeus, give up the Law, eat pork, and abandon circumcision. They were expected to frequent the theater and gymnasium, receive a Greek education, and enter athletic contests naked, an abomination to them. When the faithful revolted, Antiochus entered Jerusalem and profaned the Holy of Holies. We have met the leaders of the revolt, the Maccabees. They engineered an alliance with the Senate (c. 161 B.C.) which supported the independent Jewish state.

The policy of merely restricting an enemy was abandoned in the mid-century for one of outright annexation. First to receive attention was Carthage. Despite its tremendous losses it remained the western Mediterranean's greatest commercial center. Honest financial administration and scientific exploitation of North African agricultural resources largely balanced the loss of Spain. But Carthage met its evil genius in the Numidian Massinissa, ambitious to found an empire from Libya to the Atlantic. With boundless energy and fine organizing skill he converted one nomadic tribe after another to agriculture. He urbanized and civilized Numidia and Mauretania. From demilitarized Carthage he snatched several of its border lands; when it protested to the Senate, he called its defensive measures acts of aggression. Largely because of him, Cato (234–149 B.C.), now extremely influential, voted to destroy Carthage as a troublemaker bent on vengeance. For years Cato ended every speech in the Senate with the declaration: *Delenda est Carthago* (Carthage must be destroyed). He finally convinced the Senate of the danger both of the proximity of Carthage and of its agricultural competition by displaying a ripe fig plucked in Carthage only three days before.

When a Roman army sailed for Africa in 149 B.C., Carthage could only submit. Its government complied with a number of progressively harsher orders until the city was completely disarmed. Then the inhabitants were ordered to abandon their homes and settle as farmers inland. For a maritime people this was a death-sentence. The angry desperation of men and women resisting to their last breath made the Roman undertaking most difficult. The record of the collective heroism of a people betrayed into extinction shines beside the page recounting the aggressor's methods and aim. The women allegedly cut off their hair to make ropes for the blockade-running food-ships. The city held out until 146 B.C. Five-sixths of its 300,000 inhabitants died fighting or were massacred when the Roman soldiery entered. Fifty thousand men defending the citadel, who were promised their lives if they surrendered, were sold into slavery. The once proud metropolis was razed, the site cursed and sown with salt lest it ever rise again. Scipio Aemilianus, the destroyer of Carthage, wept to think that Rome might some day suffer a similar fate. Since the octogenarian Massinissa could not himself become master of Carthage, he was reluctant to aid Rome. Rome in turn, to forestall any Numidian act of aggression, annexed the Carthaginian domain as the province of Africa.

Then came the turn of Greece. Of its many feuds, that between Sparta and the Achaean League was the worst. Though a mere ghost, rattling the bones of its former glory, Sparta had for fifty years thwarted the Achaeans' efforts to incorporate in the League. Their endless quarrels endlessly brought before the Senate became a nuisance. After one Senatorial decision had favored Sparta, the League, aided by the Corinthian proletariat, took up arms. Rome retaliated by dissolving the League, razing Corinth (146 B.C.), and enslaving its inhabitants. Although Greece was not made a province, every state was reduced virtually to a municipality, nominally sovereign, but actually subservient to the governor of Macedonia. This measure, reinforced by the exclusion of democrats from Greek city government, finally produced a lasting peace.

This chapter has described the hesitant stages whereby the Roman Republic created a great empire. At first, nervousness in the face of real or fancied menaces from Carthage and the east prompted wars which did not often result in annexations, partly because the Senate realized that Rome's city-state machinery was inadequate to administer an empire, partly because it was reluctant to undermine its own monopoly by the increase in magistracies which more annexations would entail. But later, after 146 B.C., promagistracies increased and annexation became more common, less at the instance of the Senate than to satisfy the ambitions of military magnates and perhaps of the rising capitalist class. With annexation came, sometimes, exploitation; Roman moralists like Sallust and Cicero looked back upon the period after 146 B.C. as the time when the old-fashioned Roman virtues were corrupted by wealth and greed, held to have brought in their train the Republic's decline and fall.

Chapter 37/ IMPACT OF CONQUEST ON THE GOVERNMENT

*

The Provincial System: The Governor

Whereas the Italian peoples were allies of Rome, the overseas and trans-Alpine ones were subjects. Exceptions were few. Annexed territory was organized as a province under a charter (*lex provinciae*) from the Senate, guaranteeing rights and prescribing duties. The first provinces were Sicily and Sardinia-Corsica (227 B.C.), and Hither and Farther Spain (197 B.C.). Each was governed by a praetor, elected by the comitia centuriata. A rebellious or threatened province was put under a consul with one or more legions to back him. Like other magistrates the provincial praetors took office in Rome on March 15. But as endemic warfare in Spain required the governor's arrival in time for the spring campaign, the inaugural date was advanced (153 B.C.) to January 1, which therefore became New Year's Day in pagan and Christian Rome and in the modern world.

The provincial governor, as praetor or consul, held the imperium, which he needed especially because the Senate was too far away to con-

* Terra-cotta bust of unknown Roman, 1st century B.C. (Boston. Museum of Fine Arts)

sult. His orders and regulations had, of course, to be within the framework of the provincial charter. On assuming office he announced in an edict, again like his fellows in Rome, his general administrative and judicial policy. Extant edicts give an idea of the problems confronting the average governor and how he met them.

As chief executive the governor was responsible for tax payments, law and order, and provincial loyalty. His office was a clearinghouse for a stream of business, chiefly petitions, from the provincial cities, villages, tribes, and cantons.

As chief judge he rode the provincial circuit to preside over important lawsuits. Wherever he went, a small number of resident Roman citizens sat with him as jury. In less important cases he made a memorandum of what the law was in the case, leaving the examination of the facts and the verdict in the hands of one or more Roman citizens. Provincial justice thus followed the pattern of that obtaining in Rome.

As chief of the armed forces the governor kept the highways and countryside clear of bandits and the sea of pirates, maintained the public peace, and especially protected the border. He headed a contingent of Roman troops, the size of which depended on the degree of peace or turmoil within the province or at the border. He relied also on a native militia furnished by the different provincial communities.

A small staff accompanied the governor to his province. First came the quaestor, who supervised revenues and disbursements and might look after a part of the province or be in charge of the militia or the fleet. Three or more officials (*legati*), taken usually from among the younger men of the senatorial class, but not infrequently including older ex-magistrates, went along as advisers or deputies. Besides six lictors who accompanied the governor wherever he went, there came also secretaries, bookkeepers, messengers, slaves, a physician, and perhaps even a soothsayer. A governor might also take along impoverished friends or relatives to put them in the way of a little easy money.

The province supported the governor's establishment in cash or in kind. Communities entertained him and his staff on their tours through the province, a courtesy enjoyed also by Roman senators passing by. Whether this obligation was a pleasure or a burden depended on the demands of the officials involved. Sometimes lasting friendships resulted; sometimes rapacious officials would extort from their hosts any heirloom, art object, furniture, plate, or other item that caught their fancy. When experience revealed administrative malpractices, the Senate worked out rules to protect the provincials. Thus, for example, governors were forbidden to buy silverware or domestic slaves in the province; they could only replace a slave who died.

In the governor's capital met the provincial Commons, a sort of parliament of representatives from each city or tribe. They assembled annually to discuss problems of common concern, renew their oath of allegiance, petition for favors, or vote statues or gold crowns in the governor's honor. Under a vain or unscrupulous governor this last practice might become a heavy burden.

Lastly, the governor's court was a social center for great provincial ladies and gentlemen. Here they met their rulers and their rulers' guests —among others, artists, writers, or actors. Frequently these meetings fostered good feelings between the imperial masters and their subjects.

A good governor would retain for life the friendship of his subjects. If they were in Rome on business, he would give them introductions or act as counselor-at-law. Every province had its patron in Rome, usually a descendant of the general who conquered it or the chairman of its Charter Commission. The patron felt a sense of responsibility toward his provincial clients, since his family's honor and the preservation of family tradition were involved. Sicilians always looked to the Claudii Marcelli for help, Africans to the Scipiones, Greeks to the Mummii, and so on.

Since a governor had no Senate or tributes to restrain him, he had considerably more power in his province than had a consul in Rome. While in office he could be neither impeached, deposed, nor superseded. If his administration had been scandalous, he risked prosecution in Rome before the Assembly when his term was over. But this method was ineffective, since a town meeting grasps with difficulty the intricacies of evidence, and politics easily sways its judgment. Dissatisfaction with the provincial system, chiefly because of extortions, was widespread; and for fifty years after 197 B.C. the Senate created no new provinces, despite wide military successes. In 149 B.C. a tighter check on the governors was devised, a permanent Extortions Court (*quaestio de repetundis*) before which aggrieved provincials could sue their governor for damages.

Then the Senate established two new provinces, Macedonia, including Macedon and Greece (147 B.C.), and Africa, out of Carthaginian territory (146 B.C.). Pergamum, willed to Rome by Attalus III, became the province of Asia (129 B.C.). Southern Gaul became (121 B.C.) Provincia Narbonensis, named after its principal city.

No new praetors were created to send as governors to these new provinces, for the Senate was unwilling to multiply candidates for election and thus add fuel to the already hot political strife. The new governorhips went to ex-consuls and ex-praetors. Although it was assumed that older and wiser men would get the office, politics, not ability, dictated the choice. Before long the governors of the older provinces also were chosen from outgoing consuls and praetors.

The Extortions Court failed to guarantee good provincial government, for its jurors were all senators, whose colleagues the governors had been. So senatorial courtesy and logrolling made conviction practically impossible.

Provincial Taxation

Although the governor ruled a province as a whole, enclaves within it enjoyed varying degrees of autonomy. A few "contractual cities" (*civitates foederatae*) preserved their original freedom by entering into a formal treaty or contract with the Roman People. A treaty was a bilateral agreement, unchangeable without both parties' consent; juridically it was perpetually binding. In practice, however, it lasted only as long as the community concerned fulfilled its obligation to Rome. A contractual city enjoyed complete internal self-government; its foreign affairs were under Roman jurisdiction. It had to furnish soldiers or sailors at Rome's call, but paid no taxes. In short, a contractual city's obligations were the same as an Italian city's. Another class of communities were free and tax-exempt (*civitates liberae et immunes*). They enjoyed all the rights of the contractual cities and were subject to the same limitations. But since their privileged status was a grant of the Roman People, witnessed by a charter, it might be terminated by the grantor at will. The Sicilian ratio of five free and tax-exempt cities to three contractual ones may be viewed as representative. All other communities (*civitates stipendiariae*) paid annual tribute, a tax on their crops. This category too enjoyed autonomy except in foreign affairs. The proportion of such cities to contractual ones in highly urbanized Sicily was twenty to one. Of course all cities, irrespective of status, levied taxes to run their municipal governments. All furnished troops for the provincial militia and men, ships, or money for the provincial fleet. Rome's control of their foreign affairs implied their renunciation of war both against Rome and against each other.

Less advanced provinces contained many native tribal groups judged incapable of republican self-government. These communities were the governor's most direct charge. The self-governing groups he merely supervised or coordinated, maintaining peaceful intercity relations and seeing that the natives got on well with resident Roman citizens.

Rome did not garrison a pacified province. It sent its soldiers instead to guard the frontiers from invasion. But it would interfere to guarantee that local governments be run by aristocracies or men of property. Essentially conservative and aristocratic, the Roman government had no sympathy for the radical masses.

Unlike the Italian federated cities which contributed contingents to defend the Republic, the provinces paid tribute (*stipendium* or *decuma*, tithe). In Sicily and Sardinia-Corsica, it was 10 percent of the grain crop and 20 percent of the fruit crop, both payable in kind. When Asia was annexed, its *stipendium* was reckoned in the same proportions but paid in cash. Since provincials did not complain about the fruit tax, we infer that it was nominal, probably because it was hard to collect. What mattered was the grain tax, but since it was always 10 percent of the crop, it was light in a poor year and increased only as the farmer prospered. Most provinces however paid a money tribute originally calculated at roughly 10 percent of the crops. In Greece, Macedon, and practically everywhere, Rome's tax was half that exacted by previous regimes. In Sicily it was even smaller.

The tribute was the only tax paid by a province as mark of dependency. It paid an indirect tax also, the customs-dues (*portoria*), but this was not discriminatory since it was also levied in Italy. In addition some provincial communities or individuals paid rent, as Italians did also, to the state for mines, salt-fields, forests, and ranches. The ranch rent (*scriptura*) was a head tax on cattle.

The largest revenue from this source was the rent of expropriated lands. We know, for example, that ten or twelve cities in Sicily had their lands confiscated during the Second Punic War in punishment for desertion. Every farm therein became Roman government property and was rented to its former owner at a price fixed by the censors. Such leaseholders had thus a double obligation: rent and the usual tithe. Africa was unique: an entire province confiscated by the Roman People. The usual practice however was to leave all a conquered province's property in its owners' hands.

Lacking a state machinery for the purpose, Rome farmed out tax collection to joint-stock companies of capitalists (*publicani*), the publicans of the Gospels. Their profit came in part from a percentage of the sums collected, but mostly from side operations like banking and wholesale buying of commodities. These corporations, greedy for quick returns, gave the tax-collecting system the bad name which annoyed the government and maddened the provincials. The system contributed to the degeneration of the Roman ruling classes. The provincial governors themselves often gave the publicans free rein in return for a share of the loot.

Apart from these abuses, the Romans did not rush into the provinces to buy land, engage in business, or otherwise exploit their subjects. The publicans were almost all *Italici,* business men from the federated Italian cities. Those few Roman citizens who farmed in the provinces paid the decuma like the provincials as well as rent if they leased state properties. They were also subject to municipal taxes.

Although Roman tax rates were comparatively low, the serious drawback was that too much provincial wealth left the province. But the

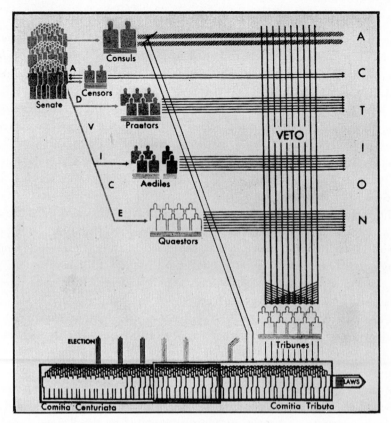

Fig. 37a. Chart to illustrate the machinery of government in Rome, 150 B.C.
(F. R. Cowell, *Cicero and the Roman Republic,* London, 1948. Chart XIII.)

prosperity or misery of the provinces depended in fact upon the personality of the governor, who was sometimes cruel, rapacious, and oppressive. The establishment of the Extortions Court was a straw in the wind.
Yet most Roman governors appear to have been honorable men; the
evil ones appear in history not as typical but as exceptional.

Empire and Politics

The empire had incalculable effects on Roman society. For example, it
accelerated the drive of the higher plebeian strata to political office.
Plebeians had served their country as legionary tribunes, cavalrymen,
even as generals-in-chief. They had become respected landowners, large-
scale lessees of public lands, and patrons of *clientes.* Education and intermarriage with the patricians gave, as we saw, these upper plebeians little
in common with the rest of their class. Their social and economic interests lay with the patriciate.

This mixed class of patricians and rich plebeians had become, with
Rome's expansion, a compact oligarchy controlling the national wealth

and monopolizing the higher magistracies and military commands. It alone could acquire broad administrative and political experience. Its members, whom we first meet as early as the beginning of the First Punic War, were first called *nobiles* and later *optimates,* the distinguished or best part of the nation as against the *populares,* or plain people. If we think of the fathers of the American Constitution—southern aristocrats and northern merchant-princes with traditions and interests setting them off from small farmers, merchants, mechanics, and laborers—we have a fair picture of the second-century B.C. Roman nobiles and what they stood for.

However hard the nobiles tried to bolt the gate to their preserve, outsiders kept pounding for entrance. Expanding agriculture and banking were making more *nouveaux riches* who could afford to run for unpaid office. Contracts for building public works, constructing fleets for overseas wars, and supplying the armies of three continents were making fortunes. The campaigns for the praetorship or consulship were enlivened by the candidates' knowledge that a lucrative propraetorial or proconsular year in the provinces would recoup the electioneering expenses of a lifetime. Then too if parvenus (the Romans called them *novi homines,* "new men") got to be consuls, they became ex-officio nobiles. They might at first be snubbed by the more pedigreed nobiles, but in the end distinctions disappeared and all nobiles clubbed together against newer new men.

Even so, factions often rent the nobility. In the political scramble the newer nobiles stood small chance against the privileged remnants of either the ancient patriciate or the noblest plebeians: the scions of the heroic families with a brilliant record on a hundred battlefields in Italy and abroad—the Fabii, Cornelii, Fulvii, Claudii Marcelli, and so on. Yet the shrewd Roman electorate could see advantages for itself in the leveling struggle of the newer against the older nobility. For in Roman politics as in our own, every issue had infinite ramifications, and candidates made more promises than they could redeem. The old guard's power was further curtailed when the lesser nobiles and the would-be novi homines combined to restore an old statute forbidding a man to hold the consulate more than once in ten years. Incidentally this explains why Scipio Africanus directed the war against Antiochus as his brother's adviser and not as general.

Increased public business now required six praetors. With the forming of the Italian Federation the lone praetor of the early Republic had been given a colleague. The senior praetor (*praetor urbanus*) heard litigation between citizens; the junior (*praetor peregrinus*) settled disputes between citizens and aliens or among resident aliens. Two more praetors were elected annually, beginning in 227 B.C., as governors of

Sicily and Sardinia-Corsica, which up to then had been administered rather casually. Another pair was created (197 B.C.) to govern the two provinces of Hither and Farther Spain. Similarly while four quaestors had sufficed in 421 B.C., by 197 B.C. twelve were required. Four new ones were created to supervise levies of men and money from the Federation; and four more as treasurers of the four new provinces, a precedent which was followed whenever new countries were annexed. Thus if more new men now sought admission to the ruling class, the new magistracies born of the needs of empire could satisfy their demands without appreciably diminishing the prestige of the old nobiles. The pressure was heaviest on the consulship, where the annual vacancies were only two, and much coveted. For while the other magistracies gave prestige to a parvenu, only election to the consulship or its equivalent exalted him to the nobility.

The relations between the Scipios and Cato, the foremost new man before Cicero, well illustrate party wrangling and knifing. While the Scipionic circle tried to impeach Cato forty-four times, Cato drove from public life the hero of the Hannibalic War, Scipio Africanus himself. But though they played party politics with a ferocity unknown even in the United States save perhaps in the Jacksonian era, the Romans were the world's most gifted empire-builders. Since the consulship was both a civil and military office, any consul in any year and any crisis might see active service as general. Actually, from the time Hannibal crossed the Alps, every year had its war. Ruling-class ability may be gauged by the consuls' record. Only a few were incapable; the average consul was a good general; some were great, especially those of the Republic's last century: Marius, Sulla, Lucullus, Pompey; at least two, Africanus and Julius Caesar, rivaled in genius Hannibal or Napoleon.

Sticklers for the constitution but also practical men, the Romans circumvented the law limiting the magistracies to one year. They kept a successful general in the field overseas, although his consular term had expired, by proroguing his office, that is, by letting him finish his job *pro consule* in lieu of the regular consul, who was given some other charge either in Rome or Italy. So too a praetorial governor might be retained for one more year or longer as propraetor if some difficulty arose requiring the benefit of his experience, or if the newly-elected praetor was needed in another assignment.

Thus under the Roman Republic a mixed patricio-plebeian ruling class governed its empire oligarchically, closing ranks against all but the inner circle of dynastically intermarried nobiles and passing office from one to another by prearrangement. Though certain biased ancient sources suggest a progressive democratizing, Rome was never in fact a democracy. In theory the People was sovereign over the *nobilitas,* but in fact the plebs was subservient to ruling-class interests.

Enhanced Prestige of the Senate

The demands of war and empire changed the essence if not the form of the constitution. Appearances deceived even the historian Polybius. He spent years in Rome, a friend and adviser of Scipio Aemilianus, a friend also of Cato and many other senators, and was a trained and talented student of politics. But, being a Greek, seeing history as the fulfillment of philosophical concepts, he accepted Aristotle's theory that a balance of monarchy, aristocracy, and democracy was the best possible government. Polybius thought that this ideal was realized in Rome, and that therefore Rome was stable at home and powerful abroad. The consuls, he wrote, were monarchic; the Senate a wise, conservative aristocracy; the People under their tribunes represented democratic experimentation and mobility. In their interdependence and interplay these elements produced the perfect state.

Now Polybius was not blind to signs of Roman deterioration. But his neat division of powers fails to record that the Senate had the lion's share from the Republic's foundation, for it was the mouthpiece of the patriciate and its organ for ruling the state. True, the plebs had challenged it, with apparent success. The *Lex Hortensia* of 287 B.C., abolishing the Senate's right to veto plebiscites, seemed to free the plebs from aristocratic checks. But the war emergency all but nullified these gains. The years from 218 to 168 B.C. were a period of national crisis. World War meant that the Senate needed unity of all classes if the constitution —that is, the governing class—was to survive. The Senate achieved this unity courageously, energetically, on the whole wisely. It asked for no sacrifices it was not willing to make itself: a higher proportion of senators than of any other class died at Cannae. This record gave the Senate moral authority and new powers, which it was reluctant to lay down when peace came. By then, too, the People had come to take senatorial control for granted. Elsewhere war begets or perpetuates kings; in Rome it was the Senate that benefited.

Senatorial powers in this period were wide-ranging. Throughout the Republic, but especially after 218 B.C., the Senate could make or break a magistrate; even a consul rarely challenged it. Theoretically any citizen might run for the consulship. In practice, however, the People usually elected only members of the hereditary senatorial nobility. Likewise the People might vote any laws; yet it never saw a bill that the Senate had not first approved. Even in the review of capital cases, a prerogative of the People, the Senate made the preliminary investigations and presented the charges. It fixed revenues and determined expenditures— and who controls the purse usually controls the state. It controlled the judiciary, for only senators were appointed to juries. It controlled policy by issuing imperative decrees to city-magistrates, provincial governors, and generals. Its over-all legislation applied also to the states of the Italian Federation. In foreign policy it received ambassadors, sent commissioners to treat with foreign powers, and in effect usurped the People's right to make war and peace. It became the dispenser of the most coveted honors.

In earlier times a magistrate was elected specifically for one job or province, for instance, as praetor for Hither Spain or as consul to command in a specific campaign. A little later his province came to be determined by lot. But after the Hannibalic War the will of the Senate supplanted the lot, so that an amenable consul's reward might be an important command to bring him wealth and glory, whereas an independent one might be relegated to an insignificant task. The Senate succeeded in taming even the tribunes of the plebs. At one time the tribunes had watched its proceedings from the door of the House, ready to interpose their veto. Allowed a little later to sit with the Senate, although still as observers, gradually they came to be regarded as members, nobles in the making. Hence they easily succumbed to senatorial blandishments and interests. Lastly, senatorial decisions acquired the force of law. This prerogative, practically born with the Republic, became fixed in the half century under discussion when the Senate had to make quick—and generally wise—decisions, which the people accepted without the formality of ratification. Thus precedent and necessity gave the Senate power to issue without the people's concurrence instructions or regulations binding on the commonwealth.

The Electorate

Our ancient sources on Roman constitutional history regard the electorate as a rubber stamp. Theoretically the magistrates were elected by the People; consuls, praetors, and censors by the comitia centuriata presided over by the outgoing consul; curule aediles and quaestors by the comitia tributa, also under the consul; plebeian aediles and tribunes by the Concilium Plebis—the traditional plebeian parliament antedating the comitia tributa, which was a patrician creation.

In the comitia centuriata, though after 241 B.C. the two top classes were deprived of a clear majority, the knights, not the common people, became the decisive voice. And in a military assembly, an old commander's influence on a veteran was considerable. Furthermore, favors economic, legal, and political, done by noble patrons for plebeian clients, put the plebeians in the nobles' debt. Voting was oral, representatives of the nobles were at the polls: the chance for intimidation or future reprisals is obvious. The final announcement of the vote was also controlled by the presiding magistrate. Thus from start to finish the nobiles controlled the elections. Though the size of the electorate between 220 and 150 B.C. has been variously estimated as from 40,000 to 90,000, attendance at the comitia was one-tenth that, and it was feasible to bribe directly or indirectly, in cash, bread, and circuses, a bare majority of 4,000 to 9,000 voters.

The comitia tributa reached in 241 B.C. its final total of 35 tribes. Here, as voting was in Rome only, representatives of rural tribes in Rome, though representing only a tenth of the population of the rural tribes, were important. One farmer's vote was worth ten times an urban one, especially under the system of group voting, where one tribe had one vote.

In the period 220–150 B.C. the make-up of the electorate had changed. The rapidly growing city population now included freedmen and dispossessed farmers, the one group bound sentimentally, the other economically, to the propertied class. These were fair game for bribery. Apart from bribery in cash, gifts of grain from surplus-producing areas were passed on to the populace, and revenues from provincial taxation provided free oil and wine. Indirect bribery by the giving of games increased; five new sets, each lasting from five to fourteen days or even longer, were introduced between 220 and 173 B.C. The games enhanced the importance of the aediles who gave them, often largely out of their own pockets, a contribution which proved to pay off handsomely in automatic election to higher office.

The Lex Aelia and the Lex Fufia, of about 150 B.C. provided the nobiles with another control, this time an indirect veto, over popular legislation. These laws gave magistrates the right to obstruct the holding of assemblies by announcing that the omens were unfavorable. Thus religion, or superstition, was made to operate in favor of the nobiles, though as time went on the tribunes came to use this device also, to obstruct legislation deemed unfavorable to the People. But another provision which the laws probably contained, forbidding assemblies to be held for the passing of laws during the period of election campaigns, operated in all probability in the nobility's favor.

In the mid-second century B.C. the electorate was still subservient to the nobility. But the Senate, though outwardly as unshaken as ever, had inward ills, and Scipio Aemilianus' gloomy reflections over the ruins of Carthage were symbolic of the nobility's realization of them. After 146 B.C. the Roman ruling class, faced with no further external challenge, fell prey to internal discords, which with the rise of the Gracchi (133 B.C.) came to a head and dispelled forever the nobiles' sense of security; henceforward the only choices were military dictatorship or mob rule.

Chapter 38/ IMPACT OF CONQUEST ON CULTURE

The City of Rome

When the rustic town on the Tiber became the capital first of Italy, then of the whole world, it underwent profound change. As our great-grandfathers dug canals, built railroads, and strung telegraph wires centering on Washington, so the Romans of the Republic built roads converging on Rome from the rest of Italy, Narbonese Gaul, Spain, and the Balkans. Over these roads went messengers, ambassadors, governors with their retinues, senatorial investigating commissions, and Roman grandees, patrons of cities and whole provinces. Over these roads came envoys seeking friendship, peace, or mercy, nobles as hostages, even kings to adorn the triumphs of Roman generals. And over them departed and returned Roman legionaries and Italian auxiliaries, each bringing home gold and silver coins to hoard or invest, jewelry, plate, trinkets, often two or three slaves. These veterans brought something else, intangible yet real: knowledge of the world and new ideas to compete with their ancestral prejudices. This broadened experience, plus a vague restlessness, was to contribute to the undermining of old beliefs and conventions.

The state itself brought in hordes of enslaved prisoners of war, sturdy

Fig. 38.1. Roman triumph, model. Based on Plutarch's description of Aemilius Paulus' triumph after Pydna (167 B.C.). The triumphator, dressed in gold, with eagle scepter and laurel branch, rides in a chariot drawn by four white horses. Lictors bearing the fasces precede him, magistrates follow; behind them, wagon after wagon loaded with spoils: trophies, silver and gold coin, plate, and crowns; captives in chains, oxen for sacrifice. Religion, dignity, pride, greed, pomp, and tragedy—all play their part in Roman history, and all are symbolized in the triumphal processions. Three hundred twenty are recorded from Romulus to Vespasian. (Rome, Museo della Civiltà Romana; J. Felbermeyer photo)

western barbarians, sensitive and educated artisans or intellectuals from the east, the latter sometimes wealthy and cultured aristocrats, doctors, apothecaries, public officials, educators, writers, architects, engineers, sculptors, painters, workers in gold, silver, or bronze, carpenters, masons or stonecutters, and other master craftsmen. Their talent was bound to leave an imprint on Roman society.

By 200 B.C. Rome had become Europe's largest city. As its population grew, real estate speculators improvised thousands of apartments. The ensuing slums were as crowded and filthy as those in any modern metropolis. Flimsy frame firetraps with wobbly floors and rickety stairs rose four to six stories high, row on row and block after block. Fires were frequent and costly, for the Republic never organized a fire department. Inadequately policed, the unlighted alleys of these forgotten neighborhoods harbored broken men and lost women, beggars and criminals as well as poor workingmen.

The privileged classes lived in houses which in plan symbolized the merging of Roman with Greek culture. The early Roman or Etruscan great house consisted of a few rooms on the ground floor, built around a patio (*atrium*) with insloping roof and central pool to collect rain water. In the developed house this area held the public rooms, while

Fig. 38.2. Praeneste. Sanctuary of Fortune, model. Axially symmetrical terraced treatment of a steep slope, based on daring use of hydraulic concrete. *Circa* 150 or 80 B.C. From bottom to top: ramps, hemicycle terrace, terrace of half-columns, Cortina terrace, hemicycle surmounted by portico. The round building containing the cult statue, at the very top, is not shown in the model, but its actual interior walls, in *opus incertum,* are visible behind it. (Praeneste, Italy, Archaeological Museum)

sumptuous living quarters were grouped at the rear, sometimes more than one story high in Hellenistic fashion round a rectangular or square peristyle enclosing a garden.

Civic architecture expanded even more. The early Republic had been too poor for much public building, but after the First Punic War victorious generals began to earmark booty for baths, triumphal arches, and temples, none as large as Tarquin's Capitoline temple, but impressive on their high podia and colorful in their polychrome terra-cotta decoration. These temples were usually of wood; when tufa was used, it was often stuccoed white. After the Hannibalic War public buildings increased in number for public business and private leisure. Between 184 and 169 B.C. the Forum acquired a new look, as three successive censors, Cato, Aemilius, and Sempronius Gracchus, each built basilicas, for social, commercial, and legal purposes. These were in Hellenistic style, with one or more entrances on the long side, interior columns producing longitudinal naves, and an interior colonnade forming a roofed peristyle. A portico or shaded walk was built in 193 B.C. and later (174 B.C.) extended to two-thirds of a mile along the river from the Emporium or commercial docks to the Campus Martius, or Field of

Mars, the drill-ground and voting place. A double portico, built in 168 B.C. with spoils from the war with Perseus, had bronze Corinthian capitals, the first in Rome. In some porticoes captured works of art were displayed as in a museum. Roman art itself developed, with certain Hellenistic influences, as historical, practical (for example, the paintings carried in triumphs), and realistic. In the Campus Martius (Largo Argentina) rose a group of tufa temples, one of which is round, in adapted Hellenistic style, while close by were erected Lysippus' equestrian statues of Alexander's companions fallen at the Granicus. These were but a fraction of the innumerable masterpieces brought to Rome as booty. From the day Marcellus brought the spoils of Syracuse to Rome,

Fig. 38.3. Roman road construction, model. 1. Field engineer aligning road with *groma*. 2. Stake man. 3. Field engineer running levels for road with *chorobates*. 4. Rodman assisting field engineer. 5. Loosening earth and marking road margins with a plow. 6. Excavator digging marginal trenches to the depth of the solid foundations. 7. Laborers shoveling loose earth and removing it in a basket. 8. Workmen consolidating roadbed with a tamper. 9. *Pavimentum:* a bedding of lime mortar or sand to form a level base. 10. *Statumen:* the first course: stones fist-size, cemented together with mortar or clay. Thickness, 10 inches to 2 feet. 11. *Rudus:* the second course: lime concrete, grouted with broken stone and pottery fragments. Thickness, 9 inches. 12. *Nucleus:* the third course: concrete made of gravel or coarse sand mixed with hot lime, placed in layers and compacted with a roller. Thickness, 1 foot at sides, 18 inches at crown of road. 13. *Summum dorsum:* the top course: polygonal blocks of hard stone carefully fitted and set in the *nucleus* while the concrete is still soft. Thickness, 6 inches or more. 14a & b. Side curbs, about 2 feet wide and 18 inches high. 15a & b. Paved footpaths. 16. Inlet to surface-water drain. 17. Outlet to surface-water drain. 18. *Milarium:* milestone. (U. S. Department of Commerce)

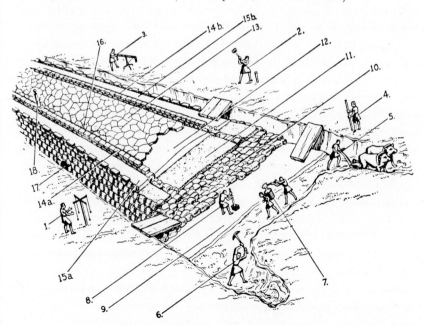

works of art flowed endlessly in as loot in wartime, as faked purchase or forced gift in peacetime. In the second century, too, Roman engineers discovered how to make imperishable, cheap cement by mixing lime with volcanic ash. The process revolutionized architecture and engineering. Perhaps about 150 B.C. was built, with cement footings, arches, and vaults, the impressive, terraced, axially symmetrical Sanctuary of Fortune at Praeneste, 24 miles east of Rome. This technique influenced architecture and engineering under the Empire, in the Renaissance, and in our own age, with its stadiums, dams, and skyscrapers.

Streets formerly graveled were now paved with blocks of hard lava, which is plentiful near Rome. The drainage system was extended and modernized at a cost of 20,000,000 sesterces, in purchasing power equivalent to about the same sum in dollars. Rome was indeed thinking grandiosely, and Cato's censorship (184–179 B.C.) was largely responsible. Forty years later an aqueduct raised on arches over part of its course brought pure water from mountains 61 miles away. The first arched bridge over the Tiber dates from 142 B.C.

Farming and Population

The Second Punic War had for over fifeen years devastated Italy's lands and killed its people. Reclamation proceeded slowly; the census records a drop in population. Rebellious cities like Capua and Tarentum were sacked, their lands confiscated, and their anti-Roman citizens sold into slavery. The appalling loss of manpower resulted in an unprecedented redistribution of land throughout Italy, but especially in the south. Some of the older towns were resettled and new ones were founded with Roman, Latin, or allied colonists. But not many Romans were willing to migrate far from the voting privileges and the bread and circuses of home. The large tracts the Roman government found on its hands, however, did not go to waste altogether, for ambitious investors leased large blocks of it for capital farming. The lessors raised sheep for wool, meat, milk, and cheese; cattle which could be driven to market more easily than grain could be freighted; horses for farming, transportation, the public games, and the army; pigs, especially in Calabria where extensive oak forests supplied acorns as cheap fodder. These ranches could be worked almost wholly with slaves, a cheap commodity in this period of constant wars. Small farmers in southern Italy, except along the seaboard, could not compete, and so arose big plantations (*latifundia*) with attendant evils: a sparse and dependent population and a barbarized countryside.

Similar conditions developed in central Italy. Such small farmers as survived the Hannibalic War, unable or unwilling to rehabilitate their properties, glutted the market with abandoned farms. Wealthy senators, prevented by custom and law from engaging in business, eagerly bought these parcels for conversion into large estates. Businessmen followed suit, to gain as gentlemen farmers that prestige which business success could not give. Averaging 60 to 160 acres, a large Italian estate employed twelve to fifteen men. Since profit was a planter's principal concern, he tried to figure income and outgo down to the last penny. The best evidence of this is Cato's *De Agricultura,* a practical manual of farm management. A business-minded farmer with a Calvinistic conscience, Cato farmed from his elders' instructions handed down in proverbs, his own experience, and his readings in translated Carthaginian treatises. His work is a milestone both in agricultural history and in the development of Latin language and literature. Cato wrote that top profits come from cattle breeding, viticulture, and olive culture, in that order. Wheat raising he describes as not worth the bother. Even when cattle were fed on the stubble, profits from wheat were smaller than those from olive orchards. Clearly central and southern Italian agriculture was being revolutionized. Only the small or uncapitalized farmer still raised wheat and other cereals for sale.

While ranches and plantations were driving the free farmer from central and southern Italy, he was coming into his own in Cisalpine Gaul. There was more rainfall there, the alluvial soil was virgin except for those sections exploited by the Gauls, and abundant land could be had for the asking. The pioneer settlements, established in the third century B.C. as garrisons against the Gauls, by the second century had become urban centers, while individual homesteaders were increasing almost as fast as they were being squeezed out of other regions. The increase of opportunities in the Po valley recalls, on a smaller scale, the early-nineteenth-century growth of the American Middle West. Before the end of the Republic, Patavium, the largest town of the region, boasted more knights than any other city but Rome. Furthermore, whereas the Rome of the Gracchan revolution (133–123 B.C.) harbored a dispirited cosmopolitan crowd of Greek immigrants, Spanish and African slaves, bankrupt Italian farmers, and impoverished Latins, the Roman towns and villages dotting Cisalpine Gaul were old-fashioned Roman. Romanism in the Po valley was to prove its vitality in the last century of the Republic in the writings of three immortals, Catullus of Verona, Vergil of Mantua, and Livy of Patavium.

Statistics on ancient population or wealth must be based on inadequate data. Even so we can estimate that in about 150 B.C. the citizen population of Italy was probably close to 1,000,000 men, women, and children. The Italian allies numbered perhaps 4,000,000, and the slaves about 1,000,000. The citizens' property, reckoned in today's purchasing power, amounted to some $6,000,000,000, or $6000 per capita. Large as this amount is, it looms greater when we remember that the Roman paid no property tax except in war emergencies. Even then the tax was only nominal and was really a loan to be repaid in full from the spoils of war.

No data are available on the wealth of the Italian allies. But we know that, although poorer in real estate than the Romans, they had more liquid capital. For they were the merchants and bankers of the expanding Republic. The wars of Rome in Africa, Spain, or the East did not profit its own businessmen—before 150 B.C. it had almost none. The considerable profits went almost wholly to southern Italian industry and business. Campania especially benefited from Roman domination of the East. Campanian forges had long furnished Latium with farm and household implements in bronze and copper, and the legions with weapons and armor. Naval vessels were built almost exclusively in Campania. Its cities, especially Cales, Minturnae, and Suessa, were prosperous industrial centers. Puteoli was Rome's chief port before Ostia was developed. Rome itself in the second century B.C. had no houses as large or splendid as those of the great merchants of Campanian Pompeii. There the Italic atrium was combined with the Hellenistic peristyle, and for a second-century Pompeian house was executed one of the most magnificent extant specimens of classical mosaic—the already mentioned flight of Darius before Alexander. The profits from the little city's vineyards and orchards cannot alone explain its opulence; most of its wealth came from manufacturing, shipping, and banking.

Roman domination of the Aegean helped these Campanian cities to double or triple their trade, for the inexperienced Romans were quite willing to leave business affairs to their Italian allies. On bustling Delos, for instance, made a free port, as we saw, to punish Rhodes for disloyalty, Rome's Italian allies, granted preference over Greek and Levantine merchants, descended to do business personally. In a Campanian business family, one member ordinarily managed the Delos branch and one or two managed the home offices. Sometimes the entrepreneur directed the whole enterprise from Italy while trusted freedmen executed his orders in Delos. In joint-stock companies, some of the directors stayed in Italy while others ran operations in Delos or elsewhere in the East. Banking was lucrative, and its profits gave some Romans leisure for literature and philosophy.

Literature

Language, literature, and culture generally reacted to imperial expansion. Early Latin usage, although sonorous, lacked grace and elegance. It could express a law or a constitutional principle clearly and directly but it was too flat and unwieldy to put across abstract thought. To be sure,

Fig. 38.4. The *Arringatore* (Orator). Bronze, found near Lake Trasimene. A Roman name, Aulus Metellus, is inscribed in Etruscan letters on the hem of the toga. Date uncertain, but the figure symbolizes the conscious power, the calm firmness, based as much on oratorical skill as on military might, of the Roman ruling class at the Republic's height (mid-2nd century B.C.). (Florence, Archaeological Museum)

certain native circumstances tended to elevate and refine it—for example, the political struggle, which stimulated and sharpened the Roman mind. More effective was the contact with the world of Theocritus, Archimedes, Polybius, and the sculptor of the *Venus* of Melos. The simple Roman peasant who had seen the quays of Carthage, the busy streets of Syracuse, the majestic temples of Corinth, the luxury of Asia, returned home with lifted horizons. The upper classes especially were touched by the enlightenment, pouring in first from the Greek cities of Italy, then from Greece itself. Becoming aware that their language could not reproduce philosophical and esthetic ideas, they set to work to reshape it. But it took almost 200 years to change a rigid tool into one flexible enough to convey the subtleties of philosophy or the surge of lyrical emotion.

In literature there was the national material to start with. A mass of heroic lays recounted the birth and growth of the Republic in Saturnian verse, an accentual ballad meter. Banter at the harvest and vintage produced licentious "Fescennine" dialogue in verse. From it grew the ribald songs sung at a marriage or a triumph. The Via Appia, which reached the Oscan cantons of the south, like Atella, carried to Rome the *fabula Atellana*, a riproaring rustic farce whose stock characters Pappus the graybeard, Bucco the glutton, Dossennus the humpback, Maccus the clown—all wearing characteristic masks—made a tumultuous appeal to the populace. Closer connections with Greek literature produced the *fabula palliata,* an urbane drama simplified from classical tragedy. The actor used only gestures and facial expression, while a singer chanted the part and a musician played the flute.

The Roman desire for public order and social discipline was expressed in precise laws austerely written. The priestly colleges and, especially, the Pontifex Maximus kept most state documents and succinctly recorded important events—a famine, plague, or flood, the birth of a heifer with two heads, or other wonders. The aediles and the censors kept records from which the second-century annalists drew for their scarcely less crude chronicles. Although stiff and monotonous, this national repertory contained the germs of the literary forms of the Golden Age—satire, history, and epic.

Politics demanded public speaking which was brief, direct, and factual, like the Roman character. A second-century orator, grave and authoritative, is portrayed in the bronze *Arringatore* in the Archaeological Museum in Florence. Speeches, not being considered literature, were never published. The first oration to be written down was Appius Claudius' against peace with Pyrrhus (280 B.C.) .

The Roman mind in the third century B.C. came under the spell of Greece, deeply stimulating in ideas and art, yet discouraging fruitful native tendencies. The pioneer in spreading Greek literature was Livius Andronicus (*c.* 284–204 B.C.), who at twelve was brought as a slave to Rome when his native Tarentum fell. He was given his freedom and during his long career influenced Roman education as schoolmaster, Latin translator of the *Odyssey,* and playwright. The rendering of Homer's masterpiece into an imperfectly developed language which he did not know well was, to judge from the fragments, not entirely successful, but it started better poets on the way to creative imitation of Homer. His finest opportunity came in old age, when the aediles, to relieve the tensions of Hannibal's war, commissioned him to write a play like those which increasing numbers of Romans had seen in the cities of Magna Graecia. It was the first of several tragedies and comedies he adapted from the Greek. Such plays as *Achilles, Ajax,* or *The Trojan Horse* had a special fascination, for the Romans had begun to believe certain legends fabricated by Greek antiquarians and genealogists which made them descendants of the Trojan hero Aeneas.

Naevius (*c.* 270–201 B.C.) , probably a native Roman, imitated Andronicus in adapting Greek plays, but handled also Roman and Italian subjects. A freeman born, he could speak to his fellow-citizens as an equal. He turned his critical and independent mind to a new literary genre, satire, later to be developed by Lucilius, Horace, Persius, and Juvenal. His blunt language allegedly offended powerful personages, and he landed in jail. His military experience in the First Punic War inspired him to an epic. He was Roman even in his Saturnian verse, to which he gave beauty, dignity, variety, and pith. Proud of his literary achievement and resentful of new Greek fashions, he wrote in his own epitaph that with his death "Folk lost the power of Latin at Rome."

The Romans regarded Quintus Ennius (239–169 B.C.) as the father of Roman poetry. Although he too translated or adapted Greek plays, like Naevius he handled national themes—for example, the Sabine women. His greatest work was the *Annales,* an epic, celebrating the national glories from the coming of Aeneas to the Hannibalic and Macedonian Wars, in hexameters, a Greek meter to which he imparted rugged Roman qualities and, occasionally, magnificence. Vergil was to owe him much. He was a fine example of that integrated nationality Rome was to forge from Italic stocks. Born of Oscan blood and educated in Greek Tarentum, when he became a Roman citizen he expressed his deep admiration of Rome in essentially Roman verse, emphasizing old-fashioned Roman incorruptibility and ascribing Roman greatness to the old-fashioned ways and the old-fashioned heroes.

But Ennius brought a new note into Roman literature. He wrote moral and philosophical treatises introducing his readers to such Greek thinkers as the mystic Pythagoras and the Syracusan skeptic Epicharmus.

The Umbrian comic poet Plautus (*c.* 254–184 B.C.) gave to Greek New Comedy a bracing Roman savor. Having been himself a worker with his hands—legend says for a time a slave—and perhaps a stage-hand, he acquired a practical knowledge of lower-class life and of stage-craft which comes out refreshingly in his twenty-one surviving plays. His swashbucklers, misers, stuffy Roman matrons, and clever slaves are life-like and hilariously funny. His technique is mature and sophisticated, involving complete command of language and meter, foreshadowing, irony, and double plots. He has influenced Molière, Shakespeare, and even modern musical comedy. In English, Dickens and Wodehouse characters like Sam Weller and Scrooge, Jeeves and Bertie Wooster have the Plautine touch.

The refined and intellectual comedies of Terence (*c.* 195–159 B.C.), of which six survive, mostly based on Menander, have little of the Plautine verve. A freed African slave in a Roman senator's household, Terence was a part of the political and intellectual circle surrounding Scipio Aemilianus. He was especially good at portraying romantic and sentimental young men. He is serious and urbane where Plautus is farcical and realistic. Yet he is subtle, intricate, and dignified, the genius of thoughtful laughter. Among moderns, E. M. Forster has his flavor and

Thornton Wilder has exquisitely imitated his *Woman of Andros*. Terence's intellectualized comedies did not please the Roman mob, and after him there was no more Roman comedy.

Philosophy and Law

Educated Romans were beginning to read Ennius' philosophical writings when, in consequence of the Third Macedonian War, a thousand educated Greeks were brought hostage to Italy. Far more cultured than their Roman hosts, they were at once employed as lecturers, teachers, advisers to consuls and town councils, and leaders of discussion groups. Several schools of thought now developed, the Stoic first. Throughout the third-century Hellenistic world, Stoicism had remained vital chiefly because of its adaptability. It dealt cogently with both speech, grammar, and literature, and the main contemporary intellectual problems, especially pseudoscientific divination and the study of nature. While some Stoics believed that the world is periodically destroyed and re-created, others held that if God's providence looks after the world—as all Stoics agreed —it must be indestructible. For if it ended and was then remade, in the interval God would be idle. More important was the Stoic contribution to ethics. Archedemus, for instance, taught in simple language that the good life consists in doing one's duty.

Epicureanism influenced Ennius; and by 173 B.C. the school was influential enough to be considered dangerous; in that year two Epicurean philosophers were expelled from Rome. But Epicurus' advice to abstain from politics was uncongenial to the Roman mind, and even when the school reached its height with Lucretius in the next century, it appears to have had more—or at least louder—detractors than adherents.

The Skeptic school was almost as important; Carneades (214–129 B.C.) was its most distinguished representative. Although he specialized in the theory of knowledge, he used practical illustrations. Denying the absolute, he reduced knowledge to three progressive stages from probability to practical certainty. The first occurs when a thing or situation in the context appears probable when one has neither time nor means for further investigation. Thus, if in war you see a presumed enemy approach, you will either kill him or seek safety. In the second stage a situation which appears convincing to you is not challenged by others. In the final stage a thing, both convincing and unchallenged, is examined in all its aspects. Carneades discredited both vulgar prophecy and divination, and Stoic providence and fate; he argued for free will. In political theory he contradicted Plato, defining justice as mere convention. In brief, while the Stoics offered ordinary men a moral standard, Carneades, their critic—paradoxically reinforcing their work—sought to place that standard on the solid ground of the probable and the reasonable. In 155 B.C. Carneades came to Rome as an envoy from his native Athens with two other philosophers, Critolaus the Peripatetic and Diogenes the Stoic. An embassy made up of philosophers may well imply that the Athenians knew the Roman ruling class was interested in philosophy. For two generations Greek plays in Latin adaptations had exposed the Roman mind to iconoclastic ideas, like the Epicurean doctrine of the gods' indifference to man's troubles. Philosophers and rhetoricians were banished from Rome in 161 as well as in 173 B.C.

But when the Stoic Panaetius of Rhodes (c. 185–109 B.C.) came (c. 144 B.C.) he received a warm welcome and soon joined the Scipionic circle. Within it, he adapted Stoic ethics to fit the Roman ruling class, preaching the duty of magnanimity, benevolence, and generosity to slaves, provincials, and foreigners, and arguing Rome's need for leaders of intellectual and moral authority to keep society in line. The result would then be *concordia* (harmony). Since his ideas strongly influenced Cicero, and probably also Augustus, he was in a sense a founder of the Roman Empire.

Greek influence also humanized Roman law: arbitration forestalled many suits both public and private; the praetors' annual edicts gave birth to a jurisprudential equity less rigid than the letter of Roman law; with Sextus Aelius Paetus Catus (censor 194 B.C.) began a long line of distinguished Roman jurists. The law began to protect the weak—minors, orphans, and women.

Greek influence was accused by Cato and others of corrupting Roman society. But far more corrupting was the influence of vast new wealth, which emphasized the gap between rich and poor and caused widespread discontent which was to culminate in a century of revolution.

Religion

Roman religion in the second century B.C. with its fixed rituals continued to prove itself profoundly conservative. But in its accommodation to the cults of the motley racial groups now crowding into Italy, it was also enormously innovating. This paradoxical combination was possible because Roman religion had always emphasized two things: cult and practicality.

The relation between worshiper and god was held to match that between patron and client; it was, as we saw, a contractual thing; the Roman worshiper said in effect to the gods, "*Do ut des*," "I give (sacrifices) that you may give (benefits)." This religious idea is of course not confined either to Rome or to antiquity. Practically speaking, it did not matter at first to what god a worshiper was devoted, especially if political considerations like raising morale in wartime made it wise for the state to accept a foreign cult, convert public festivals into public amusements to mollify the plebs, or sanction the political manipulation of the auspices. Later, certain mystic and exotic cults, like the secret society of Bacchanals, were abolished (186–181 B.C.) on the ground that they might harbor subversives.

The Roman not being by nature given to abstract speculation, his religion was ready to use the myths, the symbols, and the gods of other religions, equating Greek Hermes with Roman Mercury, Greek Athena with Roman Minerva. Before the end of the third century B.C. the process was complete, and Etruscan, Greek, and Italic Gods, such as Venus from Mt. Eryx in Sicily in 217 B.C. and, the Great Mother Cybele from Asia Minor in 204 B.C., were naturalized in Rome; in the following century the great spurt of temple building provided homes for them all. Generalizing, one might say that however closely a Roman god might be identified with a Greek one, he still preserved his own personality; and conversely, no Greek god failed to be influenced by local traditions and to assume local functions—Demeter, for example, became patroness of the plebs.

The native Roman or Italic gods like Quirinus, Janus, Saturn, Faunus, the Lares, Penates, and Manes, held their own tenaciously against the new divinities, which only enriched, without despoiling, the hospitable Roman pantheon. Ancestral religious practices developed further, but without revolution or crisis. In the midst of its evolution, Roman religion preserved its national character.

And yet fashions in cults changed so much, so many new gods were accepted or created, so many concepts changed, that one might say no religion, while preserving its fundamental utilitarian characteristics, ever underwent such various and complex changes as the Roman between the fourth and second centuries B.C. Two tendencies are especially noteworthy; the first toward atomizing, the development of multiple cults of a single divinity, like the goddess Fortune; the other toward humanizing, as in the deification of heroes, which in time was to lead to emperor worship.

However tenacious the state cults proved, a religion as formal and contractual as the Roman, without dogma or ethical code, gave no moral support against the temptations that came with wealth and empire. Indeed it was a shaky façade behind which growing skepticism and new cults made constant progress. The new class of merchants, bankers, and contractors, without traditions of its own, was to contribute to the toppling of that façade; so too were the freedmen and artisans from the Greek East. Men like Fabius, Africanus, and Cato still held staunchly to the faith of their fathers, but when members of their class fell to reading

Greek poets and philosophers or to watching the gods caricatured by comic poets, faith was shaken. Yet in the second century B.C. Polybius was still impressed by the scrupulous Roman observances of their state cult and their fidelity to their plighted oath. But it was a state religion better suited to prosperity than to decline, and doomed to fall with the ruling class that made it, despite such repressive measures as the expulsion from Rome of astrologers and Jews (139 B.C.).

Such was Roman culture in the mid-second century B.C., on the eve of the grave conflicts which were to destroy the Republic. The picture, in architecture, art, and literature as well as in religion, is of a people adjusting, for the moment successfully, to the violent impact of Hellenistic influences. In architecture these influences simply facilitated the expression of innate strivings toward solidity and grandeur. Combining Hellenistic decor with Roman engineering skill in the use of concrete in arch and vault, the Romans created a new Hellenistic-Roman amalgam. So too in art, Roman artists fruitfully combined Greek influence with native Etrusco-Italic realism. In literature, abandoning their rough native meters, authors used Greek techniques to express Roman attitudes and prepared the way for the flowering of a Golden Age. Hellenistic philosophers adapted their theories to the Roman scene; Roman praetors interpreted Hellenistic law with Roman lucidity and concrete practicality. Roman religion proved prodigiously receptive to foreign cults, but remained at bottom primitive and indigenous, without spirituality or exalted mysticism. The gods who gave the triumphs were conservers of the *mos maiorum,* the ancient ways. The state religion became ossified, and behind the façade was a spiritual void. And so it proved inadequate in the face of the troubles of the Gracchan age and after.

Chapter 39 / REVOLUTION AND REACTION

The old Rome, with the Senate controlling legislation and supplying from its membership consuls, provincial governors, and successful generals, came to an end in 133 B.C., when the people's tribune Tiberius Sempronius Gracchus invaded senatorial prerogatives with an unprecedented impetuosity and idealism. A great humanitarian, Tiberius made it his life's goal to turn the unemployed and landless into useful citizens. To carry his program he made a political revolution. After a senatorial mob killed him, his younger brother Gaius carried on, and under Gaius' fiery leadership the program was expanded beyond its original aims. Although Gaius too fell victim to senatorial opposition, the political revolution wrought by the Gracchan reforms could not be undone. With the Gracchi, a new era began in Rome.

The Agrarian Problem

The small farmer's decline, caused mainly by Hannibal's devastation of Italy and the endless Spanish wars, worried many a Roman but none so much as Tiberius Gracchus. A constructive reformer bent on arresting this decline, he has been misunderstood by his own and succeeding ages. He has been variously described as a knight in shining armor battling for social justice, a narrow patriot tampering with vested interests only to restore to Rome its vanishing military strength, a misguided politician if not a self-seeking demagogue. Birth and education combined to fit him for the intelligent leadership required to deal with the pressing agrarian evils. His father was Sempronius Gracchus, a plebeian nobilis, an old-fashioned, upright conservative who was yet progressive enough to study Greek and appreciate Greek culture. As governor of Spain the elder Sempronius, by his honest and capable administration, had raised Roman prestige, which his negligent predecessors and a demoralized army had sadly reduced. As censor (169 B.C.) he again distinguished himself by building great public works and striving to restore the ancient mores, recognized by Ennius as the pillars of the state.

Through his mother, Cornelia, daughter of the renowned Scipio Africanus, the young Tiberius enjoyed the highest social standing. One of the most gifted of thirteen children, he met in his mother's salon distinguished resident or visiting philosophers and men of letters. One of his tutors was Blossius of Cumae, a Stoic deeply concerned with Italian social problems. He was influenced also by Panaetius. Stoicism, as we have seen, taught that all men are brothers. Though it was not always interpreted democratically, this egalitarian doctrine helped to spread through the Hellenistic world the principle of state aid including, if necessary, outright grants to the unemployed. Tiberius no doubt absorbed some of these humanitarian ideas.

Tiberius distinguished himself for heroism as junior officer at the siege of Carthage. Some time later, by diplomatic skill, he saved the army which an incompetent general had allowed to be trapped in Spain. His army service opened his eyes to widespread insubordination in the ranks which during the siege of Numantia (137 B.C.) had become open mutiny. Seeking the causes of this decay in Roman character, he realized that underlying the people's aversion to the draft was the larger social evil of the dispossessed yeomen, now idlers in Rome, but ineligible for army service because they were propertyless. To keep society sound and the army strong, he thought that the city idler should be resettled on the farm. This in its simplest terms was Tiberius' goal. But its interlocking political, social, and economic aspects made it a dangerous cause to espouse, for the propertied class, entrenched in the Senate, opposed it solidly.

Tiberius was not the first Roman troubled by Rome's social decay. Men as pre-eminent as Laelius the Wise, the protagonist of Cicero's *De Republica,* and Scipio Aemilianus, the destroyer of Carthage, had recognized the need for reform. Yet, fearing to loose the storm, they had proposed no remedial legislation. Well-intentioned but timorous like the French Louis XV, they resemble him also in foreseeing *"après nous le déluge."* It was thus left to Tiberius Gracchus to translate their hopes

Fig. 39a. Map of Rome and the

Mediterranean World to 133 B.C.

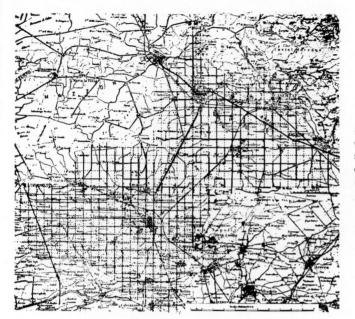

Fig. 39b. Quarter-sections (centuriation) laid out by ancient surveyors perhaps as early as 209 B.C. In the 225-square-mile area northwest of Naples, shown here, modern farm boundaries follow the ancient survey lines. (*Archaeology* IX, 1956, p. 132. Fig. 11.)

into law. Elected tribune of the plebs (133 B.C.), he brought to that office not only assets of lineage and education, but determination and an innate idealism only catalyzed by Greek philosophy. Though it had become the Senate's instrument for obstructing magistrates, the tribunate never forgot its revolutionary traditions, which Tiberius carried on. Besides, his land reform received the support of enlightened but powerful political figures like Appius Claudius Pulcher, his father-in-law and dean of the Senate; Publius Licinius Crassus, the wealthiest Roman capitalist; and the distinguished jurist, Publius Mucius Scaevola.

To swell the dwindling ranks of small farmers, Tiberius proposed to open to homesteaders the public domain. But its long-standing lessors, large-scale ranchers and cultivators, had, in good faith or bad, come to regard their holdings as private property and had accordingly made costly improvements and stopped the payment of rent. Tiberius proposed to let them each retain 500 iugera (262 acres) plus 250 iugera for each of two sons. This last provision recognized the squatters' rights of some who under the old laissez-faire policy had leased more than their legal allotment in their sons' names. They were now to be allowed to hold as much as 1000 iugera in perpetuity subject to no rent or lien whatever.

The land returned to the state was to be assigned in inheritable homestead allotments of 10 to 30 iugera (5 to 16 acres) to volunteers from among the landless, who were to pay the state a nominal quitrent. But to perpetuate the revived small-farmer class, Tiberius provided that these holdings should be inalienable. A special commission was to be created to investigate which lands were actually public domain, to return to the state all excess acreage, to assign the recovered portions to eligible citizens. To legalize its decisions, the commission was given judicial and executive authority. Finally the bill named its own backers as commissioners: Tiberius himself, his brother Gaius, and his father-in-law. Unfortunately this setup could lead to misinterpretations of the tribune's intent.

There was nothing revolutionary in this bill, and it might have passed without much opposition. But either to save time or to prevent rejection, Tiberius took the bill directly to the People—in keeping with Hortensian law of 287 B.C. which made plebiscites binding, but contrary to custom—instead of first submitting it to the Senate. When the Senate interpreted this as a flagrant insult, an economic measure became a constitutional crisis. The Senate met the challenge deviously by having another tribune, Octavius, veto submission of the bill to the People. Tiberius then, after a vain attempt to conciliate the Senate, spiked the opposition by having Octavius deposed by popular vote as a traitor to the People. This was revolution indeed, for constitutionally no elected official could be removed during his incumbency. Octavius once removed, the land bill became law, the aroused landless swarming from every corner of Italy to vote for the measure. Tiberius had relegated the Senate to second place and proved that, given proper leadership, legislation for the People could be passed despite senatorial opposition.

Fig. 39.1. A Gracchan boundary stone. Cast of original in Naples, National Museum, of a marker from Atena Lucana, in Campania, bearing names of commissioners (132–131 B.C.) responsible for land redistribution under the Gracchan law. The figure on top represents the *cardo* and the main east-west line, the *decumanus*. (Rome, Museo della Civiltà Romana)

Besides his farm, a homesteader needed financial assistance to build a hut and buy seed, a plow, and an ox or two to pull it. Realizing this, the Senate now tried to hamstring the land commission by refusing to appropriate it funds. The whole law would have been nullified except for a stroke of luck. The last king of Pergamum, being without heirs, had just bequeathed his kingdom to Rome to avoid squabbles over the succession. When the strange inheritance had been accepted as the Roman province of Asia, Tiberius and the people threatened to use part of the legacy to finance the land commission, whereupon the Senate voted the needed funds. This incident demonstrated again that under an able tribune the People could get its way.

Tiberius Gracchus knew that, given the opportunity, the Senate would destroy his work. To prevent that, he sought re-election, but this proved to be the last straw. It had not been customary for a tribune to succeed himself, and the senatorial party decided it was unconstitutional. A mob of senatorial hotheads caught the reformer unguarded and killed him, a stupid crime that betrayed the bankruptcy of senatorial morality. The sacrosanctity of the tribunes once violated and the example set of deciding political issues by murder, Rome was never again quite the same.

The Senate feared to repeal the popular land law, and land grants continued awhile unmolested. But, bent on vengeance, it established a special court which on flimsy pretexts condemned some of Tiberius' followers to death. Yet Tiberius became more dangerous dead than alive. Intent on freeing the popular assembly from senatorial influence, the martyr's successors as tribunes legalized the secret ballot, already in use for electing magistrates, for voting on new laws as well. More important still, in 128 B.C. re-election to the tribunate was legalized.

First Reforms of Gaius Gracchus

The passions and forces released by Tiberius threatened to swamp the Optimate (conservative) camp when his brother Gaius became tribune (123 B.C.). Devoted to his brother's ideals and determined to avenge his death, Gaius Gracchus swayed the masses with his personal magnetism, his oratorical power, and the appeal of his radical program. And since he was re-elected and allowed to succeed himself in 122 B.C., he had time to carry out most of his program, large and revolutionary though it was.

Though Tiberius had confirmed the People's right to pass laws without the Senate's consent, Gaius perceived that popular sovereignty and tribunician leadership would be only an illusion as long as the Senate could bribe one of the ten tribunes into vetoing a measure. Accordingly he proposed a bill barring from further office a magistrate deposed by the People. This measure would not only have discouraged a tribune from betraying his trust; it would have established implicitly the People's right to depose magistrates other than tribunes. A storm of opposition convinced Gaius that his bill had no chance, and he wisely withdrew it.

He evened the score by another move. The Senate had all but destroyed Tiberius' party by the tribunal which sent his most energetic followers to death. Gaius now had passed a law forbidding any court to inflict capital punishment without allowing an appeal to the People. In reaffirming this old constitutional right he notified the Senate that he and his party were ready for positive action.

Adopting the current Hellenistic principle that it was the government's duty to secure a cheap and adequate food supply, Gaius had a law passed authorizing the state to purchase cheap wheat overseas at harvest time, when prices were lowest, to store it in new granaries at Ostia and by the Tiber below the Aventine, and to sell it at cost to Roman citizens, poor and rich alike. This was not a dole, and it involved little drain on the treasury.

Tiberius' land commission, with additional powers, resumed land distribution energetically, and the number of farmers increased by many thousands. Air photography has recently revealed traces of Gracchan allotments near Luceria, in Apulia. But Gaius, viewing individual allotments as inadequate, devised a wider plan. He had the People approve the planting of colonies in Capua and Tarentum and seemingly elsewhere in Italy, these to be surrounded by homesteads of 120 iugera (about 62 acres), four to six times larger than Tiberius' lots. Gaius apparently aimed at attracting small capitalists, as well as farmers with means, to set up a pattern of prosperous town life. His boldest colonial project (Junonia) was planned in Africa on the domain which once had been Carthage. This idea of transmarine colonization marks Gaius as a statesman of vision. It contributed to his undoing and its charter was revoked, but the colonists held their allotments and a new phase in world history had opened.

Gaius pursued his brother's program of revitalizing the army. A law requiring the state to issue soldiers clothing brought into the legions a new propertyless class, hitherto excluded. When Marius implemented it fully some fifteen years later, it produced a social and political revolution.

Gaius and the Equestrian Order

Gaius bid for support from the now powerful Roman knights (businessmen and bankers) with a law on the collection of the provincial tribute from Asia, which turned out to be thoroughly bad.

Men had been engaged for two or three centuries in industry and commerce, with lucrative returns from state franchises and contracts, for Republican Rome had no civil service, no trained administrative personnel hired by and responsible to the state. Individually or in joint stock companies they had exploited public properties on lease: mines, salt-pans, forests, fisheries, grazing lands. During the Punic War they had built warships and transports for the government and provided legionary supplies. City improvements were a bonanza for them, for there was the Tiber to bridge, streets to pave, and aqueducts, markets, porticoes, temples, and basilicas to build. In brief, by 123 B.C. Rome had a capitalist class reaching out for new fields to exploit.

Syndicates of investors and bankers had long collected customs dues and grazing rents from lessees of the public domain. But Tiberius' land law had reduced the public domain and these syndicates claimed they had been unfairly deprived of their ancient rights. Gaius Gracchus tried to compensate them by a law providing that the contract for collecting tithes in Asia was to be bid for in Rome. Since provincial bidders could hardly compete with local cliques, Roman knights were given a practical monopoly. Although the tax rate of Asia remained substantially the same as under the Attalids, the successful bidders would make their profit from savings through efficient collection methods and from side activities like banking and wholesale trade, not to mention gouging the provincials.

This was the Roman capitalists' greatest windfall. Their enormous profits they invested in wholesale wheat and other commodities, in loans throughout the eastern provinces at 12-percent interest or higher, and in real estate operations. Reinvestment in Italian plantations enabled the knights to rival the senatorial class as princely landowners, with corresponding influence on their estate peasants and the pauperized Roman slum-dwellers. Quite apart from these advantages, the knights' prestige had so risen that Gaius officially recognized them as next to senators in dignity. He had laws passed empowering these businessmen to wear the cavalryman's ancient marks of distinction, the toga with a narrow purple stripe and the gold ring, and to sit in reserved seats at the theater. Hence Rome had two regularly established upper classes, the senatorial and the equestrian.

Gaius recognized the knights politically as well as socially, giving them a place in government. But to understand this problem we must go back in time. We saw how the Senate, after the two Spains became provinces (197 B.C.) had created no more provinces, being dissatisfied with administrative abuses and seeing in unrestrained provincial governors potential tyrants. We saw too how, after the Extortions Court was established (149 B.C.) the two new provinces of Africa and Macedonia were created under the belief that the problem had been solved. Experience proved, however, that a dishonest governor could almost always escape conviction as long as juries contained none but senators. Although there were honest men among them, senators as a class did not rise above party and family considerations, logrolling, or plain bribery. To end this scandal, Gaius transferred the Extortions Court jury to the knights' class, the closest to the Senate in wealth and education. Gaius' aim to weaken the Senate was not incompatible with an honest desire to protect the provinces nor with his hope of establishing a balance of political power, always the aim of the plebs and always observed by the Senate in form but denied in substance. His reform was to be travestied into an instrument of tyranny; the knights were to use their new privilege as a club over a governor's head. As matters developed, if a conscientious governor forbade their gouging a province under the guise of collecting taxes, extending loans, or engaging in business, the knights would at once prosecute him and their juries convict him on trumped-up charges, destroying his career. Under this vicious system, even honorable governors were forced to connive at thievery.

The Senate retaliated with a familiar political weapon. It had a tribune, Livius Drusus, thwart every Gracchan bill with a rival bill promising the people something more attractive. By thus stealing Gracchus' thunder, they hoped to lose him the voters' support. Perhaps the Senate and Livius intended to carry out their proposals, but the fact remains that Livius' laws, when enacted, remained a dead letter. Whereas Gaius, like Tiberius, had levied a quitrent on the lots distributed under his law, Livius made his rent-free. Again, Gaius had proposed two colonies in Italy and one in Africa; Livius' bill called for twelve, probably all in Italy, and therefore more attractive to colonists than accursed, barbaric, and distant Carthage.

Paradoxically, Gaius' most constructive measure led to his downfall. The Land Commission had antagonized several Italian communities when, with questionable jurisdiction, it had begun to convert into homesteads portions of the public domain they had long leased from Rome. In compensation Gaius proposed to make all Latins Roman citizens and to raise all other Italians to Latin status. But the Senate opposed this project, the knights were wary, the electorate unwilling to share its privileges with aliens. When Livius, like a hound at his heels, interposed his veto to this bill, Gaius had to acknowledge defeat, knowing he lacked the votes to depose his rival as Tiberius had once deposed Octavius. Despite spirited electioneering for a third term as tribune, he failed to overcome the powerful opposition combine. We may only surmise his reflections on being deserted by his erstwhile friends, the knights.

Gaius' death came soon after, early in 121 B.C., while the Senate was trying to repeal the law establishing the colony of Junonia. In protest against repeal, his followers seized the Aventine, long the seat of popular sedition. Manufacturing a state of emergency, the Fathers empowered the consuls "to see to it that no harm befell the Republic." The intent was to brand the Gracchans public enemies subject to martial law, and so the consuls construed it now and every time this decree was passed thereafter. But by applying this "last decree," a consul violated the constitutional guarantee against citizens' being executed without trial followed by an appeal to the People. Although Gaius tried hard to restrain his followers, the consul Opimius lusted for his blood. Gaius fell in the general butchery, not indeed by the enemy's hand, but dispatched by a faithful slave who followed his orders not to let him be captured alive. After the carnage came mass trials dooming 3000 more to death. The Senate was again master, but, as in 133 B.C., by recourse to violence. The national character had decayed not only among the masses, but also among the classes once proud of their wisdom and virtue. Unable to solve political problems by the ballot, the Senate had used the sword. A precedent had been set, and the popular party was not slow to see it.

Chapter 40 / THE FIRST
INDISPENSABLE ROMAN

A Period of Maladjustment

Their ideals did not die with the Gracchi. The popular leaders' determination to preserve the hard-won supremacy of the Concilium Plebis led to new strife with the Senate. The knights' monopoly of juries was still a bone of contention. Not merely homesteads, but whole colonies for the landless were yearly a more acute need. The Senate's recourse to assassination and martial law infuriated the People, and the Italian question was perhaps the most difficult of all. Henceforth the struggle turned on these burning issues.

A changing set of values was producing something different from the ancestral ways. The nobiles, corrupted by wealth misused, were questioning the earlier simple virtues. The destruction of Corinth and Carthage brought back vast quantities of silver and gold, fine furniture, *objets d'art,* and myriads of slaves. The nobles turned connoisseurs, built larger town and country houses, museums for their loot, and as provincial governors were willing to steal to get more of it. Sprawling seaside villas mushroomed all the way to the Bay of Naples. Hills were leveled, valleys filled, streams diverted to landscape country retreats.

Large estates still swallowed up small farms and paid no revenue to the state. Money talked; the still small voice of conscience was silent. Fraud and deceit became a fine art. The Senate passed more and more laws to stop electoral corruption, forgetting that morality cannot be legislated.

The knights became more money-mad than ever. Among them, as among the nobiles, there were honest patriots, but the average knight put profit above principle, becoming especially adept at cheating the government and robbing the provinces. The new province of Asia enriched the tax-farmers and increased banking and wholesale and retail trade. The day of the financier had arrived. Bourgeois plutocrats began to overshadow the nobiles and supplant them in politics. The Italici made fortunes in the Delian slave trade. Expanding business and banking opportunities gave sons of knights from small Italian towns, young men like Sertorius, M. Aemilius Scaurus, Marius, and later Cicero, the money for the legal education which would bring them wealth and distinction. Estates once owned by aristocrats and groups of small holdings once owned by yeomen fell into the hands of rich merchants, financiers, loansharks, or country squires. Freedom of movement, commerce, intermarriage, and business opportunities stimulated all over Italy the rise of this *bourgeoisie,* shrewd, grasping, aggressive, and now equipped with an education to rival that of the aristocrats. With their wealth, knights with political ambitions could buy elections, or procure new fields of plunder for the class as a whole. And all the while developing jealousy in Rome of Italian aspirations to political equality was fanned by the propertied class and by the natural prejudice of the proletariat.

The lower classes, despite the agrarian reforms, lived on the edge of starvation, in the country as seasonal hired hands of the great estates, in the city slums living on the crumbs thrown them by the state or by noble patrons. Skilled and unskilled slaves from the foreign wars displaced free labor on ranch and plantation, in trade, domestic service, and the crafts. Naturally, then, rural workers gravitated to the cities where though life was still poor, it was not drab and where at worst they could beg or steal a loaf of bread. Crowding in Rome accentuated an old problem. While busy farmers failed to come to Rome to vote, their fellow tribesmen, now irresponsible city idlers, sold their votes to decide elections and pass new laws.

Breezes from the East were affecting the Roman climate, bringing with them a loosening of traditional restraints as well as appreciation of the arts. Even what was good in these influences was still alien and bound to produce maladjustments. This clash in values put the Roman character under strain, as evidenced by loose morals among rich and poor alike, deepening skepticism about religion, and the worship of a new goddess, Fortuna, patroness of "go-getters" who believed that nothing succeeds like success. Shocked puritans demanded their victims; Vestal Virgins were executed for unchastity, and human sacrifices are recorded. Even more symptomatic was violent class hatred. The Gracchan revolution itself, though born of Roman conditions, was a Hellenistic movement with a time-lag, a movement related to the revolution of Agis and Cleomenes in Sparta. For all these reasons old-fashioned men shook their heads, muttering, "To learn Greek is to learn knavery."

War against Jugurtha

Ever since the knights had captured the juries, the Senate had sought to detach them from the proletariat, at first without success, but the knights soon proved willing to shift to suit their interests. They got the Senate to suppress the pirates, operating from Balearic bases. Against them two colonies were planted, one on the island of Majorca, the other at Narbonne. The Riviera's likeness to Italy in climate and natural resources soon attracted thousands of Italian settlers; it became a new Italy rather than a province. Other homeseekers settled in Numidia, where Massinissa's successors continued to promote agriculture and to foster urbanization. Here, since there was no native commercial class, business fell to the Italians, who were just beginning to prosper when Jugurtha, an able and ambitious ruler, ascended the throne. For a while he ruled with two step-brothers, but soon he assassinated one and besieged the other in the capital, Cirta. On capturing the city, he killed the second brother and all the Italian residents, mostly merchants, for allegedly supporting his brother.

Jugurtha had long been for Rome a problem child. During his quarrel with his brothers, the Senate had sent two or three commissions to Numidia to suggest a peace settlement. Each commission failed, and some Romans suspected he had bribed the envoys, resented his continuing disregard of their help, and feared a Carthaginian empire revived under him to expel Rome from Africa. The popular leaders capitalized on these fears. They stressed the Senate's ineptitude (though in fairness they might have allowed for its preoccupation with the German menace) : there would have been no Jugurthas if Gaius Gracchus had been allowed to found his colony at Carthage. News of the massacre of the Italian merchants at Cirta had, in this charged atmosphere, the impact of a national disaster. The whole equestrian order demanded revenge. A punitive expedition was sent to Numidia, but the commanding general gave Jugurtha a truce instead of a beating. Whatever his military reasons for this apparent leniency, in Rome men assumed the barbarian had bought off another Roman.

The tribune Memmius, demanding an investigation, got Jugurtha to

Fig. 40.1. So-called Marius. (Rome, Vatican Museum; Anderson photo)

Rome on a safe-conduct to testify he had bribed certain senators. But another tribune vetoed the proceedings. The king, for his part, took advantage of his visit to Rome to instigate the murder there of his cousin, a potential rival. The Senate regarded this un-guestlike act as a declaration of war, and sent Jugurtha home. The struggle that followed proved extremely difficult, chiefly because the Romans could not cope with the fast Numidian cavalry. For three years (110–108 B.C.) the war brought the Romans nothing but disappointment and shame. Again the Popular leaders made political capital, accusing the Senate of incompetence in war on top of corruption in diplomacy. They supported for the consulship one Gaius Marius. A 'new man,' a knight from the municipality of Arpinum, Marius was a thorough *popularis*. His anti-senatorial instincts turned to implacable hatred after a personal humiliation. In 108 B.C. he was an officer on the staff of the optimate Metellus, commanding in Numidia. When he asked leave to go to Rome to canvass for the consulship, the insolence with which it was finally granted was something Metellus and the whole nobility lived to regret. The plain people took it personally, and artisans, peasants, and laborers combined to insure Marius' election.

In addition, Marius' campaign promises to bring Jugurtha to Rome dead or alive elected him by a landslide. Then, defying the Senate and long-established custom, the electorate itself gave him command of the war not for the usual year, but until Jugurtha should be captured. In power-hungry hands this could lead to monarchy or perpetual dictatorship.

It is convenient here to violate strict chronology in order to pursue a political question. Unreconciled to defeat, the Optimates in 106 B.C. succeeded in passing a law restoring senators to juries in extortion cases. The knights retaliated by recombining with the plebs as in Gaius Gracchus' day. Chief instrument of this realignment was a clever demagogue of whom we shall hear more, Gaius Servilius Glaucia. As tribune, probably in 101 B.C., he swept away the Senate-sponsored repeal of the Gracchan law. The knights acquired once more a monopoly on extortion juries, but with increased powers, for Glaucia's law provided that Latins successfully prosecuting governors should receive Roman citizenship. This was shrewd politics; Glaucia was strengthening the equestrian-Popular alliance with the support of Italian public opinion. The Popular party had repeatedly re-elected Marius to the consulship; with this broadened base, it now did so for the sixth time.

But to return to Marius' first consulship. His command was a great success. His energy and skill, after the senatorial generals' mediocrity, restored Roman morale. He took charge in 107 B.C. and by September

Fig. 40.2. So-called Sulla. Recently this portrait head has been branded not ancient, but baroque. (Munich, Germany, Glyptothek; Fototeca)

105 B.C. he had taken Jugurtha prisoner. The capture was wildly hailed in Rome and later immortalized by the historian Sallust. When Marius celebrated his triumph, Jugurtha was led behind his chariot in chains and subsequently strangled. There was, however, one disturbing note. The king had actually been captured through the diplomatic finesse of one of Marius' lieutenants, Lucius Cornelius Sulla, an aristocrat out of sympathy both with his chief and with the Populares.

Rise of a Professional Army

Marius reorganized the army. Unimaginative though he was in politics and human relations, in enlisting fellow-citizens for Numidian service he boldly broke with tradition. He called for volunteers, disregarding the property qualification. This both revolutionized the army's social composition and had far-reaching political consequences. Gradually during the second century B.C. property qualifications for legionary service were reduced until citizens worth as little as $100 in land were admitted. As men of this class could not afford to buy equipment, the state began to supply it to them and to every man indiscriminately. Citizens with no property to fight for (*proletarii*) had always been considered unfit and unsafe for service. Once Marius removed this stigma, the proletarii were soon a majority in the legions. Rome had never seen so great a social revolution.

The poor could at last find steady and honorable employment. Before Marius, they had hated army service, for service interfered with farming or trade. Moreover, since overseas war meant absence from farm or shop for years on end, the second-century soldier had become sullen and mutinous. But after the Marian reform, the longer the service, the better the men liked it, since for most of them discharge would mean again poverty and unemployment. For these men war became an industry. So a new trend developed; service in the legions was later lengthened to sixteen to twenty years or longer, and Rome had for the first time a volunteer professional army.

Nor was this all. These men felt closer to their general than they ever had to the impersonal state. They took their oath of allegiance to him, not to the Republic; and, beginning with Marius, each general felt obliged to procure for his veterans substantial economic rewards. Hence generals had to join or head political groups, for only the ballot could secure the pensions the veterans came to expect. In sum, as the Gracchan period saw the political rise of the knights in league with the tribunes, the age of Marius saw the rise of the proletarii in league with their generals.

Fully as important were a number of tactical reforms. Marius grouped the old basic legionary units, the maniples, into larger units, or cohorts.

By fixing the number of cohorts at sixty, and putting 100 men in each, he increased the size of the legion from 4200 men to 6000. Erasing the previous differences in armor and weapons among *principes* (front-rank fighters with two spears and a sword each), *hastati* (middle-rankers, with a spear), and *triarii* (light-armed rear-rankers), he armed and equipped each man identically, with a new type of *pilum,* or hurling javelin, and a short sword or dagger for in-fighting. He placed each cohort under a centurion, and as most centurions came from the middle or lower *bourgeoisie,* this class too rose to new importance.

By these reforms the army became both more democratic and more cohesive. Whereas the old maniples had been individualized by age, wealth, and equipment, the new cohorts embraced men of all ages—20 to 45—and of every economic status. This leveling produced a new spirit of camaraderie in the legions. Now too, with longer service the legions could perfect more complicated maneuvers, become more hardened to fatigue, work better as a team. This was the material with which Marius, Sulla, Pompey, and Caesar won their famous victories.

The Germans at the Border

No sooner had Marius settled accounts with Jugurtha than he was called on to meet more redoubtable foes, the Cimbri and Teutones, two tribes of the many-branched Germanic people who had first appeared on the north German coast and in south Scandinavia after the last Ice Age. Of mixed stock as far back as can be traced, when they began to expand southward (about 1000 B.C.) the Germans were preponderantly tall, blonde, blue-eyed men and women. The Celts in central Europe kept them at bay for a time, but from the fifth to the third century B.C. they dispersed the Celts, as we have seen. The Cimbri and Teutones left their homes in and around southern Denmark late in the second century, driven out by invading seas. They roved freely, the vanguard of many tribes which were to invade Roman territory repeatedly and finally to submerge the Empire in the fifth century after Christ. It was Rome's mission to stem the tide for nearly 500 years, just long enough to Romanize Western Europe.

Rome had tried, a year before the Jugurthine War, to stop the barbarians beyond the Julian Alps, only to have a consular army cut to pieces (113 B.C.). Despite the slaughter and Italy's peril, the Fathers forbade the widows to wear mourning. The enemy crossed into Switzerland (Helvetia) to appear in south France. Here near Arausio (Orange) they annihilated two more Roman armies (105 B.C.), but, although the road to Italy lay open, they did not advance. The Cimbri passed into Spain, the Teutones into central Gaul.

Throughout the summer of 105 B.C., even before the Arausio disasters, everyone looked to Marius, who was about to finish the Jugurthine War. Perhaps other Romans were qualified to command the German war, but the political situation made no other choice practical, for the Populares were in full ascendancy, and Marius was the man of the hour. He was elected consul for 104 B.C. and, unprecedentedly, every year thereafter through 100. Five successive terms served both Popular interests and Marius' ambition. But whether this helped Republican institutions, Rome, and the Empire, is something else again.

Probably on the advice of friends with an eye for the dramatic, Marius celebrated his triumph over Jugurtha on the inaugural day of the second term, January 1, 104 B.C. The callousness to Roman sensibilities he displayed the next day, by attending the Senate in his general's uniform, was doubtless his own. Though a warning to the senatorial nobility the people had found their master was probably not intended, just the same it was a portent. Another unwritten law had been broken: a general had appeared within the pomerium in uniform on a day other than that of his triumph.

During his long tenure Marius consolidated his army reforms and, sure that the Germans would return to assault Italy itself, prepared to take the initiative in the attack. At Aquae Sextiae in Narbonese Gaul (autumn 102 B.C.) he decimated the Teutones. Tradition speaks of 100,000 killed and as many prisoners. Very few escaped, for Marius slaughtered the very guards protecting the women and children in their wagons. Those he was unable to take were waylaid by the natives, burning for revenge on their invaders. The Cimbri meanwhile, backtracking through Switzerland and Austria, debouched in vast numbers—exaggerated tradition reports 200,-000—through the Brenner Pass into the Po valley. They pillaged the valley from Venetia to Piedmont, where near Vercellae, despite the valor of their 15,000 horsemen, they were crushed (101 B.C.) by Marius' far smaller army. Probably never before had the Romans taken so many prisoners. 150,000 were sold as slaves. A danger when free, these people were a problem as slaves, for they replaced free citizens and free Italians as farmhands. The proletariat in helping to conquer the world was destroying itself.

During his German campaign, Marius, to facilitate the movement of supplies in southern France and apparently also to stimulate trade, had a canal dug bypassing the silted mouth of the Rhodanus (Rhone). Seagoing ships could now go far up river. Arelate (Arles) owed its commercial growth to this canal, and doubtless the equestrian class gained from it.

Many competent generals watching strategic points in the Po valley and Gaul contributed to the German defeat. Sulla was one. Marius' war leadership was such that Optimate commanders could work harmoniously with him. Not only that: the confidence inspired by his appointment to the German command enabled Rome to divert troops to other danger points: to Macedonia, for years a prey to the raids of the trans-Danubian Celtic Scordisci, and to Cilicia, now a cluster of pirate fortresses. After destroying the Hellenistic navies, Rome had so neglected policing the seas that several eastern cities could carry on commerce only by paying the pirates tribute. Marcus Antonius the Elder, in Cicero's opinion the greatest orator of his age, wiped out the pirates' nests and annexed Cilicia as a province (102 B.C.).

But Sicily, still Rome's breadbasket, was the gravest danger. There a serious slave revolt had been put down in 132 B.C., and now 30,000 slaves took up arms in east and central Sicily, 10,000 in the west. Eventually the two armies merged. The Romans faced desperate men, whom the indignities of slavery had turned into uncompromising rebels. Their defeat became possible after the victory of Aquae Sextiae allowed the transfer of seasoned troops to the island. So bitter was the resistance that only 1000 men surrendered (100 B.C.). As they gave themselves up unconditionally, they were thrown to the wild beasts in the amphitheater. The destruction of 40,000 human lives had a sobering effect. Large-scale slavery was never revived on the island and more acreage was leased to native farmers.

If Marius' German command was a shining period of civil concord, the period immediately following was one of unrelieved darkness. The Popular leaders again found it profitable to run for the consulship the willing Marius who wanted to secure pensions for his veterans. Against the Optimate opposition he felt obliged to join with two Popular leaders who had repeatedly secured his re-elections, C. Servilius Glaucia, whom we have met, and L. Appuleius Saturninus. All three advocated cheaper grain for the masses and homesteads for the veterans. Glaucia ran for the praetorship, Saturninus for the tribunate.

The campaign was turbulent. The oligarchic opposition, fighting to end perpetuation in office, rallied all conservative elements. But it could not surmount the magic of Marius' name and Saturninus' organizing ability. The victor of Aquae Sextiae was a great public hero and, to the Populares, the very symbol of their group, a knight, a foe of the nobility and a friend of the lower classes. Because the Senate had deposed Saturninus from his quaestorship in 104 B.C., charging him with responsibility for a rise in the price of wheat, he had become its sworn enemy. All three Popular candidates won the elections for the year 100 B.C. This would be Marius' sixth consulship and his fifth consecutive term, an ill-omened development.

But, Marius failed to duplicate in politics the qualities he had displayed in war. He let Glaucia and Saturninus snatch away the leadership. They governed like tyrants, flouting time-honored constitutional practices, keeping the city in turmoil, spiking opposition by their control of the proletarian vote.

Ironically, Saturninus alienated the proletariat when he proposed a good bill to plant overseas colonies for Marius' veterans, both Roman civilians and Italian allies. The mob, unwilling as ever to share its privileges with noncitizens, rejected the measure. The situation worsened toward election time, when the knights, tired of political gangsterism and of public disorder, which was bad for business, began to veer toward the Senate. The demagogues overreached themselves in the elections for 99 B.C. when Glaucia, running for the consulship, caused his closest rival's murder. As civil war seemed imminent, the Senate passed the "last decree." Glaucia and Saturninus barricaded themselves on the Capitoline. Marius, charged as consul with executing the decree, was in a dilemma. Was he to put his own friends to death or be false to his duty to the state? He stood by duty. After some bloodshed he succeeded in arresting his friends, only to see them murdered. These bloody events produced a reaction. The senatorial group, with the knights' help, regained power and Marius went into eclipse.

Chapter 41 / BIRTH OF THE ITALIAN NATION

The Irrepressible Conflict

Though Rome calmed down after Glaucia's and Saturninus' excesses, Italy still seethed. Indeed, Saturninus' bill to plant colonies open equally to Italians and Romans started a chain reaction ending in a civil war not unlike the American one. But whereas the United States, for years after the conflict itself, was rent between North and South—two worlds mutually hostile—Rome and Italy were soon welded into one indissoluble nation.

Numerous forces favored cultural and ethnic interpenetration. First, the Italic tribes had started with a similar Indo-European legacy of stock, speech, religion, and government. Second, Indo-Europeans and non-Indo-Europeans exposed to the higher cultures of Etruria and Magna Graecia had leveled off differences and developed common traits. A more powerful catalyst was Roman influence. By promoting commerce and intermarriage it knit together hundreds of ethnic and political groups. The widespread planting of Roman or mixed Roman and allied colonies, and still more the raising of many communities to full Roman, half Roman, or Latin citizenship, produced a wider interchange of ideals and interests. (A Latin citizen might [1] marry a Roman without either party's forfeiting inheritance or paternity rights, [2] have contracts protected by Roman law, [3] become a Roman citizen if permanently resident in Rome, a right later restricted to Latin magistrates only, [4] vote in the Concilium Plebis while temporarily resident in Rome, and [5] appeal from conviction on capital charges.) Besides, there was mutual borrowing, especially through the praetor for foreigners, of legal principles and procedures. His influence simplified business and strengthened social relations. These centripetal forces were focused by the Italian and Roman need for mutual defense against the Gauls, Hannibal, the Teutons and Cimbri. Lastly, Italian levies, as large and as brave as its own, had helped Rome build its empire. But despite these unifying experiences Rome and Italy were not yet one people, for Rome now treated its allies not as equals, but as political vassals.

A few examples will illustrate this. Although the Italians furnished half the troops in every one of Rome's wars, they were denied their traditional half of the spoils. They complained that the growing corporations of Roman knights were crowding them out of business opportunities they had long enjoyed throughout the Roman empire. More than one Roman senator, traveling through an Italian city, would order its officials whipped for not receiving him with proper pomp and circumstance. Roman generals offended also by too-frequent scourging or execution of disobedient Italian soldiers.

Tiberius Gracchus had unwittingly sparked Italian resentment when his agrarian commission, apparently without authority, reclaimed blocks of Roman public land leased to allied cities or citizens. Unwilling to relinquish this long-standing privilege, the allies persuaded Scipio Aemilianus to argue their case. The great general accepted, the more readily because, in his various campaigns, he had seen and admired their bravery. He managed to delay the commissioners until the Senate would investigate the matter, but his sudden death (129 B.C.) the night before the scheduled debate, with its sequel of suspicions and rumors, prevented a practical solution.

The Romans too had complaints. They objected to Italian pressure on their internal affairs—in particular to the usurpation of the ballot in nearly every election by nonvoting Italians living in Rome. Incensed public opinion actually caused the Assembly to vote (126 B.C.) the expulsion of all noncitizens. This measure, a clear violation of treaties guaranteeing the right of residence, had strong repercussions throughout Italy. When in 125 B.C. Fregellae revolted, Rome razed it to the ground.

On the positive side, the consul M. Fulvius Flaccus offered a statesmanlike proposal to give all Italians, both Latins and allies, full Roman citizenship. Unfortunately, both social extremes opposed the measure: the nobiles fearing the new citizens would join the populares and thus jeopardize their own continuance in power, and the urban proletariat refusing to share its privileges with foreigners. Faced with this opposition,

Flaccus abandoned his plan. Gaius Gracchus revived it in more conservative form, proposing to grant the full Roman franchise only to the Latin communities, elevating the Italians to Latin status. But the uncompromising attitude of the electorate forced him, too, to drop his project.

Although clearly neither the Senate nor Assembly would do them justice, the Italians stood loyally by Rome against the German menace. The expulsion law became a dead letter, and thousands of Italians came to Rome to vote for Saturninus' bill (100 B.C.) creating colonies which should include Italians. At this new attempt by noncitizens to sway the Roman vote, the Senate and the People closed ranks, and once more expelled the Italians from the city. The allies, however, found a friend in Livius Drusus, son of the tribune who had hounded Gaius Gracchus. Drusus revived the plan to confer Roman citizenship on every free inhabitant of Italy, Latin or "Italian." On the night before the bill's introduction into the tribal Assembly the courageous tribune was assassinated. This black parallel with the fate of their other friend, Scipio Aemilianus, thirty years before left the Italians no choice but to secede. War began in the spring of 90 B.C.

The rebels established a separate independent state, choosing their own rulers, forming their own senate, appointing ambassadors to foreign countries, founding a capital significantly named Italia, and coining money portraying the Italian bull goring the Roman she-wolf. The rebels won the battles but lost the war. Despite their bravery, the odds were against them. For Rome was richer, controlled the industrial centers, was mistress of the sea, and had wider experience in government, diplomacy, and strategy. Its able generals included Marius (now restored to grace), Lucullus, Sertorius, and Sulla. Then too, its colonies, studding the peninsula, were invaluable advance bases. Lastly, Rome controlled the local aristocracies, especially in Umbria and Etruria. But Rome's best weapon was the classic policy of divide and rule. Soon after the war began, it gave full citizenship to all non-rebel communities. In 89 B.C. it extended this privilege to all cities which would surrender and to every freeman inside a rebellious city who would apply for it. Thus Rome sowed the seeds of discord and division among the rebels. Lastly it won over Transpadane Gaul by giving it Latin citizenship; Cispadane freemen apparently received full citizenship. The revolt then collapsed, and Italy became a nation.

But Rome caused further Italian resentment by restricting new citizens to eight of the thirty-five tribes. Since the Assembly voted by a majority of the tribal, not the popular, vote, this cunning device nullified the Italians' vote, since Romans still outbalanced them. This injustice was exploited by the Popular leader, the tribune Publius Sulpicius Rufus. Realizing the value of the Italians to him and his faction, but also wanting to see justice done, he persuaded the Assembly to enroll the new citizens evenly in all thirty-five tribes. To defeat the inevitable senatorial reaction he strengthened his position by allying himself with Marius; for Marius, although now an old man, was still a popular hero.

The First Civil War

The old general and the young tribune ran into unexpected trouble. While the Italian rebellion was preoccupying Rome, King Mithridates of Pontus in northwest Asia Minor had incited Greece and Asia Minor to throw off the Roman yoke. His real purpose, as his earlier career had abundantly proved, was to establish an empire of his own. He had already occupied the north shore of the Black Sea, to his great profit in money and men, expanded his kingdom westward to Colchis, and was only with difficulty prevented by Rome from reaching southward to Paphlagonia and Cappadocia. Few Asian Greeks supposed that Mithridates would be gentler than Rome. But insolent and rapacious Roman governors, merchants, and soldiers had so alienated them and Roman bankers had so involved them in a vicious circle of debt, unpaid interest, and new credits, that Mithridates' signal for revolt (88 B.C.) found ready and universal response. At his command the provincials butchered numbers of Romans overestimated at 80,000 to 150,000. Rome declared war, and the Senate, then dominant, placed the aristocratic consul L. Cornelius Sulla in command.

Sulla's was a dynamic success story. Although patrician, he was impoverished and reduced to living in the slums. But his rise began after he had ensnared Jugurtha for Marius. His reckless courage, his bluff comradely ways, and his brilliant leadership bound his men firmly to him, even when he called on them to attack their own country.

After Sulla had left for Campania to train his recruits for the eastern campaign, thus giving the Populares a clear field, Sulpicius introduced his bill to incorporate the new citizens in all the tribes. Then Sulpicius had the Assembly pass also a mischievous transfer of Sulla's command to Marius. The enraged consul resolved to settle for good the long-standing struggle for supremacy between Senate and Assembly. Since Sulpicius controlled the electorate, Sulla could overcome him only by leading his army upon Rome. Never before had such flaming partisanship been seen in Rome. Never before had Roman soldiers put their general above their government. Taken by surprise, Rome fell into Sulla's hands. The sword now supplanted the ballot, and with the sword suspended over its head the Assembly was coerced into declaring Marius, Sulpicius, and the other Popular chieftains public enemies with a price on their heads. Marius and a few others escaped, but Sulpicius was killed and his laws, including his pro-Italian measure, declared invalid. Sulla's full reactionary intent

Fig. 41.1. King Mithridates VI of Pontus, adversary of Sulla, Lucullus, and Pompey. The portrait deliberately copies, presumably at the king's order, the personal appearance of Alexander the Great. (Paris, Louvre: Giraudon photo)

was revealed when he rammed through the Assembly constitutional reforms designed to hamstring the tribunate. Having thus restored the Optimates to power and insured his own position, Sulla left for the East.

With Sulla's departure the political kaleidoscope turned rapidly. A new leader, Cinna, rallying the Populares, was elected consul; the Senate deposed him; he raised a force of Italians and blockaded Rome. Meanwhile Marius, back from his African refuge, collected his own army, in his lust for vengeance enrolling even slaves. As both he and Cinna promised to revive Sulpicius' pro-Italian law, they gained more Italian adherents than the Senate. Like Sulla, they took Rome by assault. For five days and five nights Marius' slaves butchered real or fancied enemies. To cap this revolting carnival of blood and violence Marius declared himself elected consul for the seventh time and Cinna for the second.

Marius' replacement of Sulla in the Mithridatic command was on the point of confirmation when, luckily for the country, the old war-horse died, a great general but a poor politician (January 86 B.C.).

For the next four years, Cinna and the Populares produced constructive legislation. By reincorporating the Italians in all thirty-five tribes, they guaranteed the political coalition between the Italians and the Roman proletariat and made plain to the Optimates that this issue could not forever be evaded. They also relieved the burden of debt. Tempting farm and business investments had led many to borrow heavily, at high interest. Even the little fellow was caught, even more tightly because he was a greater risk and had to pay higher interest. The evil was long-standing. A monetary crisis during Drusus' tribunate had been partially met by debasing the currency. But whatever good this had done vanished under the multiple stress of the Italian War, the Sullan and Marian terror, and the massacre of Roman bankers and traders in Asia. Cinna had to attack the problem anew, especially since by now many more citizens had become debt-ridden. He passed a truly revolutionary law, enabling debtors to settle their accounts in full by paying only 25 percent. All in all Cinna ruled wisely, but his time was running out.

Meanwhile Sulla was winning successes in the East. Even with smaller forces, he and his Roman generals defeated the enemy in Greece, on the Aegean, and in Asia. When Mithridates sought peace (84 B.C.), he was forced to withdraw to Pontus, surrender part of his fleet, and pay an indemnity. But rebellious provincial cities experienced all the horrors of a war without quarter. The price of peace was the astronomical sum of 20,000 talents, to be paid collectively. The war-impoverished cities had to borrow from those very Roman capitalists who had systematically stolen their wealth, and borrow at 4 percent per month. This was bondage in perpetuity. Even Athens was mercilessly sacked, for the first time since Xerxes.

Victorious over Mithridates, Sulla started for home, ready for trouble. Rome was not big enough to hold both him, champion of senatorial rights, and the Populares, vowed to the subordination of the Senate. Convinced that only force could resolve the issue, he exacted from his army a new oath of loyalty to him personally, without reference to the welfare of the Republic. No force improvised by the Populares could withstand his seasoned veterans. Then in a master stroke he announced that he would not interfere with the incorporation of the Italians in the thirty-five tribes. He thus isolated the Populares, for large numbers of Italians, correctly assessing Sulla's military strength, went over to him. Even so, he needed a year to overcome the Popular armies in central and northern Italy. He fought his way to Rome inch by inch. The bloodiest contest was fought under the very walls—the third time in seven years that the city was taken by its own sons. For several months the carnage went on unabated. The chief Marian leaders were executed at once. Then proscription lists were issued, outlawing every senator and knight sympathetic to the Populares. Uncounted hundreds of families were wiped out by legalized murder, or disfranchised and their property confiscated. Fortunes changed hands overnight, and "carpetbaggers" descended like harpies on their newly-acquired estates. To punish his enemies, Sulla emancipated their slaves. Ten thousand such freedmen took the name of their liberator, Cornelius, ready in their own interest to defend his person and policies with their lives.

The Sullan Constitution

But Sulla had other aims than mere revenge. He hoped to eradicate what he thought were the causes of the political and social upheavals since the Gracchi. So he had himself appointed (82 B.C.) "dictator to rewrite the laws and re-establish the Republic." Intent on securing political stability under senatorial control, he left to the tribunes only their ancient power to protect individual citizens from arbitrary imprisonment or execution without appeal to the People. He restricted their right of veto, and they might no longer initiate plebiscites. To stop ambitious men from using the tribunate as a step to greater power, tribunes were disqualified for any other office. Clearly only insignificant men would care henceforth to be tribunes. The Council of the Plebs had its powers cut by two other important provisions: it could be summoned only by a curule magistrate, that is, an official controlled by the Senate; and it could consider only such business as the Senate laid before it.

The Senate thus regained sovereignty. But since this body was no longer the anti-Popular clique of the past, Sulla added 300 of his partisans to its membership, drawing on the nobility, the recently enfranchised Italians, and the upper strata of the knights, once the chief support of the Gracchan revolution. This was good statesmanship, good politics too, since it split the knights into two factions, of which the more influential would now favor the Senate.

Sulla also took measures to apportion honors and insure stability. He raised the number of quaestors to twenty, making them all ex-officio life members of the Senate. Despite the general air of arch-conservatism, the election every year from scores of candidates of twenty younger men, each appealing to a different group, did at least reflect the current mood of the electorate. In this sense, the Popular forces were not completely suppressed. But the Senate was now single-minded and became more of a gentlemen's club than at any time before. Another law provided that no man might be quaestor before the age of thirty, praetor before forty, or consul before forty-three, and that consuls must be out of office ten years before seeking re-election. Thus the dictator hoped to prevent a new Marius from overwhelming or overshadowing the club. He raised the number of praetors from six to eight and the provinces to ten by creating the new province of Cisalpine Gaul. Thus each outgoing consul and praetor would be assured of a provincial governorship, and ambitious politicians, he hoped, might abide by the rules of the game. Lastly, Sulla restored the extortion juries to senators, in order to free governors from organized equestrian blackmail.

Even more important were the provisions for the general peace. There must be no extraordinary commands the abuse of which might enable a new Marius or a new Sulla—at the head of a large army loyal only to him —to overthrow the government. Therefore provincial governors were forbidden to wage unauthorized wars beyond their frontiers or to retain office after their year was up, on pain of prosecution for treason. Thus Sulla hoped to prevent an ambitious governor from becoming a warlord. But by his creation of Cisalpine Gaul as a tenth province, its commanding promagistrate was put in a position decisively to influence the situation in Italy.

Besides these constitutional measures, which on paper seemed admirable, Sulla introduced a number of administrative reforms, chiefly of criminal law. Rome had long since become a bustling metropolis where heterogeneous elements struggled for existence or for power. Old families rubbed elbows with parvenus. Each group was spiritually torn, since for every man clinging to the ancestral religion, there was another one converted to Greek philosophy. The native middle class, in the main sound, found itself competing with clever resident tradesmen from the East. The lot of the lower classes, ill-fed, ill-clothed, ill-housed, deteriorated still further with the expansion of slavery. While the rich lived in ostentatious luxury and the poor in extreme want, increasing numbers of men and women from every station flouted the principles of personal and public morality which once had been Rome's strength. Sulla faced this social maladjustment and crime not with preventive but with punitive methods. He created several criminal courts, some to try private offenses such as forgery, assault, or murder; some to try public offenses such as embezzlement of state funds, extortion by public officials, electoral bribery, or treason. He relieved the strain on the treasury by abolishing the sale of cheap grain by the state, but thus created a new political and social problem which was to underlie the struggle between reactionaries and demagogues. He even tried, though in vain, like the ancient censors, to legislate against extravagance at weddings and funerals and against immorality. In the main, however, his administrative reforms were so soundly conceived that they outlasted his constitutional ones.

As dictator, Sulla contributed much to the growth of the Italian nation. By accepting the Italians into all 35 tribes, he enabled them to influence the future course of politics. His unequivocal recognition of Italians as citizens equal to Romans and Latins was a step toward the unification of Italy. He inadvertently helped the equestrian order to expand, since Italy's integration with Rome opened larger opportunities for individual business men, who would thus eventually rise to equestrian rank. Sulla had never intended to destroy the knights, but only to restrict them to the economic sphere. Within a dozen years, however, the reborn high *bourgeoisie* again entered politics.

Whatever his impact on the Senate, the knights, or the constitution,

Sulla's mark on the Roman state went deep. For, despite new revolutions and civil wars, the merging of Rome with Italy which he loyally accepted brought forth a new nation.

Having restored the old regime, Sulla at the peak of his power retired to a villa in Campania where he died in 78 B.C. The Senate decreed him a public funeral and the title "Father of His Country." In characteristic spirit he had these words inscribed on his tomb:

HERE LIES SULLA THE FORTUNATE
HE NEVER FORGAVE AN ENEMY
NOR FORGOT A FRIEND

Chapter 42/COALITION OF PLUTOCRATS

The Rise of Pompey

In 70 B.C. the Sullan constitution fell to pieces. The powers transferred by the dictator from People and knights to the Senate were restored to their former holders. This upset was caused less by the ambition of the consuls Pompey and Crassus than by social forces reviving after the Sullan reaction.

Pompey's meteoric rise was itself a proof that the Sullan constitution was unrealistic. Paradoxically it was the Senate which, faced with a military problem insoluble under Sulla's rules, undermined that constitution. Its instrument was the young Gaius Pompeius. When not yet twenty-four, Pompey had declared for Sulla, just then returning from the East. Raising three legions on his own, a forerunner of later private armies, and putting them at Sulla's disposal, he helped to defeat the Marian forces. Soon afterwards Sulla assigned to him the fight against the Marians in Sicily and Africa. His success led him (81 B.C.) to demand, and be grudgingly given, the grandiloquent surname *Magnus* (the Great). In 77 B.C., after a consular army had failed against Sertorius, a capable Marian leader who had taken Spain—and ruled there with exemplary justice—the Senate, against Sulla's regulations on promotions and assignment of provinces, gave Pompey the command. He fought a war of

Fig. 42.1. Pompey. According to the owner of this bust, an assured, benevolent, fearless, decisive, good-humored face, from which we may derive some notion of the statue at whose feet the murdered Caesar fell. (New Haven, Connecticut, private collection; F. E. Brown photo)

attrition, which ended, luckily for him, with the murder of Sertorius by one of his own officers.

Meanwhile a new danger appeared in Italy. Thousands of slaves, led by a gladiator, Spartacus, rose to spread terror and chaos, especially in central Italy. Disciplined and resourceful, they defeated two consular armies, whereupon the Senate appointed a younger commander, the praetor M. Licinius Crassus. In six months Crassus wiped out the rebels (71 B.C.). The few survivors fell foul of Pompey returning from Spain. Crassus and Pompey, acclaimed as national heroes, confidently campaigned for the consulship.

Crassus had made millions from buying cheap the properties of Sulla's proscribed victims. He could count on the support of the influential equestrian order and the *bourgeoisie*. Pompey controlled the masses, chiefly by promising to restore the tribunes' powers. Since he had filled none of the lower offices, Pompey could not legally run for the consulship, but with his Spanish army at the gates of Rome he was above the law, as the Senate, fearing another Sullan siege, readily agreed, thereby abdicating the powers Sulla had given it. Crassus and Pompey paid for the support of the knights and the proletariat with interest. The knights were again restored to the juries, though now under a compromise whereby they shared their seats with senators and with another class, the *tribuni aerarii*, whose economic status just below the knights made them handy counterweight against both senatorial and equestrian interests. Good

Fig. 42.2 (left). Caesar. (Pisa, Italy, Camposanto) Fig. 42.3 (right). Cicero. (Mantova, Italy, Ducal Palace)

government required that senatorial control of juries cease, for senatorial juries had proved as corrupt as the equestrian ones. Some of the credit for this reform was due to an ambitious, intelligent, and patriotic young lawyer, Marcus Tullius Cicero, a knight himself and the knights' consistent champion.

In his late twenties Cicero had courageously if indirectly attacked the Sullan dispensation. He began his public career as quaestor for Western Sicily, where he personally witnessed the evils of provincial exploitation. The Sicilians, finding him honest and sympathetic, engaged him as attorney in their prosecution of Verres, the worst governor they ever had. Verres used his Sicilian appointment to make three fortunes: one for himself, another for friends in need, and a third to buy off his judges if he should be indicted. He was certainly symbolic of the provincial spoils system at its worst, but evidence does not bear out Cicero's contention that juries of knights kept governors better in line and dispensed more even-handed justice. At any rate, Cicero's overwhelming evidence and masterly presentation forced Verres into voluntary exile before the trial had well started.

By dramatizing senatorial corruption, especially by giving the trial a sharp political twist—"if knights sat on juries corruption would not be condoned"—Cicero facilitated the passage of Crassus and Pompey's reform bills. It all worked out as planned: the senatorial class once again faced hostile juries; the tribunes once again received in theory the right to initiate plebiscites and to veto the acts of the magistrates. Again they could undermine the Senate by blocking its resolutions and, most of all, by electing through thinly-veiled class legislation generals who, with their personal armies, could dominate or supersede the government. Thus was the Sullan constitution abrogated. But the re-emergence of the tribunate was quite artificial. Henceforward the tribunes were merely the (usually paid) agents of the military magnates or the reactionary nobles.

Pompey drew handsome profits from his "restoration" of the tribunate. The circumstances were as follows. Though Rome was mistress of the Mediterranean, only a crisis could cure its neglect of its navy. Pirates had taken full advantage of the unpatrolled seas and had even established a state of their own on the Cilician coast. They preyed unmolested on commerce until businessmen, especially the knights, pressed for action. The populace, threatened with famine, joined their plea. A tribune, Gabinius, carried a law (67 B.C.) making Pompey admiral extraordinary, with both land and sea powers. Pompey did a fine job, clearing the Mediterranean of pirates within ninety days, then settling thousands of them as farmers in Italy and the provinces.

Logrolling brought Pompey still higher returns. Lucius Licinius Lucullus, highly competent, just and humane, Sulla's successor against Mithridates, had for a number of years held down graft in his province. He had decisively defeated his wily adversary in the Second Mithridatic War (73–71 B.C.). Lucullus, the Republic's last great general (as opposed to military magnate), was the real conqueror of the Roman East. Provincials considered themselves blessed by the gods if they came under Lucullus' jurisdiction. But the knights whose operations he had blocked thought differently. They made a deal with Pompey: they would get him appointed to Lucullus' eastern command if he would agree not to interfere in their affairs. When in 66 B.C. the tribune Manilius proposed a law to change commanders, Cicero, the knight, supported it. His speech survives to acquaint us with practical Roman politics, the magic of Pompey's name, and his own conservative bias. Though Pompey served the Republic well in the east, reaping the harvest Lucullus had sewn, the Gabinian and Manilian laws were a step toward constitutional breakdown. Again, as in Marius' day, the electorate usurped the power of appointing generals. This practice, politically manipulated, continued until, thirty years later, it cost Pompey his life and the Republic its existence.

Pompey proved characteristically swift and thorough. He dethroned Mithridates, reduced Armenia to a Roman protectorate, and forced various peoples south of the Caspian Sea into the Roman orbit. This series of blows deprived the expanding kingdom of Parthia of allies. Pompey's most significant feat was to annex Syria and Palestine, ending the Seleucid Empire. He thus placed all Asia from the Black Sea to the Euphrates and down to the Sinai desert directly or indirectly under Roman control. When in 62 B.C. he returned to Italy, no other man had so much extended Rome's empire.

The following data suggest the magnitude of Pompey's achievement. After distributing among his soldiers a bonus of nearly 400,000,000 sesterces, he turned into the treasury almost 500,000,000. And through him Rome's annual revenue rose from about 200,000,000 to about 350,-000,000. The East was not entirely the loser. In return for heavy taxes it received peace and eventual prosperity. Most important, Rome's policy was to foster Greek culture there. In consequence, the Asian provinces became a single block, culturally, spiritually, and economically so cohesive that when centuries later the Western Empire fell the Eastern continued for a thousand years longer.

Cicero Pater Patriae

Rome meanwhile continued to be plagued by widespread social maladjustments, chiefly an impoverished proletariat and an unrepresentative electorate. Residents of Rome controlled elections and legislation, because the 90 to 95 percent of Roman citizens spread over Italy and the provinces would not come to Rome to vote. The leaders' lust for power, in particular their ability to manipulate the city vote, increased the unrest.

Discreetly concealed behind the intrigues of 63 B.C. was Crassus, jealous of Pompey and intent on matching his rival's following. Crassus' right-hand man was the brilliant and anti-senatorial Julius Caesar.

A scion of the patrician Julian gens, which claimed descent from Venus and the Trojan hero Aeneas, Caesar was to make political capital of this myth. But he had also close Populares connections, for his aunt had married Marius and he himself was Cinna's son-in-law. Caesar, not yet nineteen, dared defy Sulla's orders to divorce the radical's daughter, well aware that what Sulla really wanted was his divorce from the Popular party. For to young Caesar the senatorial oligarchy seemed irreparably bankrupt, whereas the Populares, with all their faults, might yet satisfy his ambition and save the state. Popularis votes and Crassus' money won Caesar two elections in 63 B.C., to the office of Pontifex Maximus, at an unusually early age, and to that of praetor, which guaranteed a provincial governorship. The profits of this office he badly needed to repay to Crassus his astronomical debt incurred for the lavish shows by which he all but bought his double election.

One of the consuls for the year 63 B.C. was Cicero. To gain this pinnacle had not been easy for the son of an obscure country knight. Shrewdness and oratorical skill combined with luck to win Cicero the election. Luck gave him Catiline as his opponent. Born and reared in poverty like Sulla, Catiline had joined him and the Optimates. Praetor in 68 B.C., propraetor in Africa in 67 B.C., he was tried for extortion but acquitted. In 65 B.C., even with Crassus' support, he failed to win the consulship. His bad record prevented his nomination for 63 B.C., when Optimates preferred the upstart Cicero to the blackest sheep in their fold. Before Cicero's consulship was over, he and Catiline were to play opposites in one of the tensest dramas of Republican Rome.

On his first day as consul Cicero was offered the opportunity to go on record as protector of Pompey's interests and leader of the confused conservatives. The tribune Publius Servilius Rullus presented in a bill an ambitious agrarian program actually conceived by Crassus and Caesar. It outlined unprecedently large banking and land transactions, ostensibly to alleviate the poverty of the Italian masses. Crassus and Caesar aimed to make respectable political capital of the discontent of the poor, possibly to ward off Catiline's forthcoming conspiratorial program. Perhaps they wanted to make Cicero, elected as a coalition candidate, show his hand as a conservative. At all events, they proposed a land commission on the Gracchan model but much wider in scope, with armed authority to dispose of the Italian and provincial public domain by allotment to homeseekers or sale to investors. The commission would be empowered to buy new lands anywhere in the empire, to be assigned, resold, leased to individuals, or used for colonies at will. Apparently Rullus' bill also proposed a bank to finance these operations.

This program's humanitarian aspects concealed an attack on the absent but all-powerful Pompey. It was to be supported chiefly out of revenues from Pompey's newly conquered provinces and protectorates. The scheme, if realized, would have completely undermined his influence, for the wide network of farms, ranches, and colonies, of spoils, special interests, and favors created by the bill would have placed under obligation to Crassus and Caesar hundreds of thousands of citizens and millions of provincials. Moreover Pompey's veterans would owe their land-pensions, not to their general, but to his political enemy. Crassus, experienced in buying cheap and selling dear, may have aimed to corner all available land to sell later to Pompey for his veterans on terms politically advantageous to himself.

Cicero saw through this trickery and attacked the bill with all the re-

Fig. 42.4. Cato the Younger. Bronze bust found at Volubilis, Morocco. Splendid example of Roman portrait sculpture, well expressing the aristocratic breeding, bitterness, and irony of the doctrinaire who committed suicide at Utica. (Fototeca)

sources of Roman invective. Perhaps he was meant to; at any rate the people defeated it. His three speeches against it (*De lege agraria*) are masterpieces; they persuaded the people, on the ground that it was a stab in their hero Pompey's back, to vote against a bill ostensibly concerned in their interest. Cicero was now identified as Pompey's friend, exponent of senatorial conservatism, and Crassus' rival.

Before the year was over Cicero was to reach the pinnacle of his career. For a third time Catiline campaigned for consul, advocating in his platform a reduction of debts which would help him and other impoverished aristocrats, but also relieve bankrupt or nearly bankrupt capitalists and small farmers. Cicero, loyal as always to the equestrian creditor class which would have taken the loss, battled valiantly for the *status quo*. As consul he turned public opinion against Catiline, representing him as a threat to the propertied classes, and by a discreet show of force on election day he frightened thousands of Catiline's followers out of casting their ballots.

Defeated at the polls, Catiline went underground, organizing in a powerful conspiracy debt-ridden knights, Sullan veterans who had failed as farmers, common debtors, cultured women unsympathetic to the *status quo,* in short all who had nothing to lose from revolution and perhaps something to gain. Even senators joined. He planned the forcible overthrow of the government. But Cicero, the politician, was palpably unfair and Sallust, the historian, was less than objective, in charging that the conspirators were all disreputable: thieves, debauchees, ruffians, murderers, perjurers, gangsters. Cicero, well served by spies and *agents provocateurs,* waited until he had irrefutable proofs of Catiline's guilt. On receiving them, the Senate voted to empower the consuls to execute the culprits. Caesar's plea to the Fathers that it was politically unwise to execute citizens availed nothing, and that very day such rebel leaders as were still in Rome were executed. In an impromptu torchlight parade a hysterical people acclaimed Cicero "Savior of the Republic." When, shortly after, the Senate voted him the title "Father of His Country," he became the first Roman to be so honored in his lifetime. This unprecedented distinction so tickled Cicero's vanity that he later wrote an epic about himself.

Catiline and his staff escaped to their armed followers near Florentia (Florence) to face the Senate's legions. Here leaders and men alike fought and died like men of conviction and character. Almost every man covered with his dead body the position he had taken when the battle started. Misguided though they were, they reflected widespread despair. Catiline's address to his army before the battle powerfully indicted a system which, while permitting extreme wealth to a few, left the many with "destitution at home, debt without, present and unendurable misery, and a still more hopeless future." The next year Cato the Younger, as tribune, tacitly confessed the justice of their grievance by distributing public wheat more widely and cheaply than ever before. And Cato, who had advocated most strongly in the Senate the execution of the traitors, was an arch-conservative who believed in a balanced budget and warred against corruption, especially in the Popularis ranks.

The First Triumvirate

Rome had just shaken off the Catilinarian incubus when Pompey and his victorious army returned from the East. Pompey expected three things from the government: a well-earned triumph, land pensions for his veterans, some of whom had served for over a dozen years, and senatorial ratification of his administrative and diplomatic dispositions in the East, where he had dethroned kings, organized provinces, and set up satellite states as far away as the Caucasus. Roman politicians passed sleepless nights, fearful that, like a new Sulla, Pompey would seize the city. But Pompey was of different stuff. On reaching Italy (62 B.C.), he disbanded his army, apparently out of sincere desire to abide by the constitution. But the moment his demands had no force behind them, the Senate ignored him. So Pompey was reduced to impotent rage until Caesar, back from his Spanish governorship (60 B.C.), produced a workable solution, a masterpiece of practical politics.

Caesar's plan was a realistic version of a Ciceronian idea. In the heyday of his influence when the Catilinian crisis had enabled him to unite the parties of law and order, Cicero had considered a permanent end to the long-standing differences of senators and knights. The mutual interests of these two classes should enable them, he thought, to unite in a solid front against radicalism. He conceived himself as brain truster in this "coalition of classes" (*concordia ordinum*), and he thought of the conservative Pompey as Lord Protector to guarantee the compact with his sword. But Cicero's concept was beyond Pompey, and cooperation with an unfriendly Senate was impossible. Caesar's solution was simpler. For Cicero's coalition of orders he substituted a coalition of leaders— himself, Pompey, and Cicero. Cicero was to have been liaison man with the Senate, but he balked, instinctively distrusting Caesar. Caesar then took on as third partner Pompey's old rival, Crassus. His program divided power among the three "bosses." He himself was consul for 59 B.C., Pompey got his Eastern settlement ratified and pensions for his veterans, Crassus got for his equestrian friends in a banking firm a reduction in the amount they had agreed to pay for the privilege of collecting taxes in Asia.

Caesar as consul proved extremely highhanded. M. Calpurnius Bibulus, the other consul, and the uncompromising Cato obstructed him with every known device. So did other Optimates, who saw in the triumvirate a danger to themselves and to the Republic. Bibulus swore that he would block Caesar's proposed land pensions for Pompey's veterans by declaring the auspices unfavorable. Few in that sophisticated age believed any longer in auspices, but Bibulus' act had constitutional precedent and Caesar's legislation was technically invalid.

Finally, disgusted with this abuse of constitutional power, Caesar paid his colleague back with interest. He let loose some gangs of Pompeian veterans, and Bibulus shut himself up in his house in real or feigned fear for his life. Friendly tribunes, flouting the omens, got Pompey's Eastern settlement ratified in the Council of the Plebs. To secure the publicans' rebate of their debt to the treasury, Caesar silenced Cato by having him hustled off the floor, some say to prison, still speaking his lines to his fellow-senators who followed him in a body. While conservatives stood aghast at these rough methods, the Populares applauded. But neither side could yet foresee that the abuse of constitutional usages by entrenched special interests and ruthless shortcuts by opportunists or impatient reformers would shape history's course for a generation.

Crassus, Pompey, and their followers profited much from Caesar's consulship; Caesar profited more. For he got assigned to himself over the Senate's head and for five years a provincial command calculated to make his reputation rival Pompey's. That command was in Cisalpine Gaul plus Illyricum, to which a little later was added Narbonese Gaul. The two Gauls were to be a springboard to the conquest of Gaul proper. The triumvirate's efficiency and its practical results clearly proved the Senate's political and administrative impotence. Yet it was no simple spoils system, for even thus early Caesar revealed that concern for provincial welfare which emerged more fully later. He tightened regulations to insure honest provincial government; his effective measures remained the basic provincial law for centuries.

One of Caesar's means of assuring the coalition's efficiency was to get temporarily rid of Cicero. Grieving over the wreck of his "coalition of orders" and over the defection to the enemy of his hero, Pompey, Cicero finally declared against the triumvirate. His removal was managed with neat indirectness: an assembly act outlawing any ex-magistrate who had executed a Roman citizen without trial. Thus Cicero paid for the execution of Catiline's accomplices. After vain attempts to stop the enactment of this law, he went into voluntary exile. The agent of his eclipse was a personal enemy, the tribune Clodius, colorful, loose-tongued, conscience-less, a tool of Caesar. Actually a patrician Claudius, Clodius for reasons of practical politics had cynically had himself adopted into the plebeian class by a young man half his age. Clodius won the mob by a law to distribute grain entirely free—a law never repealed which guaranteed the degradation of the city proletariat. He maintained his power for half a dozen years by means of gangster squads legalized by being incorporated as artisan clubs. In Caesar's interest Clodius also removed Cato, the triumvirate's most formidable enemy, by having him made governor of a new province, Cyprus. With the oligarchy's watchdogs out of the way, the triumvirate's ascendancy was assured.

Caesar next engineered a five-year renewal of the coalition. Since a Sullan law prevented his leaving his province, he invited his partners (56 B.C.) to Luca, on the border of Cisalpine Gaul; here gathered not only Crassus and Pompey but from 200 miles away magistrates, office seekers, and over 100 senators. Under the new agreement Crassus and Pompey got the consulship for 55 B.C. and would sponsor laws increasing the powers of all three. Caesar was to be reappointed proconsul for another five years to finish his conquest of Gaul. After his consulship Crassus was to be governor of Syria, whence he would attack the Parthians. Crassus hoped thus to rival his colleagues' achievements. Pompey's share in the deal was the governorship of Spain and supervision of Rome's food supply. (Some powerful speculators had virtually starved the city by cornering the grain market.) Each proconsul would be empowered to raise seven to ten legions and to make war and peace in the lands bordering his province. The coalition thus controlled the country by its controlling war patronage. To keep power even, it was arranged that their commands were to expire in five years from 54 B.C.

Cicero had meanwhile been allowed to return to Rome on the tacit understanding that he would behave. Eliminated from active politics, he published a book of political theory, *De Republica*. Here he argued that the old balance of consular power, senatorial direction, and popular sovereignty—lost in the recent stress and strain—might be recaptured by creating an extra-constitutional official, a "moderator of the commonwealth," wise, upright, inspiring confidence—in short a Platonic "philosopher-king," who could re-establish political harmony, suppress anarchy, and preserve the machinery and spirit of the old constitution. His candidate for moderator may have been Pompey, but was more likely himself. In any case, the *De Republica* was a critique of existing conditions, and a vivid proof that the old order was gone. What the future held no one could foresee (though perhaps Cicero's book provided a rationalization for the Augustan principate), but thoughtful Romans were uneasy. Cicero's young friend, the poet Catullus, who also distrusted Caesar, shot metaphorical arrows at him. But neither poetry nor philosophy could save the crumbling edifice.

The triumvirate disintegrated rapidly. Pompey's marriage to Caesar's daughter Julia had cemented the original coalition. This union, though political, proved a happy one, but when Julia died (early 54 B.C.), the strongest bond between the two men was broken. Crassus' death after Carrhae (53 B.C.), in retreat before the Parthians, spelled the end of the triumvirate. When Pompey married the daughter of a conservative nobleman, a Scipio, and through her was drawn more firmly into the oligarchic orbit, Caesar's influence was severely weakened.

The trend of events too moved in Pompey's favor. Clodius and a rival tribune, Milo, in pursuit of their own factional ends, inaugurated a cycle of arson, assassinations, and anarchy. In the resulting confusion the consular elections for 53 B.C. were postponed for six months. Meantime Rome had a government of dubious legality. From his suburban villa Pompey saw anarchy grow. As administrator of the food supply he must stay close to Rome, but as proconsul with an army he could not constitutionally dwell within the city limits. Actually, unlike Caesar who had been in Gaul since 58 B.C. and Crassus who had gone to Syria in November of his consular year, Pompey never went to Spain, but ruled it through a legate. Living within walking distance of the Forum, he perhaps viewed with satisfaction the mounting chaos, confident that eventually he would be called on to clean house. Once more in 52 B.C. Clodius and Milo prevented the consular elections. When in an encounter with Milo's gangs Clodius was slain and the Senate House was burned as his symbolic funeral pyre, the Fathers took the initiative to name Pompey sole consul. He introduced needed reforms and administered justice impartially. For a few months Rome enjoyed peace, freedom, and good government—the blessings hoped for in the *De Republica*. Unfortunately for him, before the end of 50 B.C. he was persuaded to join a fanatical group bent on destroying Caesar.

The Conquest of Gaul

Central and northern Gaul had lived apart from civilization, its rich resources untapped, its people, the Celts, torn by bloody tribal feuds, and its Rhine border beset by German tribes. For Caesar this fertile land meant personal glory; for Rome, a new empire. A realist, Caesar knew that lasting political influence needed more support than a fickle electorate could give. Accordingly he chose to occupy Gaul, where he could test his generalship and build lasting prestige. Down to 51 B.C. he almost certainly contemplated no armed clash with either Pompey or the Senate. But he was foresighted enough in the early fifties to consolidate a following which would back him to the hilt if he ever needed to pit his strength against a Roman enemy. His army, built into a war machine out of citizen and provincial levies, showed unprecedented loyalty to its general. If Pompey's generalship and Pompey's army in the coming civil war were good, Caesar's genius and Caesar's men were better. Caesar himself later said that in Spain he conquered armies without a general, and that Pompey was a general without an army.

Caesar took eight years to conquer Gaul from the Alps to the North Sea and from the Rhine to the Atlantic. He was often on the brink of disaster, sometimes dubious about his next step. He employed in turn terrorism and gentleness, candor and duplicity, vengeance and forgiveness. He executed bold strategy with breath-taking speed. He shared all dangers with his troops, so that they came to accept him as one of themselves. They joked both with him and about him, coarsely and good-naturedly, and Caesar cannily let them do it.

The Gauls were emerging out of barbarism into the virtues and vices of civilization. Successful horse breeders, they developed fine cavalry squadrons which often imperiled Caesar's strategy, and built wagon roads to link their excellent river communications. They had improved their agricultural methods, produced the best utilitarian pottery outside civilized countries, and produced keen, tempered swords. They had preserved the secular spirit by limiting their Druid hierarchy to its traditional concerns with excommunications, executions, and the sacrifice of war prisoners.

Politically the north and the center had begun to go separate ways. In the north the Belgae, of mixed Celtic and German strain, enjoyed fairly stable government, having generally retained their tribal kings. But central Gaul, where tribal aristocracies had ousted the kings, inevitably suffered the twin consequences, perennial warfare and the reduction of the masses to serfdom. Even so, villages, towns, and tribes had begun to consolidate into states.

These states, however, could not assert authority over the tribal

Fig. 42.5. Avaricum. Caesar's siege-works, model. Note *agger* (dike) across ditch, surmounted by a double approach-way covered with wet skins against burning arrows. The two scaling-towers outside the wall were movable, with roofed

chieftains, jealous of their traditional privileges. Basing their power on large groups of free and serf retainers, the nobles aped the chiefs in thwarting the states' authority. By the time of Caesar's invasion the Gauls had abandoned their old chariot tactics, relying instead largely on cavalry. Except in two or three states, their infantry lacked staying power. Unless it won the field on the first encounter, it usually disintegrated.

Caesar's war in Gaul went through four phases. He first intervened in 58 B.C. when a powerful Celtic tribe, the Helvetii, tried to migrate from western Switzerland to the Atlantic coast through the Roman province of Narbonese Gaul. Blocked by Caesar's legions, they tried to make a detour northward around the Roman province. But here again they met Caesar's legions, called in by the native Aedui, long allied to Rome. Defeated near Bibracte (Autun), the Helvetii returned to their homeland.

The Helvetian exodus had been partly the result of pressure from the Suebi, a group of German tribes. They, led by the soldier-statesman Ariovistus, had occupied the region of Alsace and begun to raid central

battering rams in the bottom. The whole vast construction was completed in less than a month, in the face of bad weather and enemy action. (Rome, Museo della Civiltà Romana; J. Felbermeyer photo)

Gaul. Impressed by Caesar's success over the Helvetii, the Gallic chieftains now invited his intervention against this greater menace. Caesar wanted no part of Gallo-Germanic feuds, especially since Ariovistus too was an ally of Rome. Actually Caesar had himself recommended that alliance to the Senate. Therefore he tried conciliation, but in vain. Ariovistus' reply that he would talk peace after reaching the Atlantic coast could have no other reception at the tent of a Roman proconsul than a declaration of war. One bloody encounter decided the issue, and Gaul was promptly cleared of Germans west of the Rhine.

In pushing the Germans back behind the Rhine, Caesar finished his uncle Marius' epic work. When Ariovistus rejected Caesar's overtures, his attempt to reach the Atlantic looked like the old Cimbric-Teutonic menace revived. No Roman could tolerate a German occupation of Gaul which would encircle Italy from the Pyrenees to Trieste and threaten Rome's existence. The wall of steel Caesar put up along the German front from the Alps to the Low Countries kept the barbarians off the Empire for five hundred years.

The two operations of 58 B.C. opened Caesar's eyes to Gallic weakness and disunity and to his own military talents. Temptation followed. Fully exploiting the local situation, in 57 B.C. he subjugated virtually the whole country, with great economy of effort, marching rapidly from Belgium to Brittany and from Brittany south along the Atlantic seaboard. The following year he spent consolidating his gains. At this point, apparently to protect Gaul's borders, he made two excursions. In 55 B.C. he crossed the Rhine on a wooden bridge which his engineers had built in ten days, made threatening demonstrations, and after eighteen days returned to Gaul, destroying the bridge behind him and making the Rhine the boundary between Rome and the barbarian. That same year he explored Britain and in 54 B.C. invaded it, defeating the Britons in the field, but withdrawing after their nominal submission. He apparently did not relish the prospect of British guerrilla warfare. His real intention in venturing beyond the Rhine and the Channel is still in doubt.

Caesar had only overawed, not conquered, the Gauls. During his German and British diversions they lay low, but in 54–53 B.C. serious revolts broke out, on one occasion destroying fifteen Roman cohorts almost to a man. The last uprising (52 B.C.) proved the most formidable, for in it the Gauls, led by the able Vercingetorix, finally rose above sectionalism. For once the Romans met their equal. Repeatedly the Romans were saved from imminent disaster by their own steadfast discipline and by Caesar's skill in saving apparently hopeless situations. They had technological advantages as well, knowing how to span rivers, scale walls, batter down fortifications with siege artillery, above all the ability to construct that incomparable system of moats and ramparts which bottled Vercingetorix up in Alesia and prevented reinforcements from reaching him. With his surrender, Gaul's independence was threatened but its peace assured.

Caesar's Gallic wars had far-reaching results. His prestige and command of patronage now equaled Pompey's. His discovery of his own military genius stiffened his resolve to insist on fair play from his political enemies. His achievements had won over thousands of political neutrals and even conservatives. His position indeed had begun to rise above faction; he was the man on horseback.

The consequences of Caesar's conquest for Rome, for Gaul itself, and for mankind were incalculable. Rome acquired not only stores of gold— at least Caesar and his men did—and rich mineral deposits, but opportunities for its bankers and merchants and millions of acres for its land-hungry proletariat. This conquest, unlike that of the Greek East, brought Rome neither works of art nor an effete civilization, but a virile and gifted race which in time took eagerly to Latin culture. Within a century Gaul was sending senators to the Curia, giving Roman society new blood,

Roman minds new vigor, and by the fourth century A.D. Gaul was to be the most cultured land in Europe. The addition of Gaul made all Western Europe Roman in speech, law, thought, religion, and culture. Indeed, in the late Empire Gaul embodied the best in Roman civilization. Even the barbarian invasions which ended the Empire in the West could not undo the Romanization of Western Europe. Western Europe has remained essentially Latin to this day, and after Caesar the British Isles too were Romanized. But that tells only half the story. Borne by the Spaniards, the Portuguese, and the French, and in a more diluted form by the British, the Latin or classical inheritance was to take root and spread also over the American continent from Hudson Bay to Tierra del Fuego. The world has seldom seen an event so pregnant for history as Caesar's conquest of Gaul.

The Kingdom of Parthia

Crassus' military ambitions had involved Rome with the Hellenized Oriental kingdom of Parthia, which was to plague it for another five generations. Originally Iranian nomad invaders from east of the Caspian, the Parthians were formidable horsemen and archers; in 247 B.C. they founded a kingdom which gradually expanded over Iran and by 141 B.C. had embraced Mesopotamia, replacing the Seleucids as the dominant power in the Middle East. Their expansion made conflict with western powers inevitable. They also established trade relations eastward as far as China and derived great wealth from their control of the overland trade routes.

Setting up puppet kings and making dynastic marriages, the Parthians dominated Armenia and formed an alliance with Mithridates of Pontus (about 94 B.C.). Two years later, disturbed by the Parthians' rapid advances toward their frontier, the Romans sent Sulla to seek a solution, and the result was a Roman alliance with Parthia, to which the latter remained loyal until Pompey bungled, offending Parthia unnecessarily by partitioning certain disputed territory between it and Armenia instead of keeping his promise to guarantee Parthia a frontier on the Euphrates. Henceforward Parthia was antagonistic to Rome.

Crassus' appointment to his Syrian command occurred while two contenders were struggling for the Parthian throne, supplying an apt occasion for a Parthian war. After first plundering the temple at Jerusalem and the temple of Atargatis at Hierapolis in Syria to obtain funds for his campaign, Crassus crossed the Euphrates (53 B.C.) with 44,000 men and marched across Mesopotamia to Carrhae, where he allowed himself to be surrounded by a Parthian force of highly mobile mounted archers which he in fact outnumbered. Both Crassus and his son were killed; the son's widow later married Pompey. Of the 44,000 troops that had set out with Crassus, half were killed, 10,000 were taken prisoner, and only a fourth escaped. Carrhae was one of the world's decisive battles: it stopped the Romans dead and imposed on them a frontier which lasted until the Islamic conquest. The victory was announced to the Parthian king (while he was attending a performance of Euripides' *Bacchae*) by throwing the severed head of Crassus upon the stage. Crassus' battle standards, captured by the Parthians, were for a quarter of a century a symbol of Rome's degradation in the Middle East, until they were finally surrendered (20 B.C.) to Augustus' stepson Tiberius. Even after that, Parthia continued at intervals to be a thorn in Rome's flesh, and though Trajan finally added its fringes to the Empire, it was immediately abandoned by Hadrian.

But our concern for the moment is with the death of Crassus. It marked, as we saw, the end of the triumvirate. Caesar's conquests in Gaul were making him a dangerous rival to Pompey, and the stage was now set for a second civil war.

Chapter 43 / CAESAR, DESTROYER AND BUILDER

The Die Is Cast

Caesar's Popularis leanings, his flouting of constitutional precedents, his high-handed pursuit of his and the triumvirate's aims had made him anathema to the Optimates. Knowing that the moment he returned to private life they would prosecute him for his administration of Gaul, he resolved to prevent the day of reckoning by stepping from his Gallic proconsulship directly into the consulship. As consul he hoped to get the Assembly to ratify his proconsular acts and make them unassailable. But two requirements hampered him, one that a candidate for office be actually present in Rome, the other that a governor might not leave his province during his term. But Pompey and Crassus had agreed at Luca to help Caesar get special permission to seek the consulship *in absentia*. Despite Crassus and Julia's deaths, which, as we saw, estranged Pompey and Caesar, Pompey in 52 B.C., with help from Cicero and others, got the special law passed: the ten tribunes proposed it unanimously, for Caesar's hold on the public was strong. But within a few months other interests and influences began to pull Pompey away from Caesar. Somewhat slow-witted, he let Caesar's enemies use him.

Embarrassed at first by his own small disloyalties, he tried to blame them on forgetfulness. But after the special law was passed he did nothing to help implement it. Caesar could sink or swim—Pompey looked the other way.

Caesar's real enemy, however, was not Pompey, but a little group of willful men in the Senate who, resentful at the triumvirate's usurpation of their power, were determined to destroy its founder by suing him in criminal court. If convicted, he would lose his prestige, his property, and his citizenship and go into permanent eclipse. Cato even wanted him tried for treason, a capital charge, and urged the Senate to hand him over to some German tribes with whom he had broken faith. Having Pompey on their side emboldened these men, for Pompey had lately championed law and order and upheld senatorial authority. Pompey for his part was grateful to the Senate for renewing his Spanish proconsulship. The Senate's gift tied the recipient to the giver. This appointment, for a term of years, still not entailing Pompey's actual presence in Spain, meant that Pompey would still be near Rome, and in command of an army, when Caesar's term in Gaul ended in 50 B.C.

Every compromise proposed by Caesar to save his honor and his neck was spurned. Even so his position was not hopeless, for he had bought the services of a shrewd tribune, Scribonius Curio, until now an Optimate. Since Caesar would be legally governor of Gaul and immune from prosecution until a successor arrived, Curio vetoed every move to have a successor appointed. Having demoralized the Optimate camp by this cold war, Caesar then had Curio propose that both Caesar and Pompey relinquish their commands simultaneously. The Senate accepted this compromise 370 to 22 (December 1, 50 B.C.). But Pompey sabotaged it through a familiar device, a veto by another tribune. The next day the consul Marcellus took a fatal step: he appointed Pompey commander for the defense of Italy. Caesar must now fight or surrender. Pompey may not have wanted war, but the senatorial minority, led by Cato, forced the issue. On January 1, 49 B.C., the Senate, yielding to the diehards, decreed that Caesar must immediately give up his command or be outlawed. When Mark Antony, who meantime had replaced Curio as tribune, interposed his veto, the Senate passed the last decree, and he and a fellow tribune fled at once to Caesar's camp. Caesar claimed the sacrosanctity of the tribunes had been threatened. With this issue, which for centuries had rallied the liberal forces of the Republic, especially the masses, Caesar and his legions on January 10 crossed the Rubicon, the boundary river between Italy and Cisalpine Gaul, to dislodge his own, and the People's, enemies from Rome. The Senate supposed that most Roman citizens would take the march on Rome as treason. On the contrary they hailed Caesar as champion of the People's rights and as a faithful public servant who had been wronged, his sincere offers of compromise treated with haughty and undeserved contempt. Then when he followed victories with clemency—so unlike Marius and Sulla—he appeared as a great patriot putting his country's good above personal considerations.

Other facts were in his favor. He had not, like time-serving Pompey, waited upon events, but had favored from his earliest youth the Popular cause. He had sympathized with Catiline's aims if not his methods. This alone drew to his camp debtors of high and low degree, and they were many, for usury, debt, mortgage, bankruptcy were endemic in Roman society in this age. As consul he had indebted thousands of Pompey's veterans to him for obtaining their pensions. We saw how he won the knights over from Pompey and Crassus, by rescuing one of their banking firms. But most important was the friendship of Cisalpine Gaul, which was culturally and economically one with Italy even though it did not enjoy full citizenship rights. Three hundred thousand small-property owners lived there in Caesar's time, brave Latin yeomen and sturdy Romanized Celts. It was sending into Italy and the empire men who won distinction in business, politics, war, and letters. Catullus, Vergil, Livy, all born there, had made or would make their mark. Caesar understood better than most the importance for Rome of the broad Po valley, and on becoming master of the Republic he promptly raised its inhabitants to citizenship. Ever since, the Po valley has been the most vital and progressive section of the unified peninsula. North Italy, first in expectation, then in gratitude, remained loyal to Caesar to the end.

He found support also in Narbonese Gaul, which since its annexation (120 B.C.) had been Romanized into a second Italy. Here too Caesar, as a humane and dependable governor, had won the devotion of the people. Nor was he without influence in Spain. Although this had been Pompey's province for five years and contained six or seven of his legions, Pompey had not set foot in it during all that time. On the other hand Caesar, who had administered this province well in 61 B.C., had made lasting friends with local leaders and important communities. From all these sources Caesar drew strength rivaling or outweighing Pompey's and the Senate's. His greatest source was naturally his legions, which had stood with him in Gaul, in Germany, in Britain, often in peril but always in the end victorious. Lastly he had faith in himself, for he had discovered his own genius.

The Second Civil War

Caesar crossed the Rubicon without opposition. Almost the entire Senate, the anti-Caesarian magistrates, Pompey, and his army fled from the

Fig. 43.1. Cleopatra (?). Photo from cast. (Rome, Museo della Civiltà Romana; photo from A. Ferrabino, *Nuova Storia di Roma*, Vol. III, p. 87. Padua, 1942. By permission of the publisher, Tumminelli.)

Italian mainland, though it was they who had asked for a showdown there. For Italy, disappointing Pompey's hopes, rushed to Caesar's camp. Numbers of Pompey's own troops deserted to the People's champion. The fleeing government in its panic even left the treasury behind. Thus 15,000 bars of gold, 30,000 bars of silver, and 300,000,000 sesterces in currency fell into Caesar's hands. Within sixty-five days Caesar was master of Italy. Even now he offered reconciliation repeatedly but in vain.

Pompey withdrew east of the Adriatic, for his influence in the East gave him good prospects of raising funds and forces. He had the fleet and the naval experience, while Caesar as yet had not a single warship or transport. Pompey therefore depended upon seapower to give him ultimate victory, though Caesar should win every land battle. The fleet too might cut Italy off from its overseas wheat supply and starve it into submission. Pompey's best legions were in Spain, and with these he expected to immobilize Caesar's forces in Gaul.

But Pompey's every calculation miscarried. The ex-tribune Curio, Caesar's aide in the field as he had been at the rostra, immediately occupied Sardinia and Sicily. Curio proved to be only too energetic. When he crossed to Africa, his impetuosity boomeranged to annihilate his army. This was the Senate's only success.

In possession of Italy, but lacking a fleet to pursue Pompey, Caesar decided to invade Spain. There Pompey's competent generals, with the provincial organization behind them, caused him some anxiety, but a desperate campaign centering on Ilerda finally resulted in their surrender. Caesar's veterans, their rear now fully secured, could now pursue Pompey himself.

Requisitioning a scratch transport fleet, Caesar moved his army across the Adriatic to meet Pompey's army at Dyrrhachium (Durazzo), opposite the Italian heel. He found Pompey unexpectedly shrewd. After months spent maneuvering for position, Caesar was forced to march southeast to Thessaly in a vain attempt to keep two Pompeian forces from meeting. Pompey followed, and at Pharsalus Caesar finally forced him to give battle. Caesar had 22,000 men, Pompey nearly twice as many, but Caesar's tactics turned his enemy's attack into irreparable disaster. Pompey's camp, even his tent, were taken, he barely saving himself by flight. Thousands of his soldiers were slain, 24,000 surrendered, the rest melted away. In a day Caesar had become master of the world. He followed Pompey into Egypt to find him slain by Ptolemy XIII's traitorous chief minister. If the Egyptian had hoped by his deed to earn Caesar's gratitude, he was soon undeceived, for Caesar, grieving that a great man and his own son-in-law should have met so base an end, had the murderer put to death.

What followed in Egypt made a legend for the ages. Although the contest was far from ended, Caesar took time out to relax. For one of the spoils of Egypt was Cleopatra, its queen.

Caesar the conqueror now conquered also Cleopatra. Or was it the other way around? Barely twenty-two years old, beautiful, willful, she appealed to the Roman thirty years her senior. While for her sake he dallied several months in Alexandria, Egyptian elements resentful of foreign interference bottled him up in the city. Only by desperate street fighting was Caesar able to hold out until help arrived. Cleopatra's brother Ptolemy XIII having died in battle, Caesar placed Cleopatra more firmly on the throne, associating with her a younger brother Ptolemy XIV, a weakling with whom she soon did away. Throughout his Gargantuan holiday Caesar kept pleasure and business strictly apart. Cleopatra's Egypt was a Caesarian vassal-state.

Before returning to Italy, Caesar sought out in Asia Minor Pharnaces, the son of the great Mithridates, who was fishing in the troubled waters of the Civil War, and brought him to his knees in a five-day campaign culminating (47 B.C.) in the battle of Zela. This victory he later commemorated in a triumph with a proud laconic placard reading *Veni, vidi, vici*. Then he returned to Rome to tackle administrative and constitutional problems more difficult than war. But war called him away again, this time to end the Pompeians' control in Africa. In a single battle, at Thapsus (46 B.C.), Africa fell into his hands. When Cato, now the Optimates' leader, saw his cause lost, he killed himself. Although a doctrinaire who mistook the interests of the ruling class for the cause of liberty, he was sincere and incorruptible.

"What God abandoned, he defended,
And took the sum of things for pay." [1]

Cato's suicide has fired the imagination of Western man. Dante admired him for refusing to live when liberty was gone, and he inspired the American Patrick Henry.

Routed from Africa, the remnants of the senatorial army went to Spain to join their comrades, whom Caesar's incompetent legates had allowed to regroup and even to raise new legions. At Munda (45 B.C.) Caesar completely crushed the combined forces. Lenient in every other case—so much so that people had deified his clemency—Caesar was ruthless towards those Spanish and African towns which had remained stubbornly Pompeian. He confiscated their domain or increased their tribute: for instance, Lepcis was forced to pay 3,000,000 pounds of olive oil. The beneficiary in every case was the treasury. Previously Caesar had treated generously all his opponents who were Roman citizens, giving to officers their liberty unconditionally and to enlisted men the choice of a discharge or joining his army. But he put to death the leaders of the last-ditch Pompeian resistance in Spain.

Caesar brought no fundamental change to the Roman art of war, but he applied to it an unequaled genius. Realizing, as Roman tacticians generally did, the importance of a balanced correlation between men and supplies, he preferred to operate with small forces, which he fashioned into a machine with unique mobility and striking power. He never struck too late, and when he struck, the blow was deadly. His greatest strength, as always, was faith in himself.

Our knowledge of both the Civil War and the Gallic War is derived chiefly from Caesar's own *Commentaries*. A simple style makes these works possibly the easiest introduction to Latin study. It is a pity that, sweating over grammatical details, students often fail to appreciate the lucidity and grace of Caesar's prose. But the chief merit of the *Commentaries* lies in their historical value—both as a primary source and as propaganda. Underlying the apparently objective and simple account is a fascinating piece of self-justification by a great and highly-trained intellect who seldom needed to distort the facts.

Caesar's Administration

When Caesar defeated Pompey, the old guard hoped that he would simply take Pompey's place, supervising the commonwealth to see that

[1] Paraphrased from A. E. Housman's "Epitaph on an Army of Mercenaries," *Last Poems:* New York, 1922.

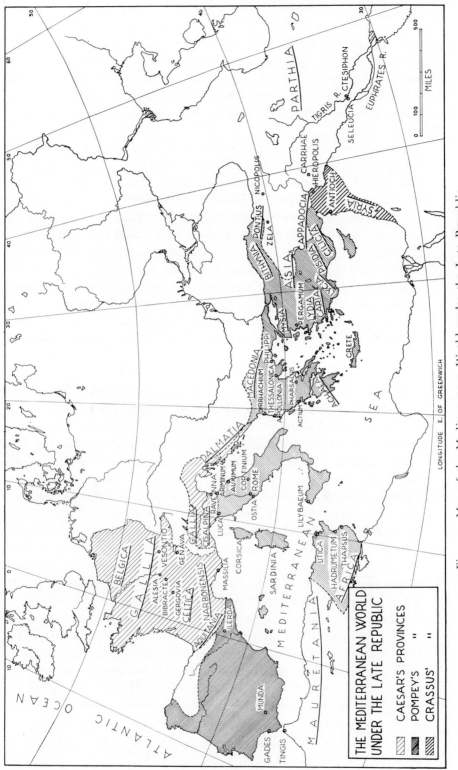

Fig. 43a. Map of the Mediterranean World under the Late Republic

every magistrate performed his task and was in due time promoted at the polls. They apparently had no idea that reform was the Roman world's first need, a need with which "business as usual" was incompatible. They hoped that Caesar would stop the revolution and renounce any program for modernizing the administration. But Caesar had no desire to benefit a class which since the Gracchi had repeatedly dishonored itself and imperiled the nation. He was an efficient administrator, impatient with privilege, incompetence, and corruption. Of the desperate need for economic reform he had been aware since he first entered politics. His long absences from Rome had widened his perspective. He now saw that social justice must be sought, and that the healthy, stable State must use all talent, not that of the oligarchy alone, but of other classes too, including provincials. Caesar's convictions, loyalties, and ambitions would not let him abandon his program to accommodate his enemies.

What was that program? First of all, by making Cisalpine Gaul a component part of the sovereign Republic, he at last unified Italy, nearly as epoch-making an accomplishment as the annexation of Gaul. He recalled all political exiles, victims of senatorial rule, and he reduced every debtor's obligations by one-fourth. He suppressed gangsterism and guarded against anarchy by prohibiting all clubs and associations, except those of respectable antiquity or religious purpose. (The Jews were incidental beneficiaries of this policy.) He reduced the number on the grain-dole from 320,000 to 150,000, not merely to relieve the budget, but to restore dignity to men degraded by that institution. Instead of charity he provided employment. He began or planned useful public works: new roads, a harbor at Ostia, reclamation of the Fucine Lake and the Pomptine Marshes, both realized in modern times, and dikes to curb the destructive Tiber. He further planned to cut the Isthmus of Corinth. He adorned Rome with a new forum and temple, and projected a theater, a library, and a new city plan. Attacking unemployment at its root, he passed a law that one-third of all ranch and plantation hands, hitherto almost entirely slave, must be free-born citizens; he proposed to reduce unemployment further in a broad colonization plan.

He planted probably 80,000 civilians in overseas industrial and commercial communities all over the Roman world: in Carthage and Corinth, both natural trading centers; in Sinope on the Black Sea, in six or eight places in Africa, and as many in Spain. Then there were 20,000 to 30,000 veterans, both his own and Pompey's, pressing for land pensions. They expected the usual land-grants, but in overcrowded Italy such grants would have dislodged either Sulla's veterans or those of Pompey's Eastern campaigns. Unwilling to disturb either group, Caesar settled few in Italy; the majority he sent to the provinces.

The benefits of this great colonization project were many. The relief of overpopulation meant less poverty throughout Italy, and less degradation and crime in the Roman slums. Colonization produced political stability also, since many went to colonies who otherwise would have sold their vote in Roman elections. Men hitherto dependent on charity got the chance to become self-supporting and self-respecting. Cities grew in the wilderness, spreading civilization into the surrounding barbarian world.

Caesar organized his colonies as self-governing corporations. Their charters prescribe the form of government, the magistrates' function, the town council's composition and mode of election. They regulate the town's social and economic life—requiring of the colonists five days' work annually on roads, limiting their output of pottery and tiles (lest they compete with the Italian market), requiring the worship of the Capitoline triad and Caesar's patroness, Venus. In brief, they sketch the main lines of public administration. As in Rome's older colonies, Caesar's colonists—both veteran and civilian—enjoyed the same political liberties, except for voting in Rome, as citizens in Rome. There was no social and political discrimination in the civilian settlements: all charter members were equal, slaves, freedmen, or free. Lastly, the colonial magistrates and senate formed a local bourgeois ruling class, comprising the ambitious or talented from different occupations, and destined to be the basic cells of the Empire-wide *bourgeoisie* which for more than two centuries proved the backbone of Roman society.

Every Roman general commanding an army abroad could grant citizenship to provincials, usually local leaders and property-owners of proven or purchasable loyalty. Caesar's liberality with this prerogative dismayed conservatives; his apparent intent was to raise his own conservative bloc as a counterweight to the old regime. Continued by the emperors, Caesar's colonization and franchise policy made the western provinces, especially Spain, Gaul, and Africa, Roman to the core.

Of Caesar's other reforms, realized or planned, two more had world significance. He put into effect the calendar devised by the Greek Sosigenes of Alexandria. To make the civic match the solar year, he added 67 days to the year 46 B.C. and decreed henceforward the addition of days to the shorter months to bring the total to 365, plus one more day in leap year. He allowed the month Quinctilis to be renamed Julius (July). His reconstructed calendar, slightly improved by another Roman pontiff, Gregory XIII (1582), is still the calendar of the civilized world. He planned the codification of Roman law, but death interfered. This vast and complex project discouraged even the emperors until Justinian completed it some 600 years later.

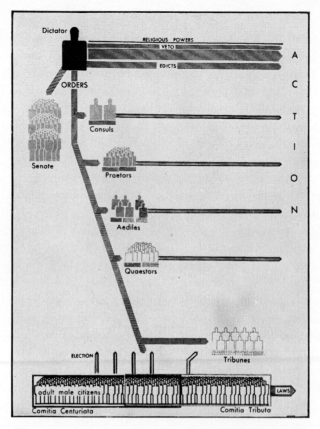

Fig. 43b. Chart to illustrate the machinery of Roman government under Julius Caesar, 45 B.C. (F. R. Cowell, *Cicero and the Roman Republic,* London, 1948. Chart XIV.)

Caesar's Constitutional Position

The constitutional problem was by far the most difficult Caesar had to face. His sword empowered him to take his choice of magistracies. From 48 B.C. to his death in 44 B.C. he was consul every year but one, but to avoid a colleague or tribune's possible veto, he preferred to be also dictator. He assumed this office first in 49 B.C. in the Civil War emergency, and again in 47 B.C. In his absences Mark Antony, his master of horse, governed. Cicero and other moderates, impressed by Caesar's generosity in preserving the estates, the lives, and—most important—the dignity of his erstwhile enemies, were willing to grant him a special constitutional place provided control was vested in the old senatorial ruling class. His third dictatorship (46 B.C.), however, disturbed them: not the office itself, which the need for major reconstruction justified, but its announced duration, which was ten years. When finally in 44 B.C. he was made dictator for life, they felt that the Republic they had known had ended.

Some said—and Shakespeare has immortalized the story—that Caesar wanted to be king. But Caesar was too canny for that: the Tarquins had given Roman kingship a bad name. Nor probably did he intend to establish a world monarchy, uniting East and West, on the now discredited Hellenistic model. For such a monarchy would require him to be worshiped, like the Ptolemies, as a living god, a notion still repugnant to Republican Romans. True, his image was struck on coins, his statues were placed in the temples, he built a temple to Venus Genetrix, his legendary ancestress, and planned one to "Caesar's Clemency," and other religious and semi-religious titles were conferred upon him. But other Republican generals had received such honors, and though his were more numerous, they hardly imply that he was considered a divine being either by himself or by his fellow citizens. He knew of course no other Roman could match him as an organizer and administrator, in war or peace. Practically speaking, then, he had to keep the power, not simply because a revolution had taken place, but because his humane and enlightened rule was to the advantage of the greatest number. Lastly, he could not shirk the responsibility of victory, namely, to build upon the ruins of the edifice he had destroyed. But he founded his rule neither on foreign models nor on theological formulas, but on Roman conceptions and methods, though, since he knew how much of a screen and a sham the "constitution" was, he probably never tried to rationalize his constitutional position.

The grant of two other powers gave Caesar a tighter control over both the state and the people. He established a new precedent by assuming for self-protection the tribunician sacrosanctity without the actual tribunate. Secondly, as "prefect of morals" he held a censor's power to supervise the morals of plain citizens, knights, and senators, and thereby to overhaul the Senate. Many senators had died in the Civil War; many others, seeing the futility of opposition, had voluntarily retired. Caesar replaced them with younger aristocrats. But he also made the Senate more representative by enlarging it to 900 members, including new men from the *bourgeoisie,* the plebs, and, for the first time, distinguished men from parts of Italy hitherto unrepresented, from the more Romanized provinces and even from the newer ones. Needless to say, a majority of this revamped Senate was friendly to him. But while the Senate would give him any laws he wanted, theoretically it abdicated none of its rights, nor did Caesar revoke any of its traditional powers. His dominance of the Assembly was complete—and not because he was the man on horseback. With patronage to dispense, with his power and influence, with the right the Senate gave him of nominating candidates for the magistracies, he controlled elections and Assembly legislation. And he could dispense with the Assembly at will, for, like Sulla, he was given power to remake the constitution and rewrite the laws as he saw fit.

Caesar's rule outside Italy was based on his proconsular office, which extended over every province. To the army he was *Imperator,* not Emperor, but commanding general, the same title that other Republican commanders had borne. The title did not come to connote absolute monarchy until years after Caesar was dead. As long as he lived, both proconsular and imperatorial offices kept their traditional Republican connotations.

Caesar's packing of the Senate and the unprecedented accumulation of powers which made him greater than any branch of government or any combination of men infuriated conservatives. They saw him, now dictator for life, as a tyrant over the Republic they had so long controlled. Threescore and more men plotted against his life. Caesar was planning a war against Parthia to avenge the death of Crassus. Fearing lest new military laurels should place his power beyond challenge, they decided to strike. Honest conviction, misguided idealism, common envy, personal grudges all helped to motivate the conspirators. Many among them owed Caesar much: office, honors, friendship. Their plans leaked out, and Caesar was warned not to attend the meeting of the Senate on the Ides of March (March 15, 44 B.C.), the time and the place chosen by the conspirators. Caesar, confident in his lucky star, disregarded the warnings. Struggling against the assassins' daggers, he fell dead at the foot of Pompey's statue. Perhaps a victim of his own ambition, he was also the victim of his determination to reform the rotten Republican government. Extortion in the provinces, coteries for control of the government at home, could not go on forever. Neither could the sanguinary class and factional struggle nor the chaotic clash of rival tribunes nor the attacks of ambitious proconsuls on senatorial or popular authority. The champions of the old order got rid of the champion of reform. Yet they did not triumph, for Caesar's heir Augustus was to frustrate them and give Italy and the world, at the price of freedom, a new era of peace, order, and justice.

Chapter 44/ THE END OF

THE REPUBLIC

Caesar's Inheritance: The Second Triumvirate

The conspirators were soon to discover that although they had made away with Caesar they could not nullify his acts, his laws, or his provisions for the future. The Dictator had designated several of them, including Marcus and Decimus Brutus and Gaius Cassius, as magistrates, governors, or army officers. Without apparent qualms of conscience all were willing to fill these positions. They compromised again when, to secure the consul Antony's agreement not to prosecute them, they voted in the Senate to give Caesar a state funeral—as if he had been a faithful servant of the state instead of the public enemy they had professed to see.

Their greatest mistake was imagining that Caesar's death would mean the rebirth of the free Republic. It did not. This was not merely because they had made no plans for handling the Senate, magistrates, people, or army, nor yet because Caesar's machine continued to function without him, but because public opinion stood unshaken for his ideals. A hero and a martyr, Caesar became to the people a personal benefactor when his will, which Mark Antony read at the funeral, revealed that he had left each citizen 1000 denarii and the use of his sumptuous gardens.

Within a month after Caesar's death, Antony had so roused public frenzy that the assassins dared not remain in Rome.

Antony won over the mob by posing as champion of Caesar's program. While his stand was doubtless sincere, it was also profitable, since it was his surest way to become a second Caesar. The dash and resourcefulness he had early shown, which closely resembled Caesar's, made him seem a worthy successor. And he could justly claim to have been Caesar's right hand from the beginning, loyal through thick and thin, in Forum, Senate, and military campaign. Above all, everyone knew that Caesar had made him his most trusted lieutenant. In short, both as a personality and as Caesar's self-proclaimed understudy, Antony was the natural heir to Caesar's mantle. A masterly combination of firmness and compromise confirmed his position and gave him the ascendancy in the Senate. Caesar's death left him in a strong position as sole consul, with the constitutional right to give orders and exact obedience.

Another man was angling for some of Caesar's political heritage, Lepidus, Antony's successor as his master of horse. But since this office lapsed with Caesar's death, Lepidus was in no position to cross Antony. In return for a pledge of support, Antony, perhaps irregularly, got him made Pontifex Maximus. Lepidus' power waxed until he became one of Rome's three most important men.

The third to claim the succession was an eighteen-year-old boy, Octavius, son of a niece of Caesar's. Intelligent, though not brilliant, and uncommonly handsome, he had received an old-fashioned Roman education, to which he added literary and philosophical tastes. He had a born ruler's hard common sense. Precociously mature, he early displayed that combination of decisiveness and dignity of carriage which the Romans called *gravitas*. In two things only was Octavius deficient—health and military capacity. Late in 45 B.C., Caesar had sent him to Apollonia to serve his apprenticeship with the legions training there for Parthia, and there he received news of the assassination. Realistic, ambitious, he at once conceived notions of revenge. With a cool calculation befitting an older man, he laid his plan. Concealing his real intentions, he moved to allay suspicions and throw potential opponents off guard.

Quietly crossing to Brundisium, where the garrison welcomed him, he learned for the first time that his great-uncle had adopted him as his son. Conceiving high hopes at the news, he prepared the ground for assuming his role as the successor to Caesar's power and took his adoptive name of Gaius Julius Caesar Octavianus—even before the adoption was legally confirmed.

Octavian's path to success was an obstacle course. He could expect no help from conservatives. Brutus, Cassius, and the other conspirators; Cicero, again influential after the Ides of March; Pompey's son Sextus, the

Fig. 44.1. The young Octavian. (Rome, Vatican Museum)

natural leader of the resurgent Pompeians, in brief, all who were Republicans by conviction or interest stood against him. Among the Caesarians, Lepidus, who had his own schemes, would hardly befriend him, and Antony, brooking no rivals for the succession, was openly hostile. The rank and file were confused and divided: the majority committed to Antony, the rest to Lepidus. The odds were against Caesar's inexperienced heir.

But Octavian had one strong asset. His name was Caesar. He was tactful, shrewd, capable. And Caesar had given him able friends, especially Marcus Agrippa, as young as Octavian, but unusually competent, a prime example of a first-rate man who out of loyalty accepted second place. There was also Maecenas, only a few years older, a polished diplomat with two absorbing interests, unselfish service to his friend and the cultivation of the arts. Octavian was fortunate in having this descendant of Etruscan kings as counselor and as liaison with the personages and factions of the opposition. Equally important was Maecenas' success in enlisting writers and artists to swing public opinion toward Caesar's adopted son. In 38 B.C. the statesmanlike Livia came into young Caesar's life. When she divorced Tiberius Claudius Nero to marry him, she carried with her aristocratic support, and thus respectability.

The Third Civil War

The game Octavian played was cleverness itself. He cajoled whole legions of Caesar's veterans to desert Antony and enroll with him. When Antony tried to block his official adoption as Caesar's son, he made an unnatural alliance with the Senate. Antony meantime had broken with the Senate, embezzled public funds with documents bearing Caesar's forged signature, even secured for himself the proconsulship of Gaul. Upon this last *démarche*, which might eventually lead to a new crossing of the Rubicon, the Senate declared him a public enemy. Octavian at once placed himself and his troops at their service. The ensuing civil war (the third since Sulla and Marius) deflated Antony's military prestige. The Senate, though victorious in the field, politically fared no better. Both consuls having died at Mutina (43 B.C.), Octavian took over by duress the unexpired term. As consul he could deal with the ex-consul Antony as equal with equal.

Now Caesar's adopted son began to show his hand. He outlawed his father's assassins, which for political reasons Antony had been unwilling to do, and he persuaded his rivals that all Caesarians must stand together. Thus was formed (43 B.C.) the second triumvirate, of Octavian, Antony, and Lepidus. They carved the western provinces into three spheres of influence, seized the central government, and, ostensibly to avenge Caesar, declared war on the Republican forces. They re-enacted abrogated Caesarian laws and swore to restore Caesar's entire program, including the establishment of veteran colonies. They even had him declared officially a god, building him a temple in that hallowed part of the Forum where his body had been cremated. They legalized their own positions by a law of the comitia tributa which put them above the regular magistrates for five years and made their acts valid without Senate approval. The Republic was not the only casualty: they proscribed 300 senators and some 2000 knights, thus destroying all opposition at one stroke and raising sorely needed funds from the victims' confiscated estates. Cicero was among the first to fall, sacrificed to Antony's hatred. No such madness had been unleashed since Sulla's day.

As in Pompey's time, the senatorial or Republican force got control of the eastern provinces. Rallying around Brutus, Cassius, and Sextus Pompey, they awaited (42 B.C.) the supreme test near Philippi on the Thracian-Macedonian border. Though the armies were evenly matched, the Caesarians had the better general in Antony. In two battles three weeks apart, first Cassius and then Brutus was defeated, and both committed suicide. With Brutus, "the noblest Roman of them all," perished the Republic.

Sextus Pompey continued the struggle, not for the sake of the Republic, but to establish a personal rule. Assembling a fleet, he seized Sicily and Sardinia, which controlled Rome's food supply, and thus forced the triumvirs to accept him for the moment as partner. But once they had assembled a fleet, they moved to freeze him out, and Agrippa swept the Pompeian fleet off the seas. Lepidus unsuccessfully attempted to claim Sicily, but Octavian won over his legions and deposed him from the triumvirate.

Sextus' defeat and Lepidus' peaceful elimination ended the Third Civil War. Almost twice as long as Caesar's war with Pompey, it had spilled more blood and done more damage to the empire's economy. Italy, which had suffered most, especially from famine, was grateful to the victorious Octavian. Maecenas' superb propaganda helped persuade Italy that its welfare depended on Octavian's fortunes. Octavian now sought to conciliate public opinion, which looked to him as an innate conservative who would bring peace and reconstruct a world shattered by a century of revolution. Public order, political security, opportunity for all to work in peace, the settlement of thousands of veterans on farms, the re-establishment of the old ways, but not real liberty, were the cornerstones of his policy. At Maecenas' suggestion, Vergil, a young poet from Mantua, once Octavian's fellow-student, formulated these ideas in an immortal epic on country life, the *Georgics*.

The East and Cleopatra

While Octavian had been dealing with Sextus, Antony was in the East, receiving the submission of its provinces and preparing the long-postponed Parthian war. With Sextus and Lepidus finally disposed of, the two chiefs divided the empire, Antony taking the East, and Octavian the West. Probably both sincerely intended to keep this new bargain, which was sealed by Antony's marriage to Octavian's sister, Octavia. But the marriage failed to bring unity: Octavia soon became a symbol over which Antony and the East clashed with Octavian and the West in one of history's decisive battles.

Antony's enemies claimed that his military capacity had begun to fail. Parthia had given renewed cause for war by taking advantage of Rome's Civil War to invade Syria and parts of Asia Minor. Roman morale was high, but Antony gambled and, as it turned out, failed by attacking Parthia from the rear, through Armenia. The Armenian king deserted him, and he found himself cut off on the outskirts of Parthia. But he skillfully saved his army and marched back into Roman territory amidst the rigors of the Armenian winter (36 B.C.). He never again had the men, money, or opportunity to make a second attempt. Crassus' death was still unavenged.

He made another and more costly mistake. As Rome's representative in the East he had seen much of Cleopatra, thus far without yielding to her charms or putting infatuation before duty. But after his Parthian reversal, when he planned a new expedition and needed the rich Egyptian treasury, he became enmeshed in her clever schemes. She hoped to reconquer her ancestral empire by diplomacy and personal charm. Therefore she gave herself to Antony as she had given herself to Caesar. According to Octavian's propaganda bureau, Antony, like an Oriental despot for whom the state is personal property, actually made over, to her and her children by Caesar and himself, Rome's vassal border states, plus Media and Parthia if and when conquered, and even Roman provinces, Cyprus, Cyrene, Cilicia, and Syria. Antony may have seen these donations as in the Roman interest: a strong Ptolemaic buffer state between Rome and Parthia. But according to Octavian's propagandists he was handing Rome's empire over to a foreign woman who had once vowed she would reign from the Capitol as mistress of the empire. Fanned indignation grew apace when Antony divorced Octavia, the chaste Roman matron, to marry the loose Greek woman. The propagandists used his own will, forcibly taken from the Vestal Virgins' archives, to prove his wish to be buried in Alexandria at the side of the Egyptian queen.

The shrewd Octavian exploited these blunders to the full. As Octavia's brother, he posed as champion of injured Roman womanhood; as consul, he vowed not to let the empire be presented to a foreigner; as a hundred-percent Roman, he feigned alarm, lest the East overcome the West. The propaganda was successful. Italy to a man swore allegiance to him, and the subservient Senate declared war, not on Antony, for this must not look like a quarrel between Romans, but on a foreign potentate, harlot and sorceress—so the propaganda bureau pictured the Egyptian queen. It influenced Antony's troops also; they deserted to Octavian by thousands. When Agrippa trapped Antony and Cleopatra's fleet at Actium (31 B.C.), she fled and he followed. Trapped again in Egypt by the legions, the couple committed suicide. So ended Cleopatra's dream and Antony's once-promising career. A reunited empire lay at Octavian's feet. Italy was ecstatic. Peace would be real now, and Rome would still be mistress of the world. "Now we can drink," sang Horace, a converted Republican; "now, free again, we can dance."

Chapter 45 / ART AND LITERATURE IN THE CICERONIAN AGE

The cult of Hellenism underwent in the late Republic a critical reappraisal. A resurgent native Italian spirit pervaded virtually every form of artistic creation. Greek art and literature now supplied starting points or hints on technique, rather than models for uncreative imitation. Thus architecture experimented with verticality and axial symmetry, sculpture became startlingly realistic, and naturalism pervaded painting. In literature, Lucretius and Catullus borrowed Greek meters, but their spirit was Italic or Roman, while Cicero brought to prose strength, plasticity, rhythmic variety, and his own adaptation of Isocrates' periodic style, which became the standard for Latin prose. Caesar was master of the simple, apparently detached style. Sallust, a historian of rare psychological insight, wrote strongly dramatic, vivid, epigrammatic, and slightly archaic prose. In brief, stylistically Roman literature of the late Republic stands out as a first-class achievement, not unworthy of comparison with Greek.

The Arts

Rome's conquest of Greece yielded rich cultural as well as financial rewards. Many a library and work of art was carried home as prize of war, while philosophical systems, science, and literary forms were borrowed wholesale. Greek teachers lectured in Rome; young men of means, like Caesar and Cicero, finished their educations in the Greek East.

With wealth earned or stolen in the East, senators, businessmen, and tax-farmers built palaces at home, sumptuously decorated with marbles, stuccoes, paintings, and sculptures, often stolen or got by sharp practices. The city, now the largest in the Mediterranean world, built aqueducts, theaters and amphitheaters, temples and basilicas, colonnaded porticoes, race courses, baths, and other public works mostly of Greek inspiration. Thousands of Romans spoke, wrote, and even tried to think Greek. But not every Roman was captivated by captive Greece; men of old Cato's stamp had fought, and in the main successfully, against Greek fads.

Despite Greek influences, always strong and at times irresistible, Roman art retained its native Italian essence. One hundred fifty years of archeological research have shown an unbroken line of development in ancient Italian art, from the terremare, Villanovan, Etruscan, Osco-Samnite, and Campanian, to its culmination in Roman art. True, numerous Greek artists were imported, especially after 150 B.C., but they were the agents, not the obliterators of the Roman spirit. And Greece sometimes borrowed Roman artists, as when (174 B.C.) a Roman architect took in hand Pisistratus' unfinished Olympieum in Athens (finally completed under Hadrian in A.D. 132). The struggle between the Scipionic circle's philhellenism and Cato's conservatism had by Caesar's time achieved a compromise: the national element now asserted itself through borrowed and modified Greek forms.

This new direction was clearest in architecture. Greek architecture was conceived horizontally; Roman often emphasized the vertical. The Roman late Republican temple, for instance, is only apparently Greek. It is set on a high podium, is reached by a long flight of steps, usually avoids the rather squat Doric order, and has a roof more steeply pitched than Greek canons allowed. The resulting elevation is thus twice as pronounced as in a Greek temple. The side columns have become decorative, not functional, as in the temple of "Fortuna Virilis" in the Forum Boarium. Many of these features are traditional in Etrusco-Italic architecture; their persistence gives Roman architecture its national character. Even round buildings—tombs or temples—were often lineal descendants of Neolithic round huts. In fact the original form of Rome's oldest circular temple, Vesta's shrine in the Forum, antedates any comparable Greek building, perhaps by as much as two centuries.

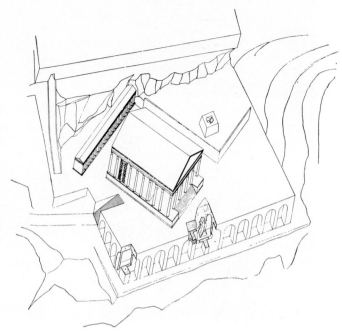

Fig. 45a. Reconstruction of Temple of Jupiter Anxur, Terracina. About 80 B.C. The temple faces seaward on its arched concrete platform. Technique and effect are as at Praeneste and Tibur. (F. Fasolo-G. Gullini, *Il Santuario della Fortuna Primigenia a Palestrina*, Rome, 1953. Tav. XXVII.)

The arch became as distinctive in Roman architecture as the column in Greek. Perhaps experience with arches in building the Sanctuary of Fortune at Praeneste enabled the Romans to adapt the arch to massive utilitarian constructions like the aqueduct and bridge mentioned in an earlier chapter. In bridges they extended the arch to great depth to form a barrel vault. Under the Empire the Romans exploited the possibilities of arch and vault to the utmost, advancing architectural engineering to the highest point possible before the invention of structural steel. And when, under the Republic, they had discovered, as at Praeneste, the technique of superimposing arches and vaults, they created the means of pushing verticality still higher.

Something else helped, as we saw earlier: the invention or improvement in the mid-second century B.C. of a new and indestructible building material, concrete. Sulla, a great builder, used it in the massive arched substructure of his temple of Jupiter Anxur at Tarracina; Lucullus in the vaults of his Tabularium, planned to house Rome's records office and to form a dramatic backdrop to the Forum. Massive concrete vaults support the Temple of Hercules at Tibur. This typical temple, centered high against the back wall of its precinct, exemplifies both verticality and axial symmetry, as does Caesar's temple to Venus Genetrix in his new Forum. We have earlier emphasized how useful to the modern world is Rome's versatile gift of concrete. After Sulla, victorious generals or ambitious politicians vied with one another in embellishing Rome with buildings. Pompey's theater (55 B.C.), the restored Basilica Aemilia

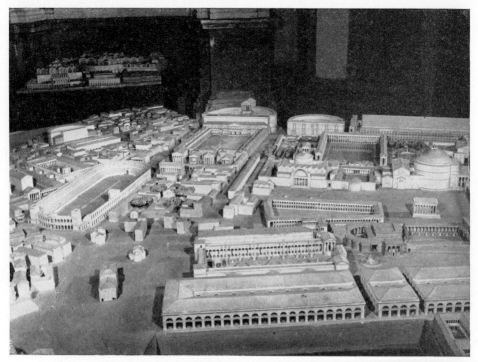

Fig. 45.1. Rome, Campus Martius, model. Left center: Circus of Flaminius (221 B.C.); upper left: Theater of Balbus (13 B.C.); upper center: Theater of Pompey (55 B.C.), with Temple of Venus Victrix and portico in which Caesar was stabbed; beside it, Domitian's Odeon and Stadium (A.D. 93); right center: Pantheon (A.D. 126); foreground: Saepta (polling place, 26 B.C.). (Rome, Museo della Civiltà Romana; J. Felbermeyer photo)

(54 B.C.), and Caesar's basilica (called Julia; finished after his death) and Forum are examples.

Roman originality is evident also in sculpture and painting. Etruscan and Italic antecedents do not by themselves account for the Roman urge to portray the human face with stark fidelity. Of more consequence was the instinct for realism and the appreciation of the individual's role in war, government, and family life. In each generation the ruling class habitually added more images to those of their ancestors kept in their home chapels or erected, with or without authority, in the Forum. By 159 B.C. they so cluttered the Forum that the censors removed the unauthorized ones. Death masks and realistic Egyptian portraits of pharaohs were other sources for Roman sculptors. Greek sculptors in the late Republic reinvigorated the realistic style from Hellenistic models. A late Republican terra-cotta head in Boston is a fine realistic portrait of a magistrate or businessman, worldly-wise, stern, self-disciplined, tenacious, unshakable though the world fall in ruins about him.

Realism in sculpture was paralleled in painting. Pictures arranged in panels commemorated the deeds (*res gestae*) of Rome's heroes, in battle and in victory. Vivid coloring and animated movement make the compo-

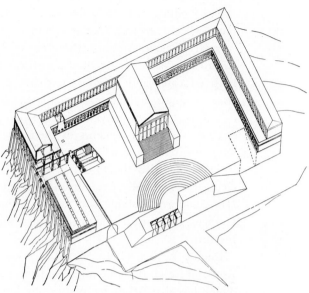

Fig. 45b. Reconstruction of Temple of Hercules, Tivoli (Tibur). About 63 B.C. Concrete substructure, as at Terracina, with buttresses on side toward Anio (left). The hemicycle and U-shaped portico, which give a theatrical effect, are elements found also at Praeneste. (F. Fasolo-G. Gullini, *Il Santuario della Fortuna Primigenia a Palestrina*, Rome, 1953. Tav. XXIX.)

sition dramatic. Such story-telling panels adorned tombs and the public buildings, were carried in triumphs or displayed as votive offerings in the temples. Some of these paintings are in the new "continuous" style, depicting as on an unrolled scroll successive episodes of the subject's career. Whereas the Parthenon frieze, for example, depicted a single occasion, Roman art might portray scenes from several different times and places.

The Romans adapted the new Hellenistic technique of architectural mural painting which by perspective created the illusion of space. By portraying painted columns supporting arches or architraves and opening the intervening space, as it were, to the light of day, Roman painters produced the effect of removing the wall to reveal a street or some monumental city quarter. But they preferred to see arbors, trees, gardens, and vistas of their countryside, whose peaceful beauty seemed more attractive the deeper they plunged into the business of empire.

Poetry

Like the artists, men of letters in the late Republic felt a pull towards Hellenism countered by an urge to go their own way. On the whole, poets followed Greek models more than did prose writers, who had native examples like Cato to follow. More than ever before, young Romans were turning to intellectual pursuits, some for esthetic reasons, others to find in history, philosophy, and poetry examples and precedents useful in oratory. Oratorical talent was, as we saw, the open sesame to political success, especially for the "new men" who had nothing but talent to help them rise.

Every educated Roman dabbled in poetry. Even politicians and states-men—Cicero, Brutus, Caesar—yielded to the temptation. In his defense of a Greek poet, Archias, whose citizenship was contested in the courts, Cicero speaks movingly of the virtues of such things as poetry, which both educates and delights, enriches and consoles, provides diversion from business and occupation for leisure.

The best-known poets of the age preceding Cicero were Lucilius and Accius, but only fragments of their work survive. Lucilius (*c.* 180–102 B.C.) originated a new literary form, the *satura,* a mocking review of the social scene with the intent of improving human behavior. His mood changed continually, here droning like a bee, there stinging like a wasp. His unadorned style was rather colloquial than literary. Through Horace, Lucilius bequeathed this whimsical genre to every Western literature.

Lucius Accius (170-*c.* 85 B.C.) wrote about fifty tragedies, two on Roman historical themes, the rest from the repertory of Greek mythology. These blood-and-thunder plays drew large audiences. Except for a brief revival by Seneca, Roman drama virtually died with him. Its place was taken by the mime, which, though born in Alexandria, reached its fullest scope in Rome. The plots were often erotic and usually scurrilous; the language was a fresh and spicy vernacular. The lure of the mime turned the Romans away from the ancient Atellan farce, whose char-acters, masks, and peasant humor died a casualty to Hellenism.

Accius was the last really old-fashioned poet. Of the brilliant follow-ing age, the greatest poet, indeed one of the greatest of all time, was T. Lucretius Carus (*c.* 94–55 B.C.) . His *De Rerum Natura* (*On The Nature of the Universe*) , a didactic poem in six books, treats of philos-ophy, religion, cosmology, psychology, anthropology, and ethics. For Lucretius, knowledge of atomic physics served a humanistic purpose, the freeing of mankind from superstitious fear of the gods and of death. He treated his weighty theme with the creative art of high poetry and a prophet's sense of liberating mission. Death might well obsess the Roman mind, in which the old disquieting influence of Etruscan demonology had been early intensified by the frightful death-toll of the Hannibalic War. In Lucretius' own time, the Social War, the First Civil War, and the Sullan proscriptions visited nearly every Roman and Italian family with death. A few years after Lucretius, Cicero too was impelled to write com-forting pages about death. Believing with Pythagoras, Socrates, and Plato in the soul's happy immortality, Cicero did not fear death; even if his belief be delusion, he wrote, it is a comforting one, to which he will cling to his last breath.

Lucretius' line was bolder. Away with your fear of death, he told his readers, for death is not an evil, but a blessed release from life's miseries. Nor fear the gods. Epicurus, his master, had argued that they neither made nor govern the world nor concern themselves with men's lives; life and the universe are the product not of the gods, but of mechanistic natural forces. The universe is composed of void and of atoms, invisible and indivisible particles, which unite fortuitously to make up matter or Being. Even the soul is atoms. Happiness is life's aim; it is attainable only through wisdom which rises above superstition and accepts with equanimity the laws governing the universe.

Every book of *De Rerum Natura* contains passages of flaming poetry. At the outset, for example, the poet invokes Venus, symbol of nature's creative power, the eternal miracle by which the earth bears fruits and flowers, the sea laughs and the sky sends out his light, the birds sing, the herds frisk in the fields or swim through rushing rivers:

> Each one with eager longing follows thee
> Whithersoever thou, Goddess, lurest them.

The praise of Epicurus, man's benefactor, whose doctrine has dethroned the gods and swept away superstition, is filled with overwhelming fervor. Book five is stirring revelation; it traces civilization's rise from savagery to man's intellectual mastery over Nature and captaincy of his soul, achieved by passing from error to error and from crisis to crisis— by the skin of his teeth. The evolution of the species and the survival of the fittest, the Social Contract, the triumph of mind over matter are all there, in this amazing book.

Lucretius made Latin poetry stand on its own feet, forging new words out of "the poverty of his native language" (his own phrase) or bending old ones to new meanings. A rough-hewn style, neither archaic like Ennius' nor polished like Vergil's, gives his poetry freshness. For sheer inspiration, majesty of hexameters, and toughness of thought, he has no equal in Latin literature. The first Roman to aim at bringing equilibrium and peace to the human mind, he was followed by a distinguished company: Cicero, Seneca, and Marcus Aurelius, and by missionaries and zealots from the Church Fathers onward.

While Lucretius tried to interpret life and the cosmos, Gaius Valerius Catullus (*c.* 84–54 B.C.) was equally intent on revealing his inner self. He belonged to a circle of brilliant young poets, self-styled *neoteroi*, or "moderns," because they composed in meters which were new to Rome (but old in Greece). They prided themselves on introducing certain Alexandrian genres, chiefly the epigram and love elegy, both symmetrically constructed and overflowing with erudition. But they gave Roman poetry a new spirit: romantic sentiment and a psychological approach, pointed up by the individualism of the day. For this was a time of revaluations and revolt in poetry as in politics. Catullus' poetry shows these moderns as a merry group of bohemians, in a chronic state of financial embarrassment and of excitement, over friends, over poetry, over love.

Catullus went to Rome from his native city of Verona in about 62 B.C. There he fell madly in love with a married woman whom he called Lesbia. Her real name was Clodia, and she was a sister of the colorful tribune Clodius, famous for her brilliance and for the number of her lovers. Rising above Alexandrian pedantry, Catullus reveals himself in sensitive lyrics, rich, warm, simple, and fresh, like those of no other Roman poet. He sang of the joys of friendship, the beauty of nature, especially of his native countryside, his profound love for his brother. He painted unforgettable scenes of family life, of joy in children, the more pathetic because it was a joy he was never to know. He wrote of the happiness of returning home from abroad, the dream come true, the homesickness assuaged, the rest in the bed one longed for. He bared his soul in describing his love for Lesbia and the hatred that burned his vitals after her many infidelities. Though he tried to renounce her, he could not:

> I hate and love, but why I cannot tell;
> I only know I feel the fires of Hell.

Few poets have matched his intensity of emotion, his poetic color and music. Poets ever since have tried to speak with his freshness—for instance, Herrick and Landor, to mention only two, in England, and Ronsard and the Pléiade in France. His fame rests on 116 poems, mostly short, probably all that he wrote. He died at thirty, in the fullness of his creative power.

Prose

Prose too came into full flower. Its greatest master was Cicero, who created a rolling period, more rhythmic and resonant than any Greek achievement. Words in majestic sweep came to him as easily as breathing; indeed his problem was self-restraint. He learned from two older contemporaries, Lucius Licinius Crassus, admired for his finished style and delivery, and Marcus Antonius, grandfather of the triumvir, famous for his cold factual reasoning. He profited even more from the strictures of his best teacher, Molo of Rhodes, who ruthlessly mocked his young pupil's infatuation with words. In maturity Cicero struck a balance between two contemporary and competing schools of composition, the Atticists, like Brutus, simple and direct like the Athenian speech-writer Lysias (c. 459–380 B.C.), and the Asianists, votaries of emotional appeal and verbal fireworks. While the Attic style sounded flat and boring to Roman ears, the Asianic seemed lacking in decorum, especially in Senate debates. Though to modern readers Cicero frequently seems turgid, it was he who expelled Asianism from Roman oratory and prose in general. Neglected, chiefly for political reasons, under the early Empire, he has since influenced all Latin prose. The Christian Fathers Ambrose, Jerome, and Augustine imitated his style. Revived by the Renaissance humanists and by them transmitted to every Western language, that style is nowhere more alive than in modern papal encyclicals. Its influence on successive centuries of English prose is especially evident in the prose of Burke and Gibbon, Macaulay and Daniel Webster, and in our own time Winston Churchill.

Cicero's literary fame rests chiefly on fifty-eight speeches written for delivery before the Senate, the Assembly, or the courts. Most famous are his defense of Archias, and his attacks on Verres, Catiline, and Antony (the latter called *Philippics*). Worth noting too are his critical works on oratorical technique, which illumine the history of Roman eloquence, and long guided Western literary criticism. His letters are delightful. Addressed to family, friends, or the politically and socially great, these letters—931 remain—constitute our best history of Ciceronian society and politics, not least because of their spontaneous and intimate tone, seldom formalized by thought of publication. They reveal the man's generosity, his domestic relations, his ideals, his political motives, his vacillations and compromises, his triumphs, frustrations, and failures.

In his maturity, when the first triumvirate eclipsed him politically, he found outlet for his energies in philosophical writing. Modestly, he claimed no originality, only adaptation from the Greeks. This understatement has led unwary historians of philosophy to ignore him, except for his contribution to philosophical vocabulary. Premier representative of the Roman or the Western utilitarian mind, Cicero had an instinct for freeing Greek thought from its seeming remoteness and presenting its essence clearly to the ordinary man. His active participation in politics and the sense of responsibility he developed from holding office (Greek philosophers never had that experience) enabled Cicero to transmute Greek abstraction into concrete cases immediately relevant to his generation, especially in *The Republic* and *The Laws,* where he recast Plato's ideal commonwealth into a Roman political reality which, as we saw, perhaps affected the Augustan principate.

Cicero has left his mark on Western political thought. For example, his thesis that the state is valid and legitimate only if it insures justice was incorporated by St. Augustine into the Christian concept of government and followed by enlightened eighteenth-century political thinkers. The philosophy of the Declaration of Independence rests wholly on that proposition. Cicero's ideal of high moral standards in government and international relations may well serve as a guide today.

His ideas on the individual's duties towards society have come into the

Christian heritage. Sketched in three books he wrote as guidance for his son, they range widely, but are based, like the theory of Augustus' principate, on the cardinal virtues of wisdom, justice, courage, and temperance. In Book One, for instance, Cicero defines man's final good, the search for truth; stresses man's duty to conduct himself according to rules of order, decency, and propriety of word and deed; condemns inordinate ambition for empire, honors, and glory; reminds us that repentance is not enough; exhorts us to combine good faith with our peacemaking; tells us that war is no excuse for injustice, cruelty, or rashness; comments on the judge's duty to punish the guilty, but to spare the many, and on the duty of *decorum*, which, for example, forbids obscene jesting but allows that which is urbane. The whole is illumined by examples chosen from Roman history. If active politicians had heeded this book, the Republic need never have fallen.

So timeless were Cicero's ideas on the moral duties of man that four centuries later St. Ambrose coupled them with Christ and the Apostles' teachings as a code of conduct for churchmen and laymen. St. Ambrose could evaluate Cicero's high standards; he too was a high Roman official before he became Bishop of Mediolanum (Milan). The very title of his book, *De Officiis Ministrorum*, is copied from Cicero.

Mastery of style and experience before audiences helped to make Cicero the earliest European popularizer of philosophy and to extend his influence over the thought of succeeding generations. Take the case of humanism. Conceived by the Greeks, principally Socrates and Plato, as an emphasis on self-realization through reason, humanism became a living force in Western history only when Cicero elaborated it. He fecundated even science. Copernicus himself related that it was from reading Cicero that he evolved the theory of the revolutions of the earth. Perhaps Cicero's greatest gift to Western man in search of good government are his ideals of liberty (under conservative law) and humanity, of attachment to constitutional processes, and of decency and moderation in politics.

In contrast to Cicero, who dramatized himself in his work, Caesar (*b.* 102 B.C.), whose life was perhaps the greatest drama in Western European history, eschewed all drama in his writings. His literary fame rests on his *Commentaries* on the Gallic and Civil Wars. Their apparent simplicity and directness is the art that conceals art. His style is "Attic" and lean, his artistic perception is sharp, but the true secret of his literary success lies in his quality of mind that got, at a glance, to the heart of a problem—in war, politics, or art. For Caesar anything but the kernel of a question was confusion and waste. The purpose of the *Commentaries* was not a random discussion of political and social issues; they were a terse military account written to justify a commander politically. Both works are masterpieces of understatement. Style, content, and the appearance of detachment combine to make them memorable as documentation and art.

Sallust (86-c. 34 B.C.), a historian of considerable talent, wrote the *War of Catiline* somewhat in Thucydides' spirit and style. He had a keen eye for the social ills that produce a Catiline. In him objectivity failed before admiration for Caesar, who, he thought, was the sole cure for the Republic's ills. His *Jugurthine War* is again biased, this time toward the Populares. Fragments, including speeches and letters, survive from his *Histories,* which in five books covered the years 78–66 B.C. He was the earliest Roman historian with psychological insight. His archaism, his vivid character sketches, and his Attic terseness give some readers more pleasure than do the works of either Cicero or Caesar.

Practically all the works of Marcus Terentius Varro (116–27 B.C.), Rome's greatest scholar, have been lost. At seventy-eight he had written 490 books; at eighty he published a surviving work on agriculture, important for its treatment of farming after Cato. Especially unfortunate is the loss of two of his historical works: *A Social History of the Roman People* (*De vita populi Romani*), and forty-one books on *Civil and Religious Aspects of Roman Civilization* (*Antiquitates rerum humanarum et divinarum*). Although as a Roman he held that religious institutions were a creation of the state, he believed that the Romans' Jupiter and the Jews' Jehovah were the same god, of whom all other gods were but aspects. Like the Hebrew prophets, he opposed image-worship and sacrifices, as detracting from the purity of religion. He hated superstition for its effect on the state religion. A pietist and a patriot, he feared that religious indifference would bring on the twilight of the gods, a fear shared by Vergil, Horace, and the Emperor Augustus. Like Lucretius he believed in progress. His place in literary history is fixed by his *Menippean Satires* (in 150 books). Though inspired by Menippus, a third-century Cynic philosopher, the satires are original in spirit and subject matter. They are humorous essays, part prose, part verse, lampooning contemporary mores, especially luxury and ostentation. Later Romans and Christian writers were awestruck at Varro's encyclopedic mind. Moderns find in his few surviving works a mine of information ranging from the nature of God to the market price of fresh eggs and flowers. A partisan of Pompey, forgiven by Caesar, outlawed by Antony, he died, an epitome of his age, in the year in which Octavian first called himself Augustus.

Part V/THE ROMAN EMPIRE

Chapter 46/AUGUSTUS:

THE CONSTITUTION

Underlying Philosophy

When the victorious Octavian entered Alexandria after Actium, he refused to see the city's greatest tourist attraction, the tomb of Alexander the Great. His alleged reason is illuminating: Alexander was not truly great, for greatness consists not in conquering countries, but in rehabilitating them. Rehabilitating the Roman empire, reconstructing society, government, the economy, religion, and morals was to be Octavian's special gift to civilization.

He founded his new structure on a pragmatic political settlement. He had no intention of abdicating his supreme authority. Ambition and duty combined to persuade him of his own indispensability. Had he stepped down, citizens and provincials alike would have faced renewed and intolerable chaos. Not retirement, then, was the question, but how much authority he wanted to retain. His innate conservatism and the lessons of Sulla and Caesar's regimes warned him against dictatorship. Instead he must appear to strike a balance, between himself and the Senate, between revolution and tradition.

The Senate was willing to compromise. It was no longer the reactionary body of 60 or 50 B.C. Many of the old guard had fallen in the civil wars or the Second Triumvirate's purges; many new men, less reactionary, had been given seats by Caesar and his successors; establishment of a New Order did not appear difficult.

Octavian himself wrote in his *Res Gestae* that he restored constitutional government to the Senate and the Roman People. The question is in what form. The current view is that under the guise of a dyarchy or joint rule of himself and the Senate, Augustus fashioned, amid popular enthusiasm and extremely modified transports from the Senate, a new monarchical form of government, perfectly constitutional, but not the old Republic.

The people were the more willing, and the Senate less reluctant to accept a monarch because the spirit of unity with which Italy had fought Cleopatra still survived. After Actium peace was the desideratum; who but Octavian could assure it? Propaganda operated, too: had not Octavian saved the nation from the despotism of an Egyptian queen and the Roman traitor she had ensnared? From Octavian, despotism was not to be feared: the spirit of conciliation was inbred in him; he would relinquish his war powers as soon as he safely could. Propaganda spoke too in marble and on coinage: an arch was erected in his honor in 30 B.C. "for having saved constitutional government"; a coin issue of 28 B.C. (from an imperial mint in Ephesus) reads "Protector of the Liberty of the Roman People." The people were grateful; the monarch's good intentions were assumed.

The Princeps: Search for an Acceptable Formula

On January 13, 27 B.C., Octavian announced to the Senate his resignation to them and the People of all powers. The Senate refused to accept it and pressed upon him proconsular powers for ten years in Spain, Gaul, and Syria. Elsewhere in the provinces, proconsuls responsible to the Senate were to govern as before, and Senate, People, and magistrates were to carry on as in the past, with "constitutional" government theoretically restored. In Rome and Italy the basis for Octavian's authority was to be the consulship, which he held every year until 23 B.C. Thereafter he was to seek his power from another source.

Octavian's new proconsular powers were the sort of commission traditional in the last two centuries of the Republic. Since these were the provinces whose peoples needed watching and where most of the legions were accordingly stationed, this commission showed that the Senate had no objection to his continuing as sole head of the army.

Octavian's proconsular *imperium* was in fact a grim necessity. If the supreme command was to remain under one head, it was unthinkable to take it away from Octavian to give it to another. Every sensible man shuddered at the alternative of splitting the office between two or more individuals. World catastrophe since Marius and Sulla was a warning against that. The historian Tacitus hated Octavian but saw the point: "after the conflict at Actium . . . it became essential to peace that all power should be concentrated in the hands of only one man."

Octavian needed the Senate: his powers depended upon it; the legitimacy of his regime required the support of solid men of property in it. Therefore to the Senate also proconsular powers were reserved. While provinces in need of defense went to Octavian as head of the army, the more civilized and peaceful ones were left in the Senate's hands. With Pompey's absentee rule in Spain (55–48 B.C.) as precedent, Octavian ruled his provinces through legates chosen by and responsible to him personally. But the Senate was sovereign over its own provinces, which it continued to administer, as in Republican times, through governors chosen by and responsible to itself though often nominated by Octavian-Augustus. Since their mandates were peaceful (for example, Sicily, Africa, Asia), Octavian did not think it necessary to give the senatorial provinces an army, only a militia to keep law and order; otherwise the governors kept the old Republican role of executives, legislators, and judges.

The point of this division of powers is obvious. The victor of Philippi and Actium knew that strength based on an army was incomplete without the support of the Senate, the moral force of legitimacy. The Senate, not he, was the living embodiment of the basic Roman moral and political forces, constitutionalism and the *mos maiorum,* the ways of their fathers. Octavian knew he must control these forces; he was willing to give them a *quid pro quo.*

These forces were certainly eating out of his hand when (January 16, 27 B.C.) the Senate granted him a new name, AUGUSTUS, by which he has been known ever since. It became at once a dynamic and mystical title, expressing something more than human. Its connotations include the ideas of increasing, innovating, taking the initiative, being revered. Octavian or his advisers chose the title to make manifest that he represented a new idea in government, not Tarquinian tyranny nor Sullan or Caesarian dictatorship, but a benevolent monarchy sprung from the synthesis of revolution and tradition. Men saw in it a good augury, and with it indeed a new historical era began.

Augustus received further tokens of public esteem: a laurel wreath for his house-door, to symbolize his having saved Roman citizens' lives; a golden shield to be hung in the Senate House inscribed with his virtues —the virtues of Cicero's *On Duty*—valor, clemency, justice, piety. Another mark of honor has lived for two millennia: the eighth month, formerly called Sextilis, was renamed *Augustus,* as the seventh had been for Julius.

Augustus, however, preferred the inoffensive and traditional name of

Fig. 46.1. The *Gemma Augustea*. Augustus, heroized, with scepter and *lituus* (augur's crooked staff), is seated on a tribune's chair beside the goddess Roma. Their feet rest on trophies of conquered tribes, with the Roman eagle beside them. Above is Augustus' lucky constellation, Capricorn. A female figure personifying the Empire holds a crown over his head. Behind him are Earth and Ocean. At left, Tiberius, with crown and scepter, steps from his triumphal chariot in which Victory rides. To Tiberius' right is Germanicus. Below, Roman soldiers, in unconscious anticipation of the flag-raising on Iwo Jima, are building a trophy, while their Pannonian prisoners strike despondent attitudes. Note the Roman soldier dragging a woman by the hair. (Vienna, Kunsthistoriches Museum)

princeps, which implied that he was the most prominent man in the state, *princeps civitatis.* The Romans had for centuries looked to their prominent men, their *principes,* to guide them. Cicero had written, perhaps with Pompey in mind, that the old Republican constitution needed an unselfish first citizen to guide it. In 27 B.C., the practical basis of Augustus' rule was his imperium, the theoretical basis was this Ciceronian moral authority, so different from Caesar or Sulla's naked military might.

By the settlement of 27 B.C. Augustus monopolized one consulship, thereby robbing the Republican politicians he wanted to conciliate of one-half of their traditional field of honors. He found a more satisfactory basis for ruling Rome and Italy in the tribunician power. In 36 B.C. he had received the tribune's inviolability, in 30 B.C. the tribune's right to protect citizens' life and liberty. Now, in 23 B.C., he assumed the tribune's remaining functions without actually holding the office; he could summon the Assembly for legislative purposes, initiate bills in the Senate, and veto acts of magistrates, Senate, or tribunes. His regime thus protected from attack, Augustus could safely step down from the consulship (July 1, 23 B.C.).

This resettlement did not affect Augustus' authority in the provinces, which he continued to govern through regular renewal of his proconsular imperium, for five- or ten-year terms. It was last renewed in A.D. 12. But that imperium was now made *maius;* that is, superior to that of any and every provincial governor, even in senatorial provinces.

On the twin bases of the tribunician power and the proconsular imperium, Augustus and his successors built another pillar of power: supreme judicial authority over citizens and provincials. By an extension of tribunician prerogatives his court became the highest appellate tribunal even for provincial citizens. On this ground, probably, the Roman citizen St. Paul stood when he petitioned the Procurator of Judaea for trial in Caesar's (Nero's) court. But he might equally well have appealed to Caesar as proconsul and *ipso facto* chief justice for his provincials. The Apostle who wrote so profoundly on Jewish and on natural law may be assumed to have known his Roman law as well. As citizen and man of learning he would have known that the Imperial legates and procurators, before one of whom he stood, were but agents of the Lord Proconsul on the Palatine.

To fix his hold on the eastern provinces Augustus adopted the Hellenistic concept of the divinity of the living ruler. Under Roman constitutional law, his proconsular imperium, which made him *Imperator* (Greek: *Autocrator*), was enough to extract their obedience and loyalty. But as lawful heir of the Hellenistic kings, who were gods to their subjects, he let himself be worshiped as god. Indeed the East, used to ruler worship, revered the Roman Republic, successor to its kings, as the Goddess Roma. Not only that; Pompey as proconsul had been hailed as Savior *(Soter)*, Caesar as God *(Theos)*. The East granted these titles also to Augustus as bringer of the divine gifts of good government, prosperity, and peace.

In the western provinces altars and temples were built and invocations addressed to *Roma et Augustus,* especially in the provincial capitals.

In Italy, the land of citizens, and in Rome itself, Augustus was not a god but the Princeps. But even here, gratitude was expressed in a form of religious recognition, the worship of his Genius or Numen, as it were, his Good Angel. Only after his death did the Senate declare him a god.

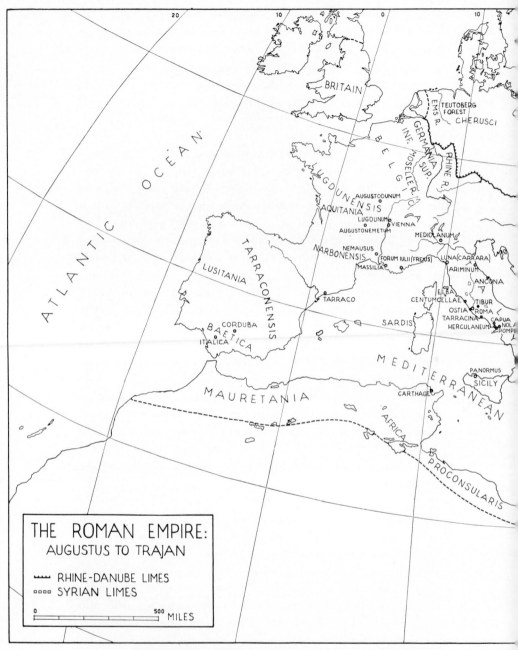

Fig. 46a. Map of the Roman Empire: Augustus to Trajan.

As the years went on Augustus received other significant privileges: the consular insignia and a chair between the consuls as if he were their superior; the right to assemble the Senate; and priority for his motions therein. These prerogatives, plus the tribunician initiative and veto centered legislative powers within less than 100 years in the emperor.

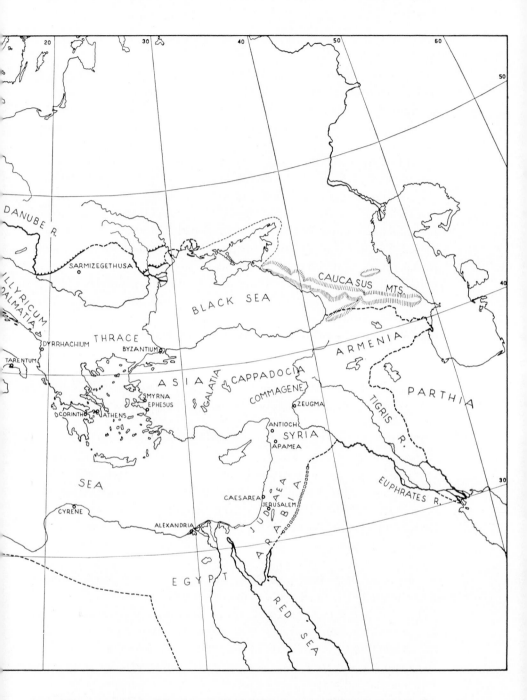

Republican Rome had had no police, fire, or water departments. Early Rome had not needed them; when the need arose the Senate and magistrates had larger matters to preoccupy them. Now the Senate appealed to Augustus' organizing genius and staff of experts to set up and supervise these services. He set up a pratetorian guard and a corps of *vigiles* (firemen) and appointed Agrippa a water-commissioner with a trained staff of 240 slaves.

Augustus acquired also a wide range of censorial powers aimed at reviving the state religion, purifying morals, rebuilding temples, and strengthening the family—in a word, legislating morality. This under the Republic had been the censor's business, but Augustus resolutely refused to hold that office himself, although it was pressed upon him. Presumably he wished to avoid the imputation of dragooning the Senate. His other powers sufficed to get his sumptuary legislation passed, and two of his partisans were appointed censors in 22 B.C.

Revision of the Senate was Augustus' most ticklish problem. Revolution and civil war had altered its composition and made it unwieldy. Caesar had added many senators, the Second Triumvirate more, not always with the good of the commonwealth in mind. Augustus ultimately reduced it to 600 members, filling it with his own partisans, often rich middle-of-the-road Conservatives from the colonies and municipalities of Italy. The Senate had always been oligarchic. Augustus made it an oligarchy of "new men" broadly representative of Rome and Italy, possessed of a property qualification of a million sesterces. This was the core of the comprehensive, traditional, and conservative Augustan group that replaced the old bankrupt aristocratic ruling class. This was the group that was to vote his projected moral reforms into law. It was more like a propaganda machine or a rubber stamp than a sovereign body.

Lepidus' death (12 B.C.) left the office of Pontifex Maximus vacant. Although Augustus had long ago refused to expel Lepidus and take over this priesthood, he was now the logical successor. All Italy agreed. From every corner of Italy, from towns, hamlets, and farms, scores of thousands of citizens flocked to Rome to cast their vote in a spontaneous endorsement of their ruler. Of course the Supreme Pontiff's office had more than sentimental value: its ramifications in appointments, in law, and in religious and civil matters gave its holder a formidable array of powers. Augustus was thus able to join spiritual and temporal powers to an extent unequaled in medieval or modern times.

The last honor came in 2 B.C., when Augustus was over sixty. As first in war, he had long been *imperator;* as first in peace, *princeps;* now he was saluted first in the hearts of his countrymen, *pater patriae*. He had come a long way from the conspiratorial days of four decades past. Propaganda had helped, but peace and reconstruction had helped more. That liberty did not exist under Augustus' principate was beside the point to the distinguished ex-Republican and veteran of Philippi, won over by the Augustan program, who proposed the *pater patriae* motion in the Senate. This conversion was living proof that Augustus had in fact turned civil discord into harmony. It might also justify the arrogance of the brash young man who had once refused to honor a conqueror because he did not know how to reorder a state.

The Senate

A study of the Senate shows clearly that Augustus took the lion's share in the division of power, since he controlled the army. But that control was what guaranteed stable government, the century-long object of Rome's longing. Opportunist that he was, he always limited the powers he accepted to what he needed at the time. A traditionalist, he was motivated in part by the old Polybian ideal of balanced government, though he never forgot the propaganda value of the myth of his glory.

His tact and his partisans in the Senate facilitated relations with that body. Opposition by and large was stilled. The sturdy freedom of speech of an Asinius Pollio was the exception that proved the rule. Such personal enemies as the Princeps had, held their peace, realizing the folly of keeping discord alive.

Augustus kept the Senate cooperative by depriving no senator of his traditional honors, rights, and offices. Senators still, as they had for centuries, filled magistracies, priesthoods, military commissions, and administrative boards. Above all they still filled the governorships which, as in Republican times, crowned a public career. But now the Princeps made policy and took responsibility. His legates, and the legionary commanders as well, were merely his lieutenants.

While individual senators lost none of their ancient honors, the Senate collectively both lost and gained. It lost heavily in administrative power, but gained elsewhere.

Chiefly the Senate gained an empty and harmless prestige, because the Princeps needed it as a legislative body. Augustus and his successors wanted their decisions, rubber-stamped by the Senate, regarded as binding law, not as mere advice to the magistrates as in Republican times. They needed the highest moral authority of tradition for the things they wanted done. Accordingly they funneled their administrative and policy proposals into the Senate House. The decadent Popular Assembly was no alternative: the Roman masses had become a rabble with only the slightest ties to the Italian electorate; the reconstituted Senate, it was argued, was a more genuine and enlightened representative of the national will. So the Princeps allowed legislative authority, under him, to reside in it. This authority extended over public and private law, administration, religion and morals, Italian and provincial affairs. Only in foreign relations did the Princeps fail to go through the form of consulting the Senate.

Second, the Senate became a high court of justice. Individual senators had acted as jurors under the Republic, but the Senate itself had never been a court of law. As a high court of justice it alone now had the right to try its own members for treason, sacrilege, fraud, adultery, or minor offenses. It therefore tried governors accused of maladministration, since, as we have seen, all governors, except of Egypt, were senators. It tried generals and legates if they abused their trust or otherwise ran foul of the law. It acted also as a supreme court on appeal from the governor's court of a senatorial province. Lastly it had jurisdiction over the princes and princesses of the reigning family and the women of the senatorial order. Some of Tacitus' most fascinating pages describe trials of aristocratic ladies by their senatorial relatives, friends, and enemies.

Third, the Senate helped to select an imperial successor. To be sure, the reigning emperor named the successor, and the praetorian guard, quartered just outside the pomerium, acclaimed him, sometimes selecting their own candidates. In any case the nominee petitioned the Fathers to recognize him as princeps. Legally and constitutionally, the Senate's consent was election, although in effect the Fathers' hands were tied, and their so-called election merely a decorous confirmation.

Fourth, after Caesar and Augustus had been posthumously deified, every emperor was anxious for like honor. The Senate alone had the constitutional power to canonize him.

Whether the emperor or his contemporaries really believed in the Senate's god-making powers is beside the point, which is that after such formal declaration he was god in law, eternally living, so that his judgments, laws, appointments, and all his public acts were assumed to be living too, still in force unless specifically revoked. Therefore every emperor, to assure the permanence of his acts, hoped to be deified. Other interested parties included his family and friends, his appointees, and every person or group whom he had benefited: enfranchised provincials, army and navy veterans, provinces, cities, villages, families, corporations, or sects.

The Senate's power to bestow or refuse deification may have exerted some restraint on the average princeps. To be deified he had to be either friendly to the Fathers or not particularly obnoxious. Augustus was the best example. The Senate might damn the memory of hated emperors—Nero, Domitian, Commodus—a fearsome fate, since it nullified an emperor's acts. Some emperors, like Tiberius and Gaius, were neither deified nor damned.

The Senate: Qualifications for Membership

The Imperial Senate, like the Sullan, admitted annually as life members all twenty quaestors. In addition the princeps admitted other men by special appointment. Though some emperors exercised these rights capriciously, evidence is rare of their packing the Senate with friends, or of their excluding enemies. Beginning with Claudius, they used this prerogative to give representation to men, classes, and districts that would never have received it under the Republic. Admitting these new elements profited the Emperor by diluting antagonistic old-guard elements. Nevertheless it was a liberal step, embodying a broader concept of political justice.

A senator had to be wealthy. He had expensive social obligations: a town house, at least one villa, entertainment of his fellow-senators, support of clients. As a peer of the princeps, he could scarcely afford to do less. Hence the property qualification of 1,000,000 sesterces ($50,000). Though custom and law still forbade a senator to engage in trade, industry, or banking, he could be a lawyer, for eloquence, although no longer concerned with politics, was still in high repute. A learned, literary or legally talented senator commanded respect.

Whereas administrative experience was required only theoretically under the Republic, Augustus insisted on it for candidates for quaestor. He ordained an apprenticeship of at least one year as legionary cavalry officer; then service as a junior magistrate—for example, as overseer of the street-cleaning department, supervisor of police, mint-manager, or judge of the manumissions court. Experience at a higher level began with the quaestorship, increased as a man advanced to aedile, praetor, or consul, and was further enriched with appointment as a legionary commander, city prefect, or member of the water, grain, or road commission.

Ideally, besides experience and wealth, moral character was needed. Not that every senator was a model of political or personal honesty; but rather that, in the absence of scandal, he was presumed to be a gentleman. We know much about senators who disgraced themselves, for scandal makes news. But for every scapegrace or pervert in Tacitus' or Suetonius' pages, there were ten whose lives and ideals would have satisfied a Cato.

So senatorial prestige was still high. Membership was as coveted as under the free Republic, and for the same reasons: desire for public service, power, honor, a position not below one's ancestors, and, among *novi homines,* the ambition to attain nobility for themselves and their posterity.

The princeps had enormous influence with the members, and not alone those whom he had elevated. Since he controlled a well-organized machine, his candidates had an advantage at the polls. Actually he inherited the consul's right to cancel a candidate simply by failing to enter his name in the list. He usually endorsed two candidates for quaestor and occasionally one running for a higher magistracy. Caesar's candidates were usually sure of election, especially after a law of A.D. 5 set up an ingenious electoral machinery which, without apparently dictating to the comitia, invited it to take its lead from ten centuries mainly drawn from the class which Augustus had wanted elected to curule offices. Lastly he had a vast patronage to dispense. Therefore a senator who had benefited or hoped to benefit from his endorsement would cultivate his friendship, or at least not oppose his views.

The very rules of procedure stacked the cards in the princeps' favor. One consul presented a bill; the other was the first to discuss it. Both were the voice of the princeps, and he himself was usually present to shed further light if needed. Indeed as dean of the Senate (*Princeps Senatus*) he was consulted first after the consuls. But he did not need to depend on the consuls; he had been given the right to initiate motions as an automatic first order of business. If he could not attend, any motion of his in writing received automatic priority. Finally, since apparently he never used his tribunician veto, the inference is warranted that he had the Senate in his pocket.

The Senate developed ways of restraining the princeps. If he was sole master of the army, the actual commanders were senators, and usually the legions' loyalty depended on their generals. Every emperor, even Augustus, constantly feared rebellions headed by generals.

Though the princeps ruled the most important provinces, the legates were senators, so that imperial authority over a province depended on the legate's loyalty.

In dispensing patronage a senator got the juiciest plums. The princeps would of course favor his personal friends in the Senate, but they in turn had friends among the opposition (as the opposition grew after Augustus), friends whom no imperial favor could induce them to abandon. In general, senators after Augustus were senators first, and the emperor's men next. Senatorial solidarity grew again after the first princeps died. Even a new man, owing his elevation to the emperor, aspired to recognition by the older aristocracy despite that group's dislike of creatures of the emperor.

The Senate came to assert its legislative independence fearlessly, as when it voted unanimously against a measure advocated by the Emperor Tiberius. Measures originated in a Privy Council, consisting entirely of senators, whose origins went back to 27 B.C. and which continued through Tiberius' reign: the two consuls, one from each board of magistrates, and fifteen senators chosen by lot, all changing semiannually. Later, princes of the imperial family were admitted, and occasionally experts for consultation. We shall never know how many imperial proposals died in this committee, or how many were amended to make them acceptable to a majority in the House. The point is that the princeps' ideas came in practice to be reshaped by the senatorial mentality, which could assert itself in the Privy Council because the lot and the rotation feature were as likely as not to produce opposition senators.

The princeps relied on another council, recruited from his personal friends, and hence called *amici Caesaris*. Some were knights, but most (less than half under Augustus, three to two under Tiberius, four to one under Gaius and Claudius) were senators. They were in almost constant attendance, as advisers, even when the princeps traveled.

The princeps as judge was assisted by senatorial jurymen. No doubt a despotic ruler could influence them, but ordinarily they reviewed the facts and interpreted the law impartially and honorably as Roman officials, despite abuses and lapses, usually did.

Lastly, the princeps himself was a member of the senatorial nobility. Except for Vespasian, the father of an emperor had been senator, his mother a senator's daughter, his childhood playmates, his schoolmates, the friends of his youth all of senatorial families. The men who shared his formative years were almost all of them senators. His first step in the public career was watched and influenced by senatorial superiors. He married into a senatorial family. After he was raised to the throne he sought his pleasures among men and women of the senatorial order. He invited them frequently to dinner, took them with him on his travels, and was wined and dined by them more often than was good for either his health or theirs. (The history of the Julio-Claudian emperors is proof of the strong influence which wives, relatives, in-laws, or friends wielded or tried to wield.) Lastly, senators surrounded him as priests in religious services, as counselors in inspections of the provinces, as strategists in war. Since imperial policies are not necessarily made in legislative halls or throne rooms, it was in all these ways, after Augustus, that senatorial influence made itself felt.

Two observations are now in order. The form of government founded by Augustus and perfected by his successors was not imported from the Hellenistic East, but sprang wholly from the old Republican principle that a magistrate was simultaneously executive, legislator, and judge. No amount of administrative detail borrowed from the East in the Roman Empire could affect retroactively the early emperors' purely Roman theory and practice.

The second observation concerns the view that Augustus established a military despotism in disguise. This thesis does not commend itself to American students who know that, although their president has exclusive control of the army, the American government is no military despotism. The power of Augustus and his successors increased and multiplied not because they controlled the army, but because they were efficient and enlightened. Such an executive, governing through a centralized administrative machinery, could be dynamic quite apart from the fact that he also controlled the legions. Augustus was a constitutional monarch, and after his death constitutional elements other than the monarch came to the fore. He himself aimed at a balance of classes and ethnic groups, with preponderance for Roman tradition and Italian men. He was the prince of peace, the fosterer of empire, the promulgator of the myth of his own glory. Rome and the Empire owed him much; they did not owe him freedom, for he gave them none.

Chapter 47/AUGUSTUS: SOCIAL CLASSES AND IMPERIAL ADMINISTRATION

The Equestrian Order

Augustus' government made room for the two citizen classes long hostile to the Senate, the knights and the proletariat. He aimed to canalize their ambitions and stabilize the state by giving them government functions. With senators, knights, and proletariat serving the state, each according to capacity and rank, he built up a uniquely efficient public administration. Social advancement from the lower ranks furthered his vision of a progressive society renewing itself from below.

Under the Augustan principate the knights' old antagonism toward the Senate virtually disappeared. The Augustan peace guaranteed their investments and fattened their profits. Augustus enlarged and revitalized their order but, wiser than Gaius Gracchus, gave them only those government posts for which they were peculiarly fitted or in which they would collide least with senatorial interests.

But who were the knights in the first two centuries of the Empire? Rome, Italy, and the provinces, expecially in the West, had numerous upper-middle class citizens, landowners or businessmen, worth at least 400,000 sesterces ($20,000 uninflated). All these were eligible for official registration as knights. On reaching military age, a young man aspiring to knighthood was given a horse by the state and, in addition, the traditional privilege of wearing the gold ring and the toga with the narrow purple band. Once a year these ambitious cadets, some five thousand strong, rode their horses before the emperor. Through a special bureau Augustus and his successors kept a discreet eye on them and expelled the unworthy from the order. A young prince of the imperial family (*princeps iuventutis*) served as their patron.

The high *bourgeoisie* had no monopoly on the honors of knighthood. Lower-middle class persons might rise by merit to equestrian status—likewise proletarians who had served as first centurions; distinguished freedmen like Augustus' court physician Antonius Musa; as the century advanced, free businessmen of servile ancestry, and, with increasing liberality, Romanized provincial aristocrats. As with the Senate, membership in the equestrian order was hereditary.

Even sons of senatorial families were included in the equestrian order. Usually a senator's son remained a knight until the quaestorship gave him a Senate seat. If he never attained a magistracy he remained in the equestrian order for life.

Such was then the class which Augustus called into government service. Besides strengthening the imperial administration with its talent and business experience, it also served the emperors as a political counterweight to the Senate. Actually, the emperor had to use the knights as civil servants, since senators, being his peers, would not accept subservient posts, and slaves or freedmen, though for lack of a civil service they had been used by Republican magistrates for administrative work, seemed inappropriate for a reformed imperial administration. Augustus used knights usually as private secretaries, often employing freeborn proletarian citizens in the numerous departmental posts of the Imperial Civil Service. But as a rule he placed a knight in charge, only exceptionally a freedman.

Equestrian posts parallelled the senatorial *cursus honorum*. At the bottom were junior officer posts: first, in an auxiliary or noncitizen company (*praefectus cohortis*); next, in a legionary cohort (*tribunus militum*); last, in a cavalry squadron (*praefectus alae*). Although this experience qualified him for the civil service, the young knight might continue a while longer in a military or semi-military job. In Rome, he might command in succession an urban cohort, a fire brigade, and a praetorian cohort. In the provinces, he might fill a technical assignment, commanding legionary engineers or other technicians.

The civil service offered the knight three categories of procuratorships: managerial, financial, and quasi-magisterial. As managerial procurator he might administer the emperor's personal estates, state-owned mines, forests, and pastures, crown lands, or other property. A manager might expect promotion to a financial procuratorship as collector of rents from state properties, customs at ports of entry, tithes in almost every province, or poll, sales, manumission, or inheritance taxes. At the top stood the quasi-magisterial procurators, minor governors of isolated districts such as an Alpine canton, or a small country like Judaea or Noricum (Austria).

Exceptionally able procurators were promoted to a great prefecture. Augustus arranged these prefectures too, in a hierarchy starting with the fire prefecture in Rome. The fire department had long been a problem. As finally reorganized (A.D. 6), it was managed by an equestrian prefect (*praefectus vigilum*), commanding seven cohorts of 1000 men each, later increased to 1200, a pattern preserved for centuries. For religious, eleemosynary, and other administrative purposes the city was divided into fourteen districts, with one fire cohort for each two districts. The firemen (vigiles) were freedmen who, having a stake in property, would, Augustus apparently thought, make a more reliable force. A quasi-military force, they served also as night patrol, and were commanded by military tribunes.

More important was the prefect of the grain supply. When Augustus took over the service developed by the Republic, he put in charge an experienced administrator who was to assure that wheat and other provisions arrived on schedule. The prefect's task involved sending agents to the provinces to encourage production, collect wheat, barley, and other commodities due as tithes, and purchase wholesale lots at the farm or on the open market. It involved also transportation from the farm to a nearby provincial port, hence to Italy where adequate wharf facilities were installed or enlarged in Puteoli, about a hundred miles from Rome, and later at Ostia at the Tiber mouth. The prefect also had charge of building and maintaining warehouses in both places, supervising the organization of stevedores, and chartering fleets of wagons and river craft to freight the cargoes to Rome. Here again other docks and warehouses were erected, stevedore gangs organized, markets built, and bakeries regulated. About the middle of the first century A.D. the prefect of the grain supply took over from senatorial officials the distribution of grain to some 200,000 recipients. Last but not least, he regulated prices and supervised grain dealers, ever ready to form pools or monopolies to corner the market.

Still higher in equestrian hierarchy stood the prefect of Egypt. No other province produced more revenue. Of wheat alone, it sent every year 5,000,000 bushels, enough to feed the City for four months. The Roman conquest changed little in Egypt. The gods, the cult, the priests, the public administration, the culture of native villages and Greek cities remained the same as under the Ptolemies. The only difference was that Augustus was now king. He ruled the land of the pharaohs from his modest house on the Palatine, the same hill from which Cleopatra had allegedly planned to rule the world. Only in Egypt, among the great provinces, did Augustus place a nonsenatorial governor. A senatorial viceroy might easily turn rebel, counting on senatorial support and rich Egyptian resources. He could starve Rome by stopping wheat shipments. Augustus therefore placed a knight in charge. To keep Egyptian agriculture and industry efficient; to maintain order in Alexandria, the Empire's most turbulent city, where Greeks, Jews, and Levantines living at close quarters made for an explosive situation; and to keep up appearances among a people accustomed to Ptolemaic splendor would challenge even the best administration. Three full legions were needed to keep order throughout the land, and—a striking anomaly!—the viceroy, though but a knight, was in command. Except for the name and the trappings, he was for the natives a king, for the Romans a true proconsul.

The highest equestrian officer was the prefect of the praetorian guard. A development of the Republican praetor or general's special bodyguard, the imperial praetorian guard was more than the princeps' bodyguard; it was a police force kept discreetly out of sight. Of its nine 1000-man cohorts, only three, until Tiberius' time, were stationed near Rome; the rest were scattered all over Italy. Since a senatorial commander winning their allegiance might well unseat the emperor, Augustus placed a pair of knights in charge; the dual command both honored Roman tradition and reduced temptation to disloyalty. But this did not remain the rule with every princeps. Repeatedly the praetorian prefect figured as the emperor's right-hand man; one, Sejanus, was actually acting emperor during Tiberius' residence at Capri.

Thus Augustus' government rested on two pillars, the Senate, which, besides legislating with him or for him, supplied the high executive personnel, and the equestrian order in charge of the civil service. Starting from different origins, the senatorial and the equestrian orders formed two parallel nobilities, each reaching to the imperial throne. Although senators could openly in the Curia or subtly in the drawing-room influence the princeps, dilute or sabotage his policies, or damn his memory, he was still their master. Frustrated, they sometimes dreamed of revolution and a restored Republic.

But the equestrian civil service was an Imperial creation. It lived in the present, loyal to the emperor who provided careers and honors. Inferior to the Senate in prestige, it had nevertheless certain advantages. It was more representative of the whole people from which it was constantly renewed. It was not restricted to Italy, but spread over the whole Empire. Imperial unity and peace from Augustus to Commodus resulted largely from the cohesion of knights: soldiers, freedmen, businessmen, miscellaneous career men—all united in serving and supporting the principate.

The Proletariat

Augustus made a humble place in the government for the poorer citizens also. Continuing the Republican practice of distributing free grain in the capital was his least constructive measure on their behalf. Such relief had become a political necessity. The dole was not limited to the unemployed, and the Roman proletariat were not all paupers, nor all slaves, freedmen, or foreigners, though aliens equaled or out-numbered natives from 170 B.C. on. Many citizens entitled to free grain were part-time laborers, but thousands of other citizens earned their living and were not on the dole. Augustus and his successors sought more positive methods of helping both these classes and the out-and-out beggars. Public works helped some; public services helped others.

Public service was more attractive to the proletariat of town and farm. Closer to the soil and to municipal business enterprises, the Italian proletariat was stronger physically and morally than the Roman. Besides, an Italian pauper's hope for free food if he went to Rome was slim, since the number or recipients of the dole there was frozen at about 200,000. The Italian and provincial proletariat, besides, was accustomed to hard work and had a long tradition of enrollment in the legions. Therefore it took to public service more readily than did the urban poor.

The legions absorbed the largest number of citizens seeking public employment—over 100,000 from both the proletariat and the least prosperous of the middle class. The rewards were attractive: a thrifty legionary could save 25 to 30 percent of his salary. The government encouraged saving, attaching a savings bank to each legion and seeing to it that each man did actually save, so that a careful private could salt away 6000 or 7000 sesterces during his twenty years' service. And since he received 12,000 sesterces bonus on discharge, he could invest or buy a house, besides putting a little sum aside for a rainy day. In any case, after discharge, but not before, he might marry and raise a family on a higher than average standard of living.

Relatively few Italian veterans retired to their native communities; still fewer bought farms in Italy. Many went to the provinces, where Imperial policy settled them in colonies. In groups or associated with other Italian immigrants, they could acquire homesteads, build businesses, or create well-to-do communities.

But usually the veteran preferred to return individually to his old army station, where he had hundreds of friends both military and civilian, and a fair idea how he could make a living. He might marry a native woman, open a tavern or an army store, ply some trade, or become a money-lender or farmer. This veteran group generally prospered: most land-owners, manufacturers, money-lenders, and merchants in the Western provinces during the first two centuries were their descendants.

We do not know how many veterans went into central or local government service, nor can we distinguish among freemen, freedmen, and slaves in those services. But veterans were probably given preference in municipal employment. The chances for municipal employment were good, for most towns had a constabulary, a water department, a courthouse, a board of public works, and sundry offices for licensing trades, supervising markets, registering deeds, and administering social welfare.

Ex-legionaries had multiple employment opportunities in the many branches of the Imperial Civil Service. There were first the treasuries: a General Imperial Treasury, the Fiscus, in Rome; a General Military Treasury which received the sales tax and other funds earmarked for the army. Apparently each army division had also a separate treasury, as did each senatorial and Imperial province. Thousands were employed in these treasuries as assessors, collectors, accountants, bookkeepers, secretaries, stenographers, and clerks. While knights occupied the responsible posts, the lower staff, when not slaves or freedmen, came from the lower middle class or were competent proletarians, preferably ex-soldiers. There were jobs also on the emperor's private estates, the public domain, and the crown lands; in the mint, the highway department, the postal service, the fleet and Egypt. In Rome one might work in the imperial household, the libraries, or the organization of games. The Senate's own civil service in Rome, Italy, and the provinces offered no such large opportunities as its Imperial counterpart, but it too gave employment to veterans.

Employment of mere numbers is perhaps less significant than the recognition of talent. Augustus' civil service favored deserving men regardless of class. For instance, towards the end of his reign, centurions were no longer chosen from among young knights, but from the legionary ranks. By A.D. 60 this had become a fixed practice. There were sixty centurions to a legion, 1500 in all. Promotion was a prize indeed, since a centurion's salary was 3750 denarii, sixteen times a private's. The social advantage was fully as important, especially since the emperors used centurions to rejuvenate the equestrian nobility.

Inscriptions enable us to follow the career of a poor but talented commoner. He enters the legions as private and is promoted to centurion. On discharge he is enrolled almost automatically as knight, thereby becoming member of the lesser nobility and eligible for the procuratorial posts outlined in the last section. He may attain even higher honors, and if he retires to a municipal town, he is sure to become a member of the local government and aristocracy. For a concrete example, C. Baebius Atticus, an obscure citizen from a little town in Northeast Italy, becomes head centurion (*primus pilus*) of his legion, with a tidy salary of 15,000 denarii ($3000 uninflated). He is then made a knight, sent as Imperial commissioner, first, to a Danubian province, then to the Maritime Alps. He returns for a while to army life, after which he is appointed governor of Noricum. We last see Baebius as chief magistrate of his native town.

One Helvidius was more significant, as illustrating the advantages of rising to knighthood for a man's children. Helvidius, from the obscure municipality of Cluviae, rose to be head centurion and was almost certainly knighted on retirement. We know nothing more about him; but his son, Helvidius Priscus, taking full advantage of the liberal imperial policy, became Roman senator and praetor in A.D. 70.

The Army

The employment of some 150,000 citizens as soldiers was but one aspect of the complex military establishment. Augustus inherited from the Republic a number of separate armies, usually improvised, handed over to political governor-generals, then if not demobilized, transferred to other political generals. This was of course a consequence of the haphazard growth of provinces administered as unrelated units. Failure to deal intelligently with the twin provincial and military problem, even more than to settle the class struggle, had caused the Republic's fall. Augustus learned the lesson well. He delimited the Rhine, Danube, and Euphrates frontiers, stationing legions along each to keep the peace. This produced three main blocks of provinces. Far more important was the problem of leadership. Following Caesar's example, he appointed to each province able men who, as under the Republic, were both civilian governors and military commanders. Taking another cue from Caesar, he made the provincials partners in Imperial defense.

At Actium no less than 300,000 men surrendered. Wisely, Augustus treated them not as a defeated enemy, but as partners in reconstruction. Reconverting these large military forces, including his own, to useful civilian life was no mean task. Each man, whether Antony's or his own, received on discharge a generous bonus. Some 150,000 of them he settled in about seventy-seven colonies in Gaul, Spain, and Africa, but chiefly in Italy.

The army he kept after Actium was largely a new organization, with three main divisions: legions, praetorians, and *auxilia*. The legions were limited to twenty-eight, each of 6000 citizens, enlisted for twenty years, under strict old-fashioned discipline, to maintain the fighting spirit. Each

Fig. 47.1. A Roman cavalryman. Model, derived from relief on Trajan's column, of horseman and horse armored Parthian fashion in cloth sewn with scales of bone, metal, or leather. (Rome, Museo della Civiltà Romana; J. Felbermeyer photo)

legion contained ten 600-man cohorts. Its spirit and its strength lay in the centurions, six to each cohort, and sixty altogether, men risen from the ranks, courageous and patriotic, kin to our own professional sergeants. Among these it was on the first centurion that the whole legion's morale depended.

Whereas most centurions were middle class, with a good sprinkling of proletarians, the young superior officers (*tribuni militum*) were usually senatorial, sometimes equestrian. But they were not vital cogs of the fighting machine. Enlisting for only a year or two, they were rather apprentices, learning the art of war in camp instead of in a military academy. A senator's son might ultimately be appointed commander of a legion (*legatus legionis*), but only after having been at least praetor. A governor-legate (*legatus Augusti*) of a frontier province held the higher command of both the legions within his provinces and those on its frontier.

The praetorian guard was recruited for a sixteen-year hitch from the highest ranks of the Italian *bourgeoisie.* Each of its nine cohorts was led by an ex-*primipilus,* and the entire force was headed, as we saw, by two equestrian prefects, usually from obscure families. Its presence near the city from the reign of Tiberius on was probably intended to forestall revolution. A smaller corps, the urban cohorts, policed the city under senatorial authority. When an emperor traveled abroad a praetorian honorguard accompanied him. Residence in Italy, relative freedom from hazardous duty, and shorter service made the praetorian guard the most desirable branch of the armed services. But its greatest attraction was its pay, for whereas a legionary received 2½ sesterces a day and 12,000 as retirement bonus, the praetorian received 8 sesterces a day and 20,000 as bonus. Service in all branches was practically always voluntary.

The *auxilia* formed a separate volunteer corps, recruited from provincial non-citizens, and mostly from Imperial provinces. Originally mustered by race or tribe and serving in their home localities, they were generally organized as 500-man foot battalions. A fourth to a third served as cavalry squadrons of the same size. The cavalry units were commanded by Roman knights called prefects, the auxiliary infantry normally by tribunes. We do not know the auxilia's pay-rate or bonus; their most prized reward was Roman citizenship after twenty-five-years' service. The entire corps contained about 150,000 men, roughly the same as the legions.

Foreign Policy

Augustus considered this army of 300,000 (about ½ percent of the entire population) sufficient to defend the Empire from the North Sea to the Euphrates and the Sahara. It proved adequate: in the next two centuries this force was not increased more than 15 percent, and that in time of war. Army size was closely related to Augustus' foreign policy. He tried for a time to bring Germany into the Empire by moving the border to the Elbe and might have succeeded but for the accidental death of the commanding general, his stepson Drusus, in 9 B.C. He failed again when three invading legions under another kinsman, the incompetent Varus, were decimated by the Cherusci near the Teutoberg Forest in A.D. 9. Augustus refrained from avenging this humiliation probably because at the age of 71 he was reluctant to entangle the Empire in a major war. Trouble, he knew, might arise at his death: legionary defections, renewed civil war, or attack from another quarter, Parthia. Therefore, subordinating prestige to safety, he held the frontier on the Rhine. In his younger days he had rejected a suggested invasion of Britain. In western Europe his major aggressive act was to annex northwest Spain—a logical sequel to an unfinished job.

Augustus changed western European frontier lines little, central and eastern ones much. His generals, often highhandedly, reduced to order Italy's Alpine frontier. His stepsons Tiberius and Drusus assured the security of the Po valley by adding to the Empire (15 B.C.) Rhaetia (the central and eastern Alps). Between 16 B.C. and A.D. 9 Augustus, Tiberius, and Germanicus annexed with ease Noricum (east Austria) and with difficulty Pannonia (west Hungary and north Yugoslavia), thus advancing Roman frontiers to the upper Danube. On the lower Danube, farther east, his generals pacified the tribes of Moesia (south Yugoslavia) and Thrace (Bulgaria). Moesia was organized as a province in A.D. 6. These major accretions to Roman territory establish Augustus as Rome's greatest empire-builder; the frontier he fixed was easily defensible, the peoples useful recruits to the Roman army.

Augustus was cautious in dealing with Parthia. Resisting pressure from would-be avengers of Crassus' death and Antony's retreat, he managed to live in peace with Parthia, simply by respecting the Euphrates boundary; threatening invasion when the Parthians seemed to get out of hand; supporting pretenders and rebels within the royal family to keep the monarchy weak and the nation divided. By such means as these he— or rather Tiberius—recovered (A.D. 20) the standards and prisoners still in Parthian hands and contrived to get the king's sons to Rome— whether as guests or hostages is not clear. One or another might always be sent back home as pretender. One was actually set up as king about A.D. 7, on request of a rebellious Parthian faction. Although he was eventually expelled, a precedent was established for Roman interference in Parthia's internal affairs. Finally Augustus chose the Syrian desert as Rome's boundary with Parthia.

The problem was bound up with that of Armenia, which was important as commanding the important China trade routes. More important, if Parthia controlled it, Asia Minor would be open to invasion, and Roman prestige beyond the Caucausus weakened. Romans in Armenia could threaten northern Parthia and offer an invasion route more vital to the powerful trans-Caucasian Sarmatians, the Parthians' hereditary enemies. But since neither Rome nor Parthia wanted the expense of occupying Armenia, each sought to set up a friendly Armenian regime. Although the situation changed twice in Parthia's favor, Augustus usually held the ascendancy. He strengthened Roman power in Asia Minor by making the hitherto independent kingdom of Galatia a province.

To sum up, a profound revolution in foreign relations occurred under Augustus. His legions along the Rhine, the Danube, and the Parthian border were purely defensive force. Except for Egypt, Africa needed little defense: the Sahara was a natural barrier. Augustus thus jettisoned, except along the Danube, the Republican expansionist policy, including Caesar's plans against Parthia. With strength and patience he resisted pressure from patriots and imperialists, including the poet Horace—

though it made the new regime look static, unspectacular, and downright un-Roman. But Augustus was convinced that peace paid off better than war, that enough blood had been shed since Caesar crossed the Rubicon. In his will he even enjoined his successor to let the frontier stay where it was.

Augustus did not wholly disband the fleet that had beaten Sextus Pompey and Antony, for he wanted to keep down piracy and protect the commerce essential to reconstruction. So he kept a standing navy on sea and river patrol. He stationed fleets at Misenum and Ravenna in Italy, along the French Riviera, off the Syrian coast, at Alexandria, in the Black Sea, and on the Danube and Rhine. The oarsmen and marines were slaves according to Republican precedent; the commanding officers were freedmen.

Finances

Civil and military expenses Augustus met less by levying new taxes than by overhauling the old Republican system. First, he periodically took census in the provinces, usually one at a time, to ascertain the number and wealth of the noncitizens. Roman citizens in the provinces were normally covered by the Italian census. By his death in A.D. 14 the Empire's population was probably 70,000,000, 20,000,000 of whom were citizens. Augustus himself spent several years in the provinces, chiefly Spain and Gaul, studying administrative details before beginning a threefold reorganization, political, economic, and fiscal.

As a second reform he restricted the old method of collecting taxes through companies of publicans. He still used publicans to collect indirect taxes, but he supervised them so closely that they never again made those profits nor wielded that influence which had been the bane of the Republic. Direct taxes he now collected through civil service officials.

Of direct taxes the most remunerative and widespread was the land tax (*tributum soli*) which fell only on provincial land, whether owned by provincials or by citizens. The *tributum capitis*, a direct tax on other forms of property, was paid only by a few, and in only two or three provinces. Egypt alone paid a poll tax.

Only two of the indirect taxes fell on citizens and provincials alike; customs dues (always for revenue, not a protective tariff) and a 1-percent sales tax. Since citizens in Italy had paid no land tax since 167 B.C., (though Caesar had planned to change this situation), Augustus assessed upon them some of the burden of running the government, in the form of a 5-percent inheritance tax and a 4-percent tax on the sale of slaves. He continued the old Republican 5-percent tax on the value of every manumitted slave. Rentals from public properties—pastures, forests, mines, and the like—can scarcely be reckoned as taxes. All revenues amounted to little more than 500,000,000 sesterces, while total expenses for the army and navy, the praetorian guard, the City police, the dole, the erection and repair of public buildings and roads, public games, and the civil service did not go much above 485,000,000 sesterces.

Little of these revenues went to the aerarium (the state treasury) in Rome. The largest part was sent to the treasury of the province from which they originated. When, as sometimes happened, the income proved insufficient, Augustus made up the deficit from his own huge private funds. No taxes went to the Emperor. Except in the Imperial provinces, all, including the Italian revenues, were handled by senatorial officers and employees. This aspect of Augustus' regime deserves special attention. Augustus neither made a budget nor established financial machinery of his own to counterweigh the Senate's, even though he knew, as Caesar had demonstrated, that control of the purse assures power. Of course from a loyal or subservient Senate he had nothing to fear, but leaving financial matters to the Senate, however servile, was good administrative policy. The Fiscus, or General Imperial Treasury, did not overshadow the aerarium until after Augustus.

Late in life Augustus established a military treasury, separate from the aerarium, with a gift of 170,000,000 sesterces of his own money augmented by earmarking the inheritance and sales taxes for military purposes. Thus he was always assured of ready cash to pay the 12,000 sesterces bonus to the 7500 legionaries discharged annually. He regarded those two imposts as repayment by citizens and provincials for the benefits of the Pax Augusta.

Considering the Empire's vast resources and the honesty and beneficence of the government, taxes were far from heavy. (Local taxes are here left out of account.) The tax burden was balanced between provincials and citizens. There is no evidence of group or class exploitation by the Augustan government, except in Egypt, where mulcting the taxpayer had been a refined system for four or five thousand years.

One of the principal reasons, besides low taxes, for the prosperity of his reign was Augustus' apparent belief in what we call nowadays "the quantitative theory of money." Here again he learned from Caesar, the true founder of the Roman Empire. Conforming to the traditional Republican practice of letting the army commander issue the currency, Augustus took over the mint. The Senate continued to strike bronze and copper for use as token money in Italy, but the issue of Imperial or international currency was reserved to the Princeps. His principal mint was in Lugdunum (Lyons), the capital of Gaul, then the largest gold producer. The active Imperial mints placed a tremendous amount of money on the market: in twenty-five years some eighty issues of gold and no less than four hundred of silver were coined. The resultant prosperity helped to produce a Golden Age in literature and art.

Chapter 48/THE GOLDEN
AGE: *NOVA PROGENIES*

Social Policy

The preservation of the Italian stock engaged Augustus' constant and active attention. He saw how interpenetration of Rome and the Italian states had been going on for centuries, only to culminate in the paradox of the fratricidal Social War. During the succeeding sixty years, Rome and Italy had taken several roads to reunion. Some were devised by Caesar or Augustus: extending citizenship to north Italians, enlisting Italy on Caesar's side, the Italian oath of allegiance against Antony and Cleopatra. Against Antony, Augustus relied mainly on Italy, where he profited by fostering political unity. Victorious, he continued his solicitude for Italy's political and economic stability, seeking also to strengthen it as a social and spiritual force capable of world leadership.

Augustus had reason to cast Italy in that role. For example, it had in his own lifetime attained a unified culture. For, while Rome gave the world a Caesar and Latium a Cicero, north Italy had given Catullus, Vergil, and Livy; central Italy, Propertius and Ovid; the south, Horace, while from the old Etruscan race came Maecenas, whose life work it was to reconcile party interests and to stimulate arts and letters. This maturity in Italy was the natural product of a centuries-long fusion of cultures.

We call the resulting culture Roman, but, as Vergil and Horace knew, the Italian element in it was strong. Augustus encouraged his subjects to think of the ideal of virtue and valor as Italian as well as Roman; hence Vergil, speaking for the regime as well as from his heart, sings in his *Georgics* of Italy as above everything else a land of men, strong-limbed and stout, of undaunted hearts; he names the roster of self-sacrificing Italian heroes, whose statues Augustus was to erect in his Forum: the Decii, Marius, Camillus, Scipio, and Augustus (himself a member of the Italian small-town *bourgeoisie*)

> Who now triumphant along the furthest Asian frontiers
> Keeps the war-worthless Indians away from the towers of Rome.
> Hail, great mother of harvests! O land of Saturn, hail!
> Mother of Men! [1]

And Augustus was presumably not displeased to read later in Vergil's epic, the *Aeneid*, that the gods willed the formation of the Italian people to bring peace and civilization to the world.

Augustus put the Italians on the same plane with Romans from Rome. To fill magistracies and to man high Imperial and senatorial offices had become their birthright. He even planned to allow balloting in the Italian municipalities for Roman magistracies, but for unknown reasons the experiment was abandoned. Veterans from the *auxilia* and Romanized provincials might gradually be granted citizenship, but Augustus was at pains to prevent the dilution of Italian blood by indiscriminate admission of foreigners.

To the same end, Augustus restricted manumissions of slaves. About 16,000 slaves had been freed yearly between 80 and 50 B.C., and the rate had steadily increased since, masters finding it cheaper to free their slaves and throw them on the dole than to keep them in bondage. The new freedmen would then by prearrangement share their wages with their former masters. Augustus wondered whether the nation could absorb so many men alien to the Roman tradition. Therefore, to curb wholesale and informal manumissions, he assigned freedmen so created to a new category of semi-citizenship called Junian Latinity. Junian Latins might not receive legacies or make wills, but their children were legally recognized as free-born Latins, a status which might eventually lead to Roman citizenship.

Finally, Augustus forbade ex-slaves convicted of certain crimes to live in Rome, to receive or assign property, or to acquire citizenship. His intent throughout was to keep alien blood from debasing the citizen body.

Except for this fixed preoccupation, he did not discriminate against slaves and freedmen. He would publicly humiliate masters cruel to their slaves. He entrusted freedmen with delicate missions, even with public

[1] C. Day Lewis, *The Georgics of Vergil*. London, Cape, 1940, p. 40.

office; naval officers, we saw, were usually freedmen. He paid his freedmen physicians well. He occasionally made special grants of Roman citizenship or even knighthood to freedmen. Freedmen's daughters might become Vestal Virgins. Though denied ambitious political careers, freedmen might lead in their own restricted circles. In each of the 265 precincts into which the fourteen city wards were divided, Augustus let freedmen supervise weights, distribute the public grain and other Imperial largesses, or lead the worship of the neighborhood Lares, chiefly the Genius of Augustus himself, in shrines at squares and crossroads. This precinct leadership by freedmen gave them a sense of importance and social distinction. The four leaders elected within each precinct doubtless took great satisfaction in appearing annually on their special feast-day dressed in the robes of a Roman magistrate and preceded by lictors.

Preservation of the Roman Family

Augustus had a more positive program for preserving the Italian stock. It consisted of encouraging marriage, marital chastity, and an increased birth rate. He discovered that men and women resented interference with their private affairs, but he persisted. He was the particular foe of loose living and unconventionality in high places. Sudden wealth and Hellenistic sophistication, the rhetoricians said, the immense booty—money, slaves, furniture, art, and property—from two centuries of wars had brought luxury and ostentation, self-indulgence and easy morals. Pleasure-seeking went to fantastic lengths. Marriage had fallen into low esteem. Husbands were openly faithless. Wives felt no restraint either of convention or of conscience. They divorced their husbands for the merest whims, often without any legal formality. Many a man preferred an open liaison with a loyal slave or freedwoman. The birth rate had fallen sharply.

But now under Augustus, adultery, long regarded as a private affair, became a statutory crime tried in a special court, and virtually all promiscuous sexual relations were decreed unlawful.

Marriage was to be restored by decree to the old-fashioned ideal, a sacred obligation to perpetuate the race. Therefore men and women who did not marry were penalized. For example, a man still unmarried at twenty-five was barred from bequests from any but his closest relatives. Rich women still unmarried at twenty were similarly penalized, and had besides to pay a yearly spinster's tax of 1 percent of the value of their property.

To increase the birth rate Augustus legalized marriage, for the common people, between free-born Romans and freed slaves. Finally to encourage the nobles to raise large families, preference in elections and in appointments to governorship was given to those with three or more children. Various revisions, mitigating the most unpopular penalties, making the inducements more attractive, produced results. The census of A.D. 14 showed a population of 4,937,000 male citizens above the age of twenty, an increase of 874,000, or about 18 percent, over that of 28 B.C. Even if we attribute part of the increase to citizenship grants, the figures still show that Augustus' marital legislation had some effect.

Religious Policy

A religious program rounded out Augustus' moral reforms. A modern constitution is secular, but Roman religion had always been closely associated with the state. Its decline during the late Republic had inevitably engaged the attention of thoughtful men like Sallust, Cicero, and Varro. Cicero advocated a close supervision over private and foreign cults, with their deviant priests and prophets. Varro claimed that national greatness was inseparable from faith in the national gods. The native gods would keep Rome powerful if it returned to old-fashioned *pietas*—that threefold loyalty to family, to country, and to gods. Horace, Augustus' laureate, reminded Romans, as Kipling reminded Englishmen, that they owed their dominion over palm and pine to an humble and contrite heart, subordinating itself to the gods, and that the wars of Italy sprang from a neglect of religion. In sum, enlightened Romans would have arrested the nation's decay by a return to ancestral faith. This was Augustus' program.

Building new temples, rebuilding old ones, re-establishing neglected festivals did not exhaust that program. To fill the need for priests of patrician blood, Augustus raised certain families to patrician status. He revived the Arval brotherhood, the rites of which were supposed to insure abundant harvests. To symbolize peace and hark back to the pious past, he closed (31 B.C.) the temple of Janus, which had not been done since 235 B.C. Later he forbade the cult of the Egyptian goddess Isis. Though, as we saw, worship of his person was confined to the provinces, Italy too regarded him as savior, and began spontaneously to honor his guardian spirit; implying no attribution of divinity to him, it was rather the citizens' way of saying, "God bless you." When he ultimately made this ceremony a national institution, he brought the ancient Italian gods, among whom were the Genii, Lares, and numina, closer to the people. The practice of family prayers was revived, adding one more old-fashioned touch to the religious revival.

A spectacular event was staged in 17 B.C. to dramatize the idea of religious restoration. By then, Senate, knights, and common people were working together under the princeps to their mutual benefit. The army had been forged into an instrument of peace, the provinces subordinated and reorganized, prosperity re-established, the purity of the Italian stock protected, that of the family fostered, temples rebuilt, reverence to the gods restored. Lastly the sufferings of the civil wars were but a memory, the benefits of the Pax Augusta a reality. Augustus thought there was enough in all this to fill Roman hearts with pride, enough for which to thank the gods.

And the gods were thanked on an unprecedented scale, with a festival signifying the end of an era and the beginning of a happier one. Led by Augustus personally, the nation went to the temples to rededicate itself to the deities who from small beginnings had made it the greatest power on earth. Twenty-seven boys and a like number of girls, model patricians all, sang, first on Apollo's—and Augustus'—Palatine Hill, then on Jupiter's Capitoline, a hymn by Horace. The hymn reveals the spirit of the new age, striving to recapture the essence of the old. It stresses, echoing Vergil's *Aeneid,* Roman descent from Trojans, and Augustus' from Venus and the Trojan Anchises; it invokes the blessing of the Roman gods on Augustus' deeds and plans, his laws on race and family, his efforts to promote prosperity, his hope of seeing the young generation brought up in old-fashioned simplicity and modesty.

Literature

In literature the Augustan revival was celebrated by Augustus' friends: Vergil in epic, Horace in lyric, and Livy in history. All, and artists as well, though subsidized to propagandize the regime, created art-forms worthy of comparison with Greek, fit symbols of a Greco-Roman empire.

Vergil (70–19 B.C.), a farmer's son from north Italy whose confiscated paternal lands were restored through the intervention of Octavian, his one-time schoolmate, expressed his gratitude in high poetry, perhaps the greatest ever written in Latin. Vergil's earliest patron was Asinius Pollio, Augustus' sturdy Republican opponent, for whom he wrote pastoral poems (*Eclogues,* written 42–37 B.C.) including one, the fourth, predicting the return under Pollio's guidance of a golden age symbolized by the birth of a child in whom some have seen Pollio's son, others Antony's and Octavia's, others Octavian's, and still others a prophecy of the birth of Christ. But during Pollio's absence governing Macedonia for Antony, Maecenas, seeing Vergil's promise and the possibility of involving him in propagandizing the regime, offered him patronage, and suggested to him the theme of his *Georgics* (37–30 B.C.) an epic of country life, grave, religious, and patriotic in tone, shot through with Vergil's love for the lovely land of Italy and his belief in the gospel of hard work, a poem

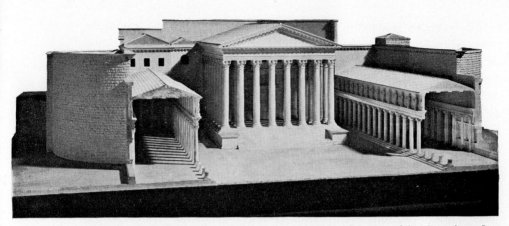

Fig. 48.1. Rome. Temple of Mars the Avenger, model. Vowed by Octavian after Philippi (42 B.C.) this was Rome's first all-marble temple. Greek in material and décor, it is Italic in its location on a high podium at the back of the precinct; it thus symbolizes the Augustan compromise. The porticoes at the sides contained statues of distinguished Romans, a Hall of Fame intended to connect the *princeps* with Rome's storied past. (Rome, Museo della Civiltà Romana)

both deeply felt and in line with Octavian's desire to resettle his veterans contentedly on farms. Vergil's masterpiece, the *Aeneid,* left unfinished at his death, is also on a theme congenial to the Augustan program; how the hero, the "pious" Aeneas, a refugee from Troy, came guided by the hand of destiny through many trials to Italy and founded the Roman race. The poem is filled with a sense of the past implicit in the present, and its culmination is in the rule of Augustus. The hero is in a sense Augustus too, idealized, endowed with the virtues Augustus desired to see reborn: *pietas,* a sense of duty, sobriety, steadfastness, tenacity. On his way the Carthaginian queen Dido—is she Cleopatra?—tempts him, but in vain: his is a higher destiny than such a marriage. In Italy he meets and overthrows Turnus, an Italian hero whose wrong-headed excesses anticipate Antony's. Aeneas has his faithful Achates as Augustus had Agrippa. In prophecy Aeneas sees the future greatness of Augustan Rome. But the poem is more than propaganda or allegory: it has been perceptively said that Aeneas in flight from Troy, holding a child by the hand, his burden his father and his gods, a city in flames behind him, is universal history; it is ourselves. There is tragedy in the *Aeneid,* perhaps all the greater if we believe that Vergil's deathbed instructions to burn the poem sprang from an ultimate disillusionment with the prince of peace.

Another beneficiary of Maecenas was Vergil's friend the south Italian Horace (65–8 B.C.) , a freedman's son. He fought on the wrong side at Philippi, was amnestied, received a minor civil service post, and used his leisure to compose poetry, at first bitter, later humane and tolerant satires. These brought him to the attention of Maecenas, who gave him a farm in the Sabine hills beyond Tibur, where he wrote his *Odes,* exquisitely wrought lyrics in Greek meters on friendship, love, a homespun philosophy, and sometimes politics. He praised frugality and virtue, hymned martial and imperial ideals. The first six odes of his Third Book, written between 28 and 26 B.C., reflect Augustus' policy of social regeneration, based on the virtues emphasized in Cicero's *On Duty,* Augustus' *Res Gestae,* and on the shield that decorated Augustus' simple Palatine house—courage, justice, clemency, *pietas,* the virtues that had made Rome great, exemplified, as the sculpture of Augustus' Forum was planned also to do, by the old Republican heroes and by Augustus himself. But the poet never sold his integrity with his Muse: he saw and flayed the iniquities of the age, and in his ode on rejoicing after Actium dared to flout the propaganda line and express admiration of Cleopatra.

Fig. 48.2. Rome. Arch of Augustus, restored to show location of *Fasti.* (A. Degrassi, *Inscriptiones Italiae* XIII, Fasc. 1, Rome, 1947. Plate IX.)

Urbane, mellow, cosmopolitan, believing in the primacy of the intellect over the emotions and in the educative function of poetry, Horace typifies the Ciceronian ideal of *humanitas* as well as Augustus' golden age.

Augustus' historian was Livy (59 B.C.–A.D. 17) from rich Patavium in the Po valley, who devoted his life to the composition of an immensely long account (in 142 books, all but 35 now lost) of Rome from its founding to 9 B.C. It is to Livy that we owe the fabulous accounts of Rome of the kings, Romulus and Remus suckled by the she-wolf, the rape of the Sabine women, the tyranny of the Tarquins. His antiquarian pages, in the rhetorical style of Hellenistic historians, suited Augustus' purpose; they are filled with old Roman types, austere, self-sacrificing, moral, patriotic. But, as with Vergil and Horace, Livy's pages are more than propaganda; his eloquence, seriousness, and humanity produced a stirring and inspiring story. As an admirer of Pompey, a commonwealth man in a monarchical age, he may have reflected the sentiments of the regime, as perhaps when he expressed in his preface his annoyance with the immoral present, when Rome could bear neither its maladies nor the remedies proposed to cure them. But these views may also be interpreted as reflecting a spirit as independent as Vergil's or Horace's.

An Augustan creative artist who certainly failed to express the spirit of the regime was Ovid (43 B.C.–A.D. 17), who lived to regret this failure. Coming from his Apennine birthplace, Sulmo, to the gay amoral atmosphere of cosmopolitan Rome, he wrote gay amoral love-poetry, including an extremely funny and irreverent manual, the *Art of Love,* on how to win girls and influence women. His *Letters of the Heroines,* addressed by jilted ladies in the angry tones of a prosecuting attorney to their faithless lovers, portrays in thin mythological disguise the amours of Augustan high society. His masterpiece, the *Metamorphoses,* a Roman *Arabian Nights,* with its 250 tales of miraculous transformations, has been called full of gods but empty of reverence. His *Fasti,* a versification on the first six months of the Roman calendar, essays, but unsuccessfully, the solemn tone of the Augustan revival; Ovid's essential lack of gravity peeps through. All this irritated the Princeps, and when Ovid was implicated in a scandal involving Augustus' own granddaughter, he was exiled to Tomi (modern Constanta in Romania) where, despite nine books of pleading poetic letters to Rome, he failed to move either Augustus or his successor to pity, and died there brokenhearted.

Opposition to Augustus is represented also, but in milder and more anemic form, by Tibullus (*c.* 48–19 B.C.), the poet of a Republican literary circle headed by Messalla Corvinus, who once refused to be Augustus' city prefect, but lived to propose for him the title of Father of His Country. Tibullus wrote charmingly of love and idyllic country life. A far more positive and tormented personality, whose spirit has been transmuted to our time by Ezra Pound, was Propertius (*c.* 50–

Fig. 48.3. Aeneas. Rome, Ara Pacis. A serious, middle-aged figure, far from a romantic type; as imagined by a sculptor working within six to ten years of Vergil's death. (G. Moretti, *L'Ara Pacis Augustae*, Rome, 1948. Plate XIX.)

16 B.C.) from Assisi, a younger member of Maecenas' circle, a poet of love and peace who sang also of Actium, of archaic religious rites, and of the need to avenge Crassus. His noblest poem is an epitaph for a noble Roman matron who epitomized the virtues Augustus was trying to revive.

Fig. 48.4. Maecenas (?) from the Ara Pacis. (Paris, Collection Rothschild; G. Moretti, *L'Ara Pacis Augustae*, Rome, 1948. Fig. 192.)

Fig. 48.5. Italy or Mother Earth, from the Ara Pacis. The relief expresses in marble what Vergil's *Georgics* express in verse: fruitfulness, in crops and in men; agriculture and grazing (bull and sheep); air (to the left), and water (to the right), all contributing to the fertility of the Italian land. (Florence, Uffizi Gallery; Anderson photo)

Architecture and Art

Augustan architecture shares two characteristics with Augustan literature: it was in the service of the Princeps, and it adapted Greek techniques to Roman themes. The theory of Augustan architecture is set forth in a treatise by Vitruvius.

Augustus dedicated in 42 B.C. the previously-mentioned temple to the deified Julius; in 29 B.C. he decorated it with the decks of ships captured at Actium. In 42 B.C. also, after Philippi, he vowed a marble temple of the Corinthian order to Mars the Avenger, not finally dedicated until forty years later. Intended as a complement to Caesar's temple of Venus, it was built at right angles to it, set in the Roman manner on a high podium centered at the back of an open area, Augustus' Forum, built in Italian travertine and tufa, revetted and paved with Greek marble. The plan of the Forum was axially symmetrical: on either flank of the temple, in semicircular *exedrae,* were set the statues of Rome's worthies which, as we saw, repeat the spirit of Vergil, Horace, Livy, and the age. Trajan later repeated in his Forum the semicircular motifs, and we find them again in Bernini's grandiose plan for St. Peter's.

Among the other eighty-two temples the building or restoration of which Augustus mentions with pride was Apollo's on the Palatine, vowed in 36 B.C. dedicated in 28 B.C., its precinct rich with gold, ivory, and polychrome marble. Connected with it, appropriately enough, since Apollo was patron of the Muses, and Augustus patron of literary artists, were two libraries, one Greek and one Latin. The temple was destroyed by fire in A.D. 363 and its precise site is not known.

In 30 B.C., to celebrate his victory at Actium, Octavian built a monumental arch in the forum, to which, in 19 B.C., after Crassus' standards were recovered from the Parthians, were added two lists, still preserved, one of consuls since the founding of the city, the other of generals who had celebrated triumphs. Here again he revealed his concern to connect his regime with the storied Republican past.

As early as 28 B.C. Augustus had begun to take thought on the manner of his burial. In that year he began in the Campus Martius his mausoleum, surrounded by groves and avenues of evergreens to make a public park. No doubt the mausoleum was intended to rival that at Halicarnassus, or even the Egyptian pyramids; but with his usual respect for the ancient traditions, the plan Augustus chose was an enormous drum, like the Etruscan tombs of Caere, but much larger—290 feet in diameter and 143 feet high—built in concentric circles of masonry with four superimposed stories of vaulted corridors. Over it was heaped a tumulus of earth planted with cypresses; before it were placed on two pillars the

Fig. 48.6. Prima Porta Augustus, detail. Statue found at the villa of Livia, Augustus' wife, on the Via Flaminia just north of Rome. The Emperor is idealized as a commander-in-chief haranguing his troops. The symbols on his breastplate commemorate what he has done for the Empire, bringing to its provinces peace and prosperity, under the gods. (Rome, Vatican Museum)

bronze tablets of the *Res Gestae,* Augustus' autobiography; within it were buried, around the central space reserved for the tomb of the Princeps, the members of the royal house: his sons-in-law Marcellus and Drusus, his sister Octavia, his lieutenant Agrippa, his grandsons Lucius and Gaius, all of whom died before him. His wife Livia, his stepson and successor Tiberius, Caligula, Claudius, Nerva and the empress Julia Domna, wife of Septimius Severus, were also buried here.

Between 27 and 23 B.C., as a part of a general plan undertaken with Agrippa to beautify the Campus Martius, Augustus surrounded the new temples of Jupiter and Juno with the Porticus Octaviae, named in honor of his sister and enriched with marbles, works of art, and Greek and Latin libraries. The total effect must have rivaled that of the Museum and Library at Alexandria, but all that survives is one of the four pedimented entrance ways. Nearby in 13 B.C. he dedicated the Theater of Marcellus, in travertine, seating about 10,000; its three superimposed arcades with engaged columns in the three Greek orders were to influence the plan of the Coliseum.

The greatest surviving masterpiece of Augustan art is the *Ara Pacis,* Altar of Peace on the Field of Mars, just outside the pomerium. It was vowed in 13 B.C., dedicated in 9 B.C., to symbolize all the basic ideas of the Augustan program. The altar itself, though the sacrificial scenes of its frieze are interesting, is of less importance than its enclosure, which portrays a double procession of Roman dignitaries among whom can be identified Augustus, Livia, his daughter Julia, Agrippa, Tiberius, Octavia, Lucius and Gaius, and perhaps Maecenas. One panel represents a grave, bearded Aeneas, sacrificing to the Penates; another, Italy or Mother Earth, fecund with fruits, children in her lap: they might be illustrations for Vergil's *Aeneid* and *Georgics.* The whole may be compared and contrasted with the Parthenon frieze. The reliefs are thoroughly Italian in their informality—the great personages in the procession chat together, and the grave Octavia puts her finger to her lips to quiet them. Tranquil, unpretentious, stately and yet intimate, delighting in nature, showing a perfect balance between land and city, expressing greatness in modest dimensions, the Altar of Peace is Roman art at its best. Few in the age of the Princeps would have been bold enough to ask the whereabouts of an Altar to Liberty.

Statues of the Princeps were everywhere; the most famous is that from Livia's frescoed villa at Prima Porta, just north of Rome, now in the Vatican, portraying him as middle-aged, austere, and as dedicated to duty as Aeneas. His armor is emblazoned with symbolic figures, Sky and Earth, Apollo and Diana, and the personified Provinces of Gaul and Spain; the central motif is the restoration of the Parthian standards. At his feet the naked child may be Cupid, a delicate reference to the Princeps' alleged descent from Venus.

Even the minor arts glorified the Princeps; a silver cup from Bosco-reale portrays Augustus as the victorious Prince of Peace, flanked by Mars and Venus, receiving the homage of seven conquered provinces. Such silverware was cheaply but charmingly reproduced in coral-red clayware called Arretine (from Arretium, modern Arezzo) cast from molds, with scenes, often erotic, of banquets or festivals taken from the Hellenistic repertory and adapted to Roman taste. Thus in clay and in silver, as on marble reliefs and in poetry and prose, a mature and amalgamated Greco-Roman art reflected the glory and the program of the founder of a New Order, a Golden Age.

Chapter 49/ERA OF
CONSOLIDATION
(A.D. 14–68)

The Succession

Augustus died quietly (A.D. 14), in the arms of Livia his wife and counselor, at 77 at Nola, in Campania. The success of his program of reconstruction planned in Alexandria forty-four years earlier had recently been attested by public devotion: at Puteoli, the passengers and crew of an Alexandrian ship, dressed in white, garlanded, and bearing incense, had chanted that through him they lived, sailed the seas, and enjoyed liberty and prosperity. His fellow citizens' conduct at his death told the same story. His body was borne from town to town in torchlight procession on the shoulders of the leading men. To Bovillae came the knights to bear it to Rome. He had prescribed the order of his own funeral: the cortège, preceded by the statue of Victory from the Curia, passed beneath his Arch, while a choir of patrician children sang a dirge. The Senate decreed that his lifetime should be called the Augustan Age, and within a month of his death deified him.

Four princes of Augustus' line, the Julio-Claudian dynasty, ruled the Empire to A.D. 68: Tiberius, Gaius nicknamed Caligula, Claudius, and Nero. Tradition has stereotyped these emperors into a Hypocrite, a Madman, a Fool, and a Rogue. Tradition admitted that the Hypocrite was an able ruler, but the Madman, the Fool, and the Rogue were conceded no redeeming feature whatever. Yet under this quartet of allegedly sinister rulers, the Empire showed steady progress. Politically, administrative efficiency increased and peace became more firmly grounded; the frontier was extended and the law humanized. Economically and socially, the Empire prospered and class distinctions tended to break down. Culturally, it was a Silver, not a Golden Age, but literature and philosophy flourished, and the arts fell not far short of the creativeness and vigor of the Augustan Age.

When Augustus decided that the principate must continue after his death, Tiberius (A.D. 14–37), son of Livia by a previous marriage, was not his first choice as successor. The Princeps outlived all the members of his family whom he successively designated to succeed him: first his nephew Marcellus whom he married to his daughter Julia; then his friend Agrippa to whom he gave her after Marcellus' death. After Agrippa's death, Augustus forced Tiberius to divorce his wife, for whom he had genuine affection, in favor of Julia. But Julia proved unfaithful, and Tiberius, a stickler for respectability, exiled himself from Italy, without giving his father-in-law any hint of his grievance. When the Emperor eventually discovered that his own daughter had flouted his laws for regulating improvement of morality he banished her and all her lovers except one who killed himself.

Tiberius had another reason for withdrawing from public affairs. He had spend his life at the outposts of civilization in the defense of his country. With his brother Drusus he had conquered kingdoms and tribes from the Low Countries to the middle Danube, thus insulating northern Italy with a crescent of peaceful lands. The endorsement of this brilliant record, apparent in his choice as heir, was canceled by the Emperor's later preference for two young grandsons, Agrippa's children by Julia. For the resentful prince this shift was injustice compounded with ingratitude.

Julia's infidelities and his own humiliation apparently affected Tiberius' character. At least they deepened his aversion for Rome, where glitter often concealed intrigue and corruption. He spent his voluntary exile in Rhodes with artists and scholars, studying sculpture, painting, and philosophy and dabbling in astrology, meanwhile stiffening his natural bent to austerity and his contempt for the vulgarities of the age. Like the patrician he was (for five centuries the Claudii had no equal in the number of statesmen given Rome), he withdrew more and more into himself under misfortune.

One of his favored grandsons having died at twenty-three, the other in his late 'teens, Augustus turned again to the forty-six-year-old Tiberius, adopted him, renamed him Tiberius Julius Caesar, and gave him tribunician and proconsular powers equal to his own. Hence Tiberius was emperor in everything but name. The heir apparent was appointed on this pattern down to the end of the Empire.

A groundless rumor that Livia (Tiberius' mother by a previous husband, Tiberius Claudius Nero) encompassed the deaths of all the Julian heirs-apparent caused a very real antagonism between the Julian and Claudian sides of the dynasty.

Tiberius desired to preserve both the spirit and the form of the Augustan principate without innovation or experiment. Augustan policy should continue in every phase of government: in the use of the Senate by the princeps, in the civil service, defense, finance, foreign relations, and the local government of Rome. Perhaps he lacked the imagination to initiate policies, and he often procrastinated in applying those he inherited, thereby confusing the Senate and damaging his own reputation. But few emperors equaled his administrative ability. Perhaps he wanted to revive the Republic, but he concluded that his historical mission was to preserve and pass on the first princeps' creation, his inheritance.

When he was confirmed as emperor, he told the Senate he hoped they would soon relieve him of this office. But that was easier said than done. Tired at last of court life and politics, he retired to the island of Capri (A.D. 26), keeping all his executive powers, but making the praetorian prefect, Sejanus, his agent. Two evils developed from this retirement. His dispatches to the Senate began to look like the orders of a distant and unapproachable tyrant. Then when Sejanus intrigued and murdered (one of his victims was Tiberius' own son) to secure the throne for himself, the Emperor, not satisfied with having him executed, developed a treason complex, instituting trials before the Senate as Supreme Court, exposing several compromised members, executing some innocent ones, and causing a general feeling of insecurity. His relations with the Senate grew impossibly strained.

Tiberius' personality was not attractive to the masses. He disapproved of the theater, expelled actors from Italy, and tried to restrict gladiatorial games as wasteful and immoral. He was thrifty; on his death he left the state coffers bulging with over 2,000,000,000 sesterces. But thrift is not a quality attractive to a restless and greedy army; nor puritanical morality to a circus-hungry mob. The news of his death brought universal rejoicing.

Decline of the Senate

While the Julio-Claudian principate kept largely to the Augustan pattern, significant modifications appeared and multiplied. Each succeeding emperor assumed more personal power at the Senate's expense.

Understandable under despots like Gaius or Nero, this is surprising under traditionalists like Tiberius and Claudius. Personality has something to do with it; the nature of the Augustan design has more. The princeps was a magnet attracting the loyalty of army, provinces, ambitious individuals and classes—and their tax money. Moreover, the princeps knew what he wanted, had always the initiative, and commanded legal and extra-legal means to weaken opposition. Even if each emperor had been a saint and the Senate a choir of angels, centralization of power in the princeps' hands, fundamental in the Augustan design, would have expanded the princeps' authority and shrunk the Senate's. Centralized power feeds on more centralization.

Tiberius at first submitted to the Senate all problems, even minor ones, not curtailing its freedom of speech or vote. But his suspicious nature led him to institute too many treason trials, in which he used the Senate as his cat's-paw. Informing, which was highly rewarded, had produced a professional class of blackmailers, and, though Tiberius' vindictiveness may have been exaggerated, the Senate's subservience gave it a bad name. Paradoxically, Tiberius was annoyed at its flattery. When a member proposed that the month November should be renamed Tiberius, he crushed him by asking, "And what will you do if you have thirteen Caesars?" Feeling the masses too irresponsible to be trusted with sovereignty, he transferred to the Senate the election of magistrates, but with the Emperor nominating the candidates this proved an empty privilege.

So, despite his good intentions, Tiberius got into difficulties with the Senate, most of them personal. His own bitter experiences probably made him incapable of cordial relations with anybody, let alone his peers. He lacked Augustus' patience and tact in dealing with politicians and winning over even enemies. But the blame is not all on his side. Many handicaps beset his efforts toward cooperation and harmony. The greatest was the invincible dislike of die-hard senators who had expected a miracle the instant Augustus died—the resurrection of the Republic. They vented their disappointment on Tiberius, making him out a hypocrite scheming to foil them. Thus started the legend of the tyrant laying traps. Much of our knowledge of Tiberius' psychology, motivation, and controversies comes from the intransigeant historian Tacitus, who misunderstood and disliked him as much as Macaulay misunderstood and disliked the Stuarts. Yet except for Agrippa and his own brother Drusus, both long dead, no man was better equipped than Tiberius to carry on Augustus' ideals. The Senate's refusal to deify him after death is a measure of its resentment and his failure.

The relations of Senate and princeps were still further upset by Gaius (A.D. 37–41). His reign began auspiciously, for he had the luck to follow

Fig. 49.1. The Claudian Aqueduct, near Rome. Finished in A.D. 52, it brought water from 40 miles away. Nine miles of its course are carried on arches like these, sometimes over 80 feet high. Once striking in the lonely Roman Campagna, it is now surrounded by Rome's expanding suburbs. (Fototeca)

an unpopular ruler, and he seemed friendly and likable. But Gaius had had practically no administrative experience. Six months after his accession he suffered a serious illness which may have affected his mind. His morbid fear of assassination bred cruelty in him. That he considered himself a younger brother of Jupiter, god in the flesh, may not have been madness, but acceptance of Hellenistic ruler-worship. He treated senators like lackeys, bringing all opposition to heel by arbitrary executive act or judicial condemnation. When to insult of the Senate he added insult of provincials, the city-mob, and, stupidly, the army itself, a conspiracy, in which senators shared, murdered him (A.D. 41).

Claudius (A.D. 41–54), owed the crown to reaction against Gaius' tyranny and reflected the general wish for a return to constitutionalism. Imitating in principle Augustus, his great-uncle, and conditioned by temperament to rely on advisers, he tried to awaken a sense of responsibility in the Senate, which his master Livy had taught him to respect. Ironically, his interpretation of the spirit of the constitution led him to advocate a reform unpopular with most senators. Claudius told the Senate that the Roman constitution had shown flexibility through the centuries, breaking down political and social barriers, admitting more men to the privileges of citizenship, adapting itself to ever-changing conditions. He thought of societies as evolving, not fixed; for example, he said, the center of gravity had shifted from Rome to Latium, later from Latium to central Italy, still later to the whole peninsula, and now it was time for a new shift from Italy to the provinces. Therefore he submitted a plan for which he claimed Augustan authority, that the Senate, now Italian, should become cosmopolitan, representing the whole Empire. Claudius' short-range objective was to open the Senate to a few wealthy, Romanized, and therefore dependable Gallic aristocrats. His long-range objective was to turn the Senate into an Empire-wide parliament. He assumed the censorship to dramatize his epoch-making reform. Regarded by the Gauls as their Magna Carta, Claudius' speech was immortalized on bronze in Lugdunum, the Gallic capital and his birthplace.

Little as they liked Claudius' provincializing of the Senate, the Fathers liked still less some of his administrative reforms, which trespassed on prerogatives left them by Augustus; for example, finances, flood control, regulation of traffic in Rome, supervision of taverns, the conduct of foreign affairs, or the administration of Ostia where Claudius was building a harbor.

But Claudius was no tyrant. He respected the Senate and tried to enhance its authority. He invited criticism and expected members to vote according to their conscience, as a surviving speech of his indicates. Although malicious gossip slandered him in life, and lampoons in death, the Senate deified him, which suggests among other things that he had not mortally wounded their pride or transgressed their rights.

Yet clearly the Senate's power and prestige were decreasing. Tyrants despised it; honest rulers found it obstructionist. It could not match the princeps' singleness of direction, bureaucratic strength, and military power. High-minded and conscientious senators found it increasingly difficult to make their voice felt. It remained for Nero (54–68), a more refined tyrant than Gaius, to place its very integrity, to say nothing of its prestige and usefulness, at the ruler's mercy. True, the Senate joined the army in a revolution which dethroned the tyrant, but that improved matters little. When Vespasian (69–79) ascended the throne, it lost such shadowy authority as even the worst Julio-Claudians had left it. And

Fig. 49.2. Rome. Porta Maggiore, model. Combines the functions of a triumphal arch, a gate, and a support for Rome's major aqueducts. Inscriptions record its construction under Claudius, with repairs by Vespasian and Titus. Aurelian

Vespasian was no despot, but an honest prince dedicated to the public welfare.

Growth of the Princeps' Authority

Augustus' regular practice of organizing new services in response to need or to requests of a subservient Senate had important consequences. His expanding staff of civil servants encroached steadily on magistrates' activities. Senatorial authority decreased when Tiberius added knights to the Privy Council. It decreased still further when his retirement to Capri forced the Imperial chancery acting with Sejanus to use discretionary powers more fully.

An Imperial cabinet was clearly in the making, since treasury and justice departments appeared under Tiberius, and a Secretary for Petitions and Letters under Gaius. So far the development was casual, but for efficiency's sake Claudius both divided ministerial labor more sharply and made the cabinet a formal institution, with Senate acquiescence if not explicit ratification. His cabinet had four secretaries: a Secretary-in-Chief whose office handled all communications to the emperor; a Secretary of the Treasury, a Secretary of Justice, and a Literary Adviser. The latter's functions, perhaps related to Maecenas' propaganda activities, may have embraced the editing of important documents and the supervision of the emperor's private library and art collection, but a more sinister possible activity was heading the secret police, for which we begin to find evidence. Apparently created by Augustus, but kept

later incorporated it into his wall. (Rome, Museo della Civiltà Romana; J. Felbermeyer photo)

prudently behind the scenes, this hated force of detectives was finally abolished by Vespasian.

The Senate disliked the cabinet, especially as Claudius' secretaries attended its meetings. The senators despised the secretaries' social status: they were ex-slaves, directing a great empire. Intelligent, cultured, and efficient they might be, but to the uncompromising Senate they were freedmen, serving a despot. The powers of the civil service were also centralized. For example, procurators who under Augustus had simply been collectors of revenues by A.D. 50 had acquired judicial authority over tax cases. Again, Ostia, for centuries administered by a quaestor, was placed, when Claudius made it a chief port, under an imperial agent. The Senate had automatically honored all foreign commitments made by the emperor. But by A.D. 50 international agreements made by imperial provincial legates were binding on the Senate as if made by the princeps himself.

Beginning with Augustus, the emperor took special interest in the provinces. Any business with social implications might be subject to imperial supervision. For example, Augustus, Tiberius, or Claudius invoked capital punishment upon anyone desecrating graves in Palestine. Augustus himself used his superior imperium to intervene in senatorial provinces. Five edicts from Cyrene show his concern for provincial welfare; one provides for including Greeks on juries and suggests that governors not assign Romans to prosecute Greeks in murder cases not involving Romans.

Behind the subservience of countless provincial inscriptions calling the Julio-Claudian emperors friends, guardians, saviors, benefactors, and father lies evidence of the emperors' winning upper-class provincial allegiance with consequent damage to the Senate's prestige. Provincials valued above all one imperial gift: Roman citizenship. Tiberius followed Augustus in rewarding military service with citizenship; under him more than 100,000 provincials became citizens. Gaius was not so liberal, but both Claudius and Nero were. Claudius equated naval with auxiliary service, thus enfranchising all honorably discharged sailors and marines, their wives, and children. In addition he enfranchised no less than twenty-five cities, and in principle advocated citizenship for all Romanized subjects.

Claudius' census of A.D. 48 registered nearly 6,000,000 citizens, an increase of more than 1,000,000 over that of A.D. 14. The largest proportionate increase was doubtless in the provinces, through enfranchisement of natives and increase in resident citizens. Thus rose in the provinces a dynamic *bourgeoisie* politically equal to Italians, grateful to an emperor for its wealth and privileges. Devoted new citizens always took the name of the emperor who enfranchised them. The Senate had no corresponding advantage.

Nero did not alter Claudius' citizenship policy. But he especially admired Greek culture, giving Greek games in Rome, demonstrating his ability as poet and harpist to Hellenized Naples, making the grand tour of Greece to compete in artistic and athletic contests. In his enthusiasm for Greek culture, he gave Greece almost complete self-government and, best of all, exemption from tribute. His projected Corinth Canal would, if completed, have profited that city enormously.

Nero marked the culmination of nearly 300 years of Rome's discipleship to Greek arts, letters, and philosophy. Greek meters had been transposed into Latin, Greek techniques borrowed in poetry and prose, Greek methods and motifs taken as inspiration for Roman art, Greek science and religion used as the foundation of the Roman. Some writers, Augustus included, as surviving letters show, despised any Latin page not salted with Greek allusions. Claudius, although he held that speaking Latin should be a prerequisite of Roman citizenship, once summarized Rome's debt to Greece by referring to Greek and Latin as "both our languages." Nero's Greek tour formally recognized the Roman debt to Greece. Within fifty years Hadrian was to make Hellenization an alternative to Romanization for acquiring Roman citizenship. Although the aristocracy, disgusted by Nero's exhibitionism, joined with the Italian *bourgeoisie* in driving him to suicide, it could not suppress upper-class Greek gratitude towards the principate. No revolution could destroy the community of interests between the princeps and his millions of Eastern subjects.

The Jews and Emperor-worship

Emperor-worship mattered little in the growth of imperial authority. Only the superstitious and ignorant took it as religion; and the emperor had other means of capturing popular devotion. It was essentially a civil amenity involving no spiritual satisfactions. As an expression of loyalty it was of course valuable. It brought a feeling of universality and unity to millions of Eastern provincials who previously had worshiped regional rulers, Ptolemies, Seleucids, or Attalids. For sophisticates it had no more meaning than saluting the flag has nowadays. Tiberius and Claudius alike discouraged grants of divine honors by Greek cities. Claudius, not wanting to be offensive to his contemporaries, deprecated to the Alexandrians, traditional ruler-worshipers, the appointment of a high priest to him and the building of temples. Neither was Nero, megalomaniac though he was, concerned with claims to divinity. His interests were esthetic, and he much preferred crowns for artistic ability to sacrifices and incense.

Gaius alone seems to have taken emperor-worship seriously, though the evidence is inconclusive. In any case, he must have been taken aback when, dressed as the god Jupiter, during a trip in Gaul, he asked a native cobbler what he thought of him. "A great humbug," was the answer. Not every provincial of course was so agnostic, and in the less-educated western provinces emperor-worship was certainly used as a political instrument, as Stalin-worship was until recently.

With one people in the Empire, the Jews, the policy of emperor-worship had to be handled with care. Augustus wisely did not require his image in their synagogues or the burning of incense to him, being satisfied with honorific wreaths on the synagogues' interior walls and with congregational prayers offered for him. Gaius incurred serious trouble by trying to reverse this policy. In Jerusalem and throughout Palestine his orders to place his statue in the Temple provoked riots which would have flamed into revolt but for Petronius, the legate of Syria, who skillfully found pretexts for postponing the execution of the order. Under these circumstances Gaius' murder appeared to the Jews as an act of Providence.

Gaius' decree caused at least equal hardship among the Jews in scores of Eastern cities where gentile trouble-makers used it as a pretext for degrading Jews. In Alexandria, where 40 percent of the 500,000 population were Jews, Greeks especially hated Jews for having welcomed the invading Caesar and Augustus. For Greeks, loyal to the Ptolemies, this was treason. Augustus fanned the flames by confirming the Jewish community as a separate self-governing body alongside the Greek community —a city within a city, with its own laws, courts, council, and assembly.

The Greeks took vengeance when the Jews resisted Gaius' order to worship him. Parading as friends of the Empire, the Greeks denounced the Jews as enemies. Anti-Semitism engulfed Egypt, involving assaults not only on life and property, but also on religion. Alexandrian intellectuals published books proclaiming the incompatibility of Judaism with gentile ideals, but they met their match in the great philosopher Philo. He headed a Jewish group sent to Gaius to counteract a Greek delegation. We still have his pamphlet, *Embassy to Gaius,* giving the Jewish viewpoint and the Jewish version of the Alexandrian pogroms. The news of Gaius' assassination sparked new riots.

Claudius restored order based on the Augustan *status quo.* He ordered the Greeks to respect the liberties Augustus had guaranteed to the Jews, and he warned the Jews neither to agitate for more privileges nor to gain Alexandrian citizenship by surreptitious methods, nor to encourage clandestine immigration of Palestinian Jews into Egypt.

Military and Foreign Policy

The security of both Empire and emperor was one of the Julio-Claudians' most delicate problems. It had three principal aspects: economical financing of the army, maintaining its morale, and combining border defense with a peaceful foreign policy.

Discipline became a problem after Augustus' death. Now that the rich countries and glamorous cities of the then known world were conquered, it was the legions' lot to guard frontier deserts and forests throughout a monotonous twenty-year enlistment. The troops endured these hardships while Augustus lived. But on hearing of his death they mutinied in Illyricum and Germany. Long service and short pay were the reasons. Tiberius' son Drusus firmly forced obedience on the Illyrian legions. Those in Germany proved more troublesome, chiefly because their commander, Germanicus, had neither clear policy nor perhaps great capacity, for he tried now fanfare, now duplicity, now merely procrastination.

This Germanicus was Tiberius' nephew, son of the Drusus who, as we saw, almost subjugated Germany. When Augustus adopted Tiberius, he had the latter adopt Germanicus, who thus became heir to the throne. In emulation of Drusus, but also to avenge Teutoberg and to restore legionary morale, Germanicus decided to resume the conquest of Germany. The strategy was sound. He transported his troops through the Dutch lakes to the Ems River to avoid the German swamp and a possible surprise by Arminius. But a storm took heavy toll of men and ships, and minor blunders made the campaign inconclusive. Although Tiberius knew the difficulties of conquering Germany, he hesitated at first to restrain his nephew, lest he antagonize Germanicus' wife Agrippina, an ambitious and hot-tempered woman who headed the jealous Julian branch of the dynasty. Tiberius tactfully stopped the project only after two more campaigns had showed the excessive effort required. Germanicus' reputation did not suffer.

Tiberius' hands-off policy toward the Germans justified itself, for when Roman pressure relaxed they immediately resumed their inter-tribal quarrels. Even the powerful Maroboduus, king of the Marcomanni, lost control of his people. Luckily for him, he was accorded refuge in Italy, where he spent nineteen years as a royal hostage. But the hero of Teutoberg, Arminius, was assassinated by his own Cherusci. By subtly widening tribal rifts Tiberius prevented united action and kept the Empire's Rhine frontier secure.

The North heard the drums of war once more, under Claudius. The scene was Britain. Augustus had considered Britain more profitable as a friendly commercial ally than under military occupation. The situation, however, changed in his last years when a local chieftain, Cunobellinus, built up an extensive and cautiously nationalistic kingdom. His sons quarreled and split the chieftains into two factions, one of which sought Roman intervention. Gaius, then emperor, ordered the invasion of Britain, but it was Claudius who actually occupied it (A.D. 43).

Why conquer Britain? Perhaps the British Druids were collaborating with the national party, undertaking to stir up their Gallic kinsmen. An appeal to the Gauls to return to their ancestral religion and to revolt from Rome contradicted Imperial interests. British mineral resources must have been attractive. Lastly, Claudius, Drusus' son and Germanicus' brother, may have wanted the military achievement fate had denied them. At any rate he made the occupation good.

Able generals led the expedition. Claudius personally and the regime profited from this success. While the army, flushed with victory, drew closer to the principate than at any time since Augustus, civilians were also stirred. Poets glorified the conquest in song, architects with altars and arches, cities with festivals and congratulatory embassies to the Emperor, plain folk with votive tablets. Britain itself raised temples to Claudius the god, while the Senate decreed him a triumph and styled him Britannicus. The Emperor commemorated the event on his coins and named his son Britannicus.

Claudius annexed two other provinces, Mauretania and Thrace. Gaius had planned to occupy the former. When Claudius completed the task, Rome ruled all North Africa from the Red Sea to the Atlantic. Thrace was an enclave client-kingdom, which a powerful anti-Roman party, sometimes including the kings themselves, had kept distracted and weak. This internal strife, though not dangerous in itself, left the Danube border poorly guarded. Finally the patriots solicited barbarian help against a Romanizing king. Claudius thereupon annexed the kingdom outright and assigned the Danube frontier patrol to the Imperial army.

The greatest threat to the Pax Romana came from Parthia. The Parthians themselves were a minor menace, but their internal disorders and inability to prevent incursions into Roman territory made life insecure along the border. Tiberius and Claudius, like Augustus, supported rival kings, thus inexpensively keeping Parthia preoccupied, no difficult task, for strife was endemic in the royal house and the nobility. In Armenia too the emperors supported friendly kings, usually one of the trans-Caucasian princes whose independence Parthian control of Armenia would imperil. Tiberius strengthened Rome's position in Asia Minor by annexing Cappadocia and Commagene. Claudius went further; he stationed a legion at Zeugma on the Euphrates bend to consolidate Rome's control of the desert and put the Roman army within striking distance of Parthia.

Vologeses I (52–80) showed how dangerous Parthia could be under a tough king. In 54 he seized Armenia for his brother Tiridates. Though Nero's general Corbulo invaded Armenia and enthroned a pro-Roman king, Vologeses recaptured it and spread the war into the Roman provinces. Only after Nero made Corbulo generalissimo over every province from the Black Sea to the Arabian border and gave him 50,000 men did Vologeses agree to peace terms whereby Tiridates must receive his crown from the Emperor. Nero staged this ceremony in Rome in 66 with master showmanship. Although this seemed an honorable compromise, some felt that Nero had given too much too fast, lest a resounding victory make Corbulo a national hero and possibly a rival for the throne. The compromise however lasted almost fifty years, until Trajan's accession.

The Jewish Rebellion

In a more rebellious mood than Parthia was Judaea. Though Claudius had restored order between Jews and gentiles in Alexandria, he failed to rescue Judaea from the disorder caused by Gaius. Perhaps no emperor could have succeeded here, given the chasm between Jewish and Greco-Roman ideals. Augustus had kept the shrewd Herod I on the throne of Judaea, but Herod was not popular, being Jewish only in religion, not in blood nor in culture. Although patron of the Jews of the Diaspora, in Judaea he championed Hellenization, which for Jehovah's people was apostasy and treason. He even enacted laws at variance with those of the Bible. It was Herod who, according to St. Luke's Gospel, caused the slaughter of the innocents.

Affairs in Judaea took a turn for the worse when, after Herod's death,

Rome decided to administer it directly as a procuratorial province. Although the procurators, usually freedmen or knights, were generally incapable, they failed chiefly because the population scorned them as heathen dogs. After Judaea's violent reaction against worship of Gaius, Claudius made it semi-autonomous again as a vassal kingdom, placing over it his friend Herod Agrippa, Herod I's grandson. At his death three years later (A.D. 44) —much mourned, for he was popular—Claudius annexed the kingdom, perhaps lest left to itself it might become a Parthian satellite.

The Jews held Romans guilty on many counts. For one thing, they were conquerors. Their policy of Hellenizing the coastal cities disgusted patriots. Though Romans boasted of giving their subjects freedom of worship, they kept a garrison in the fortress dominating the Temple. Even the grant of dispensation from Imperial cult practices and from military service did not satisfy the Jews. Roman high taxes, the Jews claimed, made farming unprofitable and drove the peasants to brigandage. Romans were reproached, with some justice, for sending unsympathetic procurators who needlessly antagonized the people, but the trial of Jesus shows what extraordinary demands the Jews made on their governors. The procurator Pontius Pilate had no authority to crucify Jesus and he was reluctant to do so. He probably had power to save him, but if he had the Jews would have charged him with interfering with their religious freedom.

Lastly, the Romans upheld the landowning aristocracy, the core of the Sadducee party which controlled the priesthoods. In return the Sadducees made certain compromises in liturgy and law. The other party, the Pharisees, had popular support because it emphasized ritual, was strongly nationalist, and challenged the rich and the nobles. Jesus went outside of both parties. But he may have seemed to endorse the Sadducees both by saying, "Render unto Caesar the things that are Caesar's," and by his tireless denunciation of the Pharisees for their empty formalism.

A succession of incompetent governors after Agrippa's death played into the hands of the fiery Zealots, of false prophets and false Messiahs who incited civil disorder. An underground bandit organization systematically robbed the estates of the rich. Dispersed by the Roman militia, they reappeared as the "Men of the Knife." Their bloody deeds fully justified that title. The pro-Roman landowners retaliated and the high priest connived at judicial murders and summary executions, of which James, the brother of Jesus, was one victim.

Nero exploded the situation by decreeing that Caesarea was a Greek city, which by implication denied citizenship to Jewish residents unless they went to Greek schools, took oaths to the emperor, and worshiped heathen gods. Hotheads called this proof that the emperor himself, not

Fig. 49.3. Rome. Arch of Titus. Relief showing seven-branched candlestick from spoils of temple in Jerusalem, sacked in A.D. 70.

merely his procurators and soldiers, was Judaism's enemy. Widespread rebellion flared, Jews and non-Jews, nationalists and pro-Romans attacking and killing each other. Nero had to suppress the revolt. Early in 67 he sent an able general, Titus Flavius Vespasianus, a veteran of British service, to Palestine with over 50,000 troops. Vespasian soon reduced all Palestine except Jerusalem. A prey to religious fanatics and to groups who could expect no mercy if taken alive, the city barricaded itself while the Romans remained inactive, first, because in the summer of 68 they learned of Nero's fall and suicide, then because in 69 Vespasian himself was made emperor. His son Titus, who took over the command, did not begin siege operations until 70. In six months the city was taken and practically destroyed, and the Temple burned. In Titus' triumph the seven-branched candelabrum from the Temple was carried; its likeness in marble relief still adorns his Arch in the Roman Forum.

Nero and the Fall of the Julio-Claudians

Nero's death ended the Julio-Claudian dynasty. Some aspects of his conduct in life justify the legend of the monster come to the throne through the intrigues of his mother Agrippina, Claudius' third wife. He sent to their deaths Claudius' son Britannicus, whom he feared as a rival; his wife Octavia, to make way for the beautiful Poppaea; and even his own mother, who would not willingly resign her regency and whose advice he resented. His opponents, his fancied enemies, men and women whom he disliked or feared, and suspected conspirators Nero disposed of by peremptory orders to commit suicide. Thus he made away with Petronius, the most original writer of the age, whose social graces and exquisite artistic taste he could not hope to equal. Thus too he got rid of his counselor Burrus, to whom his reign owed its vigor and efficiency, his teacher Seneca, and the poet Lucan, among others. Outstanding generals, including the brilliant Corbulo, received the fatal order on the flimsiest suspicion of disloyalty. Several of his victims set examples of fortitude that will forever inspire mankind.

Nero is most execrated as the emperor who caused Christians to be burned alive or thrown to the wild beasts of the arena as scapegoats for the destructive Roman fire of 64, which he himself was accused of setting. But the mass punishment was too horrible even for a Roman audience. When Nero turned the execution into an elaborate carnival, and moreover built his Golden House, an imperial palace and park, in the devastated area, he was more than ever suspected of arson.

Therefore a nobleman, Calpurnius Piso, formed a conspiracy in which many illustrious Stoics participated. These men, even more than the old-fashioned aristocracy, were shocked by the tyrant's villainies, for to them a monarch should have been the father and friend of mankind. But the conspiracy was discovered and ruthlessly suppressed.

Much of Nero's tragedy lay, however, in the nature of the principate, which had tended inevitably to absolutism. More than any other Julio-Claudian, he was caught by the inner contradictions of the regime. He made minor good-will gestures towards the Senate, but kept firm hold on administration. Therefore old-line Republicans naturally considered the Princeps a despot. Nero's reign brought out the ambiguities because his character was contradictory. He was both mean and magnanimous, cruel and sensitive, vulgar and refined, amateurish and capable. His talent for poetry and music and his dilettantism proved his undoing. For when, with blood on his hands, he toured Greece competing as poet, singer, player, dancer, or charioteer, a wave of indignation swept over Italy and the conservative West. Both to the older nobility and to the respectable middle class, the matricide and arsonist had become a buffoon.

Another conspiracy was organized in Rome, which reached the provincial proconsuls and generals, and finally the soldiery. Fatally, Nero had never cultivated the army, never visited the men fighting for the Empire, either in Britain where the colorful Queen Boudicca had struck for independence, on the sun-parched Parthian border, in the rugged Armenian mountains, or on Judaea's desert hills. But he went to decadent Greece, his rancorous enemies argued, exhibiting himself as an actor and collecting prizes which no judge could refuse an emperor. When news reached Rome that the army in Spain and Gaul had proclaimed another emperor, and the Senate declared him a public enemy, the frightened Nero killed himself, exclaiming, "What an artist dies in me!"

Paradoxically, although Nero's memory was damned and his acts voided, the principate as an institution and the sovereignty of the princeps were strengthened under him. His philhellenic policy caused the East to regard him, and through him succeeding emperors, as friend and champion of culture and justice. His splendid court, his dazzling festivals, his magnificent buildings gave the principate a hitherto lacking royal air. The West too had felt the effulgence of a *roi soleil*. Senate, army and *bourgeoisie* by now regarded the principate too highly to have it occupied by a rogue. Nero fell, but the principate stood, more dynamic than ever.

Chapter 50/EARLY
IMPERIAL SOCIETY

Imperial Economic Policy

Good government has seldom paid quicker dividends than did the Augustan principate. The Italian public's conviction that Octavian's triumph meant peace, and the business community's confidence that the radical era was over created favorable employment and investment conditions. A government midway between Republican conservatism and Caesar's reforming ideals seemed to create the basis for a sound economy. The provinces too welcomed the end of organized oppression and the establishment of responsible government. Business was materially aided by a policy of plentiful sound money, public spending, good roads, and safe travel and transportation.

One of the first improvements was the conversion of Egyptian gold into Roman coins. Their wide circulation brought interest rates down from 12 percent to 4 percent per annum. The aerarium circulated the 400,000,000 sesterces annually in public expenditures, and Augustus put on the average 65,000,000 sesterces a year into circulation as salaries, donatives, bonuses, and purchases, chiefly of land for his veteran colonies.

All the Julio-Claudian emperors adhered to a sound money policy. Both Augustus and Nero reduced the weight of the aureus, a standard gold piece, apparently to make the currency keep step with a rising market. Toward the end of the Republic the aureus had weighed one-fortieth of a pound; Augustus reduced it to one forty-second, Nero to one forty-fifth, manipulations too slight to hurt business.

We lack sufficient data to appraise Nero's monetary policy. Whereas the late Republican (one-fortieth of a pound) aureus had been worth 84 silver denarii, the new (one forty-fifth of a pound) aureus was worth 96. But silver did not become cheaper; officially the ratio of gold to silver changed from 1:12.5 to 1:11.7. Actually it remained almost the same, for Nero lowered the silver content of the denarius, too, by substituting a fractional amount of copper for the silver removed. This debasement enriched the treasury without apparent harm to business.

Tiberius, while preserving the metallic fineness of the Augustan aureus, minted less money—16 emissions of gold and 36 of silver for his whole reign as against 80 of gold and 400 of silver for the first twenty-five years of Augustus'. Business was left without an adequate money supply, and the result was a financial crisis in A.D. 33. Tiberius' nearly three-billion-sesterces' reserve was practically so much money taken out of circulation. A third upsetting item was the mounting loss of gold to China and India, since imports of silks, spices, and other luxury goods were not balanced by exports. The silks and spices have perished, but the gold and silver coins that bought them have survived in hoards, especially in India.

All this made money tight. The Senate's attempt at corrective measures only made matters worse. In the scramble for ready cash propertied people had the advantage, but when they glutted the market with farm lands and real estate for immediate sale, values collapsed. Tiberius met the emergency with a donation of 100,000,000 sesterces, with which a bank was set up to make three-year interest-free loans against land collateral. Before long confidence was restored, but the business community had learned a lesson. Gaius' spending spree was possibly not unaccountably insane, but deliberately calculated to put money back into circulation.

Public works engaged thousands of artisans and myriads of unskilled workers in reconditioning Italian roads and bridges, repairing Roman streets, building or rebuilding temples, constructing aqueducts, porticoes, arches, theaters, basilicas, wharfs, fountains, and fora, and developing new urban regions. Julio-Claudian vigor in road-building was unprecedented and not matched again in Europe until the nineteenth-century railroad boom. Augustus laid down a magnificent road network for Gaul, connecting its principal centers. Tiberius displayed even greater energy. He did for Spain what Augustus had done for Gaul; and he linked it with Gaul and Italy in one broad system. He used the legions to build another road network, partly rock-cut, from Dalmatia to the upper and middle Danube, a daring and imaginative piece of engineering.

Gaius and Nero were scarcely less active. Claudius reconstructed the

Mediterranean coastal highway connecting Italy with Spain, improved the Iberian system to open up the mining districts, linked the Po with the Danube across the Alps, and repaired many Eastern highways and secondary roads. Most important of all, he reconditioned the roads from northern Italy to the English Channel, to facilitate communication with his new province of Britain.

Ancient historians tell us practically nothing about the Roman emperors as roadbuilders, but luckily the emperors themselves left their names on the milestones of every new or repaired road. From surviving milestones modern historians can reconstruct a given emperor's roadbuilding activity. Spanish milestones—15 for Tiberius, 7 for Gaius, 16 for Claudius, 9 for Nero—give some index of their comparative roadbuilding activity there.

Claudius and Nero built other public works. The former spent 1,500,-000,000 sesterces on utilitarian projects: aqueducts, flood control, and harbors. The latter rebuilt spectacularly large sections of Rome. We have mentioned his projected Corinthian canal, a work so ambitious that it was not resumed until 1882. Possibly the confiscation of large estates from Gaius to Nero was the emperors' way of diverting idle wealth, by accident or design, to the public treasuries, whence it was circulated as salaries, wages, donatives, or payments for public works. The money Claudius put on the market, however, came chiefly from mining in Spain, Gaul, Britain, Germany, and the Danube valley.

Private business kept pace with public spending, especially in Italy. Trade prospered, shipping was more active than ever, imports increased, while exports of wine, olive oil, perfume, ceramics, glass, bronze, and silverware reached wider markets. Fortunes were made not only in Rome but in almost every town and plantation; farming methods were improved, real-estate values doubled, and mortgages were liquidated. The rich built luxurious town houses and landscaped suburban gardens; the towns in a lively building program contributed materially to the waves of spending.

Talent was amply rewarded. Horace's income from his Sabine farm gave him leisure for poetry. Vergil was assigned a total of 10,000,000 sesterces. The principal court physicians were paid 250,000 a year; court tutors 100,000. A Massiliot physician in private practice received 200,-000 from a patient for the cold-water cure. Another Marseilles doctor left a fortune of 20,000,000. These were obviously exceptional cases, but they show that the times favored men of industry and talent.

Italian prosperity was not secured at the provinces' expense. Augustus aimed to knit Italy and the provinces, including the border kingdoms, into an integrated but not regimented economy. Tampering little with local methods, he aided chiefly by removing the debris left by the civil wars and creating an atmosphere where peaceful arts might flourish.

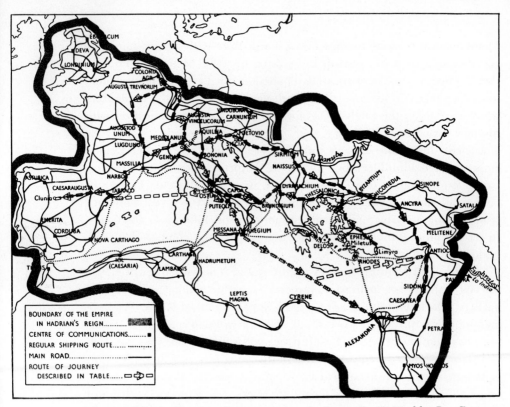

Fig. 50a. Map to illustrate Roman communications. (L. H. Waddy, *Pax Romana and World Peace*, London, 1950. Facing p. 122.)

EXPLANATORY TABLE

(*The routes shown are partly conjectural*)

DATE	DETAILS OF JOURNEY (Approximate distances in English miles)	AVERAGE SPEED FOR HOW LONG	FACILITIES	REFERENCE
9 B.C.	Tiberius: 180 miles in 1 day	180 for 1 day	Exceptional	Valerius Maximus, *Facta Memorabilia*, v, 3
A.D. 4	Special Messenger: Lycia–Rome: 1300 + miles in ?36 days	45–50 for 36 days	Exceptional	Inscription (D. 140)
A.D. 41	Imperial Courier: Rome–Antioch by sea, bad weather: 3 months	—	—	Josephus, *Bell. Jud.* ii, 10, 5
?A.D. 49	St. Paul: Troas–Neapolis (port near Philippi): 140 miles by sea in 2 days	70 for 2 days	—	Acts xvi, 11
?A.D. 56	St. Paul: Philippi–Troas: by sea, 5 days	30 for 5 days	—	Acts xx, 6
?A.D. 56	St. Paul: Mitylene–Miletus: by sea, 3 days	—	—	Acts xx, 15
?A.D. 62	St. Paul: Rhegium–Puteoli: by sea, 1 day	200 for 1 day	—	Acts xxviii, 14
A.D. 68	Special Messenger: Rome–Clunia, ?6½ days (including Tarraco–Clunia, 332 miles in ?1½ days)	190 for 1½ days	Exceptional	Plutarch, *Galba* 7; see map
A.D. 68	Imperial Courier: Rome–Alexandria by sea, 28 days or less	—	—	Inscription
A.D. 69	Special Messenger: Mainz–Cologne: 100 miles in ?12 hours	200 for ½ day	Exceptional	Tac. *Hist.* i, 56
A.D. 69	Special Messenger: Mainz–Rheims–Rome: 1300 + miles in ?9 days	145 for 9 days	Exceptional	Tac. *Hist.* i, 12
A.D. 193	Imperial Courier: Rome–Alexandria: by land, distance uncertain, 63–64 days	—	Exceptional	Inscription
A.D. 238	Imperial Courier: Aquileia–Rome: 470 miles in 3–4 days	120 for 4 days	Exceptional	S.H.A. *Duo Max.* 25

The result was everywhere the same: no evidence of offended national or tribal honor, but rather a general contentment. Let two examples suffice.

Egypt enjoyed greater stability at home and on its borders and a better administration than in the last two centuries of Ptolemaic rule. Civil order was re-established in Alexandria, the commercial center of the East, whereby Greeks, Levantines, and Jews lived again at peace and put their energies into the production and export trade which made theirs the Empire's richest city. The legions were set to rebuild the irrigation system, thus putting new lands under cultivation and making larger crops possible. Egyptian houses under Augustus were more substantial than they had been for a century past, and the average family was better off. Quasi-municipal government in the nome-capitals invigorated communal life and strengthened Greek culture, as greater refinement in the arts shows.

Augustus favored Gaul particularly. From 27 to 8 B.C. he visited it five times. He lived there continuously from 16 to 13 B.C. He founded or colonized no less than thirty-three cities and towns. The monuments of his reign—arches, theaters, amphitheaters, and temples, the *Maison Carrée* of Nimes among others—proclaim prosperity. The architecture and culture of the Roman settlements inspired the old Gallic villages to rebuild themselves into cities. Following Agrippa's comprehensive plan, periodic censuses were taken, the entire country surveyed, the town and tribe domains carefully mapped. The delimitation of each village area and each farm boundary helped to create the industrious and stable farming population and vigorous parish community still traditional in France. Gaul so prospered that there were no adverse effects when Augustus quadrupled Caesar's low tribute of 10,000,000 sesterces. Now began that steady advance which in fifty years made Gaul the Empire's richest province. Spanish Cadiz might boast more knights than any city outside Italy, but Lugdunum, the Gallic capital, became under Augustus the West's most important city after Rome. At the hub of the Imperial highways between the Atlantic and the Rhine, it was probably the busiest center of Imperial provincial administration. Its mint issued most of the gold for the whole Empire and it was the seat of an urban cohort.

Farming and Farmers

Agriculture formed the core of Roman economy both in the Empire at large and in Italy. The latter did not produce enough wheat for a population which by the end of the Julio-Claudian dynasty was close to twenty million. The deficit was met by imports from Egypt, Sicily, Spain, Africa, and other provinces. Only a part was tribute; the rest represented purchases. To stimulate imports Tiberius gave dealers a bounty of eight sesterces for every bushel sold, while Claudius' harbor at Ostia was provided with grain elevators; Claudius also devised insurance for ships and cargoes against losses from storms. He even offered Roman citizenship to shipowners of Latin status who would import grain.

Wheat imports were partly paid for with profits from fruit culture. Grapes were raised all over the peninsula, and viticulture even on the poorest soil generally paid better than the best wheat farms. A careful grower could net as high as $68 per acre, a good return, even compared with California. This meant of course that the value of vineyard land was high: $105 for an unimproved acre to $1150 an acre for the best. The choicest Italian wines drove the Greek from the market.

Olive culture brought the next highest farm profits, partly because Italian soil was perfect for it, but chiefly because the Western provinces were not yet competitive. Not until the second century of our era was Spanish oil plentiful and excellent enough to capture the Roman market.

Cereals, fruits, nuts, and various vegetables were raised for local consumption, forming, as they still do, the staple diet of even the poorest people. Figs were cheap and nourishing. Quinces, jujubes, peaches, pears, cherries, and apples had recently been acclimated. Alfalfa was prized as fodder, but clover as better for milk production. Native forests probably supplied all the timber and lumber needed for industry. Florists throve in the neighborhood of the larger cities; so did poultrymen and bee-keepers. Cattle, sheep, goats, and pigs were carefully bred. Horse-raising was remunerative, since horses were the fastest means of transport and racing a national craze. Italians plowed with oxen, while practically all overland freight was carried on mule-back. An exceptionally fine ass stud sold for $27,500. Pack asses which could carry 200 or 300 pounds cost an average of $7. A mule, probably old, cost about $5 in Pompeii. Small talk among the dinner guests of Trimalchio, a rich freedman probably of Nero's time, throws light on the scientific management of farming, stock-raising, and husbandry. His rams came from Tarentum, his bees from Athens, he trafficked with India, and his mules were especially bred.

Most farmers found their occupation worth their while. We hear nowhere that the 200,000 men whom Augustus settled on farms drifted back wholesale to the cities, like Sulla's unsuccessful veterans. Their holdings were modest, but in Italian climate and soil a ten- or twenty-acre farm could support a family comfortably, since it could yield at once wheat, forage, varied garden products, olives, fruits, grapes, and honey. Consequently a farmer scarcely purchased anything except manufactured goods. The small peasant was indeed well-to-do if he lived near a city where he could sell his surplus at good prices; and Italy was, we know, studded with prosperous towns.

Campania especially was heavily industrialized, and the Po valley was a land of prosperous farmers, of increasing numbers of artisans called in to develop local industries, and of retired tradesmen, soldiers, and Imperial civil servants. The rich soil of the Po valley gave more generous rewards than other parts of Italy. Its growing industries profited from the great highways which on one side connected it with the capital, on the other with Spain, Gaul, the Rhineland, Switzerland, Bavaria, Austria, and the other Danubian provinces. The roads caused innkeeping to flourish: property-owners along the great trunk roads might build inns with their own slaves as managers and helpers, and sell their own products there.

The small farm was the rule everywhere except in extreme south Italy, parts of Campania, Etruria, Latium, and the highest mountain regions where ranching or shepherding paid best. The hill districts were more profitably worked by small-scale owners or tenants, working between 50- and 20-acre farms. A farm of 100 to 130 acres was considered to be a medium-sized property. Absentee landlordism was developing only sporadically, nowhere justifying Pliny's remark that large estates were the ruination of Italy. That large estates did exist however is clear from Columella's *On Agriculture,* a work on scientific farm-management, written in Nero's reign for the guidance of the planter of a thousand acres. Even so, the fortune of 300,000,000 sesterces amassed by the freedman Volusius from large-scale farming operations was altogether exceptional.

The typical large estate was run with slave labor and needed little outside help, even at harvest time. The hordes of paupers moving from estate to estate to cultivate or to harvest had decreased since Gracchan days; now sections of an estate were more often rented to freeman sharecroppers or to cash tenants working the land either themselves or with the help of slaves.

As compared with the late Republic, the trend was towards more free labor and free small enterprise. Cato the Elder knew no way of working a large estate except slave labor. A hundred years later this was still the custom, but Varro wanted the more important work done by free workers, specifically because they used their wits. Still later Vergil romanticized the small free landowner: the word "slave" is not in the *Georgics.* Finally towards the end of the Julio-Claudian period more voices, including Columella's, proclaimed the advantages of free labor, while Seneca recorded that free tenants were on the increase. Humanitarian philosophers advocated the spread of free peasantry. Unfortunately the movement was towards free tenantry rather than free ownership. In practice, however, the distinction was unreal, especially on the imperial domains where the cultivators were owners in everything but name.

While life for the farmer and his hands was not easy, still in terms of adequate food and shelter, and especially human dignity, it was infinitely better than the urban worker's. If Horace, Tibullus, and Vergil romanticized its joys, that does not mean that the joys were a myth, or that they existed only for the gentleman farmer. The poets, especially Vergil, could not have spoken with such conviction if they had not actually observed such a way of life.

Industry and Trade

Most manufacturing was done in small industrial shops. There was house-industry too, especially in rural districts, but cheap goods produced in regular industrial establishments made it uneconomical. The small shop operated by its owner-craftsman with one, two, or three apprentices was the general rule. Iron tools were manufactured in small shops chiefly in Campania, Venetia, and Etruria near Elba where there are still iron mines. Although Campania was paramount in the manufacture of bronzeware and copper utensils, bronzesmiths and coppersmiths were numerous enough elsewhere, in Rome and Milan for instance, to form guild associations. Lead water-pipes were made in shops by smiths who were also plumbers. Many have been found in Rome, fewer in other large cities. Evidently more households in Rome than elsewhere had running water. Small shops produced gold and silver ornaments. Jewelers, pearl dealers, cameo cutters, and intaglio workers found much employment in an ostentatious society. One section of the Sacred Way in Rome was lined with jewelry shops. The jewelry, bronzeware, furniture, and luxury trades did not use mass production, but filled individual orders. In the small shop were combined both production and sales, a practice rare in the modern world. The man at the bench served also behind the counter, being owner, craftsman, and retailer in one. This aspect of ancient industry doubtless gave the men engaged in it a sense of satisfaction and dignity.

The Roman Empire had nothing like the modern factory system— that is, no industrial establishments owned by absentee capitalists, employing hundreds of workmen solely to tend machines. But there were large shops employing scores or hundreds—some even say thousands— of workmen and owned by individual industrialists or even by joint-stock companies. The "factory system" was most used in industries requiring specialization and division of labor and in those involving mass production.

The manufacture of bronzeware, used in the Empire as universally as aluminum today, is a case in point. Platters, bowls, and kitchen utensils in rich homes were made of bronze. Every well-to-do household had bronze lamps, lampstands, tripods, and braziers, prized for their durability and admired for their artistic merit, as well as bronze tables, couches, bedsteads, and strong-boxes, such as now adorn our museums. Bronze was also more used than nowadays in casting busts, statues, and statuettes. The large capital investment and the fine division of labor indispensable in this industry seem to postulate a near-factory system. Capua in Campania was the largest bronze manufacturing center.

The "factory system" likewise is implied in the rapid changes in silver-ware fashions in the early Empire, attested by the objects themselves; by the division of the silversmith's craft into casters, polishers, engravers, and embossers; and by Pliny's statement that the industry was equipped to satisfy the ever-changing public taste.

Glassware too was apparently manufactured in factories. The invention of the blowpipe, probably in Augustus' time, made it possible to produce purer and cheaper glass, individual molds being no longer necessary. In the hot Roman summer the genteel served food in glass dishes. Poets call water "glass-like," which suggests that the use of glass was common. In Tiberius' time, unbreakable glass bowls were invented. When the inventor proved his claims before the Emperor by dashing a bowl on the floor, Tiberius allegedly ordered him executed, for if he marketed his wares gold would lose its value and an economic collapse ensue. Ordinary and stained-glass windows have been found in Pompeii.

In textiles, homespun was produced everywhere, as in every age before our own. Enterprising fullers (the ancient dry-cleaners) bought the homespun, then processed it for the market. Fullers were numerous enough to form local guilds in most large cities. Rich ones donated large sums to their towns or erected guild and market halls. The factory system, run with slave labor, seems to have prevailed in the Po valley, whence came fine woolens and carpets, and also in Tarentum, where special equipment and highly trained workmen produced sheer fabrics. Cheap clothing, worn especially by slaves, was apparently a specialty of the "factory system."

The factory technique prevailed in brick and tile production, where the market was inexhaustible, especially in Italy, throughout the first century A.D. The devastating fire of 64 in Rome further increased the demand. Since weight made a long haul of brick and tile too costly, nearly every city had its own brickyards. But transmarine shipments were not unknown; for instance, brick made at Ariminum was sold in Dalmatia, while river shipments on the Po and the Tiber were not unusual. Trademarks stamped on bricks and tiles make it possible to trace the number, location, and distribution-points of factories and to calculate their output—for instance, over a million bricks a year by one Annius Verus' factory.

Many manufactures showed advances in techniques. The chemical industries discovered how to process better colors at a lower cost; how to substitute new substances for the perfumes of the East; how to compound better alloys, for example, in soldering, or converting iron to steel. Echoes of Roman pride in these achievements have reached us in

Fig. 50.1. Pompeii. House of the Tragic Poet, model. The model is split longitudinally to show structure: a long narrow entrance flanked by shops and paved in mosaic; atrium with stairs to servants' quarters; on the ground floor, porter's room and bedrooms. The atrium (right center) is painted with scenes from the Trojan legend. Next comes the *tablinum,* with paintings of scenes from tragedy and the theater, and finally (left), the peristyle, with its family shrine, and, opening out of it, the dining room frescoed with mythological scenes. (Rome, Museo della Civiltà Romana; J. Felbermeyer photo)

Pliny the Elder's encyclopedic *Natural History.* The progress in glass-blowing was part of this mild industrial renaissance. So also was the development of central heating, the use of cranes for loading and unloading ships and of derricks for heavy hoisting, a wider application of levers, blocks, and pulleys, and the perfecting of the water-wheel.

The fullest documentation of Julio-Claudian industry and trade is in the ruins of Pompeii, destroyed by the eruption of Vesuvius in 79, eleven years after the dynasty's end. Every object there testifies to prosperity, art widespread rather than refined, many and diverse local manufactures, vigorous import trade, wide distribution of wealth, and an efficient municipal administration. Although not every Italian city was so flourishing, there would certainly have been no prosperous Pompeii without an equally healthy economy elsewhere.

Slaves and Freedmen

The slave's lot was improving. He still had to work from dawn to dark, but he was better treated, since fewer wars meant fewer slaves, and those raised in farm or household were the chief source of supply and therefore an expensive and valuable commodity. Slave women who had borne three children were regularly freed: Romans of the early Empire aimed, not to increase the slave population, but to keep it substantially at the same level.

The rural slave, like his city brother, received shoes, clothing, and five pecks of wheat a month for his keep, but apparently no pocket money. But he probably got other gratuities, chiefly wine, oil, and fruits. He was allowed to join his master and the free peasants in the frequent neighborhood festivals, especially at harvest time. We have no certain proof that slaves were a majority in agriculture or small industry. The shoemaker, tailor, baker, and in general every artisan who sold the wares manufactured in his own small shop was ordinarily freeborn in the towns and villages, but more likely a freedman in the cities, especially in Rome. But even there the jewelers were mostly Italians or naturalized immigrants; freedmen were a minority. If the shop needed two or three assistants, the free master ordinarily employed first his sons, then slaves. There were of course more slaves in medium-sized establishments.

Only the "factory" employed all slave labor. We know of one ceramics concern employing fifty-eight slaves, and a brick factory employing fifty. Certain industries used only slave labor, for instance, the quarrying of Luna (Carrara) marble, which occupied 5000 to 6000 men, or mining, which used slaves or sometimes the forced labor of condemned criminals. Large-scale ranching too employed slaves almost entirely.

While the condition of "factory" and ranch slaves must have been wretched, slave life in small businesses was much better. First, in the Roman Empire there was apparently no race or minority intolerance. Second, a broad camaraderie prevailed between master and worker both inside and outside the shop. Third, incentives like profit-sharing, bonuses on output, and sales commissions spurred both thrift and talent. The number of slaves who bought their freedom out of savings or, more frequently, were given it by appreciative masters must have been considerable. Normally a freed artisan would go into business for himself.

Does slavery lead to character deterioration? Funeral inscriptions testify that in the Roman Empire slaves were often admired for their character. On stone after stone are recorded industrial and business workers and household servants who won freedom for honesty, gentleness, affection, or faithful service.

Roman society of this time shows an improvement in both private and social morality. The slave's lot was being bettered by an increased social consciousness, both among the educated, as Seneca testifies, and among the lower classes, as witness the teaching of St. Paul and the Apostles. Laws recognized slaves as human beings, granting them rights never dreamed of under the Republic: to inherit property, to have their evidence in court accepted like a free man's, and most of all the right to the inviolability of the human body—rights which extended to the slave the concept of the dignity of man. Augustus forbade the torture of slaves to force testimony against their masters; Tiberius ruled that a slave under indictment must be given all legal benefits granted to freemen; Nero forbade masters to continue, without a court order, the practice of making slaves fight wild beasts in the arena, as a punishment or for profit; Claudius legalized the marriage of a slave with a free woman and ordered that sick or aged slaves exposed by their masters become automatically free.

Imperial legislation was thus following public opinion. Even an esthete like Propertius made his Cynthia plead from her grave in behalf of two women slaves. While St. Paul was affirming that freemen and slaves were one in Christ, Petronius claimed that slaves were human beings and Seneca argued that class distinctions are snobbish and that slave birth is no bar to Heaven. Thousands of epitaphs referring to slaves testify to their improved status and suggest that they deserved it. One reads: "Florentina, my sweet wife, mistress of my heart, modesty and purity and a loyalty which kept inviolate the marriage couch have made thee dear to thy husband."

Julio-Claudian Art

Before Caesar's time the West had appropriated from the East taxes, possessions, arts, and ideas, but had given little in return. With Augustus this one-way system was reversed. The West still borrowed more heavily than ever in art, philosophy, and letters, but of material assets it took nothing more than fair taxes. In return it gave the East unprecedented peace and justice. The resulting prosperity gave congenial employment to ability and skill. Eastern peoples rebuilt and enlarged their cities; they also brought their skills to the West, where new colonies and older towns were competing in civic architecture, and especially to Rome, now fast becoming the ancient world's most imposing capital. Although perhaps the artists and artisans who beautified Italian cities were mostly Hellenistic immigrants, Romans provided the moving ideal which inspired these workers to create statues, reliefs, and buildings not merely Hellenistic but thoroughly Roman in spirit.

Julio-Claudian achievements in art were remarkable. Money was spent freely, and each emperor tried to equal or outdo his predecessors as builder. Tiberius built the *Castra Praetoria,* an immense (1380 by 1200 foot) brick and concrete barrack-fortress. He lived on the Palatine, not in Augustus' modest house, but in a magnificent new palace, with spacious atrium, fish-pond, and library, the earliest of the sumptuous

Fig. 50.2. Rome. Circus Maximus (and Palatine), model. For chariot races. Over 2,000 feet long, said to have seated 250,000. The central parapet (*spina*) was decorated with obelisks. The emperor could enter his box direct from his palace on the Palatine. (Rome, Museo della Civiltà Romana; J. Felbermeyer photo)

mansions which were to make that hill the Empire's most imposing residential center. Architects and engineers joined forces in executing Claudius' public works. The harbor at Ostia was his most spectacular achievement. He expanded the aqueduct system and monumentalized with splendid gates, like the surviving Porta Maggiore, the points where main highways passed beneath it. During his reign was also built, probably by a neo-Pythagorean cult, a subterranean basilica, forerunner of Christian types, with narthex or vestibule, a barrel-vaulted nave supported by piers, two lateral aisles, and an apse decorated in stucco with a scene in which the poetess Sappho triumphs over death.

The energetic Julio-Claudian building activity culminated under Nero, who on land cleared after the conflagration of 64 built his incomparable Golden House, a combined imperial palace and country estate in the heart of Rome, twice the size of the modern Vatican City, with pavilions, villas, gardens, orchards, parks, and lakes. A colonnaded avenue connected it with the east end of the Forum. Nero's two chief architects, Severus and Celer, also opened broad monumental vistas elsewhere in the city and cut straight boulevards through some of the slums.

Official sculpture, idealized and dignified under Augustus, was often

Fig. 50.3. The Altar of Piety. The three figures at the left have been identified with some uncertainty as Propertius, or Livy, Vergil, and Horace watching the Secular Games (17 B.C.). The frontal figure (right center) is probably Claudius officiating as *flamen* at the dedication of the altar. (Rome, Villa Medici; Fototeca)

frigid, but in private portraits Republican naturalism persisted. The bust of Nero's general Corbulo in the Conservatori reveals a firmness of character which Nero did well to respect. The bronze Julio-Claudian youth in the Metropolitan Museum of Art, with its delicately fashioned body, its sensitive face, and meditative mood incarnates the elusive transition from boy to man.

Official reliefs continued to commemorate key events in the emperor's reign or to symbolize his cardinal policies. The originals from Rome were adapted for propaganda purposes in the provinces: thus Carthage had a smaller version of the Ara Pacis. A Roman original, a free development of the Ara Pacis technique, is the Claudian Altar of Piety now in the Villa Medici, which was probably surrounded with an enclosure bearing a processional frieze like the Ara Pacis, the occasion being perhaps Claudius' installation as *Flamen Augustalis*. Three highly individualized spectators of the procession may just possibly be Livy, Vergil, and Horace. The relief portrays temples (probably of Mars the Avenger, the Great Mother, and the Palatine Apollo) of the same height as the human figures. This departure from realism for narrative's sake foreshadows the technique of Trajan's Column. The absence of allegory or legend differentiates this altar from the Ara Pacis. The regime could now stand on its own feet without need of props from the past. Here Augustan ideals were set forth to edify a new generation, which paid little heed, for sixteen years after the Altar of Piety was dedicated, a new and impious civil war broke out.

Chapter 51 / THE
BOURGEOIS EMPIRE

The Flavian Dynasty (69–96)

Only after Galba, the legions' candidate, had said he would accept the throne, did the Senate declare Nero deposed. This sequence underscores Senate subservience; the army called the tune. But discord rent the army when the praetorians, on the pretext of Galba's incompetence, supported another candidate, Otho, whom Nero had made governor of Lusitania as compensation for stealing his beautiful wife Poppaea. Confusion became worse confounded when the German legions hailed as emperor their own commander Vitellius.

Otho's and Vitellius' simultaneous emergence was no mere accident of faulty army liaison. It reflected jealousy between branches, but still more, a social difference between the higher *bourgeoisie* of the praetorian guard and the middle and lower strata in the legions. The legions envied the praetorians their better pay and quarters, shorter enlistment and urban duty, by virtue of which last they had usurped the privilege of nominating the Imperial successor. Now the provincial legions were challenging this privilege by proclaiming first Galba and then Vitellius. These internal differences opened the way to military anarchy and civil

Fig. 51.1. Cancelleria relief. The figure at the right center is the Emperor Vespasian, greeting his son Domitian, in the presence of the Genius of the Roman People (beardless) and of the Roman Senate (bearded). At this symbolic moment the Flavian dynasty is founded and Rome is relieved of the troubles of the Four Emperors' Year (A.D. 69). Rome, Vatican Museum; Fototeca)

war, especially in north Italy where the Empire's main highways met.

The Eastern legions did not at first play at kingmaking, perhaps because of better discipline or a higher sense of duty, or more likely because half of them were preoccupied with the Jewish revolt. They swore allegiance to Galba; after Galba was slain (January 69) to Otho, and on Otho's suicide to Vitellius. But when the last-named, too, proved weak and incompetent, the Eastern and Danube legions elevated Titus Flavius Vespasianus, the general of the Jewish war, the fourth emperor to reign in 69. A bloody battle at Cremona between the Vitellians and the Danubian legions marked the height of a brief but fratricidal war.

The new emperor (69–79) embodied all the virtues of the middle class. Of farming ancestry, a centurion's son who rose by his bootstraps to be a knight, he had reached the highest peacetime posts, a seat in the Senate, a general's commission, and the consulship. He exemplifies the open society, the opening of careers to talent, fostered by Caesar and his successors. His marble portrait confirms the ancient descriptions of him as middle-class, thrifty, shrewd, witty, unimaginative and unemotional, impervious to intrigue or flattery, accustomed to life's rough-and-tumble and taught by his father, a moneylender, to drive a hard bargain. His character therefore qualified him well for the difficult task of restoring prosperity, justice, and order and controlling the army. He rehabilitated north Italy and the provinces, refilled the treasury emptied by Nero's extravagances, reinforced the frontier, aided farmers, established colonies —in short, re-energized the administration and revitalized the Empire. As a result, in his lifetime men began to feel quietly confident of the "Eternity of the Roman People," and at his death the Senate deified him.

However stereotyped the act, the appreciation of his beneficent rule was genuine.

To legitimize his position, Vespasian took the name "Augustus." To counter the Senate (which despite its many accretions still considered itself the embodiment of the old Republican nobility and regarded him as a usurper of the highest office which had always been held by a patrician) he needed constitutional and legal authority higher than his nomination by the army or even his election by the Senate. He sought this authority directly from the People. Although since Tiberius, as we saw, the People's Assembly no longer elected magistrates, it could still legislate. Vespasian now had the Assembly give him the fullest rights of initiative, execution, and interpretation of the laws, and of discretion and final decision in every department of government—civil, military, and religious. This law became the basis for all his successors' powers to the end of the Empire.

This did not imply that Vespasian was authorized to be an autocrat, or that the principate was licensed to change its Augustan nature. Rome was too conservative for that. For the law specified that his powers were to be exercised "constitutionally," as they had been by Augustus, Tiberius, and Claudius. The omission of the tyrannical Gaius and Nero served notice that arbitrary rule would not be tolerated.

But statutes alone do not explain a government's nature nor prescribe its limits, even where the constitution has been written down as in the United States. Above, beneath, and around the founding fathers' explicit directions is their inner spirit, which lives on from generation to generation, never fully stated and never fully realized. To define it is impossible. It manifests itself in the agreement of public opinion, permitting certain actions, prohibiting others, or fostering certain trends. To it every branch of government, including the courts, is responsive. In the Roman Empire too, the princeps was expected to act within the compass of educated opinion and never to go beyond the spirit of the laws and the unwritten constitution. In short, constitutionalism was the rule from Augustus to Vespasian and from Vespasian down to the third century. Absolutism was the exception; a despotic princeps paid for it with his life. The bourgeois Emperor's principal merit was to revive and insure for another 150 years the idea of the Augustan principate, of limited constitutional powers.

While the Assembly's grant legalized Vespasian's succession, it did not help his social status. If nobility depended on consulships, Vespasian knew how to acquire it. In his short ten-year reign he and his sons, Titus and Domitian, were consuls twenty-one times; thus no other Roman family could compare with the Flavians in nobility. He further improved his standing by raising his family, and others of ancient or recent distinction, to patrician rank, chiefly to fill priesthoods reserved to patricians.

Vespasian carried his program despite sabotage by the senatorial aristocracy. To emphasize the legitimacy of his succession to the Julio-Claudian line he had the Senate confer on his sons the title "Caesar" as advance notice that both were heirs apparent and would succeed him without break. He lived modestly and restored the gardens of Nero's Golden House to public use to emphasize that his government was to be not Neronian but Augustan, not centered in a royal palace and a megalomaniac's whims, but lodged in a modest household and dedicated to the Empire's welfare.

Titus duly succeeded his father, and like him was deified, for his short reign (79–81) appeared even more beneficent. He counted that day lost on which he had done no good deeds, and he died, Suetonius tells us, "the darling of the human race." Only the Jews did not mourn his loss.

Domitian (81–96) matched his father and brother in efficient administration of the provinces and, at first, in sense of obligation for the public welfare. Indeed Vespasian, Titus, and Domitian in his early years made the word "princeps" synonymous with "first servant." And they successfully translated this ideal into actuality by choosing as public servants at all administrative levels able and honest men. But Domitian required poets and courtiers to address him as *Dominus et Deus* (Master and God), and his domineering taciturnity caused him to lose credit for his good qualities.

Domitian, like Gaius, was suspicious, fearful, and therefore cruel. He never recovered from the shock of a revolt by the lower Rhine legions which set up a rival emperor. Exiles and executions quickly followed, and the Senate, thoroughly cowed, became the partner of his judicial murders of senators and high officials. When his reign of terror began to endanger even the lives of the praetorian prefects and his own household, a palace conspiracy murdered him.

Flowering of the Adoptive System (96–180)

The conspirators against Domitian had been careful to choose beforehand a successor acceptable to the Senate, the elderly Marcus Cocceius Nerva (96–98), twice consul, whose poetry Nero had admired. Kindly and colorless, Nerva was esteemed by his senatorial colleagues. He swore on accession to execute no senator; it was expected of him to be the reverse of Domitian. Tacitus praises him for harmonizing two hitherto irreconcilable opposites, Imperial authority and individual liberty, and for inaugurating an era of good feeling, without thought control. But in fairness the revolutionists who assassinated Domitian deserve some of the credit,

Fig. 51.2. Burning the tax rolls. Members of the Praetorian Guard bring to be burned the records of arrears of provincial or Italian taxes, at the order of Trajan or Hadrian. From a balustrade formerly in the Forum. (Rome, Curia; Fototeca)

for serving notice that public opinion would no longer tolerate a tyrant. Furthermore the new freedom apparently stemmed rather from the Emperor's weakness than from any fundamental political theory. For Nerva permitted excesses: in the desecration of Domitian's memory, in the wreaking of senatorial vengeance. He allowed confusion, indecision, and fear so to invade the government that thoughtful men remarked that mob license is a worse evil than tyranny. He died after reigning seventeen months.

Nerva's greatest service to the Empire was to adopt as son and successor Marcus Ulpius Traianus (98–117), whom he hardly knew, but who was to prove one of history's most successful rulers. Having chosen a military career, Trajan came to know in detail frontier topography and provincial needs. His courage and unaffected comradeship won the soldiers' confidence. Vespasian had elevated his father to patrician rank. Modest, open-hearted, affable, but dignified and strong-minded, Trajan won his people's trust. His immense successes in war and peace as administrator, statesman, increaser of the Empire's might, above all, as humane and democratic ruler, won him the title *Optimus Princeps,* the Best of Emperors.

Trajan was a native of Spain, but that fact did not carry the modern connotation of different nationality. Italica, his birthplace, was a Roman city, founded by Scipio Africanus long before (206 B.C.); Trajan's ancestors had been among its earlier settlers. The settlers of a Roman city within a province were not provincials either in law or in culture. The provincials were natives, conquered and dominated by Rome. Two separate and different worlds lived thus side by side in each province, the Italians or Roman citizens and the provincials or *peregrini.* But Spain was specially privileged. The Italian cities there—Italica, Corduba,

Tarraco, and scores of others—had Romanized the natives so thoroughly that Vespasian had given the whole province Latin status, which meant Roman citizenship in the not-too-distant future.

The Spaniard Trajan's accession was therefore significant, not because Spaniards were taking Imperial rule away from Italians, but because Romans from overseas were sharing that honor with homeland Romans. Caesar's system, expanded by Claudius, of careers open to talent, had now extended to the Imperial throne itself. Within fifty years of Claudius' opening of senatorial careers to provincials, Trajan, a provincial of the senatorial class, rose to justify Caesar's, Augustus', and Claudius' faith in the average educated man.

Whatever hopes of renewed influence the Senate had at Nerva's accession vanished during Trajan's reign. It still shared in administration, but exerted little effect on the Emperor's decisions and plans. The Emperor was still master, and with finesse Trajan made that mastery palatable. His powers were no less sweeping, his responsibilities no less firmly held, than Domitian's. But he was no suspicious, cruel despot; he was simply convinced that the Senate was incapable of intelligent action. Nevertheless he was politely attentive to the Fathers and they came to regard him as one of themselves. Of course by Trajan's time at least half the Senate was recruited from Italian and provincial families without Republican traditions or prejudices, and therefore more in step with political realities. Trajan's fine tact and high purpose disarmed hostility. He regularly consulted senatorial leaders in friendly informal meetings and although he seldom took their advice, the Fathers' pride was saved. In the hope of increasing the Senate's freedom and dignity he introduced the secret ballot for elections of magistrates. He was shocked when, on the first occasion, a number of votes were returned scribbled with obscene remarks.

Trajan's deathbed adoption of his townsman and kinsman Publius Aelius Hadrianus brought another extraordinary man to the throne of the Caesars. Hadrian (117–138) was the most intellectual of Roman emperors. His ancestors had moved to Italica at its founding. One of them had been sponsored for the Senate by Julius Caesar. Hadrian had received the best Latin and Greek education from tutors selected by Trajan. Then he entered the military career, took part in Trajan's major wars, became general of legions and governor of provinces, and consul at thirty-two. Thus he had experience of most of the Empire and of administration before reaching the throne.

Hadrian was even more solicitous than Trajan and the Flavians for the Empire's welfare. But whereas Trajan had expanded the Empire by war, Hadrian's policy, like Augustus', was contraction, consolidation, and peace. Like Augustus too, he visited every province, developing as he went a comprehensive plan of economic rehabilitation. A real connoisseur, he promoted the fine arts and subsidized a revival of Hellenistic culture in art, philosophy, and literature. Half facetiously, half contemptuously, his fellow-Romans dubbed him "the Greekling."

Haunted by the siren voice of the arts, striving to create beautiful things around him—temples, mansions, porticoes, gardens, libraries, statues, as well as a living world of music, fine speech, high thought—in a feverish quest for ever new sensual and intellectual experiences, Hadrian in his last years lost contact with the world of simple human beings. Politically he earned thereby the Senate's profound dislike; psychologically the chills of loneliness closed in more tightly on his ever-seeking spirit. As he lay waiting for the end, he composed this resigned, sentimental, mannered little poem to his soul

> Anima vagula, blandula,
> Hospes comesque corporis
> Quae nunc abibis in loca
> Pallidula, rigida, nudula,
> Nec, ut soles, dabis iocos . . .

> Little soul, gentle and drifting, guest and companion
> of my body, now you will dwell below in pallid places,
> stark and bare; there you will abandon your play of yore.[1]

Thanks to Hadrian's wise husbanding of the Imperial resources, shrewd management of public affairs, and modernizing of the Empire, no trouble, either political or economic, beset the reign of Antoninus Pius (138–161), Hadrian's chosen son and co-emperor. Handsome, cheerful, of simple tastes and unassailable integrity, kind, devout, patient in the face of malice, happiest in the simple life of his rural estates, and distrustful of the glitter of power, Antoninus symbolized the Empire's tranquillity and developed culture in his day. For this was paganism's loftiest age, and Antoninus embodied the pagan virtues. He lacked Trajan's or Hadrian's originality and restless energy, but he was as industrious in his quiet if prosaic way and he ruled as wisely, surrounding himself with capable and virtuous men and consistently following their advice.

Next came Marcus Aurelius (161–180), chosen as Antoninus' heir by Hadrian himself, a pagan saint, Stoic philosopher, and persecutor of Christians—the latter a part of his duty as he saw it. He devoted his life, in his early years to the point of endangering his health, to seeking and understanding the truth and to living in accordance with reason. Among other things, reason told him that men were made to work together, not

---

[1] From *Hadrian's Memoirs* by Marguerite Yourcenar, coypyright 1954 by Marguerite Yourcenar. Used by permission of the publishers, Farrar, Straus and Cudahy, Inc.

against each other; and that war, even a war of defense, was "robbery." Yet war dominated his reign, and influenced his *Meditations,* wherein he day and night examined and strove to improve his intellectual and moral life. He never forgot Antoninus' example, to live so that he might die at any hour with his conscience clear.

As emperor he personified Plato's philosopher-king. Conceiving of the state as literally a *res publica,* a commonwealth, the property of the people, and of himself as the people's servant, he concluded that he must own nothing personally but should live on what the state allowed him. When disasters—earthquakes, plagues, wars, and famine—rendered the public treasury inadequate to alleviate suffering, Marcus did not raise the taxes, but sold the imperial plate, gems, art treasures, and furniture to obtain funds for relief work. Familiar, from his study of history, with the principate's theoretically liberal character and the violence done to it by Nero and Domitian, he strove to make his an enlightened monarchy. Lastly, he cultivated a higher concept of civilization, not only the One World of the Roman Empire, but a kind of City of God. His contemporaries called this philosopher-king the most god-fearing and philanthropic Emperor, and his reign "the holiest of times."

Cosmopolitan Bourgeoisie

Although the historian Tacitus presented Nerva and Trajan as a new breed, he conceived the history of the Empire as a conflict between virtue and the emperors, virtue being embodied in the aristocracy and the Senate, while the emperors personified corruption and tyranny. His passionate advocacy and irresistible literary power have led every historian of Rome to see the Roman Empire from Augustus to Domitian as nothing but a struggle between the Senate, all sweetness and light, and the emperors, all crossness and perversion. Only recently has Imperial history emerged as both nobler and more complex. Documents make this even clearer for the second than for the first century.

Though even in Trajan's reign cities were encountering serious financial and economic difficulties, the Empire as an institution and a way of life gained wider support wherever it could demonstrate its ability to promote the general welfare. Provincial aristocracies, in return for knighthood, were willing enough to become cogs in the Imperial administrative machine. Religious sects, except Christians and sometimes Jews, stood staunchly by a government that gave them freedom of worship, freedom of movement, and the right to proselytize. Intellectuals, the Stoics if not the Cynics, were happy in a well-ordered and humane society. Common people, free or slave, urban or rural, for whom the Empire meant peace, work, and an opportunity to rise in the world, saw in the emperor a savior and a god. The Moselle vinedresser who exported his product to Syria; the Alexandrian glassmaker or the Capuan bronzesmith whose wares were sold in Britain; the Gallic potter whose products are found in the remotest corners of the Roman world; the Spanish farmer whose olive oil went to Egypt, whose wine was drunk in Roman and provincial taverns, whose cherries were eaten in Belgium, whose truffles, honey, figs were sought in every city; the Sicilian and African planter who raised wheat for export; the Austrian and Hungarian metalworker who supplied the Danubian legions; the Asian and Syrian merchant who profited from highways free of brigands, and seas free of pirates; the actor, the clown, the public lecturer, the missionary, the miracle worker, the huckster, and the prostitute, free to travel and ply their trades in every city on three continents—all these and thousands of others found the Empire good, and worth their loyalty.

The equestrian order deserves special notice. The opening of careers to its talent reinvigorated the middle class and consolidated the Imperial regime. Its ranks grew steadily from Augustus to Marcus Aurelius with the growth of cities, the acquisition of new provinces, the expansion of industry and trade, and greater use of natural resources. Wealth, population, and revenue increased, and so did administrative personnel at all levels, from modest procuratorships of an imperial estate, a mine, a remote customs station, a small provincial town, or a provincial capital, to the highest level in Rome itself.

By the end of the Julio-Claudians, when a century of successful service had strengthened their awareness of their dignity and potentialities, the knights were eying the state secretaryships, until then occupied by freedmen. Vitellius and Otho, to strengthen themselves politically, took them into the cabinet. The bourgeois emperors naturally employed them in more responsible posts. Domitian especially, who made honest and efficient civil-service appointments, promoted knights to top levels, to the Privy Council along with Senators, to command of the Dacian War, even, though it shocked the Senate, to the governorship of Asia, formerly the perquisite of the noblest and most distinguished senators. Knights reached their peak in government under Hadrian, when they held a majority of the cabinet posts. A knight experienced in jurisprudence was even made chairman of the Privy Council, a precedent which continued unbroken as long as the principate lasted. This is a significant honor, for the Privy Council was legal and administrative adviser to the Emperor and its rulings were for all practical purposes final.

Lastly, Hadrian confirmed and extended another Augustan policy, the reorganization of the equestrian order as a lesser aristocracy, a bourgeois counterpart of the senatorial nobility. Its prestige had grown with its usefulness to the Imperial government; and its political power grew as the

Senate's declined. Hadrian formalized this dignity of office and reinvigorated the order's competitive spirit by dividing it into four ranks (*trecenarii, ducenarii, centenarii, sexagenarii*) with salaries of 300, 200, 100, and 60 thousand sesterces respectively. Hadrian's reforms probably produced the new titulature, whereby an ordinary knight was "vir egregius" (man of distinction), the highest among them "viri perfectissimi" (most excellent gentlemen), while the praetorian prefects were "eminentissimi" (Your Eminence).

Equestrians under the bourgeois Empire increasingly married into senatorial families, especially after Hadrian's reforms increased the knights' prestige and power. Equestrian ability, usefulness, and moral worth were signally recognized when Marcus Aurelius chose equestrian husbands for his three daughters. He, a uniquely conscientious and enlightened ruler, honored men not for wealth, birth, or political considerations, but for merit alone.

The equestrian order was more than a social group. It was of course the top of the bourgeois pyramid; it represents the talented and aspiring middle class. But it was also a cosmopolitan force with roots in every city and town and every part of the Empire. It brought to the Imperial government the most varied aptitudes and capacities, first-hand acquaintance with every regional need, a trained ability to gauge public opinion, above all an Empire-wide outlook. Its unanimity in supporting the reigning emperor was a new type of informal plebiscite, voluntarily recorded in countless inscriptions. Its support, therefore, and its contribution in ability and vision gradually made the Empire no longer narrowly Roman, Italian, or Western, but cosmopolitan and universal.

Equestrian recognition inevitably affected the senatorial nobility. By promoting knights and their sons to senatorial seats, Augustus and his dynasty started a chain reaction. The emperors from Vespasian on were of bourgeois origin, and the Senate itself was more and more recruited from the middle class. Its most illustrious members came from the *bourgeoisie*. Pliny the Elder, admiral of the fleet, and his nephew Pliny the Younger, a famous advocate and provincial governor, were of north Italian bourgeois descent. Julius Agricola, promoted to patrician status for consolidating Rome's conquest of Britain, was the grandson of knights from southern France. Pertinax, whom fortune was to raise to the purple, was a freedman's son. Greeks and Orientals were given more Senate seats when Trajan began to prefer natives as provincial governors, and still more when Hadrian placed Greek-speaking people on a political par with those speaking Latin. Hadrian's Senate contained barely thirty descendants of the old Roman nobility, while under Marcus Aurelius 42 percent of the members were of provincial origin. The second-century "good emperors" got along well with the Senate partly because it had become less tradition-bound, less Roman and Italian, and contained more and more new men brought in by the emperors. The recurring names in second- and third-century senatorial rosters are Julius, Claudius, Flavius, Ulpius, Aelius, Aurelius, each denoting a freedman or provincial enfranchised by the emperor whose name he bore. These senators of bourgeois origin furnished more and more of the generals, governors, members of the emperor's staff, and great jurists who were to enrich the law.

Government with a Social Conscience

The stirrings of a new social conscience are evident in Cicero's writings, in Caesar's new deal for the provinces, and still more in Stoic humanitarianism. The emperors, responsive to this trend, instituted various reforms to protect more effectively life, liberty, and property. This tendency is clear in the changing punishment of debtors. The Twelve Tables had empowered creditors to sell defaulting debtors as slaves; next, imprisonment replaced slavery; then, Caesar enabled debtors to file a bankruptcy declaration, thus preserving both their good name and their freedom. Legal humanitarianism grew under the Empire. Tiberius, for example, extorted from a recalcitrant Senate a law forbidding executions within ten days of the sentence. In the interval new evidence might turn up in favor of the victim.

Claudius' reign shows the variety of humanitarian legislation. To keep women from being cheated, he forbade them to stand surety for anybody, even their husbands. He enabled mothers, previously disqualified, to inherit their children's estate under certain conditions. He allowed a free woman to contract a legal marriage with a slave and still retain her freedom. He forbade usurers to make loans to minors payable on their coming into their inheritance. Likewise, to save the estates of orphaned minors, he prohibited the latter's adoption by their guardians. He decreed that legal confiscation of a man's estate should not encumber his son's also. Finally, a statute of limitations applied after five years on unpaid inheritance taxes. As we saw, Claudius declared aged or sick slaves exposed by their masters to be *ipso facto* free, and regarded the killing of a slave by his master as common murder, therefore punishable by the state.

The emperors, as practical men, held that government is a commodity for which the public must pay, yet they kept taxes low. The freedman Licinus, Augustus' tax-collector in Gaul, is a case in point. He collected higher taxes than his master directed, but, though he scrupulously turned the surplus in to the Fiscus, Augustus ordered him to keep within the law, and would have none of his arguments, which were true, that Gaul was too lightly taxed anyway. Tiberius frowned on petty extortions in Egypt, stating dryly that he wanted his sheep sheared, not skinned.

Taxes have become as inevitable as death ever since the modern state took from the executive the right of making exceptional cases. Examples of humanity towards the taxpayer, impossible in modern times, are abundant in the Roman Empire. To cite only a few, when an earthquake devastated Sardis and eleven other Asian cities, Tiberius exempted them from tribute for five years. Claudius gave similar relief to earthquake-stricken Apamea, Ephesus, Smyrna, and the cities of Crete, and also exempted Byzantium, exhausted from border warfare.

But public calamities were relieved by more positive steps. Thus, Tiberius donated 10,000,000 sesterces to Sardis, hardest hit by the earthquake of 19; gave 100,000,000 to the homeless after an Aventine fire, and another 100,000,000 to relieve the panic of 33. In the eruption which destroyed Herculaneum, Pompeii, and other towns, the fleet evacuated some of the inhabitants, while Titus organized large-scale relief work, among other measures applying unclaimed legacies to the rebuilding of the buried cities. He sold the furnishings of his villas, using the proceeds to restore Roman temples and public buildings damaged by fire; we have seen how religiously he tried to serve his people by a daily act in the public welfare.

The "five good emperors" left a shining record of public benefactions. Nerva sold his personal property for 60,000,000 sesterces, with which he bought land to allot to Rome's poor. Trajan, Hadrian, and Marcus Aurelius remitted all tax arrears, burning the pertinent records in a welcome symbolic gesture. Hadrian is said to have remitted 900,000,000 sesterces.

Cheap bread was undoubtedly the emperors' chief concern. They tried various means, for instance, bringing more provincial land under cultivation, organizing maritime transportation, constructing harbors and harbor installations, or building up a vast distribution service. The princeps, as we have seen, regarded himself as a patron with the entire citizen community as his clientele and, more narrowly, as a paterfamilias with the city as his own family. The Roman government, Republican as well as Imperial, may have been organized on the model of the Roman family. In any case, the emperors absorbed along with the Hellenistic monarchies the familiar Hellenistic postulate of the state's inherent duty to feed the poor.

We have mentioned Augustus' organization of the grain supply. Nearly every emperor expanded and improved the system. Tiberius, we saw, kept the price of bread down in the famine of 19 by granting grain dealers a bounty of eight sesterces (40¢) for every bushel they sold. Claudius' anti-inflationary contributions we have also reviewed: the harbor at Ostia, political concessions to provincials who would transport grain from overseas, and new and better government insurance on ship and cargo. Nero had the same objective in exempting ships engaged in the grain trade from taxation. Antistius Rusticus, Domitian's governor of Galatia-Cappadocia, typifies the official view. On being informed by the city council of Pisidian Antioch that winter grain scarcity had brought unmanageable high prices, he ordered all inhabitants to declare their holdings of grain and to sell their surplus at a slight markup, to be fixed by him, "as it is most unfair," his proclamation reads, "that men should make a profit from their fellow-citizens' hunger."

Doubtless on the advice of his eminent ministers Burrus and Seneca, Nero considered a bold attack on the cost of living—no less than the repeal of all indirect taxes, especially the sales tax and the customs dues. This would of course have made him popular with the masses. The propertied classes' dismay is clear from opposition in the Senate, where the old clichés half-humorously appeared: what had been good for their grandfathers should be good enough for the present generation; this was the thin end of the wedge: the next to go would be the direct tax. The fact was that since senators were traditionally barred from business, their wealth was in real estate, and they feared that what the treasury lost in indirect taxes it would eventually make up by taxing real estate. The project was indeed revolutionary, as is apparent when one recalls that real estate had seldom been taxed in Italy since 167 B.C. The whole idea collapsed under senatorial opposition. Only two or three mild measures came out of it: a stricter holding to account of the revenue-collecting corporations and a lowering of transportation costs, perhaps made possible by the exempting of merchant ships from taxation.

Aside from considerations of piety or pride in beautifying Rome, the Julio-Claudian emperors were guided by utilitarian motives in building roads, aqueducts, dikes, canals, harbors, and libraries. Vespasian, generally regarded as a frugal emperor, spent fantastic sums on public works, chiefly the Coliseum, not to win prestige as a builder, but from a keen sense that it was his duty to keep men employed. To this end he even rejected labor-saving devices.

Even Domitian, who was even more frugal than his father, spent huge sums on public works. It was Trajan, however, that left the most imperishable record of public works producing employment. He enlarged the harbor at Ostia, built harbors also at Ancona, Centumcellae (Civitavecchia), and Tarracina, an aqueduct for Ravenna and a new one for Rome, endeavored to drain the Pomptine Marshes and the Lacus Fucinus (after an earlier attempt by Claudius), improved the Italian highway system, and gave Rome a new theater, a new amphitheater, a *naumachia* (basin for mock naval battles), and the largest baths designed up to that time. He gave also an enormously expensive new Forum complex that bore his name, a complement to Augustus' Forum, with its great docu-

Fig. 51a. Plan of Ostia and its ports. Left to right, the Claudian port, the hexagonal Trajanic port, the Isola Sacra (site of a necropolis), and Ostia proper, where decumanus, theater, and Forum can be seen in the plan. Work on an airport on the filled-in site of the Claudian port has revealed ancient footings which will modify the plan. (*Archaeology* I, 1948, p. 34.)

mentary column depicting his Dacian wars, its gorgeous basilica, its library, and its market rising five stories and containing more than 150 shops, perhaps intended for the wholesale distribution of government grain, oil, and wine. And he gave to about 300,000 persons sums aggregating 2600 sesterces ($130) per head.

While Trajan concentrated his benefactions mainly in Italy, Hadrian and Antoninus embraced the provinces also, with the same objective of making work. In and near Rome Hadrian kept numbers of building tradesmen employed throughout his reign on the Pantheon, the Temple of Venus and Rome, his mausoleum and his villa near Tibur, to mention only his most grandiose projects. We still have an inscription of his reign recording a contract for repairing fifteen miles of the Via Appia. Government contributed two-thirds of the cost and the adjacent property owners one-third, each mile costing 100,000 sesterces, or more than $10 per square yard in today's values. On his extensive journeys, Hadrian took along architects and engineers to survey and make plans for provincial needs. Since a list of public works which he donated to cities and smaller towns would fill pages, we will mention only a harbor for Ephesus and aqueducts for Corinth, Antioch, Dyrrhachium, and Sarmizegethusa. His benefactions to Athens were as great as those to Rome: he finished the Olympieum started by Pisistratus, built a library, a gymnasium, public porches and porticoes, temples, an aqueduct in use until recent times, and a whole new city beside the old one. And to Athens, mother of the arts and thereby entitled to the gratitude of civilized man, he extended the Roman Imperial dole.

Marcus Aurelius probably surpassed every other emperor in his concern for the general welfare. But by his time prosperity had dwindled, chiefly because of the Parthian and German wars, new earthquakes, and most of all the plague. Brought into Italy by the Euphrates army, the plague spread over all the provinces. It lasted almost twenty years, at its worst carrying off 2000 persons daily in Rome alone. The provinces rioted, angered that taxes were not reduced to compensate for decreased business. It was now, when the surplus of nearly 3,000,000,000 sesterces left by Antoninus had melted away, that Marcus sold his valuables, as we saw, in a gigantic auction which lasted two months. On seven occasions he distributed in largesses a total of 3400 sesterces per head. Reckoned in today's purchasing power, this would amount in all to $1,250,000,000.

A broad imperial plan of grants-in-aid (*alimenta*) to indigent boys and girls excites our interest. Nerva began it, as the government's version of earlier private trusts for poor boys and girls' education. Expanded by Trajan and Hadrian, it continued well into the third century. The State provided 2,000,000,000 sesterces out of which loans were made to farmers at 5 percent interest, lower than the market rate. Thus far the system had the advantage of making the farmer independent of moneylenders, or at any rate of enabling him to make needed improvements. The interest was used to support freeborn boys and girls throughout Italy. The aim was apparently to increase the birth rate. But since boys received 16 sesterces (80¢) a month, and girls only 12, in the ratio of seven boys to one girl, the intent may have been also to provide recruits for the army and civil service. The *alimenta* were widely advertised in sculpture, reliefs, and coins. Probably for a generation or two they stimulated agriculture, raised living standards, and enabled more young people to get an education. To keep Rome and Italy in balance, Trajan granted free grain and largess to 5000 Roman children. Later Antoninus Pius set up a fund in honor of his wife Faustina to support 5000 Roman girls.

Paternalistic commercial banks (*kalendaria*) benefited small merchants or city people in general. Apparently the emperors turned over to the cities certain revenues of the Fiscus, the local governments making loans at low interest out of this yearly rising fund. Two such banks, probably established by Hadrian, existed in Panormus (Palermo) in Sicily.

The glitter of this picture is mainly superficial. Every remedy conceals an evil. Cities received the chief benefit; workers and farmers, especially in the provinces, suffered increasing distress. The Empire proved unable to afford the expense of frequent wars, and with the death of Marcus Aurelius was already declining to its fall.

Chapter 52/PROVINCIAL GOVERNMENT

The Provinces

The bourgeois Empire realized to the fullest Vergil's admonition to Rome, "To rule mankind and make the world obey." An aggregate of lands so vast that it still excites our wonder lay like a constellation around Italy. After Hadrian withdrew from Armenia and Mesopotamia, the Empire included the following administrative divisions:

Italy, still a privileged land, where most Roman citizens lived.

Two provinces in the central Mediterranean (starred provinces were senatorial) :

*1. Sicily

*2. Sardinia and Corsica (became Imperial under Vespasian)

Nine provinces in Western Europe:

  3. Britannia (England)

  4. Belgica (northeast France)

  5. Lugdunensis (northwest and central France)

  6. Aquitania (southwest France)

*7. Narbonensis (southeast France)

  8. Germania Inferior (lower Rhineland)

  9. Tarraconensis (north and central Spain)

*10. Baetica (south Spain)

11. Lusitania (Portugal)

Seven provinces in Central Europe:

12. Germania Superior (upper Rhineland or southwest Germany)
13. Rhaetia (east Switzerland, west Austria, and parts of south Germany)
14. Noricum (east Austria and parts of south Germany)
15. Pannonia Superior (Hungary closer to Austria)
16. Pannonia Inferior (Hungary south of Budapest)
17. Dacia (Romania)
18. Illyricum or Dalmatia (west Yugoslavia)

Six provinces in Southern Europe:

19. Moesia Superior (south Yugoslavia)
20. Moesia Inferior (north Bulgaria)
21. Thracia (south Bulgaria and European Turkey)
*22. Macedonia
23. Epirus (northwest Greece and parts of Albania)
*24. Achaea (Greece)

Six provinces in Asia Minor:

*25. Asia
*26. Bithynia and Pontus
27. Pisidia, called also Lycia-and-Pamphylia
28. Cilicia
29. Galatia
30. Cappadocia

Four provinces in the eastern Mediterranean:

*31. Cyprus
32. Syria
33. Palestine
34. Arabia Petraea

Five provinces in North Africa

35. Mauretania Tingitana (Morocco)
36. Mauretania Caesariensis (Algeria)
*37. Africa Proconsularis (Tunisia and Tripolitania)
38. Numidia (west and south of Tunisia)
*39. Cyrenaica and Crete

Egypt, the 40th and economically the most important province.

The list excludes the outlying protectorates and smaller procuratorial districts like the Maritime, Cottian, or Pennine Alps. Augustus' assignment of the peaceful provinces to the Senate, those requiring policing to the emperor was still adhered to.

Several agencies operated to spread, not to force, Romanization. The revenue collectors in every province, although few, could influence the natives. Merchants helped to transmit ideas as well as goods. Italian

Fig. 52a. Map of the provinces of the Roman Empire. Insets

peasants seeking land in the wake of armies, scores of government-spon-
sored colonies, above all, the legions stationed along thousands of miles
of frontier, were so many carriers of cosmopolitanism, if not Romanization. The most important agent of all was hope for Roman citizenship, a

THE ROMAN EMPIRE

☐ PROVINCES AT AUGUSTUS' DEATH (A.D. 14)
▨ PROVINCES ANNEXED A.D. 14-98
▧ TRAJAN'S CONQUESTS (A.D. 98-116)
---- SENATORIAL
—— IMPERIAL

0 _____ 500 MILES

show Britannia and Germania Superior and Rhaetia.

privilege available to every foreigner deemed worthy of it. Any man anywhere in the Empire could aspire to that honor.

Although the governor's powers had not changed since the Republic,
provincial administration was now, for several reasons, more efficient and

honest. First, to lessen the temptation to steal, each governor was paid, usually a million sesterces. Second, whereas senatorial governorships were still political appointments, the principal qualification for governors of Imperial provinces was military and administrative ability. Moreover these Imperial employees knew that promotion depended on achievement. Third, every emperor from Augustus to Marcus Aurelius was personally interested in good provincial government. Fourth, senatorial governors competed with imperial ones in promoting their subjects' welfare, or took the consequences. More senatorial governors than under the Republic were tried and convicted for malfeasance. The emperor seldom had his legates or imperial governors tried; he simply dismissed those he mistrusted.

New institutions were created to link emperor, provincials, and governors. Nearly every emperor built roads. Augustus established an Imperial Postal Service, while Claudius' Department of Correspondence was among other things a clearing house between the emperor and his provincial officers. The lively official correspondence between Trajan and his governor of Bithynia, Pliny, shows how minutely an emperor could know local problems.

The emperors sought to make the provincials feel like co-proprietors of the Empire. Augustus and his successors encouraged the formation of provincial councils or parliaments. Meeting annually in the provincial capital, at the temple of the deified Augustus or of Augustus and Rome, the provincial parliament began its session by worshiping the Emperor-god, a token of loyalty like our saluting the flag. The formalities over, it moved its thanks to the emperor, and often a petition. These resolutions were forwarded directly, probably through a deputation, whereas under the Republic no provincial might communicate with Rome except through the governor. The parliament could send complaints even against the governor. It could also appoint investigators of alleged gubernatorial misdeeds or go to Rome as prosecutor. When Claudius opened the Senate to native provincial leaders, he gave them not merely the right to discuss Imperial affairs, but virtual partnership in the Empire.

The provinces got a new deal in taxation. They all paid the *decuma,* now called *tributum soli* (land-tax), but now the tax was collected by civil service officials responsible to the emperor, who were expected to be both more efficient and more humane. As in Republican times this tax fell also on resident citizens who were now much more numerous; indeed many cities, especially in the western provinces, contained none but Roman citizens. Only rarely was such a city granted the *ius Italicum,* the right to regard its territory as Italian, and therefore tax-free.

A few provinces, as we saw, owed the *tributum capitis,* an excise tax on individual businesses. Finally the provinces were occasionally subject to *aurum coronarium,* a gift to the emperor at his accession. Noncitizens had no inheritance tax to pay. All other imposts fell impartially on Italians as well as provincials: the previously-mentioned customs dues of from 2½ to 5 percent ad valorem, the 5-percent manumission, and the 1-percent sales tax.

Increase in the number of citizens improved provincial status most. Individual emigrations of Italians accounted only in part for this change; positive imperial policy was more important. Since the emperors had an Empire-wide rather than an Italian point of view, they adopted various methods of granting Roman citizenship to natives, even in senatorial provinces. One was reward for military service. Legionary recruits from a self-governing community, who were already civilized and accustomed to liberty, were enfranchised on the day of enrollment. Those with a barbaric background, presumed to be incapable of free or civilized living, could join only the *auxilia.* Since twenty-five years of service taught them Latin and Roman ways, they were given citizenship papers, as we saw, on being honorably discharged. Their wives and children were enfranchised with them. Beginning with Claudius, the same privilege was extended to sailors and marines. Thus military service alone enabled 15,000 to 20,000 men annually to become Roman citizens. Tiberius offered the franchise to freedmen enrolling for six years in the fire and patrol department at Rome. Despite senatorial criticism he upheld the princeps' right to confer legal free status and citizenship on men born in slavery. Every succeeding emperor honored these precedents.

Besides these individual enfranchisements, there were other mass methods. The emperors revived the Republican policy of granting Latin status to entire communities, thus putting their inhabitants, slaves excluded, on the way to attaining full Roman citizenship. Vespasian went further; he conferred this honor on the whole of Spain. Since a "Latin" city's annual magistrates became Roman citizens on assuming office and this privilege applied also to their fathers, sons, grandsons, and the women of the respective households, in a decade or two all such local aristocracies received the full franchise. Hadrian made citizens of more of the *bourgeoisie* by enfranchising the municipal councilors of such communities. Eventually communities that Romanized themselves—for instance, St. Albans in Britain or certain cantons around Tridentum in the Alps— were enfranchised en masse. Claudius alone rewarded nine such cities with the citizenship. Trajan and Hadrian were even more generous, but more generally it was the wealthy only who received preferment.

The more energetic emperors planted citizen colonies in practically every province, either on virgin territory or in decayed towns like Syracuse and Syrian Ptolemaïs to give them new blood. In Ptolemaïs the older inhabitants were also promptly enfranchised to avoid discrimination. Caesar and Augustus between them established over a hundred colonies. More were established between the Claudian and the Hadrianic ages.

Lastly, many army camps became active centers radiating Roman culture and fitting natives for Roman life. Such were especially the legionary headquarters, like Lindum (Lincoln) and Eboracum (York) in Britain and Lambaesis in Africa. Such were also the *canabae,* the business centers which grew up close to legionary encampments, inhabited by men and women catering to soldiers' needs: tailors, cobblers, armorers, moneylenders, peddlers, tavern keepers, fortunetellers, concubines, or prostitutes. In time both types of settlement were organized as full-fledged municipalities.

In conclusion, millions of provincials in Europe, Asia, and Africa became citizens from Augustus to Marcus Aurelius. As the Republic made Italy a Greater Rome, so the Empire made the whole inhabitable world the home of Roman citizens. A third-century jurist, the Syrian Modestinus, referring to this achievement, called Rome *communis nostra patria,* our common fatherland. In the fifth century the Gallic poet Rutilius Namatianus echoed the same idea:

> Fecisti patriam diversis gentibus unam . . .
> Urbem fecisti quod prius orbis erat.

> Of all the nations you have made one country.
> You made one city what was once a world.

To be sure the path of Romanization was not always smooth. Powerful native forces—princes, politicians, priests, legal systems—opposed Roman encroachments. But testimonials from poets and lawyers from Syria to Gaul prove the Romans' success in establishing a one-world community. For 2000 years various states had tried but failed to unify nations. For 2000 years since, great minds and powerful princes have tried but failed to realize that dream.

The Cities

A province was the sum of its local units. Some of these, consisting of civilized free men, had local autonomy; others, still in a tribal stage, hence incapable of self-government, were administered by chieftains. Rome preferred to deal with self-governing units, but tolerated the tribal system pending its evolution towards civilization. Thus, for example, eighty years after Vespasian had given Latin status to Spain, it had 248 free or self-governing cities against 27 non-free tribal communities.

Free cities abounded, especially in areas of Italian, Greek, Hellenistic, or Phoenician culture. Tribes were the rule in the Asia Minor hinterland

and the newer parts of Europe, that is, Gaul, Britain, Germany, Dacia, Thrace, and other Danubian provinces. To be sure, towns existed even in a tribal district—for instance, Paris was a little tribal capital—but such towns were merely an agglomeration of buildings. To the Romans, however, the word "town" or "city" meant a way of life, an association of free men governing themselves, theoretically through a nice balance of popular assembly, selective council, and annually elected magistrates.

The empire in its prime urbanized the underdeveloped sections of Asia and other parts of the ex-Seleucid Empire. Under the system which Rome inherited, hamlet, plantation, and village communities were ruled by royal officials, by nearby cities to which the king had assigned them, by temple authorities, or by feudal lords. Egypt had only three self-governing cities; Naucratis, Ptolemaïs, and Antinoöpolis, the last founded by Hadrian. The nomes, rural districts of innumerable tiny villages, were ruled by Imperial procurators, responsible to the prefect in Alexandria. In Africa, where the whole land was Roman government property, the natives of Berber or Phoenician descent were likewise governed from above. Nomads were relegated beyond the frontier, or made to settle down under Imperial supervision. Whatever gradations these non-free communities had, Imperial policy helped hundreds of them, everywhere except in Egypt, to become free and autonomous cities, for the emperors identified local freedom and local republican life with three characteristics of civilization: law and order, prosperity, and culture. They preferred to deal with free men of the wealthier class who, understanding civilization's meaning, could assume responsibility and cooperate in keeping the peace.

New or old, east or west, of citizen or noncitizen status, a city had three obligations toward the central government, dating from Republican times: it let Rome control its foreign affairs (that is, it renounced war) ; it paid taxes to Rome, to defray Imperial administrative expenses and as an insurance premium for peace; it furnished volunteer troops for the common defense. Otherwise a city might freely regulate its own affairs, administer justice, maintain its official cult, levy local taxes, and conduct local elections as it saw fit. Noninterference with the political, religious, cultural, or economic life of the cities was for the Romans a basic principle, even when a city had received the Roman franchise, for though Rome was working for universality and unity, it seldom practiced regimentation.

Thus Rome dealt with foreigners without chauvinism. If they wanted Roman citizenship, the central government encouraged them; if not, and they were friendly, they were left alone. This policy existed because the Romans had no feeling of race superiority and no delusion of divine or historic mission, except world peace. The Hellenistic East with its superior culture benefited especially from this policy. For whereas in the West knowledge of Latin was a prerequisite to citizenship, Greeks and Greek-speaking Orientals faced no such requirement, at least not after Nero and Hadrian.

This attitude produced harmony out of diversity. Rome allowed its peoples and tribes their choice of a way of life, of a place in the changing conditions wrought by Roman supremacy. More explicitly, the Roman emperors superimposed no rigid scheme, but left all peoples free to weave the twin strands of Roman elements and local tradition into their own cultural pattern. Thus the speech, arts, institutions, and social life of Libyan or Phoenician Africa were a mixture, Roman borrowings grafted onto local traditions. What is now France was "Gallo-Roman," and every other province showed a similar blend. This cultural *laissez faire* was even more conspicuous in the third century, after Caracalla—partly for fiscal reasons—enfranchised every freeman in the Empire. By that act every community—Syrian, German, Jewish, or Greek—became Roman in one jump.

In sum, Rome successfully united into a world-wide community men of diverse races and cultures through its genius for striking a balance between two sets of loyalties, Imperial and local. The stimulus came from above; the working out came from below: the upper class, at least, of the nations composing the Roman Empire was universally contented and the Imperial structure solid.

In Greece, the Hellenistic East, Sicily, and every other place of Greek origin, the form of local government was inherited from the *polis*. Each community had the ecclesia, boule, archons, courts, and priesthoods familiar to us from Greek history. In such cities the Romans felt most comfortable if the local magistrates were pro-Roman oligarchs, and indeed the social structure within all the cities of the Empire was profoundly oligarchical and timocratic.

The typical city of the West was a *municipium* of Latin or Roman status, in either case organized after the Roman Republican pattern. Its popular assembly or *plebs*, besides electing the magistrates, voted on proposals brought before it. Alongside the assembly was the council or senate, usually of a hundred life members, called *centumviri, decuriones,* or more simply *ordo* (*the* Order) . Finally, either two or three pairs of officers constituted the board of magistrates or city commission. The *duoviri iure dicundo,* the highest authority, presided over meetings of both plebs and ordo and, as their names imply, administered justice. A pair of quaestors handled finances. Where the city charter named no quaestors, the other four officers performed their functions. Although nominally independent, the magistrates had to consult the ordo and follow its directives just as Roman Republican consuls consulted and obeyed the Senate.

The council of a western city was recruited from propertied ex-magistrates, after the pattern of the Roman Senate, or rather of the early Italian town-councils of which the Roman Senate was one. Since the rich and the gentry always had the advantage at elections, municipal government throughout the West soon became aristocratic. This development was assured by having duoviri act quinquennially as censors. The *quinquennales,* as the duoviri of that particular year were called, ratified the entrance of ex-magistrates into the local senate, renewed leases of city properties, and examined each individual's personal and property qualifications and fixed his place in city's political structure. The result of the census was then transmitted to Rome.

The master model of the municipal constitution just sketched was the *Lex Julia Municipalis,* a collection of various statutes, drafted for Julius Caesar, who is therefore regarded as the father of the urbanization of Europe, and later incorporated into a single bill and carried by Antony. With the usual clarity and precision of Roman law, this charter prescribes the setting up of a municipal government. It defines each magistrate's jurisdiction and the council's and electoral body's authority. It empowers appropriate authorities to prepare the budget and to raise local taxes to support public services. It provides for public worship. It enumerates the qualifications for municipal citizenship, chiefly birth, age, character, and occupation (for example, actors, gladiators, and bankrupts were ineligible) . It defines, as we saw in Chapter 43, the community's and the individual citizen's responsibilities in building and maintaining streets or constructing and defending the city wall. Principles are even laid down for the civic education of rustics or barbarians dwelling in the town domain. Indeed, to every emperor after Caesar, a *municipium* was what the geographer Strabo called Greek Massalia, "a school for barbarians." Whenever an emperor issued a municipal charter, he applied, to a particular case and with suitable amendments, Julius Caesar's fundamental law.

The Frontier in Europe

A turbulent world of barbarians across the Rhine, Danube, Black Sea, and Euphrates frontiers required armed vigilance. The Romans retired to the Rhine after Germanicus withdrew from the Elbe. But to the east much of Holland was a Roman protectorate; Roman settlers occupied a large district in Germany itself and minted silver in the Taunus Mountains further up the river. Temporary garrisons, moreover, were stationed well inland in emergencies. Eight legions, close to 50,000 men, not counting the German and Gallic auxiliaries, guarded the border from the North Sea to Switzerland, while a fleet patrolled the river. We have seen how skillfully the Romans protected themselves by egging on the German tribes, which had neither national unity nor national consciousness, to internal strife.

The German frontier engaged Vespasian's close attention; he replaced earthworks with permanent stone-built legionary fortresses, symbolizing the Julio-Claudians' abandonment of further expansion. With the wisdom of hindsight we can see the danger of these comfortable, almost civilian quarters, which softened and immobilized the army.

Domitian revamped all the defenses of upper Germany and Switzerland. To protect the agriculturally rich Rhine valley he fortified a line southeastward from Bonn, which then turned east and north to near Giessen, whence it plunged southward to Lorch north of the Danube. This big wedge was incorporated into the Roman system to restrain the Chatti, who had replaced the Cherusci as a major nuisance. While the principal legionary camps remained far to the rear—at Moguntiacum (Mainz), Argentoratum (Strasbourg), and Vindonissa (Windisch)—over sixty auxiliary forts, comprising the limes, averaging seven miles apart— in some sectors in two parallel lines—protected upper Germany and Switzerland. The new, shorter frontier required fewer soldiers. An intricate road network facilitated emergency troop movements from Gaul and Britain to Bavaria, Austria, and Hungary. In military science this fortified communications system, until the crumbling of the Maginot Line, was considered classic.

Before Domitian had finished the limes he had to face the Dacians, a menace to the Romans since the second century B.C. when the Macedonian conquest required them to defend civilized Europe south of the Danube. Under a capable king, Burebistas, with a force of perhaps 200,000, the Dacians, beginning about 60 B.C., had plundered several Greek cities northwest of the Black Sea, reached out for Thrace, conquered Hungary east of the Danube, and even occupied Slovakia. Burebistas' empire disintegrated into several kingdoms after his assassination in 44 B.C.

In fixing on the Danube the defense line between civilized and barbarian Europe, Augustus devastated a strip several miles deep beyond the river, a no-man's land barred to barbarian settlement, "making a wilderness," as Tacitus makes a British chieftain say, "and calling it peace." Even so, the Dacians repeatedly invaded the Danubian provinces. In A.D. 85, unified under a new and imperialistic king, Decebalus, they killed the governor of Moesia and besieged the legions in their camps. Domitian himself marched with the praetorian guard into Moesia to supervise the counterattack. He cleared the province without difficulty, but in 86 a Roman army which had bridged the Danube in search of Decebalus was decisively defeated. Finally in 88 a Roman victory compelled Decebalus

Fig. 52.1. Roman bridge over the Danube, model. Derived from a relief on Trajan's column. (Rome, Museo della Civiltà Romana; J. Felbermeyer photo)

to sue for peace. In return for acknowledging Rome's overlordship, he received an annual subsidy, and masons, engineers, and other skilled workers to rebuild his capital, Sarmizegethusa. Domitian's enemies called this a Roman surrender, though Romans regularly subsidized one barbarian state against another. The subsidized Dacians kept in order other Roman enemies, like their traditional foes the Iazyges, and the restless Marcomanni and Quadi in Bohemia.

Trajan, preferring more direct methods, undertook a war to end all wars in that part of Europe. Perhaps he also hoped to win prestige with an easy conquest. He began by improving communications between Pannonia and Moesia, building bridges over the Danube and two new roads into Dacia. Despite a brave and well-planned opposition, Decebalus had to yield. He was treated leniently and left as a vassal king, but required to dismantle the fortifications of Sarmizegethusa, deliver his engineers and artillery, and admit Roman garrisons (102). But his stubborn revolt two years later ruled out considerations of mercy. Sarmizegethusa was recaptured, the whole kingdom conquered, and when all was lost Decebalus committed suicide (106). Trajan commemorated the conquest on his famous column.

Dacia was made a province and opened to settlers from the whole

Fig. 52.2. Rome. Trajan's column, reliefs on lower part of shaft. In the lowest band the god of the Danube presides benignly over the crossing (A.D. 101) of Trajan's army on a bridge of boats; in the second, the soldiers are building a walled camp with moat and drawbridge.

Empire; a high proportion of the immigrants was from Dalmatia. Roads were opened; gold, iron, and salt mines were exploited; and several villages were organized as self-governing municipia and agents of Romanization. Dacia was so thoroughly Romanized that it still speaks a Romance language and calls itself Romania. The conquest affected the entire Balkan area: cities multiplied, industry and commerce developed, and prosperity reigned from Austria to the Black Sea.

Sixty peaceful years after the conquest of Dacia the Empire felt the first repercussions of a mass movement of peoples far beyond the frontier. Romanization had turned Germans from nomads into a settled agricultural people. In the process came the Goths, the chief element of an entirely separate and distinct branch of the Germanic peoples, the East Germans, who now enter world history and all but dominate it down to the fall of the Western Empire. The Goths, searching for fertile lands, trekked all the way from northeast Germany to southwest Russia, thereby setting up a chain-reaction among other German tribes of Central Europe, including the Chatti, Chauci, Bergundi, Longobardi, and Vandals, and most of all the Quadi and Marcomanni. These displaced tribes endangered the Roman frontier from Belgium to Romania; some actually crossed the middle Danube, invading Illyricum and Italy itself, besieging Aquileia and coming within sight of Verona.

A turbulent Germany, threatening the Pax Romana more seriously than ever, caused Marcus Aurelius' staff to revise Rome's whole defense strategy, so as to push the border outward to the Oder, then link it with Dacia through the Carpathian Mountains. Shortened by three-fourths, the new frontier could have been more easily and cheaply defended, and most of Germany, Czechoslovakia, and east Hungary would have been annexed as provinces and gradually Romanized. Thus barbarian invasions might not have overthrown the Empire, and all European history might well have taken a different course. After thirteen years of hard fighting Marcus had crushed the tribes' resistance. Only one more summer was needed to complete the plan when the Emperor died in his camp at Vienna (March 180). With his death and the accession of his weak son Commodus his whole plan collapsed. Once more the Rhine, the Danube, and the Dacian salient marked the frontier. In Rome Marcus Aurelius' imitation of Trajan's Column unfolds the main episodes of this Marcomannic war.

Only one near-disaster in Nero's time slowed the Romanization of Britain. The East Anglian dowager-queen Boudicca had capitalized on a number of popular grievances; unaccustomed taxes, greedy moneylenders, encroachment on private property by colonists, and restrictions on Druidic rites aggravated the general native restlessness in the face of Roman attempts to impose their ideas of law and order. To protect the British lowlands the Roman general Agricola felt he must conquer the rest of Britain, Scotland, and perhaps Ireland. Deterred by Domitian from such costly adventures, he employed his talents in Romanizing Britain and consolidating its economy. Hadrian, who retrenched wherever it did not affect the Empire's defense, withdrew all forces south of a 73-mile line from Solway to Tynemouth. He then built from sea to sea a string of some seventy castles and forts, defended by Welsh militia and connected by a masonry wall. Hadrian's successor Antoninus built a forward defense line from the Firth of Forth to the River Clyde, which was easier to defend, being thirty-seven miles shorter, and closer to the Scottish Highlands, a perennial source of raiding parties.

Britain began to be Romanized, first in the south, which was closer to the continent, then in the north and west: London, Colchester, St. Albans, Bath, Silchester, Caerleon, Chester, Lincoln, York were the most important centers. Mines were exploited and Roman farming and sheep-raising methods widely introduced. Wool was to shape British history down to the seventeenth century. Shops, schools, and shrines, farms and social institutions followed Roman models. The poet Martial mentioned a young Romanized British woman who moved at ease in Rome's highest social circles. Archeological excavations all over Britain have begun to revise the nineteenth-century view that Rome touched the British little or not at all.

Fig. 52.3. Rome. *The Miracle of the Rain,* column of Marcus Aurelius. The rain, represented as a benevolent bearded god with arms and wings spread, refreshed the Roman army and ruined the barbarians; the miracle was later attributed to Christian soldiers' prayers. Dramatic date A.D. 172 or 173. (C. Caprino and others, *La Colonna di Marco Aurelio,* Rome, 1955. Fig. 24.)

The Frontier in Asia and Africa

After Nero's diplomatic success in Armenia, the Flavian emperors increased Roman preponderance over Parthia by annexing every kingdom from Cappadocia to Palestine and the no-man's land between Syria and the Euphrates. Only Arabia Petraea retained semi-independence, but Trajan annexed it as a province almost without striking a blow. With his instinct for empire-building, he opened a highway from Damascus southward to the principal cities of the new province: the capital, Bostra, Hellenized Philadelphia, and the old capital Petra, with side roads to less important points. He supplied water, reclaimed land, built cities, and made the desert flower.

A nationalistic Parthian king, Chosroes, upset the Eastern *status quo* in Trajan's time. He closed the caravan route from India where it entered the Empire at the Euphrates bend nearest Syria and overran Armenia and dethroned its king. To this clear violation of the Neronian treaty Trajan's reply was swift. He extended the Damascus-Petra road to the Gulf of Aqaba as an alternate route to India; and in a swift campaign he tried to settle the Armenian question permanently by annexing the country. (However, as we saw, his successor Hadrian immediately abandoned it.) Then he finished the Parthian War which, 160 years before, death had prevented Caesar from undertaking. He easily conquered northern Mesopotamia, annexed it (temporarily) as a province, and marched south toward the Parthian winter capital, Ctesiphon. His organization of river transport for his army down the Euphrates and the Tigris is a classic of Roman logistics. But although Ctesiphon fell and the king's daughter and his golden throne were captured, Chosroes himself escaped. Trajan, after visiting the Persian Gulf to reorganize the Indian trade route, tarried in Babylon to organize a southern Mesopotamian province. Suddenly Chosroes counterattacked, and both north and south rebelled.

The revolt was connected with a serious Jewish uprising in Palestine and throughout the East. Religious and racial resentment, mounting since Titus' destruction of Jerusalem, broke into open violence. In Egypt Jewish fanatics went on a rampage of murder and arson. They devastated Cyrenaica, destroyed the capital of Cyprus, and killed almost the whole population. Chosroes, who had fanned these flames, encouraged their spread into Mesopotamia, which, since the Babylonian exile, contained a large Jewish population. Although many had returned to Palestine when the Persian Empire took over, many had remained to multiply and acquire wealth and power. With the Empire in turmoil from Cyrene to the Tigris, Trajan decided against annexing southern Mesopotamia, making it instead a client kingdom under a friendly Parthian prince. But he retained, though his successor abandoned, northern Mesopotamia, which, with Dacia, Armenia, and Arabia made four new provinces added to the Empire in only nineteen years. Trajan thus ranks next to Caesar and Augustus as a conqueror.

Hadrian however was another Augustus, a man of peace. Doubting the Empire's resources for further expansion, he withdrew from both Mesopotamia and Armenia, at the risk of open revolt, since Trajan's appointees controlled the army and the administration. This retrenchment produced a frontier easier and cheaper to defend.

Relations with Parthia continued unsatisfactory. When next a powerful Parthian king seized Armenia for a kinsman, Marcus Aurelius, though even more peace-minded than Hadrian, had to intervene. The Parthian spurned compromise, and Roman armies destroyed Artaxata, Ctesiphon, and Seleucia-on-the-Tigris and gave Armenia to a pro-Roman king. Marcus made the ex-Parthian dependency of Osrhoene a client-kingdom, thus straightening the Euphrates arc. Elsewhere he restored the frontier where the Parthians had pierced it. Though his Parthian war was a military success, his armies brought back, as we saw, a stubborn and disastrous plague that spread misery and death from Syria to Gaul, decimating Imperial armies and destroying prosperity. The Empire never quite recovered.

North Africa remained peaceful. Since Augustus' time Roman troops had protected Egypt from the Nubians up to the first cataract. Cyrenaica and Libya were safe behind the forbidding Sahara; so were Africa Proconsularis and Numidia. One legion stationed by the Flavians at Theveste in Numidia, then moved by Trajan to Lambaesis 100 miles west, sufficed to guard civilization from Tunis to the Atlas Mountains, the more easily since the camps were the centers of an excellent road network. Even the petty Berber forays on the two Mauretanias practically ceased after Hadrian extended the occupation south towards the Atlas. The whole world basked in the Roman peace.

Chapter 53/THE SILVER AGE

(I): URBANISM AND ART

The City of Rome

Silver Age culture, a product of the cities, may be better understood from a glance at their physical aspect. First, of course, was Rome. Capital of the world, Rome boasted an architectural grandeur never equaled in ancient and seldom in modern times. Republican monuments, many still in use, were venerated by nostalgic residents and tourists; Augustan ones had begun to mellow with age.

At the close of the Silver Age majestic temples had been erected to the deified emperors: to Claudius on the Caelian, to Vespasian at the head of the Roman Forum, three columns of which are still standing; to Hadrian, the philhellenist, in the Greek style; to Antoninus Pius and his wife Faustina, beside the Basilica Aemilia.

To Hadrian we owe three other sacred edifices. First, the temple of Venus and Rome, the two apsidal cellae built back to back so as to form one structure, its unity accentuated by a surrounding colonnade. Next his own mausoleum on the west bank of the Tiber, to rival Augustus', a great drum with a spiral ramp leading to the central tomb chamber. In the medieval era it was used as a fortress, and its crowning bronze sculpture, a four-horse chariot, replaced by the archangel Michael; hence the modern name, Castel Sant' Angelo. Lastly, the Pantheon. Retaining

Fig. 53.1. Rome. Temple of Venus and Rome. Probably designed by Hadrian himself, with two apses, back to back, perhaps an architectural pun (AMOR-ROMA). Its gilt bronze roof-tiles were removed to cover an early phase of St. Peter's. The plantings in the foreground represent columns of the surrounding colonnade; some of the actual columns of the side of the colonnade appear at the left. (Photo by Laura Voelkel)

Agrippa's name on the portico, Hadrian's architects replaced Agrippa's rectangular temple with a rotunda, 140 feet wide and 140 feet high. Light pours down from a 30-foot aperture at the center of the coffered dome, to deepen the sense of space resulting from the perfect balance of floor, wall, and ceiling. Unparalleled in art history for its harmony of form, the Pantheon is a living witness to Roman architects' imagination and technical skill. Perhaps Hadrian himself designed it, setting himself the pretty problem of inscribing a sphere in a cylinder. It has been a constant challenge to architects, among others Michelangelo (the dome of St. Peter's) and Jefferson (the Rotunda of the University of Virginia; Monticello.)

Specialized buildings served the comfort and recreational needs of the leisure-loving Romans. Every emperor, except the ultraconservative Tiberius, left his memorial in such constructions. But no more theaters were built after Trajan, and fewer plays were given in Pompey's or Marcellus' theater. Mime and pantomime were now the fashion. In pantomime the chief actor conveyed ideas, plot, dialogue, and characterization exclusively by posture, gesture, and subtle facial expression. Speaking actors, a chorus, and an orchestra supported him. The mime portrayed stock characters; the ragged clown, the pickpocket, the adulterer, the cocotte, the procurer exhibited a broad licentiousness. The best actors made large fortunes. Not even Christianity could abolish the mime; medieval itinerant minstrels may have derived from Roman traveling mime companies.

Chariot races competed with the theater in popularity. Rome had two racecourses, the Circus Maximus, since regal times in the valley between Palatine and Aventine, and the Circus Flaminius, built in 221 B.C. in the Campus Martius. Gaius built a more sumptuous one in the Vatican valley, beside the site of St. Peter's. The Circus Maximus alone accommodated at least 140,000 spectators. To idle and pleasure-bent Romans the circuses were as essential as the Tiber warehouses bulging with wheat and staples.

The king of sports was one of blood and death. War prisoners and convicted criminals were made to entertain the public by fighting, usually in pairs, until one was killed. Buying slaves and having them trained professionally as gladiators was good business. Even poor freemen hired themselves out as gladiators, and the time came when knights or nobles, including women, joined them. Despite denunciations by humanitarians like Cicero and Seneca and occasional disapproval in high places, the taste for gladiatorial combats grew so bloodthirsty that in Trajan's triumph over Decebalus 10,000 war prisoners fought in the arena. The best society, including the emperor and empress, joined the rabble at these gory games, calling for blood, though occasionally they spared the

Fig. 53.2. Rome. Pantheon. Entirely Hadrianic. A massive concrete drum, 140 feet high and 140 wide, supporting a concrete dome. It imposes a hemisphere upon a cylinder, a neat exercise in solid geometry. Over the porch Hadrian had inscribed the name of Augustus' lieutenant Agrippa, who had dedicated a humbler Pantheon on this site in 27 B.C. (Anderson photo)

vanquished in recognition of bravery. Combats of men against wild animals and of animal against animal—Trajan had 11,000 slaughtered in a single show—accompanied gladiatorial games.

For gladiatorial spectacles Roman architects designed a special building, the amphitheater, combining two theaters into an oval. The most famous was the Roman Coliseum, dedicated under Titus. Its oval façade contains four stories of superimposed arches. From the protective wall encircling the arena rose seats for 50,000 spectators, tier on tier to the very rim. Superimposed vaulted concrete galleries lightened the mass and, connected by ample double stairways, facilitated the flow of traffic. Modern stadiums and Mexican and Spanish bull rings reproduce Roman amphitheaters.

The Coliseum symbolizes the revolution that destroyed Nero. The great fire of 64 destroyed Rome's central slums, the Suburra, haunt of the poor and of immigrants, between the Viminal and the Caelian Hills. The Suburra housed also some industrial establishments, at least one synagogue, and several shrines of illegal cults. Nero built in the devastated area, as we saw, his Golden House, the Versailles of the Roman Empire. Intended as a fitting home for the *roi soleil* and a center of artistic and literary life, the Golden House was resented by Romans as the extravagance of a mad despot. The bourgeois emperors therefore considered it good politics to do away with it. On the site rose the Coliseum, the Baths of Titus and Trajan, the Temple of Venus and Rome, a corner of Vespasian's Forum—and still it was not wholly exploited. The discovery during the Renaissance of some of the buried rooms created a sensation. Raphael reproduced the ceiling decorations in his famous Vatican rooms.

But Nero also turned the fire to public advantage. His architects and town planners gave the Suburra a new look. The new wide straight avenues were lined with multi-storied apartments (*insulae*) built around an arcaded courtyard with windows and balconies looking out on the street, and porticoes giving access to luxury shops. A new day had dawned for Roman architecture, and the insula-plan was to influence medieval monasteries and Renaissance palaces as well.

The 100,000 people rendered homeless by the fire probably moved to the city's periphery, many across the Tiber, most to the outer slopes of the seven hills. Here too new apartment houses went up, perhaps not quite so squalid nor so congested as those of the old Suburra.

Few ancient peoples equaled the Romans in personal cleanliness. Bathing establishments were characteristic of Roman civilization. Rome had hundreds, private and public, but the Baths of Agrippa, Nero, Titus, and Trajan were the finest of their time.

The imperial baths served for more than bathing. They developed

Fig. 53.3. Rome. Republican and Imperial fora, model. Rome outgrew its earliest civic center, and Julius Caesar, Augustus, Vespasian, Nerva, and Trajan successively built fora on a grand scale, using axially symmetrical plans and incorporating temples, basilicas, libraries, and shops. (Rome, Museo della Civiltà Romana; J. Felbermeyer photo)

into huge complexes enclosing a central hall with room for thousands, a swimming pool (heated by tile conduits in walls and floor), warm and steam baths, and changing rooms. They also had libraries, lecture rooms, gardens, promenades, a track for foot races, courts for wrestling and boxing, and a small theater. They were lavishly ornamented with marbles, reliefs, stuccoes, and mosaics. The best artists painted murals there, while originals or copies of Greek statues were placed at vantage points as in modern museums. Freemen and slaves, grandees and paupers not only bathed and exercised at the baths, but exchanged news, imbibed culture, or whiled away the time. Most baths were open part of the day to women.

To supply the baths with water required engineering skill. For the pools and fountains in rich houses also needed water, as did the tall apartment houses and the many public fountains. The abundant Roman water-supply astonished visitors. Nowadays only New York City surpasses Imperial Rome in per-capita water consumption. Claudius solved the water problem by tapping two mountain streams. Trajan's aqueduct—Rome's eleventh—supplied the region across the Tiber, especially the Janiculum Hill. This one was technologically significant; it powered the

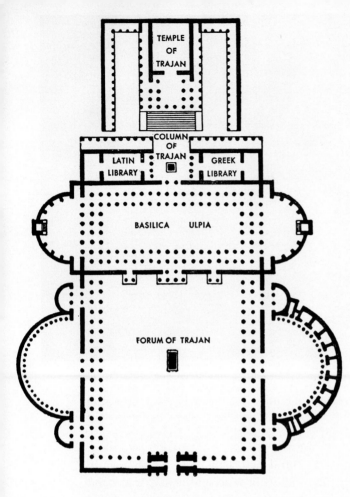

Fig. 53a. Plan of Trajan's Forum, Rome. The lower right apse is a part of Trajan's market. The library balconies gave a good view of the reliefs on the Column. The temple is a Hadrianic addition. (W. Fleming, *Art and Ideas,* New York, 1955. Fig. 3.4.)

West's—perhaps the world's—earliest water-driven grist mills. Both emperors wrestled with technical problems of conservation and distribution. They expanded or organized more efficiently the maintenance crews, put competent engineers in charge, installed water meters, sought to stop pilfering from the water mains. One of the Silver Age's most interesting books is a technical treatise, *The Waters of Rome,* by Frontinus, Trajan's water commissioner. The scale and engineering complexities of this public service is revealed by the surviving aqueducts, above all the majestic structure of the Porta Maggiore, the heart of Rome's water system, linking seven aqueducts (see Fig. 49.2).

The Imperial Fora contained far the most spectacular buildings. Nero's great avenues were the first attempt at facilitating pedestrian traffic. Although carriages were forbidden in the city and carts for essential services allowed only at night, the main streets were choked with people. One cause of congestion was the resurgence of an ancient institution, the patronate. Restricted politically, Roman nobles kept a sense of self-importance by surrounding themselves with droves of clients. The poorer the clients, the more eager they were to pay morning calls on their patron, lingering in and outside the house until they received the customary basket of food. Occasionally they were invited to dinner. As they followed their patron to the courts, the baths, the theater, the market, or wherever he went, they actually slowed or blocked traffic.

A partial remedy was the construction of the Imperial Fora, which when completed, formed a promenade through the heart of Rome. A man walking northwest from the Coliseum would first cross the site of the Golden House, keeping the Temple of Venus and Rome on his left. He next entered the Forum of Vespasian with its Temple of Peace housing a library-museum where the temple-treasures from Jerusalem and a marble plan of Rome were permanently displayed. On leaving its colonnaded square he crossed the Forum of Nerva, or *Forum Transitorium*, built to expedite pedestrian transit from the Suburra to the Roman Forum. Then, passing the Forum of Augustus, the Temple of Mars to his right and Caesar's Forum to his left, he entered the Forum of Trajan.

Trajan's architect, Apollodorus of Damascus, conceived grandiose architectural projects worthy of his master. The area of his Forum with its annexes, already mentioned in Chapter 51, is twice that of Rockefeller Center. The Forum proper was flanked by two colonnades, and these in turn by two semicircular complexes repeating similar ones in Augustus' Forum and housing shops and government offices. The eastern market area, against a steep hill, had six stories, terraced like the Sanctuary at Praeneste. Next was the Basilica (called the Ulpia after Trajan's family name), the largest and most ornate in the Greco-Roman world. Its conventional central nave had two aisles on each side. At each end was an apse as large as a large modern theater, serving as a law court. North of the Basilica rose the column commemorating the Emperor's Dacian War. It was flanked by two libraries, one Greek, the other Latin, from whose balconies the reliefs on the column could be read like a great scroll. The last unit in this complex plan was Hadrian's Temple of the Deified Trajan.

Trajan's Forum was an engineering triumph. It tied together all the Imperial Fora in a logical plan. A ridge between the Capitolium and the Quirinal, as high as an eleven- or twelve-story building, separated the two halves of the city. Trajan removed it to make room for his Forum and to link the Campus Martius with the other Imperial Fora, the Coliseum, and the quarters beyond. Thus he solved the traffic problem in the center of the city. An inscription at the base of the famous column informs posterity that its top marks the height of the ridge that was excavated. The column's original crowning statue of Trajan has been replaced by one of St. Peter, a symbol of pagan Imperial Rome's yielding to Christianity.

Italian and Provincial Cities

Of the thousands of Italian and provincial cities that flourished under the Empire we choose to describe three where recent excavation has cast new light, Ostia in Italy, London in the West, and Dura-Europus—already mentioned in Chapter 30—in the East. Ostia is, after Pompeii, the most important source of our knowledge of Roman life. At its peak under Trajan its population was 40,000 to 50,000; it had 800 years of history behind it. Lying only 20 miles from Rome, but, as a port town, reacting to cosmopolitan influence, it housed shops of every known trade and temples of exotic religions from Mithraism to Christianity. Its plan combined utility, monumental quality, and the scenic. It is soberer and more austere than Pompeii, as befits the tenement life of a lower middle class of which we know little from elsewhere.

Augustus gave Ostia a theater and a commercial center, Tiberius a Temple of Rome and Augustus, Caligula an aqueduct. Claudius and Trajan each built artificial harbors, Hadrian a grandiose Capitolium, a firemen's barracks, and new baths, the Antonines great new warehouses.

Ostia's most important feature is its *insulae,* blocks of apartment houses, multi-storied and balconied, the best of them with a central garden-plot where many families shared the pergolas, fountains, pool, and statue-studded lawn. Yet there is a certain deadly sameness about the flats: Ostia was a lower-middle-class city, where the petty *bourgeoisie* lived much as they do in the unfashionable quarters of Rome today. Here we see complete a middle-class city at the gates of Rome, not provincial, not foreign, but on the periphery, the vestibule to the world's metropolis. Through its warehouses passed the goods to feed, clothe, and pander to the luxurious tastes of the richest city in the world.

Far-away London was a typical western provincial capital, of which we have learned much more since the bombing of World War II. Its Hadrianic walls, which underlie the East End of modern London from Blackfriars Bridge to the Tower, enclose some 350 acres (the West's fifth largest town) and imply a population of about 45,000.

Already important as a road center in Boudicca's time, it became the financial capital. Under the Flavians London boasted a gridded street plan, a huge basilica, 500 feet long, presenting its long side to the Forum on the site of Leadenhall Market. A main street connected the Forum with the river, and London Bridge probably had a Roman predecessor leading to a southern suburb. After a fire late in Hadrian's reign the city was rebuilt, and indeed did not reach its highest point of prosperity till late in the third century. The most important discovery since the war,

Fig. 53.4. Roman London. It lay entirely east of the present site of St. Paul's Cathedral. The Forum and Basilica are east of the Wallbrook, between Cornhill and Lombard Street. Thence the *cardo* led directly south to the river and bridge. (G. Home, *Roman London*, London, 1948. Betw. pp. 144 and 145.)

Fig. 53.5. Dura. Air view. Note position on rocky height dominating the
Euphrates. Main gate is to the left, agora in the center. The rectangular grid of
unexcavated streets is plainly visible. (From the files of the Yale Expedition
to Dura-Europus)

a late-second-century Mithraeum in Walbrook, is identical in plan with
many in Ostia (where at least eighteen are known), with its apse, sunken
nave, and side aisles supported by seven columns, probably related to
the seven degrees of Mithraic freemasonry. The likeness in plan suggests
how unifying a force throughout the Empire was this Eastern worship, to
which soldiers especially were devoted.

Dura-Europus, a fortified caravan city on a high bank overlooking the
Middle Euphrates, occupied by the Romans in A.D. 165, was excavated
in the 1930's by a Yale expedition; the number, importance, and well-
preserved state of the finds make it the Pompeii of the Syrian desert. It
lay on the main Seleucid caravan route from Antioch-on-the-Orontes to
Seleucia-on-the-Tigris. It had been a Hellenistic foundation, with a
typical Hippodamian grid-plan; its fortifications, with twenty-two towers
and three main gates, were also Hellenistic. About the middle of the
second century B.C. the Parthians took over and the citizens gradually
Orientalized themselves. Citizens with Greek names had wives and children with Iranian or Semitic ones; the temples and their architecture
show a syncretism of Greek and Oriental gods; there is a Mithraeum, and
in the third century there was a frescoed synagogue and a Christian
Church with a baptistery.

Though the Romans held Dura briefly under Trajan, it was soon returned to Parthian control, though Romans in it enjoyed a high prestige. About 165 the Romans took it over, made it one of the fortresses of the Syrian limes, and incorporated it in the province of Syria. At first the Roman garrison was small, with little apparent effect on local life: the bazaars, shops, and private houses show little Roman influence. It was not until after the Antonines that a fourth of the city was expropriated and walled off as a Roman camp. Up to that time the Roman policy of live and let live apparently prevailed. The result is that much evidence of native culture survives, in inscriptions, *graffiti,* parchments and papyri, including fragments of a Seleucid code, contracts in Greek giving evidence of Oriental feudalism, and Roman military archives.

The evidence of Ostia, London, and Dura suggests that the chief bond of the Empire was religious, and the cult which appears in all three places is an Oriental one which appealed especially to the army. Yet the apartment houses of Ostia, the Basilica and Forum of Roman London, and the Oriental bazaars of Dura all existed and in their time flourished under the widespread protection of the Roman peace.

City Life

The great fact of the Silver Age is the rise of towns. Urban life made possible more amenities than the Republic had known, more luxury for high society, more public festivals for high and low.

Upper-class luxury is illustrated by the extraordinary specialization of slave duties. The emperor had a separate valet for every kind of attire: civilian, formal civilian, military, formal military, the theater and the gladiatorial shows. There were separate dishwashers for drinking glasses, plates, silver, gold, rock-crystal, and ware encrusted with precious stones. Besides bathmen, masseurs, and barbers, there were special slaves for levees: to lift the entrance curtain, to escort the visitors, to announce the names. The kitchen swarmed with cooks, bakers, pastry cooks, and confectioners; and there were butlers, waiters, busboys, stewards for each kind of wine, choristers, musicians, dancers, dwarfs, buffoons, and slaves to test the emperor's food and drink for poison.

The frivolity and extravagance of Nero and his court was especially notorious. We hear of golden fish-nets and silver horseshoes, a year's supply of Arabian incense burned at Poppaea's funeral. The Emperor had a private racetrack in his Vatican gardens, where in 64 his night races were lit by Christian bodies dipped in pitch and hung on crosses. Though he did not precisely fiddle while Rome burned, he is said to have played on that occasion, with lyre accompaniment, a poem of his own composition on the fall of Troy. He watched gladiatorial shows

Fig. 53.6. Tivoli. Hadrian's Villa, model. The grandest of the Roman villas, built beginning *c*. A.D. 126 south of Tibur, the modern Tivoli, about 17 miles from Rome. It was allegedly intended to reproduce various buildings which had impressed the Emperor on his travels. In the foreground, a vast porticoed area (700 × 500 feet) for the Emperor's walks; behind, a stadium; to the far right, a reflecting pool and Serapeum. The palace proper is in the background. (Rome, Museo della Civiltà Romana; J. Felbermeyer photo)

through a monocle made of a single emerald, collected vases of alabaster, crystal, and amber, hung the rooms of his Golden House with Babylonian tapestries. Among the statues adorning his palace and villas were the *Apollo Belvedere* and the *Laocoön* now in the Vatican Museum, and the *Girl from Anzio* now in the Terme. By night he enjoyed roaming the streets in disguise, committing assault on unoffending citizens.

Villas also illustrated upper-class luxury. Pliny in a letter describes his own seaside villa near Ostia, landscaped, with meadow and pine grove. It had a D-shaped portico and a dining room running out to sea, with windows on three sides. His bedroom faced the morning light and had a bay-window and bookcases. There were lower bedrooms also offering magnificent views of landscape and the sea. There were paths for walks in shade and sun, and flower and vegetable gardens—a pleasant retreat within a day's journey of Rome.

The most famous villa of the period was Hadrian's near Tibur, a vast complex of palaces, state chambers, baths, theaters, libraries, exercise grounds, porticoes, banqueting halls, private apartments, barracks, and slave quarters, over a half-mile from end to end. For meditative walks Hadrian had built about a reflecting pool a rectangular peristyle, one-seventh of a mile around. Nearby a walled enclosure contained a tiny circular artificial island, with moat and drawbridge, where the Emperor could retire for rest, study, and writing. A valley to the south contained the Canopus, imitating a sanctuary of Serapis near Alexandria; beside its central pool were placed copies of the Caryatids from the Erechtheum in Athens; at the end of the pool rose the vaulted Temple of Sarapis, crammed with Egyptian sculpture. The temple may have been a memorial to Hadrian's favorite, Antinous, who died young, tragically and mysteriously, near Alexandria. The architectural plans, which may be by Hadrian himself, are full of baroque exaggerations, alternations of light and darkness, straight lines and curves, plays of water, works of art. The key to the whole is vastness, sweep, and richness; the complex was built without regard to limitations, technological or financial. It mirrors the personality of the man himself, restless, dilettante, formal, unapproachable, tense, and self-conscious, a far cry from the rough simplicity of the old Republic. In its grandiose and ruined spaces one can catch the flavor of decline and fall.

The Silver Age was dedicated to great public spectacles to which 159 days a year were devoted under Claudius as compared with 59 in Sulla's time. The race-mad Roman crowd idolized the charioteers and were fervent partisans of one or another of the four racing syndicates, the red, the white, the blue, and the green. Inscriptions record charioteers'

Fig. 53b. Schematic drawing of beast elevator, Coliseum, Rome. Before the show the portcullises (a) were raised, admitting a beast from the dens (1) into the tunnel (2), built purposely too narrow for him to turn around and retreat; he was then forced to enter the elevator cage (3), whose gates shut automatically. At the moment of the show, the trainer threw a lever (near A) disengaging a counterweight and raising the cage to position (4). The gate opened automatically and the beast emerged on level (5), passed along the platform (6) to the ramp (7), and emerged into the arena through the trapdoor (8). (G. Cozzo, *Ingegneria Romana*, Rome, 1928. Tav. 90.)

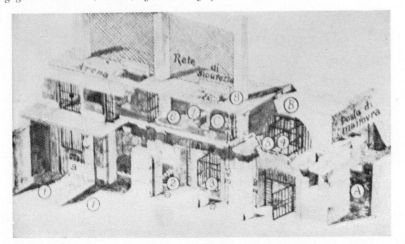

victories; one, a Spaniard, in a twenty-four-year career raced 4257 times, and won 1462 victories worth 35,863,120 sesterces. Gladiators were romantically admired; a graffito from the amphitheater at Pompeii describes how the girls sigh for one of them: *"suspiria puellarum."* Refinements of gladiatorial combat introduced fighting blindfolded, with nets, two swords, or lasso. There were even contests between dwarfs and women. In the beast fights, the most exotic animals were pitted sometimes against each other, sometimes against men. We hear of panthers, bears, bulls, lions, elephants, hippopotami, and even crocodiles. The Coliseum had an ingenious system of counterweighted elevators designed to discharge the beasts into the arena. It is hard not to see in these meat markets of human and animal flesh serious symptoms of the decadence that was to bring the Roman Empire to its fall.

Chapter 54 / THE SILVER AGE (II): LITERATURE AND PHILOSOPHY

The Background

Literature lagged behind the other arts. Yet many conditions were favorable. Free trade, easy communications, extensive travel by merchants, tourists, soldiers, philosophers, and missionaries stimulated the exchange of ideas. The Roman laissez-faire policy promoted tolerance Empire-wide. Social clubs and burial societies offered amenities, especially to the lower classes. Wealth had reached unprecedented heights, and though the masses lived wretchedly, the *bourgeoisie* were more prosperous than ever. Some of the upper class had a deeper sense of social responsibility than in the Republican or Augustan eras, and this mitigated the lot of the poor, including struggling authors. To cite examples, the rich commonly helped to support clients and neighbors, saw promising young men through school, financed festivals, or built burial places for artisan guilds. Perpetual charitable trusts provided dowries for indigent girls. Generous patrons gave millions to provide one city with baths, another with a theater, to repair an aqueduct, a temple, or a bridge, to build facilities for the improvement of the mind: lecture

Fig. 54.1. Inscription, showing lettering of Trajan's time. It records thanks of the people to Trajan for allotting them more space at the chariot races. (Rome, Capitoline Museum; Joyce Gordon photo from *Greece and Rome* XX, 1951. Plate CVII [III a].)

halls, art galleries, covered halls (*odea*) for music and poetry recitals, libraries, and schools.

Elementary education was mostly private, financed by student fees or by a patron. Imperial *alimenta* indirectly subsidized elementary schools with public funds. By the mid-second century, and largely through Imperial legislation, the cities had become responsible for maintaining schools. Whatever the method, urban illiteracy at least was practically wiped out. Evidence is provided by thousands of graffiti on walls of shops and private houses, taverns, barracks, and brothels. These impromptu inscriptions tell much more than why gentlemen preferred blondes. They cover a wide range of moral precepts and religious ideas, bits of home-spun philosophy, many-sided human interests, and a creditable general education. They reveal especially a knowledge of books, particularly the poetry of Vergil, Propertius, and Ovid. Vespasian started a new trend when he gave professors of Greek and Latin rhetoric salaries with a modern purchasing power approximating $20,000. Before the second century was over, the Imperial government was financing practically all higher education.

Books, then as now the most effective vehicle of education, by 100 had come within the average man's means. Best-sellers could be purchased in provincial towns, and public and private libraries accommodated all sorts of readers. That of Timgad, a small city, had 23,000 volumes. Epaphroditus, one of Claudius' freedmen, had a collection of 30,000 volumes. Though no original of any Silver Age book survives (our oldest Latin literary manuscript is a fourth-century Vergil), inscriptions in this period were handsomely cut and are the basis of many modern type-faces.

Despite these favorable conditions, literature did not maintain the high levels of the Augustan age. Tacitus (*c.* 55–*c.* 117) traced its decline to the suppression of political liberty after Augustus' victory at Actium. This is an attractive view, especially in a democracy. But how then explain why great literatures flourished under Tudor and Stuart absolutism or under such despots as Louis XIV or the nineteenth-century czars? Vergil too and his contemporaries overcame the handicap alleged by Tacitus; indeed Tacitus himself became one of the world's greatest writers.

Fig. 54.2. A Latin papyrus letter. An estate bailiff reports to a decurion (town-councilor) the governor's authorization to reimburse the decurion for expenses incurred during the governor's visit to estates in the nome Arsinoë in Egypt. (Madison, Wisconsin, University Memorial Library; University of Wisconsin Photo Laboratory)

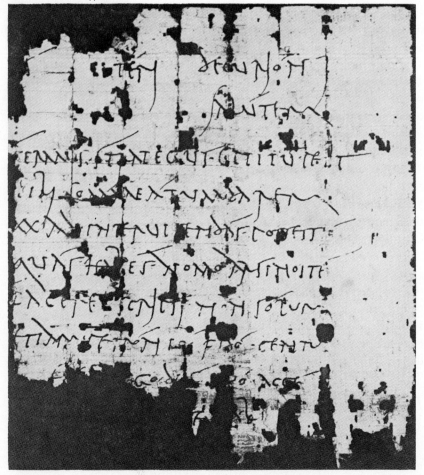

Some seventy years before Tacitus, a third-rate historian, Velleius Paterculus, had offered a more plausible explanation—that the worship of tradition choked off creative power. Greco-Roman literature usually followed models; what makes a great age is *creative* imitation. Perhaps Vergil's reputation dazzled his successors and a return to Greek originals would have helped. But the fact is that the best writers were precisely those who owed least to the Greeks: Petronius, Lucan, Tacitus, Juvenal, and Martial.

The educational system combined with the uncreative worship of tradition to produce the decline from the Golden Age. Rhetors made their pupils specialize too narrowly in declamation, slavishly following inferior handbook models. They classified situations and characters into types carefully packaged and labeled for their pupils' convenience, and encouraged them to reinforce their assigned themes with reckless arguments, lurid motivations, and purple patches, so that school declamations became verbal pyrotechnics.

This method, originally intended to prepare lawyers, was unfortunately carried over into creative writing. The habit grew among poets and prose-writers of reading their compositions to friends and admirers. The drawing room became an extension of the classroom. Fashionable salons were thrown open to authors whose chief intent was to win applause for flashiness. Sometimes they read in competition, intoxicated with the exuberance of their own verbosity. The natural result, in this unnatural atmosphere, was not creative art—though there were exceptions—but precocious academic exercises.

Even apart from these causes, demographic changes explain the difference between Silver Age style and vocabulary and that of Cicero or Vergil. Claudius' census of 48 registered 5,984,072 citizens, over 17 percent more than that of 14. The citizen body increased further after Claudius, chiefly through the assimilation of peoples different in race, culture, and level of education from Cicero's or Augustus' contemporaries. To reach this larger audience writers adopted more pointed and colorful diction and shorter, simpler sentences, somewhat as the nineteenth-century American daily press did to reach semi-literate non-English speaking immigrants. But Silver Age literature suffers only by comparison with that of the Golden Age. The best of it lived on to teach, delight, and inspire Western man.

Latin Literature

A brief survey of the principal Silver Age writers is now in order. Tacitus is its great historian. His major works are the *Annals,* on Roman history from the death of Augustus to the death of Nero, and the *Histories,* from 69 to Domitian's death in 96. Tacitus was the master, not the servant, of rhetoric. He developed a unique, spare style, note-worthy for its use of innuendo. Imbued with a Roman gentleman's ideas of public rectitude and private morality, he wrote history as in duty bound to exalt virtue and consign evil to infamy and is the more fascinating as he never achieves the objectivity to which he lays claim.

Tacitus' political bias warped him as a scientific historian. To him the principate was an evil system headed by evil men who would not permit the existence of good, but dragged men down to do, speak, and think evil. Tacitus did not knowingly misrepresent the facts, for he was a gentleman of unimpeachable integrity. Rather, his deep-seated politi-cal passions distorted his whole point of view.

Thus he missed the essence of Imperial history. The court was the center of his story, his subject a jumble of backstairs intrigue with lurid overtones of murders, suicides, and executions, the stuff of irresponsible journalism, with emperors jealous of pretenders, good and able men neglected, unworthy men appointed to high office, frustrated aristocrats and high-flying parvenus. He never suspected that the significant history of the period was being enacted away from Rome by legions protecting and advancing the front line of Roman culture, colonists clearing forests and peasants turning deserts into orchards, entrepreneurs expanding the Italian and provincial economy, sea-captains, sailors, and cart-drivers supplying the demand for goods, artisans busy at a thousand crafts to make life comfortable and the cities beautiful, engineers laying roads from the English Channel to Arabia Petraea, school teachers in towns and villas, roving lecturers, philosophers preaching the brotherhood of man, missionaries of new religions, the local upper and middle classes building or expanding civilized communities on three continents, and the sharecroppers and slaves carrying on their backs much of the load of civilization. The emperors' private lives or squabbles with the aristocracy had less to do with this epic than did their policies, which, unfalteringly pursued, assured to citizens and subjects freedom to work, live, and prosper under an enlightened law, and the benefits of universal peace. Of this, the essence of the Roman Empire, Tacitus had no inkling. Yet, despite his bias, his writings touched the peak of genius, achieving their purpose of stirring the conscience of mankind and forming one of Rome's most important bequests to posterity.

Suetonius (69–c. 140) wrote the *Lives of the Twelve Caesars*—Julius to Domitian. Though his style is clear and crisp and usually free from rhetorical encumbrances, his biographical method uncritically combines irresponsible muckraking with material favorable to the Emperors. He was blissfully unaware that even the most uncomplicated characters are problems in psychology. His *Lives* are therefore travesties rather than accurate pictures, but they make fascinating reading.

Invaluable for our knowledge of ancient life is the *Natural History* of Pliny the Elder (23–79). He died the victim of his own scientific curiosity. Admiral of the Tyrrhenian fleet, after ordering the ships to evacuate the terrified populations of Pompeii and Herculaneum, he was asphyxiated when he ventured too close to Mt. Vesuvius to investigate the eruption. His prodigious industry produced 102 volumes. The *Natural History* deals in thirty-seven books with the physical universe: geography, ethnology, anthropology, physiology, zoology, botany, pharmacology, mineralogy, metallurgy, the arts, and thousands of lesser subjects. Pliny consulted 2000 books by 473 authors, mostly Greek, and, a rarity among ancient authors, he cited his authorities. His work is an encyclopedia—a treasure-house, he called it. (A later encyclopedic work is the *Attic Nights* of Aulus Gellius [*c.* 123–165]). Unscientific criteria produced inaccuracies and misconceptions on almost every page, but perhaps no more than in the celebrated eighteenth-century *Encyclopédie*, the first comparable modern work. Pliny tells us more than any other ancient writer about the Greco-Roman cultural evolution. The Silver Age would be significant had it bequeathed posterity nothing more than the *Natural History*.

Seneca (5 B.C.–A.D. 65), Seneca the rhetorician's son, was his age's most representative and versatile writer. He made the Ciceronian period obsolete by bringing into vogue his own short vivid sentences and the use of colloquialisms. As a philosopher his sanity in ethics commended him to the Church Fathers; the medieval era regarded him as a Christian. His tenets are contained in his *Letters to Lucilius,* in some *Dialogues* or essays on human behavior, and in his *Physical Investigations,* which, despite its title, deals with philosophical and ethical problems. But his thinking is neither profound, systematic, nor consistent. Worse yet, his life was quite at variance with his preaching.

Seneca wrote nine tragedies—to be read, not acted. The plots were derived from Greek drama, the characters vehicles for Stoic preaching. The meter is a monotonous staccato; the rhetoric overflows. Even so, his plays stimulated early modern tragedy in England and France. A famous passage in his *Medea* sounds like a prophecy of the discovery of America; another in the *Physical Investigations* shows that he possessed, like Lucretius, the idea of progress, so often denied to the ancients.

Pliny the Younger (61/2—113/4) was a letter-writer. Ten books survive; their polish and charm reflect his own kind, unselfish nature and the moral idealism and high cultural standards of his distinguished friends. Particularly touching are the letters to his wife, showing a Roman couple's deep love and chaste marital relations. Two letters to Tacitus describe Vesuvius in eruption and the death of his uncle, Pliny the Elder. One book, written to Trajan while Pliny was governor of Bithynia, is a precious record of conscientious provincial administration.

The Silver Age's most original work is Petronius' novel, the *Satyricon,* of which only two incomplete books remain. (The only complete Latin novel extant is the *Golden Ass* of Apuleius [born *c.* 123]). The author was probably the man described by Tacitus as Nero's "arbiter of good taste," driven to an elegant suicide by Nero's envy. The longest connected fragment, "Trimalchio's Banquet," gives us a taste of this earliest known picaresque novel, presumably Petronius' own invention, since Greek examples of the genre are later. The novel recounts three freedman-rogues' shady adventures; its climax is the *nouveau riche* Trimalchio's banquet. The uncouth millionaire is ruthlessly caricatured, the rogues treated, sometimes almost sympathetically, as young men of a lost generation. Petronius was a master of the nuances of vulgar Latin; his objective narrative style leaves open the question whether he intended serious social criticism.

The Silver Age produced technical works of interest for their influence on the Renaissance. Columella wrote two treatises, *On Agriculture* and *On Arboriculture,* expanding Vergil's *Georgics.* We have mentioned an Augustan work, Vitruvius' *On Architecture,* a storehouse of information on architecture, civic, religious, and domestic, on paving and building materials, surveying, town-planning, water-supply, and machines, including a kind of speedometer or taximeter. Frontinus' *Waters of Rome,* also mentioned earlier, is both a history and a description of the administrative and technical problems of hydraulic engineering. Celsus, a layman, wrote an encyclopedia, of which the books *On Medicine* alone have survived, a complete treatment, especially strong on theory and on the history of medicine from the Greeks to his own time. All these, honest works by honest scientists, are distinguished by lucidity and absence of rhetoric.

The Training of the Orator by Quintilian (*c.* 35–*c.* 95) is both technical and humanistic. By oratory or eloquence Romans meant composition in general; hence Quintilian's work is a guide to good writing. It does much more than give good advice on grammar and the improvement of memory, on wit, humor, and emotional appeal, on artistic structure and the art of delivery. As a humanist convinced that character matters more than knowledge of techniques, Quintilian strove to inculcate in the reader—as he did in his pupils—the Roman ideal of character, an amalgam of practical wisdom, spiritual strength, and honorable living. In Quintilian's day Romans still paid at least lip-service to Cato's belief that a good orator must first be a good man. Quintilian's theories, especially his penetrating criticism of the great Greek and Roman writers and his discussion of elementary education, profoundly influenced Western literary taste and education from the discovery of the manuscript early in the fifteenth century through most of the nineteenth. A writer of impeccable taste, Quintilian combined the virtues of Cicero's opulent periods with those of Silver Age baroque prose. In recognition of his merit, Vespasian appointed Quintilian to the first Imperial chair of rhetoric. A few years later Dòmitian made him a consul.

In poetry Seneca's nephew Lucan (39–65) wrote the *Pharsalia,* an epic on Pompey and Caesar's Civil War. To match a subject so recent, he discarded old-fashioned epic machinery, giving his work a modern ring. He tried to replace the Homeric gods with the naturalistic and romantic folklore of ancient Italy. His old-fashioned Republicanism made him seek to awaken his contemporaries to their loss of political liberty and involved him in Piso's conspiracy, and he was condemned to die. But he failed to fuse his novel ingredients into sustained exalted poetry, for he was too passionately fond of rhetorical epigram, and his scenes, although often of absorbing human interest, lack unity. Maturity might have corrected this fault, but he died at 26, executed, after torture, by Nero. Despite some harsh criticism, ancient and modern, Dante equates him with Homer and Vergil—and himself—and recently his reputation has grown.

Satire was the most successful and original poetic genre of the Silver Age. Good-natured in Horace's hands, with the Stoic Persius (34–62) it became merciless, humorless, unsympathetic invective. This young puritan fanatic was fervently addicted to high ideals and deadly seriousness —more preacher than artist.

An even more blistering critic and a better artist was Juvenal (*c.* 50– *c.* 130). Indignation, he said, made him a satirist, indignation at poets spouting rubbish, at sexual perverts and hypocritical morality-peddlers, at society cold-shouldering honest men, at Rome with its peril from fire, falling houses, and predatory men. He described with savage acidity, yet with some relish, the immorality of women. He lashed out, perhaps from bitter experience, against the rich as niggardly patrons; against snobs as valuing pedigree over virtue; against men's stupidity in praying to Heaven for worldly favors when the greatest blessing is *mens sana in corpore sano,* a healthy mind in a healthy body. But although he fired round after round of invective, he was always the observer, not the preacher.

Juvenal's satires have fixed for posterity the picture of a Roman society steeped in sin. But satire, like the yellow press, feeds on the abnormal and sensational. The chaste wife, the faithful husband, the hard-working and law-abiding citizen are not news; crime, sin, corruption are. Other sources, especially Pliny's letters, show a different world; upright men and women, model families, kind masters, honest and devoted slaves, public-spirited noblemen. The historian must of course look at both sides of the picture, weighing the effect of poverty on Juvenal and prosperity on Pliny. Juvenal has influenced post-Renaissance satire, especially in eighteenth-century England.

Finally there was Martial (*c.* 40–*c.* 104), craftsman supreme in literary miniatures. He added wit to the graceful Greek epigram. His more than 1500 epigrams reveal every type and every aspect of Roman life. And each poem, though often only a line or two long, gives a complete picture. Few ancient writers are more delightful, either for artistic technique or understanding of human nature. When Coleridge defined the epigram as a full-rounded composition, "its body brevity and wit its soul," he had Martial in mind.

Greek Literature

Roman men of letters spoke also in Greek. But while some writers in Latin were creative in their imitation, or even original—though originality is not a classical virtue—writers in Greek, with two or three exceptions, were academic and pedantic. Classical tragedy and comedy were dead; the mime was an unpalatable substitute. A simple Attic style was the ideal, expressed in the so-called "Second Sophistic" movement, but only Lucian's essays attained it with any vitality. These new Sophists became jacks-of-all-trades: political orators, dabblers in philosophy, scholars, antiquarians, and artists. Eastern genteel society esteemed them highly, but never did so many well-intentioned men waste so much time on such trivial stuff. An exception is the medical work of Galen (*c.* 129–199).

The earliest "Sophist" of note was Dio of Prusa (*c.* 40–after 112), called Chrysostom (Golden-mouthed), who could occasionally paint a vivid scene and stood for social reform. Equally respected was Aelius Aristides (117–189), also from Asia Minor, the author of a eulogy *To Rome,* extravagant at times, but on the whole a just appreciation of its civilizing role. Aristides' life illuminates the religion and psychology of the age. When a chronic illness baffled his doctors, he turned to the god Asclepius who, he records, helped him in a number of dream-visits.

Lucian of Samosata on the Euphrates (*c.* 120–after 180) was both the greatest "Sophist" and the most creative post-classical Greek prose-writer. Born of Syriac-speaking parents, he learned his Greek in school, yet wrote it idiomatically. His 136 works are mostly varied and original comic dialogues. He traveled widely, lecturing in both East and West, then settled as a teacher in Athens. An enemy of superstition and humbug, he aimed his choicest shafts at orthodox mythology, especially in his rollicking *Dialogues of the Gods.* In the *Dialogues of the Dead* he exposed the complacency and pretense of time-wasting, absurd philosophers, of the rich, the lecherous, even the athlete. The fantastic inventions and inexhaustible wit of this second-century Voltaire have inspired many a modern satirist, including Swift and Rabelais.

Greek writers made solid contributions to history. Arrian (*c.* 95–175) a Bithynian, wrote, in Xenophon's straightforward style, the *Anabasis of Alexander* (the Great). Based chiefly on Ptolemy I's memoirs, this is the most authoritative account of the conqueror, free of romantic frills and rhetoric. A Lydian, Pausanias (*fl. c.* 150) has left a *Description of Greece,* a serviceable Baedeker for that age of tourism. His special concern with historical monuments has made him an invaluable guide to modern archeologists who, following his footsteps, have located important ancient buildings; for example, in Olympia, Delphi, and the Athenian Agora.

Plutarch (*c.* 46–after 120), Boeotia's greatest writer after Pindar, wrote the *Moralia,* some 270 collected essays on an amazing variety of topics. A few titles show how wide were his interests: *Alexander: Luck or Genius?, Can Virtue Be Taught?, On Music, The Face of the Moon, Advice to Married Couples, Monarchy, Democracy and Oligarchy, The Luck of the Romans.* The *Moralia's* intrinsic interest is heightened by the author's delightful way of rambling over all fields of knowledge. Principally through Montaigne, the *Moralia* have shaped the modern essay; in America they influenced Emerson.

Another of Plutarch's works, the *Parallel Lives,* was constantly read down through the nineteenth century. The *Lives* too have a transparent moral purpose. Arranged in Greek and Roman pairs (for example, Alexander and Caesar, Demosthenes and Cicero), they were designed to show Greeks and Romans alike exemplifying the public virtues—love of justice, love of liberty, military prowess, or devotion to duty—or justly chastised for vice. They imply that the two nations, one with the nimble mind, the other with the capacity to rule, molded the world society in which men like Plutarch could live content.

Philosophy

In this age philosophical schools blended. While Stoicism was the most vital force, with Cynicism a close second, there were still Platonists and Aristotelians; eclectics like Plutarch picked and chose among systems. Neglecting its earlier metaphysical emphasis, Stoicism became a lay religion aiming at self-improvement. Since to the Stoics the moral life was the life according to Nature, they centered their inquiry around Man, Nature, and God, the creator and preserver of Nature. To live according to Nature was for them to live according to God's will. Seneca emphasized God's fatherly goodness. His view of the struggle between good and evil in man is not unlike St. Paul's. And while St. Paul was writing in his epistle to the Romans, "In Him we live and move and have our being," Seneca was saying, "God is near you, with you, in you." Medieval scholars regarded him as a Christian and forged a correspondence between him and St. Paul.

Epictetus (c. 55–135), who as a boy slave in Rome was given opportunity to hear the great masters of the day, developed further two related Stoic ideas: the brotherhood of man and the goodness of Divine Providence. For him, happiness depends not on outside circumstances but on the inner man, and is best attained by renouncing worldly pomps and desires. Compare the saying of Jesus, "The Kingdom of Heaven is within you." To Epictetus, suffering was a necessary step to understanding; and criminals and evil-doers were to be pitied rather than punished. He opened a successful school; unlike most philosophers, he made his teaching clear and homely in order to be understood by the masses.

Marcus Aurelius felt the influence of Epictetus. Most of his *Meditations* were written (in Greek) at the front during the Marcomannic War as escape from uncongenial soldiering. He found being a philosopher-king an agonizing experience. As philosopher he disapproved of war; but as emperor he owed it to his people to wage it unremittingly. A greater tragedy for this pagan Hamlet was his conviction, derived from Cynic influences, that life, property, worldly values, and all human institutions were not, philosophically speaking, worth preserving, yet as emperor he was forced to preserve them. Overcoming his personal feelings, he did his duty like an old-fashioned Roman. Although he did not believe in immortality, he tried as hard as any Christian to guard against sin and every form of earthly attachment. He saw only death and ashes—the vanity of vanities of *Ecclesiastes*—behind every mortal pleasure. He found spiritual comfort in contemplating the "City of Zeus" where neither Athens, Rome, nor social divisions had place, but all men were brothers.

Chapter 55 / RISE OF

CHRISTIANITY

Mystery Cults

As far back as Augustus' reign a variety of cults held the allegiance of various peoples of the Empire.

The Eastern cities, especially those in the polis-tradition, had their own official cults—of Zeus, Apollo, Athena, and the rest. The cities of the Latin West followed the Roman state religion imported by the Roman pioneers. Observed as state ceremonial by the public authorities, none of these cults was compulsory for private citizens.

The East without exception and the West in varying degrees worshiped the living Emperor, both as a symbol unifying the Empire's peoples and as a visible Providence insuring universal welfare. There was no conflict whatever between the imperial cult and the worship of the gods.

There was a third type of pagan religion, the cult of the family gods, especially those of the hearth and the health of the household and of the gods protecting a rural hamlet's welfare: the gods of sowing, growing, harvesting, the health of the cattle, favorable weather conditions, and the like. In this category also belong the patron divinities of various occupations; of bakers, barbers, blacksmiths, stevedores, and soldiers,

Fig. 55.1. Ostia. Mithraeum. The photograph shows the cult statue as reconstructed where found, in the Mithraeum under the Baths of Mithras (2nd-3rd centuries A.D.), one of 18 Mithraea known at Ostia. Light from overhead illuminated the cult statue, which was mutilated by the Christians, who threw its fragments in a drain. (Ostia, Italy, Museum; Fototeca)

for example. Obviously such gods would enlist greater devotion than the gods of the state or those of poetic tradition.

The mystery cults or Oriental religions, so widespread in the Hellenistic world—of Egyptian Isis and Phrygian Attis in an earlier wave, of Persian Mithras and Jupiter Dolichenus in a later—during the Silver Age invaded Italy and the West. By offering the convert personal salvation they provided an intimate appeal no pagan god could match, yet they did not exclude the other gods. For example, an Athenian, as citizen, worshiped Athena and other official Athenian gods; as an Imperial subject, the living emperor; as, say, a demesman of Marathon, its ancient local divinities; and, besides, his family gods and those of his guild. But as an individual with a conscience, with spiritual problems, and with freedom to choose among cults, he might adopt Isis or Mithras as his favorite. Thus in the Silver Age cults competed but they did not clash.

Brought to the West by Oriental immigrants, chiefly slaves, and by returning soldiers, the mystery cults followed a common pattern. The god, as we have seen, undergoes suffering or some heroic trial, dies young, and descends to the nether world, then is resurrected to enjoy everlasting life and endow his votaries with immortality. He has a consort—Attis with Cybele, Osiris with Isis. He makes moral demands on his followers. His annual feast is a cult-drama re-enacting his trials, death, and resurrection. By following these holy episodes, the faithful die with the god in spirit, rise with him, and are purified of sin, their hearts uplifted by initiation and other sacramental rites. A professional clergy wearing special street garb and wielding great authority over the votaries' lives and minds dispensed grace. The divine service they conducted, rich in priestly vestments, torches, and incense, appealed powerfully to the senses and to the mind trained to see in these media the meaning of life and death and the purpose of creation.

Cults differed. In that of Attis the priests worked themselves into a frenzy, emasculated themselves in imitation of the god, and begged for alms, all of which repelled Westerners. Isis was more attractive, having, as wife, mother, and widow, strong human appeal, especially for women, who were granted the honor of serving as her priestesses. The ritual, beautiful and dignified, combined congregational singing and sacramental symbols, penitence, meditation, and sacred bathing. Mithras' devotees were exclusively male, especially soldiers, as we have seen. Originally a servant of Ahura-Mazda, god of light, Mithras came to the Greco-Roman world from Iran via Asia Minor. He gradually became identified with the sun. He was the enemy of Ahriman, the source of death and evil. Countless reliefs represent him as a handsome youth slaying the bull whose blood brings renewal to the crops and immortality to the believer baptized with it. Another important rite was a congregational meal, symbolic of spiritual bond. The cult's mysteries and moral demands were revealed in seven successive degrees of initiation. Those of the highest degree, the Fathers, acted as clergy.

A few pagan divinities had become Oriental salvation gods—for example, Adonis, Dionysus, and Zeus himself syncretized with certain Syrian divinities. As the mystery cults, by embracing rich and poor, free and slave, Oriental and Westerner, produced a leveling of classes and races, so too similarities in rites and doctrines led to blending with each other and even with the more mystic pagan myths. Isis "of the thousand names" was, for example, equated with Cybele, with the Syrian Atargatis, with the Punic Moon goddess, and even with Aphrodite and Demeter.

Philosophy showed a parallel syncretism. Plutarch believed in divine unity—for example, of Osiris, Dionysus, and Jehovah. There was a common ground among devotees of Attis, Mithras, and Sabazius, and between them and the Christians. Philosophers perceived truth everywhere, in the classical gods, the mystery cults, Judaism, and its offshoot, Christianity. Philosophy, for example, the Neo-Pythagoreanism of the subterranean basilica at the Porta Maggiore, had by this time deserted rational inquiry to search for one universal mystic formula—call it Providence or divine father—quieting the conscience and satisfying the heart.

Judaism

Only the Jews refused to accept any god but their own. Jupiter, the god-emperor, and the salvation gods were mutually accommodating; Jehovah exacted undivided allegiance. When the emperors fought the Jews, they saw it as political and military, not religious, battle. Tiberius and Claudius expelled the Jews from Rome not out of religious discrimination, but for infringing law and order. The First Jewish War was fought to crush Judaea's armed bid for independence. And Trajan likewise ruthlessly suppressed a Jewish revolt in the provinces of Cyprus and Cyrene because, in bitter race conflicts with the Greeks, the Jews had devastated Cyrenaica and destroyed Salamis, the Cypriot capital (115). Defensive also was a second war (131–134). Under the Pax Romana Greco-Roman civilization had flourished over the Jewish homeland. The magnificent ruins of Gerasa testify to the advanced urban life the Romans had established there up to the desert's very edge. To expand the economy and promote urbanism, as Imperial policy dictated, Hadrian rebuilt Jerusalem, settling it with Greek-speaking elements. Renamed Aelia Capitolina, the city was intended as a center of gentile culture. But the Palestinian Jews upset Hadrian's calculations by revolting at this sacrilege. Guerrillas fought in open country, from cavern and mountain fastness. Led by Barcochba (Son of the Star), in whom they saw the Messiah and whose signature appears in the famous Dead Sea Scrolls, they took Aelia and almost annihilated the garrison. The emergency demanded Hadrian's personal attention. The Romans, suffering heavy losses, destroyed a thousand villages and killed more than 500,000 people. To prevent renewed bloodshed Syria and Palestine were reorganized.

But the Jews of the Diaspora prospered both materially and spiritually. Tolerated by Imperial policy, they propagandized through written works and itinerant preachers. Greek was their mother tongue, their teaching incorporated Greek ideas, and they used Greek to instruct sympathetic gentiles and enlighten the ignorant or prejudiced. Philo (c. 30 B.C.– A.D. 45), a leader of the Alexandrian Jewish community but intellectually Hellenized, devoted his life to reconciling Greek philosophy and

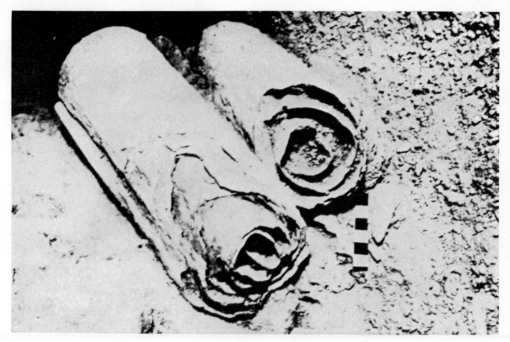

Fig. 55.2. Copper scrolls from the Dead Sea Caves. The Dead Sea scrolls, first discovered in 1947, cast light upon the manuscript tradition of the Old Testament and on a Judaic sect, the Essenes, which flourished at the time of Christ. (*Archaeology* IX, 1956, p. 43.)

Jewish revelation. He borrowed from Aristotle, Stoicism, and Neo-Pythagoreanism, but most of all from Plato. Taking Plato's "ideas" in their original sense of realities antedating man and matter, Philo incorporated them into Jewish revelation. God, he taught, engenders the Logos, his First Thought or Self-Manifestation (a Being in and by itself) which acts as creative Force between God and the World. But He engenders secondary, intermediary Forces through which the Logos operates in creating and preserving the world. Philo's theory, borrowed for Christian doctrine, shaped Western thought. Two other Philonic beliefs affected Christian thinking: that man cannot of his own wish know God or commune with Him, but only by God's grace; and that God destroys the persecutors of His people as He destroyed the Emperor Gaius.

A Palestinian Jew, the historian Josephus (b. *c.* 38), continued the work of reconciling Jew and gentile. Captured while commanding in Galilee in the First War, he went over to the Roman party, and he wrote the *Jewish War* to tell the Palestinian, Syrian, and Babylonian Jews the harsh fact that resistance to the Romans was hopeless. But despite his Roman bias he remained fiercely proud of the Jewish religion. His *Jewish Antiquities,* a history of the Jews since the Creation, was written to acquaint the gentiles with the wonderful works of Jehovah and the spiritual superiority of his people. In *Against Apion* he brilliantly argued that Jews could match every Greek moral or intellectual achievement. He also wrote an autobiography. Despite inventions and distortions his colorful and dramatic style makes for exciting reading.

Philo's and Josephus' works did more than add variety to Silver Age literature; they satisfied a growing Greek and Roman curiosity about Jewish religion. There were proselytes or God-fearing gentiles, as they are called in *Acts,* who, though they objected to circumcision and Jewish taboos, worshiped the Jewish God. They liked especially the Sabbath sermon, which both explained the Law and lifted men's hearts to God. The mystery cults had nothing like it; their appeal was chiefly emotional. Judaism won the respect of educated gentiles both for its moral tone, akin, though superior, to their own Stoic or eclectic precepts, and for the Hellenic imprint it had received from Philo. This Hellenized Judaism entered the noblest Roman families and the Imperial court itself. Jewish counselors had the Empress Poppaea's ear; Epaphroditus, Nero's and Domitian's state secretary, was either a Jew or a proselyte; and some of the Flavians were, if not proselytes, at least sympathizers.

St. Paul

The philosophical and religious situation just sketched favored the spread of Christianity. An offshoot of Judaism (Jesus said He came "not to destroy the Law but to fulfill it"), Christianity had behind it the authority and prestige of the Old Testament. It preached a god who suffered, died, and was resurrected. It satisfied sacramental hunger as a mystery cult with the comfort and inspiration of baptismal initiation, eucharistic meal, and other mystic rites. Its doctrine of spiritual rebirth and immortality was superior to that of other salvation cults, and its explanation of evil was acceptable to the Hellenic mind: "Blessed are ye when men shall revile and persecute you . . ." Nor is this all. In it morality and mysticism, philosophy and historicity, fervor and common sense combined to command more reverence than did any other Oriental cult or any pagan myth.

The central figure of Christianity was Jesus of Nazareth, born in 4 B.C. (the traditional chronology is based on an inaccurate sixth-century computation.) Some scrolls found in 1947 in a cave near the Dead Sea contain the doctrines of an earlier Jewish sect, the Essenes, whose organization may have influenced that of the early Christian church, and whose beliefs anticipate or agree with some of Jesus' teachings. Jesus' life and doctrine are recounted in the Gospels which, after describing certain miraculous events attending His birth, recount His last three years. Beyond all earlier prophets He spiritualized the concept of God as loving

Father and maintained that the essence of religion is faith and goodness, not outward observances. The brotherhood of man was for Him a vital tenet, and love the cornerstone of human relations. He sought out the poor and repentant sinners, whom He comforted, called specially beloved of God, and assured of their reward in heaven. He planted securely in men's hearts the belief in a future life. The Gospels tell us that through faith in His healing powers the blind were able to see, the deaf hear, the crippled walk, the sick recover. The conviction spread that He was the Messiah, King, and Son of God.

The Pharisees whom He bitterly denounced as hypocrites, the priests whose authority He undermined, in short, all religious conservatives saw in Him a dangerous revolutionary. The Sanhedrin, the supreme Jewish council, acted swiftly when, as He entered Jerusalem for the Passover, the masses acclaimed Him son of David. He was then in His early thirties. The council saw two issues involved. By accepting the title Son of God, He committed or tolerated blasphemy; a claim to kingship might look treasonable to the Romans, especially since many Jews were waiting for the liberating Messiah. The council put its case to the procurator Pontius Pilate, who did his utmost to save Jesus, but the priests, the Sanhedrin, and the fickle mob left him no choice: mercy to Jesus the King was treason to Caesar. Pilate, no hero, sentenced Jesus to death by crucifixion. A handful of disciples laid the body in a nearby grave. The Gospels relate that on the third day Jesus rose from the dead, that later various friends saw, heard, and ate with Him, and that forty days after His resurrection he ascended into Heaven. The belief soon spread, and became of enormous and decisive importance in the victory of Christianity over paganism, that He would return with power and glory to judge the living and the dead.

Jesus' disciples, though faithful to His doctrine and convinced of His divinity, continued to worship as pious Jews in the Temple. The twelve who had been closest to Him were moved to become Apostles to the gentiles, and according to the book of *Acts* were miraculously endowed to that end with fluency in various languages. They became leaders of the disciples, preaching, making converts, and curing the sick. When the high priests rejected them as heretics they set up against the orthodox a separate religious society, for which they claimed authenticity. The converts, moved too by Jesus' spirit, pooled their properties to support the poor among them. Persecution drove the nascent church out of Jerusalem, first into Judaea and Palestine, then through Syria and other Roman provinces, where they instructed gentiles in Judaism as modified by Jesus, making circumcision an indispensable rite, then baptizing them.

A convert, St. Paul, changed this narrow view. His missionary zeal and intellectual power found him first a place, then the primacy, among the Apostles. It was he who made Christianity a completely independent religion—universal in its appeal—by eliminating Judaism as a precondition for membership. To tell the pagans of Jesus he traveled widely, even to Rome itself. He epitomized in himself the universality he gave to the new religion. A Jew, he clung tenaciously to the Jewish wisdom of the Old Testament. He was born in Hellenized Tarsus, learned Greek early, studied Greek philosophy and poetry in the local school. He was a Roman citizen—at home anywhere in the Empire and aware of a status transcending national, racial, and social boundaries. This happy combination crystallized in Paul's mind in the concept of an all-inclusive spiritual society where "there is neither Jew nor gentile, Greek nor barbarian, nor bond nor free, but all are in Christ."

The Influence of Hellenism

Hellenism, however, had begun to affect Judaism long before St. Paul, through Socrates' belief in the immortality of the soul and through Cleanthes' sublime poetic statement of man's obligation to do God's will, which anticipates the Lord's Prayer by nearly 300 years.

When the Old Testament was translated into Greek in the third century B.C., Greek shadings could hardly be kept out of the original Hebrew thought. Christian thought was also affected, for Paul and his fellow missionaries preached to the gentiles and the Jews of the Diaspora in Greek, the only language those prospective converts understood. Thus they created the familiar Christian vocabulary; sin, grace, repentance, baptism, eucharist, faith, hope, charity—all the basic terms of Christian theology and Christian mystic experience. But, translated into Greek, out of Jesus' and the Apostles' Aramaic, some terms shifted slightly in emphasis or color. For instance, Jesus was called in Aramaic Master or Teacher, which becomes in Greek *Kyrios,* Lord; while Messiah—the Expected Deliverer—became *Christos* (Christ)—the Anointed One. And the original language of the entire New Testament, except St. Matthew's Gospel, was Greek, so that Hellenism shaped the first systematic presentation of Christian thought, if not Christian thought itself.

Hellenism affected Christianity in other ways. Since the gentiles believed in many gods and in men whose fathers were gods, they accepted Christ's divine sonship more readily than did the strictly monotheistic Jews, and Paul preaching on the Areopagus could quote the Hellenistic astronomical poet Aratus on man's kinship to God, or writing to the Colossians in Asia Minor, could use the Platonic "ideas," elaborated by Philo, to accentuate the prior existence and prime importance of Christ and the setting up of the hierarchy of creation through him. Platonism inspired also the language of St. John's Gospel: the Word that was God is Platonic Reason.

The Christian sacraments themselves were touched by Hellenism. We saw how sacramental ideas had crept into Greek religious experience since Orpheus and spread through the influence of Oriental cults. They had even entered Judaism: witness John the Baptist's call to repentance and the immersion of converts in the river Jordan. By the second century the many similarities between Christian and pagan sacraments were embarrassing to the Church Fathers: St. Justin Martyr and St. Irenaeus, bishop of Lyons, explained the mystery cults as a cheap imitation of Christian rites, invented by the devil to confuse men and turn them away from Christ.

This necessarily brief and inadequate treatment of Christianity may close with some remarks on its hierarchical organization, which safeguarded the new religion from dissension within and attack from without. The Apostles felt divinely commissioned to teach, to found and govern congregations, and to transmit Christ's grace to the faithful. At the outset they appointed helpers (deacons) to administer the moneys and properties donated to care for the poor. For the first sixty years or so, several other offices were in existence: apostles, bishops (*episcopoi*), elders (*presbyteroi*), shepherds, teachers, miracle-workers, and prophets who spoke "with tongues." These last were a problem. While some were inspired preachers, others set out to rouse mass hysteria. A few were impostors; some permitted or even taught loose morals. Some, Gnostics or intellectuals, contended that only knowledge, not faith, piety, or good works could bring salvation. To control such anarchy one undisputed authority was needed in every community. Thus by the early second century one bishop in every city had become supreme priest, teacher, and ruler. In the process all other offices were eliminated, except presbyters and deacons. Dedicated to perpetuating Christ's and the Apostle's teachings, the bishops developed a close mutual understanding which planted orthodoxy, weeded out heresy, and helped the Catholic and Apostolic Church to grow.

Christian Literature

Christianity was more than a way of life or an ecclesiastical establishment. It was a dynamic force that produced the New Testament, the first century's most significant literature. Simple in style, sincere in conviction, the New Testament is both a sacred book and timeless literature. Its art is different from Petronius' or Tacitus', but in content it is the most creative literary production since Plato. It contains Christ's and the

Apostles' teaching, written expressly to guide and edify the faithful; it reassesses human values. For Greco-Roman individualism and state-centered civilization, it substituted a Christ-centered philosophy founded on personal purity, love of God, and love of man, even enemies. Intent on imitating Christ's other-worldly love, Christians tended to withdraw from government, business, and all earthly ambitions, leaving such things to the wicked. To them, Imperial Rome was the Babylonian harlot, organizer and preserver of corruption. They scorned human affairs because they believed that the Lord's second coming and the end of the world were imminent. As Christian ideas took hold, history changed its course and a new era dawned.

The year 100 divides Christian literature's creative or Apostolic period from the Patristic. Holy and learned bishops and sometimes priests strove to purge Apostolic doctrine of what seemed to them vicious aberrations or simply misguided tendencies. In this they followed St. Paul's angry denunciations of false prophets and false teachings. What they accepted was orthodoxy; what they rejected, heresy. They and their successors in the next few centuries are called Fathers of the Church, because of their special service in preserving and consolidating the faith. The greatest second-century Father was St. Irenaeus (c. 125–202), pre-eminent in influence among Catholics to this day, among Protestants until about a hundred years ago, when historical method was applied to theology. He systematized Christian beliefs in five books *Against Heresies,* the model of all subsequent works on this subject. Seeking for an authority capable of harmonizing discords and commanding respect and obedience, he settled on the Church of Rome because Peter and Paul had founded it. Roman Catholics see in Irenaeus the earliest explicit witness of the Bishop of Rome's primacy.

Controversy among Christians, as reflected in second-century exegetical literature, was paralleled by controversy with outsiders: philosophers, the non-believing masses, and the public authorities. The mob had hated, suspected, and feared Christians ever since Nero had accused them of arson. For 250 years Christians were regarded as perpetrators of public calamities or used as scapegoats. Their self-imposed aloofness produced rumors that they were organized criminals and traitors, their prayer-meetings orgies, their eucharist—partaking of Christ's body and blood—cannibalistic. In particular, their abstention from pagan worship marked them as dangerous "atheists"; Tacitus calls them haters of the human race. But for two centuries persecutions were sporadic and local, arising from emergency or hysteria in a single city or province. While some officials might go witch-hunting, others painstakingly ascertained the facts. One of the latter was Pliny the Younger, while he was governor of Bithynia. After diligent investigation, Pliny concluded that

Christians were law-abiding and their meetings harmless; they gathered before dawn to worship their God Christ, with prayers, hymns, and a simple common meal. But they would not obey the order to renounce their religion—and Roman law made civil disobedience a serious offense. Trajan instructed Pliny that public functionaries should do no witch-hunting nor heed anonymous accusations. Only when denounced openly should Christians be subjected to trial. If found guilty, they were to be pardoned on recanting, but punished if they refused. Trajan's attitude set the pattern in the provinces throughout the second century. Even so persecution afflicted the Church during the otherwise enlightened reign of Marcus Aurelius.

This antagonism to the faith produced the apologetic literature of the second and following centuries, essentially a reasoned defense against outside attack. The greatest second-century apologist was Justin Martyr (c. 100–165), who emphasized that Christians were decent, law-abiding people, described their beliefs and worship, and insisted on their loyalty to the emperor for whose preservation and power they prayed. Another point of Justin's deeply impressed the later Church Fathers, and incidentally shows Hellenism's impact on Christianity—that Christ, the Logos or Word of God, is God's agent for creating the world, inspiring the Jewish prophets and gentile holy men, including Greek sages like Socrates and Plato, that where Greek philosophy is true, it is in itself Christian and part of the Christian inheritance. Thus began the systematic effort to prove what St. Paul had first seen, that Christianity was not alien to the best traits of Greco-Roman culture nor dangerous to the Roman Empire.

Chapter 56 / END OF
ITALIAN SUPREMACY

*

The Disastrous Rule of Commodus

His nineteen-year-old son Commodus succeeded Marcus Aurelius in 180. The change from a philosopher-king to a young voluptuary and mystic ended the era of the "five good emperors." Some historians, noting how Commodus abandoned his predecessors' policies—principally concern for the people's welfare, respect for public opinion, and insistence on border security—hold him chiefly responsible for the Empire's decline and fall.

Apparently Marcus Aurelius was forced to swallow his misgivings about his son's fitness, for had he adopted one of his experienced collaborators, Commodus almost certainly would have precipitated a civil war. And of course the young man might develop a sense of responsibility once he was in office. But Commodus disappointed this hope: he dismissed those able associates who had helped his father administer the Empire so conscientiously.

Incredible as it seems, Commodus jettisoned his father's German policy, almost successfully concluded at Marcus' death, with the new Oder-Carpathian frontier almost secured. But Commodus did not bother to

* Coin of Septimius Severus (enlarged). (Ashmolean Museum)

garner the fruits of thirteen years of labor. He granted peace on terms his father had refused some years earlier, before the barbarians had felt Rome's full strength. In the context of Marcus' solid victories, public opinion judged Commodus' peace dishonorable, even treasonable. Apparently Commodus, after years of military campaigning, was impatient for Roman high life. His cheap showmanship showed how shallow was his understanding of a ruler's obligation. He drank and made love in public and played the toreador in the amphitheater. Believing himself Hercules reincarnate, he built a new imperial mystique around the lion-slaying demigod, delighting the mob and disgusting the conventional.

He allowed his praetorian prefect, Perennis, to act like an Ottoman vizier and run the Empire while the Roman sultan, gossip said, lived in an endless orgy with 300 mistresses and 300 boys. Although Commodus eventually struck down Perennis and his friends, the vizier pattern was repeated. A Phrygian ex-slave, Cleander, was promoted prefect; he sold honors and court holdings for cash, allegedly at the rate of twenty-five consulships a day. The allegation reflects as much discredit on decadent aristocrats as on the venal freedman. When a popular uprising suppressed Cleander, his successor conspired to murder the despot. Even Marcia, Commodus' mistress, who was apparently a Christian, joined the plot. They acted on December 31, 192, to prevent the disgrace of an Emperor's celebrating the New Year by playing gladiator in the Coliseum.

Commodus had no sense of duty. The Empire carried on, at home and abroad, by the momentum of an efficient civil and military machine. Commodus left inoperative some of his predecessors' finest social legislation, taking no interest in the general welfare. We have no record of his grappling at all with major contemporary problems. He lived in an unreal dream world; though he broke every law of morality and decency, he felt neither guilt nor stain. He fancied he was establishing a new epoch, a new civilization where the radiance from his handsome face and his brute strength and passions assumed mystic significance. Even the months were to be renamed after his principal titles, while Rome itself was to be rechristened *Colonia Commodiana*.

A Semitic Dynasty: The Severi

Although the praetorian guard had grown corrupt and undisciplined under Commodus, it followed good advice in nominating for the succession the experienced Pertinax. The Senate ratified the nomination and damned Commodus' memory. Eighty-seven days later the guard paraded through the City, displaying to a dumfounded populace the head of Pertinax. They had slain him for trying to effect economies, enforce discipline, and end graft. The guard then auctioned off the Imperial crown to one Didius Julianus for 25,000 sesterces per man.

As in 69, the legions now took over, abetted by ambitious generals. The armies of Syria and the East, of Southeast and of Western Europe, proclaimed their respective commanders emperor. Five years of civil war brought Septimius Severus to power. He had the largest army, the twelve Danube legions, and from his station in Pannonia, closest to Italy, he got to Rome first, seizing the treasury and the administration. A nimble and original mind, inspired military leadership, and a capacity to make and execute quick decisions seemed to guarantee that he could reestablish law and order. He proved himself a talented administrator, preferring, like his successors until Elagabalus, equestrians over senators for government posts. He sought at first to conciliate public opinion by posing as Pertinax' avenger and upholder of Marcus Aurelius' policies. As such and in virtue of a promise, soon broken, to put no senator to death without trial by his peers, he secured ratification from the Senate, overawed by the presence in Rome of his Danubian army.

Septimius' boldest feat once he seized power was to discharge without bloodshed the kingmakers, the praetorian guard, made up until then of middle-class Italians and some contingents from the more civilized provinces. His reconstituted guard, now of 15,000 men, was hand-picked from the legions; that is, from citizens of the frontier provinces. In brief, whereas Augustus had chosen Italians to guard their country and his person, Septimius transferred this honor to frontiersmen, mostly Illyrian and Thracian peasants from his Danubian legions. Public opinion which had accepted the old guard's dismissal was outraged by this roughshod disregard of Italian privilege. Tension mounted when Septimius condemned twenty-nine senators to death at once.

Septimius' very appearance and personality showed that a new strain ruled the Empire. Born in Lepcis Magna in the Tripolitanian desert, he was of Libyan-Phoenician descent, spoke Latin with a Punic accent, and, though educated as an upper-class Roman, was alien to the spirit of Roman tradition. His wife, the Syrian Julia Domna, concurred in his radical policies. She was beautiful, witty, brilliant, well educated, endowed with insatiable intellectual curiosity. But although she cultivated philosophers and savants (Galen, for instance), she remained addicted to Oriental superstitions, and was deeply impressed by the claim of some of her entourage to supernatural power. She inspired a muddle-minded philosopher, Philostratus, to write a pagan counterblast to the Christian Gospels, the *Life of Apollonius of Tyana,* a wandering Pythagorean mystic, a contemporary of the Apostles and like them a miracle-worker. Septimius' conquering legions "of savage aspect, foreign accent, and boorish manners," as his earliest biographer says, completed the picture— semi-barbarians had become the Empire's masters.

Septimius founded a new dynasty, a monarchy resting on army support. To keep that army loyal he gave it pay increases and other favors at the expense of the prosperous urban middle class. His son and successor Caracalla (212–217) is quoted by the contemporary historian Cassius Dio as saying that no one but himself should have money. To secure the soldiers' good will, Caracalla took money from the upper and middle class by confiscations and legalized executions. Like his father he got rid of senators and officials suspected of disaffection. But this high-handedness involved more danger than profit. It was no accident that some unruly legions murdered Caracalla while he was preparing an expedition against Parthia. He was briefly succeeded (217–218) by Macrinus, the first equestrian to become emperor.

The gap between Italy and the civilized provinces on one side and the throne on the other was further widened when an adolescent, the Syrian Elagabalus (218–222), acceded to the title through the schemes of his grandmother Julia Maesa, a sister of Julia Domna. Hereditary priest of the Baal of Emesa, Elagabalus had the black conical stone representing this sun-god brought to Rome and enshrined on the Palatine, after being taken through the streets in a dazzling procession, surrounded by Syrian priests singing Syrian hymns and performing Syrian rites, in which dazed Roman senators were forced to participate. The god's wedding to the Punic goddess Tanit was symbolized by that of Elagabalus, his high priest, to a Vestal Virgin. The sight of a circumcised emperor consecrating in the Rome of Augustus the obscenities of a Syrian cult revolted public opinion. Shortly afterwards the young Emperor was assassinated, his body dragged through the streets and thrown into the Tiber. The black idol was sent back to Emesa.

Julia Maesa may have acquiesced in this business, sacrificing a hopeless grandson to keep the crown in the family. In any case she managed to put another grandson on the throne, the promising Severus Alexander. Of good character and disposition, intelligent and well-educated, Alexander (222–235) followed her good advice and that of his mother Mamaea to the satisfaction even of conservatives, for, while Alexander maintained the emperor's supremacy, he pointedly deferred to the Senate and to public opinion. He restored no golden age, but he tried to reduce taxes on the middle and lower classes and to make the laws less harsh even to Christians. Mamaea, who resembled Domna intellectually and was abreast of the spiritual currents of the time, helped foster religious tolerance. She invited Origen (185/6–254/5), head of the Alexandrian Christians, to her court to teach her Christian theology. And her fondness for or openmindedness toward the new religion was such that Hippolytus of Rome dedicated to her his treatise on the Resurrection. Alexander apparently included Christ among the deities honored in the Palace chapel. But despite their enlightenment and their effort to ameliorate social conditions, Alexander and his mother were murdered by the soldiers near Mainz while preparing to defend the German border. To understand what motivated this crime we must analyze further the Severan dynasty's basic policies.

The Severan Revolution

Septimius Severus' rise entailed Italy's decline. His placing of men from the less civilized provinces in the praetorian guard was the first of many acts against Italian supremacy. The second was to station a legion near Rome, to keep either Italy or the new guard under surveillance. In either case the result was to lower Italy's status to that of a province, or less, for the policing legion was less civilized than the new guard itself.

Septimius discriminated also against the older and more civilized provinces with interests akin to Italy's. They had acquired political and economic importance under the principate and suspected an emperor intent on changing its character. Like Italy, therefore, they had favored the other pretenders, believing that these would preserve the privileges they had acquired under Augustan constitution. Septimius sought to overcome antagonism by pretending that the revered Marcus Aurelius had adopted him. Hence he took and passed on to his dynasty the Antonine name, to legalize his usurpation and convey the impression that he would carry on the Antonines' policy.

But few were fooled. The Senate and the cosmopolitan *bourgeoisie* never forgave him for liquidating every man of note suspected of favoring his rivals. Even after his five-year civil war he continued his persecutions for another five years until the opposition was thoroughly destroyed. By confiscating the estates of thousands of real or fancied enemies he acquired more wealth than any preceding emperor. This immense fortune he organized as his private treasury.

Septimius solidified legionary support by economic and political concessions. He raised each man's annual pay from 375 denarii to 500. His successors increased it to 750. These were not bribes but steps required by the debasement of the currency and the resulting inflation. But the political concessions were revolutionary, for eventually they raised semi-barbarian soldiers and veterans to ruling-class status. We saw how Vespasian, to prevent civil wars, discouraged Italians from enlisting, entrusting Imperial defense to volunteers from the more civilized provinces. When by Marcus Aurelius' time this class lost taste for legionary service, men from the outer provinces replaced them: Germans, Syrians, and Egyptians. What ancient history repeatedly shows, that the defenders of the state ultimately get political preferment, now occurred under the Severi.

One reform was to legalize soldiers' marriage. When the army became chiefly defensive, it took up permanent quarters along the frontier, where, as we saw, the men had taken to marrying local women, even though such unions were illegal and the children illegitimate. But this reform, humane though it was, undermined morale, since now the soldiers lived in the *canabae* instead of in barracks. Noncommissioned officers were permitted to form social clubs. Privates were allowed to wear the gold ring, symbolizing their potential society equality with the knights. They were given land-grants near the camp on condition that they cultivate them. On discharge they were exempted from "liturgies" (municipal compulsory services). They received other rewards; for example, scores of urbanized villages—in Algeria, Tripolitania, Syria, Asia Minor, and especially in the Danubian provinces—where they had married and settled after their discharge were raised in juridical status.

Military zones were converted into civil communities in the following way. Villages, both civilian (canabae) and military (*castra*) with no previous political freedom were made self-governing cities (*municipia*) ; if municipia, they were promoted to *coloniae,* and especially favored by the Emperor; if coloniae they got the *ius Italicum,* which meant exemption from real-estate taxes. Lambaesis, the road center in Algeria, exemplifies a legionary camp raised to municipal freedom; Severus' birthplace, Lepcis Magna, received the ius Italicum and was adorned with magnificent buildings.

The few freemen left without citizenship acquired it in 212 when Caracalla granted it, by the *Constitutio Antoniniana,* to freemen universally, partly, as we saw, to raise revenue (from the 5-percent inheritance tax on citizens), partly to simplify administration, but perhaps chiefly in accordance with the age-old precedent, inherited from the Republic, of granting citizenship on a steadily wider scale. Now only slaves and serfs remained outside the world-wide citizen body.

The change in the legions' composition led the Severi to promote frontiersmen to noncommissioned rank, now and then even to general. The Imperial system of naming ex-service men to desirable positions in civil administration, whether in the cities or around the emperor, profoundly affected the Empire's culture and even its stability. African or Oriental veterans increasingly manned the lower civil-service echelons.

The Senate no longer embodied Italian and cosmopolitan public opinion. Representatives of the traditional values of the enlightened upper and middle classes were being liquidated. New stocks and a new mentality largely alien to Greco-Roman culture came to the fore. Incentives to Romanization like requirement of knowledge of the official languages, Latin or Greek, broke down under the Severan dynasty. Permission to the peripheral provinces to use native languages like Punic or Celtic in legal documents is clear evidence that classical culture had lost its power of assimilation and that barbarism was reasserting itself.

Almost as important as the above concessions to the semibarbarian fringe was the Severan policy of befriending the underprivileged. Industrial workers, farm tenants, and the poor generally were allowed, without petition to the government, to form *collegia tenuiorum* (corporations of humble folk) for social and recreational purposes and for mutual assistance. Provincial eleemosynary organizations—until then private in character—were given official standing and placed under the emperors' personal protection. Elementary schools were founded even in the smallest villages. Hadrian's policy of enabling tenants on imperial estates to become independent landowners was intensified, while Egyptian peasants who had fled from the tax collectors were restored to their lands.

Foreign Relations

Imperial defense engaged the Severan dynasty on three fronts, Parthia, Germany, and Britain. Vologeses IV of Parthia took advantage of the civil wars to add to Severus' troubles. First, he encouraged some districts closest to the Syrian frontier, hitherto loyal to Rome or neutral, to revolt. Septimius thereupon temporarily annexed the vassal kingdom of Osroëne beyond the Euphrates and invaded Adiabene across the Tigris. When Vologeses again intervened, Septimius, as soon as the civil war was over, organized an expedition as formidable as Trajan's ninety years before. The victory was easy. Every city he approached surrendered, including Babylon and Seleucia-on-the-Tigris, while the capital itself, Ctesiphon, offered only token resistance. Again it was proven that while Parthia could inflict pinpricks, it could not withstand a mass attack. Septimius now set up an improved defense of Syria by re-creating and enlarging Trajan's province of Mesopotamia. Rome's victory had considerable repercussions. In Parthia it so discredited the age-old Arsacid dynasty that a rival house, the Sassanids, soon took over. In the East it taught every ruler from Arabia to Armenia new respect for Roman power. In the Empire itself it stirred up a wave of patriotism which helped to heal the wounds of the civil war.

Caracalla had little reason to resume the Parthian war except a megalomaniac's desire to repeat Trajan's and his own father's triumphs. But factions within the army resulting from his assassination turned the enterprise into a fiasco; the Romans were forced to withdraw to the Euphrates.

The Sassanid Revolution was religious and national; the Persian element reasserted itself over the Parthian, and the Persian empire was reborn, strong, intensive, and warlike. The new king and his followers were Zoroastrian fanatics bent on re-establishing the purity of the old national religion by the sword. To stop Sassanid aggression Severus Alexander, with his mother, organized an adequate army. But, doubting the loyalty of some unruly contingents, he followed Mamaea's advice, relied on negotiations rather than action, and let the initiative pass to the enemy.

The campaign was a stalemate. But Sassanid Persia became progressively stronger, a real and present danger to subsequent Greco-Roman civilization. Even after the Empire dissolved the Sassanids kept its Byzantine successor on the alert for three or four more centuries.

The Sassanid forces lay quiet for a few years, but then there was trouble on the Western front. The Germans took advantage of the withdrawal of considerable forces from the Rhine to the Euphrates. The resulting uprisings became serious when the Alemanni joined in. In 234 Severus Alexander, again accompanied by Mamaea, from his headquarters in Mainz again tried parley, even attempting to buy a peace. The Pannonian legions rose in disgust, murdered Alexander and his mother, and hailed as emperor their general Maximinus, inaugurating the Roman Empire's blackest hour.

The danger to Britain's peace was briefer and less serious. When Septimius' rival Albinus withdrew three British legions to fight Septimius in Gaul (197), the Scottish tribes took the withdrawal as an open invitation to raid with impunity. Though in 208 Septimius took personal charge of British operations, he could never catch up with the main body of Scots. Abandoning the Antonine Wall, he again made Hadrian's Wall the principal Roman defense, after which north Britain enjoyed a long period of peace. Septimius died in 211 in his camp in York on the eve of a major campaign against the Scots. Like Marcus Aurelius' death in Vienna, this event foreshadowed the shape of the future. More and more emperors were to die on the battlefront, East or West, trying to stem the barbarian tide: some by the hands of their own troops, others by the enemy's sword. The frontier was becoming more important than the old centers of civilization, more important than Rome itself.

To sum up, the Severi based their power on support from the lower classes and the outer, less civilized provinces. Humanitarian considerations aside, they had a political motive: to counterbalance the hostility of the cosmopolitan *bourgeoisie,* which was being systematically eliminated. The outer provinces furnished the army, whose veterans soon constituted the equestrian order, hence also the civil administration. They even began to supply the Senate, which, despite the dynasty's enmity, was still considered necessary to legalize the emperor's acts. It was left to the last representatives of the dynasty, Alexander Severus and his mother, to discover that a government based on the supremacy of an unruly soldiery was like a house built on quicksand. They therefore set out to cultivate the old upper classes and the old *bourgeoisie,* including the Senate. But their hope that a united public opinion might restrain the army's caprice proved abortive, for the army had discovered that it was indispensable and, as such, need have no regard for public opinion. This phase will be the subject of Chapter 58.

Chapter 57/ROMAN LAW

Roman Contributions to Civilization

Before undertaking the study of Rome's decline and fall, let us recall its principal contributions to Western civilization.

1. By trial and error, but always with an instinct for justice, it developed the art of world government. It united first the communities of Italy, then the nations of the known world, into a federation happily balanced between local self-government and imperial unity.

2. It took up the torch of Hellenism from decadent Greece to carry its light to the whole of "the inhabitable world."

3. It created on these Greek foundations a literature which has inspired every major Western literary experiment.

4. It produced an art, especially a portrait sculpture, of unsurpassed realism and individuality, and an architecture, great in itself, which influenced Byzantine, Romanesque, Gothic, and baroque church design.

5. It accomplished a feat never realized before nor since, the attainment of peace within the civilized world for as long as a quarter millennium.

6. It gave its stock and its speech, its social and political organization to every country from the middle Danube to the Atlantic and the North Sea. This Romanization of Europe, this casting of the European mind into its distinctive mold, is a major historical development.

* Manuscript page of Justinian's *Digest.*

7. Although its social structure was riddled with injustice it built, and for more than 300 years maintained, an open society, releasing its people's constructive forces to work, plan, and prosper along with the Empire.

8. Likewise in politics it was nonexclusive. Foreigners and even slaves could become citizens. The descendants of petty bourgeois could rise to command legions, govern provinces, or ascend the Imperial throne.

9. It indulged religion as it indulged thrift and talent. It tolerated new creeds and foreign cults. Though it was sometimes hard on Christianity, Roman law and policy tended to foster rather than oppose it./The emperors who tried to suppress the Church were few. The official Church view is that God established the Roman Empire purposely to facilitate the spread of Christianity.

10. Lastly, Rome evolved, partly from Hellenistic sources, a legal system generally regarded as ancient man's most successful instrument for securing justice. Indeed, for many scholars Rome's law stands out as its greatest achievement. Experts emphasize in Roman law a spirit of honor, good faith, and equitable firmness unsurpassed in modern systems, even in the English common law. We have generally abandoned the nineteenth-century belief that Roman law promoted tyranny whereas common law fosters liberty, that liberty was born among the Germanic tribes. For this is a part of the exploded myth of the superiority of the Germanic or Anglo-Saxon peoples. It might clarify the issue to note that while many reasonable men throughout history have upheld despotism and while most thoughtful men in modern Western society champion liberty, both sides agree that justice is the goal of the state. And that was the goal of Roman law.

A few illustrations should help us to evaluate the civilizing influence of Roman law. Roman law has laid down the principle that no man should be judge in his own trial, nor be adjudged guilty until after an examination of the facts. As St. Paul knew, it was not the Roman custom to condemn a man without giving him the opportunity to face his accusers and defend himself from their charges. In some cases both plaintiff and defendant had to deposit with the court as bond the same amount of money. The winner of the case got his money back; the loser forfeited his. To lay equal legal responsibility on both parties implies the principle that a man is presumed innocent until proven guilty; in American criminal cases bail is imposed on the defendant and returned if trial fails to prove the charges against him. The principle prevailed that the courts should limit whatever tends to damage the defendant and enlarge whatever works in his favor. The theory expressed in the Declaration of Independence that all men are created equal is a tenet of Roman law. The Roman jurisprudents' view that no law is binding unless it be founded on reason is still valid, and, incidentally, was used as an argument against prohibition in the United States. In constitutional law the Romans adopted the rule followed by modern parliaments, except in the United States, that in a conflict of laws the latest one is binding. They established another principle always fundamental to democracy, that the people is the foundation of sovereignty, the emperor's powers being delegated to him by the people. In the words of the Declaration of Independence, governments derive "their just powers from the consent of the governed."

Early Roman Law

Roman law sprang from three main sources: the *ius civile* (civil law), the *ius gentium* (law of nations), and the *ius naturale* (natural law). These were not three successive stages, since by Cicero's time the three cycles were running concurrently.

The earliest source was represented by the Twelve Tables as interpreted and supplemented in the course of centuries. The Twelve Tables, as we saw, were a fifth-century B.C. codification (tradition said with Greek help) of legal customs mostly inherited from the monarchy. Their precise language, clarity of style, brevity, and forcefulness postulate long experience in the science of jurisprudence. Undertaken for the convenience of Roman citizens (*cives*), this codification became the cornerstone of the *ius civile,* to be reinterpreted and supplemented in response to economic and social changes and the shifting balance of political power. During the Republic these supplements came as laws from the Centuriate Assembly, as plebiscites from the Council of the Plebs, as resolutions from the Senate, or as edicts from the magistrates. During the Empire they emanated from the Senate as laws or resolutions, or from the emperor as edicts, decrees, decisions-in-court, rescripts (answers on points of law), or instructions (*mandata*) to officials, chiefly on administrative matters.

When the urban praetor ceased being third consul and became administrator of the judicial system (366 B.C.), his became the task of interpreting the law. Eventually the praetor began, on entering office, to promulgate his edict, that is, he listed the legal principles and criteria he intended to follow. To him the law now meant both the Twelve Tables and later Republican legislative enactments.

The praetor was not a trial judge but rather a chief justice to whom both plaintiff and defendant submitted their cases. After a brief hearing he asked both parties to agree on the particular point of law on which they wished the case to be tried. Where they could not agree, he himself did the choosing, by which both parties were bound. Then a trial judge was named, not a professional lawyer—the class did not yet exist—but a senator or, in later times, a knight. The parties to the suit selected him;

only if they could not agree did the praetor appoint a judge. He was assisted by a *consilium,* a group of advisers somewhat like our petty jury, and was subject to punishment for corruption or carelessness. His function was to determine whether the facts revealed in the trial fell under the particular point or principle of law indicated by the praetor. If they did not, the defendant was adjudged not guilty. Procedure was rapid; a case took only a few days or at most a few weeks. Thus Roman legal actions differed from American ones, where a case may be appealed to a higher court and ultimately to the Supreme Court, which does not examine the facts, but only declares what the law is in respect to the case, remanding it to a lower court where it is retried in the light of that law.

Freedom in selecting the principles and criteria of this edict enabled the urban praetor to modernize the law as the electorate's social conscience deepened. Supplements to the law by the people, the Senate, and the magistrates were generally humanitarian and liberal. Other factors tended in the same direction. One was that praetorship was elective. In campaigning, a candidate for praetor announced the substance of the edict he would follow if elected, and the more liberal program had some chance of drawing more votes. The other factor was the opening of the praetorship to plebeians, who might be more responsive to popular aspirations.

Lastly, the praetor sought the guidance of the best legal minds of the day. Although the early and middle Republic had no professional lawyers, an authoritative class of jurisprudents had grown up. Most of them had been pontiffs, magistrates, or judges, advisers to praetors or judges, and usually also defenders of their own families' clients in trouble with the law. And since practically all were senators, their experience helped to formulate senatorial enactments and influence magistrates' judgment. Some of these jurisprudents recorded their own pragmatic approach to legal questions or their recollection of elder statesmen's views and sayings. Others published collections of court decisions or of their own observations on statutes and on magistrates' edicts. They even composed treatises and textbooks. Especially important was the formulation of *regulae,* the theory and principles distilled from precedents. A legal philosophy thus replaced the memorizing of thousands of decisions. Aelius Paetus Catus (consul 198 B.C.) published the first such key to legal science. These were the various origins of Roman jurisprudence, which continued to help Roman law develop down into the late Empire.

Ius Gentium

The appointment (*c.* 242 B.C.) of the praetor peregrinus for foreigners opened a new era in the development of Roman law. Whereas the modern state subjects all immigrants or visitors to its own laws, the Romans created for such persons a new legal system (wisely incorporating legal elements from Greek sources), which combined simplicity with fairness. They regarded it as unfair to subject a foreigner to the formalism of the *ius civile,* where one slip would lose him his case. Since in Rome litigants pleaded their own cases, it seemed unreasonable to expect a foreigner to master the language, let alone the complex details or the spirit of Roman national law. Clearly a cultivated foreign litigant, a south Italian Greek, for example, would consider childish a Roman verdict based on the Twelve Tables. The conquest of new provinces complicated the problem; now an illiterate Spaniard might sue a sophisticated Greek or a nimble-witted Syrian.

The praetor peregrinus met this challenge with remarkable imagination. In a case of contract, for example, involving a Roman and a Phoenician, he ignored the stereotyped phrases, oaths, and religious rites prescribed by Roman or Phoenician custom, knowing that what was sacrosanct to one party might be strange or meaningless to the other. Instead, he sought some easily understandable formula, some broad or universal standard—in this case the concept of intent. If the parties had intended to sell and to buy, and later one of them changed his mind, the praetor peregrinus considered the act binding. Or, in litigation between a Syracusan and a Neapolitan over rent, lease, loan, or barter, the praetor peregrinus might inquire whether the contract was entered into in good faith, regardless of its conformity to Syracusan custom or Neapolitan law. In a third case he might invoke another new principle, fair play, acceptable to reasonable men anywhere. Thus intent, good faith, fairness gradually superseded the maze of national legal practices to create a new philosophy of law, just and equitable to all, the *ius gentium* or law of nations. Thus was invented a new legal concept, equity: the spirit of enlightened justice, sensitive to circumstances, assisting rather than dictating, protecting rather than punishing, flexible and humane as against the rigid letter of the law.

The praetor peregrinus did not choose one good legal practice from, say, Capua, another from Tarentum, a third from somewhere else, until his total selections crystallized as the *ius gentium.* Certainly he profited from a growing acquaintance with Hellenistic jurisprudence. He borrowed from other peoples commercial customs commendable for their simplicity; for example, from Rhodes admiralty laws inherited from the Athenian Empire and proved eminently workable by long experience. But this legal eclecticism was limited; it was the philosophy behind these customs and laws that the praetor peregrinus tried to grasp. In sum, he did not collect or codify good foreign laws; he did not import the *ius gentium;* he created it.

The *ius gentium* had its impact on the Romans themselves. Gradually the praetor urbanus applied to Roman citizens the simpler formulas and superior principles evolved by his colleague, until under the Empire the *ius civile* and the *ius gentium* were inextricably interwoven and what was called *ius civile* was an amalgam of the two systems. Indeed every Roman jurist, legislator, and official after the second century B.C. regarded the *ius gentium* as superior to the *ius civile*. Henceforth *ius gentium* meant no longer law for foreigners but the law applied to foreigners and Romans alike. The *ius gentium* was applied not only in Rome and Italy but in every land under Roman jurisdiction. For the new legal system grew steadily throughout the first two centuries of the Empire, fostered by the provincial governors along lines set in Rome. It continued as a separate code as long as there were provincials, that is, until 212 when the Antoninian constitution made all foreigners citizens. Thereafter the whole Empire lived under the *ius civile,* as penetrated by the philosophy and provisions of the *ius gentium.*

Natural Law

A third factor in the growth of Roman law was the concept of natural law. On this the clearest statement was Cicero's, derived from his study of Greek philosophy. Antigone had appealed to eternal, unwritten Heavenly laws, which take precedence over human laws. Socrates, going further, taught that not even the gods could change those everlasting precepts. An action is good not because the gods command it; rather they command it because it is good. Plato added that, as a compelling expression of God's intellect, the law imposes itself on man's intellect, which reflects God's. Even though Plato's chief interest was to prove that the highest human intellect—the philosopher's—should rule the ideal commonwealth, he strengthened the Socratic tenet that ordinary human intelligence perceives and is naturally attracted to truth and goodness. Aristotle identified man as a rational (that is, intellectual) being and every human act as good if in harmony with his rational nature. Law, then, is essentially reason or the rule of reason.

But the Stoics popularized the idea of natural law by identifying Nature with God, and Cicero made this idea current in the Latin West. Combining Sophocles with Plato, he said that law is no mere piece of human ingenuity or ordinary legislation, but something eternal which rules the whole universe; that true law is right reason, agreeing with nature, universal in application, unchanging, everlasting. St. Paul echoed Cicero, for both had absorbed Stoicism. St. Paul as a Jew saw an affinity between the natural and the Mosaic law. For him, when a gentile, though ignorant of the Jewish moral code, yet by nature acted morally, the existence of a universal, natural law which moves the conscience of Jew and gentile alike to approve moral acts and disapprove immoral ones was proved.

Cicero profoundly influenced Christian as well as Roman thought. St. Augustine and Thomas Aquinas, the two main medieval Roman Catholic philosophers, repeated him almost verbatim. So did the Protestant Blackstone, whose *Commentaries* are as the Bible of common law. He spoke of the law of nature, as old as man, dictated by God, and more binding than any other, always and everywhere; human laws are invalid if they contradict it; their validity derives, directly or indirectly, from natural law. The Declaration of Independence bases its "self-evident truths" on "the Laws of Nature and of Nature's God," while the United States Supreme Court has repeatedly affirmed the principle that reason and natural law are the ultimate standards of legal judgment.

The concept of natural law reinvigorated the Romans' quest for higher principles of justice. A concrete example is the evolution of slavery's juridical standing. At first the Romans considered slavery legitimate, since their civil law had always sanctioned it. When, as they extended their empire over the known world, they discovered legalized slavery everywhere, they concluded that at least in the matter of slavery the civil law and the law of nations were in harmony. The concept of natural law changed all this, by taking the position that "in so far as Nature is concerned all men are equal," so that slavery as an institution could no longer be justified. Admittedly it was never abolished. But the force of enlightened public opinion weakened it as did the practice of unrecorded thousands of masters who freed their slaves, sometimes en masse, as did Imperial legislation, Imperial legal decisions, and, later, Christian influence.

The concept of natural law, though never explicitly adopted as practice, subtly humanized Imperial laws and Imperial justice. The imperium proconsulare, the maius imperium, and the right to initiate measures in the Senate allowed the emperors to legislate for the whole Empire. Their tribunician power gave them also the right to review trials involving citizens from anywhere in the Empire. Their normal guide was the philosophy of government and the legal procedures developed by the praetor's edict. Although under the Republic this was valid only during a praetor's term, such of its provisions as experience had proved equitable or generally satisfactory were retained year after year and decade after decade, so that the edict as a whole became self-perpetuating. Hadrian ordered a definitive edition published about 130 in which all praetorian laws and procedural rules were collected, amended, revised, and brought up to date by the famous jurist Salvius Julianus. This *Edictum Perpetuum* became the cornerstone of Roman legal science and judicial procedure.

The Jurists and the Code

In their judicial capacity the emperors sought guidance from the best legal minds of the day. Roman jurisprudence developed steadily for 500 years—from the middle Republic to the middle Empire. It flowered in the second and early third century A.D., mostly in the hands of Easterners, primarily Syrians. Learning and teaching the tricks of the legal profession was only a small part of jurisprudence; its chief purpose was to acquire a deeper understanding of the spirit or philosophy of the law, to create the science of the just and the equitable.

Roman jurists successfully developed law as a science not so much because they were gifted teachers as because magistrates, especially praetors and trial judges, regularly invited them to sit as advisers in their councils. This was a new achievement in the history of civilization; not even the Greeks had ever made such an attempt. Another instrument which made Roman law scientific was the penetrating Roman legal mind that could extract theory or general principles from masses of individual enactments. Moreover the art of government was in the Roman blood, and a set of rules was a practical help.

Jurists advising trial judges helped to shape individual edicts and other legislation and to guide the court's verdict. The jurists were thus in a position to harmonize the past and the present, to accommodate old laws and interpretations to the changing present. Specifically they could reorient the *ius civile* towards the liberalism of the *ius gentium* and the higher morality of the *ius naturale*. Indeed by Ulpian's death (228) these three divisions of Roman law existed only in theory, being in practice fused, as we saw, into the single stream of the *ius civile,* in which the old and the new, the historical and the philosophical had merged into an indivisible whole. *Ius civile* since the Republic had been transformed by a pragmatic feeling for higher principles of justice, by reason, and by persistent idealism into something universal.

Jurisprudents reached their highest usefulness under the Empire. Indeed the time from Augustus to about 250 is the period of classical Roman jurisprudence. In the first place, they produced an enormous number of scientific works—*Digests, Institutes, Manuals, Rules, Commentaries, Notes, Opinions, Questions, Definitions, Disputations, Responses* and the like. Invaluable for the history of legal institutions and the exposition of the spirit of the law, written lucidly, forcefully, and concisely, these works constitute the most original branch of Silver Age secular literature. They bear the imprint of the penetrating mind, of scholarship; without arrogance, they seek always those formulas or opinions most conducive to the attainment of justice.

Then too, like their Republican predecessors, but more actively, the

Imperial jurisprudents drafted laws and formulated judicial verdicts. They regularly achieved magistracies and sometimes membership in the Emperor's Privy Council. The presence in Hadrian's Privy Council of Salvius Julianus (c. 100–169), codifier of the Edictum Perpetuum, indicates the emperors' increasing dependence on jurists, though Salvius' prolific younger contemporary, Gaius, held no government post. His *Institutes*, a textbook for beginners, served as model for the Emperor Justinian's *Institutes* four centuries later.

The Privy Council's importance rose when the early Severi turned it into a legislative body as a handy device to weaken the Senate's power. Determined to change the principate into a family despotism, they also assigned the Council greater judicial powers. The dynasty partly redeemed this reactionary policy by appointing able jurisconsults as praetorian prefects. By this time the prefect was general of the praetorian guard, lieutenant-emperor, and, as head of the privy council, chief justice. Septimius' praetorian prefect was Papinian; Paul, and Ulpian of Tyre, Council members under Septimius, became prefects under Severus Alexander. These luminaries of Roman jurisprudence could thus translate their enlightened philosophy into official Imperial legislation and supreme judicial decisions. The immediate beneficiaries were the lower classes, whom the Severi favored on principle. The law as a whole benefited from the broadmindedness of these jurist-statesmen. They were not of course wholly innovators; they owed much to Hellenistic legal theory. But it is to their credit that as despotism advanced, they extended, or at least reasserted, that benevolent political attitude we have called government with a conscience. At the same time it would be uncandid not to emphasize that these hardheaded lawyers recognized rigid class distinctions, between *honestiores* ("the better people") and *humiliores* ("the baser sort") ; the world would have to wait many centuries before there would cease to be one law for the rich and another for the poor. Jurisconsults were especially influential under Severus Alexander; of his seventy Privy Councilors twenty were jurisprudents. Papinian combined in his numerous legal treatises originality, amazing scholarship, respect for others' opinions, and devotion to the principles of ethics; the works of Paul and Ulpian supply half the contents of Justinian's *Digest*.

The 900 legal treatises produced by these fine jurists was only a fraction of the prodigious quantity of juristic literature produced in Rome since the middle Republic. Augustus founded a special law library and the juristic literature produced after him may have tripled or quadrupled its size. With the onset of the third-century military anarchy and the Augustan principate's transformation into Diocletian's "dominate," Roman jurisprudence declined. The attempt of Diocletian's successors to arrest economic collapse and social disintegration produced an endless stream of administrative enactments. These, from Constantine's reign to 438, the thirtieth year of Theodosius II, were collected in the *Codex Theodosianus.*

Justinian (527–565) decided to codify the whole body of Roman Law, the *Corpus Juris Civilis,* entrusting the work (530–534) to a commission headed by Tribonian, an immensely learned scholar and judge. Justinian's *Corpus* consists of the *Digest,* the *Codex,* and the *Institutiones.*

The *Digest* (*Pandects* is its Greek synonym) is a classified collection of rules, principles, opinions, interpretations, and comments handed down by classical jurists. Tribonian and his commission condensed 2000 books (3,000,000 lines) of law into a manageable 150,000 lines. For the phrasing and sometimes for the substance of thousands of statutes, judges' verdicts, and jurists' opinions, they substituted modern idiom or a new, and sometimes false, interpretation. The historical background and motivation of great areas of Roman law have thus been obscured, sometimes hopelessly. The sources of classical Roman law are very much more complex than this brief chapter can adequately bring out. The great problem, not yet solved, is to determine which elements are Roman and which Hellenistic and, as to the latter, which elements are Greek and which Oriental. But doubts about sources do not obscure the fact that civilization owes Justinian an immeasurable debt. But for his compendium Roman juristic literature would have been lost; sheer magnitude made it unmanageable and impossible to preserve. The *Digest* is our chief source for the growth of Roman jurisprudence from about 100 B.C. to A.D. 250. It stops with Ulpian's pupil Modestinus, the last classical jurist, and ignores the creative period of early Republican law.

The *Code* too gives only a partial picture. It is a collection of Imperial laws from Hadrian to Justinian. It avoids the pre-Hadrianic age, already covered by the Edictum Perpetuum. But since sometime after Justinian the Edictum Perpetuum was lost, its contents can be gathered only indirectly through historical and philological research. The *Code* and the *Digest* are complementary. The former preserves the Empire's laws; the latter shows how the jurists interpreted and applied them. Of scarcely less value are the *Institutes,* which Justinian called "Basic Elements of the Science of Law," an elementary manual for law students. Based largely on Gaius' classical arrangement of Persons, Things, and Actions, the *Institutes* has introduced generations of students to legal science and is still a standard text. To these works was added a fourth, the *Novels,* mostly in Greek, a collection of Justinian's own laws issued after the final edition of the *Codex.*

In spite of gaps and inadequate treatment, Justinian's codification stands out as possibly the ancient world's richest secular legacy to modern times. It forms the core of the law of continental Europe, Scotland, and of former European colonies in North and South America, including Louisiana and Quebec. Together with the Bible and Church tradition, it is the foundation of canon law, which imitates its methodology, its inner spirit, and thousands of its provisions, especially those on marriage, legitimacy, inheritance, and ecclesiastical administration. Through it the wisdom of old Rome and old Rome's power to assimilate Greek theory still guide modern society.

Even common law, this finest Anglo-Saxon creation, owes much, historically and substantively, to Roman law. Superior to Roman criminal law, it is held inferior in the civil sphere. But even at its best it is elusive and cumbersome, for whereas Roman law judges individual cases on rock-bottom rational principles, common law looks back to precedent, which is many-faced, discordant, frequently confused, even contradictory. Moreover, common law is so inadequate to meet legal problems arising in world trade and commerce that the English-speaking countries have substituted for it the commercial law handed down by Rome. In fact modern international law is based on the *Corpus Iuris Civilis*. Lastly, in default of any common-law precedent and any Federal statute, the United States Supreme Court has been known to go to Roman law for guidance in deciding litigation between the states.

When Justinian issued his code the Empire had been Christian for more than two hundred years. Just as Greek philosophy had been incorporated into Christian thought, so Greco-Roman jurisprudence became the foundation of the Christian legal system. To enlightened churchmen, Roman law was a kind of progressive revelation; the *ius civile* of the early and middle Republic had been smelted in the crucible of the *ius gentium*, further refined by the *ius naturale,* and Christianity came to correct whatever flaws remained. The Christian Empire embraced the Pagan Empire's law with filial devotion. Justinian prefaced his edition of the *Corpus Iuris Civilis* with the words, "In the name of our Lord Jesus Christ." No higher endorsement could be given to pagan legal wisdom than the seal of Christian approval.

Chapter 58/BREAKDOWN AND REHABILITATION

Military Anarchy

From Severus Alexander's murder in 235 to Diocletian's unchallenged domination fifty years later, various disasters brought the Roman Empire, even civilization itself, to the brink of extinction. Not since the collapse of Mycenaean culture under the Dorian attacks had there been a period of similar disintegration. To be sure the Empire survived, still Roman in name, but its nature was changed. A new era was emerging from the debris of the classical world; we call it the medieval period.

The causes of this cataclysm were interpenetrating and complex. One was an act of God, a twenty-year plague. Undiagnosed and unchecked, it swept from province to province, killing hundreds of thousands, one of the Emperors among others. It left armies too weakened to defend the border and civilians too numb to face man-made calamities: inflation, economic chaos, civil wars, military anarchy, and famine. Barbarian invasions, cutting deep into several provinces, threatened for a time to break up the Empire, while paganism fought Christianity to disrupt its spiritual unity.

Estrangement from the traditions and standards of value which make up a way of life produced the greatest evil of all, inability to repair the breakdown of constitutional government. Whereas five emperors had reigned in the century from Augustus' victory at Actium down to Nero's

Fig. 58.1. Rome. Baths of Caracalla, model. Original built A.D. 211–216, enclosing an area 1080 feet square. Besides dressing-rooms and rooms for hot and cold baths, the central building contained large halls veneered with colored marble. There were a porticoed court for exercise and sports, lecture rooms, library, and gardens. New York's Pennsylvania Station is modeled on this plan. Nowadays, outdoor opera is presented in the summer in the ruins of the Baths. (Rome, Museo della Civiltà Romana; J. Felbermeyer photo)

death, and six in the century after Domitian's accession, no less than nineteen held power between 235 and 285. Of these all but one died violently, slain by their own troops or by the barbarians. Besides these emperors, formally recognized by the Senate, there were scores of usurpers and lesser pretenders. One emperor alone, Gallienus (253–268), put down eighteen.

The army was responsible for this situation. When Septimius and Caracalla reduced the Senate's power, the army alone determined the succession. But since each army faction wanted its general on the throne, the result was anarchy, an aggravated repetition of A.D. 69. A pernicious practice, as old as Augustus, now proved a major cause of instability, the cash gift by each new emperor to every soldier. Loyalty was thus for sale. Generals ambitious to be emperor competed in offering larger and larger grants. The soldiers sold their support to new aspirants every year or so, sometimes every few months. A vicious circle set in: a general proclaimed emperor had to meet in battle a rival pretender; his own men would slay the weaker and for a higher price declare for the stronger; the victor in turn had to meet another and yet another usurper. Such is the history of this period with all sections of the army from the Rhine to the Euphrates. The worst period was from 251 to 270.

Sometimes, however, genuine loyalty or faith in a commander's ability motivated the troops' proclamations. And some of the commanders were strong personalities, efficient at Imperial defense or administration. Even Maximinus, who in 235 started the plunge to anarchy, had a patriotic purpose, to fight the Germans instead of bribing them like Severus Alexander, then emperor.

A peasant, risen from the ranks, Maximinus was a good soldier who won his troops' admiration. Though harassed by two pretenders, he invaded German territory and had re-established order from the middle Rhine to the upper Danube when serious senatorial opposition compelled him to turn against Italy. He had overstrained his treasury by doubling the army's pay. To raise funds he had confiscated private fortunes, impoverishing the rich and bankrupting most cities. In 238 the Senate called a halt. Declaring Maximinus a public enemy, it made two of its own members joint emperors, colleagues like the old Republican consuls whose spirit the Senate thus hoped—vainly—to recapture.

This resurgence of senatorial leadership inspired the Italians, including the regular troops of provincial origin, successfully to resist Maximinus' march on Rome. Maximinus' own men killed him and went over to the senatorial emperors, whom in turn the praetorian guard assassinated, expecting no favors from a conservative regime. Senatorial resurgence had lasted only ninety-nine days.

The Praetorians' nominee was Gordian III (238–244), a boy of fifteen, grandson and nephew of the two senatorial emperors. Wise counselors conciliated the Senate which was still backed by public opinion. New laws halted army excesses, restricted military judges to military cases, curbed tax-collectors and moneylenders. The Germans, even the Goths, were kept firmly in hand. Parthia was now the trouble spot.

Parthia had once been a Persian satrapy. In 63 B.C. its local lord Arsaces subjected the other vassal-kings, but his successors, though each called himself King of Kings, could never organize the Parthian Empire, then a loose feudal confederation, into a strong centralized monarchy. Dissension and treason, as we saw, so rent the royal court that though the Arsacids could raid Roman territory, they could not sustain a war of attrition. But in A.D. 224 the usurper Ardashir (Artaxerxes), from the province of Persis, revolted and killed the Great King, and was shortly proclaimed King of Kings. He soon subjected all the kings, satraps, and priestly potentates eastward to the Punjab, north to Chorasmia (Khwarezm), and south to the Persian Gulf. He then turned west, to consolidate his power as far as the Roman frontier on the Euphrates.

The advent of the Sassanids, so-called from Ardashir's grandfather,

Sassan, brought epoch-making changes. The undiluted and rugged old Persian stock resumed leadership, and greatly strengthened the army and the central government. Zoroastrianism was made the state religion, and its holy books, the *Avesta,* collected in a new canonical edition. Accompanying these reforms, a wave of expansionist nationalism, under Ardashir's son Shapur I (241–272) and for centuries thereafter, threatened to engulf the Roman East.

Gordian attacked Shapur I as he was threatening Antioch-on-the-Orontes, key to Roman eastern defenses. But Gordian's competent general Timesitheus died when victory was imminent. His successor, Philip, son of an Arab sheik, straightway had Gordian murdered and himself proclaimed emperor by the Eastern army (244). Although Philip, eager to get to Rome, made a premature peace, he retained Mesopotamia and Lesser Armenia.

A good administrator, Philip tried to protect his subjects from fiscal and military extortions and opposed special privileges. For example, he would not exempt poets from taxation, not from scorn of culture but to prevent abuses, since Rome was full of poetasters. His reign's most memorable event was the celebration of Rome's thousandth birthday on April 21, 248, a year late, since the preceding April had seen him campaigning beyond the Danube. The dazzling festival renewed public faith in Rome's eternity. It signalized the culmination of one of man's most fruitful political experiments. The cluster of primitive villages on the Tiber had become a universal empire of free citizens. If the Roman character, spreading over distant provinces and absorbing alien stocks, had been diluted, it still typified many of the traditional public and private virtues.

Barbarian Invasions

The festivities celebrating Rome's millennium were barely over when the Goths and other German tribes spilled across the Danube. Almost simultaneously several Eastern provinces revolted against oppressive taxation. Only one senator, Decius, opposed the dejected Philip's offer to abdicate. The Emperor rewarded his trust and complimented his efficiency by assigning him the invaded Danubian provinces.

The tall, fierce, east German Goths were the most formidable German league ever to attack the Empire. Several decades back they had migrated from their original home, Scandinavia, to south Russia. Restless energy and greed for gold drove them into the Empire, not land-hunger, for they had more than enough fertile land in Russia. As they multiplied prodigiously and every man was a trained warrior, they outnumbered the legions. Besides, the more civilized Empire was no match for primitive, violent, war-loving hordes. As by Gresham's law bad money drives out good, so the primitive east Germanic culture ultimately overbore the superior Greco-Roman civilization.

Decius' Danubian troops proclaimed him emperor (249), reportedly to his dismay, almost immediately after he took command. He proved a poor strategist, but fought the Goths determinedly and died heroically in battle. Thereupon the enemy pillaged Thrace and the Dobrudja, carrying off jewels and money, gold and silver plate and furniture, and thousands of men and women, especially the young. Only a promised annual subsidy for staying outside the frontier induced them to withdraw. The Emperor's death abruptly ended his recently ordered persecution of Christians. His motive was apparently not hatred of Christianity, but desire to restore the Empire's spiritual unity in the face of perilous times. Christian writers saw in him a "bloodthirsty tyrant" and "detestable beast," and God's hand in his death. Pagan literature however makes him an exemplar of the old Roman virtues.

After Decius' death, conditions suddenly deteriorated Empire-wide. The plague broke out; treason, often inside the general staff, struck down every emperor; usurpers multiplied; and while Romans fought Romans, barbarians pierced the ill-guarded frontiers. These invasions were ominous; over a twenty- or twenty-five year-period, Imperial armies were now first to fight on three fronts, western, eastern, and middle.

The western front was the hardest hit. In 256 another group of German tribes, the Franks, from beyond the lower Rhine, burned and slaughtered their way across central Gaul into northeast Spain. Simultaneously the Alemanni overran the *Agri Decumates,* the wide fortified Rhine-Danube triangle, to plunder the Rhone valley, while the Marcomanni forced the Brenner Pass to overrun north Italy as far as Ravenna. Italy and Gaul escaped greater devastation thanks to Gallienus, who became emperor with his father Valerian in 253. Valerian commanded the East; Gallienus undertook the Rhine defense. Intent on saving Gaul, Rome's key province and the hinge of western defenses, he kept his forces together, letting the Danubian provinces shift for themselves until 258, when he felt that Gaul could be left safely to subalterns. At his departure, the Saxons and their kinsfolk from the north German coast began the first of many raids on Britain and Gaul.

In Gaul the general Postumus now (260) had himself proclaimed emperor over an "Empire of the Gauls," from the Scottish border to Gibraltar, with a capital, a senate, magistrates, praetorian guard, and armies. Defense of its territories was its excuse for being; though Postumus did not think of it as politically a separate state, it was so administratively.

Gaul's drift away from the Empire's central authority was paralleled in the Danubian provinces. Their sufferings from raids by Quadi, Marcomanni, Sarmatians, and Vandals ever since Caracalla's time had multiplied while Gallienus was concentrating on saving Gaul. The Goths reappeared, forgetting their pledge. Year after year crops were stolen or burned, moneys extorted, homes wrecked, farms ruined, cities sacked, men's lives at the marauders' mercy. The Danubians blamed Gallienus and revolt flared, extending to the army. Though the troops were native, their mutiny stemmed not from sympathy with their civilian kinsmen but from plain insubordination. Gallienus' eventual arrival had no reassuring effect. Indeed, most of the usurpers who plagued his reign now arose. He had to fight barbarian invaders, Roman citizens, and Roman armies simultaneously. But he re-established a semblance of order, crushing the usurpers, conciliating civilians and soldiers, smashing the Alemanni near Milan, and crippling several Gothic bands. Through it all he contrived to promote the liberal arts; his was a Gallienic Renaissance whose chief representative was the Neo-Platonist Plotinus (205–269), to whom we shall have occasion to refer again. His staff officers murdered Gallienus in 268. He had won the praise of friends and enemies, including Christians. His endeavors to preserve the Empire and his tactics for containing the invader stand as models of patriotism and generalship.

The Goths saw in Gallienus' death their chance to enter the Empire en masse. In two main waves they rolled in with wives, children, cattle, flocks, and baggage, determined to settle permanently in the Danube valley. But Gallienus' successor, Claudius II (268–270), stopped them, annihilating one wave just within the frontier, then rushing back to cut to pieces the other, already deep in Roman territory. The crushing blows intimidated the Goths for a century.

The elevation of Claudius, surnamed Gothicus after his victories, marks a turning point in third-century history. It opened the period of liberation and started a new line of good emperors: Aurelian, Probus, Diocletian, and Constantine, all from Illyricum, like Claudius, and all dedicated to shoring up Roman civilization. Though far removed from Vergil's and Horace's vision and Augustus' political idea, they considered themselves true heirs of the Roman spirit. Illyricum was then becoming the paramount province. Its peasants were the Empire's best soldiers, early recognizing the evils of anarchy and acclaiming and upholding able emperors. Their patriotism, reminiscent of Rome's better days, restored Imperial unity. Pannonia too, a neighboring province and home of Decius, was as Romanized as Illyricum. So were Noricum, Dacia, and other Danubian provinces. Hence, despite centuries of Byzantine and Turkish rule, most Danubian countries have preserved a Western outlook.

The Empire's other two fronts suffered almost as severely as the western. The middle front, Greece, Macedonia, and Asia Minor, lost abruptly in 253 the uninterrupted peace it had enjoyed for more than three centuries. Crossing the Black Sea from south Russia, the Goths devastated the northern Asia Minor coast, then plundered the ancient cities of Ionia, including Smyrna and Ephesus. Meanwhile a Gothic fleet terrorized the Aegean as far south as Egypt. Other Gothic bands pillaged Macedonia and Greece. Athens itself was besieged and nearly captured.

On the eastern front reborn nationalist Persia threatened. In 253 Shapur I captured Antioch-on-the-Orontes, the former Seleucid capital and, after Alexandria, the largest and richest city in the East. Probably no Hellenistic-Roman community was ever so systematically sacked. And Shapur escaped Valerian's vengeance. Shapur saw that to exert any lasting pressure on the Empire he must first drive out its forces east of Syria. Accordingly in 255 he destroyed the advanced base garrison at Dura.

The conquest of Dura enabled Shapur to recapture Antioch and make a supreme effort to drive the Romans from Syria and Asia Minor. But he lost Antioch, three times in all. New Persia, like old Parthia, could hit and run, or hold briefly; it could not dig in permanently. To divert Shapur from Asia Minor, Valerian in 259 marched on Mesopotamia. But Shapur gained by deception what he could not win with the sword. Having invited the Emperor to a parley, Shapur kidnaped him; Valerian died in captivity within a few months. An irresolute general and mediocre statesman, he is remembered for his persecution of Christians, whom he blamed for plague, invasions, and other calamities that afflicted his reign. Shapur abandoned Asia Minor permanently when Gallienus, to avenge his father, encouraged Odaenathus, ruler of the desert city-state of Palmyra, to attack Mesopotamia.

The oasis of Palmyra, some 150 miles southeast of Antioch and about as far west of Dura, dominated the principal caravan route to India and China. The city had prospered from the tolls the Empire had permitted it to collect on goods in transit. In return the Palmyrene dynasts protected traffic over the desert route from the Persian to the Roman border. When the turbulent Sassanids interrupted this traffic, thus imperiling Palmyra's prosperity, Odaenathus made the Empire's cause his own. Leading a joint Roman-Palmyrene army into Mesopotamia, he regained the whole Euphrates valley (264). Gallienus set him up as "King of Kings," rival to the king of Persia, and gave him command of Rome's Eastern armies, thus effectively containing Sassanid expansion.

On Odaenathus' death two years later, nominally his son, actually his widow Zenobia, succeeded him. Talented and cultured, this new Cleopatra reversed Palmyra's tradition of friendship with Rome, allied herself with Persia, and then conquered the Roman East for herself, not by war but by shrewd diplomacy. For example, by opening her court to Greek writers, she both gratified her taste and won the support of Greek-speaking cities. By intervening in the contest for the bishopric of Antioch she intensified division among the Christians of Syria. In half a dozen years she extended her empire to the Hellespont and possibly to Alexandria. Only the great Aurelian's accession (270) kept her from ejecting Rome bodily from the East.

Claudius Gothicus' chief lieutenant and idol of his fellow-Illyrian soldiers, Aurelian (270–275) seemed sent by destiny to save the crumbling Empire. He mopped up whatever Gothic stragglers remained after Claudius' death. He strengthened the Danubian border defenses, withdrawing to this end from Dacia, now too thoroughly Romanized to be dangerous.

Aurelian saved Italy from two sets of Germanic invaders who had swept down the Alps from western Austria. Under previous emperors invaders had been bribed to return to their homes; under Aurelian they were lucky to escape with their lives. Convinced that barbarian attacks would recur for generations, Aurelian built permanent defenses for Italian cities. Rome he encircled with a twelve-mile brick wall, twenty feet high and twelve thick, with 381 towers. Sixteen gates gave passage to the principal highways. Aurelian's Wall is today among Rome's most picturesque sights, running through slums and parks, boulevards and princely estates. Its towers are a home for vagrants and for artists.

Aurelian's greatest accomplishment was to reunify the Empire, though the price he paid was the abandonment of Dacia. First he recovered from Zenobia the Eastern provinces, including Egypt. He smashed two of her armies, one at Antioch, the other near Emesa. Though Zenobia speedily prepared Palmyra for siege, both she and the city were captured. The Emperor had returned to the Danubian provinces when he learned late in 272 of another Palmyrene revolt, this time without Zenobia, who was already his prisoner. Aurelian mercilessly reduced Palmyra to a heap of rubble, and called himself Restorer of the East. In 274 he reconquered the Empire of the Gauls. Tetricus, its last ruler, and Zenobia, both in chains, graced the Emperor's triumph; the crowd hailed him "Restorer of the World." Tetricus was soon given an Italian administrative post; Zenobia was permitted to live regally in Hadrian's villa.

Aurelian sought a solution for anarchy and invasions in a mystic-political concept. In honor of a divine being, Elagabal, the Sun-God of Emesa, who supposedly had aided his victory there, he built a magnificent temple in Rome and founded a new college of senatorial priests. He promoted his cult of the "Invincible Sun" as a unifying force for the whole Empire: for Syrians, whose own god it was, for the East where the related cult of Mithraism was popular, for Greeks and Romans who identified the new sun-god with Apollo. Aurelian fostered his new cult especially in the army, hoping that if the soldiers would believe that the god, not they, conferred the Imperial power, anarchy would be halted and discipline restored.

Yet some disgruntled officers, moved not by ambition but by fear of execution, murdered the "Restorer of the World." Discovering that they had been duped by a lying secretary who feared Aurelian's anger, they and the whole army, in remorse, begged the Senate to appoint a successor. A weak Senate, having no mind for a strong emperor, elected the seventy-five-year-old Tacitus, who soon collapsed under the strain.

The army, resuming the imperial nomination, chose Probus, another able Illyrian general (276). His friend Aurelian had reunited the Empire militarily; he would restore it internally to peace and prosperity. But invasions still raged from the North Sea to the Euphrates, and there were revolts. His death in one of these (282) prevented his executing his program. Yet he implanted a new public confidence, a hope for a better day.

That better day came with Diocletian in 284. An army appointee, he first had to defeat the last of three emperors who reigned after Probus. His magnanimity to the defeated (285), which ended civil war, was the first of many statesmanlike acts by which he reconstructed both the state and society. But before we tell this last Roman Titan's story we must deal with another aspect of the third century, the economic and social ordeal.

Economic Collapse

By 235 Roman economy had reached the point of no return. It had expanded briskly over Italy and the older provinces from the early days of Augustus to about 100, thereafter across the frontier provinces, where older cities were enlarged, new ones founded, agriculture and industry developed, and roads built. Hence down through the early third century the Empire prospered, but Italy lost its economic pre-eminence.

For this the emperors were principally responsible. Failure to discriminate in its favor destroyed Italy's economics as it had destroyed its political supremacy. The emperors gave the Empire first place, Italy second. Imperial policy was usually not positive or protectionist; it was essentially negative, economic *laissez faire*. The provinces were left free to develop industries, commerce, and agriculture chiefly on their own, not through Imperial legislative assistance.

Consequently central and southern Italian prosperity declined. Only the Po valley and Istria held their own as sources of industrial supplies for prosperous provinces nearby. Ironically, the Pax Romana also contributed to Italian economic decay. War-prisoners had supplied slave labor, the very foundation of the Italian economy. Hard times produced emigration and depopulation; land went uncultivated; capitalists, big and little, emigrated to exploit greater opportunities in the provinces and compete with Italy.

Economic expansion ceased in about 235 with the last of the Severi. Stagnation which had troubled some areas since Hadrian's time now became general. A dead level of scarcity descended on Roman society:

scarcity of imagination and talent, of output per man and per workshop, of mass purchasing power, and of wealth, decimated by taxation and civil war. The frequency of third-century coin-hoards testifies to a general sense of insecurity. Coinage was devalued; from 256 to 280, prices rose 1000 percent. There was no longer income to support charities like the *alimenta,* nor pagan religion, though Christianity prospered, not depending on income from the same sources.

Both agriculture and industry suffered. The few remaining wealthy landowners bought up derelict lands to add to their latifundia farmed by tenants bound to the land—the ancestors of the medieval serfs. In industry too artisans and their sons were tied to their trades. In troubled Gaul and Germany industry declined; cities shrank in size until they became too small for their walls. Only in Britain was a gradual recovery noticeable after 250. Shrinkage of imperial trade is evidenced by the stamped amphora handles in the Monte Testaccio, a great pottery dump by the Tiber in Rome, where the latest jars are dated about 255. The situation cried aloud for reform and reorganization.

Diocletian and the Reconstruction of the Empire

The reformer and reorganizer was Diocletian (284–305), who came to power by killing a praetorian prefect who stood in his way. Diocletian entrusted the command in Gaul to another Illyrian, Maximian, an Agrippa to his Augustus, though both called themselves Augusti. In 288 they met at Milan to work out a program of administrative reform, based on the premise that civil and military powers should be separate. At the same time was decreed for the Imperial court the Persian practice of prostrating oneself before the monarch, which had so annoyed the Macedonians when Alexander had tried to introduce it.

At Sirmium (293) the two Augusti adopted two Caesars. Diocletian adopted the Dacian Galerius; Maximian adopted his praetorian prefect, Constantius Chlorus, probably also an Illyrian. The resulting tetrarchy divided its powers territorially. Constantius, with his impressive capital at Augusta Trevirorum (Trèves), reconquered Britain, where the Batavian Carausius had set up an independent empire, and defeated the Alemanni. Maximian, based at Aquileia, pacified Spain and Africa. Galerius, with headquarters probably at Sirmium, fought the Goths on the lower Danube. Diocletian himself, with his seat at Nicomedia in Bithynia —he never saw Rome till 303—besieged Alexandria to put down an Egyptian usurper and summoned Galerius to undertake a successful campaign against Persia, which extended Rome's frontiers beyond the Tigris to the Armenian border.

The frontiers secured, Diocletian turned to domestic reforms. Far from

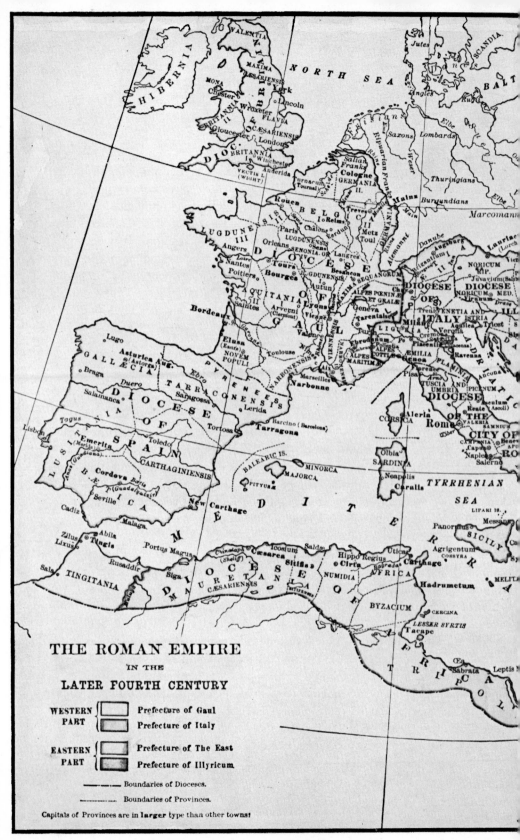

Fig. 58a. Map of the Roman Empire in the later fourth

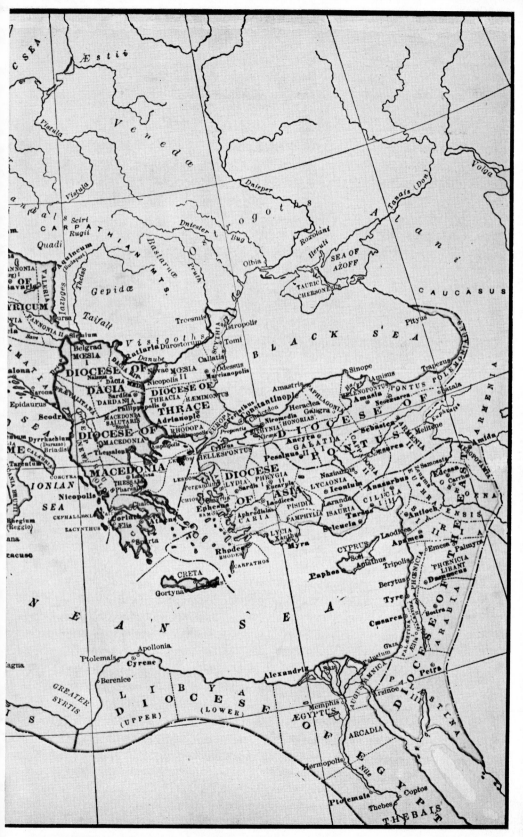

century. (E. Dow, *Atlas of European History*, New York, 1907.)

Fig. 58.2. Piazza Armerina, Sicily. Mosaic from imperial hunting lodge. 4th century A.D. A hunter's banquet under a red awning. On the table, a trussed bird. In the foreground, wine and food in wicker baskets. The hunter on the right is feeding a dog. (Photo by Dorothy MacKendrick)

restoring the municipal autonomy, senatorial liberalism, and economic *laissez faire* of the Empire from Augustus to the Antonines, he imposed a massive uniform paternalistic system of Imperial controls. Latin was decreed the sole official language; the administration of the provinces, now increased from about 50 to 100 or more, was standardized; from his Privy Council, now called the *Sacrum Consistorium* or Consistory, laws emanated in prodigious numbers. The Empire was divided into four prefectures, each under a praetorian prefect; the prefectures were in turn divided into dioceses, 12 in all, each under a vicar responsible to the prefect. In the west they foreshadowed the nations of modern Europe. The 100-odd provincial governors, now called *praesides* or *rectores,* were responsible to the vicars. The army was enlarged to about 400,000 men by conscription, enlistment, and a hereditary obligation to serve, and two legions stationed in each frontier province; the Emperor had his own élite corps, the *comitatenses.*

Diocletian attempted economic reforms. He standardized the coinage, and introduced new denominations. This tampering with the currency inevitably produced inflation, which he vainly attempted to curb by a price-control edict (301) which still survives, with its preface condemning blackmarket profiteers, and its list of over a thousand items on which a maximum price is fixed, to exceed which was punishable by death. It is the most valuable document we possess on ancient economic history. To standardize tax collection he invented a new form of census, attempting to set up equations between real and personal property. Taxes in kind (*annonae*) were imposed for the first time on part of Italy (the Diocese of Milan, then first called *Italia Annonaria*.) He devised for Egypt a municipal system on the Italian model, in the hope of encouraging the municipal economy, but the heavy liturgies imposed on the municipal ruling class resulted in decline, not prosperity. Colleges of artisans became state-controlled economic rather than religious organizations. Finally, Diocletian's economic policy encouraged public works, built or maintained by forced labor, of which the most grandiose survivors are his palace at Spalato and his baths in Rome. A villa recently excavated at Piazza Armerina in Sicily, remarkable for its mosaics, may have been a palace of Maximian. Yet the fixing of capitals away from Rome undermined the very Romanism which Diocletian intended to foster.

Diocletian's hardheaded awareness of the usefulness of lip service to Rome's ancient traditions, and his desire to unify the Empire under a

Fig. 58.3. Split (Salona). Diocletian's fortified palace, model. Built after the abdication in 305. It follows the plan of a walled Roman camp with towers and monumental gates. Its octagonal mausoleum has become the cathedral of the modern city. (Rome, Museo della Civiltà Romana)

single absolute ruler, law, and religion prompted savage attacks on Christianity. The first Edict of Persecution (303) ordered Christian churches closed and Christian sacred books confiscated. When the Christians resisted, he issued two more edicts, decreeing compulsory sacrifices to the emperor first by the clergy, then by Christian congregations. But the blood of the martyrs proved the seed of the church, and the fury of the persecutions soon abated.

In 305 Diocletian, ill and perhaps mentally deranged, abdicated. He had saved the Empire, but the price was absolutism.

Chapter 59 / FALL OF THE ROMAN EMPIRE

From Constantine to Odoacer (306–476)

Maximian having abdicated along with Diocletian, their two Caesars, Galerius and Constantius, became Augusti. Before their abdication Diocletian and Maximian had appointed two new Caesars, bypassing Maximian's son Maximinus and Constantius' bastard Constantine. The resentment of the snubbed heirs caused disorders which broke down Diocletian's system. Out of these disorders Constantine (306–337) emerged triumphant over Maximinus, after a battle (312) near the Milvian Bridge just north of Rome, rendered famous by the legend that during this battle the sign of the cross and crown appeared to him, and from Heaven resounded the magic words "In hoc signo vinces" (In this sign thou shalt conquer). Whatever the truth of the legend, Christians could breathe again, for by an Edict of Toleration signed at Milan (313) they were restored freedom of worship and their confiscated properties. Though Constantine was not himself baptized until the eve of his death, his later pro-Christian legislation repealed Augustus' laws against celibacy, made Sunday a holy day, authorized manumission by declaration in churches, permitted the Church to receive legacies, and allowed transfer of trials from civil to ecclesiastical courts. This leniency toward

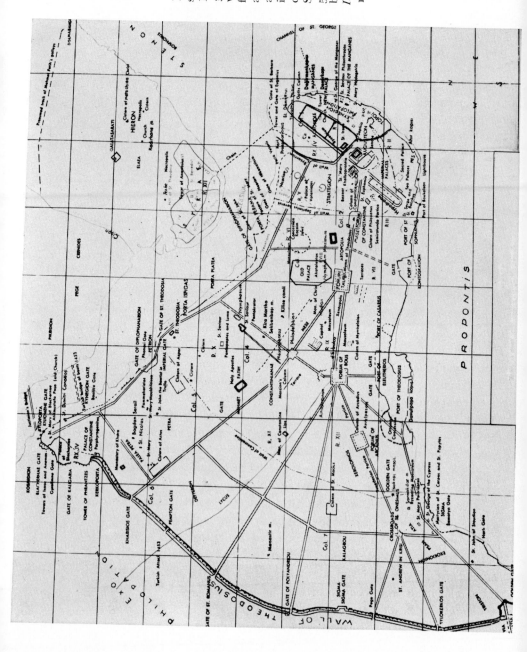

Fig. 59a. Plan of Constantinople. Built as New Rome A.D. 324–330, famous for its walls, harbors, palaces, fora, Hippodrome, and aqueducts, and above all for Justinian's great domed church of Hagia (or Sancta) Sophia (A.D. 532–537). (E. Mamboury, *The Tourists' Istanbul*, Istanbul, 1953. Facing p. 64.)

the Christians embroiled Constantine with his brother-in-law and rival Licinius, whom he defeated and had put to death (324). In this year also began the building of a new capital at Byzantium, to be renamed Constantinople. To resolve theological quarrels, he called a council at Nicaea (325), whose decision that the Son is of one substance with the Father forestalled a split in the Church.

Constantine correctly believed that the lower Danube was Rome's most vulnerable frontier, and his new capital (inaugurated as a new Rome in 330) was perhaps chosen as an operating base convenient to it. The Goths made peace in 332 and were rapidly Christianized; the Sarmati of the middle Danube were defeated and 300,000 of them dispersed through the Balkans and Italy; the Rhine frontier was guarded; only the Persians were a menace, taking ill Constantine's insistence that they should cease persecuting Christians. But though he hoped at his death (337) to see the Empire pass peacefully to his heirs, he left it menaced by a Persian war, religious quarrels, and court intrigues.

Under Constantine the central government continued as bureaucratic as under Diocletian, with an especially complex and expensive organization of the emperor's court, and a corresponding opportunity for flattering courtiers to influence the emperor. The Consistory continued important; to it all department heads reported; the Roman Senate was a shadow, whose prestige was still further reduced when a new Senate was set up in Constantinople. But the senatorial order, its members now called *clarissimi*, remained the highest and richest social class. Constantine dissolved the praetorian guard, made the praetorian prefects purely civil officers, multiplied their number, and divided Imperial administration among them as vice-emperors, with independent budgets and the right to hear cases on appeal; the result was to make the Empire a federation. The power of the vicars lapsed.

The reformed army consisted of peasant soldiers (*ripenses* or *limitanei*, commanded by *duces*) and an élite reserve (*comitatenses,* commanded by *comites*), whose cream were the *palatini*. Barbarian auxiliaries gained prestige, but the Roman cavalry (*vexillationes*) held the place of honor. Corresponding to the old centurions were the *protectores,* a picked corps of whom formed the Emperor's bodyguard.

All this was expensive; the state payroll contained more names than the tax-rolls. Recourse was had to ruinous surtaxes on large landowners, merchants, and municipal *decuriones*. The Emperor's private fortune was so large that it required two ministers to superintend it. His lavish public works program had an inflationary effect. The aerarium was reduced to the paltry municipal revenues of Rome itself.

Constantine's death touched off a new series of civil wars which kept the Empire divided, though his son Constantius held it together for a time (353–360). The history of his reign was written in crabbed Latin by Rome's greatest neglected historian, the Syrian Ammianus Marcellinus (b. *c.* 330). Constantius emerges as a cruel bureaucrat, head of a spy-ridden police-state. His brother and successor Julian the Apostate (360–363) held the Empire together, but is chiefly famous for abjuring Christianity; hence his nickname. He tried to organize the pagan clergy in imitation of the Christian hierarchy, wrote vigorously against the Christians, excluding them from public employment, taxed them excessively, and condoned persecution. Wounded in a campaign against the Persians, he died, like Socrates, conversing with philosophers on the immortality of the soul.

Soon after Julian's death two Pannonian brothers, Valentinian (364–375) and Valens (364–378), divided the western and eastern Empires. Valentinian in the West, aided by his great general, the Spaniard Theodosius the Elder, saved Gaul and Britain for the Empire and tried to stem barbarization by forbidding marriages between Romans and barbarians. Hating the rich, he established in rural areas a *defensor plebis* (defender of the people) to harass them. Under him Diocletian's sharp division between civil and military functionaries became blurred; in the new hierarchy both appeared in the same list. Under him, too, Christians returned to favor; he confirmed (373) Ambrose as Bishop of Milan. Meanwhile in the East Valens had to contend with Goths, Persians, and Huns; hoping to use the latter as peasants and soldiers, he unwisely permitted them to settle in Thrace, where they welcomed the invading Goths. Ammianus, historian also of this reign, described the invaders cracking their whips as they drove troops of captive Roman women before them. When Gothic cavalry defeated and killed Valens before Adrianople (378) and threatened Constantinople itself it was the beginning of the end; the Empire was never again to be rid of them.

To counteract the disastrous effects of the battle of Adrianople, Theodosius I (379–395), son of Valentinian's general, was called in. His remedy for the Gothic problem, enrolling Goths in the legions, was to prove worse than the disease, for it barbarized the Eastern army. A famous incident of his reign is his punishment of the people of Thessalonica for revolt; he assembled them in the Circus and for three hours had them systematically slaughtered. For this barbarism Bishop Ambrose excommunicated him, taking him back into the fold only after a public penance. In the West, Theodosius restored unity after two civil wars; the Western capital was transferred from Trèves to Milan.

At Theodosius' death the Empire was divided between his sons, Arcadius in the East (395–408), Honorius in the West (395–423), with the Vandal general Stilicho as regent (395–408). This division proved to be permanent. In the East, courtiers and bureaucrats combined with ecclesiastics to resist the barbarian; in the West, generals and feudal lords, in collusion, often compromised with them. Both groups oppressed the common people; the buffer state of *bourgeoisie* was no longer a social force. Factional quarrels weakened the central government, and nationalist movements sprang up in Mauretania, Gaul, and Egypt.

Stilicho was immediately called to the East to withstand the Visigothic raids of Alaric I, against whom he was indecisive, being hampered by conflict among the policy makers of Arcadius' court. Alaric escaped to Illyricum and invaded Italy; Stilicho's enemies poisoned Honorius against him and procured his execution on a trumped-up charge of high treason. His is a tragic story of great statesmanship and generalship unrewarded. Honorius was left to reign by himself, at Ravenna; Alaric appeared at the gates of Rome, which he subjected to a three-day sack (410). Not for 800 years had the city so suffered. No wonder the priest Orosius could argue, in his *Universal History* (417), that the Empire was falling, in punishment for its vices. Three years after the sack Augustine began his *City of God,* contrasting the spiritual with the temporal power and foreshadowing the medieval conflicts between pope and emperor.

After two years of conflict between East and West, Honorius' nephew Valentinian III (425–455) assumed the Western throne, though the actual power was in the hands of the rival generals Boniface, "the last of the Romans," and Aetius. In this reign Africa was lost to the Vandals under Gaiseric, Aquitania became an independent Visigothic state, and the Saxons in Britain, the Suebi in Spain, and the Alani and Salic Franks in Gaul were virtually uncontrolled. In 452 the Hun Attila threatened Milan. The Western Empire was ruined, and the poor preferred barbarian inroads to imperial taxation. Soon after Valentinian's assassination Gaiseric swept down upon Ostia by the sea and sacked Rome (455).

The Suebian Ricimer held a fifteen-year protectorate (456–472) over the Western Empire. In 475 the Pannonian Orestes, who had been Attila's secretary, had his son, Romulus Augustulus, proclaimed emperor, but he was put down by the army at Milan in favor of the German Odoacer (August 23, 476) and the Roman Empire in the West, as a political entity, ended.

But the Eastern Empire survived. Arcadius' son and successor, Theodosius II (408–450), presided over a rebirth of Hellenism, Constantinople received new walls and a new university, the law was codified, a passion for the circus seized the new capital. The Huns laid the city under tribute, but the Eastern Empire contrived to divert the barbarians toward the West, leaving the East in the comparative tranquillity out of which grew the "stabilized vitality" of the Byzantine Empire.

External and Internal Pressures

The wonder is, not that the Western Empire fell, but that it was able to withstand so long the pressures of barbarians from without and of usurpers and intriguers, both pagan and Christian, from within.

Against the barbarian stood the limes and the legions. But 400,000 men, recruited with difficulty from a diminishing population, must be spread thin to defend a 1500-mile frontier, and even when levies could be exacted from the powerful landed proprietors, it was naturally the worst qualified who were the first to go. The government in consequence accepted instead cash payments with which it hired mercenaries, setting barbarians to fight barbarians, thus making of the "Roman" army a barbarizing rather than a Romanizing instrument and placing perforce on the shoulders of those with the smallest stake in the commonwealth the burden of defending it. This largely barbarian army fought with barbarian weapons and armor: the dagger, the bow, the coat of mail; cavalry came to occupy the pride of place it held from the medieval period to World War I. More and more, as the principle of separating civil and military functions prevailed, command came to be vested in the equestrian, not the senatorial, order; rising from the ranks became commoner, and men like Stilicho, on the extraordinarily competent general staff, were recruited from barbarian career officers. The emperors themselves, at least until Theodosius' death in 395, were perforce soldiers, whose very lives, and the Empire's existence, depended on their military competence. The navy, neglected and despised, proved in the end no match for the African-based Vandal pirates.

But the pressure of the barbarians beyond the frontiers proved too great for the Imperial army and for the intrigue-ridden, underpopulated, and demoralized Western Empire itself. Julian the Apostate fell in 363 in the vain defense of the eastern frontier against Shapur and his Persians; Valens in 378 at Adrianople before the Goths. In the west, Roman legions never crossed the Rhine after 388, while Germanic tribes repeatedly invaded Gaul and Spain. Along the Danube ranged Visigoths, Vandals, and Ostrogoths, lusting for the wealth, fertility, and civilized comforts of the Roman side of the frontier and feeling in their turn always behind them the pressure of the Huns, whom Ammianus called "wild beasts with two legs." In Africa, the nomads swooped down from the Sahara and the Atlas, and cut the Empire's grain supply-line, aided from within, sometimes deliberately, by Donatist schism and government clique. In Britain, Picts and Scots pierced Hadrian's Wall and forced the Romans to evacuate the island (407). Thus the West, with its longer frontier, menaced by fiercer tribes, felt its strength overtaxed and was eventually submerged; the East precariously survived, somewhat

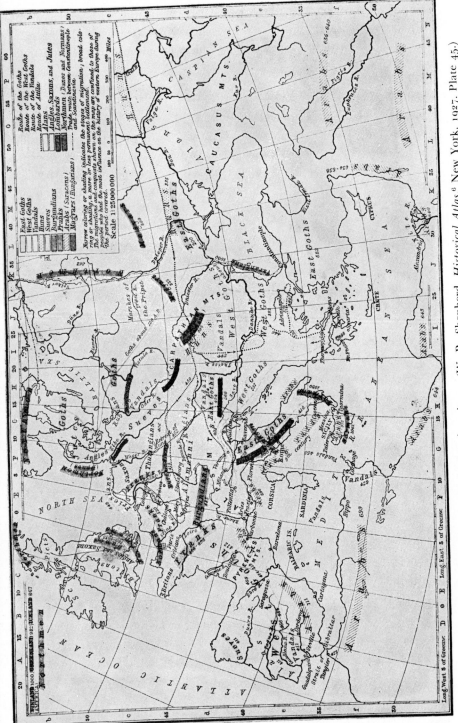

Fig. 59b. Map to illustrate the barbarian invasions. (W. R. Shepherd, *Historical Atlas*,[6] New York, 1927. Plate 45.)

protected by the Black Sea and the beetling walls of Constantinople and facing the less predatory and more civilized Ostrogoths, with whom, and with the Vandals, its emperors contrived to come to terms, playing off one barbarian faction against another and even encouraging the enemy to attack the West.

Within, the Empire was menaced by civil wars and religious conflicts. We have seen how civil wars and usurpations had been endemic in the Empire, which had never worked out a smooth system of succession from one emperor to another. The anarchy of the third century had proved once more that secure tenure of the throne depended on army support, which was fickle and unpredictable, supporting a usurper in one part of the Empire while the distracted emperor was busy in another. Diocletian's ingenious attempted solution, the tetrarchy with enforced abdication after a fixed term, fell prey to its own inherent over-rigidity and failure to allow for human ambition, and did not last. Constantine's division of the Empire among his sons and nephews bred only disunity, inefficiency, multiple bureaucracy, dissatisfaction, and new usurpers. Yet Constantine founded a dynasty, Valentinian another, and Theodosius a third, and, though the course of the dynasties ran far from smooth, they did enlist a certain loyalty and prevent usurpers from reaching power as often as they had in the third century or even in the first. Still, they did not wipe out the perennial evil of civil wars and treasonable appeals for enemy intervention, which distracted the Imperial troops from their prime duty of guarding the frontiers and thus made the barbarian menace still more formidable.

The Empire's other major internal disease was religious conflict. The very religious enthusiasm which carried men through this time of troubles produced also divisive heresies and schisms. Impatience with these explains in part Diocletian's persecution of the Christians. The Edict of Milan and Constantine's conversion brought a respite, but, by making Christianity the state religion, opened the Church to political ambitions and subjected its hierarchy to the temptation of increasing its power by heresy-hunting. And Church-state relations were not always happy: though Bishop Ambrose might force Theodosius to do penance for the massacre of Thessalonica, the humiliation rankled; the independence of the secular power was at stake as it was often to be in the conflicts between pope and emperor which racked the medieval era. Meanwhile, the continuing paganism of the army and the intellectual and senatorial classes still held, as Julian the Apostate's reign proves, the seeds of conflict. When an edict of Theodosius (392) abolished pagan cult practices, conflict continued within the Christian Church, which, as the state religion, appealed to the secular arm for help against heretics. Of the heresies, the most vexatious were two. In Africa, a Donatist bishop, whose sect rigorously condemned those who had yielded in the face of persecution, held the see of Carthage at the very moment of Constantine's conversion, while in the East, Arius, offering a monotheistic solution to the problem of reconciling the unity of the Father with the divinity of the Son, was accusing his bishop of heresy. Though Constantine referred the controversies to Church Councils, he was not above intervening in their deliberations, and it was he who was responsible for exiling Arius and for favoring the Athanasian party, which championed the compromise of the Nicene Creed, declaring, as we saw, the Son to be of one substance with the Father. Under pressure from rival bishops, Constantine more than once changed his mind, recalling Arius, exiling his rival Athanasius, and alternately persecuting and forgiving the Donatists. His successors followed his example, both in imposing orthodoxy and in veering with the winds of doctrine which attempted to define it. These interventions, however well-meant, prolonged the Donatist conflict into the sixth century and the Arian-Athanasian controversy until 381, when Theodosius finally unseated all Arian bishops. Not until 385 was the first execution for heresy (the Priscillian, an ascetic mysticism) by the secular arm recorded: this again was to have grim echoes in the medieval era. Undeniably the link between church and state infused new life into the Empire, helped to civilize and Christianize the barbarians, formed the mind of the medieval period, and helped preserve the classical heritage. But these interventions by the state in Church affairs, plus civil difficulties with usurpers and the constant threat from the barbarians, combined to force the fourth-century Empire further into absolutism.

Absolute Monarchy

The anarchy of the third century and the spiritual revolution which was Christianity forced Diocletian and his successors to extreme measures. The result was an absolute, bureaucratic monarchy which operated with equal rigor in the economic life and in the local, regional, and central administration of the Empire. The liberal Antonine age had been able to afford the luxury of granting home rule to responsible municipalities: now, financial and military crises forced intervention and control by the central government. At the center, such powers as the Imperial Senate had ever had passed more and more to the emperor and the increasingly complex bureaucracy which surrounded him. The absolute monarchies of the East, especially Egypt, their autocracy disguised as paternalism, supplied a precedent. Faced with the external and internal pressure described above, plus poverty, depression, and insecurity, especially in the cities, Diocletian and his successors inevitably had recourse to a concentration of powers.

In the economic sphere, inflation and the need to maintain the various

Imperial courts, the army, and a large civil service required high taxes, in cash, in kind, and in forced labor, to defray the expenses of palaces, camps, supplies, offices, warehouses, roads, the postal service, the dole, and the circus games; and all this had to be paid for out of a declining economy. Caracalla's grant of universal citizenship in 212 had provided more persons to tax; Diocletian tried to make the burden fall fairly. He based the tax on a complicated census, revised every fifteen years. Constantine levied a tax in gold on senators; Valentinian changed the levy of "coronary gold" upon municipal dignitaries from an occasional to a regular exaction. The state domains and the emperors' private estates, increased by proscriptions, produced some revenue. By the fourth century, the state was taking two-thirds of the income of cities and forcing municipal authorities to exact local taxes regularly on pain of paying the ruinous arrears themselves. Though theoretically fair, the system of local tax-collection was inefficient; surtaxes were frequent, and bribery to escape full payment more frequent still. It proved impossible to keep the census up to date, to avoid inequities, unfair exemptions (especially through the granting of sinecures), and tax evasion. All this increased the burden upon the honest and the humble, and finally ruined what had been the hard core of the Empire, the municipal ruling class.

Hence the decline of the cities, which had been the glory of the Greco-Roman world. Though still theoretically autonomous, local administration ruined itself trying to meet Imperial exactions. Power and wealth now were centered, at any rate in the West, on the great self-sustaining estates, tilled by serfs, enlisting perforce the loyalty of neighboring free farmers who had to look to the lords of these estates, if to anyone, for protection. Evading Imperial taxes with impunity and levying their own, dispensing their own justice, supporting their own private armies, dwelling in fortified villas, these large landowners, sumptuously clothed and richly fed, were reminiscent of the nabobs of the end of the Republic and foreshadowed the barons of the feudal era.

They were growing to power in the face of the largest, most pompous, and most powerful hereditary bureaucracy the Empire had ever known: over 10,000 civil servants in the provinces, 4500 in the dioceses, and hundreds more in the various capitals. A rigid hierarchy and an Imperial espionage system sapped initiative; promotion, theoretically by merit and seniority, was often assisted by intrigue; yet, inefficient and venal as it was, the bureaucracy helped to hold the Empire together.

In the provinces, the bureaucrats fell under the jurisdiction of the civil governor, shorn of his former military powers and assisted by a provincial assembly with the right of appeal to the emperor, which it occasionally exercised. The dioceses in the fourth century were increased from twelve to fifteen. Of praetorian prefects there were now usually three, stationed at Constantinople, Milan, and Trèves (later Arles), with vice-regal powers. The absence of a praetorian prefect for Rome is significant: Rome's political (but not religious) importance declined as that of Constantine's richly-bedecked, strategically placed new Rome on the Bosporus grew. Both cities had a Senate, with purely honorific functions; there were still consuls, still a *cursus honorum,* its offices nominal but costly, involving chiefly the supervising and underwriting of the games. Each capital had its own city prefect (to be distinguished from the praetorian prefects), who presided over the Senate, acted as trial judge, kept public order, and administered the dole. But though the capitals had more superficial grandeur than the provincial cities, they had no real independence.

The sole independent spirit was the emperor, though even he was subject to personal influences and court intrigues. At his right hand stood his *comites* (companions; modern "counts"). The absolute monarchy was the emperor's personal affair, and these were his personal friends, like the staff that had surrounded Alexander, trustworthy for special missions and "trouble-shooting." The emperor presided over the Consistory: in his absence, the Quaestor of the Sacred Palace did so; this official also drafted laws and answered petitions. Chiefs of departments, with senatorial rank, attended the Consistory: these included the Grand Chamberlain (often a eunuch), the Chief Notary (who kept the civil and military lists), the Count of the Sacred Largesses (the treasurer; he had 834 clerks), the Count of the Private Estates, the Master of the Offices (head of the secretariat and of the secret police). Fearing rivalry or treachery, the emperor had no prime minister or grand vizier; only under Theodosius did commanding personalities like Stilicho, Rufinus, or Eutropius come to the fore, and they were the emperor's personal choice, Stilicho his guardian, his cousin by marriage, and later his father-in-law.

Prudence dictated a completely separate military command, whose highest officers were the Masters of the Soldiers, eventually eight. Beneath them were some 35 dukes, of whom the senior ten were *comites.* Besides, there were two counts of the domestics (the palace guard, made up of veteran *protectores* and domestics proper, aristocratic cadets). Among all these functionaries the emperor naturally had his favorites, and intrigue was rife among both the men and the women of the court. The court was a hotbed of denunciation, treachery, jealousy and rivalry, the natural result of an absolutist regime.

The emperor in his purple general's cloak was commander-in-chief of the army. His diadem, scepter, and globe symbolized belief in him as God's representative, under obligation to construct the City of God on earth and to watch with paternal benevolence over his subjects' morals and welfare. In fact, the emperor's sacred status gave him unlimited powers: he was the living law above all law. His sanctity was reflected in court ceremonial and nomenclature: everything concerned with him was "sacred," he was portrayed with a halo, courtiers kissed the hem of his jewel-encrusted robe; his bodyguard, his horse, his chariot glistened with gold and precious stones. Here is the pomp and circumstance of medieval Byzantium. This absolute status was defended by the secret police, ever ready to bring charges of treason, to elicit confession by the most exquisite tortures, to execute its victims with the most refined cruelty. The emperor was no longer "first citizen"; he was *Dominus,* "Lord," and his subjects were his humble slaves, without freedom, either of thought or of action.

Economic, Social, and Intellectual Life

Three principal traits have been distinguished in the economic and social life of the late Empire: state intervention, the gulf between rich (*honestiores*) and poor (*humiliores*), and the special place of the Church. In literature and art, too, the Church dominated; only in architecture was the massiveness of the secular authority strongly marked.

The economy adapted itself in various ways to reduced circumstances. Coined silver and gold was still fairly sound money, and indeed the ancient world now for the first time went on the gold standard, but gold was scarce and hoarded, and bronze was deeply debased. The result was a mixed economy, based partly on barter. Depreciation of the bronze money led of course to inflation; hence Diocletian's abortive Price Edict, from which, among other things, we can derive the information that in 301 a pound of pork or mutton cost a rural day-laborer a day's pay. Inflation proceeded apace: it has been calculated that in the fourth century it would have taken 16 metric tons of bronze money to buy 50 pounds of wheat. In these circumstances, only the authority of the state kept the economy going. The state's needs had priority; it owned the mines and quarries, held monopolies in some industries, especially the luxury trades, and controlled guilds and transport. But the social consequences of this regimentation were more serious than the economic, for the economy was not ruined. Famines were less frequent than in the Empire's prime; there were technical improvements: mechanical harvesters, wider use of watermills, new wine-producing areas along the Garonne and Moselle, new glassworks along the Rhine. Some Eastern provinces reached in the fourth century new heights of prosperity, from the profits of traffic in luxury goods, which passed through Antioch, Tyre, and Alexandria on their way to Arabia, India, and China. But the picture should not be painted in too glowing terms, for most cities retrogressed, especially Rome, bypassed by the major trade-routes.

Late Imperial society, which this economy affected, must be treated under two heads, lay and ecclesiastical. Lay society was full of new citizens, especially barbarians. Whereas the earlier Empire had facilitated gradual rise in the social scale, the needs of the state now encouraged social mobility at the higher levels, while the lower classes were increasingly bound to their trades. The major sufferers were the municipal *bourgeoisie,* bound, from father to son, to their obligations to the state, doctors, lawyers, and teachers alone excepted; as for the others, they led completely regimented lives, without initiative or prospects. As for the upper class, the crisis of the third century and pressing needs of the state in the fourth had produced a new hierarchy of state nobility, graded from *illustres* through *spectabiles* and *clarissimi* to *perfectissimi;* these filled the higher bureaucratic offices, degree of nobility depending on responsibility of function. They enjoyed exemption from taxes and favor before the law (one law for the *honestiores,* a harsher law for *humiliores*). Some grew fabulously rich and invested chiefly in land, embellished with sumptuous fortified villas and worked by slaves. Slaves, however, were fewer than in earlier centuries, and their lot sometimes somewhat improved by their masters' conversion to Christian standards of morality, though the wretches in the state-owned mines were still treated with unspeakable cruelty. There grew up a rural proletariat of migratory workers turned brigand, ever ready, especially in Africa, to use civil strife and religious conflict as an excuse for agitation. There grew up, too, a class of serfs (*coloni*), bound to the land, neither slave nor free. Even free peasants, placing themselves under the patronage of large landowners, became indistinguishable from serfs, despite sporadic efforts on their behalf, more frequently effective in the East than in the West, by the imperially-appointed *defensores plebis.* From the labor of their serfs and their free dependents, the large landowners grew progressively richer and more powerful, while the peasants, as always, lived lives of more or less quiet desperation.

Linked to the laity and yet distinct was the ecclesiastic hierarchy. Since Constantine's conversion Christianity had gained converts on both sides of the frontier: the Abyssinians and Goths had bishops; the Gothic bishop Ulfila translated the Bible into his native tongue. Within the Empire, by the end of the fourth century Christianity was supreme and the Church the largest landowner, having been remembered in the wills of many wealthy communicants, especially ladies. Though it dispensed much of its wealth in charities, the Church was not tax-exempt. It has been held responsible for serious loss of secular manpower through the attractiveness to many of the solitary or monastic life. In the fourth century the Egyptian desert was peopled by several thousand hermits, their withdrawal from the world prompted by mystic exaltation or a desire to escape the Imperial tax-collector. Elsewhere in the East, ascetics practiced extremes of self-denial: St. Simeon spent thirty-seven years atop a column. Some, both male and female, preferred the community to the solitary life: monasteries and convents sprang up, each under the rule of a Superior; their members devoted their lives to prayer, study, and farm work. But the monasteries were somewhat apart from the central organization of the Church, which stemmed from the bishops, with their seats in the principal cities. Aided by a large staff, they appointed and supervised an ever-growing clergy; their authority was curbed by the pressure of opinion, or, at need, by a Council of bishops called by the emperor. In each province, the metropolitan (bishop of the chief city) came to hold primacy over the other bishops. Certain cities—Alexandria, Antioch, Constantinople, Jerusalem—had patriarchs, whose prestige was greater still. Tradition gave the Bishop of Rome the greatest prestige of all, expressly recognized as early as the Council of Nicaea, and enhanced by his stand against the Huns and Goths. But his prestige was challenged by the Patriarch of Constantinople, with the backing of the Emperor of the East, and at the Western Empire's fall, the future of the papacy was still undecided. So was the problem of harmonious relations between Church and state.

The Church, especially in the East, played a prime role in the intellectual life of the age. Dying paganism received its last impetus from the Eastern cult of Mithras and from the Eastern philosophy of Neo-Platonism, expounded by the Egyptian Greek Plotinus (205–269/70), who combined pantheism, monotheism, and ascetic Platonism with a subtlety and exalted fervor which appealed strongly to intellectuals like Julian the Apostate, though in the fourth century it also harbored charlatans on its fringes. In the East, too, partly through the Neo-Platonic schools, pagan Greek literature, science, and philosophy were kept alive. Christians used pagan Greek philosophy, as Origen (185–255) had done, in erecting theology into an intellectual system which could reconcile the controversies of Arians and Athanasians and resolve other heresies which racked the Eastern church. In the matter of heresies the West, meanwhile, except for the Donatists, remained comparatively calm. Not until the fifth century do we find controversy again active there, with Augustine's vigorous attack upon the Pelagians' denial of original sin. Augustine himself had been a Manichee, disciple of a strange religion born in Babylonia in the 240's, which united to the dualism of Mazda-worship elements borrowed from Buddhism, Gnosticism, and Christianity itself. The hierarchical, proselytizing Manichaean clergy, expecting the end of the world, practiced celibacy and refused to serve the state. But Christianity triumphed over all heresies, not without certain compromises

Fig. 59.1. Venice, Basilica di San Marco. The Emperors of the Tetrarchate. Porphyry. 4th century A.D. Possibly portraits of Diocletian, Maximian, Valerius, and Constantius. In Venetian popular tradition, these are four Saracens turned to stone for having tried to rob the treasure-house of San Marco.

with them and with paganism, the latter symbolized, for example, by the coincidence of Christmas with the pagan Saturnalia, or the popular belief in amulets and the cult of relics. With its triumph was associated a sumptuous setting in large, richly-decorated basilica churches, and a ritual which high and low alike found impressive, accompanied as it was by rich vestments, solemn music, and sacramental objects in gold and precious stones. Paganism had never been so impressive, nor brought equal promise of salvation, nor set so high a standard of morality.

Literature remained what it had been since Hadrian: conventional, rhetoric-ridden, banal, devoted to flattery, controversy, and propaganda, but its barrenness was sometimes relieved, for example, by the charm of Ausonius' (d. c. 395) description of the beauties of the Moselle, or the genuineness of Ammianus' affection for Julian the Apostate. Some have seen in the mediocrity of the literature a reflection of the outmoded rhetorical education. But this had withstood even the Christian revolution, despite the sarcasms leveled against it as long ago as the second

Fig. 59.2 Rome. Arch of Constantine. A.D. 312. The medallions are Hadrianic, recarved; the reliefs in the attic, of the time of Marcus Aurelius, "a confession of inferiority to the past." In the frieze sculpture there is already something medieval.

century by the fiery and intense African heretic Tertullian (*c.* 160–225). The pagan classics still supplied to Christians the canons of taste and the rules of reason, and the professors of rhetoric were Christians, except briefly during Julian's reign. The quality of their teaching is indicated by Servius' commentary on Vergil, and Donatus' on Terence. On the Greek side, the most distinguished names in rhetoric are those of Themistius of Constantinople (*c.* 317–388) and Libanius of Antioch (314–393), Ammianus' teacher. Despite a busy life and an early death, the Emperor Julian, too, distinguished himself by a rhetoric marked by satiric intolerance. The languages of instruction in the East were both Greek and Latin, but in the West Greek was dying out. While science stagnated, the law flourished: a glory of the fourth century is the Theodosian Code. This century saw also the publication by the learned and lovable Illyrian St. Jerome (*c.* 348–420) of a careful Latin version of the Bible which was to become the standard ("Vulgate"). Other Christian authors were Lactantius (*c.* 250–317), "the Christian Cicero," apologist and historian of Diocletian's persecution, and Eusebius (*c.* 260–340), friend and biographer of Constantine and historian of the Church. Poetry is represented, besides Ausonius, by the Latin encomia upon Rome and Stilicho of the Greek Claudianus of Alexandria (*fl.* 395) and by the Christian verse of the Spaniard Prudentius (b. 348) and Ausonius' pupil Paulinus of Nola (b. *c.* 353). But the Church Fathers were the fourth century's particular glory: eloquent defenders of the faith like Libanius' pupil St. John Chrysostom (the Golden-Mouthed; *fl.* 398) in Greek and St. Augustine (354–430) in Latin. Augustine, bishop, moralist, polemicist, autobiographer, theologian and philosopher, was the greatest intellect of his age, deeply moving in his *Con-*

fessions, profoundly inspired in his *City of God.* To such a man, secure in his hope of the Heavenly kingdom, the fall of Rome would have little importance. His otherworldliness was the ideal of the medieval ages.

Art, like literature, was in this period traditional and classicizing, and beginning to fail in technique. Sculpture is crude in its rigid frontality, as witness the contemporary reliefs of the Arch of Constantine in Rome or the rigid porphyry Tetrarchs of St. Mark's in Venice. But from the East was coming a decorative exuberance which was to issue in the golden magnificence of Byzantine mosaic and painting. In architecture, villas and imperial palaces were more luxurious than ever, the concrete vaults of baths and basilicas still more massive and imposing. To adorn Constantinople, the Roman world was stripped of treasures; there the emperor had his choice of three palaces, and the Hippodrome was as large as the Circus Maximus in Rome. But other cities declined, pillaging their own monuments to build hasty walls against the ever-present barbarian menace. The chief architectural activity became the building of churches, not yet typed as to plan, but often adapting to Christian uses the pagan basilica with nave, apse, and two side aisles. Severe with-

Fig. 59.3. Constantinople. Walls. Built 413–448, enlarging the Constantinian circuit, and often added to or repaired. Concrete faced with squared limestone, bonded with courses of brick. (*Archaeology* VI, 1953, p. 130; photo by S. Weinberg)

Fig. 59.4. Constantinople. Hagia Sophia. Dedicated A.D. 537. A daring experiment in late Roman architecture, successfully solving the problem of carrying a dome over a square floor plan. The minarets were added after the capture of the city by the

Fig. 59c. Reconstruction of the Basilica of Maxentius. About A.D. 313. Derived from the vast vaulted concrete central halls of baths. Note clerestory and buttresses. Early Christian basilica churches were influenced by this plan. Nowadays, outdoor concerts are played in the summer in the ruins. (J. I. Sewall, *A History of Western Art,* New York, 1953. Fig. 7.28.)

out, they were decorated within with rich marbles and mosaics gleaming with gold, foreshadowing yet again the medieval era, when all art was to be dedicated to the glory of God.

Possible Causes of the Fall

The external and internal pressures we have been describing, the dead weight of absolute monarchy and bureaucracy, economic decline, social inequality, intellectual stagnation, all predisposed the Western Empire to its fall. Many allegations of the causes of the fall tell us more about the analyst than about the problem: thus an eighteenth-century rational-ist like Gibbon lays the responsibility at the door of the Christians, a Californian sees the decline of rainfall as the root of the matter; a certain sort of German is depressed by the late Empire's persistent extermination of its élite; a great White Russian detects a class-conscious alliance of ignorant soldiers and peasants to overthrow the aristocracy, and civilization therewith; a Frenchman, writing after World War II, singles out the renunciation of compulsory military service as the prime cause. Now, while complete historical objectivity is impossible, and application of the causes of Rome's fall to one's own time desirable, we may perhaps face the problem less subjectively if we remember that only the Western Empire fell and inquire which of the alleged causes applied more to the West than to the East. Scholars have isolated four: (1) Failure of manpower in the Western army's regular recruiting area, Illyricum and Pannonia, which led to filling the ranks with barbarians without the Roman tradition or the feeling for Rome's past. (2) The greater pressure of barbarian invaders upon West than East, preventing the free interchange of ideas and things which is civilization, and which can only occur within a unified and reasonably prosperous area safeguarded from violence. This the whole Empire had once provided; the barbarians broke it down in the West, where their splinter kingdoms destroyed Western unity and prosperity. Constantinople was not to know until 1453 the disaster that befell Rome in the fifth century. (3) The preponderance among high Imperial officials of the West of large landowners tending to grant to their own class exemptions ruinous to the Empire, whereas in the East the senior officials were likely to be middle-class lawyers who played no such favorites. (4) Finally, the greater frequency in the West of military dictatorship over civilian government, so that the Western rulers enlisted less loyalty and encountered more apathy than those in the East.

Two final points should be made: first, the collapse was not so sudden as the compressed account in this chapter might suggest; and, second, the modern world's heritage from Rome is so great that the political collapse of the West is less important than the intellectual and spiritual continuity of the millennium and a half that separate us from Odoacer.

First, the collapse was not sudden. The Romans themselves were aware of this; Cicero, Sallust, Livy, and Horace wrote as though theirs was an age of decline, which they attributed to the growth of luxury and irresponsibility since a Golden Age which they place in the middle of the second century B.C. before Rome destroyed Carthage and Corinth. Part of this is pure rhetoric, but behind it is a great truth: ancient civilization was a minority civilization, kept by slavery at a low level of technical development, with a regrettable divorce between intellectuals and manual workers and lamentable extremes of wealth and poverty. Half a millennium before Odoacer, some Romans knew they were faced with a choice which their ruling class declined to make; between reforming their society from within and accepting the ruthless regimented absolutism of the bureaucratic state. The Roman *bourgeoisie* might have abandoned their privileges, paid higher wages, developed technology. One alternative, a revolt of the masses, was rendered impossible by poverty and disunity, and if it had been possible, would hardly, to judge by the record of the Roman *plebs* in the early Republic, have produced an equalitarian society.

And so the other choice was taken, and the absolutist state arose, containing within it the seeds of its own destruction. Politically, absolutism, which became inevitable once the Roman ruling class had refused to reform itself, had to force a decaying social system to work at the expense of mass happiness and freedom, using as the agents of compulsion a progressively more barbarized professional army, without roots, without sense of tradition, making and unmaking emperors with cynical self-interest.

Socially, the Empire presents the depressing picture of extreme upper-class luxury beside lower-class poverty and hardship. Seneca preaching the simple life beside his fabulous collection of citron-wood tables, Hadrian building his gigantic folly, the villa at Tivoli, Maximian ordering the extravagant mosaics of his palace at Piazza Armerina, may be set beside Juvenal's picture of the lot of the poor in a great city or Philostratus' description of the mob in Aspendus threatening to burn their chief magistrate alive in a bread riot, in order to obtain a graphic understanding of the social and economic causes predisposing to decline and fall.

Intellectually, we must consider under the Empire the decline of rationalism and scientific thought, the increase of superstition, and the use of literature for propaganda. All these considerations taken together produce a picture of what we nowadays call totalitarianism, and men of good will are laboring manfully to see that no such picture may ever be drawn of our society.

Second, the important thing is not what fell but what lasted: the transmission of Greek thought, of Roman law and equity; the political ideal of "one world-wide family all akin to Rome," living under law and order, under a regime which shall curb individual power and protect collective activity by a just administration; the intellectual ideal of the rule of reason, proof against excesses alike of preciosity, pedantry, and mysticism; the unselfish moral and religious ideals of paganism and Christianity at their best. That the Roman world did not always live up to its ideals this survey has abundantly shown, but it stated them, and its failures can still provide a challenge to our time.

Conclusion

These soberly optimistic considerations bring us to the end of a long story, and one worth the telling if it has brought us to think beyond yesterday. It will have served its purpose if it has persuaded us that man's story is not one of continuous progress, that material progress matters less than spiritual advance, and that spiritual advance is not the product of wishful thinking but of dedicated unselfish work by many minds of many men of good will. It will have served its purpose if it induces in us a proper sense of humility in the face of man's successes— and his failures—in the past, a decent sense of perspective, of knowing our place in space and time, combined with a high resolve to learn from the triumphs and profit from the shortcomings of our past.

The tale may seem to many to be one of unrelieved violence, woe, and pain, of man's inhumanity to man, and indeed this is an aspect of history that needs to be contemplated seriously, not least by those who aspire to make the future better, in more than a material sense, than the past. We need, to this end, to reflect upon Egyptian rigidity, Jewish fanaticism, Assyrian cruelty, Spartan military despotism, Athenian narrowness and apathy, Republican Rome's rapacity, the Empire's fiddling while Rome burned. We need too to reflect upon the sorry history of war, violence and persecution and assassination: war prisoners in chains working upon the pyramids, Jews deported, Troy in flames, Athens fallen, Hannibal ravaging South Italy, the Parthian dipping Crassus' severed head in blood, Christians smeared with pitch and crucified. For all this is a part of man's past, and, if it seems to us a sorry business, we may be goaded into the high resolve to do our part to make the history of the next millennia a less tragic story.

But this is negative. There have been triumphs and exalted moments to record also, moments of victory for the human mind. We remember the humanitarian Code of Hammurabi, the idealism of Ikhnaton, the fervor of the Hebrew prophets; the *joie de vivre* of Minoan art, the democratic greatness of Periclean Athens, the keenness and courage of Socrates, Alexander's dream of the brotherhood of man, the foursquare sturdiness of old Cato, the humanity of Tiberius Gracchus, the gentle sadness of Vergil, the fiery conviction of St. Paul, the Stoic intensity of Marcus Aurelius, the logic and equity of the Roman jurists. These are men and ideas to make us proud to belong to the human race, and they are part of the living heritage of antiquity, a perpetual positive challenge to us to equal or surpass these achievements.

And so we come to the end of our inquiry into the deeds of man's past which have made his present and will shape his future, knowledge of which we arrive at by interpreting evidence, often equivocal, to the end that we may know ourselves, may know where we have been so that we can chart where we are going. Now, not being ignorant of our past, we are not doomed to repeat it. More positively, we know now that we stand heirs to a great tradition, that we need to make ourselves worthy of man's past achievements, proud of man's past successes, alert against the causes of his failures. The achievements are of mind, working out the greatest good of the community as a whole. The failures come from an emotional atmosphere of hysteria, fear, thought-control, jealousy, ambition, and ignorance. Ancient man at his best rose above these pettinesses, and so can we. If we learn from ancient history the lesson of mind's capabilities, it will give more wisdom to the wise, more human sympathy to those capable of it, and new opportunities of admiring and renewing in fruitful action some of the greatest achievements of mankind. We cannot do better than to end with the words of Pericles, one of the ancient world's greatest statesmen, "Knowing freedom to be happiness, and courage the creator of freedom, let us fear no risks, but rival what these men have done."

CHRONOLOGICAL TABLE

DATES FOR PREHISTORY are approximate and in a state of flux. Ancient Near Eastern absolute dates, especially before 2000 B.C., are still the subject of debate; the table follows Pritchard (see *Suggested Additional Reading*, p. 758). Greek and Roman dates are firmer, but slight variants due to different interpretations of ancient calendars still occur. In the list below an attempt has been made to follow the latest and best authorities. For an alternative survey of ancient history by dates, see W. L. Langer, ed., *An Encyclopedia of World History*, rev. ed., Boston, 1956.

B. C. (all dates approximate)

6000	Neolithic Age in the Aegean
4500–4000	Earliest habitation at Ugarit
3100	Merger of Two Kingdoms of Egypt
3100–2650	Dynasties I–III
3000–2200	Early Minoan Age in Crete
2650–2500	Dynasty IV in Egypt
2600	Ur-Nanshe King of Lagash
2500–2350	Dynasty V in Egypt
2400	Bronze Age begins in Crete
2375	Urukagina King of Lagash
2350	Sargon I King of Akkad
2350–2200	Dynasty VI in Egypt
2200	End of Egyptian Old Kingdom
2200–2000	Dynasties VII–XI in Egypt
2200–1600	Middle Minoan Age in Crete
2070	Gudea King of Lagash
2060–2038	Ur-Nammu King of Ur
2038–1990	Shulgi King of Ur
2000–1800	Middle Kingdom in Egypt (Dynasty XII)
1991–1961	Amenemhet I Pharaoh in Egypt
1972–1947	Ibbi-Sin King of Ur
1929–1894	Amenemhet II
1900	Alphabetic writing devised by Semites working Sinai mines
1878–1840	Senusret III Pharaoh in Egypt
1730–1570	Hyksos rule in Egypt
1728–1686	Hammurabi King of Babylon
1700	Earthquake devastates central Crete
1685–1648	Samsu-Iluna King of Babylon
1600–1200	Late Minoan Age in Crete
1570–1545	Ahmose I Pharaoh in Egypt (Dynasty XVIII)
1545–1525	Amenhotep I
1525–1495	Thutmose I
1525–1500	Telepinus King of Hittites
1495–1490	Thutmose II Pharaoh in Egypt
1490–1436	Thutmose III
1465–1165	Egyptian Empire
1459	Thutmose III takes Carchemish
1450	Mainland Greeks attack Knossos
1439–1406	Amenhotep II Pharaoh in Egypt
1398–1361	Amenhotep III
1390–1354	Suppiluliumas King of the Hittites
1369–1353	Amenhotep IV (Ikhnaton) Pharaoh in Egypt
1352–1344	Tutankhamen
1350	Height of Mycenaean civilization: Treasury of Atreus
1302–1290	Seti I Pharaoh in Egypt (Dynasty XIX)
1300	Hebrew Exodus from Egypt

1293–1270	Hattusilis III King of the Hittites
1290–1224	Ramses II Pharaoh in Egypt
1286	Battle of Kadesh
1279	Treaty of friendship between Hatti and Egypt
1247	Assyrians sack Babylon
1224–1214	Merneptah Pharaoh in Egypt
1195–1164	Ramses III
1180	Destruction of Troy
1114–1078	Tiglath-Pileser I King of Assyria
1100	Dorian invasion of Greece
1020–1005	Saul King of the Hebrews
1005–965	David
1000	Villanovans invade Etruria and Umbria; Latins settle Alban Hills and Palatine
1000–800	Etruscans settle in Etruria
965–925	Solomon King of the Hebrews
883–859	Ashurnasirpal II King of Assyria
873–852	Elijah prophet in Israel
852–781	Elisha
814	Tyre founds Carthage
800–500	Period of Greek colonization
800	Homer flourishes; Hesiod's *Works and Days* Sabine village on Esquiline Hill, Rome
798–753	Amos prophet in Israel
781	Hosea
776	First Olympic Games
767–686	Isaiah prophet in Judah
753	Legendary date of founding of Rome
753–716	Romulus
750	Cumae founded
745–727	Tiglath-Pileser III King of Assyria
739–693	Micah prophet in Judah
734	Tiglath-Pileser III invades Syria and Israel
725–705	Sparta's First Messenian War
722–705	Sargon II King of Assyria
722	Sargon II destroys Samaria Merodach-baladan unifies Chaldeans
715–672	Numa Pompilius King of Rome
711	Archilochus of Paros, satirist, flourishes

709	Sargon II drives Merodach-baladan from Babylon
708–655	Deioces chieftain of Medes
707	Taras (Tarentum) founded
704–681	Sennacherib King of Assyria
701	Sennacherib besieges Jerusalem
691	Battle of Halule
683	Gyges usurps Lydian throne
680–669	Esarhaddon King of Assyria
676	Esarhaddon destroys Sidon
672–640	Tullus Hostilius King of Rome
671	Esarhaddon destroys Memphis
668–633	Ashurbanipal III King of Assyria
664	Sea battle between Corinth and Corcyra
663–609	Psamtik Pharaoh in Egypt
661	Ashurbanipal sacks Egyptian Thebes
654–611	Alcman, lyric poet, flourishes in Sparta
650	Earliest official coined money in Greece Zaleucus of Locri, lawgiver, flourishes
650–550	Tyranny flourishes on Greek mainland
649	Ashurbanipal burns Babylon
646	Ashurbanipal destroys Susa
641–586	Jeremiah prophet in Judah
640–620	Sparta's Second Messenian War
640–616	Ancus Marcius King of Rome
633–584	Cyaxares King of Medes
631 or 628	Curse of the Alcmaeonidae at Athens
630	Dorians found Cyrene
629–553	Stesichorus of Himera, dithyrambic poet
628–625	Arion of Lesbos, dithyrambic poet, flourishes
625–605	Nabopolassar King of Chaldean Babylon
621	Josiah destroys last tribal shrines
621	Draco lawgiver in Athens
620	Alcaeus of Lesbos, lyric poet, born
616–578	Tarquin I King of Rome

612	Fall of Nineveh	514	Hipparchus assassinated in Athens
	Sappho of Lesbos, lyric poetess, born	512	Darius' Scythian expedition
610	Anaximander of Miletus, philosopher, born	510	Tyrant Hippias expelled from Athens
609–594	Necho Pharaoh in Egypt	509	Founding of Roman Republic
608–597	Jehoiakim King of Judah		
608	Battle of Megiddo	508	Cleisthenes' reforms ratified in Athens
605	Battle of Carchemish; end of Assyria	500–428	Anaxagoras of Clazomenae, philosopher
604–562	Nebuchadrezzar II King of Chaldean Empire	500	Marzabotto, Etruscan city, flourishes
597	Nebuchadrezzar invests Jerusalem; Jedekiah King of Judah		Hecataeus of Miletus, geographer, flourishes
594/3 *	Solon archon in Athens		Alcmaeon of Croton, medical writer, flourishes
586	Jerusalem besieged and taken: "Babylonian exile"		Heraclitus of Ephesus, philosopher, flourishes
Before 585	Thales of Miletus, philosopher, flourishes	499	Ionian revolt
582–507	Pythagoras of Samos, philosopher	498	Burning of Sardis
		496–406	Sophocles of Athens, tragic poet
580	Acragas, in Sicily, founded	494	Greek navy defeated at Lade; Miletus falls to Persia
578–534	Servius Tullius King of Rome		First secession of plebs in Rome
570	Xenophanes of Elea, philosopher, born	493	Foedus Cassianum
	Anacreon of Teos, lyric poet, born	493–433	Empedocles of Acragas, philosopher
569–546	Croesus King of Lydia	490	Battle of Marathon
565	Naucratis founded		Zeno of Elea, philosopher, born
560–527	Pisistratus tyrant in Athens		
556–468	Simonides of Ceos, lyric poet	490–417	Phidias of Athens, sculptor
550	Beginning of Peloponnesian League	487/6	First recorded ostracism in Athens; archonship by lot begins
549–529	Cyrus I King of Medes and Persians		
546	Anaximenes of Miletus, philosopher, flourishes	485–465	Xerxes King of Persia
		484–428	Herodotus of Halicarnassus, historian
544–541	Theognis of Megara, elegiac poet, flourishes	481–411	Protagoras of Abdera, "sophist"
539	Cyrus takes Babylon	480	Battles of Thermopylae, Salamis, and Himera
535	Battle of Alalia		
534	Thespis wins prize for tragedy in Athens	480–445	Myron, Greek sculptor, flourishes
534–509	Tarquin the Proud King of Rome	480–406	Euripides of Athens, tragic poet
529–522	Cambyses King of Persia	479	Battles of Plataea and Mycale
525	Death of Croesus		
525–456	Aeschylus of Athens, tragic poet	478/7	Delian League established
521–486	Darius I King of Persia	476/5	Eion captured
518–438	Pindar of Thebes, lyric poet	474	Etruscan naval defeat at Cumae
515	Parmenides of Elea, philosopher, born	474/3	Athens conquers Skyros

* Attic civil year began in midsummer; hence fractional dates.

470	Themistocles ostracized
469	Athens subjects Naxos
469–399	Socrates of Athens, philosopher
468 or 467	Battle of the Eurymedon
465–463	Athens subjects Thasos
465	Aeschylus' *Prometheus Bound*
464	Earthquake destroys Sparta
462/1	Ephialtes assassinated in Athens
461/0	Cimon ostracized
460	Temple of Zeus, Olympia, dedicated
460–400	Thucydides of Athens, historian
459	Athens settles Messenians at Naupactus
459–380	Lysias of Athens, speech-writer
458	Aeschylus' *Oresteia*; Athens builds Long Walls; Corinth declares war on Athens Cincinnatus, dictator in Rome, defeats the Aequi
458/7	Archonship in Athens open to Zeugites
457	Athenian defeat at Tanagra; Aegina surrenders to Athens
454	Delian League treasury moved to Athens; Tribute Lists begin (to 414); Athens has friendly diplomatic relations with Naples; Athenian naval disaster on the Nile
454	Phidias' chryselephantine statue at Olympia
452–415	Polyclitus, Greek sculptor, flourishes
451	Twelve Tables at Rome Law of Pericles restricting Athenian citizenship
450–385	Aristophanes of Athens, comic poet
449/8	Peace of Callias between Athens and Persia
448–446	Abortive Athenian attempts at hegemony over central Greece
447	Pericles proposes Panhellenic Congress; Parthenon begun
446	Athens signs Thirty-years' Peace with Sparta
445	Syracuse defeats Acragas

443	Thucydides son of Milesias ostracized from Athens; Thurii colonized Censors instituted in Rome
442	Sophocles writing *Antigone*
437	Propylaea begun in Athens
436–338	Isocrates of Athens, rhetorician
435	Rome captures Fidenae
432	Parthenon finished
431–421, 414–404	Peloponnesian War
431	Euripides' *Medea*; Pericles' *Funeral Oration*
430	Athens takes Potidaea
430–354	Xenophon of Athens, historian
429	Sophocles' *Oedipus the King*; Pericles dies in the plague
429–347	Plato of Athens, philosopher
427	Gorgias of Leontini, rhetorician, comes to Athens
425	Jury pay raised in Athens; Cleon takes Sphacteria
424	Conference of Gela; Aristophanes' *Knights*
424–405	Darius II King of Persia
423	Aristophanes' *Clouds*
422	Aristophanes' *Wasps*; Cleon killed in battle
421	Peace of Nicias; Aristophanes' *Peace*
420–406	Erechtheum building in Athens
418	Nicias elected general; Alcibiades the defeated candidate
417	Hyperbolus ostracized
416	Athens destroys Melos
415–413	Sicilian Expedition
413–399	Archelaus King of Macedon
412–411	Constitution of the Four Hundred at Athens
411	Aristophanes' *Lysistrata* and *Thesmophoriazusae* Peloponnesian fleet crippled at Cynossema and Abydos
410	Peloponnesian fleet annihilated at Cyzicus
409	Carthaginians attack Himera
406	Lysander defeats Athenians at Notium; Athenians defeat Spartans at Arginusae. Aristophanes' *Frogs*
406–367	Dionysius I tyrant of Syracuse

405	Dionysius makes peace with Carthage
404	Athenians defeated at Aegospotami
404–358	Artaxerxes II King of Persia
404–403	Thirty Tyrants: reign of terror in Athens
401–399	Expedition of the Ten Thousand
397	Carthaginians threaten Syracuse Great Harbor
396	Romans capture Veii
395	Sparta declares war on Thebes; Battle of Haliartus; Lysander killed
395–386	Corinthian War
394	Battles of Cnidus and Coronea
390	Gauls capture Rome
	Isocrates founds school in Athens
387	Plato's Academy founded
386	The King's Peace
384	Demosthenes and Aristotle born
380	Isocrates' *Panegyricus*
379	Dionysius I conquers Croton
377	Second Athenian Confederation founded
371	Peace of Callias; Sparta defeated at Leuctra; Epaminondas Boeotarch
370	Megalopolis founded
369–285	Theophrastus of Athens, philosopher
366–345	Dionysius II tyrant of Syracuse
366	First praetors and curule aediles in Rome
362	Battle of Mantinea
359–336	Philip II King of Macedon
358–338	Artaxerxes III King of Persia
357–355	Social War
357	Isocrates' *Areopagiticus* (or 355)
355	Isocrates' *On the Peace*
354	Dion of Syracuse murdered
353	Mausoleum of Halicarnassus begun
348	Olynthus destroyed
346	Peace of Philocrates
345–337	Timoleon active in Sicily
343–341	Rome's First Samnite War
343	Artaxerxes III of Persia conquers Egypt
	Hermes of Praxiteles
342–291	Menander of Athens, comic poet
342–271	Epicurus of Samos and Athens, philosopher
341	Demosthenes' *Third Philippic*
339	Isocrates' *Panathenaicus*
338	Battle of Chaeronea
	Rome dissolves Latin League
336–330	Darius III King of Persia
336–323	Alexander III (the Great) King of Macedon
335	Alexander destroys Thebes; Aristotle teaching in Lyceum at Athens
335–263	Zeno of Citium, Stoic philosopher
334	Battle of the Granicus
333	Battle of Issus; Alexander's siege of Tyre; conquest of Egypt
331	Battle of Gaugamela; Alexandria founded in Egypt
330	Demosthenes' *On the Crown*; Alexander has Philotas executed
330–327	Alexander in central Asia
327–325	Alexander in India
326–304	Rome's Second Samnite War
322	Demosthenes and Aristotle die; battle of Crannon
319	Death of Macedonian general Antipater
318–307	Demetrius of Phalerum strategos in Athens
317	Philip Arrhidaeus murdered
317–289	Agathocles tyrant of Syracuse
313	Zeno comes to Athens
312	Appian Way begun
310–250	Theocritus of Cos and Syracuse, pastoral poet
310	Alexander IV of Macedon murdered
310–230	Aristarchus of Samos, astronomer
307–303, 297–272	Pyrrhus King of Epirus
306	Epicurus opens school in Athens; battle of Salamis (Cyprus)
304–283	Ptolemy I Soter King of Egypt
301	Battle of Issus
300	Euclid of Alexandria, geometrician, flourished

298–290	Rome's Third Samnite War	243	Achaean League takes Acro-
295	Battle of Sentinum		corinth
295–247	Apollonius of Rhodes, epic	242	First praetor peregrinus ap-
	poet		pointed in Rome
293–261	Antiochus I Soter ruler of	241	Battle of Aegates Islands
	Seleucid Empire	241–197	Attalus I King of Perga-
291	Rome founds Latin colony		mum
	at Venusia	241	Roman comitia tributa
289	Mamertines seize Messana		reaches total of 35 tribes
288	Demetrius I Poliorcetes loses	239–229	Demetrius II King of Mace-
	Greece		don
287	Lex Hortensia abolishes Ro-	239–169	Ennius, Roman epic poet
	man Senate's right to veto	235–222	Cleomenes III King of Sparta
	plebiscites	234–149	Cato the Elder, Roman
284–204	Livius Andronicus, Greek		statesman
	writer of epic in Latin	230	Attalus I routs the Gauls
283	Demetrius I Poliorcetes dies	229/8	Athens transfers sympathies
283–239	Antigonus II Gonatas King		to Egypt
	of Macedon		Rome establishes protector-
283–246	Ptolemy II Philadelphus		ate over coastal belt in Al-
	King of Egypt		bania
281	Lysimachus, tyrant of	227–221	Antigonus III Doson King
	Thrace, dies		of Macedon
280–198	Achaean League flourishes	227	Sicily, Sardinia, Corsica be-
280	Appius Claudius' oration		come Roman provinces; 2
	against peace with Pyrrhus		praetors added
279	Gauls invade Macedon	223–187	Antiochus III King of Syria
277	Antiochus I defeats the	222	Battle of Sellasia: Antigonus
	Gauls		crushes Cleomenes
275–194	Eratosthenes of Cyrene,	221–179	Philip V King of Macedon
	polymath	221	Circus of Flaminius dedi-
273	Egypt offers Rome a friend-		cated in Rome
	ship treaty	218–201	Second Punic War
272	Pyrrhus of Epirus killed in	218	Battles of Ticinus and Tre-
	Argos		bia
271–213	Aratus of Sicyon, general of	217	Battle of L. Trasimene; bat-
	Achaean League (from 245)		tle of Raphia
270–189	Aetolian League flourishes		Worship of Venus Erycina
270	Death of Queen Arsinoe II		introduced into Rome
	of Egypt	216	Battle of Cannae
270–215	Hiero II reigns in Syracuse	214–129	Carneades of Cyrene, phi-
270–201	Naevius, Roman epic poet		losopher
266–262	Chremonidean War	214–205	First Macedonian War
264–241	First Punic War	206	Scipio Africanus founds
263–241	Eumenes I ruler of Perga-		Italica in Spain
	mum	204	Worship of Cybele intro-
262	Romans capture Agri-		duced into Rome
	gentum	203–120	Polybius of Megalopolis,
260	Carthaginian naval defeat		historian
	off Mylae	202	Battle of Zama
258	Antigonus Gonatas sweeps	200–197	Second Macedonian War
	Egyptian fleets from the	198	Seleucids conquer Palestine
	Aegean		and southern Syria
254–184	Plautus, Roman comic poet	197–160	Eumenes II King of Perga-
249	Battle of Drepana		mum
247	Kingdom of Parthia founded	197	Roman praetors increased to
244–241	Agis IV King of Sparta		6; provinces of Two Spains

	created; battle of Cynoscephalae
196	Flamininus declares "freedom" of Greece
195–159	Terence, Roman comic poet
194	Sex. Aelius Paetus Catus, distinguished Roman jurist, censor (cos. 198)
193	Porticus Aemilia built in Rome
192–189	Roman war with Antiochus
191	Battle of Thermopylae
189	Battle of Magnesia
188	Peace of Apamea; Rome gives most of Seleucid Asia Minor to Pergamum
186–181	Roman Senate stamps out Bacchanals
185–109	Panaetius of Rhodes, philosopher
184–169	Basilicas (Porcia, Aemilia, Sempronia) built in Rome
183	Hannibal commits suicide
180–102	Lucilius, Roman satirist
175–163	Antiochus IV Epiphanes Seleucid King
174	Roman architect plans Olympieum at Athens
173	Philosophers and rhetoricians banished from Rome
171–167	Third Macedonian War *
170–85	Accius, Roman tragic poet
169	Ti. Sempronius Gracchus the Elder censor; Achaean hostages taken to Rome
168	Battle of Pydna
166	Rome makes Delos a free port
161	Maccabean alliance with Rome; philosophers and rhetoricians again banished from Rome
161–126	Hipparchus of Nicaea, astronomer, working
159	Unauthorized statues removed from Roman Forum
153	Inaugural date for Roman provincial praetors advanced from March 15 to January 1
150?	Upper Sanctuary of Fortune at Praeneste (or Sullan)
150	Leges Aelia et Fufia, on use of auspices by Roman magistrates
149–148	Third Macedonian War; province of Macedonia created

* See text.

149	Extortions court set up in Rome
146	Romans destroy Carthage and Corinth; province of Africa created
144	Panaetius comes to Rome
142	First arched bridge over Tiber
141	Parthians in Mesopotamia
139	Astrologers and Jews expelled from Rome
137	Hostilius Mancinus besieged in Numantia (fell 133)
135–51	Posidonius of Apamea, philosopher
133	Ti. Gracchus tribune
132	Slave revolt in Sicily
129	Scipio Aemilianus dies; province of Asia created
126	Law bars noncitizens from Roman towns
125	Revolt and razing of Fregellae
123–122	Tribunate of C. Gracchus
122	L. Drusus tribune
121	Province of Narbonensis created; C. Gracchus dies; colony planted on Majorca
118	Colony planted at Narbo
116–27	M. Terentius Varro, Roman polymath
113	Cimbri defeat Romans at Noreia
111–105	Jugurthine War
107	First consulship of Marius
106–43	Cicero, Roman statesman and orator
105	Cimbri defeat Romans at Arausio
104–100	Marius consul
102	Marius defeats Teutons and Ambrones at Aquae Sextiae; Julius Caesar born; Cilicia made a Roman province
101	C. Servilius Glaucia tribune; Marius destroys Cimbri at Vercellae
100	Slave revolt put down in Sicily; second tribunate of Saturninus; bill proposed for colonies to include Italians; murder of Saturninus and Glaucia
94–55	Lucretius, Roman philosophical poet

94	Parthian alliance with Mithridates		50–16	Propertius, elegiac poet
91	Livius Drusus the Younger, tribune, murdered		49	Caesar crosses Rubicon
			48	Battle of Pharsalus; Pompey murdered at Alexandria
91–88	Social War		48–19	Tibullus, elegiac poet
89–85	First Mithridatic War		47	Battle of Zela
87–84	Cinna consul		46	Battle of Thapsus; Cato suicide; Julian calendar begins
86	Marius' seventh consulship and death		45	Battle of Munda
86–34	Sallust, Roman historian		44	Caesar murdered; Dacian King Burebistas murdered
84–54	Catullus, lyric poet		43–A.D. 17	Ovid, poet
82–79	Sulla dictator		43	Second Triumvirate; battle of Mutina; Cicero murdered
81	Pompey successful against Marians in Sicily and Africa		42	Battle of Philippi; Octavian dedicates Temple of Deified Julius, vows temple to Mars the Avenger
80	Lower area at Praeneste built			
78	Sulla dies; Tabularium built in Rome		36	Mark Antony in Armenia; Octavian receives tribunician power
77	Pompey's command in Spain			
73–71	Revolt of Spartacus and the gladiators		31	Battle of Actium
70–19	Vergil, epic poet		30	Octavian assumes tribune's right to protect citizens
70	Fall of Sullan constitution; Pompey and Crassus consuls; Cicero *Against Verres*		30–A.D. 45	Philo, Jewish philosopher
			29	Arch of Octavian; Temple of Janus closed
67	Gabinian Law gives Pompey extraordinary command against pirates		27	Octavian assumes title of **Augustus;** first Privy Council
66	Manilian Law gives Pompey Eastern command		27–23	Porticus Octaviae built
65–8	Horace, lyric poet		23	Augustus assumes full tribunician power
63	Cicero consul; conspiracy of Catiline; Caesar praetor and pontifex maximus; Octavian born; Syria organized as province; Temple of Hercules, Tibur		22	Augustus revives censorship
			20	Tiberius regains Crassus' standards from Parthians
			19	Fasti added to Arch of Augustus in Roman Forum
			17	Secular games
62	Pompey returns to Italy		16–13	Augustus resident in Gaul
61	Caesar propraetor in Spain		16–A.D. 9	Noricum and Pannonia annexed
60	First Triumvirate			
59–A.D. 17	Livy, historian		15	Tiberius and Drusus add Rhaetia to Empire
59	Caesar consul			
58–50	Caesar's conquest of Gaul		13	Theater of Marcellus dedicated; Altar of Peace vowed
58–57	Cicero in exile			
56	Conference of Luca		12	Lepidus dies
55	Pompey's theater dedicated in Rome		9	Drusus dies; Altar of Peace dedicated
54	Cicero *De republica;* Julia dies; Basilica Aemilia restored		5–A.D. 65	Seneca, philosopher
			4–A.D. 30	Jesus of Nazareth
53	Crassus dies at Carrhae; Parthians capture Roman standards		2	Augustus saluted as Father of His Country
			A. D.	
52	Clodius murdered; Caesar permitted to seek consulship *in absentia*		5	Lex Valeria Cornelia gives prerogatives to 10 chosen centuries

6	Rome's fire department organized; Moesia organized as a province	114–117	Parthian War
		115	Jewish revolt destroys Salamis (Cyprus)
9	Battle of Teutoberg Forest	117–138	**Reign of Hadrian**
14	Augustus dies	117–189	Aelius Aristides, "sophist"
14–37	**Reign of Tiberius**	120	Pantheon building
19	Earthquake devastates Sardis	120–after 180 Lucian, satirist	
		123–165	Aulus Gellius, encyclopedist
23–79	Pliny the Elder, encyclopedist	123	Apuleius, novelist, born
		125–202	St. Irenaeus
26	Tiberius retires to Capri	129–199	Galen, medical writer
33	Financial panic in Rome	130	Hadrian promulgates *Edictum Perpetuum*
34–62	Persius, satirist		
35–95	Quintilian, rhetorician	131–134	Jewish War
37–41	**Reign of Gaius**	135	Temple of Venus and Rome
38	Josephus, Jewish historian, born	138–161	**Reign of Antoninus Pius**
		150	Pausanias, traveler and geographer, flourished
39–65	Lucan, epic poet		
40–104	Martial, epigrammatist	160–225	Tertullian, apologist
41–54	**Reign of Claudius**	161–180	**Reign of Marcus Aurelius**
43	Britain a province	162–166	Parthian War
44	Death of Herod Agrippa; Judaea annexed	166	Great Plague
		170–244	Flavius Philostratus Verus, biographer
46–after 120 Plutarch, biographer			
48	Claudius holds census	180–192	**Reign of Commodus**
50–130	Juvenal, satirist	185–254	Origen, theologian
54–68	**Reign of Nero**	193	**Reigns of Pertinax and Didius Julianus**
55–117	Tacitus, historian		
55–135	Epictetus, philospher	193–211	**Reign of Septimius Severus**
61–113	Pliny the Younger, letter-writer	195–198	Parthian War
		197	Clodius Albinus' revolt in Gaul
64	Great Fire in Rome		
67	Nero sends Vespasian to Palestine	200	Paulus, jurist, flourished
		203	Papinian becomes praetorian prefect
69	**Reigns of Galba, Otho, Vitellius**		
		205–269	Plotinus, philosopher
69–79	**Reign of Vespasian**	208–211	War in Britain
69–140	Suetonius, biographer	212–217	**Reign of Caracalla**
70	Titus sacks Jerusalem; Helvidius Priscus praetor	212	*Constitutio Antoniniana* universalizes Roman citizenship
75–82	Coliseum building		
79–81	**Reign of Titus**		
79	Eruption of Vesuvius destroys Pompeii	217–218	**Reign of Macrinus** (first equestrian emperor)
81–96	**Reign of Domitian**	218–222	**Reign of Elagabalus**
85	Dacian revolt under Decebalus	222–235	**Reign of Severus Alexander**
		224–636	Sassanid dynasty in Parthia
95–175	Arrian, historian	224	Revolt of Ardashir
96–98	**Reign of Nerva**	228	Ulpian, jurist, dies
98–117	**Reign of Trajan**	234–235	War with Alemanni
100–165	Justin Martyr, writer of Christian apologetics	235–285	Military anarchy
		235–238	**Reign of Maximinus**
100–169	Salvius Julianus, jurisconsult	238–244	**Reign of Gordian III**
101–102 ⎱	Dacian Wars	241–272	Shapur I King of Parthia
105–106 ⎰		244–249	**Reign of Philip the Arab**

248	Celebration of millennium of Rome	348	Prudentius, poet, born
249–251	**Reign of Decius**	348–420	St. Jerome
250–317	Lactantius, theologian	353	Paulinus of Nola, poet, born
253–260	**Reign of Valerian**	353–360	**Reign of Constantius**
253–268	**Reign of Gallienus**	354–430	St. Augustine
253	Gothic invasion of Macedonia, Greece, and Asia Minor Shapur I captures Antioch	360–363	**Reign of Julian the Apostate**
		364–375	**Reign of Valentinian**
255	Shapur I destroys Dura garrison	364–378	**Reign of Valens**
		373	Ambrose Bishop of Milan
256	Franks invade Gaul and Spain	378–395	**Reign of Theodosius I**
		381	Council of Constantinople; Theodosius unseats all Arian bishops
259	Valerian marches on Mesopotamia		
260	Postumus proclaims Empire of the Gauls	385	Priscillian, Bishop of Lusitania, executed for heresy
		390	Massacre of Thessalonica
260–340	Eusebius, church historian	392	Edict of Theodosius forbids practice of pagan cults
264	Odaenathus of Palmyra regains Euphrates valley for Rome		
		395–408	**Reign of Arcadius in the East**
268–270	**Reign of Claudius II Gothicus**	395–423	**Reign of Honorius in the West**
269	Zenobia of Palmyra conquers Egypt	395–408	Stilicho regent
		395–430	Augustine Bishop of Hippo
270–275	**Reign of Aurelian**	395	Ausonius, poet, dies; Claudianus, poet, flourishes
270	Romans withdraw from Dacia		
271–275	Aurelian's Wall built round Rome	407	Romans evacuate Britain
		408–450	**Reign of Theodosius II in the East**
274	Aurelian reconquers Gaul		
275	**Reign of Tacitus**	410	Alaric sacks Rome
276–282	**Reign of Probus**	413–426	Augustine writing the *City of God*
284–305	**Reign of Diocletian**		
286–305	**Reign of Maximian**	417	Orosius' *Universal History*
293	Diocletian and Maximian adopt Galerius and Constantius Chlorus	425–455	**Reign of Valentinian III in the West**
		429	Vandals under Gaiseric invade Africa
301	Diocletian's Price Edict		
303	Edict of Persecution	438	Theodosian Code promulgated
306–337	**Reign of Constantine**		
307–324	**Reign of Licinius**	452	Attila and the Huns threaten Milan
312	Battle of Milvian Bridge		
313	Edict of Milan recognizes Christians	455	Gaiseric and Vandals sack Rome
314–393	Libanius, rhetorician	456–472	Suebian Ricimer Protector of Western Empire
317–388	Themistius, rhetorician		
324–330	Constantinople building	475–476	**Romulus Augustulus Western Emperor**
325	Council of Nicaea		
329–389	St. John Chrysostom	476	Odoacer proclaimed king in Italy
330	Ammianus Marcellinus, historian, born		
		527–565	**Reign of Justinian in the East**
332	Peace with Goths		
340–348	Ulfila Bishop to the Goths	530–534	Tribonian's commission edits *Corpus Juris Civilis*

SUGGESTED ADDITIONAL READING

THIS BOOK-LIST stresses recent books in English. Where older books and books in foreign languages are cited, they may be assumed to be of unusual importance, or, where marked with an asterisk, to have proved especially helpful in writing this book. For fuller bibliography, see the *Cambridge Ancient History;* Hermann Bengtson, *Einführung in die alte Geschichte* [2] * (Munich, 1953); Jean Marouzeau and Juliette Ernst, *L'année philologique* (Paris, annually); and John A Nairn, *Classical Hand-List* [3] (Oxford, Blackwell, 1953). More important than any of the books listed here are the primary sources, the ancient authors themselves. More and more of these are appearing in translation in cheap paperbound reprints; for a list, see *Classical Weekly* LI (1958), 100–110. The fullest series is the Loeb Classical Library (Harvard University Press).

General

Barker, Ernest, *From Alexander to Constantine.* Oxford, 1956.
———, G. N. Clark, P. Vaucher, *The European Inheritance.* 3 vols. Oxford, 1955.
*Bengtson, H., *Grosser Historischer Weltatlas.* Erster Teil: *Vorgeschichte und Altertum.* Munich, 1954.
Breasted, James H., *Ancient Times.*[2] Boston, 1935.
Bury, John B., and others (eds.), *Cambridge Ancient History.* 12 vols., 5 vols. of plates. Cambridge, England, 1923–39.
Caldwell, Wallace E., W. C. McDermott, *Readings in the History of the Ancient World.* New York, 1951.
Cary, Max, and others (eds.). *Oxford Classical Dictionary.* Oxford, 1949.
Cochrane, Charles N., *Christianity and Classical Culture.*[2] New York, 1944.
Collingwood, Robin G., *The Idea of History.* Oxford, 1946.
Daniel, Glyn E., *One Hundred Years of Archaeology.* London, 1950.
Eyre, E. (ed.), *European Civilization.* Vols. I and II. Oxford, 1934.
*Fraccaro, Plinio, *Atlante Storico.* Fasc. I: *Evo Antico.* Novara (reprint), 1956.
Grant, Michael, *Ancient History.* London, 1952.
Harvey, Sir Paul, *Oxford Companion to Classical Literature.* Oxford, 1937.
Highet, Gilbert, *The Classical Tradition.* New York, 1949.
Langer, William L., *Encyclopedia of World History.* Revised ed. Boston, 1956.
Marrou, H. I., *A History of Education in Antiquity.* London, 1956.
Muller, H. J., *The Uses of the Past.* Oxford, 1952.
Toynbee, Arnold J., *A Study of History.* Abridgment by D. C. Somervell. 2 vols. Oxford, 1948–57.

* Superior numbers refer to editions.

Westermann, W. L., *The Slave Systems of Greek and Roman Antiquity*. Philadelphia, 1955.

Primitive Man

Bataille, Georges, *Lascaux, or the Birth of Art*. Lausanne, 1955.
Braidwood, R. J., *Prehistoric Men*. Chicago, 1948.
Childe, V. Gordon, *What Happened in History*. Harmondsworth, 1942.
———, "Prehistory," in Barker, E., *Eur. Inher.* (cited above), I, 3–86.
Clarke, J. G. D., *From Savagery to Civilization*. London, 1946.
Hawkes, Christopher F. C., *The Prehistoric Foundations of Europe to the Mycenaean Age*. London, 1940.
Howells, William, *Mankind So Far*. New York, 1945.
Zeuner, Frederick E., *Dating the Past*.[2] London, 1950.

The Ancient Near East

Chiera, Edward, *They Wrote on Clay*. Chicago (reprint), 1956.
Childe, V. Gordon, in Barker, E., *Eur. Inher.*, I, 87–132.
*Delaporte, L., *Les peuples de l'orient méditerranéen*. Vol. I: *Le proche orient asiatique*. Paris (reprint), 1948.
Dentan, R. C. (ed.). *The Idea of History in the Ancient Near East*. New Haven, 1955.
*Drioton, E., J. Vandier, *Les peuples de l'orient méditerranéen*. Vol. II: *L'Egypte*.[3] Paris, 1952.
Frankfort, Henri, *The Birth of Civilization in the Near East*. New York (reprint), 1956.
Frankfort, H., and others, *The Intellectual Adventure of Ancient Man*. Chicago, 1946. Reprinted as *Before Philosophy*. Harmondsworth, 1949.
Gaster, Theodor H., *The Scriptures of the Dead Sea Sect*. London, 1957.
*Gurney, O., *The Hittites*. Harmondsworth, 1952.
Kramer, Samuel N., *From the Tablets of Sumer*. Indian Hills, Colorado, 1956.
Marek, K. W. (pseudonym, C. W. Ceram), *The Secret of the Hittites,* New York, 1956.
*Orlinsky, H. M., *Ancient Israel*. Ithaca, 1954.
Pritchard, James B., *Ancient Near Eastern Texts Relating to the Old Testament*.[2] Princeton, 1955.
———, *The Ancient Near East in Pictures*. Princeton, 1954.
*Speiser, Ephraim A., *The United States and the Near East*.[2] Cambridge, Mass., 1950.
*Wilson, John A., *The Burden of Egypt*. Chicago, 1951. Reprinted as *The Culture of Ancient Egypt*.[3] Chicago, 1956.

Greece: General

Botsford, George W., E. H. Sihler, *Hellenic Civilization*. New York, 1920.
Hammond, N. G. L., *A History of Greece*. Oxford, 1958.
*Whibley, Leonard (ed.), *Companion to Greek Studies*.[4] Cambridge, 1931.

Greece: Minoan and Mycenaean Civilization

Forsdyke, J., *Greece Before Homer*. London, 1956.
Lorimer, H. L., *Homer and the Monuments*. London, 1950.

Mylonas, George, *Ancient Mycenae*. Princeton, 1957.

Nilsson, Martin P., *Homer and Mycenae*. London, 1933.

Pendlebury, J. D. S., *The Archaeology of Crete*. London, 1939.

——, *A Handbook to the Palace of Minos at Cnossos*. London, 1954.

Ventris, Michael, J. Chadwick, *Documents in Mycenaean Greek*. Cambridge, 1956.

Wace, A. J. B., *Mycenae*. Princeton, 1949.

Greek Political and Constitutional History

Andrewes, A., *The Greek Tyrants*. London, 1956.

*Bury, John B., *A History of Greece*. 3rd ed., revised by Russell Meiggs. London and New York, 1951.

Cary, Max, *A History of the Greek World 323–146 B.C.*[2] London, 1951.

Childe, V. Gordon, in Barker, E., *Eur. Inher.*, I, 133–148.

Chrimes, K. M. T., *Ancient Sparta*. London, 1949.

*Cohen, Robert, *La Grèce et l'hellenisation du monde antique.*[3] Paris, 1948.

De Ste. Croix, G. E. M., "The Character of the Athenian Empire," *Historia,* III (1954), 1–40.

Dunbabin, Thomas J., *The Western Greeks*. Oxford, 1948.

Gomme, Arnold W., "Greece," in Eyre, E., *European Civilization,* I (Oxford, 1934), 971–1245.

Grote, George, *History of Greece,* condensed and edited by J. M. Mitchell and M. O. B. Caspari. London, 1909.

Havelock, Eric A., *The Liberal Temper in Greek Politics*. New Haven, 1957.

*Hignett, C., *The Athenian Constitution*. Oxford, 1952.

Jones, A. H. M., *Athenian Democracy*. Oxford, 1957.

Laistner, M. L. W., *A History of the Greek World 478–373 B.C.* London, 1936.

Larsen, J. A. O., *Representative Government Amongst the Greeks*. Berkeley, 1955.

Tarn, William W., *Alexander the Great*. 2 vols. Cambridge, 1948.

Toynbee, Arnold J., *A Study of History,* III (London, 1934), 50–79 (on Sparta).

Zimmern, Alfred E., *The Greek Commonwealth.*[5] Oxford, 1931.

Greek Social and Economic History

Blakeway, A., "Prolegomena to the Study of Greek Commerce with Italy, Sicily, and France in the Eighth and Seventh Centuries B.C.," *Annual of the British School at Athens,* XXXIII (1935), 170–208.

Glotz, Gustav, *Ancient Greece at Work*. New York, 1926.

——, *The Greek City*. New York, 1929.

Gomme, A. W., *The Population of Athens*. Oxford, Blackwell, 1933.

*Gulick, Charles B., *The Life of the Ancient Greeks*. New York, 1902.

Meritt, Benjamin D., H. T. Wade-Gery, M. F. McGregor, *The Athenian Tribute Lists*. 4 vols. (esp. vol. III). Cambridge, Mass., 1939–52.

Rostovtzeff, M. I., *Social and Economic History of the Hellenistic World*. 3 vols. Oxford, 1941.

Seltman, C., *Greek Coins.*[2] London, 1955.

Greek Cultural History (Literature, Art, Architecture, Philosophy, Religion, and Law)

Agard, Walter R., *The Greek Mind*. Princeton, 1957.

Beazley, John D., B. Ashmole, *Greek Sculpture and Painting to the End of the Hellenistic Period*. Cambridge, 1932.

Bieber, Margarete, *The Sculpture of the Hellenistic Age*. New York, 1955.

Bonner, Robert J., Gertrude E. Smith, *The Administration of Justice from Homer to Aristotle*. 2 vols. Chicago, 1930–38.

Bowra, C. M., *The Greek Experience*. New York, 1958.

Dinsmoor, William B., *The Architecture of Ancient Greece*.[3] London, 1950.

Festugière, André J., *Epicurus and his Gods*. Cambridge, Mass., 1956.

Guthrie, William K. C., *The Greeks and their Gods*. London, 1950.

Hadas, Moses, *A History of Greek Literature*. New York, 1950.

Hamilton, Edith, *The Echo of Greece*. New York, 1957. (The fourth century).

Hatch, Edwin, *The Influence of Greek Ideas on Christianity*[2] (ed. F. C. Grant). New York, 1957.

Higham, Thomas F., C. M. Bowra (eds.). *The Oxford Book of Greek Verse in Translation*. Oxford, 1938.

Hill, Ida T., *The Ancient City of Athens*. Cambridge, Mass., 1953.

Jaeger, Werner, *Paideia* (tr. Gilbert Highet). 3 vols. Oxford, Blackwell, 1944–45.

Jones, J. Walter, *The Law and Legal Theory of the Greeks*. Oxford, 1956.

Kitto, H. D. F., *The Greeks*. Harmondsworth, 1951.

Lawrence, Arnold W., *Classical Sculpture*.[2] London, 1944.

MacKendrick, Paul, H. M. Howe, *Classics in Translation*. Vol. I (Greek). Madison, 1952.

Nilsson, Martin P., *Greek Piety*. Oxford, 1948.

Parke, Herbert W., D. E. W. Wormell, *The Delphic Oracle*.[2] 2 vols. Oxford, Blackwell, 1956.

Pfuhl, E., *Masterpieces of Greek Drawing and Painting*. London, 1926.

Pickard-Cambridge, Arthur W., *The Dramatic Festivals of Athens*. Oxford, 1953.

Plommer, Hugh, *Ancient and Classical Architecture*. London, 1956.

Richter, Gisela M. A., *The Sculpture and Sculptors of the Greeks*.[3] New Haven, 1950.

Robertson, Donald S., *Greek and Roman Architecture*. 2nd ed., corrected. Cambridge, 1954.

Seltman, Charles T., *Attic Vase Painting*. Cambridge, Mass., 1933.

Tarn, W. W., G. T. Griffith, *Hellenistic Civilisation*.[3] London, 1953.

Ure, Percy N., *The Greek Renaissance*. London, 1921 (Age of the Tyrants).

Webster, Thomas B. L., *Greek Art and Literature*. Oxford, 1939.

*———, *Art and Literature in Fourth Century Athens*. London, 1956.

Wycherley, R. E., *How the Greeks Built Cities*. London and New York, 1949.

Rome: General

Jones, Henry S., *Companion to Roman History*. Oxford, 1912.

Lewis, Naphtali, M. Reinhold, *Roman Civilization*. 2 vols. New York, 1951–55.

Sandys, Sir John E., *Companion to Latin Studies*.[3] Cambridge, 1921.

Early Italy

Pallottino, Massimo, *Etruscan Painting*. Lausanne, 1952.

*———, *The Etruscans*. Harmondsworth, 1955.

Randall-MacIver, David, *Italy Before the Romans*. Oxford, 1928.
Whatmough, Joshua, *The Foundations of Roman Italy*. London, 1937.

Roman Political and Constitutional History

*Aymard, André, *Rome et son empire*. Paris, 1954.
Broughton, T. Robert S., *The Magistrates of the Roman Republic*. 2 vols. New York, 1951–52.
Buchan, John, *Augustus*. Boston, 1937.
Burn, Andrew R., *The Government of the Roman Empire from Augustus to the Antonines*. London, 1952.
*Cary, Max, *A History of Rome*.² London, 1954.
Charlesworth, Martin P., *The Roman Empire*. London, 1951.
Collingwood, Robin G., J. N. L. Myres, *Roman Britain and the English Settlements*.² Oxford, 1937.
*Debevoise, N. C., *A Political History of Parthia*. Chicago, 1938.
von Fritz, Kurt, *The Mixed Constitution in Antiquity*. New York, 1954.
Gibbon, Edward, *The Decline and Fall of the Roman Empire*. Condensed ed. by Dero A. Saunders. New York, 1952.
Gomme, Arnold W., "The Roman Republic," in E. Eyre, *Eur. Civ.* (cited above), II (1935), 1–158.
Grant, Michael, *From Imperium to Auctoritas*. Cambridge, 1946.
Hammond, Mason, *City-State and World State*. Cambridge, Mass., 1951.
Haskell, H. J., *The New Deal in Old Rome*. New York, 1947.
Katz, Solomon, *The Decline of Rome and the Rise of Medieval Europe*. Ithaca, 1955.
Marsh, Frank B., *A History of the Roman World 146–30 B.C.* 2nd ed. rev. by H. H. Scullard. London, 1951.
McDonald, Alexander H., *The Rise of Roman Imperialism*. Sydney, 1940.
Miller, S. N., "The Roman Empire in the First Three Centuries," in E. Eyre (cited above), II, 283–521.
———, "The Church, the Later Empire, and the Barbarians," in E. Eyre (cited above), II, 603–672.
Parker, Henry M. D., *A History of the Roman World 138–337 A.D.* London, 1935.
*Piganiol, A., *L'Empire chrétien*. Paris, 1947.
*Piganiol, A., *Histoire de Rome*.⁴ Paris, 1954.
Previté-Orton, C., *The Shorter Cambridge Medieval History*. Vol. I. Cambridge, 1952.
*Salmon, Edward T., "The Evolution of Augustus' Principate," *Historia*. V (1956) 456–478.
———, *A History of the Roman World 30 B.C.–138 A.D.*² London, 1950.
Scramuzza, Vincent M., *The Emperor Claudius*. Cambridge, Mass., 1940.
Scullard, Howard H., *A History of the Roman World 753–146 B.C.*² London, 1951.
———, *Roman Politics, 220–150 B.C.* Oxford, 1951.
Sherwin-White, Adrian N., *The Roman Citizenship*. Oxford, 1939.
Smith, R. E., *The Failure of the Roman Republic*. Cambridge, 1955.
Starr, Chester G., *Civilization and the Caesars*.² Ithaca, 1954.
———, *The Emergence of Rome*. Ithaca, 1953.
*Stein, Ernst, *Geschichte de spätrömischen Reiches*. Vol. I. Vienna, 1928.
*Syme, Ronald, *The Roman Revolution*. Oxford, 1939.

*Tarn, William W., "Rome," in Barker, E., *Eur. Inher.* (cited above) I, 197–249.

Taylor, Lily R., *Party Politics in the Age of Caesar.* Berkeley, 1949.

Roman Social and Economic History

*Baynes, N. H., "The Decline of the Roman Power in Western Europe: Some Modern Explanations," *Journal of Roman Studies,* XXXIII (1943) 29–35.

Barrow, Reginald H., *The Romans.* Harmondsworth, 1949.

Boak, Arthur E. R., *Manpower Shortage and the Fall of the Roman Empire in the West.* Ann Arbor, 1955.

Cowell, F. R., *Cicero and the Roman Republic.* London, 1948. Reprint, with the excellent photographs but without the valuable charts, Harmondsworth, 1956.

Fowler, W. Warde, *Rome.* 2nd ed. rev. by M. P. Charlesworth. New York, 1947.

Frank, Tenney, *An Economic Survey of Ancient Rome.* 6 vols. Baltimore, 1933–40.

Johnston, Mary, *Roman Life.* Chicago, 1957.

Mattingly, Harold, *Roman Coins.* London, 1938.

Oliver, James H., "The Ruling Power," *Transactions of the American Philosophical Society,* XLIII (1953), 871–1003. Fascinating analysis of the panegyric of Rome by Aelius Aristides.

Rostovtzeff, Mikhail I., *Social and Economic History of the Roman Empire.* 2 vols. 2nd ed. rev. by Peter M. Fraser. Oxford, 1957.

*Walbank, Frank W., *The Decline of the Roman Empire in the West.* London, 1946.

Roman Cultural History

Anderson, William J., R. P. Spiers, T. Ashby, *Architecture of Ancient Rome.*[3] London, 1927.

Bigot, P., *Rome antique.*[2] Paris, 1955. Photographs of models of Imperial Rome.

Brendel, Otto, "Prolegomena to a Book on Roman Art," *Memoirs of the American Academy in Rome,* XXI (1953), 7–73.

Calza, Guido, *Ostia.*[3] Rome, 1955.

Clarke, M. L., *The Roman Mind.* Cambridge, Mass., 1956.

Curtius, Ludwig, A. Newrath, *Das antike Rom.* Vienna, 1944. Pictures; authoritative introduction and text.

Duff, J. Wight, *Literary History of Rome to the Close of the Golden Age.*[2] London and New York, 1953.

———, *Literary History of Rome in the Silver Age.*[2] London and New York, 1953.

Hadas, Moses, *Roman Literature.* New York, 1952.

Haskell, H. J., *This Was Cicero.* New York, 1950.

Jolowicz, H. F., *Historical Introduction to the Study of Roman Law.*[2] Cambridge, 1952.

———, *The Roman Foundations of Modern Law.* New York, 1957.

Laistner, M. L. W., *The Greater Roman Historians.* Berkeley, 1947.

MacKendrick, Paul, H. M. Howe, *Classics in Translation.* Vol. II (Roman). Madison, 1952.

———, *The Roman Mind at Work.* Princeton, 1958.

Maiuri, Amadeo, *Roman Painting.* Lausanne, 1953.

Mattingly, H., *Roman Imperial Civilization*. London, 1957.

Nash, Ernest, *Roman Towns*. New York, 1944.

Perret, J., *Virgile*. Paris, 1952.

Plommer, Hugh, *Ancient and Classical Architecture*. London, 1956.

Richter, Gisela M. A., *Ancient Italy*. Ann Arbor, 1955.

Robathan, Dorothy M., *The Monuments of Ancient Rome*. Rome, 1950.

Robertson, Donald S., *Greek and Roman Architecture* (cited above).

Rostovtzeff, M. I., *Caravan Cities*. Oxford, 1932.

————, *Dura-Europus and its Art*. Oxford, 1938.

Ryberg, Inez Scott, *An Archaeological Record of Rome from the Seventh to the Second Centuries B.C.* London, 1940.

————, *Rites of the State Religion in Roman Art,* Mem. Am. Acad. in Rome, XXII (1955).

*Sanctis, Gaetano de, *Storia dei Romani*. Vol. IV, Part ii, Vol. i. *Vita e pensiero nell' età delle grandi conquiste*. Florence, 1953.

Schulz, F., *Classical Roman Law*. Oxford, 1951.

Scott, Inez, "Early Roman Tradition in the Light of Archaeology," *Mem. Am. Acad. in Rome,* VII (1929), 1–116.

Strong, Eugénie, *Art in Ancient Rome*. 2 vols. New York, 1928.

Wolff, Hans J., *Roman Law: An Historical Interpretation*. Norman, Okla., 1951.

Index

Dancing girls, Temple of Hera, *168*
Darius, Alexander and, *330, 331*, 351, 352; attacks Greece, 209, 212–214; Ionians and, 209; Persian Empire of, 110–114, 346
Darius's audience hall, *112*
David, 79, 80
Dead Sea scrolls, *684*, 685
Decebalus, 648, 649
Decius, 714
Deioces, 103
Delian League, 224–227, 232, 234
Delphi, 171, 327, 328
demes (Attica), 202
Demeter, 144, 472; cults of, 171, 196–197, 328
Demetrius, of Phalerum, 360, 372
Demetrius, "Sacker-of-Cities," 372
democracy, Athenian, 200–207, 271, 275–276; beginnings of, 194–195; Cleisthenes and, 202; drama and, 257; growth of, 234–236; oligarch opposition to, 240–242; ostracism and, 281; post-Periclean, 277–278
Demosthenes, *311*, 312, 335, 338–339; in Peloponnesian War, 277–278, 285; Persian bribery of, 345; Philip and, 313–314, 339; Sacred War and, 312–314
Descent of Ishtar, 42
dialectic, 267
Diana, of the Ephesians, 331–332
Diaspora, 100–101, 683
diet, Achaean, 138; Greek, 173
Dio, Cassius, of Prusa, 677
Diocletian, absolute monarch, 733; army under, 722; Christianity and, 723–724; as emperor, 715, 718; empire reconstructed by, 719–724; provinces and, 722; tax policy of, 734
Diocletian's palace, *723*
Diodotus, 277
Diogenes, 471
Dion, 322, 323
Dionysia, Rural and City, 256, 257, 258, 259, 260, 328
Dionysius the Elder, 321–322
Dionysius the Younger (II), 322, 323
Dionysus, 137, 301; Theater of, *259*
Discobolus (Myron), *248*
Dodona, oracles at, 328
Domitian, *623;* eastern defenses by, 648–649; as em-

peror, 625; public works by, 634
Domna, Julia, 693, 694
Dorians, Achaea invaded by, 140–141, 154; Italian colonization by, 404; Laconia invaded by, 178
Doric order, *196*
Doryphorus (Polyclitus), *248*, 250, 268
Draco, 191
drama, Greek, 198–199, 256–260, 385; mime and pantomime as, 656–657; Roman, 469, 470
Drepana, 437
Druids, 428
Drusus, Livius, 483, 497, 573, 574, 591, 600
Dura-Europus, 368, 664–665, 716
Duris, 268
Dying lioness, Assyria, *91*

Ea, 39
Eannatum, 34
Ecbatana, 368
Ecclesia, Areopagus and, 235; capital punishment by, 268; Cleon and, 278; duties and powers of, 195, 204–205; paid attendance at, 326
economy, Achaean, 137–138; Athenian, 194, 326; of Carthage, 318; Cretan, 119, 123–124; of Greece, 175–176; Hittite, 63; money, 149; of Roman allies, 465–466; of Roman Empire, 607–611, 718–719, 723, 734, 736; of Sparta, 181–182; Sumerian, 32
Edict of Toleration, 725
Edictum Perpetuum, 705, 707
education, in Greece, 173–174, 266–267; in Persian Empire, 113; in Roman Empire, 670; Spartan, 182–183; Sumerian, 40–41
education, adult, Greek theater as, 258
Egypt, agriculture in, 16, 22; Alexander's conquest of, 351–352; ancient, 14–26, *map, 15;* Antiochus III defeated by, 441; army of, 50, 54; architecture of, *24*, 26, *46*, 48–49, *54*, 78; art in, 18, 48–49, 67, 116; Assyria and, 96–98; Athenian expedition to, 231; burial customs of, 19, 24–25; clans in, 16, 17; clothing in, 22–23; Caesar in, 525; commerce of, 21, 50, 70; culture of, 69–71, 116; decline of, 69; dynasties of, 18–19; empire of, 53–59;

feudal, 46–47; Golden Age of, 47; government of, 18–19, 21–22; Greeks in, 365; Hittites and, 66–69; Hyksos' capture of, 52–53; Jews in, 365, 366; law in, 19; life in, 23; literature of, 49–50, 71; mercenaries in, 365; migrations into, 50–51, 69, 101, 365, 366; Middle Kingdom of, 46–50; Neolithic and Paleolithic, 16; Old Kingdom of, 21–25; peoples of, 17; Persia and, 110, 346; under the Ptolemies, 364–366; religion in, 17–19, 23, 53, 55–56, 71; under Roman emperors, 611; sculpture in, *25*, 26, *57;* Semites in, 17; slaves in, 48; society of, 70; taxation in, 19; unification of, 20–21
Egyptian women weaving, *70*
Elagabalus, 694; temple of, 717
electorate, Roman, 458–459
Elis, 178
Empedocles, 265, 268
Enlil, 36, 39
Ennius, Quintus, 469, 470
Entemena, 34
Eolithic period, 6
Epaminondas, 303–306, 308–309
Ephialtes, 228, 234–236
Epic of Gilgamesh, 42
Epicharmus, 469
Epictetus, 679
Epicurus, 379, 470, 545
Epidaurus, theater at, 333–334, *336*
equestrian order, Augustus and, 565–568; Gaius Gracchus and, 481–483; growth of, Julio-Claudians, 630–632. *See also* knights
Eratosthenes, 380–381, 384; map by, *382*
Erechtheum, 254
Eretria, 212
Esarhaddon, 95, 97
Essenes, 684, 685
Eteobutadae, 171
Etruscans, city-planning by, *400;* civilization and culture of, 398–402; Gauls and, 428–430; language of, 403; literature of, 402; metals used by, 402, *403;* music of, 402; religion of, 400–402; Roman monarchy of, 409–414; women's status among, 400
Eubulus, 312, 339
Euclid, 380
Eumenes I, 371
Eumenes II, 372, 391, 443
Eupatrids, 189–190, 193, 196, 200–201

tian and, 715, 718, 719–724; division of, 728; of East, 728, 729; economy of, 607–611, 718–719, 734, 736; education in, 670; Egypt and, 611; European frontier of, 647–651, 714–715; family in, 579–580; festivals of, 413, 581, 713; during Flavian dynasty, 622–625; Hellenism spread by, 156, 699; housing in, 666; industry and trade in, 614–616, 719; Jewish rebellion against, 602–604, 653, 683; under Julio-Claudian dynasty, 590–606, 607–621, *see also* Claudius, Gaius, Nero, Tiberius; law, *see* Roman law; libraries in, 670; literature of, 581–585, 672–677, 739; living costs in, 634; money in, 576, 736; Parthia and, 574, 602, 652–653, 712–713; Persia and, 716, 727; plague in, 710; politics in, 454–456; population of, 575, 580, 598, 611, 672; princeps during, 554–558, 561–563, 596–598, 624; provinces, *see* provinces; public works of, 528, 596–597, 609–610, 634–636, 723, *see also* architecture, building; religion in, 665, 732–733; religious tolerance of, 700; roads of, 608–609; senate, *see* Senate; social classes in, 565–571, 737–738; social welfare in, 632–637; society of, 454–456, 607–621, 737–738; succession in, 625–629, 719; taxation in, 575–576, 590–598, 632–633, 723, 727, 734; temples of, 582, 586–587, 655; tetrarchy in, 719; under Vespasian, 595, 622, 623, 634, 648, 670; Western, 729, 730; world government of, 699

Roman Empire, *maps, 556–557, 720–721*

Roman law, achievement and influence of, 700–701, 709; on assembly, 459; civil, 701, 704; under Claudius, 632; codification by Hadrian, 705, 707, by Justinian, 708, by Theodosius, 708, 740; and emperor's constitutional powers, 624; for foreigners, 702–704; on free grain distribution, 513; Gabinian, 507; Greek influence on, 471; humanitarianism in, 632, 705; interpretation of, 701–702; Manilian, 507; on mar-

riage, 579–580; natural law as, 704–705; slaves protected by, 617–618; sources of, 701; Sulla and, 502; Twelve Tables of, 423, 632, 701

Roman triumph, model, *461*

Romanization, of Britain, 651; of Europe, 699

Rome, city of, bathing establishments in, 658–659, *711;* during the Empire, 618–621, *619,* 655–661; entertainment in, 656–658; Etruscan, 409–410; fire of 64 in, 658; founding of, 405–408; Jews expelled from, 473, 683; during the Republic, 460–464; rebuilt, 430; sacked by Visigoths, 729; Sulla captures, 500; water supply for, 409, 659–660

Rome, monarchy of, absolute, 733–735; Etruscan, 405–415

Rome, Republic of, annexation by, 446–448; Antiochus III and, 443, 444–446; architecture in, 462–464, *462, 473,* 539–541, *541, 542, 543;* army of, *see* Roman army; art of, 473, 540–543; astrology in, 473; building in, 462–464; Carthage and, 435–438, 438–441, 446–447; city-planning in, *429;* civil war in, First, 498–500, Second, 498–500, Third, 536–537; conquered peoples and, 426, 427; and Gaul, 429, 433, 518–519; contributions of, to civilization, 699–700; Corinth and, 448; culture of, 460–473; electorate in, 458–459; end of, 533–538; Etruscan influence on, 403; and Etruscan monarchy, 409–414; government of, 415–419, 457–459, chart of, *454, 530;* Greek influence on, 403–404, 461, 463, 467, 470–471, 473, 539, 540, 598; housing in, 461–462; Italy and, 495–498; Jugurtha and, 487–490; Latin League and, 426, 430, 431; literature in, 466–470, 473, 539, 543–549; Macedonia and, 441–444; magistrates in, 415–418; painting in, 542–543; Parthia and, 519–520, 537; provincial government of, 449–452, 513, 529; philosophy in, 470–471, 473; religion in, 411, 412–413, 471–473, 680–683; roads in, 432, 460, *463,* 464; Sabines and, 425, 426;

Samnite Wars and, 430–433; sculpture in, *367, 505, 506, 510, 524, 535, 542, 585, 586, 587, 623, 739,* 741, *741;* Senate, *see* Senate; social classes in, 418–422, 454–455, 502; Spain and, 438–441, 442; status of women in, 426, 563; temples of, 472, 540, *541, 543*

Rome and Italy, *maps, 396, 436*

Rome and Latium, *map, 407*

Rome and Mediterranean World, *map, 476–477*

Romulus and Remus, 402, *403*

Romulus Augustulus, 729

Rosetta Stone, 20

Roxana, 356, 360

Rufus, Curtius, 384

Rufus, Publius Sulpicius, 497, 498

ruler-worship, 378, 555, 590, 599–600, 680

Rullus, Publius Servilius, 509

Sabellians, 397–398

Sabines, Latins and, 408; Rome and, 425, 426

Sacred Precinct, Delphi, *177*

Sacred War, 312–314

Saga of Aqhat, Son of Daniel, 74, 75

St. Ambrose, 548, 728

St. Augustine, 705, 740–741

St. Irenaeus, 689

St. Jerome, 740

St. John Chrysostom, 740

St. Paul, 686–687, 700, 704–705

Salamis, battle of, 214–219, 234; *map, 218*

Sallust, 490, 510, 539, 549

Samnite Wars, 430–433

Samsu-Iluna, 52

Sanctuary of Fortune, *462,* 541

Sappho, 165

Sardinia-Corsica, 449, 452–456

Sardis, conference at, 300

Sargon I, 38, 89

Sargon II, 86, 90, 92, 95; palace of, *93*

Sassanid Revolution, 697, 698, 713

satire, 468–469, 676

Saturn, 472

Saturninus, L. Appuleius, 493, 494

Saul, 80

Scaevola, Publius Mucius, 478

Schliemann, Heinrich, 118, 133

science, Alexander and, 358–359; beginnings of, Greece, 164–165; of Hellenistic era, 380–383; under Pericles, 268